1000 RECIPE COOKBOOK

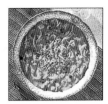

1000 RECIPE COOKBOOK

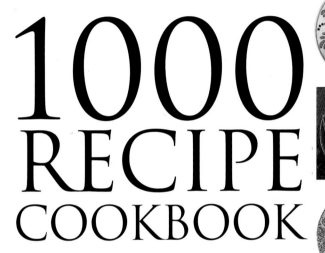

the ultimate collection of delicious dishes
for all occasions, from snacks and
light lunches to gourmet meals, with over
1000 fantastic photographs

consultant editor: martha day

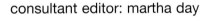

LORENZ BOOKS

This edition is published by Lorenz Books

Lorenz Books is an imprint of Anness Publishing Ltd
Hermes House, 88–89 Blackfriars Road, London SE1 8HA
tel. 020 7401 2077; fax 020 7633 9499
www.lorenzbooks.com; info@anness.com

© Anness Publishing Ltd 1997, 2005

UK agent: The Manning Partnership Ltd, 6 The Old Dairy, Melcombe Road, Bath BA2 3LR
tel. 01225 478444; fax 01225 478440; sales@manning-partnership.co.uk

UK distributor: Grantham Book Services Ltd, Isaac Newton Way, Alma Park Industrial Estate
Grantham, Lincs NG31 9SD; tel. 01476 541080; fax 01476 541061; orders@gbs.tbs-ltd.co.uk

North American agent/distributor: National Book Network, 4501 Forbes Boulevard, Suite 200
Lanham, MD 20706; tel. 301 459 3366; fax 301 429 5746; www.nbnbooks.com

Australian agent/distributor: Pan Macmillan Australia, Level 18, St Martins Tower, 31 Market St
Sydney, NSW 2000; tel. 1300 135 113; fax 1300 135 103; customer.service@macmillan.com.au

New Zealand agent/distributor: David Bateman Ltd, 30 Tarndale Grove, Off Bush Road
Albany, Auckland; tel. (09) 415 7664; fax (09) 415 8892

Publisher: Joanna Lorenz
Senior Cookery Editor: Linda Fraser
Project Manager: Anne Hildyard
Designer: Siân Keogh
Photographers: Karl Adamson, Edward Allwright, David Armstrong, Steve Baxter, James Duncan, John Freeman
Michelle Garrett, Amanda Heywood, Tim Hill, Don Last, Patrick McLeavy, Michael Michaels
Recipes: Alex Barker, Carla Capalbo, Maxine Clark, Frances Cleary, Carole Clements, Roz Denny, Christine France,
Sarah Gates, Shirley Gill, Rosamund Grant, Patricia Lousada, Norma MacMillan, Sue Maggs, Janice Murfitt,
Annie Nichols, Louise Pickford, Katherine Richmond, Jenny Stacey, Liz Trigg, Hilaire Walden,
Laura Washburn, Steven Wheeler, Elizabeth Wolf-Cohen
Additional Photography: Sopexa UK
Food for Photography: Carla Capalbo, Joanne Craig, Carole Handslip, Wendy Lee,
Sarah Maxwell, Angela Nilsen, Jenny Shapter, Jane Stevenson, Liz Trigg and Elizabeth Wolf-Cohen
Home Economists: Carla Capalbo, Jenny Shapter
Stylists: Madeleine Brehaut, Carla Capalbo, Michelle Garrett, Hilary Guy, Amanda Heywood,
Maria Kelly, Blake Minton, Kirsty Rawlings, Rebecca Sturrock, Fiona Tillett

Previously published as *1000 Great Recipes*

Front cover main picture shows *Pasta with Tomatoes and Rocket*–for recipe see page 156

1 3 5 7 9 10 8 6 4 2

NOTES

For all recipes, quantities are given in both metric and imperial measures and, where appropriate, measures are
also given in standard cups and spoons. Follow one set, but not a mixture because they are not interchangeable.
Standard spoon and cup measurements are level.
1 tbsp = 15ml, 1 tsp = 5ml, 1 cup = 250ml/8fl oz
Australian standard tablespoons are 20ml. Australian readers should use 3 tsp in place of 1 tbsp for measuring small
quantities of gelatine, cornflour, salt etc.
medium eggs should be used unless otherwise stated.

CONTENTS

Introduction

In the modern world's quest for innovation and new taste sensations, it's often easy to forget just how delicious and fulfilling a classic recipe can be. This volume contains a definitive selection of best-ever recipes which will serve as an essential reference point for beginners and as a timely reminder to the experienced cook when planning the perfect meal.

These cosmopolitan creations have gained worldwide status through their harmonious balance of fresh ingredients, herbs and spices. Stemming from justified popularity in their homelands, they have attained universal appeal as part of the international chef's repertoire. Even more appealing is the fact that many traditional recipes are based on a natural nutritional equilibrium that was taken for granted before the days of "fast food" and a high intake of saturated fats. Many of these dishes excel when analyzed in the light of today's vogue for healthy eating. Others are unashamedly sinful (chocoholics, beware!).

The dishes presented in this book are tailored to every season and every event: you can mix and match cooking styles and influences to suit the mood and the occasion, not to mention your pocket. There is a fine selection of hearty soups such as Red Pepper Soup with Lime, which are satisfying enough for a light meal yet attractive enough to serve as an impressive dinner party appetizer. Sophisticated appetizers include Smoked Salmon and Dill Blinis or Chicken Liver Pâté with Marsala, Avocados with Tangy Topping or Pears and Stilton.

Fish and shellfish are increasingly popular in today's health-conscious society. Flavoursome dishes such as Smoked Trout with Cucumber or Grilled Fresh Sardines are classics that will

always provide a light, fresh main course to tantalize your tastebuds.

Present directions in menu planning may point away from a truly carnivorous way of life, yet there are many occasions when a sumptuous meat course will win the day. This volume will arm you with the confidence and conviction needed to present a perfect Roast Beef with Yorkshire Pudding or a melting Cottage Pie. Also included is a variety of more unusual dishes such as Duck with Chestnut Sauce, a simple yet impressive dinner party presentation, and economical yet nutritious main courses that will appeal to adults and children alike, such as Sausage and Bean Ragoût. Whether we choose western fare such as Tuna Fishcake Bites or an exotic Kashmir Coconut Fish Curry, these recipes are characterized by a distinctive depth of flavour created by a judicious blend of herbs and spices.

The vegetable dishes in this book are delicious concoctions that can be prepared at short notice as an accompaniment or a complete, well-balanced meal. Some are long-standing favourites of vegetarian fare, such as Chick-pea Stew; others are innovative versions of world-famous dishes such as a Chunky Vegetable Paella, which combines a colourful appearance with satisfying texture and harmonious flavours.

Desserts feature prominently in this collection, ranging from from light, fluffy mousses and cool, super-smooth sherbets to the richest trifles, dream puddings made from fruit, cream and chocolate, and a fabulous array of all kinds of baked treats.

Baking is one of the most satisfying of all the culinary arts. It fills the house with the most wonderful aroma, gives ample reward for minimal effort and always meets with approval, especially from younger members of the family. Bake a batch of brownies, a fresh fruit pie, a crusty loaf of bread or a luxurious gâteau, and watch your rating rise!

Included here is a wide range of recipes, from simple treats like drop scones and basic biscuits to elaborate cakes for special celebrations. The step-by-step instructions are so simple and straightforward that even a novice will find them easy to follow.

In fact, novice cooks often make the best bakers, preheating the oven in plenty of time, taking care to measure ingredients accurately and following recipe methods to the letter. All these elements are important in baking, which demands more precision than many other types of cooking. With a soup or stew you can happily sling in extra ingredients or cheat a little when it comes to exact quantities, but the balance of ingredients, the temperature and the timing are all very important when you are baking a cake or pastry. It is worth reading the chosen recipe carefully before you begin, doing any advance preparation such as browning almonds or softening butter, then setting out the ingredients in the style of the TV cook.

Advice on lining tins is given in individual recipes. Greaseproof paper is the traditional lining material, but non-stick baking paper is even easier to use and gives excellent results. To base-line a tin, place it on the paper and draw around the outside edge, then cut out the shape. Grease the base of the tin with a dab of oil or butter to hold the paper in place, then fit it in the tin.

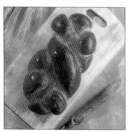

Grease the paper (if using greaseproof) and the sides of the tin.

Whether or not to grease tins used for pastry is a matter of choice. If the pastry is high in fat, such as shortcrust, flaky or puff, it is not usually necessary; however, spills from fillings may stick. When in doubt, grease the tins lightly.

If you are a novice baker, start with some of the simpler recipes, such as Chocolate-chip Cookies, Chive and Potato Scones or a Quick-mix Sponge. Try some of the delectable breads, from a traditional Plaited Loaf to the contemporary Saffron Focaccia.

You'll find every occasion amply catered for, from Valentine's Day through to a wedding. There are cakes for christenings, anniversaries and every possible birthday, from novelty teddies to telephones - including a mobile! For the family, the collection includes wonderful ways of keeping the cake tin and biscuit barrel brimming with healthy snacks, including a selection for those with dietary restrictions. With vegans in view, there's a special chocolate gâteau and a Dundee cake, and an entire chapter is devoted to low-fat cakes and bakes.

There's a sweet or savoury treat for every moment of the day, from breakfast Blueberry Muffins to a late-night slice of Pecan Tart.

This collection of 1000 classic recipes has been drawn together from the combined talents of some of the world's most respected cooks and food writers. With the help of this authoritative guide, your cooking will not only withstand the scrutiny of your most demanding critic – be it yourself or a fierce rival – but will win them over in style.

Carrot and Coriander Soup

Use a good home-made stock for this soup – it adds a far greater depth of flavour than stock made from cubes.

Serves 4

50g/2oz/4 tbsp butter
2 leeks, sliced
450g/1lb carrots, sliced
15ml/1 tbsp ground coriander
1.2 litres/2 pints/5 cups chicken stock
150ml/¼ pint/⅔ cup Greek-style yogurt
salt and ground black pepper
30–45ml/2–3 tbsp chopped fresh coriander, to garnish

1 Melt the butter in a large saucepan. Add the leeks and carrots and stir well, coating the vegetables with the butter. Cover with a tight-fitting lid and cook for about 10 minutes, until the vegetables are beginning to soften but not colour.

2 Stir in the ground coriander and cook for about 1 minute. Pour in the stock and season to taste with salt and pepper. Bring to the boil, cover and simmer for about 20 minutes, until the leeks and carrots are tender.

3 Leave to cool slightly, then purée the soup in a blender until smooth. Return the soup to the pan and add about 30ml/2 tbsp of the yogurt, then taste the soup and adjust the seasoning again to taste. Reheat gently but do not boil.

4 Ladle the soup into bowls and put a spoonful of the remaining yogurt in the centre of each. Scatter over the coriander and serve immediately.

Leek, Potato and Rocket Soup

Rocket, with its distinctive peppery taste, is wonderful in this filling soup. Serve it hot with ciabatta croûtons.

Serves 4–6

50g/2oz/4 tbsp butter
1 onion, chopped
3 leeks, chopped
2 potatoes, diced
900ml/1½ pints/3¾ cups light chicken stock
2 large handfuls rocket, roughly chopped
150ml/¼ pint/⅔ cup double cream
salt and ground black pepper
garlic-flavoured ciabatta croûtons, to serve

1 Melt the butter in a large heavy-based saucepan, add the onion, leeks and potatoes and stir until all the vegetable pieces are coated in butter.

2 Cover with a tight-fitting lid and leave the vegetables to sweat for about 15 minutes. Pour in the stock, cover once again with the lid, then simmer for a further 20 minutes, until the vegetables are tender.

3 Press the soup through a sieve or food mill and return to the rinsed-out pan. (When puréeing the soup, don't use a blender or food processor, as these will give the soup a gluey texture.) Add the chopped rocket, stir in and cook gently for about 5 minutes.

4 Stir in the cream, then season to taste with salt and pepper. Reheat gently. Ladle the soup into warmed soup bowls, then serve with a few ciabatta croûtons in each.

Cook's Tip
To make the croûtons, cut the bread into 1cm/½ in cubes, without the crust if you wish, and either fry or bake in a roasting tin in oil until golden and crunchy.

Tomato and Basil Soup

In the summer, when tomatoes are both plentiful and cheap to buy, this is a lovely soup to make.

Serves 4

30ml/2 tbsp olive oil
1 onion, chopped
2.5ml/½ tsp caster sugar
1 carrot, finely chopped
1 potato, finely chopped
1 garlic clove, crushed
675g/1½lb ripe tomatoes,
*   roughly chopped*
5ml/1 tsp tomato purée
1 bay leaf
1 thyme sprig
1 oregano sprig
4 fresh basil leaves,
*   roughly torn*
300ml/½ pint/1¼ cups
*   light chicken or*
*   vegetable stock*
2–3 pieces sun-dried
*   tomatoes in oil*
30ml/2 tbsp shredded
*   fresh basil leaves*
salt and ground black
*   pepper*

1 Heat the oil in a large saucepan, add the onion and sprinkle with the caster sugar. Cook gently for 5 minutes.

2 Add the chopped carrot and potato, cover the pan and cook over a low heat for a further 10 minutes, without browning the vegetables.

3 Stir in the garlic, tomatoes, tomato purée, herbs and stock, and season to taste with salt and pepper. Cover the pan with a tight-fitting lid and cook gently for about 25–30 minutes, or until the vegetables are tender.

4 Remove the pan from the heat and press the soup through a sieve or food mill to extract all the skins and pips. Season again with salt and pepper to taste.

5 Reheat the soup gently, then ladle into four warmed soup bowls. Finely chop the sun-dried tomatoes and mix with a little oil from the jar. Add a spoonful to each serving, then scatter the shredded basil over the top.

Corn and Shellfish Chowder

Chowder comes from the French word *chaudron*, meaning a large pot in which the soup is cooked.

Serves 4

25g/1oz/2 tbsp butter
1 small onion, chopped
350g/12oz can
*   sweetcorn, drained*
600ml/1 pint/2½ cups
*   milk*
2 spring onions, finely
*   chopped*
115g/4oz/1 cup peeled,
*   cooked prawns*
175g/6oz can white
*   crabmeat, drained and*
*   flaked*
150ml/¼ pint/⅔ cup
*   single cream*
pinch of cayenne pepper
salt and ground black
*   pepper*
4 whole prawns in the
*   shell, to garnish*

1 Melt the butter in a large saucepan and gently fry the onion for 4–5 minutes, until softened.

2 Reserve 30ml/2 tbsp of the sweetcorn for the garnish and add the remainder to the pan, along with the milk. Bring the soup to the boil, then reduce the heat, cover the pan with a tight-fitting lid and simmer over a low heat for 5 minutes.

3 Pour the soup, in batches if necessary, into a blender or food processor. Process until smooth.

4 Return the soup to the pan and stir in the spring onions, crabmeat, prawns, cream and cayenne pepper. Reheat gently over a low heat.

5 Meanwhile, place the reserved sweetcorn kernels in a small frying pan without oil and dry-fry over a moderate heat until golden and toasted.

6 Season to taste with salt and pepper and serve each bowl of soup garnished with a few of the toasted sweetcorn kernels and a whole prawn.

Spiced Parsnip Soup

This pale, creamy-textured soup is given a special touch with an aromatic garlic and mustard seed garnish.

Serves 4–6

40g/1½oz/3 tbsp butter
1 onion, chopped
675g/1½lb parsnips, diced
5ml/1 tsp ground coriander
2.5ml/½ tsp ground cumin
2.5ml/½ tsp ground turmeric
1.5ml/¼ tsp chilli powder

1.2 litres/2 pints/5 cups chicken stock
150ml/¼ pint/⅔ cup single cream
15ml/1 tbsp sunflower oil
1 garlic clove, cut into julienne strips
10ml/2 tsp yellow mustard seeds
salt and ground black pepper

1 Melt the butter in a large saucepan and fry the onion and parsnips gently for about 3 minutes.

2 Stir in the spices and cook for 1 minute more. Add the stock, season to taste with salt and pepper and bring to the boil, then reduce the heat. Cover with a tight-fitting lid and simmer for about 45 minutes, until the parsnips are tender.

3 Cool slightly, then place in a blender and purée until smooth. Return the soup to the pan, add the cream and heat through gently over a low heat.

4 Heat the oil in a small pan, add the julienne strips of garlic and yellow mustard seeds and fry quickly until the garlic is beginning to brown and the mustard seeds start to pop and splutter. Remove the pan from the heat.

5 Ladle the soup into warmed soup bowls and pour a little of the hot spice mixture over each. Serve at once.

Cook's Tip
Crushed coriander seeds may be substituted for the mustard seeds in the garnish.

Pumpkin Soup

The flavour of this soup will develop and improve if it is made a day in advance.

Serves 4–6

900g/2lb pumpkin
45ml/3 tbsp olive oil
2 onions, chopped
2 celery sticks, chopped
450g/1lb tomatoes, chopped
1.5 litres/2½ pints/6¼ cups vegetable stock
30ml/2 tbsp tomato purée

1 bouquet garni
2–3 rashers streaky bacon, crisply fried and crumbled
30ml/2 tbsp chopped fresh parsley
salt and ground black pepper

1 With a sharp knife cut the pumpkin into thin slices, discarding the skin and seeds.

2 Heat the oil in a large saucepan and fry the onions and celery for about 5 minutes. Add the pumpkin and tomatoes and cook for a further 5 minutes.

3 Add the vegetable stock, tomato purée and bouquet garni to the pan. Season with salt and pepper. Bring the soup to the boil, then reduce the heat, cover and simmer for 45 minutes.

4 Allow the soup to cool slightly, remove the bouquet garni, then purée (in two batches, if necessary) in a food processor or blender.

5 Press the soup through a sieve, then return it to the pan. Reheat gently and season again. Ladle the soup into warmed soup bowls. Sprinkle with the crispy bacon and parsley and serve at once.

Jerusalem Artichoke Soup

Topped with saffron cream, this soup is wonderful to serve on a chilly winter's day.

Serves 4

50g/2oz/4 tbsp butter
1 onion, chopped
450g/1lb Jerusalem artichokes, peeled and cut into chunks
900ml/1½ pints/3¾ cups chicken stock
150ml/¼ pint/⅔ cup milk

150ml/¼ pint/⅔ cup double cream
large pinch of saffron powder
salt and ground black pepper
snipped fresh chives, to garnish

1 Melt the butter in a large heavy-based saucepan and cook the onion for 5–8 minutes, until soft but not browned, stirring occasionally.

2 Add the artichokes to the pan and stir until coated in the butter. Cover with a tight-fitting lid and cook gently for 10–15 minutes; do not allow the artichokes to brown. Pour in the stock and milk, then cover again and simmer for about 15 minutes. Cool slightly, then process in a food processor or blender until smooth.

3 Strain the soup back into the pan. Add half the cream, season to taste with salt and pepper, and reheat gently. Lightly whip the remaining cream and saffron powder. Ladle the soup into warmed soup bowls and put a spoonful of saffron cream in the centre of each. Scatter over the snipped chives and serve at once.

Broccoli and Stilton Soup

A really easy, but rich, soup – choose something simple to follow, such as plainly grilled meat, poultry or fish.

Serves 4

350g/12oz/3 cups broccoli florets
25g/1oz/2 tbsp butter
1 onion, chopped
1 leek, white part only, chopped
1 small potato, diced
600ml/1 pint/2½ cups hot chicken stock

300ml/½ pint/1¼ cups milk
45ml/3 tbsp double cream
115g/4oz Stilton cheese, rind removed, crumbled
salt and ground black pepper

1 Discard any tough stems from the broccoli florets. Set aside two small florets for the garnish.

2 Melt the butter in a large saucepan and cook the onion and leek until soft but not coloured. Add the broccoli and potato, then pour in the stock. Cover with a tight-fitting lid and simmer for 15–20 minutes, until the vegetables are tender.

3 Cool slightly, then purée in a food processor or blender. Strain through a sieve back into the pan.

4 Add the milk, cream and seasoning to the pan and reheat gently. At the last minute add the cheese, stirring until it just melts. Do not boil.

5 Meanwhile, blanch the reserved broccoli florets and cut them vertically into thin slices. Ladle the soup into warmed bowls and garnish with the broccoli florets and a generous grinding of black pepper.

Cook's Tip
Be very careful not to boil the soup once the cheese has been added.

Minestrone with Pesto

This hearty, Italian mixed vegetable soup is a great way to use up any leftover vegetables you may have.

Serves 4

30ml/2 tbsp olive oil
2 garlic cloves, crushed
1 onion, sliced
225g/8oz/2 cups diced lean bacon
2 small courgettes, quartered and sliced
50g/2oz/1½ cups French beans, chopped
2 small carrots, diced
2 celery sticks, finely chopped
bouquet garni
50g/2oz/½ cup short cut macaroni
50g/2oz/½ cup frozen peas

200g/7oz can red kidney beans, drained and rinsed
50g/2oz/1 cup shredded green cabbage
4 tomatoes, skinned and seeded
salt and ground black pepper

For the toasts
8 slices French bread
15ml/1 tbsp ready-made pesto sauce
15ml/1 tbsp grated Parmesan cheese

1 Heat the oil in a large saucepan and gently fry the garlic and onions for 5 minutes, until just softened. Add the bacon, courgettes, French beans, carrots and celery to the pan and stir-fry for a further 3 minutes.

2 Pour 1.2 litres/2 pints/5 cups of cold water over the vegetables and add the bouquet garni. Cover the pan with a tight-fitting lid and simmer for 25 minutes.

3 Add the macaroni, peas and kidney beans and cook for 8 minutes more. Then add the cabbage and tomatoes and cook for an additional 5 minutes.

4 To make the toasts, spread the bread slices with the pesto, sprinkle a little Parmesan over each one and gently brown under a hot grill. Remove the bouquet garni from the soup, season to taste and serve with the toasts.

French Onion Soup

Onion soup comes in many different guises, from smooth and creamy to this – the absolute classic from France.

Serves 4

25g/1oz/2 tbsp butter
15ml/1 tbsp oil
3 large onions, thinly sliced
5ml/1 tsp soft brown sugar
15g/½oz/1 tbsp plain flour
2 x 300g/10oz cans condensed beef consommé
30ml/2 tbsp medium sherry

10ml/2 tsp Worcestershire sauce
8 slices French bread
15ml/1 tbsp French coarse-grained mustard
75g/3oz/1 cup grated Gruyère cheese
salt and ground black pepper
15ml/1 tbsp chopped fresh parsley, to garnish

1 Heat the butter and oil in a large saucepan and cook the onions and brown sugar gently for about 20 minutes, stirring occasionally until the onions start to turn golden brown.

2 Stir in the flour and cook for a further 2 minutes. Pour in the consommé plus two cans of water, then add the sherry and Worcestershire sauce. Season with salt and pepper, cover and simmer gently for a further 25–30 minutes.

3 Preheat the grill and, just before serving, toast the bread lightly on both sides. Spread one side of each slice with the mustard and top with the grated cheese. Grill the toasts until bubbling and golden.

4 Ladle the soup into bowls. Pop two croûtons on top of each bowl of soup and garnish with chopped fresh parsley. Serve at once.

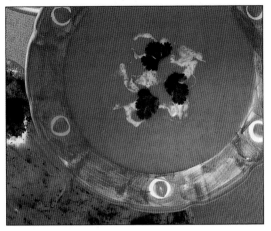

Curried Parsnip Soup

The spices in this soup impart a delicious, mild curry flavour which brings back memories of the Raj.

Serves 4

25g/1oz/2 tbsp butter
1 garlic clove, crushed
1 onion, chopped
5ml/1 tsp ground cumin
5ml/1 tsp ground coriander
450g/1lb (about 4) parsnips, sliced
10ml/2 tsp medium curry paste
450ml/¾ pint/scant 2 cups chicken or vegetable stock

450ml/¾ pint/scant 2 cups milk
60ml/4 tbsp soured cream
good squeeze of lemon juice
salt and ground black pepper
fresh coriander sprigs, to garnish
ready-made garlic and coriander naan bread, to serve

1 Heat the butter in a large saucepan and fry the garlic and onion for 4–5 minutes, until lightly golden. Stir in the spices and cook for a further 1–2 minutes.

2 Add the parsnips and stir until well coated with the butter, then stir in the curry paste, followed by the stock. Cover the pan with a tight-fitting lid and simmer for 15 minutes, until the parsnips are tender.

3 Ladle the soup into a blender or food processor and blend until smooth. Return to the pan and stir in the milk. Heat gently for 2–3 minutes, then add 30ml/2 tbsp of the soured cream and the lemon juice. Season well with salt and pepper.

4 Serve in bowls topped with spoonfuls of the remaining soured cream and the fresh coriander accompanied by the warmed, spicy naan bread.

Cook's Tip
For the best flavour, use home-made chicken or vegetable stock in this soup.

Red Pepper Soup with Lime

The beautiful rich red colour of this soup makes it a very attractive starter or light lunch.

Serves 4–6

4 fresh red peppers, seeded and chopped
1 large onion, chopped
5ml/1 tsp olive oil
1 garlic clove, crushed
1 small red chilli, sliced
45ml/3 tbsp tomato purée
juice of 1 lime

900ml/1½ pints/3¼ cups chicken stock
salt and ground black pepper
finely grated rind and shreds of lime rind, to garnish

1 Cook the onion and peppers gently in the oil in a saucepan covered with a tight-fitting lid for about 5 minutes, shaking the pan occasionally, until softened.

2 Stir in the garlic, then add the chilli with the tomato purée. Stir in half the stock, then bring to the boil. Cover the pan and simmer for 10 minutes.

3 Cool slightly, then purée in a food processor or blender. Return to the pan, then add the remaining stock, the lime rind and juice and seasoning.

4 Bring the soup back to the boil, then serve at once with a few shreds of lime rind scattered into each bowl.

Thai-style Sweetcorn Soup

This is a very quick and easy soup. If you are using frozen prawns, defrost them before adding to the soup.

Serves 4

2.5ml/½ tsp sesame or
 sunflower oil
2 spring onions, thinly
 sliced
1 garlic clove, crushed
600ml/1 pint/2½ cups
 chicken stock
425g/15oz can cream-
 style sweetcorn

225g/8oz/2 cups peeled,
 cooked prawns
5ml/1 tsp green chilli
 paste or chilli sauce
 (optional)
salt and ground black
 pepper
fresh coriander leaves, to
 garnish

Heat the oil in a large heavy-based saucepan and sauté the onions and garlic over a moderate heat for 1 minute, until softened but not browned. Stir in the chicken stock, cream-style sweetcorn, prawns and chilli paste or sauce, if using. Bring the soup to the boil, stirring occasionally. Season to taste with salt and pepper, then serve at once, sprinkled with fresh coriander leaves to garnish.

Haddock and Broccoli Chowder

This hearty soup makes a meal in itself when served with crusty, country-style bread.

Serves 4

4 spring onions, sliced
450g/1lb new potatoes,
 diced
300ml/½ pint/1¼ cups
 home-made fish stock
 or water
300ml/½ pint/1¼ cups
 skimmed milk
1 bay leaf

225g/8oz/2 cups broccoli
 florets, sliced
450g/1lb smoked haddock
 fillets, skinned
200g/7oz can sweetcorn,
 drained
ground black pepper
chopped spring onions, to
 garnish

Place the spring onions and potatoes in a pan and add the stock, milk and bay leaf. Bring to the boil, reduce the heat, cover and simmer for 10 minutes. Add the broccoli. Cut the fish into bite-size chunks; add to the pan with the sweetcorn. Season well with black pepper, then cover again and simmer until the fish is cooked through. Remove the bay leaf, scatter over the chopped spring onions and serve immediately.

Cock-a-leekie Soup

This healthy main course soup is given a sweet touch by the inclusion of prunes.

Serves 4-6

Gently cook 1.2 litres/2 pints/5 cups chicken stock and bouquet garni for 40 minutes. Cut 4 leeks into 2.5cm/1in slices, add to the pan along with 8–12 soaked prunes and cook gently for 20 minutes. Discard the bouquet garni. Remove the chicken, discard the skin and bones and chop the flesh. Return the chicken to the pan and season to taste. Heat the soup, then serve with soft buttered rolls.

Green Pea and Mint Soup

This soup is equally delicious lightly chilled. Stir in the swirl of cream just before serving.

Serves 4

50g/2oz/4 tbsp butter
4 spring onions, chopped
450g/1lb/4 cups fresh or frozen peas
600ml/1 pint/2½ cups chicken or vegetable stock
2 large fresh mint sprigs

600ml/1 pint/2½ cups milk
pinch of sugar (optional)
salt and ground black pepper
single cream, to serve
small fresh mint sprigs, to garnish

1 Heat the butter in a large saucepan and gently fry the spring onions until just softened but not coloured.

2 Stir the peas into the pan, add the stock and mint and bring to the boil. Cover and simmer very gently for about 30 minutes for fresh peas or 15 minutes if you are using frozen peas, until the peas are very tender. Remove about 45ml/3 tbsp of the peas using a slotted spoon, and reserve for the garnish.

3 Pour the soup into a food processor or blender, add the milk and purée until smooth. Then return the soup to the pan and reheat gently. Season to taste with salt and pepper, adding a pinch of sugar if you wish.

4 Pour the soup into bowls. Swirl a little cream into each, then garnish with mint and the reserved peas.

Cook's Tip
Fresh peas are increasingly available during the summer months from greengrocers and supermarkets. The effort of podding them is well worthwhile, as they impart a unique flavour to this delicious, vibrant soup.

Beetroot and Apricot Swirl

This soup is most attractive if you swirl together the two coloured purées, but mix them together if you prefer.

Serves 4

4 large cooked beetroot, roughly chopped
1 small onion, roughly chopped
600ml/1 pint/2½ cups chicken stock

200g/7oz ready-to-eat dried apricots
250ml/8fl oz/1 cup orange juice
salt and ground black pepper

1 Place the beetroot and half of the onion in a saucepan with the stock. Bring to the boil, then reduce the heat, cover with a tight-fitting lid and simmer for about 10 minutes. Purée in a food processor or blender.

2 Place the rest of the onion in a pan with the apricots and orange juice, cover and simmer gently for about 15 minutes until tender. Purée in a food processor or blender.

3 Return the two mixtures to the saucepans and reheat. Season to taste with salt and pepper, then swirl the mixtures together in individual soup bowls to create a marbled effect.

Cook's Tip
Beetroot are available ready cooked. To cook your own, simply place in a saucepan with enough water to cover, bring to the boil, then cover and cook for 1 hour. Drain, then peel the beetroot with your fingers when cool enough to handle.

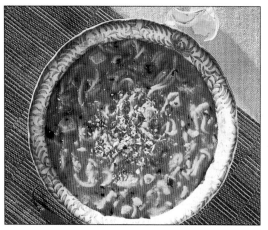

Thai-style Chicken Soup

Omit the red chilli from the garnish if you prefer a milder flavour in this soup.

Serves 4

15ml/1 tbsp vegetable oil
1 garlic clove, finely chopped
2 x 175g/6oz boned chicken breasts, skinned and chopped
2.5ml/½ tsp ground turmeric
1.5ml/¼ tsp hot chilli powder
75g/3oz creamed coconut
900ml/1½ pints/3¾ cups hot chicken stock
30ml/2 tbsp lemon or lime juice

30ml/2 tbsp crunchy peanut butter
50g/2oz/1 cup thread egg noodles, broken into small pieces
15ml/1 tbsp spring onions, finely chopped
15ml/1 tbsp chopped fresh coriander
salt and ground black pepper
30ml/2 tbsp desiccated coconut and ½ red chilli, seeded and finely chopped, to garnish

1 Heat the oil in a large saucepan and fry the garlic for 1 minute until lightly golden. Add the chicken and spices and stir-fry for a further 3–4 minutes. Crumble the creamed coconut into the stock and stir until dissolved. Pour on to the chicken and add the lemon juice, peanut butter and egg noodles. Cover and simmer for 15 minutes. Add the spring onions and coriander, season to taste with salt and pepper and cook for a further 5 minutes.

2 Fry the coconut and chilli for 2–3 minutes, stirring until the coconut is lightly browned. Use as a garnish for the soup.

New England Pumpkin Soup

For a smooth-textured soup, process all the mixture in a food processor or blender.

Serves 4

25g/1oz/2 tbsp butter
1 onion, finely chopped
1 garlic clove, crushed
15g/½ oz/1 tbsp plain flour
pinch of grated nutmeg
2.5ml/½ tsp ground cinnamon
350g/12oz pumpkin, seeded, peeled and diced
600ml/1 pint/2½ cups chicken stock

150ml/¼ pint/⅔ cup orange juice
5ml/1 tsp brown sugar

For the croûtons
15ml/1 tbsp vegetable oil
2 slices granary bread, without the crusts
30ml/2 tbsp sunflower seeds
salt and ground black pepper

1 Melt the butter in a large saucepan and gently fry the onions and garlic for 4–5 minutes, until softened.

2 Stir in the flour, spices and pumpkin, then cover and cook gently for 6 minutes, stirring occasionally.

3 Add the chicken stock, orange juice and brown sugar. Cover again, and bring to the boil, then simmer for 20 minutes until the pumpkin has softened.

4 Process half the mixture in a blender or food processor. Return the soup to the pan with the remaining chunky mixture, stirring constantly. Season to taste and heat through.

5 To make the croûtons, heat the oil in a frying pan, cut the bread into cubes and gently fry until just beginning to brown. Add the sunflower seeds and fry for 1–2 minutes. Drain the croûtons on kitchen paper. Serve the soup hot, garnished with a few of the croûtons scattered over the top, and serve the remaining croûtons separately.

Split Pea and Courgette Soup

Rich and satisfying, this tasty and nutritious soup is ideal to serve on a chilly winter's day.

Serves 4

175g/6oz/1 cup yellow
   split peas
5ml/1 tsp sunflower oil
1 large onion, finely
   chopped
2 courgettes, finely diced

900ml/1½ pints/3¾ cups
   chicken stock
2.5ml/½ tsp ground
   turmeric
salt and ground black
   pepper

1 Place the split peas in a bowl, cover with cold water and leave to soak for several hours or overnight. Drain, rinse in cold water and drain again.

2 Heat the oil in a saucepan. Add the onion, cover with a tight-fitting lid and cook until soft. Reserve a handful of diced courgettes and add the rest to the pan. Cook, stirring constantly, for 2–3 minutes.

3 Add the stock and turmeric to the pan and bring to the boil. Reduce the heat, then cover and simmer for about 30–40 minutes, or until the split peas are tender. Add seasoning to taste.

4 When the soup is almost ready, bring a large saucepan of water to the boil, add the reserved diced courgettes and cook for 1 minute, then drain and add to the soup before serving hot with warm crusty bread.

Cook's Tip
For a quicker alternative, use split red lentils for this soup. They do not require presoaking and cook very quickly. Adjust the amount of chicken stock used, if you need to.

Mediterranean Tomato Soup

Children will love this soup – especially if you use fancy pasta such as alphabet or animal shapes.

Serves 4

675g/1½lb ripe plum
   tomatoes
1 onion, quartered
1 celery stick
1 garlic clove
15ml/1 tbsp olive oil
450ml/¾ pint/scant
   2 cups chicken stock

15ml/2 tbsp tomato purée
50g/2oz/½ cup small
   pasta shapes
salt and ground black
   pepper
fresh coriander or parsley
   sprigs, to garnish

1 Place the tomatoes, onion, celery and garlic in a saucepan with the oil. Cover with a tight-fitting lid and cook over a gentle heat for 40–45 minutes, shaking the pan occasionally, until the vegetables become very soft.

2 Spoon the vegetables into a food processor or blender and process until smooth. Press through a sieve to remove the tomato pips, then return to the pan.

3 Stir in the stock and tomato purée and bring to the boil. Add the pasta and simmer gently for about 8 minutes, or until the pasta is tender. Add salt and pepper to taste, then sprinkle with coriander or parsley to garnish and serve hot.

White Bean Soup

Small white lima beans or pinto beans work well in this soup, or try butter beans for a change.

Serves 6

350g/12oz/1½ cups dried
 cannellini or other
 white beans
1 bay leaf
75ml/5 tbsp olive oil
1 onion, finely chopped
1 carrot, finely chopped
1 celery stick, finely
 chopped
3 tomatoes, peeled and
 finely chopped

2 garlic cloves, finely
 chopped
5ml/1 tsp fresh thyme
 leaves or 2.5ml/½ tsp
 dried thyme
750ml/1¼ pints/3⅔ cups
 boiling water
salt and ground black
 pepper
extra virgin olive oil, to
 serve

1 Pick over the beans carefully, discarding any stones or other particles. Soak the beans in a large bowl of cold water overnight. Drain. Place the beans in a large saucepan of water, bring to the boil, and cook for 20 minutes. Drain. Return the beans to the pan, cover with cold water, and bring to the boil again. Add the bay leaf, and cook 1–2 hours until the beans are tender. Drain again. Remove the bay leaf.

2 Purée about three-quarters of the beans in a food processor or blender. Alternatively, pass through a food mill, adding a little water if needed.

3 Heat the oil in a large saucepan and cook the onion until softened but not browned. Add the carrot and celery, and cook for a further 5 minutes.

4 Stir in the tomatoes, garlic and fresh or dried thyme. Cook for 6–8 minutes more, stirring often.

5 Pour in the boiling water. Stir in the beans and the bean purée. Season to taste with salt and pepper. Simmer for about 10–15 minutes. Serve in individual soup bowls, sprinkled with a little extra virgin olive oil.

Fish Soup

For extra flavour use some smoked fish in this soup and rub the bread with a garlic clove before toasting.

Serves 6

900g/2¼ lb mixed fish
 fillets such as coley,
 dogfish, whiting, red
 mullet or cod
90ml/6 tbsp olive oil,
 plus extra to serve
1 onion, finely chopped
1 celery stick, chopped
1 carrot, chopped
60ml/4 tbsp chopped
 fresh parsley

175ml/6fl oz/¾ cup dry
 white wine
3 tomatoes, peeled and
 chopped
2 garlic cloves, finely
 chopped
1.5 litres/2½ pints/
 6¼ cups boiling water
salt and ground black
 pepper
French bread, to serve

1 Scale and clean the fish, discarding all innards but leaving the heads on. Cut into large pieces. Rinse well in cool water.

2 Heat the oil in a large saucepan and cook the onion over a low to moderate heat until just softened. Stir in the celery and carrot and cook for 5 minutes more. Add the parsley.

3 Pour in the wine, raise the heat and cook until it reduces by about half. Stir in the tomatoes and garlic. Cook for 3–4 minutes, stirring occasionally. Pour in the boiling water and bring back to the boil. Cook for 15 minutes.

4 Stir in the fish and simmer for 10–15 minutes, or until the fish are tender. Season to taste with salt and pepper.

5 Remove the fish from the soup with a slotted spoon. Discard any bones. Place in a food processor and purée until smooth. Taste again for seasoning. If the soup is too thick, add a little more water.

6 To serve, heat the soup to simmering. Toast the rounds of bread and sprinkle with olive oil. Place two or three in each soup plate before pouring over the soup.

Barley and Vegetable Soup

This soup comes from the Alto Adige region, in Italy's mountainous north. It is thick, nourishing and warming.

Serves 6–8

225g/8oz/1 cup pearl barley, preferably organic
2 litres/3½ pints/9 cups meat stock or water, or a combination of both
45ml/3 tbsp olive oil
2 carrots, finely chopped
2 celery sticks, finely chopped
1 leek, thinly sliced
1 large potato, finely chopped

115g/4oz/½ cup diced ham
1 bay leaf
45ml/3 tbsp chopped fresh parsley
1 small fresh rosemary sprig
salt and ground black pepper
freshly grated Parmesan cheese, to serve

1 Pick over the barley and discard any stones or other particles. Wash the barley in cold water and soak it in cold water for at least 3 hours.

2 Drain the barley and place it in a large saucepan with the stock or water. Bring to the boil, lower the heat and simmer for 1 hour. Skim off any scum.

3 Stir in the oil, all the vegetables and the ham. Add the herbs. If necessary add more water; the ingredients should be covered by at least 2.5cm/1in. Simmer for 1–1½ hours, or until the vegetables and barley are very tender.

4 Season to taste with salt and pepper. Serve hot with grated Parmesan cheese, if desired.

Pasta and Dried Bean Soup

In Italy this soup is made with dried or fresh beans and served hot or at room temperature.

Serves 4–6

300g/11oz/1¼ cups dried borlotti or cannellini beans
400g/14oz can plum tomatoes, chopped, with their juice
3 garlic cloves, crushed
2 bay leaves
coarsely ground black pepper
90ml/6 tbsp olive oil, plus extra to serve

750ml/1¼ pints/3½ cups water
10ml/2 tsp salt
200g/7oz/scant 2 cups ditalini or other small pasta
45ml/3 tbsp chopped fresh parsley
freshly grated Parmesan cheese, to serve

1 Soak the beans in water overnight. Rinse and drain well. Place them in a large saucepan and cover with water. Bring to the boil and cook for 10 minutes. Rinse and drain again.

2 Return the beans to the pan. Add enough water to cover them by 2.5cm/1in. Stir in the coarsely chopped tomatoes with their juice, the garlic, bay leaves, black pepper and the oil. Simmer for 1½–2 hours, or until the beans are tender. Add more water if necessary.

3 Remove the bay leaves. Pass about half of the bean mixture through a food mill, or purée in a food processor. Stir into the pan with the remaining bean mixture. Add the water and bring the soup to the boil.

4 Add the salt and the pasta. Stir, then cook until the pasta is just done. Stir in the parsley. Allow the dish to stand for at least 10 minutes, then serve with extra olive oil and grated Parmesan cheese.

Pasta and Lentil Soup

Small brown lentils are usually used in this wholesome soup, but green lentils may be substituted.

Serves 4–6

225g/8oz/1 cup dried green or brown lentils
90ml/6 tbsp olive oil
50g/2oz/¼ cup ham or salt pork, finely diced
1 onion, finely chopped
1 celery stick, finely chopped
1 carrot, finely chopped
2 litres/3½ pints/9 cups chicken stock or water
1 fresh sage leaf
1 fresh thyme sprig or 1.5ml/¼ tsp dried thyme
salt and ground black pepper
175g/6oz/2½ cups ditalini or other small soup pasta

1 Carefully check the lentils for small stones. Place them in a bowl, cover with cold water and soak for 2–3 hours. Rinse and drain well through a colander.

2 Heat the oil in a large saucepan and sauté the ham or salt pork for 2–3 minutes. Add the onion and cook gently until it softens but does not brown.

3 Stir in the celery and carrot and cook for 5 minutes more, stirring frequently. Add the lentils and stir to coat them evenly in the cooking fats.

4 Pour in the stock or water and the herbs and bring the soup to the boil. Cook over a moderate heat for about 1 hour or until the lentils are tender. Season to taste.

5 Stir in the pasta, and cook until it is just done. Allow the soup to stand for a few minutes before serving.

Pasta and Chick-pea Soup

The addition of a fresh rosemary sprig creates a typically Mediterranean flavour in this soup.

Serves 4–6

200g/7oz/generous 1 cup dried chick-peas
3 garlic cloves, peeled
1 bay leaf
90ml/6 tbsp olive oil
pinch of ground black pepper
50g/2oz/¼ cup diced salt pork, pancetta or bacon
1 fresh rosemary sprig
600ml/1 pint/2½ cups water
150g/5oz/generous 1 cup ditalini or other short hollow pasta
pinch of salt
freshly grated Parmesan cheese, to serve (optional)

1 Soak the chick-peas in water overnight. Rinse well and drain. Place in a large saucepan with water to cover. Boil for 15 minutes. Rinse and drain.

2 Return the chick-peas to the pan. Add water to cover, one garlic clove, the bay leaf, half of the oil and the pinch of pepper.

3 Simmer about 2 hours until tender, adding more water as necessary. Remove the bay leaf. Pass about half the chick-peas through a food mill or purée in a food processor with a little cooking liquid Return the purée to the pan with the rest of the chick-peas and the remaining cooking water.

4 Sauté the diced pork, pancetta or bacon gently in the remaining oil with the rosemary and two garlic cloves until just golden. Discard the rosemary and garlic.

5 Stir the meat with its oils into the chick-pea mixture.

6 Add the water to the chick-peas, and bring to the boil. Adjust the seasoning if necessary. Stir in the pasta, and cook until just *al dente*. Serve with Parmesan cheese, if you wish.

Leek and Potato Soup

If you prefer a smoother textured soup, press the mixture through a sieve or purée it in a food mill.

Serves 4

50g/2oz/4 tbsp butter	*900ml/1½ pints/3¾ cups*
2 leeks, chopped	*chicken or vegetable*
1 small onion, finely	*stock*
chopped	*salt and ground black*
350g/12oz potatoes,	*pepper*
chopped	

1 Heat 25g/1oz/2 tbsp of the butter in a large saucepan and gently cook the leeks and onions for about 7 minutes, stirring occasionally until softened but not browned.

2 Add the chopped potatoes to the pan and cook for 2–3 minutes, stirring occasionally, then add the chicken or vegetable stock and bring to the boil. Cover the pan with a tight-fitting lid and simmer gently for 30–35 minutes, until all the vegetables are very tender.

3 Season to taste with salt and pepper. Remove the pan from the heat and stir in the remaining butter in small pieces until completely melted. Serve the soup hot with warm crusty bread and butter, if you wish.

Cook's Tip
Never use a food processor or blender to purée potatoes as the starch in the vegetable will be broken down and will create an unpleasant gluey consistency.

Scotch Broth

Sustaining and warming, this traditional Scottish soup makes a delicious winter soup anywhere in the world.

Serves 6–8

900g/2lb lean neck of	*1 large carrot, chopped*
lamb, cut into large	*1 turnip, chopped*
even-size chunks	*3 leeks, chopped*
1.75 litres/3 pints/	*½ small white cabbage,*
7½ cups water	*shredded*
1 large onion, chopped	*salt and ground black*
50g/2oz/¼ cup pearl	*pepper*
barley	*chopped fresh parsley, to*
bouquet garni	*garnish*

1 Put the lamb and water into a large saucepan and bring to the boil. Skim off the scum, then stir in the onion, barley and bouquet garni.

2 Bring the soup back to the boil, then partly cover the saucepan and simmer gently for 1 hour. Add the remaining vegetables and season to taste with salt and pepper. Bring to the boil, partly cover again and simmer for about 35 minutes until the vegetables are tender.

3 Remove any surplus fat from the top of the soup, then serve hot, sprinkled with chopped parsley.

Country Vegetable Soup

To ring the changes, vary the vegetables according to what you like and what is in season.

Serves 4

50g/2oz/4 tbsp butter
1 onion, chopped
2 leeks, sliced
2 celery sticks, sliced
2 carrots, sliced
2 small turnips, chopped
4 ripe tomatoes, skinned and chopped
1 litre/1¾ pints/4 cups chicken or vegetable stock
bouquet garni
115g/4oz/1 cup green beans, chopped
salt and ground black pepper
chopped fresh herbs such as tarragon, thyme, chives and parsley, to garnish

1 Heat the butter in a large saucepan and cook the onion and leeks gently until soft but not coloured.

2 Add the celery, carrots and turnips and cook them for about 3–4 minutes, stirring occasionally. Stir in the tomatoes and stock, add the bouquet garni and simmer the vegetables gently for about 20 minutes.

3 Add the beans to the soup and continue to cook until all the vegetables are tender. Season to taste with salt and pepper and serve garnished with chopped herbs.

Split Pea and Bacon Soup

This soup is also called "London Particular", because of the city's smog. The fogs in turn were named "pea-soupers".

Serves 4

15g/½oz/1 tbsp butter
115g/4oz smoked back bacon, chopped
1 large onion, chopped
1 carrot, chopped
1 celery stick, chopped
75g/3oz/scant ½ cup split peas
1.2 litres/2 pints/5 cups chicken stock
2 thick slices firm bread, buttered and without crusts
2 slices streaky bacon
salt and ground black pepper

1 Heat the butter in a saucepan and cook the back bacon until the fat runs. Stir in the onion, carrot and celery and cook for 2–3 minutes.

2 Add the split peas, followed by the stock. Bring to the boil, stirring occasionally, then cover with a tight-fitting lid and simmer for 45–60 minutes.

3 Meanwhile, preheat the oven to 180°C/350°F/Gas 4. Bake the bread for about 20 minutes, until crisp and brown, then cut into dice.

4 Grill the streaky bacon until very crisp, then chop finely.

5 When the soup is ready, season to taste and serve hot with the chopped bacon and croûtons scattered on each portion.

Smoked Haddock and Potato Soup

This soup's traditional name is "cullen skink". A "cullen" is a town's port district and "skink" means stock or broth.

Serves 6

1 Finnan haddock (about 350g/12oz)	600ml/1 pint/2½ cups milk
1 onion, chopped	40g/1½oz/3 tbsp butter
bouquet garni	salt and ground black pepper
900ml/1½ pints/3¾ cups water	snipped fresh chives, to garnish
500g/1¼lb potatoes, quartered	

1 Put the haddock, onion, bouquet garni and water into a large saucepan and bring to the boil. Skim the scum from the surface, then cover the pan with a tight-fitting lid. Reduce the heat and poach for about 10–15 minutes, or until the haddock flakes easily.

2 Lift the poached fish from the pan using a fish slice and remove the skin and bones. Flake the flesh and reserve. Return the skin and bones to the pan and simmer, uncovered, for 30 minutes.

3 Strain the fish stock and return to the pan, then add the potatoes and simmer for about 25 minutes or until tender. Remove the potatoes from the pan using a slotted spoon. Add the milk to the pan and bring to the boil.

4 Meanwhile, mash the potatoes with the butter, then whisk into the milk in the pan until thick and creamy. Add the flaked fish to the pan and adjust the seasoning. Sprinkle with chives and serve at once with crusty bread, if you wish.

Cook's Tip
If Finnan haddock is not available, ordinary smoked haddock may be substituted.

Mulligatawny Soup

Choose red split lentils for the best colour, although green or brown lentils could also be used.

Serves 4

50g/2oz/4 tbsp butter or 60ml/4 tbsp oil	6 black peppercorns, lightly crushed
2 large chicken joints (about 35g/12oz each)	50g/2oz/¼ cup lentils
1 onion, chopped	900ml/1½ pints/3¾ cups chicken stock
1 carrot, chopped	40g/1½oz/¼ cup sultanas
1 small turnip, chopped	salt and ground black pepper
about 15ml/1 tbsp curry powder, to taste	
4 cloves	

1 Heat the butter or oil in a large saucepan and brown the chicken over a brisk heat. Transfer the chicken to a plate.

2 Add the onion, carrot and turnip to the pan and cook, stirring occasionally, until lightly coloured. Stir in the curry powder, cloves and peppercorns and cook for 1–2 minutes, then add the lentils.

3 Pour the stock into the pan, bring to the boil, then add the sultanas and chicken and any juices from the plate. Cover and simmer gently for about 1¼ hours.

4 Remove the chicken from the pan and discard the skin and bones. Chop the flesh into bite-size chunks, return to the soup and reheat. Season to taste with salt and pepper before serving the soup piping hot.

Smoked Haddock Pâté

This easily-prepared pâté is made with Arbroath Smokies, small haddock which have been salted and hot-smoked.

Serves 6

3 large Arbroath Smokies (about 225g/8oz each)
275g/10oz/1¼ cups medium-fat soft cheese
3 eggs, beaten
30–45ml/2–3 tbsp lemon juice

pinch of freshly ground black pepper
fresh chervil sprigs, to garnish
lemon wedges and lettuce leaves, to serve

1 Preheat the oven to 160°C/325°F/Gas 3. Generously butter six individual ramekin dishes.

2 Lay the smokies in a baking dish and heat through in the oven for 10 minutes. Carefully remove the skin and bones from the smokies, then flake the flesh into a bowl.

3 Mash the fish with a fork and work in the cheese, then the eggs. Add the lemon juice and season with pepper to taste.

4 Divide the fish mixture among the six ramekins and place in a roasting tin. Pour hot water into the roasting tin to come halfway up the dishes. Bake for 30 minutes, until just set.

5 Allow to cool for 2–3 minutes, then run a knife point around the edge of each dish and invert on to a warmed plate. Garnish with fresh chervil sprigs and serve with the lemon wedges and lettuce.

Spinach, Bacon and Prawn Salad

Serve this hot salad with plenty of crusty bread to mop up the delicious juices.

Serves 4

105ml/7 tbsp olive oil
30ml/2 tbsp sherry vinegar
2 garlic cloves, finely chopped
5ml/1 tsp Dijon mustard
12 cooked king prawns, in the shell

115g/4oz rindless streaky bacon, cut into strips
115g/4oz/1 cup fresh young spinach leaves
½ head oak leaf lettuce, roughly torn
salt and ground black pepper

1 To make the dressing, whisk together 90ml/6 tbsp of the olive oil with the vinegar, garlic, mustard and seasoning in a small saucepan. Heat gently until thickened slightly, then keep warm.

2 Carefully peel the king prawns, leaving their tails intact. Set aside until needed.

3 Heat the remaining oil in a frying pan and fry the bacon until golden and crisp, stirring occasionally. Add the prawns and stir-fry for a few minutes until warmed through.

4 While the bacon and prawns are cooking, arrange the spinach and torn oak leaf lettuce leaves on four individual serving plates.

5 Spoon the bacon and prawns on to the leaves, then pour over the hot dressing. Serve at once.

Cook's Tip
Sherry vinegar lends its pungent flavour to this delicious salad. It is readily available in large supermarkets or delicatessens. However, red or white wine vinegar could be substituted if you prefer.

Hot Tomato and Mozzarella Salad

A quick, easy starter with a Mediterranean flavour. It can be prepared in advance, then grilled just before serving.

Serves 4

450g/1lb plum tomatoes, sliced
225g/8oz mozzarella cheese
1 red onion, chopped
4–6 pieces sun-dried tomatoes in oil, drained and chopped
60ml/4 tbsp olive oil
5ml/1 tsp red wine vinegar

2.5ml/½ tsp Dijon mustard
60ml/4 tbsp mixed chopped fresh herbs such as basil, parsley, oregano and chives
salt and ground black pepper
fresh herb sprigs, to garnish (optional)

1 Arrange the sliced tomatoes and mozzarella in circles in four shallow flameproof dishes. Scatter over the onion and sun-dried tomatoes. Whisk together the olive oil, vinegar, mustard, chopped herbs and seasoning. Pour over the salads.

2 Place the salads under a hot grill for 4–5 minutes, until the mozzarella starts to melt. Grind over plenty of black pepper and serve garnished with fresh herb sprigs, if you wish.

Asparagus with Tarragon Butter

Eating fresh asparagus with your fingers is correct but messy, so serve this dish with finger bowls.

Serves 4

500g/1¼lb fresh asparagus
115g/4oz/½ cup butter
30ml/2 tbsp chopped fresh tarragon

15ml/1 tbsp chopped fresh parsley
grated rind of ½ lemon
15ml/1 tbsp lemon juice
salt and black pepper

1 Trim the woody ends from the asparagus spears, then tie them into four equal bundles.

2 Place the bundles of asparagus in a large frying pan with about 2.5cm/1in boiling water. Cover with a lid and cook for about 6–8 minutes, until the asparagus is tender but still firm. Drain well and discard the strings.

3 Arrange the asparagus spears on four warmed serving plates. Make the tarragon butter by creaming together the remaining ingredients; heat it gently and pour it over the asparagus. Serve at once.

Devilled Kidneys

This tangy dish makes an impressive starter, although it is sometimes served as an English breakfast dish.

Serves 4

Mix 10ml/2 tbsp Worcestershire sauce, 15ml/1 tbsp each English mustard, lemon juice and tomato purée. Season with cayenne pepper and salt. Melt 40g/1½oz/3 tbsp butter, add 1 chopped shallot; cook until softened. Stir in 8 prepared lambs' kidneys; cook for 3 minutes on each side. Coat with the sauce; serve sprinkled with chopped parsley.

Egg and Tomato Salad with Crab

You could also adjust the quantities in this tasty salad to make a quick, light and healthy weekday meal.

Serves 4
1 round lettuce
2 x 200g/7oz cans
   crabmeat, drained
4 hard-boiled eggs, sliced
16 cherry tomatoes,
   halved
½ green pepper, seeded
   and thinly sliced
6 stoned black olives,
   sliced

250g/8fl oz/1 cup
   mayonnaise
10ml/2 tsp fresh lemon
   juice
½ green pepper, seeded
   and finely chopped
5ml/1 tsp prepared
   horseradish
5ml/1 tsp Worcestershire
   sauce

For the dressing
45ml/3 tbsp chilli sauce

1 To make the dressing, place all the ingredients in a bowl and mix well. Set aside in a cool place.

2 Line four plates with the lettuce leaves. Mound the crabmeat in the centre. Arrange the eggs around the outside with the tomatoes on top.

3 Spoon some of the dressing over the crabmeat. Arrange the green pepper slices on top and sprinkle with the olives. Serve immediately with the remaining dressing.

Stuffed Mushrooms

These flavoursome mushrooms may also be served as an accompaniment to a main course.

Serves 4
275g/10oz spinach, stalks
   removed
400g/14oz medium cap
   mushrooms
25g/1oz/2 tbsp butter,
   plus extra for
   brushing
25g/1oz bacon, chopped
½ small onion, chopped

75g/5 tbsp double cream
about 60ml/4 tbsp grated
   Cheddar cheese
30ml/2 tbsp fresh
   breadcrumbs
salt and ground black
   pepper
fresh parsley sprigs, to
   garnish

1 Preheat the oven to 190°C/375°F/Gas 5. Butter a baking dish. Wash but do not dry the spinach. Place it in a saucepan and cook, stirring occasionally, until wilted.

2 Place the spinach in a colander and squeeze out as much liquid as possible. Chop finely. Snap the stalks from the mushrooms and chop the stalks finely.

3 Melt the butter in a pan and cook the bacon, onion and mushroom stalks for about 5 minutes. Stir in the spinach, cook for a moment or two, then remove the pan from the heat, stir in the cream and season to taste with salt and pepper.

4 Brush the mushroom caps with melted butter, then place, gills uppermost, in a single layer in the baking dish.

5 Divide the spinach mixture among the mushrooms. Mix together the cheese and breadcrumbs, sprinkle over the mushrooms, then bake for about 20 minutes until the mushrooms are tender. Serve warm, garnished with parsley.

Cook's Tip
Squeeze out all the excess water from the cooked spinach, otherwise the stuffing will be too soggy.

Pears and Stilton

Stilton is the classic British blue cheese, but you could use blue Cheshire instead, or even Gorgonzola.

Serves 4

4 ripe pears	**For the dressing**
75g/3oz blue Stilton cheese	45ml/3 tbsp light olive oil
50g/2oz/3 tbsp curd cheese	15ml/1 tbsp lemon juice
pinch of ground black pepper	10ml/½ tbsp toasted poppy seeds
fresh watercress sprigs, to garnish	salt and ground black pepper

1 First make the dressing. Place the olive oil, lemon juice, poppy seeds and seasoning in a screw-topped jar and shake together until emulsified.

2 Cut the pears in half lengthways, then scoop out the cores and cut away the calyx from the rounded end.

3 Beat together the Stilton, curd cheese and a little pepper. Divide this mixture among the cavities in the pears.

4 Shake the dressing to mix it again, then spoon it over the pears. Serve garnished with watercress.

Cook's Tip
The pears should be lightly chilled in the fridge before they are used in this dish.

Potted Shrimps

The brown shrimps traditionally used for potting are very fiddly to peel. Use peeled cooked prawns if you prefer.

Serves 4

225g/8oz/2 cups shelled shrimps	fresh dill sprigs, to garnish
225g/8oz/1 cup butter	lemon wedges and thin slices of brown bread and butter, to serve
pinch of ground mace	
salt and cayenne pepper	

1 Chop a quarter of the shrimps. Melt half of the butter slowly, carefully skimming off any foam that rises to the surface.

2 Stir all the shrimps, the mace, salt and cayenne pepper into the saucepan and heat gently without boiling. Pour the shrimp and butter mixture into four individual pots and leave it aside to cool.

3 Heat the remaining butter in a clean small pan, then carefully spoon the clear butter over the shrimps, leaving behind the sediment.

4 Leave until the butter is almost set, then place a dill sprig in the centre of each pot. Leave to set completely, then cover and chill in the fridge.

5 Transfer the shrimps to room temperature 30 minutes before serving with lemon wedges and thin slices of brown bread and butter.

Leek Terrine with Deli Meats

This attractive starter is simple yet looks spectacular. It can be made a day ahead.

Serves 6
20 – 24 small young leeks
about 225g/8oz mixed
  sliced meats, such as
  Parma ham, coppa
  and pancetta
50g/2oz/½ cup walnuts,
  toasted and chopped

For the dressing
60ml/4 tbsp walnut oil
60ml/4 tbsp olive oil
30ml/2 tbsp white wine
  vinegar
5ml/1 tsp wholegrain
  mustard
salt and ground black
  pepper

1 Cut off the roots and most of the green part from the leeks. Wash them thoroughly under cold running water.

2 Bring a large saucepan of salted water to the boil. Add the leeks, bring the water back to the boil, then simmer for 6 – 8 minutes, until the leeks are just tender. Drain well.

3 Fill a 450g/1lb loaf tin with the leeks, placing them alternately head to tail and sprinkling each layer as you go with salt and pepper.

4 Put another loaf tin inside the first and gently press down on the leeks. Carefully invert both tins and let any water drain out. Place one or two weights on top of the tins and chill the terrine for at least 4 hours, or overnight.

5 To make the dressing, whisk together the walnut and olive oils, vinegar and mustard in a small bowl. Season to taste.

6 Carefully turn out the terrine on to a board and cut into slices using a large sharp knife. Lay the slices of leek terrine on serving plates and arrange the slices of meat alongside.

7 Spoon the dressing over the slices of terrine and scatter the chopped walnuts over the top. Serve at once.

Garlic Prawns in Filo Tartlets

Tartlets made with crisp layers of filo pastry and filled with garlic prawns make a tempting and unusual starter.

Serves 4
For the tartlets
50g/2oz/4 tbsp butter,
  melted
2 – 3 large sheets filo
  pastry

For the filling
115g/4oz/½ cup butter
2 – 3 garlic cloves,
  crushed

1 fresh red chilli, seeded
  and chopped
350g/12oz/3 cups peeled,
  cooked prawns
30ml/2 tbsp chopped
  fresh parsley or
  snipped fresh chives
salt and ground black
  pepper

1 Preheat the oven to 200°C/400°F/Gas 6. Brush four individual 7.5cm/3in flan tins with melted butter.

2 Cut the filo pastry into twelve 10cm/4in squares and brush with the melted butter.

3 Place three squares inside each tin, overlapping them at slight angles and carefully frilling the edges and points while forming a good hollow in each centre. Bake the pastry for 10 – 15 minutes, until crisp and golden. Cool slightly and remove from the tins.

4 To make the filling, melt the butter in a large frying pan, fry the garlic, chilli and prawns for 1 – 2 minutes to warm through. Stir in the parsley or chives and season to taste with salt and pepper.

5 Spoon the prawn filling into the tartlets and serve at once.

Cook's Tip
Use fresh filo pastry rather than frozen, then simply wrap and freeze any leftover sheets.

Smoked Salmon and Dill Blinis

Blinis, small pancakes of Russian origin, are so easy to make, yet they make a sophisticated dinner party starter.

Serves 4

115g/4oz/1 cup
   buckwheat flour
115g/4oz/1 cup plain
   flour
pinch of salt
15ml/1 tbsp easy-blend
   dried yeast
2 eggs
350ml/12fl oz/1½ cups
   warm milk

15ml/1 tbsp melted
   butter, plus extra for
   shallow-frying
150ml/¼ pint/⅔ cup
   crème fraîche
45ml/3 tbsp chopped
   fresh dill
225g/8oz smoked salmon,
   thinly sliced
fresh dill sprigs, to
   garnish

1 Mix together the buckwheat and plain flours in a large bowl with the salt. Sprinkle in the yeast and mix well. Separate one of the eggs. Whisk together the whole egg and the yolk, the warm milk and the melted butter.

2 Pour the egg mixture on to the flour mixture. Beat well to form a smooth batter. Cover with clear film and leave to rise in a warm place for 1–2 hours.

3 Whisk the remaining egg white in a large bowl until stiff peaks form, then gently fold into the batter.

4 Preheat a heavy-based frying pan or griddle and brush with melted butter. Drop tablespoons of the batter on to the pan, spacing them well apart. Cook for about 40 seconds, until bubbles appear on the surface.

5 Flip over the blinis and cook for 30 seconds on the other side. Wrap in foil and keep warm in a low oven. Repeat with the remaining mixture, buttering the pan each time.

6 Combine the crème fraîche and dill. Serve the blinis topped with the salmon and cream. Garnish with dill sprigs.

Celeriac Fritters with Mustard Dip

The combination of the hot, crispy fritters and the cold mustard dip is extremely tasty.

Serves 4

1 egg
115g/4oz/1 cup ground
   almonds
45ml/3 tbsp freshly grated
   Parmesan cheese
45ml/3 tbsp chopped fresh
   parsley
1 celeriac (about 450g/1lb)
squeeze of lemon juice
oil, for deep-frying

For the mustard dip
150ml/¼ pint/⅔ cup
   soured cream
15–30ml/1–2 tbsp
   wholegrain mustard
salt and ground black
   pepper
sea salt flakes, for
   sprinkling

1 Beat the egg well and pour into a shallow dish. Mix together the almonds, grated Parmesan and parsley in a separate dish. Season to taste, then set aside.

2 Peel and cut the celeriac into strips about 1cm/½in wide and 5cm/2in long. Drop them immediately into a bowl of water with a little lemon juice added to prevent them from becoming discoloured.

3 Heat the oil in a deep-fat fryer to 180°C/350°F. Drain and then pat dry half the celeriac chips. Dip them into the beaten egg, then into the ground almond mixture, making sure that the pieces are coated completely and evenly.

4 Deep-fry the celeriac fritters, a few at a time, for about 2–3 minutes until golden. Drain on kitchen paper and keep warm while you cook the remainder.

5 To make the mustard dip, mix together the soured cream, mustard and sea salt to taste. Spoon into a small serving bowl.

6 Heap the celeriac fritters on to warmed individual serving plates. Sprinkle with sea salt flakes and serve at once with the mustard dip.

Chicken Liver Pâté with Marsala

This is a really quick and simple pâté to make, yet it has a delicious – and quite sophisticated – flavour.

Serves 4
350g/12oz chicken livers, defrosted if frozen
225g/8oz/1 cup butter
2 garlic cloves, crushed
15ml/1 tbsp Marsala
5ml/1 tsp chopped sage

salt and ground black pepper
8 fresh sage leaves, to garnish
Melba toast, to serve

1 Pick over the chicken livers, then rinse and dry with kitchen paper. Melt 25g/1oz/2 tbsp of the butter in a frying pan and fry the chicken livers with the garlic over a moderate heat for about 5 minutes, or until they are firm but still pink in their centres.

2 Transfer the livers to a food processor or blender using a slotted spoon. Add the Marsala and chopped sage.

3 Melt 150g/5oz/generous ½ cup of the remaining butter in the frying pan, stirring to loosen any sediment, then pour into the food processor or blender and process until smooth. Season well with salt and pepper.

4 Spoon the pâté into four individual pots and smooth the surface. Melt the remaining butter in a separate pan and pour over the pâtés. Garnish with sage leaves and chill in the fridge until set. Serve with triangles of Melba toast.

Cook's Tip
This delicious pâté contains Marsala, a dark, sweet, pungent dessert wine made in Sicily. If this is not available, you could substitute either brandy or a medium-dry sherry.

Salmon Rillettes

A variation on the traditional pork rillette, this starter is much easier to make.

Serves 6
350g/12oz salmon fillets
175g/6oz/¾ cup butter
1 celery stick, finely chopped
1 leek, white part only, finely chopped
1 bay leaf
150ml/¼ pint/⅔ cup dry white wine

115g/4oz smoked salmon trimmings
large pinch of ground mace
60ml/4 tbsp fromage frais
salt and ground black pepper ·
salad leaves, to serve

1 Lightly season the salmon with salt and pepper. Melt 25g/1oz/2 tbsp of the butter in a frying pan and cook the celery and leek for about 5 minutes. Add the salmon and bay leaf and pour over the wine. Cover with a tight-fitting lid and cook for about 15 minutes until the fish is tender.

2 Strain the cooking liquid into a saucepan and boil until reduced to 30ml/2 tbsp. Cool. Melt 50g/2oz/4 tbsp of the remaining butter and gently cook the smoked salmon until it turns pale pink. Leave to cool.

3 Remove the skin and any bones from the salmon fillets. Flake the flesh into a bowl and add the cooking liquid.

4 Beat in the remaining butter, the mace and fromage frais. Break up the smoked salmon trimmings and fold into the mixture with the pan juices. Taste and adjust the seasoning.

5 Spoon the salmon mixture into a dish or terrine and smooth the top level. Cover and chill in the fridge.

6 To serve the salmon rillettes, shape the mixture into oval quenelles using two dessert spoons and arrange on individual plates with the salad leaves. Accompany with brown bread or oatcakes, if you wish.

Mexican Dip with Chips

Omit the fresh chilli and the chilli powder if you prefer a dip to have a mild flavour.

Serves 4

2 medium-ripe avocados
juice of 1 lime
½ small onion, finely
   chopped
½ red chilli, seeded and
   finely chopped
3 tomatoes, skinned,
   seeded and finely
   diced
30ml/2 tbsp chopped
   fresh coriander
30ml/2 tbsp soured
   cream
salt and ground black
   pepper

15 ml/1 tbsp soured
   cream and a pinch of
   cayenne pepper, to
   garnish

For the chips
150g/5oz bag tortilla
   chips
30ml/2 tbsp finely grated
   mature Cheddar
   cheese
1.5ml/¼ tsp chilli powder
10ml/2 tsp chopped fresh
   parsley

1 Halve and stone the avocados and remove the flesh with a spoon, scraping the shells well.

2 Place the flesh in a blender or food processor with the remaining ingredients, reserving the soured cream and cayenne pepper. Process until fairly smooth. Transfer to a bowl, cover and chill in the fridge until required.

3 To make the chips, preheat the grill, then scatter the tortilla chips over a baking sheet. Mix the grated cheese with the chilli powder, sprinkle over the chips and grill for about 1–2 minutes, until the cheese has melted.

4 Remove the avocado dip from the fridge, top with the soured cream and sprinkle with cayenne pepper. Serve the bowl on a plate surrounded by the tortilla chips, garnished with the chopped fresh parsley.

French Goat's Cheese Salad

The deep, tangy flavours of this salad would also make it satisfying enough for a light meal, if you wished.

Serves 4

200g/7oz bag prepared
   mixed salad leaves
4 rashers rindless back
   bacon
16 thin slices French
   bread
115g/4oz/½ cup full-fat
   goat's cheese

For the dressing
60ml/4 tbsp olive oil
15ml/1 tbsp tarragon
   vinegar
10ml/2 tsp walnut oil
5ml/1 tsp Dijon mustard
5ml/1 tsp wholegrain
   mustard

1 Preheat the grill to a moderate heat. Rinse and dry the salad leaves, then arrange in four individual bowls. Place the ingredients for the dressing in a screw-top jar, shake together well and reserve.

2 Lay the bacon rashers on a board, then stretch with the back of a knife and cut each into four. Roll each piece up and grill for about 2–3 minutes.

3 Meanwhile, slice the goat's cheese into eight and halve each slice. Top each slice of bread with a piece of goat's cheese and pop under the grill. Turn over the bacon and continue cooking with the goat's cheese toasts until the cheese is golden and bubbling.

4 Arrange the bacon rolls and toasts on top of the prepared salad leaves, shake the dressing well and pour a little of the dressing over each one.

Chinese Garlic Mushrooms

High in protein and low in fat, marinated tofu makes an unusual stuffing for these mushrooms.

Serves 4

8 large open mushrooms	200g/7oz can sweetcorn,
3 spring onions, sliced	drained
1 garlic clove, crushed	10ml/2 tsp sesame oil
30ml/2 tbsp oyster sauce	salt and ground black
5g/10oz packet marinated	pepper
tofu, diced	

1 Preheat the oven to 200°C/400°F/Gas 6. Finely chop the mushroom stalks and mix with the next three ingredients.

2 Stir in the diced marinated tofu and sweetcorn, season well, then spoon the filling into the mushrooms.

3 Brush the edges of the mushrooms with the sesame oil. Arrange them in a baking dish and bake for 12–15 minutes, until the mushrooms are just tender, then serve at once.

Tomato Cheese Tarts

These crisp little tartlets are easier to make than they look and are best eaten fresh from the oven.

Serves 4

2 sheets filo pastry	handful of fresh basil
1 egg white	leaves
115g/4oz/½ cup	3 small tomatoes, sliced
skimmed milk soft	salt and ground black
cheese	pepper

1 Preheat the oven to 200°C/400°F/Gas 5. Brush the sheets of filo pastry lightly with egg white and cut into sixteen 10cm/4in squares.

2 Layer the squares in twos, in eight patty tins. Spoon the cheese into the pastry cases. Season with salt and ground black pepper and top with basil leaves.

3 Arrange the tomato slices on the tarts, add seasoning and bake for 10–12 minutes, until golden. Serve warm.

Ricotta and Borlotti Bean Pâté

A lovely light yet full-flavoured pâté that can be enjoyed by vegetarians.

Serves 4

Process 400g/14oz borlotti beans, 175g/6oz/¾ cup Ricotta cheese, 1 garlic clove, 60ml/4 tbsp melted butter, juice of ½ lemon and seasoning. Add 30ml/2 tbsp chopped fresh parsley and 15ml/1 tbsp fresh thyme or dill; blend. Spoon into one serving dish or four lightly-oiled and base-lined ramekins. Chill. Garnish with salad leaves and serve with warm crusty bread or toast. If serving the pâté individually, turn each one out of its ramekin on to a plate, then remove the paper. Top the pâté with radish slices and sprigs of dill.

Avocados with Tangy Topping

Lightly grilled with a tasty topping of red onions and cheese, this dish makes a delightful starter.

Serves 4

15ml/1 tbsp sunflower oil	15ml/1 tbsp chopped
1 small red onion, sliced	fresh basil, marjoram
1 garlic clove, crushed	or parsley
dash of Worcestershire	50g/2oz Lancashire or
sauce	mozzarella cheese,
2 ripe avocados, stoned	sliced
and halved	salt and ground black
2 small tomatoes, sliced	pepper

1 Heat the oil in a frying pan and gently fry the onion and garlic for about 5 minutes until just softened. Shake in a little Worcestershire sauce.

2 Preheat a grill. Place the avocado halves on the grill pan and spoon the onions into the centre.

3 Divide the tomato slices and fresh herbs between the four halves and top each one with the cheese.

4 Season well with salt and pepper and grill until the cheese melts and starts to brown.

Bruschetta with Goat's Cheese

Simple to prepare in advance, this appetising dish can be served as a starter or at a finger buffet.

Serves 4–6

For the tapenade

400g/14oz can black	45–60ml/3–4 tbsp olive
olives, stoned and	oil
finely chopped	salt and ground black
50g/2oz sun-dried	pepper
tomatoes in oil,	
chopped	**For the bases**
30ml/2 tbsp capers,	12 slices ciabatta or other
chopped	crusty bread
15ml/1 tbsp green	olive oil, for brushing
peppercorns, in brine,	2 garlic cloves, halved
crushed	115g/4oz/½ cup soft
2 garlic cloves, crushed	goat's cheese or other
45ml/3 tbsp chopped	full-fat soft cheese
fresh basil or 5ml/	mixed fresh herb sprigs,
1 tsp dried basil	to garnish

1 To make the tapenade, mix all the tapenade ingredients together and check the seasoning. It should not need too much. Allow to marinate overnight, if possible.

2 To make the bruschetta, grill both sides of the bread lightly until golden. Brush one side with oil and then rub with a cut clove of garlic. Set aside until ready to serve.

3 Spread the bruschetta with the cheese, roughing it up with a fork, and spoon the tapenade on top. Garnish with sprigs of mixed fresh herbs.

Cook's Tip
Grill the bruschetta on a barbecue for a delicious smoky flavour if you are making this starter in the summer.

Grilled Garlic Mussels

Use a combination of fresh herbs, such as oregano, basil
and flat-leaf parsley.

Serves 4

1.5kg/3 – 3½lb live
  mussels
120ml/4fl oz/½ cup dry
  white wine
50g/2oz/4 tbsp butter
2 shallots, finely chopped
2 garlic cloves, crushed
50g/2oz/½ cup dried
  white breadcrumbs

60ml/4 tbsp mixed
  chopped fresh herbs
30ml/2 tbsp freshly
  grated Parmesan
  cheese
salt and ground black
  pepper
fresh basil leaves, to
  garnish

1 Scrub the mussels well under cold running water. Remove
the beards and discard any mussels that are open. Place in a
large saucepan with the wine. Cover and cook over a high
heat, shaking the pan occasionally for 5–8 minutes, until the
mussels have opened.

2 Strain the mussels and reserve the cooking liquid. Discard
any mussels that remain closed. Allow them to cool slightly,
then remove and discard the top half of each shell.

3 Melt the butter in a pan and fry the shallots until softened.
Add the garlic and cook for 1–2 minutes. Stir in the dried
breadcrumbs and cook, stirring until lightly browned.
Remove the pan from the heat and stir in the herbs. Moisten
with a little of the reserved mussel liquid, then season to taste
with salt and pepper.

4 Spoon the breadcrumb mixture over the mussels and
arrange on baking sheets. Sprinkle with the grated Parmesan.

5 Cook the mussels under a hot grill in batches for about
2 minutes, until the topping is crisp and golden. Keep the
cooked mussels warm in a low oven while grilling the
remainder. Garnish with fresh basil leaves and serve hot.

Nut Patties with Mango Relish

These spicy patties can be made in advance, if you wish,
and reheated just before serving.

Serves 4–6

175g/6oz/1½ cups finely
  chopped roasted and
  salted cashew nuts
175g/6oz/1½ cups finely
  chopped walnuts
1 small onion, finely
  chopped
1 garlic clove, crushed
1 green chilli, seeded and
  chopped
5ml/1 tsp ground cumin
10ml/2 tsp ground
  coriander
2 carrots, coarsely grated
50g/2oz/1 cup fresh
  white breadcrumbs
30ml/2 tbsp chopped
  fresh coriander

15ml/1 tbsp lemon juice
1–2 eggs, beaten
salt and ground black
  pepper
fresh coriander sprigs, to
  garnish

For the relish

1 large ripe mango, cut
  into small dice
1 small onion, cut into
  slivers
5ml/1 tsp grated fresh
  root ginger
pinch of salt
15ml/1 tbsp sesame oil
5ml/1 tsp black mustard
  seeds

1 Preheat the oven to 180°C/350°F/Gas 4. In a bowl, mix
together the nuts, onion, garlic, chilli, spices, breadcrumbs,
carrots, chopped coriander and seasoning.

2 Sprinkle the lemon juice over the mixture and add enough
of the beaten egg to bind the mixture together. Shape the
mixture into twelve balls, then flatten slightly into round
patties. Place them on a lightly greased baking sheet and
bake for about 25 minutes, until golden brown.

3 To make the relish, mix together the mango, onion, fresh
root ginger and salt. Heat the oil in a small frying pan and fry
the mustard seeds for a few seconds until they pop, then stir
into the mango mixture. Serve with the nut patties, garnished
with coriander.

Dim Sum

A popular Chinese snack, these tiny dumplings are now fashionable in many specialist restaurants.

Serves 4

For the dough
150g/5oz/1¼ cups plain
   flour
50ml/2fl oz/¼ cup
   boiling water
25ml/1fl oz/⅛ cup cold
   water
7.5ml/½ tbsp vegetable
   oil

For the filling
75g/3oz minced pork

45ml/3 tbsp chopped
   canned bamboo shoots
7.5ml/½ tbsp light soy
   sauce
5ml/1 tsp dry sherry
5ml/1 tsp demerara sugar
2.5ml/½ tsp sesame oil
5ml/1 tsp cornflour
mixed fresh lettuce leaves
   such as iceberg, frisée
   or Webbs

1 To make the dough, sift the flour into a bowl. Stir in the boiling water, then the cold water together with the oil. Mix to form a ball and knead until smooth. Divide the mixture into sixteen equal pieces and shape into circles.

2 For the filling, mix together the pork, bamboo shoots, soy sauce, sherry, sugar and oil. Then stir in the cornflour.

3 Place a little of the filling in the centre of each dim sum circle. Carefully pinch the edges of the dough together to form little "purses".

4 Line a steamer with a damp dish towel. Place the dim sum in the steamer and steam for 5–10 minutes. Serve on a bed of lettuce with soy sauce, spring onion curls, sliced red chilli and prawn crackers, if you wish.

Cook's Tip
As an alternative filling, substitute the pork with cooked, peeled prawns.

Sesame Prawn Toasts

Serve about four of these delicious toasts per person with a soy sauce for dipping.

Serves 6
175g/6oz/1½ cups peeled,
   cooked prawns
2 spring onions, finely
   chopped
2.5cm/1in piece fresh root
   ginger, peeled and
   grated
2 garlic cloves, crushed
30ml/2 tbsp cornflour

10ml/2 tsp soy sauce,
   plus extra for dipping
6 slices stale bread from a
   small loaf, without
   crusts
40g/1½ oz sesame seeds
about 600ml/1 pint/2½
   cups vegetable oil, for
   deep-frying

1 Place the prawns, spring onions, ginger and garlic cloves into a food processor fitted with a metal blade. Add the cornflour and soy sauce and work the mixture into a paste.

2 Spread the bread slices evenly with the paste and cut into triangles. Sprinkle with the sesame seeds, making sure they stick to the bread. Chill in the fridge for 30 minutes.

3 Heat the oil for deep-frying in a large heavy-based saucepan until it reaches a temperature of 190°C/375°F. Using a slotted spoon, lower the toasts into the oil, sesame-seed side down, and fry for 2–3 minutes, turning over for the last minute. Drain on absorbent kitchen paper. Keep the toasts warm whilst frying the remainder.

4 Serve the toasts with soy sauce for dipping.

English Ploughman's Pâté

This is a thoroughly modern interpretation of a traditional ploughman's lunch.

Serves 4

50g/2oz/3 tbsp full-fat soft cheese	15ml/1 tbsp apricot chutney
50g/2oz/½ cup grated Caerphilly cheese	30ml/2 tbsp butter, melted
50g/2oz/½ cup grated Double Gloucester cheese	30ml/2 tbsp snipped fresh chives
4 pickled silverskin onions, drained and finely chopped	4 slices soft-grain bread salt and ground black pepper watercress and cherry tomatoes, to serve

1 Mix together the soft cheese, grated cheeses, onions, chutney and butter in a bowl and season lightly with salt and ground black pepper.

2 Spoon the mixture on to a sheet of greaseproof paper and roll up into a cylinder, smoothing the mixture into a roll with your hands. Scrunch the ends of the paper together and twist them to seal. Place in the freezer for about 30 minutes, until the parcel is just firm.

3 Spread the chives on a plate, then unwrap the chilled cheese pâté. Roll in the chives until evenly coated. Wrap in clear film and chill for 10 minutes in the fridge.

4 Preheat the grill. To make Melba toast, lightly toast the bread on both sides. Cut off the crusts and slice each piece in half horizontally. Cut each half into two triangles. Grill, untoasted side up, until golden and curled at the edges.

5 Slice the pâté into rounds with a sharp knife and serve three or four rounds per person with the Melba toast, watercress and cherry tomatoes.

Golden Cheese Puffs

Serve these deep-fried puffs – called *aigrettes* in France – with a fruity chutney and salad.

Makes 8

50g/2oz/½ cup plain flour	2.5ml/½ tsp mustard powder
15g/½oz/1 tbsp butter	pinch of cayenne pepper
1 egg plus 1 egg yolk	oil, for deep-frying
50g/2oz/½ cup finely grated mature Cheddar cheese	salt and ground black pepper
15ml/1 tbsp grated Parmesan cheese	mango chutney and green salad, to serve

1 Sift the flour on to a square of greaseproof paper and set aside. Place the butter and 150ml/⅔ pint/⅔ cup water in a saucepan and heat gently until the butter has melted.

2 Bring the liquid to the boil and tip in the flour all at once. Remove from the heat and stir well with a wooden spoon until the mixture begins to leave the sides of the pan and forms a ball. Allow to cool slightly.

3 Beat the egg and egg yolk together in a bowl with a fork and then gradually add to the mixture in the pan, beating well after each addition.

4 Stir the cheeses, mustard powder and cayenne pepper into the mixture and season to taste with salt and pepper.

5 Heat the oil in a large pan to 190°C/375°F or until a cube of bread dropped into the pan browns in 30 seconds. Drop four spoonfuls of the cheese mixture into the oil at a time and deep-fry for 2–3 minutes until golden. Drain on kitchen paper and keep hot in the oven while cooking the remaining mixture. Serve two puffs per person with a spoonful of mango chutney and green salad.

Kansas City Fritters

Crispy bacon and vegetable fritters are served with a spicy tomato salsa.

Makes 8

200g/7oz/1¾ cups
canned sweetcorn,
drained well
2 eggs, separated
75g/3oz /¾ cup plain
flour
75ml/5 tbsp milk
1 small courgette, grated
2 rashers rindless back
bacon, diced
2 spring onions, finely
chopped
large pinch of cayenne
pepper
45ml/3 tbsp sunflower oil

salt and ground black
pepper
fresh coriander sprigs, to
garnish

For the salsa

3 tomatoes, skinned,
seeded and diced
½ small red pepper,
seeded and diced
½ small onion, diced
15ml/1 tbsp lemon juice
15ml/1 tbsp chopped
fresh coriander
dash of Tabasco sauce

1 To make the salsa, mix all the ingredients together and season to taste. Cover and chill until required.

2 Empty the sweetcorn into a bowl and mix in the egg yolks. Add the flour and blend in with a wooden spoon. When the mixture thickens, gradually blend in the milk.

3 Stir in the courgette, bacon, spring onions, cayenne pepper and seasoning and set aside. Whisk the egg whites until stiff peaks form. Gently fold into the sweetcorn batter mixture.

4 Heat the oil in a large frying pan and place four large spoonfuls of the mixture into the oil. Fry over a moderate heat for 2–3 minutes on each side until golden. Drain on kitchen paper and keep warm in the oven while frying the remaining four fritters.

5 Serve two fritters each, garnished with coriander sprigs and a spoonful of the chilled tomato salsa.

Spinach and Cheese Dumplings

These tasty little dumplings are known as *gnocchi* in Italy, where they are very popular.

Serves 4

175g/6oz cold mashed
potato
75g/3oz/½ cup semolina
115g/4oz/1 cup frozen
leaf spinach, defrosted,
squeezed and chopped
115g/4oz/½ cup ricotta
cheese
75ml/5 tbsp freshly
grated Parmesan
cheese
30ml/2 tbsp beaten egg
2.5ml/½ tsp salt
large pinch of grated
nutmeg

pinch of ground black
pepper
30ml/2 tbsp freshly
grated Parmesan
cheese
fresh basil sprigs, to
garnish

For the butter

75g/3oz/6 tbsp butter
5ml/1 tsp grated lemon
rind
15ml/1 tbsp lemon juice
15ml/1 tbsp chopped
fresh basil

1 Place all the gnocchi ingredients except the 30ml/2 tbsp Parmesan and the basil in a bowl and mix well. Take walnut-size pieces of the mixture and roll each one back and forth along the prongs of a fork until ridged. Make 28 gnocchi in this way.

2 Bring a large pan of water to the boil, reduce to a simmer and drop in the gnocchi. They will sink at first, but as they cook they will rise to the surface; this procedure will take about 2 minutes, then simmer for 1 minute. Transfer the gnocchi to a lightly-greased and warmed ovenproof dish.

3 Sprinkle the gnocchi with the Parmesan cheese and grill under a high heat for 2 minutes, or until lightly browned. Meanwhile, heat the butter in a pan and stir in the lemon rind, lemon juice and basil. Season to taste. Pour some of this butter over each portion of gnocchi and serve hot, garnished with the chopped fresh basil.

Tricolour Salad

This can be a simple starter if served on individual salad plates, or part of a light buffet meal laid out on a platter.

Serves 4–6

1 small red onion, thinly sliced
6 large full-flavoured tomatoes
extra virgin olive oil, to sprinkle
50g/2oz rocket or watercress, chopped
175g/6oz mozzarella cheese, thinly sliced
salt and ground black pepper
30ml/2 tbsp pine nuts (optional), to garnish

1 Soak the onion slices in a bowl of cold water for about 30 minutes, then drain and pat dry. Skin the tomatoes by slashing and dipping briefly in boiling water. Remove the cores and slice the flesh.

2 Arrange half the sliced tomatoes on a large platter or divide them among small plates.

3 Sprinkle liberally with olive oil, then layer with the chopped rocket or watercress and soaked onion slices, seasoning well with salt and pepper. Add the cheese, then sprinkle over more oil and seasoning.

4 Repeat with the remaining tomato slices, salad leaves, cheese and oil.

5 Season well to finish and complete with some oil and a good scattering of pine nuts, if using. Cover the salad and chill in the fridge for at least 2 hours before serving.

Cook's Tip
When lightly salted, tomatoes make their own dressing with their natural juices. The sharpness of the rocket or watercress offsets them wonderfully.

Minted Melon Salad

Use two different varieties of melon in this salad, such as a Charentais and a Galia.

Serves 4

2 ripe melons
fresh mint sprigs, to decorate

For the dressing
30ml/2 tbsp roughly chopped fresh mint
5ml/1 tsp caster sugar
30ml/2 tbsp raspberry vinegar
90ml/6 tbsp extra virgin olive oil
salt and ground black pepper

1 Halve the melons, then scoop out the seeds using a dessertspoon. Cut the melons into thin wedges using a large sharp knife and remove the skins.

2 Arrange the two different varieties of melon wedges alternately among four individual serving plates.

3 To make the dressing, whisk together the mint, sugar, vinegar, oil and seasoning in a small bowl, or put them in a screw-top jar and shake until blended.

4 Spoon the mint dressing over the melon wedges and decorate with mint sprigs. Serve very lightly chilled.

Cook's Tip
You could also try an orange-fleshed Cantaloupe with a pale green Ogen, or choose a small white-fleshed Honeydew for a different variation.

Garlic Mushrooms

Serve these on toast for a quick, tasty starter or pop them into ramekins and serve with slices of warm crusty bread.

Serves 4

450g/1lb button mushrooms, sliced if large	115g/4oz/½ cup low-fat soft cheese
45ml/3 tbsp olive oil	30ml/2 tbsp chopped fresh parsley
45ml/3 tbsp stock or water	15ml/1 tbsp snipped fresh chives
30ml/2 tbsp dry sherry (optional)	salt and ground black pepper
3 garlic cloves, crushed	

1 Put the mushrooms into a large saucepan with the olive oil, stock or water and sherry, if using. Heat until bubbling, then cover the pan with a tight-fitting lid and simmer gently for about 5 minutes.

2 Add the crushed garlic and stir well to mix. Cook for a further 2 minutes. Remove the mushrooms with a slotted spoon and set them aside. Cook the liquor until it reduces down to 30ml/2 tbsp. Remove from the heat and stir in the soft cheese, parsley and chives.

3 Stir the mixture well until the cheese has completely melted, then return the mushrooms to the pan so that they become coated with the cheesy mixture. Season to taste with salt and pepper.

4 Pile the mushrooms on to thick slabs of hot toast. Alternatively, spoon them into four ramekins and serve accompanied by slices of crusty bread.

Cook's Tip
Use a mixture of different types of mushrooms for this dish, if you prefer. Shiitake mushrooms will give this starter a particularly rich flavour, if you can find them.

Vegetables with Tahini

This colourful starter is easily prepared in advance. For an *al fresco* meal, grill the vegetables on a barbecue.

Serves 4

2 red, green or yellow peppers, seeded and quartered	salt and ground black pepper
2 courgettes, halved lengthways	**For the tahini cream**
2 small aubergines, degorged and halved lengthways	225g/8oz tahini paste
	1 garlic clove, crushed
	30ml/2 tbsp olive oil
1 fennel bulb, quartered	30ml/2 tbsp fresh lemon juice
dash of olive oil	120ml/4fl oz/½ cup cold water
115g/4oz Green Halloumi cheese, sliced	warm pitta or naan bread, to serve

1 Preheat the grill or barbecue until hot. Brush the vegetables with the oil and grill until just browned, turning once. (If the peppers blacken, don't worry. The skins can be peeled off when cool enough to handle.) Cook the vegetables until just softened.

2 Place all the vegetables in a shallow dish and season to taste with salt and pepper. Allow to cool. Meanwhile, brush the cheese slices with olive oil and grill these on both sides until they are just charred. Remove them from the grill pan with a palette knife.

3 To make the tahini cream, place all the ingredients, except the water, in a food processor or blender. Process for a few seconds to mix, then, with the motor still running, pour in the water and blend until smooth.

4 Place the vegetables and grilled cheese slices on a platter and trickle over the tahini cream. Serve with plenty of warm pitta or naan bread.

Haddock with Parsley Sauce

The parsley sauce is enriched with cream and an egg yolk in this simple supper dish.

Serves 4

4 haddock fillets (about
   175g/6oz each)
50g/2oz/4 tbsp butter
150ml/¼ pint/⅔ cup
   milk
150ml/¼ pint/⅔ cup fish
   stock
1 bay leaf

20ml/4 tsp plain flour
60ml/4 tbsp cream
1 egg yolk
45ml/3 tbsp chopped
   fresh parsley
grated rind and juice of
   ½ lemon
salt and ground black
   pepper

1 Place the fish in a frying pan and heat half the butter, the milk, fish stock, bay leaf and seasoning, and heat over a moderately low heat to simmering point. Lower the heat, cover the pan with a tight-fitting lid and poach the fish for 10–15 minutes, depending on the thickness of the fillets, until the fish is tender and the flesh just begins to flake.

2 Transfer the fish to a warmed serving plate with a slotted spoon, cover the fish and keep warm while you make the sauce. Return the cooking liquid to the heat and bring to the boil, stirring. Simmer for about 4 minutes, then remove and discard the bay leaf.

3 Melt the remaining butter in a saucepan and add the flour, stirring continuously for 1 minute. Remove from the heat and gradually stir in the fish cooking liquid. Return to the heat and bring to the boil, stirring. Simmer for about 4 minutes, stirring frequently.

4 Remove the pan from the heat, blend the cream into the egg yolk, then stir into the sauce with the parsley. Reheat gently, stirring for a few minutes; do not allow to boil. Remove from the heat, add the lemon juice and rind, and season to taste with salt and pepper. Pour into a warmed sauceboat and serve with the fish.

Pickled Herrings

A good basic pickled herring dish which is enhanced by the grainy mustard vinaigrette.

Serves 4

4 fresh herrings
160ml/5fl oz/⅔ cup white
   wine vinegar
2 tsp salt
12 black peppercorns
2 bay leaves
4 whole cloves
2 small onions, sliced

For the dressing
1 tsp coarse grain
   mustard
3 tbsp olive oil
1 tbsp white wine
   vinegar
salt and ground black
   pepper

1 Pre-heat the oven to 160C°/325°F/Gas 3. Clean and bone the fish. Cut each fish into two fillets.

2 Roll up the fillets tightly and place them closely packed together in an ovenproof dish so that they can't unroll.

3 Pour the vinegar over the fish and add just enough water to cover them.

4 Add the spices and onion, cover and cook for 1 hour. Leave to cool with the liquid. To make the dressing, combine all the ingredients and shake well; serve with the fish.

Herrings in Oatmeal with Mustard

In this delicious dish, crunchy-coated herrings are served with a piquant mayonnaise sauce.

Serves 4

about 15ml/1 tbsp Dijon
  mustard
about 7.5ml/1½ tsp
  tarragon vinegar
175ml/6fl oz/¾ cup thick
  mayonnaise

4 herrings (about
  225g/8oz each)
1 lemon, halved
115g/4oz/1 cup medium
  oatmeal
salt and ground black
  pepper

1 Beat the mustard and vinegar to taste into the mayonnaise. Chill lightly in the fridge.

2 Place one fish at a time on a board, cut-side down and opened out. Press gently along the backbone with your thumbs. Turn over the fish and carefully lift away the backbone and discard.

3 Squeeze lemon juice over both sides of the fish, then season with salt and ground black pepper. Fold the fish in half, skin-side outwards.

4 Preheat a grill until fairly hot. Place the oatmeal on a plate, then coat each herring evenly in the oatmeal, pressing it on gently with your fingers.

5 Place the herrings on a grill rack and grill the fish for about 3 – 4 minutes on each side, until the skin is golden brown and crisp and the flesh flakes easily. Serve hot with the mustard sauce, served separately.

Fish and Chips

The traditional British combination of battered fish and thick-cut chips is served with lemon wedges.

Serves 4

115g/4oz/1 cup
  self-raising flour
150ml/¼ pint/⅔ cup
  water
675g/1½ lb potatoes

675g/1½ lb piece skinned
  cod fillet, cut into four
oil, for deep-frying
salt and ground black
  pepper
lemon wedges, to serve

1 Stir the flour and salt together in a bowl, then form a well in the centre. Gradually pour in the water, whisking in the flour to make a smooth batter. Leave for 30 minutes.

2 Cut the potatoes into strips about 1cm/½in wide and 5cm/2in long, using a sharp knife. Place the potatoes in a colander, rinse in cold water, then drain and dry them well.

3 Heat the oil in a deep-fat fryer or large heavy-based saucepan to 150°C/300°F. Using the wire basket, lower the potatoes in batches into the oil and cook for 5 – 6 minutes, shaking the basket occasionally until the potatoes are soft but not browned. Remove the chips from the oil and drain them thoroughly on kitchen paper.

4 Heat the oil in the fryer to 190°C/375°F. Season the fish. Stir the batter, then dip the pieces of fish in turn into it, allowing the excess to drain off.

5 Working in two batches if necessary, lower the fish into the oil and fry for 6 – 8 minutes, until crisp and brown. Drain the fish on kitchen paper and keep warm.

6 Add the chips in batches to the oil and cook them for about 2 – 3 minutes, until brown and crisp. Keep hot until ready to serve, then sprinkle with salt and serve with the fish, accompanied by lemon wedges.

Trout with Hazelnuts

The hazelnuts in this recipe make an interesting change from the almonds that are more often used.

Serves 4

50g/2oz/½ cup
  hazelnuts, chopped
65g/2½oz/5 tbsp butter
4 trout (about 275g/
  10oz each)

30ml/2 tbsp lemon juice
salt and ground black
  pepper
lemon slices and flat-leaf
  parsley sprigs, to serve

1 Preheat the grill. Toast the nuts in a single layer, stirring frequently, until the skins split. Then tip the nuts on to a clean dish towel and rub to remove the skins. Leave the nuts to cool, then chop them coarsely.

2 Heat 50g/2oz/4 tbsp of the butter in a large frying pan. Season the trout inside and out, then fry two at a time for 12–15 minutes, turning once, until the trout are brown and the flesh flakes easily when tested with the point of a sharp kitchen knife.

3 Drain the cooked trout on kitchen paper, then transfer to a warm serving plate and keep warm while frying the remaining trout in the same way. (If your frying pan is large enough, you could, of course, cook the trout in one batch.)

4 Add the remaining butter to the frying pan and fry the hazelnuts until evenly browned. Stir the lemon juice into the pan and mix well, then quickly pour the buttery sauce over the trout and serve at once, garnished with slices of lemon and flat-leaf parsley sprigs.

Cook's Tip
You can use a microwave to prepare the nuts instead of the grill. Spread them out in a shallow microwave dish and leave uncovered. Cook on full power until the skins split, then remove the skins using a dish towel as described above.

Trout Wrapped in a Blanket

The "blanket" of bacon bastes the fish during cooking, keeping it moist and adding flavour at the same time.

Serves 4

juice of ½ lemon
4 trout (about 275g/
  10oz each)
4 fresh thyme sprigs
8 thin slices rindless
  streaky bacon

salt and ground black
  pepper
chopped fresh parsley and
  thyme sprigs,
  to garnish
lemon wedges, to serve

1 Preheat the oven to 200°C/400°F/Gas 6. Squeeze lemon juice over the skin and in the cavity of each fish, season all over with salt and ground black pepper, then put a thyme sprig in each cavity.

2 Stretch each bacon slice using the back of a knife, then wind two slices around each fish. Place the fish in a lightly greased shallow baking dish, with the loose ends of bacon tucked underneath to prevent them unwinding.

3 Bake in the oven for 15–20 minutes, until the trout flesh flakes easily when tested with the point of a sharp knife and the bacon is crisp and beginning to brown.

4 Serve garnished with chopped parsley, sprigs of thyme and accompanied by lemon wedges.

Cook's Tip
Smoked streaky bacon will impart a stronger flavour to the fish. If you prefer, use fresh chopped coriander in place of the parsley for the garnish.

Smoked Trout Salad

Horseradish goes as well with smoked trout. It combines well with yogurt to make a lovely dressing.

Serves 4

1 oakleaf or other red
   lettuce, such as lollo
   rosso
225g/8oz small ripe
   tomatoes, cut into thin
   wedges
½ cucumber, peeled and
   thinly sliced
4 smoked trout fillets,
   about 200g/7oz each,
   skinned and flaked
   coarsely

For the dressing
pinch of English mustard
   powder
15–20ml/3–4 tsp white
   wine vinegar
30ml/2 tbsp light olive oil
100ml/3½fl oz/scant ½
   cup natural yogurt
about 30ml/2 tbsp grated
   fresh or bottled
   horseradish
pinch of caster sugar

1 To make the dressing, mix together the mustard powder and vinegar, then gradually whisk in the oil, yogurt, horseradish and sugar. Set aside for 30 minutes.

2 Place the lettuce leaves in a large bowl. Stir the dressing again, then pour half of it over the leaves and toss lightly using two spoons.

3 Arrange the lettuce on four individual plates with the tomatoes, cucumber and trout. Spoon over the remaining dressing and serve at once.

Cook's Tip
The addition of salt to the horseradish salad dressing should not be necessary because of the saltiness of the smoked trout fillets.

Moroccan Fish Tagine

Tagine is the name of the large cooking pot used for this type of cooking in Morocco.

Serves 4

2 garlic cloves, crushed
30ml/2 tbsp ground
   cumin
30ml/2 tbsp paprika
1 small fresh red chilli
   (optional)
30ml/2 tbsp tomato purée
60ml/4 tbsp lemon juice
4 whiting or cod cutlets
   (about 175g/6oz each)

350g/12oz tomatoes,
   sliced
2 green peppers, seeded
   and thinly sliced
salt and ground black
   pepper
chopped fresh coriander,
   to garnish

1 Mix together the garlic, cumin, paprika, chilli, tomato purée and lemon juice. Spread this mixture over the fish, then cover and chill in the fridge for about 30 minutes to let the flavours penetrate.

2 Preheat the oven to 200°C/400°F/Gas 6. Arrange half of the tomatoes and peppers in a baking dish.

3 Cover with the fish, then arrange the remaining tomatoes and peppers on top. Cover the baking dish with foil and bake for about 45 minutes, until the fish is tender. Sprinkle with chopped coriander or parsley to serve.

Cook's Tip
Try different white fish in this dish, such as hoki or pollack. If you are preparing this dish for a dinner party, it can be assembled completely and stored in the fridge until you are ready to cook it.

Prawn and Mint Salad

Green prawns make all the difference to this salad, as the flavours marinate well into the prawns before cooking.

Serves 4

12 large green prawns
15g/½oz/1 tbsp unsalted
  butter
15ml/1 tbsp fish sauce
juice of 1 lime
45ml/3 tbsp thin coconut
  milk
2.5cm/1in piece of root
  ginger, peeled and
  grated

5ml/1 tsp caster sugar
1 garlic clove, crushed
2 fresh red chillies, seeded
  and finely chopped
30ml/2 tbsp fresh mint
  leaves
ground black pepper
225g/8oz light green
  lettuce leaves, such as
  butterhead, to serve

1 Peel the prawns, leaving the tails intact.

2 Melt the butter in a large frying pan and toss in the green prawns until they turn pink.

3 Mix the fish sauce, lime juice, coconut milk, ginger, sugar, garlic, chillies and pepper together.

4 Toss the warm prawns into the sauce with the mint leaves. Serve the prawn mixture on a bed of green lettuce leaves.

Cook's Tip
For a really tropical touch, garnish this flavoursome salad with some shavings of fresh coconut made using a potato peeler.

Mackerel with Tomatoes and Pesto

This rich and oily fish needs the sharp tomato sauce. The aromatic pesto is excellent drizzled over the fish.

Serves 4
For the pesto sauce
50g/2oz/½ cup pine nuts
30ml/2 tbsp fresh basil
  leaves
2 garlic cloves, crushed
30ml/2 tbsp freshly
  grated Parmesan
  cheese
150ml/¼ pint/⅔ cup
  extra virgin olive oil

salt and ground black
  pepper

For the fish
4 mackerel, gutted
30ml/2 tbsp olive oil
115g/4oz onion, roughly
  chopped
450g/1lb tomatoes,
  roughly chopped

1 To make the pesto sauce, place the pine nuts, basil and garlic cloves in a food processor fitted with a metal blade. Process until the mixture forms a rough paste. Add the Parmesan cheese and, with the machine running, gradually add the oil. Set aside until required.

2 Heat the grill until very hot. Season the mackerel well with salt and pepper and cook for 10 minutes on either side.

3 Meanwhile, heat the oil in a large heavy-based saucepan and sauté the onions until soft.

4 Stir in the tomatoes and cook for 5 minutes. Serve the warm fish on top of the tomato mixture and top with a dollop of pesto sauce.

Cook's Tip
The pesto sauce can be made ahead and stored in the fridge until needed. Soften it again before using. For red pesto sauce, add some puréed sun-dried tomatoes after the oil.

Mackerel with Mustard and Lemon

Mackerel must be really fresh to be enjoyed. Look for bright, firm-fleshed fish.

Serves 4

4 fresh mackerel (about
  275g/10oz each),
  gutted and cleaned
175–225g/6–8oz/
  1½–2 cups spinach

**For the mustard and
lemon butter**
115g/4oz/½ cup butter,
  melted

30ml/2 tbsp wholegrain
  mustard
grated rind of 1 lemon
30ml/2 tbsp lemon juice
45ml/3 tbsp chopped
  fresh parsley
salt and ground black
  pepper

1 To prepare each mackerel, use a sharp knife to cut off the head just behind the gills, then cut along the belly so that the fish can be opened out flat.

2 Place the fish on a board, skin-side up, and, with the heel of your hand, press along the backbone to loosen it.

3 Turn the fish the right way up and pull the bone away from the flesh. Remove the tail and cut each fish in half lengthways. Wash and pat dry with kitchen paper.

4 Score the skin three or four times, then season the fish. To make the mustard and lemon butter, mix together the melted butter, mustard, lemon rind and juice and parsley. Season with salt and pepper. Place the mackerel on a grill rack. Brush a little of the butter over the mackerel and grill for 5 minutes each side, basting occasionally until cooked through.

5 Arrange the spinach leaves in the centre of four large plates. Place the mackerel on top. Heat the remaining butter in a small saucepan until sizzling and pour over the mackerel. Serve immediately.

Whitebait with Herb Sandwiches

Whitebait are the tiny fry of sprats or herring and are served whole. Cayenne pepper makes them spicy hot.

Serves 4

unsalted butter, for
  spreading
6 slices granary bread
90ml/6 tbsp mixed
  chopped fresh herbs,
  such as parsley,
  chervil and chives
450g/1lb whitebait,
  defrosted if frozen

65g/2½oz/scant ¾ cup
  plain flour
15ml/1 tbsp chopped
  fresh parsley
salt and cayenne pepper
groundnut oil,
  for deep-frying
lemon slices, to garnish

1 Butter the bread slices. Sprinkle the herbs over three of the slices, then top with the remaining slices of bread. Remove the crusts and cut each sandwich into eight triangles. Cover with clear film and set aside.

2 Rinse the whitebait thoroughly. Drain and then pat dry on kitchen paper.

3 Put the flour, chopped parsley, salt and cayenne pepper in a large plastic bag and shake to mix. Add the whitebait and toss gently in the seasoned flour until lightly coated. Heat the oil in a deep-fat fryer to 180°C/350°F.

4 Fry the fish in batches for 2–3 minutes, until golden and crisp. Lift out of the oil and drain on kitchen paper. Keep warm in the oven until all the fish are cooked.

5 Sprinkle the whitebait with salt and more cayenne pepper, if liked, and garnish with the lemon slices. Serve at once with the herb sandwiches.

Sole Goujons with Lime Mayonnaise

This simple dish can be rustled up very quickly. It makes an excellent light lunch or supper.

Serves 4

675g/1½lb sole fillets,
  skinned
2 eggs, beaten
115g/4oz/2 cups fresh
  white breadcrumbs
oil, for deep-frying
salt and ground black
  pepper
lime wedges, to serve

For the mayonnaise
200ml/7fl oz/scant 1 cup
  mayonnaise

1 small garlic clove,
  crushed
10ml/2 tsp capers, rinsed
  and chopped
10ml/2 tsp chopped
  gherkins
finely grated rind
  of ½ lime
10ml/2 tsp lime juice
15ml/1 tbsp chopped
  fresh coriander

1 To make the lime mayonnaise, mix together the mayonnaise, garlic, capers, gherkins, lime rind and juice and chopped coriander. Season to taste with salt and pepper. Transfer to a serving bowl and chill until required.

2 Cut the sole fillets into finger-length strips. Dip into the beaten egg, then into the breadcrumbs.

3 Heat the oil in a deep-fat fryer to 180°C/350°F. Add the fish in batches and fry until golden brown and crisp. Drain well on kitchen paper.

4 Pile the goujons on to warmed serving plates and serve with the lime wedges for squeezing over. Hand the lime mayonnaise round separately.

Cook's Tip
Make sure you use good quality mayonnaise for the sauce, or – better still – make your own. But remember that some people, including pregnant women, should not eat raw egg.

Spicy Fish Rösti

Serve these delicious fish cakes crisp and hot for lunch or supper with a mixed green salad.

Serves 4

350g/12oz large, firm
  waxy potatoes
350g/12oz salmon or cod
  fillet, skinned and
  boned
3–4 spring onions,
  finely chopped
5ml/1 tsp grated fresh
  root ginger

30ml/2 tbsp chopped
  fresh coriander
10ml/2 tsp lemon juice
30–45ml/2–3 tbsp
  sunflower oil
salt and cayenne pepper
lemon wedges, to serve
fresh coriander sprigs, to
  garnish

1 Bring a saucepan of water to the boil and cook the potatoes with their skins on for about 10 minutes. Drain and leave to cool for a few minutes.

2 Meanwhile, finely chop the salmon or cod fillet and place in a bowl. Stir in the chopped spring onions, grated root ginger, chopped coriander and lemon juice. Season to taste with salt and cayenne pepper.

3 When the potatoes are cool enough to handle, peel off the skins and grate the potatoes coarsely. Gently stir the grated potato into the fish mixture.

4 Form the fish mixture into 12 cakes, pressing the mixture together but leaving the edges slightly rough.

5 Heat the oil in a large frying pan, and, when hot, fry the fish cakes a few at a time for 3 minutes on each side, until golden brown and crisp. Drain on kitchen paper. Serve hot with lemon wedges for squeezing over. Garnish with sprigs of fresh coriander.

Mediterranean Plaice Rolls

Sun-dried tomatoes, pine nuts and anchovies make a flavoursome combination for the stuffing mixture.

Serves 4

4 plaice fillets (about
  225g/8oz each),
  skinned
75g/3oz/6 tbsp butter
1 small onion, chopped
1 celery stick, finely
  chopped
115g/4oz/2 cups fresh
  white breadcrumbs
45ml/3 tbsp chopped
  fresh parsley

30ml/2 tbsp pine nuts,
  toasted
3–4 pieces sun-dried
  tomatoes in oil,
  drained and chopped
50g/2oz can anchovy
  fillets, drained and
  chopped
75ml/5 tbsp fish stock
pinch of black pepper

1 Preheat the oven to 180°C/350°F/Gas 4. Using a sharp knife, cut the plaice fillets in half lengthways to make eight smaller fillets.

2 Melt the butter in a pan and cook the onion and celery. Cover with a tight-fitting lid and cook over a low heat for about 15 minutes until softened. Do not allow to brown.

3 Mix together the breadcrumbs, parsley, pine nuts, sun-dried tomatoes and anchovies. Stir in the softened vegetables with the buttery juices and season to taste with pepper.

4 Divide the stuffing into eight portions. Taking one portion at a time, form the stuffing into balls, then roll up each one inside a plaice fillet. Secure each roll with a cocktail stick.

5 Place the rolled-up fillets in a buttered ovenproof dish. Pour over the stock and cover the dish with buttered foil. Bake for about 20 minutes, or until the fish flakes easily. Remove the cocktail sticks, then serve with a little of the cooking juices drizzled over.

Salmon with Watercress Sauce

Adding the watercress right at the end of cooking retains much of its flavour and colour.

Serves 4

300ml/½ pint/1¼ cups
  crème fraîche
30ml/2 tbsp chopped
  fresh tarragon
25g/1oz/2 tbsp butter
15ml/1 tbsp sunflower oil
4 salmon fillets, skinned
  and boned

1 garlic clove, crushed
120ml/4fl oz/½ cup dry
  white wine
1 bunch watercress
salt and ground black
  pepper

1 Gently heat the crème fraîche in a small saucepan until just beginning to boil. Remove the pan from the heat and stir in half the tarragon. Leave the herb cream to infuse while cooking the fish.

2 Heat the butter and oil in a frying pan and fry the salmon fillets for 3–5 minutes on each side. Remove from the pan and keep warm.

3 Add the garlic and fry for a further 1 minute, then pour in the wine and let it bubble until reduced to about 15ml/1 tbsp.

4 Meanwhile, strip the leaves off the watercress stalks and chop finely. Discard any damaged leaves. (Save the watercress stalks for soup, if you wish.)

5 Strain the herb cream into the pan and cook for a few minutes, stirring until the sauce has thickened. Stir in the remaining tarragon and watercress, then cook for a few minutes, until wilted but still bright green. Season to taste with salt and pepper and serve at once, spooned over the salmon. The dish can be accompanied by a mixed lettuce salad if you wish.

Warm Salmon Salad

This light salad is perfect in summer. Serve immediately, or the salad leaves will lose their colour.

Serves 4

450g/1lb salmon fillet, skinned
30ml/2 tbsp sesame oil
grated rind of ½ orange
juice of 1 orange
5ml/1 tsp Dijon mustard
15ml/1 tbsp chopped fresh tarragon
45ml/3 tbsp groundnut oil
115g/4oz fine green beans, trimmed
175g/6oz mixed salad leaves, such as young spinach leaves, radicchio and frisée
15ml/1 tbsp toasted sesame seeds
salt and ground black pepper

1 Cut the salmon into bite-size pieces, then make the dressing. Mix together the sesame oil, orange rind and juice, mustard, chopped tarragon and season to taste with salt and ground black pepper. Set aside.

2 Heat the groundnut oil in a frying pan and fry the salmon pieces for 3–4 minutes, or until lightly browned but still tender on the inside.

3 While the salmon is cooking, blanch the green beans in boiling salted water for about 5–6 minutes, until tender yet still slightly crisp.

4 Add the dressing to the salmon, toss together gently and cook for 30 seconds. Remove the pan from the heat.

5 Arrange the salad leaves on serving plates. Drain the beans and toss over the leaves. Spoon over the salmon and cooking juices and serve immediately, sprinkled with the toasted sesame seeds.

Red Mullet with Fennel

Ask the fishmonger to gut the mullet but not to discard the liver, as this is a delicacy and provides much of the flavour.

Serves 4

3 small fennel bulbs
60ml/4 tbsp olive oil
2 small onions, sliced
2–4 fresh basil leaves
4 small or 2 large red mullet, cleaned
grated rind of ½ lemon
150ml/¼ pint/⅔ cup fish stock
50g/2oz/4 tbsp butter
juice of 1 lemon

1 Snip off the feathery fronds from the fennel bulbs, finely chop and reserve for the garnish. Cut the fennel into wedges, being careful to leave the layers attached at the root ends so the pieces stay intact.

2 Heat the oil in a frying pan large enough to take the fish in a single layer and cook the wedges of fennel and onions for about 10–15 minutes, until softened and lightly browned.

3 Tuck a basil leaf inside each mullet, then place on top of the vegetables. Sprinkle the lemon rind on top. Pour in the stock and bring just to the boil. Cover with a tight-fitting lid and cook gently for 15–20 minutes, until the fish is tender.

4 Melt the butter in a small saucepan and, when it starts to sizzle and colour slightly, add the lemon juice. Pour over the mullet, sprinkle with the reserved fennel fronds and serve.

Cook's Tip
Grey mullet can also be cooked in this way. Look for fish with bright, convex eyes and firm, gleaming flesh and red gills.

Tuna with Pan-fried Tomatoes

Meaty and filling tuna steaks are served here with juicy tomatoes and black olives.

Serves 2

*2 tuna steaks (about
  175g/6oz each)
90ml/6 tbsp olive oil
30ml/2 tbsp lemon juice
2 garlic cloves, chopped
5ml/1 tsp chopped fresh
  thyme
4 canned anchovy fillets,
  drained and chopped*

*225g/8oz plum tomatoes,
  halved
30ml/2 tbsp chopped
  fresh parsley
4–6 black olives, stoned
  and chopped
pinch of ground black
  pepper
crusty bread, to serve*

1 Place the tuna steaks in a shallow non-metallic dish. Mix 60ml/4 tbsp of the oil with the lemon juice, garlic, thyme, anchovies and pepper. Pour this mixture over the tuna and leave to marinate for at least 1 hour.

2 Lift the tuna from the marinade and place on a grill rack. Grill for 4 minutes on each side, or until the tuna feels firm to touch, basting with the marinade. Take care not to overcook.

3 Meanwhile, heat the remaining oil in a frying pan and fry the tomatoes for a maximum of 2 minutes on each side.

4 Divide the tomatoes equally between two serving plates and scatter the chopped parsley and olives over them. Top each with a tuna steak.

5 Add the remaining marinade to the pan juices and warm through. Pour over the tomatoes and tuna steaks and serve at once with crusty bread for mopping up the juices.

Cook's Tip
If you are unable to find fresh tuna steaks, you could replace them with salmon fillets, if you wish – just grill them for one or two minutes more on each side.

Sautéed Salmon with Cucumber

Cucumber is the classic accompaniment to salmon. Here it is served hot, but be careful not to overcook it.

Serves 4

*450g/1lb salmon fillet,
  skinned
40g/1½oz/3 tbsp butter
2 spring onions, chopped
½ cucumber, seeded and
  cut into strips
60ml/4 tbsp dry white
  wine*

*120ml/4fl oz/½ cup
  crème fraîche
30ml/2 tbsp snipped
  fresh chives
2 tomatoes, peeled, seeded
  and diced
salt and ground black
  pepper*

1 Cut the salmon into about 12 thin slices, then cut across into strips.

2 Melt the butter in a large frying pan and sauté the salmon for 1–2 minutes. Remove the salmon strips using a slotted spoon and set aside.

3 Add the spring onions to the pan and cook for 2 minutes. Stir in the cucumber and sauté for 1–2 minutes, until hot. Remove the cucumber and keep warm with the salmon.

4 Add the wine to the pan and let it bubble until well reduced. Stir in the cucumber, crème fraîche, half of the chives and season to taste with salt and pepper. Return the salmon to the pan and warm through gently. Sprinkle the tomatoes and remaining chives over the top. Serve at once.

Crunchy-topped Cod

It's easy to forget just how tasty and satisfying a simple, classic dish can be.

Serves 4

4 pieces cod fillet (about
  115g/4oz each)
  skinned
2 tomatoes, sliced
50g/2oz/1 cup fresh
  wholemeal
  breadcrumbs

30ml/2 tbsp chopped
  fresh parsley
finely grated rind and
  juice of ½ lemon
5ml/1 tsp sunflower oil
salt and ground black
  pepper

1 Preheat the oven to 200°C/400°F/Gas 6. Arrange the cod fillets in a wide, ovenproof dish.

2 Arrange the tomato slices on top. Mix together the breadcrumbs, fresh parsley, lemon rind and juice and the oil with seasoning to taste.

3 Spoon the crumb mixture evenly over the fish, then bake for 15–20 minutes. Serve hot.

Fish Balls in Tomato Sauce

This quick meal is a good choice for young children, as you can guarantee there are no bones.

Serves 4

450g/1lb hoki or other
  white fish fillets,
  skinned
60ml/4 tbsp fresh
  wholemeal
  breadcrumbs
30ml/2 tbsp snipped
  chives or spring onion

400g/14oz can chopped
  tomatoes
50g/2oz button
  mushrooms, sliced
salt and ground black
  pepper

1 Cut the fish fillets into chunks; place in a food processor. Add the breadcrumbs, chives or spring onion. Season and process until the fish is chopped, but still with some texture. Divide the fish mixture into about 16 even-sized pieces, then mould them into balls with your hands.

2 Place the tomatoes and mushrooms in a saucepan; cook over a medium heat until boiling. Add the fish balls, cover and simmer for about 10 minutes until cooked. Serve hot.

Tuna and Corn Fish Cakes

These economical tuna fish cakes are quick to make. Use either fresh mashed potatoes or instant mash.

Serves 4

Place 300g/11oz/1½ cups mashed potato in a bowl; stir in 200g/7oz tuna fish, 115g/4oz/¼ cup canned sweetcorn and 30ml/2 tbsp chopped parsley. Season to taste with salt and black pepper, then shape into eight patties. Press the fish cakes into 50g/2oz/1 cup fresh breadcrumbs to coat them lightly, then place on a baking sheet. Cook under a moderate grill until crisp and golden, turning once. Serve hot with lemon wedges and fresh vegetables.

Cod Creole

Inspired by the cuisine of the Caribbean, this fish dish is both colourful and delicious.

Serves 4

450g/1lb cod fillets, skinned
15ml/1 tbsp lime or lemon juice
10ml/2 tsp olive oil
1 onion, finely chopped
1 green pepper, seeded and sliced

2.5ml/½ tsp cayenne pepper
2.5ml/½ tsp garlic salt
500g/14oz can chopped tomatoes
boiled rice or potatoes, to serve

1 Cut the cod fillets into bite-size chunks and sprinkle with the lime or lemon juice.

2 Heat the oil in a large, non-stick frying pan and fry the onion and pepper gently until softened. Add the cayenne pepper and garlic salt.

3 Stir in the cod and the chopped tomatoes. Bring to the boil, then cover and simmer for about 5 minutes, or until the fish flakes easily. Serve with boiled rice or potatoes.

Cook's Tip
This flavoursome dish is surprisingly light in calories, so if you are worried about your waistline, this is the meal for you.

Salmon Pasta with Parsley Sauce

The parsley sauce is added at the last moment to the salmon mixture and does not have to be cooked separately.

Serves 4

450g/1lb salmon fillet, skinned
225g/8oz/2 cups pasta, such as penne
175g/6oz cherry tomatoes, halved
150ml/¼ pint/⅔ cup low-fat crème fraîche

45ml/3 tbsp finely chopped parsley
finely grated rind of ½ orange
salt and ground black pepper

1 Cut the salmon into bite-size pieces, arrange on a heatproof plate and cover with foil.

2 Bring a large saucepan of salted water to the boil, add the pasta and return to the boil. Place the plate of salmon on top and simmer for 10–12 minutes, until the pasta and salmon are cooked.

3 Drain the pasta and toss with the tomatoes and salmon. Mix together the crème fraîche, parsley, orange rind and pepper to taste, then toss into the salmon and pasta and serve hot or leave to cool to room temperature.

Cook's Tip
The grated orange rind in the sauce complements the salmon beautifully in this recipe. For an alternative, try trout fillets and substitute grated lemon rind.

Monkfish with Mexican Salsa

Remove the pinkish-grey membrane from the tail before cooking, or the fish will be tough.

Serves 4

675g/1½lb monkfish tail	**For the salsa**
45ml/3 tbsp olive oil	4 tomatoes, seeded, peeled
30ml/2 tbsp lime juice	and diced
1 garlic clove, crushed	1 avocado, stoned, peeled
15ml/1 tbsp fresh	and diced
coriander, chopped	½ red onion, chopped
salt and ground black	1 green chilli, seeded and
pepper	chopped
fresh coriander sprigs	30ml/2 tbsp chopped
and lime slices, to	fresh coriander
garnish	30ml/2 tbsp olive oil
	15ml/1 tbsp lime juice

1 To make the salsa, mix the salsa ingredients and leave at room temperature for about 40 minutes.

2 Prepare the monkfish. Using a sharp knife, remove the pinkish-grey membrane. Cut the fillets from either side of the backbone, then cut each fillet in half to give four steaks.

3 Mix together the oil, lime juice, garlic, coriander and seasoning in a shallow non-metallic dish. Turn the monkfish several times to coat with the marinade, then cover the dish and leave to marinate at cool room temperature, or in the fridge, for 30 minutes.

4 Remove the monkfish from the marinade and grill for 10–12 minutes, turning once and brushing regularly with the marinade until cooked through.

5 Serve the monkfish garnished with coriander sprigs and lime slices and accompanied by the salsa.

Seafood Pancakes

The combination of fresh and smoked haddock imparts a wonderful flavour to the pancake filling.

Serves 4–6

12 ready-made pancakes	40g/1½oz/3 tbsp plain
	flour
For the filling	pinch of freshly grated
225g/8oz smoked haddock	nutmeg
fillet	2 hard-boiled eggs,
225g/8oz fresh haddock	shelled and chopped
fillet	salt and ground black
300ml/½ pint/1¼ cups	pepper
milk	sprinkling of Gruyère
150ml/¼ pint/⅔ cup	cheese
single cream	curly salad leaves, to
40g/1½oz/3 tbsp butter	serve

1 To make the filling, put the haddock fillets in a large pan. Add the milk and poach for 6–8 minutes, until just tender. Lift out the fish using a draining spoon and, when cool enough to handle, remove skin and bones. Reserve the milk. Measure the single cream into a jug, then strain enough milk into the jug to make it up to 450ml/¾ pint/scant 2 cups.

2 Melt the butter in a pan, stir in the flour and cook gently for 1 minute. Gradually mix in the milk mixture, stirring continuously to make a smooth sauce. Cook for 2–3 minutes. Season to taste with salt, pepper and nutmeg. Flake the haddock and fold into the sauce with the eggs. Leave to cool.

3 Preheat the oven to 180°C/350°F/Gas 4. Divide the filling among the pancakes. Fold the sides of each pancake into the centre, then roll them up to enclose the filling completely. Butter four or six individual ovenproof dishes and arrange two or three filled pancakes in each, or butter one large dish for all the pancakes. Brush with melted butter and cook for 15 minutes. Sprinkle over the Gruyère and cook for a further 5 minutes, until warmed through. Serve hot with a few curly salad leaves, if you wish.

Herby Plaice Croquettes

Deep-fry with clean oil every time as the fish will flavour the oil and taint any other foods fried in the oil.

Serves 4
450g/1lb plaice fillets	2 eggs
300ml/½ pint/1¼ cups milk	15g/½oz/1 tbsp unsalted butter
450g/1lb cooked potatoes	225g/8oz/2 cups white breadcrumbs
1 bulb fennel, finely chopped	30ml/2 tbsp sesame seeds
1 garlic clove, finely chopped	oil, for deep-frying salt and ground black pepper
45ml/3 tbsp chopped fresh parsley	

1 Poach the fish fillets in the milk for about 15 minutes until the fish flakes. Drain the fillets and reserve the milk.

2 Peel the skin off the fish and remove any bones. Process the fish, potatoes, fennel, garlic, parsley, eggs and butter in a food processor fitted with a metal blade.

3 Add 30ml/2 tbsp of the reserved cooking milk and season to taste with salt and pepper.

4 Chill in the fridge for about 30 minutes, then shape into 20 croquettes with your hands.

5 Mix together the breadcrumbs and sesame seeds.

6 Roll the croquettes in the mixture to form a good coating. Heat the oil in a large heavy-based saucepan and deep-fry in batches for about 4 minutes until golden brown. Drain well on kitchen paper and serve hot.

Mixed Smoked Fish Kedgeree

An ideal breakfast dish on a cold morning. Garnish with quartered hard-boiled eggs and season well.

Serves 6
450g/1lb mixed smoked fish such as smoked cod, smoked haddock, smoked mussels or oysters, if available	5ml/1 tsp medium-hot curry powder
	2.5ml/½ tsp freshly grated nutmeg
300ml/½ pint/1¼ cups milk	15ml/1 tbsp chopped fresh parsley
175g/6oz/1 cup long grain rice	salt and ground black pepper
1 slice of lemon	2 hard-boiled eggs, to garnish
50g/2oz/4 tbsp butter	

1 Poach the uncooked smoked fish in milk for 10 minutes or until it flakes. Drain off the milk and flake the fish. Mix with the other smoked fish.

2 Cook the rice in boiling water together with a slice of lemon for 10 minutes, or according to the instructions on the packet, until just cooked. Drain well.

3 Melt the butter in a large saucepan and add the rice and fish. Shake the pan to mix all the ingredients together well.

4 Stir in the curry powder, nutmeg, parsley and seasoning. Serve immediately, garnished with quartered eggs.

Cook's Tip
When flaking the fish, keep the pieces fairly large to give this dish a chunky consistency.

Spanish-style Hake

Cod and haddock cutlets will work just as well as hake in this tasty fish dish.

Serves 4

30ml/2 tbsp olive oil
25g/1oz/2 tbsp butter
1 onion, chopped
3 garlic cloves, crushed
15g/½oz/1 tbsp plain
   flour
2.5ml/½ tsp paprika
4 hake cutlets (about
   175g/6oz each)
250g/8oz fine green
   beans, cut into
   2.5cm/1in lengths

350ml/12fl oz/1½ cups
   fresh fish stock
150ml/¼ pint/generous
   ½ cup dry white wine
30ml/2 tbsp dry sherry
15–20 live mussels in
   the shell, cleaned
45ml/3 tbsp chopped
   fresh parsley
salt and ground black
   pepper
crusty bread, to serve

1 Heat the oil and butter in a sauté or frying pan and cook the onion for 5 minutes, until softened but not browned. Add the crushed garlic and cook for 1 minute more.

2 Mix together the plain flour and paprika, then lightly dust over the hake cutlets. Push the sautéed onion and garlic to one side of the pan.

3 Add the hake cutlets to the pan and fry until golden on both sides. Stir in the beans, stock, wine, sherry and season to taste with salt and pepper. Bring to the boil and cook for about 2 minutes.

4 Add the mussels and parsley, cover the pan with a tight-fitting lid and cook for 5–8 minutes, until the mussels have opened. Discard any that do not open.

5 Serve the hake in warmed, shallow soup bowls with crusty bread to mop up the juices.

Fish Goujons

Any white fish fillets can be used for the goujons – you could try a mixture of haddock and cod for a change.

Serves 4

60ml/4 tbsp mayonnaise
30ml/2 tbsp natural
   yogurt
grated rind of ½ lemon
squeeze of lemon juice
15ml/1 tbsp chopped
   fresh parsley
15ml/1 tbsp capers,
   chopped
2 x 175g/6oz sole fillets,
   skinned

2 x 175g/6oz plaice
   fillets, skinned
1 egg, lightly beaten
115g/4oz/2 cups fresh
   white breadcrumbs
15ml/1 tbsp sesame seeds
pinch of paprika
oil, for frying
salt and ground black
   pepper
4 lemon wedges, to serve

1 To make the lemon mayonnaise, mix the mayonnaise, yogurt, lemon rind and juice, parsley and capers in a bowl. Cover and chill.

2 Cut the fish fillets into thin strips. Place the beaten egg in one shallow bowl. Mix together the breadcrumbs, sesame seeds, paprika and seasoning in another bowl. Dip the fish strips, one at a time, into the beaten egg, then into the breadcrumb mixture and toss until coated evenly. Lay on a clean plate.

3 Heat about 2.5cm/1in of oil in a frying pan until a cube of bread browns in 30 seconds. Deep-fry the strips in batches for 2-3 minutes, until lightly golden.

4 Remove with a slotted spoon, drain on kitchen paper and keep warm in the oven while frying the remainder. Garnish with watercress and serve hot with lemon wedges and the chilled lemon mayonnaise.

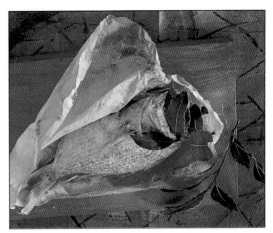

Pan-fried Garlic Sardines

Lightly fry a sliced garlic clove to garnish the fish. This dish could also be made with sprats or fresh anchovies.

Serves 4

1.1kg/2½ lb fresh sardines	salt and ground black pepper
30ml/2 tbsp olive oil	
4 garlic cloves	**For the tomato bread**
finely grated rind of 2 lemons	8 slices crusty bread, toasted
30ml/2 tbsp chopped fresh parsley	2 large ripe beefsteak tomatoes

1 Gut and clean the sardines thoroughly.

2 Heat the oil in a frying pan and cook the garlic cloves until they are softened.

3 Add the sardines and fry for 4–5 minutes. Sprinkle the lemon rind, parsley and seasoning over the top.

4 Cut the tomatoes in half and rub them on to the toast. Discard the skins. Serve the sardines with the tomato toast.

Cook's Tip
Make sure you use very ripe beefsteak tomatoes for this dish so they will rub on to the toast easily.

Sea Bass en Papillote

Bring the unopened parcels to the table and let your guests unfold their own fish to release the delicious aroma.

Serves 4

4 small sea bass, gutted	4 bay leaves
130g/4½oz/generous ½ cup butter	salt and ground black pepper
450g/1lb spinach	new potatoes and glazed carrots, to serve
3 shallots, finely chopped	
60ml/4 tbsp white wine	

1 Preheat the oven to 180°C/350°F/Gas 4. Season both the inside and outside of the fish with salt and pepper. Melt 50g/2oz/4 tbsp of the butter in a large heavy-based saucepan and add the spinach. Cook gently until the spinach has broken down into a smooth purée. Set aside to cool.

2 Melt another 50g/2oz/4 tbsp of the butter in a clean pan and add the shallots. Gently sauté for 5 minutes until soft. Add to the spinach and leave to cool.

3 Stuff the insides of the fish with the spinach filling.

4 For each fish, fold a large sheet of greaseproof paper in half and cut around the fish laid on one half, to make a heart shape when unfolded. It should be at least 5cm/2in larger than the fish. Melt the remaining butter and brush a little on to the paper. Set the fish on one side of the paper.

5 Add a little wine and a bay leaf to each package.

6 Fold the other side of the paper over the fish and make small pleats to seal the two edges, starting at the curve of the heart. Brush the outsides with butter. Transfer the packages to a baking sheet and bake for 20–25 minutes until the packages are brown. Serve with new potatoes and glazed carrots.

Chilli Prawns

This delightful, spicy combination makes a lovely light main course for a casual supper.

Serves 3–4

45ml/3 tbsp olive oil
2 shallots, chopped
2 garlic cloves, chopped
1 fresh red chilli, chopped
450g/1lb ripe tomatoes, peeled, seeded and chopped
15ml/1 tbsp tomato purée
1 bay leaf
1 fresh thyme sprig
90ml/6 tbsp dry white wine
450g/1lb/4 cups peeled, cooked large prawns
salt and ground black pepper
roughly torn fresh basil leaves, to garnish

1 Heat the oil in a saucepan and fry the shallots, garlic and chilli until the garlic starts to brown.

2 Add the tomatoes, tomato purée, bay leaf, thyme, wine and seasoning. Bring to the boil, then reduce the heat and cook gently for about 10 minutes, stirring occasionally until the sauce has thickened. Discard the herbs.

3 Stir the prawns into the sauce and heat through for a few minutes. Taste and adjust the seasoning. Scatter the basil leaves over the top and serve at once.

Scallops with Ginger

Scallops are at their best in winter. Rich and creamy, this dish is very simple to make and quite delicious.

Serves 4

8–12 shelled scallops
40g/1½ oz/3 tbsp butter
2.5cm/1in piece fresh root ginger, finely chopped
1 bunch spring onions, diagonally sliced
60ml/4 tbsp white vermouth
250ml/8fl oz/1 cup crème fraîche
salt and ground black pepper
chopped fresh parsley, to garnish

1 Remove the tough muscle opposite the coral on each scallop. Separate the coral and cut the white part of the scallop in half horizontally.

2 Melt the butter in a frying pan. Add the scallops, including the corals, and sauté for about 2 minutes until lightly browned. Take care not to overcook the scallops as this will toughen them.

3 Lift out the scallops with a draining spoon and transfer to a warmed serving dish. Keep warm.

4 Add the ginger and spring onions to the pan and stir-fry for 2 minutes. Pour in the vermouth and allow to bubble until it has almost evaporated. Stir in the crème fraîche and cook for a few minutes until the sauce has thickened. Season to taste with salt and pepper.

5 Pour the sauce over the scallops, sprinkle with parsley and serve at once.

Smoked Trout Pilaff

Smoked trout might seem an unusual partner for rice, but this is a winning combination.

Serves 4

225g/8oz/1¼ cups white
   basmati rice
40g/1½oz/3 tbsp butter
2 onions, sliced into
   rings
1 garlic clove, crushed
2 bay leaves
2 whole cloves
2 green cardamom pods
2 cinnamon sticks
5ml/1 tsp cumin seeds

4 smoked trout fillets,
   skinned
50g/2oz/½ cup slivered
   almonds, toasted
50g/2oz/generous ½ cup
   seedless raisins
30ml/2 tbsp chopped
   fresh parsley
mango chutney and
   poppadoms, to serve

1 Wash the rice thoroughly in several changes of water and drain well. Set aside. Melt the butter in a large frying pan and fry the onions until well browned, stirring frequently.

2 Add the garlic, bay leaves, cloves, cardamom pods, cinnamon and cumin seeds, and stir-fry for 1 minute.

3 Stir in the rice, then add 600ml/1 pint/2½ cups boiling water. Bring to the boil. Cover the pan with a tight-fitting lid, reduce the heat and cook very gently for 20–25 minutes, until the water has been absorbed and the rice is tender.

4 Flake the smoked trout and add to the pan with the almonds and raisins. Fork through gently. Re-cover the pan and allow the smoked trout to warm in the rice for a few minutes. Scatter the parsley over the top and serve with mango chutney and poppadoms.

Cod with Spiced Red Lentils

This is a very tasty and filling dish, yet it is a healthy option at the same time.

Serves 4

175g/6oz/¾ cup red
   lentils
1.25ml/¼ tsp ground
   turmeric
600ml/1 pint/2½ cups
   fish stock
30ml/2 tbsp vegetable oil
7.5ml/1½ tsp cumin
   seeds
15ml/1 tbsp grated fresh
   root ginger

2.5ml/½ tsp cayenne
   pepper
15ml/1 tbsp lemon juice
30ml/2 tbsp chopped
   fresh coriander
450g/1lb cod fillets,
   skinned and cut into
   large chunks
pinch of salt, to taste
fresh coriander leaves
   and lemon wedges,
   to garnish

1 Put the lentils in a saucepan with the turmeric and stock. Bring to the boil, cover with a tight-fitting lid and simmer for 20–25 minutes, until the lentils are just tender. Remove from the heat and add salt.

2 Heat the oil in a small frying pan. Add the cumin seeds and, when they begin to pop, add the ginger and cayenne pepper. Stir-fry the spices for a few seconds, then pour on to the lentils. Add the lemon juice and the coriander and stir them gently into the mixture.

3 Lay the pieces of cod on top of the lentils, cover the pan and then cook gently over a low heat for 10–15 minutes, or until the fish is tender.

4 Transfer the lentils and cod to warmed serving plates with a fish slice. Sprinkle over the coriander leaves and garnish each serving with one or two lemon wedges. Serve hot.

Mediterranean Fish Stew

Use any combination of fish you wish in this stew, which is served with an authentic rouille sauce.

Serves 4

225g/8oz/2 cups cooked
    prawns in the shell
450g/1lb mixed white
    fish, skinned and
    chopped (reserve skins
    for the stock)
45ml/3 tbsp olive oil
1 onion, chopped
1 leek, sliced
1 carrot, diced
1 garlic clove, chopped
2.5ml/½ tsp ground
    turmeric
150ml/¼ pint/⅔ cup dry
    white wine or cider
400g/14oz can chopped
    tomatoes
sprig of fresh parsley,
    thyme and fennel
1 bay leaf

small piece of orange peel
1 prepared squid, body
    cut into rings and
    tentacles chopped
12 mussels in the shell
salt and ground black
    pepper
30–45ml/2–3 tbsp fresh
    Parmesan cheese
    shavings and fresh
    parsley, to garnish

For the rouille sauce

2 slices white bread,
    without crusts
2 garlic cloves, crushed
½ fresh red chilli
15ml/1 tbsp tomato purée
45–60ml/3–4 tbsp
    olive oil

1   Peel the prawns, leaving the tails. Make stock with the prawn and fish skins and 450ml/¾ pint/1¾ cups water. Fry the onion, leek, carrot and garlic in the oil for about 6–7 minutes; stir in the turmeric. Add the wine, tomatoes, the reserved fish stock, herbs and orange peel. Bring to the boil, cover and simmer for 20 minutes.

2   To make the rouille sauce, purée all the sauce ingredients in a food processor or blender.

3   Add the fish and seafood to the pan and simmer for about 5–6 minutes, until the mussels open. Remove the bay leaf and peel; season to taste. Serve with a spoonful of the rouille, garnished with Parmesan cheese and parsley.

Salmon with Herb Butter

Other fresh herbs could be used to flavour the butter – try mint, fennel, parsley or oregano.

Serves 4

50g/2oz/4 tbsp butter,
    softened
finely grated rind of ½
    small lemon
15ml/1 tbsp lemon juice
15ml/1 tbsp chopped
    fresh dill

4 salmon steaks
2 lemon slices, halved
4 fresh dill sprigs
salt and ground black
    pepper

1   Place the butter, lemon rind, lemon juice, chopped dill and seasoning in a small bowl and mix together with a fork until thoroughly blended.

2   Spoon the butter on to a piece of greaseproof paper and roll up, smoothing with your hands into a sausage shape. Twist the ends tightly, wrap in clear film and place in the freezer for 20 minutes until firm.

3   Meanwhile, preheat the oven to 190°C/375°F/Gas 5. Cut out four squares of foil big enough to encase the salmon steaks and grease lightly. Place a salmon steak in the centre of each square.

4   Remove the butter from the freezer and slice into eight rounds. Place two rounds on top of each salmon steak with a halved lemon slice in the centre and a sprig of dill on top. Lift up the edges of the foil and crinkle them together until they are well sealed.

5   Lift the parcels on to a baking sheet and bake for about 20 minutes. Remove from the oven and place the unopened parcels on warmed plates. Open the parcels and slide the contents on to the plates with the juices.

Spanish Seafood Paella

Use monkfish instead of the cod, if you wish, and add a red
mullet cut into chunks.

Serves 4

60ml/4 tbsp olive oil
225g/8oz cod, skinned and
   cut into chunks
3 prepared baby squid,
   body cut into rings and
   tentacles chopped
1 onion, chopped
3 garlic cloves, finely
   chopped
1 red pepper, seeded and
   sliced
4 tomatoes, skinned and
   chopped
225g/8oz/1¼ cups arborio
   rice
450ml/¾ pint/scant 2
   cups fish stock

150ml/¼ pint/⅔ cup
   white wine
75g/3oz/¼ cup frozen peas
4–5 saffron strands,
   soaked in 30ml/2 tbsp
   hot water
115g/4oz/1 cup peeled,
   cooked prawns
8 fresh mussels in the
   shell, scrubbed
salt and ground black
   pepper
15ml/1 tbsp chopped fresh
   parsley, to garnish
lemon wedges, to serve

1   Heat 30ml/2 tbsp of the oil in a frying pan and stir-fry the
cod and the squid for 2 minutes. Transfer to a bowl.

2   Heat the remaining oil in the pan and fry the onion, garlic
and pepper for 6–7 minutes, stirring until softened.

3   Stir in the tomatoes and fry for a further 2 minutes, then
add the rice, stirring to coat the grains with oil, and cook for
2–3 minutes more. Pour on the stock and wine and add the
peas, saffron and water. Season to taste.

4   Gently stir in the reserved cooked fish with all the juices,
followed by the prawns, and then push the mussels into the
rice. Cover with a tight-fitting lid and cook over a gentle heat
for about 30 minutes, or until the stock has been absorbed.
Remove from the heat, keep covered and leave to stand for 5
minutes. Sprinkle with parsley; serve with lemon wedges.

Spaghetti with Seafood Sauce

The Italian name for this tomato-based sauce is *marinara*. It
is very popular in coastal regions.

Serves 4

45ml/3 tbsp olive oil
1 onion, chopped
225g/8oz spaghetti
600ml/1 pint/2½ cups
   passata
15ml/1 tbsp tomato purée
5ml/1 tsp dried oregano
1 bay leaf
5ml/1 tsp sugar
115g/4oz/1 cup peeled,
   cooked shrimps
115g/4oz/1 cup peeled,
   cooked prawns

175g/6oz cooked clam or
   cockle meat (rinsed
   well if canned or
   bottled)
15ml/1 tbsp lemon juice
45ml/3 tbsp chopped
   fresh parsley
25g/1oz/2 tbsp butter
salt and ground black
   pepper
4 cooked prawns, to
   garnish

1   Heat the oil in a saucepan and fry the onion and garlic for
6–7 minutes until softened. Meanwhile, cook the spaghetti in
a large pan of boiling salted water for 10–12 minutes or
according to the instructions on the packet, until *al dente*.

2   Stir the passata, tomato purée, oregano, bay leaf and sugar
into the onions and season to taste with salt and pepper. Bring
to the boil, then simmer for 2–3 minutes.

3   Add the shellfish, lemon juice and 30ml/2 tbsp of the
parsley. Stir well, then cover and cook for 6–7 minutes more.

4   Drain the spaghetti and add the butter to the pan. Return the
drained spaghetti to the pan and toss in the butter. Season well.

5   Divide the spaghetti among four warmed plates and top
with the seafood sauce. Sprinkle with the remaining parsley,
garnish with whole prawns and serve immediately.

Garlic Chilli Prawns

In Spain *gambas al ajillo* are traditionally cooked in small
earthenware dishes, but a frying pan is just as suitable.

Serves 4
60ml/4 tbsp olive oil
2–3 garlic cloves, finely
   chopped
1/2 –1 fresh red chilli,
   seeded and chopped
16 cooked whole
   Mediterranean
   prawns

15ml/1 tbsp chopped
   fresh parsley
salt and ground black
   pepper
lemon wedges and
   French bread, to serve

1 Heat the oil in a large frying pan and stir-fry the garlic and
chilli for 1 minute, until the garlic begins to turn brown.

2 Add the Mediterranean prawns and stir-fry for about
3–4 minutes, coating them well with the flavoured oil.

3 Add the parsley, remove from the heat and serve four
prawns per person in heated bowls, with the flavoured oil
spooned over them. Serve with lemon wedges for squeezing
and French bread to mop up the juices.

Deep-fried Spicy Whitebait

This is a delicious British dish – serve these tiny fish very
hot and crisp.

Serves 4
450g/1lb whitebait
40g/1½oz/3 tbsp plain
   flour
5ml/1 tsp paprika
pinch of cayenne pepper
12 fresh parsley sprigs

vegetable oil, for
   deep-frying
salt and ground black
   pepper
4 lemon wedges, to
   garnish

1 If using frozen whitebait, defrost in the bag, then drain off
any water. Spread the fish on kitchen paper and pat dry.

2 Place the flour, paprika, cayenne and seasoning in a large
plastic bag. Add the whitebait and shake gently until all the
fish are lightly coated with the flour. Transfer to a plate.

3 Heat about 5cm/2in of oil in a saucepan or deep-fat fryer
to 190°C/375°F, or until a cube of bread dropped into the oil
browns in about 30 seconds.

4 Add the whitebait in batches and deep-fry in the hot oil
for 2–3 minutes, until the coating is lightly golden and crispy.
Remove, drain on kitchen paper and keep warm in the oven
while frying the remainder.

5 When all the whitebait is cooked, drop the sprigs of
parsley into the hot oil (don't worry if the oil spits a bit) and
fry for a few seconds until crisp. Drain on kitchen paper.
Serve the whitebait garnished with the deep-fried parsley
sprigs and lemon wedges.

Baked Fish Creole-style

Fish fillets cooked in a colourful pepper and tomato sauce are topped with a cheesy crust.

Serves 4

15ml/1 tbsp oil	4 tail end pieces cod or
25g/1oz/2 tbsp butter	haddock fillets (about
1 onion, thinly sliced	175g/6oz each),
1 garlic clove, chopped	skinned
1 red pepper, seeded,	6 basil leaves, shredded
halved and sliced	45ml/3 tbsp fresh
1 green pepper, seeded,	breadcrumbs
halved and sliced	25g/1oz/¼ cup grated
400g/14oz can chopped	Cheddar cheese
tomatoes with basil	10ml/2 tsp chopped fresh
15ml/1 tbsp tomato purée	parsley
30ml/2 tbsp capers,	salt and ground black
chopped	pepper
3–4 drops Tabasco sauce	fresh basil sprigs,
	to garnish

1 Preheat the oven to 230°C/450°F/Gas 8. Heat the oil and half of the butter in a saucepan, and fry the sliced onion for about 6–7 minutes until softened. Add the garlic, peppers, chopped tomatoes, tomato purée, capers and Tabasco and season to taste. Cover and cook for 15 minutes, then uncover and simmer gently for 5 minutes to reduce slightly.

2 Place the fish fillets in a buttered ovenproof dish, dot with the remaining butter and season lightly. Spoon the tomato and pepper sauce over the top and sprinkle with the shredded basil. Bake in the oven for about 10 minutes.

3 Meanwhile, mix together the breadcrumbs, cheese and parsley in a bowl. Remove the fish from the oven and scatter the cheese mixture over the top. Return to the oven and bake for about another 10 minutes. Let the fish stand for about a minute, then, using a fish slice, carefully transfer each topped fillet to warmed plates. Garnish with sprigs of fresh basil and serve while still hot.

Tuna Fishcake Bites

An updated version of a traditional British tea-time dish, these little cakes would also make an elegant starter.

Serves 4

675g/1½lb potatoes	sunflower oil, for
knob of butter	shallow-frying
2 hard-boiled eggs,	salt and ground black
chopped	pepper
3 spring onions, chopped	green salad, to serve
grated rind of ½ lemon	
5ml/1 tsp lemon juice	**For the tartare sauce**
30ml/2 tbsp chopped	60ml/4 tbsp mayonnaise
fresh parsley	15ml/1 tbsp natural
200g/7oz can tuna in oil,	yogurt
drained	15ml/1 tbsp finely
10ml/2 tsp capers,	chopped gherkins
chopped	15ml/1 tbsp capers,
2 eggs, lightly beaten	chopped
115g/4oz/2 cups fresh	15ml/1 tbsp chopped
white breadcrumbs	fresh parsley

1 Boil the potatoes. Drain and mash with the butter.

2 Mix the hard-boiled eggs, spring onions, lemon rind and juice, parsley, tuna, capers and 15ml/1 tbsp of the beaten egg into the cooled potato. Season to taste, cover and chill.

3 Mix all the sauce ingredients together. Chill in the fridge.

4 Roll the fishcake mixture into about 24 balls. Dip these into the egg and then roll gently in the breadcrumbs until evenly coated. Transfer to a plate.

5 Heat 90ml/6 tbsp of the oil in a frying pan and fry the balls over a moderate heat, in batches, for about 4 minutes, turning two or three times until browned all over. Drain on kitchen paper and keep warm in the oven while frying the remainder. Serve with the tartare sauce and a salad.

Kashmir Coconut Fish Curry

The combination of spices in this dish give an interesting depth of flavour to the creamy curry sauce.

Serves 4

30ml/2 tbsp vegetable oil
2 onions, sliced
1 green pepper, seeded and sliced
1 garlic clove, crushed
1 dried chilli, seeded and chopped
5ml/1 tsp ground coriander
4ml/1 tsp ground cumin
2.5ml/½ tsp ground turmeric
2.5ml/½ tsp hot chilli powder
2.5ml/½ tsp garam masala

15g/½oz/1 tbsp plain flour
115g/4oz creamed coconut, chopped
675g/1½lb haddock fillet, skinned and chopped
4 tomatoes, skinned, seeded and chopped
15ml/1 tbsp lemon juice
30ml/2 tbsp ground almonds
30ml/2 tbsp double cream
fresh coriander sprigs, to garnish
naan bread and boiled rice, to serve

1 Heat the oil in a large saucepan and add the onions, pepper and garlic. Cook for 6–7 minutes, until the onions and peppers have softened. Stir in the chopped dried chilli, all the ground spices, the chilli powder, garam masala and flour, and cook for 1 minute.

2 Dissolve the coconut in 600ml/1 pint/2½ cups boiling water and stir into the spicy vegetable mixture. Bring to the boil, cover and then simmer gently for 6 minutes.

3 Add the fish and tomatoes and cook for 5–6 minutes, or until the fish has turned opaque. Uncover and gently stir in the lemon juice, ground almonds and cream. Season well, garnish with coriander and serve with naan bread and rice.

Mussels with Wine and Garlic

This famous French dish is traditionally known as *moules marinière*, and can be served as a starter or a main course.

Serves 4

1.75kg/4lb live mussels
15ml/1 tbsp oil
25g/1oz/2 tbsp butter
1 small onion or 2 shallots, finely chopped
2 garlic cloves, finely chopped

150ml/¼ pint/⅔ cup dry white wine or cider
fresh parsley sprigs
ground black pepper
30ml/2 tbsp chopped fresh parsley, to garnish
French bread, to serve

1 Check that the mussels are closed. (Throw away any that are cracked or won't close when tapped.) Scrape the shells under cold running water and pull off the hairy beard attached to the hinge of the shell. Rinse well in two or three changes of water.

2 Heat the oil and butter in a large pan and fry the onions and garlic for 3–4 minutes.

3 Pour on the wine or cider and add the parsley sprigs, stir well, bring to the boil, then add the mussels. Cover with a tight-fitting lid and cook for about 5–7 minutes, shaking the pan once or twice until the shells open (throw away any that have not opened).

4 Serve the mussels and their juices sprinkled with the chopped parsley and some ground black pepper. Accompany with hot French bread.

Thai Prawn Salad

This salad has the distinctive flavour of lemon grass, the bulbous grass used widely in South-East Asian cooking.

Serves 2

250g/9oz/2¼ cups peeled, cooked, extra large tiger prawns
15ml/1 tbsp oriental fish sauce
30ml/2 tbsp lime juice
7.5ml/½ tbsp soft light brown sugar
1 small fresh red chilli, finely chopped
1 spring onion, finely chopped

1 small garlic clove, crushed
2.5cm/1in piece fresh lemon grass, finely chopped
30ml/2 tbsp chopped fresh coriander
45ml/3 tbsp dry white wine
8–12 Little Gem lettuce leaves, to serve
fresh coriander sprigs, to garnish

1 Place the tiger prawns in a bowl and add all the remaining ingredients. Stir well, cover and leave to marinate in the fridge for 2–3 hours, mixing and turning the prawns from time to time.

2 Arrange two or three of the lettuce leaves on each of four individual serving plates.

3 Spoon the prawn salad into the lettuce leaves. Garnish with fresh coriander and serve at once.

Cajun Spiced Fish

Fillets of fish are coated with an aromatic blend of herbs and spices and pan-fried in butter.

Serves 4

5ml/1 tsp dried thyme
5ml/1 tsp dried oregano
5ml/1 tsp ground black pepper
1.25ml/¼ tsp cayenne pepper
10ml/2 tsp paprika
2.5ml/½ tsp garlic salt
75g/3oz/6 tbsp butter

4 x tail end pieces of cod fillet (about 175g/6oz each)
½ fresh red pepper, sliced
½ green pepper, sliced
fresh thyme sprigs, to garnish
grilled tomatoes and sweet potato purée, to serve

1 Place all the herbs and spices in a bowl and mix well. Dip the fish fillets in the spice mixture until lightly coated.

2 Heat 25g/1oz/2 tbsp of the butter in a large frying pan, add the peppers and fry for 4–5 minutes, until softened. Remove the peppers and keep warm.

3 Add the remaining butter to the pan and heat until sizzling. Add the cod fillets and fry over a moderate heat for about 3–4 minutes on each side, until browned and cooked.

4 Transfer the fish to a warmed serving dish, surround with the peppers and garnish with thyme. Serve the spiced fish with some grilled tomatoes and sweet potato purée.

Golden Fish Pie

This lovely light pie with a crumpled filo pastry topping makes a delicious lunch or supper dish.

Serves 4–6

675g/1½lb white fish
    fillets
300ml/½ pint/1¼ cups
    milk
flavouring ingredients
    such as onion slices,
    bay leaf and black
    peppercorns
115g/4oz/1 cup peeled,
    cooked prawns,
    defrosted if frozen
115g/4oz/½ cup butter

50g/2oz/½ cup plain
    flour
300ml/½ pint/1¼ cups
    single cream
75g/3oz/¾ cup grated
    Gruyère cheese
1 bunch watercress,
    leaves only, chopped
5ml/1 tsp mustard
5 sheets filo pastry
salt and ground black
    pepper

1 Place the fish in a saucepan, pour over the milk and add the flavouring ingredients. Bring to the boil, cover with a lid and simmer for 10–12 minutes, until the fish is almost tender. Skin and bone the fish, then roughly flake into a shallow ovenproof dish. Scatter the prawns over the fish. Strain the milk and reserve.

2 Melt 50g/2oz/4 tbsp of the butter in a pan. Stir in the flour; cook for 1 minute. Stir in the milk and cream. Bring to the boil, stirring, then simmer for 2–3 minutes, until thickened. Remove from the heat and stir in the Gruyère, watercress, mustard, and season. Pour the mixture over the fish and leave to cool.

3 Preheat the oven to 190°C/375°F/Gas 5, then melt the remaining butter. Brush one sheet of filo pastry with a little butter, then crumple up loosely and place on top of the filling. Repeat with the remaining filo sheets and butter until they are all used up and the pie is completely covered.

4 Bake in the oven for 25–30 minutes, until the pastry is golden and crisp. Serve immediately.

Special Fish Pie

This fish pie is colourful, healthy and best of all, it is very simple to make.

Serves 4

350g/12oz haddock fillet,
    skinned
30ml/2 tbsp cornflour
115g/4oz/1 cup peeled,
    cooked prawns
200g/7oz can sweetcorn,
    drained
75g/3oz/scant 1 cup
    frozen peas
150ml/¼ pint/⅔ cup
    skimmed milk

150ml/¼ pint/⅔ cup
    low-fat fromage frais
75g/3oz/1½ cups fresh
    wholemeal
    breadcrumbs
40g/1½oz/generous
    ¼ cup grated reduced-
    fat Cheddar cheese
salt and ground black
    pepper

1 Preheat the oven to 190°C/375°F/Gas 5. Cut the haddock into bite-size pieces and toss in cornflour to coat evenly.

2 Place the fish, prawns, sweetcorn and peas in an ovenproof dish. Beat together the milk, fromage frais and seasoning, then pour into the dish.

3 Mix together the breadcrumbs and grated cheese, then spoon evenly over the top. Bake for 25–30 minutes, or until golden brown. Serve hot with fresh vegetables.

Cook's Tip
For a more economical version of this dish, omit the prawns and replace with more fish fillet.

Smoked Trout with Cucumber

Smoked trout provides an easy and delicious first course or light meal. Serve at room temperature for the best flavour.

Serves 4

1 large cucumber	4 smoked trout fillets
60ml/4 tbsp crème	salt and ground black
fraîche or Greek-style	pepper
yogurt	dill sprigs, to garnish
15ml/1 tbsp chopped	crusty wholemeal bread,
fresh dill	to serve

1 Peel the cucumber, cut in half lengthways and scoop out the seeds using a teaspoon. Cut into tiny dice.

2 Put the cucumber in a colander set over a plate and sprinkle with salt. Leave to drain for at least 1 hour to draw out the excess moisture.

3 Rinse the cucumber well, then pat dry on kitchen paper. Transfer the diced cucumber to a bowl and stir in the crème fraîche or yogurt, chopped dill and some freshly ground pepper. Chill the cucumber salad for about 30 minutes.

4 Arrange the trout fillets on individual plates. Spoon the cucumber and dill salad on one side and grind over a little black pepper. Garnish the dish with dill sprigs and serve with crusty bread.

Fish Cakes

Home-made fish cakes are an underrated food which bear little resemblance to the shop-bought type.

Serves 4

450g/1lb cooked, mashed	1 egg, separated
potatoes	1 egg, beaten
450g/1lb cooled mixed	fine breadcrumbs made
white and smoked fish	with stale bread (about
such as haddock or	50g/2oz/1 cup)
cod, flaked	pinch of pepper
25g/1oz/2 tbsp butter,	vegetable oil, for
cubed	shallow frying
45ml/3 tbsp chopped	
fresh parsley	

1 Place the potatoes in a bowl and beat in the fish, butter, parsley and egg yolk. Season to taste with pepper.

2 Divide the fish mixture into eight equal portions, then, with floured hands, form each into a flat cake.

3 Beat the remaining egg white with the whole egg. Dip each fish cake in the beaten egg, then in breadcrumbs.

4 Heat the oil in a frying pan and fry the fish cakes for about 3–5 minutes on each side, until crisp and golden. Drain on kitchen paper and serve hot with a crisp salad.

Cook's Tip
Make smaller fish cakes to serve as a starter with a salad garnish. For an extra special version, make them with cooked fresh salmon or drained, canned red or pink salmon.

Stuffed Plaice Rolls

Plaice fillets are a good choice for families because they are economical, easy to cook and free of bones.

Serves 4

1 courgette, grated	15ml/1 tbsp lime or
2 carrots, grated	lemon juice
60ml/4 tbsp fresh	4 plaice fillets
wholemeal	salt and ground black
breadcrumbs	pepper

1 Preheat the oven to 200°C/400°F/Gas 6. Mix together the carrots and courgettes. Stir in the breadcrumbs, lime juice and season with salt and pepper.

2 Lay the fish fillets skin-side up and divide the stuffing between them, spreading it evenly.

3 Roll up to enclose the stuffing and place in an ovenproof dish. Cover and bake for about 30 minutes, or until the fish flakes easily. Serve hot with new potatoes.

Mackerel Kebabs with Parsley

Oily fish such as mackerel are ideal for grilling as they cook quickly and need no extra oil.

Serves 4

450g/1lb mackerel fillets	12 cherry tomatoes
finely grated rind and	8 stoned black olives
juice of 1 lemon	salt and ground black
45ml/3 tbsp chopped	pepper
fresh parsley	

1 Cut the fish into 4cm/1½in chunks and place in a bowl with half the lemon rind and juice, half of the parsley and some seasoning. Cover the bowl and leave to marinate for about 30 minutes.

2 Thread the chunks of fish on to eight long wooden or metal skewers, alternating them with the cherry tomatoes and olives. Cook the kebabs under a hot grill for 3–4 minutes, turning the kebabs occasionally until the fish is cooked.

3 Mix the remaining lemon rind and juice with the remaining parsley in a small bowl, then season to taste with salt and pepper. Spoon the dressing over the kebabs. Serve hot with plain boiled rice or noodles and a leafy green salad.

Grilled Salmon Steaks with Fennel

Fennel grows wild all over the south of Italy. Its mild aniseed flavour goes well with fish.

Serves 4

juice of 1 lemon
45ml/3 tbsp chopped
 fresh fennel, or the
 green fronds from the
 top of a fennel bulb
5ml/1 tsp fennel seeds
45ml/3 tbsp olive oil

4 salmon steaks of the
 same thickness (about
 700g/1½lb)
salt and ground black
 pepper
lemon wedges, to garnish

1 Combine the lemon juice, chopped fennel and fennel seeds with the olive oil in a bowl. Add the salmon steaks, turning them to coat them with the marinade. Sprinkle with salt and ground black pepper. Cover and place in the fridge. Allow to stand for about 2 hours.

2 Preheat the grill. Arrange the fish in one layer on a grill pan or shallow baking tray. Grill about 10cm/4in from the heat source for 3–4 minutes.

3 Turn the steaks over and spoon on the remaining marinade. Grill for 3–4 minutes, or until the edges begin to brown. Serve hot, garnished with lemon wedges.

Cook's Tip
If you wish, remove the skin from the salmon steaks before serving. Simply insert the prongs of a fork between the flesh and the skin at one end and roll the skin around the prongs in a fluent action.

Seafood Pilaff

This one-pan dish makes a satisfying meal. For a special occasion, use dry white wine instead of orange juice.

Serves 4

10ml/2 tsp olive oil
250g/9oz/1¼ cups long
 grain rice
5ml/1 tsp ground
 turmeric
1 fresh red pepper, seeded
 and diced
1 small onion, finely
 chopped
2 courgettes, sliced
150g/5oz button
 mushrooms, wiped
 and halved

350ml/12fl oz/1½ cups
 fish or chicken stock
150ml/¼ pint/⅔ cup
 orange juice
350g/12oz white fish
 fillets
12 live mussels (or
 cooked shelled
 mussels)
salt and ground black
 pepper
grated rind of 1 orange,
 to garnish

1 Heat the oil in a large non-stick frying pan and fry the rice and turmeric over a gentle heat for about 1 minute.

2 Add the pepper, onion, courgettes and mushrooms. Stir in the stock and orange juice. Bring to the boil.

3 Reduce the heat and add the fish. Cover with a tight-fitting lid and simmer gently for about 15 minutes, until the rice is tender and the liquid absorbed. Stir in the mussels and heat thoroughly. Adjust the seasoning, sprinkle with orange rind and serve hot.

Cook's Tip
If you wish, bring the pan to the table, rather than transferring the pilaff to a serving dish, and let everyone help themselves.

Grilled Fresh Sardines

Fresh sardines are flavoursome, firm-fleshed and rather different in taste and consistency from those canned in oil.

Serves 4–6

900kg/2lb very heavy
  fresh sardines, gutted
  and with heads
  removed
olive oil, for brushing

salt and ground black
  pepper
45ml/3 tbsp chopped
  fresh parsley, to serve
lemon wedges, to garnish

1 Preheat the grill. Rinse the sardines in water. Pat dry with kitchen paper.

2 Brush the sardines lightly with olive oil and sprinkle generously with salt and pepper. Place the sardines in one layer in a grill pan. Grill for about 3–4 minutes.

3 Turn, and cook for 3–4 minutes more, or until the skin begins to brown. Serve immediately, sprinkled with parsley and garnished with lemon wedges.

Cook's Tip
Frozen sardines are now available in supermarkets and will keep well in the freezer for 6 weeks. Thaw them in the fridge overnight, then use a sharp pointed knife to slit the belly, remove the innards and cut the heads off. For a fuller flavour, you might like to leave them whole, as they do in some Mediterranean countries.

Red Mullet with Tomatoes

Red mullet is a popular fish in Italy, and in this recipe both its flavour and colour are accentuated.

Serves 4

4 red mullet (about
  175–200g/6–7oz each)
450g/1lb tomatoes,
  peeled, or 400g/14oz
  can plum tomatoes
60ml/4 tbsp olive oil
60ml/4 tbsp finely
  chopped fresh parsley

2 cloves garlic, finely
  chopped
120ml/4fl oz/½ cup dry
  white wine
4 thin lemon slices, cut
  in half
salt and ground black
  pepper

1 Scale and clean the fish without removing the liver. Wash and pat dry with kitchen paper.

2 Finely chop the tomatoes. Heat the oil in a saucepan or casserole large enough to hold the fish in one layer. Add the parsley and garlic, and sauté for 1 minute. Stir in the tomatoes and cook over a moderate heat for 15–20 minutes. Season to taste with salt and pepper.

3 Add the red mullets to the tomato sauce and cook over a moderate to high heat for 5 minutes. Add the wine and the lemon slices. Bring the sauce back to the boil, and cook for about 5 minutes more. Turn the fish over and continue to cook for 4–5 minutes more. Remove the fish to a warmed serving platter and keep warm until needed.

4 Boil the sauce for 3–4 minutes to reduce it slightly, then spoon it over the fish and serve immediately.

Cook's Tip
To peel fresh tomatoes, use a sharp knife to make a slit in their bases, plunge into boiling water for 30 seconds, or until the skins split, and then plunge into cold water. The skins should then slip off easily.

Middle-Eastern Sea Bream

Buy the smallest sea bream you can find to cook whole, allowing one for two people.

Serves 4

1.75kg/4lb sea bream or
   2 smaller sea bream
30ml/2 tbsp olive oil
75g/3oz/¾ cup pine nuts
1 large onion, finely
   chopped
450g/1lb ripe tomatoes,
   roughly chopped
75g/3oz/½ cup raisins
1.5ml/¼ tsp ground
   cinnamon

1.5ml/¼ tsp mixed spice
45ml/3 tbsp chopped
   fresh mint
225g/8oz/1¼ cups
   long grain rice
3 lemon slices
300ml/½ pint/1¼ cups
   fish stock

1 Trim, gut and scale the sea bream. Meanwhile, preheat the oven to 175°C/350°F/Gas 4.

2 Heat the oil in a large heavy-based saucepan and stir-fry the pine nuts for 1 minute. Add the onions and continue to stir-fry until softened but not coloured.

3 Add the tomatoes and simmer for 10 minutes, then stir in the raisins, cinnamon, mixed spice and mint.

4 Add the rice and lemon slices. Transfer to a large roasting tin and pour the fish stock over the top.

5 Place the fish on top and cut several slashes in the skin. Sprinkle over a little salt, mixed spice and cinnamon and bake in the preheated oven for 30–35 minutes for large fish or 20–25 minutes for smaller fish.

Cook's Tip

If you prefer, use almonds instead of pine nuts. Use the same quantity of blanched almonds and split them in half before stir-frying.

Salmon with Spicy Pesto

This pesto uses sunflower seeds and chilli as its flavouring rather than the classic basil and pine nuts.

Serves 4

4 x 225g/8oz salmon
   steaks
30ml/2 tbsp sunflower oil
finely grated rind and
   juice of 1 lime
pinch of salt

For the pesto
6 mild fresh red chillies
2 garlic cloves
30ml/2 tbsp pumpkin or
   sunflower seeds
freshly grated rind and
   juice of 1 lime
75ml/5 tbsp olive oil
salt and ground black
   pepper

1 Insert a very sharp knife close to the top of the salmon's backbone. Working closely to the bone, cut your way to the end of the steak so one side of the steak has been released and one side is still attached. Repeat with the other side. Pull out any extra visible bones with a pair of tweezers.

2 Sprinkle a little salt on the surface and take hold of the end of the salmon, skin-side down. Insert a small sharp knife under the skin and, working away from you, cut off the skin keeping as close to the skin as possible. Repeat with the three remaining pieces of fish.

3 Rub the sunflower oil into the boneless fish rounds. Add the lime juice and rind and marinate in the fridge for 2 hours.

4 To make the pesto, seed the chillies and place them together with the garlic cloves, pumpkin or sunflower seeds, lime juice, rind and seasoning in a food processor or blender. Process until well mixed. Pour the olive oil gradually over the moving blades until the sauce has thickened and emulsified. Drain the salmon from its marinade. Grill the fish steaks for about 5 minutes on either side and serve with the spicy pesto.

Roast Chicken with Celeriac

Celeriac and brown breadcrumbs give the stuffing an unusual and delicious twist.

Serves 4

1.6kg/3½lb chicken
15g/½ oz/1 tbsp butter

For the stuffing
450g/1lb celeriac, chopped
25g/1oz/2 tbsp butter
3 slices bacon, chopped
1 onion, finely chopped
leaves from 1 fresh thyme sprig, chopped

leaves from 1 fresh small tarragon sprig, chopped
30ml/2 tbsp chopped fresh parsley
75g/3oz/1½ cups fresh brown breadcrumbs
dash of Worcestershire sauce
1 egg
salt and ground black pepper

1 To make the stuffing, cook the celeriac in boiling water until tender. Drain well and chop finely. Heat the butter in a saucepan and gently cook the bacon and onion until the onion is soft. Stir in the celeriac and herbs and cook, stirring occasionally, for 2–3 minutes. Meanwhile, preheat the oven to 200°C/400°F/Gas 6.

2 Remove the pan from the heat and stir in the fresh breadcrumbs, Worcestershire sauce, sufficient egg to bind the mixture, and season it with salt and pepper. Use this mixture to stuff the neck end of the chicken. Season the bird's skin, then rub it with the butter.

3 Roast the chicken, basting occasionally with the juices, for 1¼–1½ hours, until the juices run clear when the thickest part of the leg is pierced. Turn off the oven, prop the door open slightly and allow the chicken to rest for about 10 minutes before carving.

Chicken with Lemon and Herbs

The herbs can be changed according to what is available; for example, parsley or thyme could be used.

Serves 2

50g/2oz/4 tbsp butter
2 spring onions, white part only, finely chopped
15ml/1 tbsp chopped fresh tarragon

15ml/1 tbsp chopped fresh fennel
juice of 1 lemon
4 chicken thighs
salt and ground black pepper
lemon slices and herb sprigs, to garnish

1 Preheat the grill to moderate. In a small saucepan, melt the butter, then add the spring onions, herbs, lemon juice and season with salt and pepper.

2 Brush the chicken thighs generously with the herb mixture, then grill for 10–12 minutes, basting frequently with the herb mixture.

3 Turn the chicken over and baste again, then cook for a further 10–12 minutes or until the chicken juices run clear.

4 Serve the chicken garnished with lemon slices and herb sprigs, and accompanied by any remaining herb mixture.

Chicken with Peppers

This colourful dish comes from the south of Italy, where sweet peppers are plentiful.

Serves 4

1.5kg/3lb chicken, cut
   into serving pieces
3 large fresh peppers, red,
   yellow or green
90ml/6 tbsp olive oil
2 red onions, finely sliced
2 garlic cloves, finely
   chopped
small piece of dried chilli,
   crumbled (optional)

120ml/4fl oz/½ cup dry
   white wine
2 tomatoes, fresh or
   canned, peeled and
   chopped
45g/3 tbsp chopped fresh
   parsley
salt and ground black
   pepper

1   Trim any fat off the chicken and remove all excess skin. Wash the peppers. Prepare by cutting them in half, scooping out the seeds, and cutting away the stem. Slice into strips.

2   Heat half the oil in a large heavy saucepan or casserole and cook the onion over a gentle heat until soft. Remove to a side dish. Add the remaining oil to the pan, raise the heat to moderate, add the chicken pieces and brown them on all sides, 6–8 minutes. Return the onions to the pan, and add the garlic and dried chilli, if using.

3   Pour in the wine and cook until it has reduced by half. Add the peppers and stir well to coat. Season to taste. After 3–4 minutes, stir in the tomatoes. Lower the heat, cover the pan with a tight-fitting lid, and cook for about 25–30 minutes, until the peppers are soft and the chicken is cooked. Stir occasionally. Stir in the parsley and serve.

Cook's Tip

For a more elegant version of this dish to serve at a dinner party, use skinless, boneless chicken breasts. Substitute the fresh parsley with different chopped fresh herbs, such as coriander, tarragon, rosemary, chervil or marjoram.

Golden Parmesan Chicken

Served cold with the garlic mayonnaise, these morsels of chicken make good picnic food.

Serves 4

4 chicken breast fillets,
   skinned
75g/3oz/1½ cups fresh
   white breadcrumbs
40g/1½oz/½ cup
   Parmesan cheese,
   finely grated
30ml/2 tbsp chopped
   fresh parsley
2 eggs, beaten
50g/2oz/4 tbsp butter,
   melted

salt and ground black
   pepper

**For the garlic
mayonnaise**
120ml/4fl oz/½ cup good
   quality mayonnaise
120ml/4fl oz/½ cup
   fromage frais
1–2 garlic cloves,
   crushed

1   Cut each chicken fillet into four or five large chunks. Mix together the breadcrumbs, Parmesan cheese, parsley and salt and pepper in a shallow dish.

2   Dip the chicken pieces in the beaten egg, then into the breadcrumb mixture. Place in a single layer on a baking sheet and chill in the fridge for at least 30 minutes.

3   Meanwhile, to make the garlic mayonnaise, mix the mayonnaise, fromage frais, garlic and pepper to taste. Spoon the mayonnaise into a small serving bowl. Chill in the fridge until ready to serve.

4   Preheat the oven to 180°C/350°F/Gas 4. Drizzle the melted butter over the chicken pieces and cook for about 20 minutes, until crisp and golden. Serve the chicken immediately with a crisp green salad and the garlic mayonnaise for dipping.

Chicken in Green Sauce

Slow, gentle cooking makes the chicken in this dish very succulent and tender.

Serves 4
25g/1oz/2 tbsp butter
15ml/1 tbsp olive oil
4 chicken portions (legs, breasts or quarters)
1 small onion, finely chopped
150ml/¼ pint/⅔ cup medium-bodied dry white wine
150ml/¼ pint/⅔ cup chicken stock

leaves from 2 fresh thyme sprigs and 2 fresh tarragon sprigs
175g/6oz watercress, leaves removed
150ml/¼ pint/⅔ cup double cream
salt and ground black pepper
watercress leaves, to garnish

1 Heat the butter and oil in a frying pan and brown the chicken evenly. Transfer the chicken to a plate using a slotted spoon and keep warm in the oven.

2 Add the onion to the cooking juices in the pan and cook until softened but not coloured. Stir in the wine, then boil for 2–3 minutes. Add the stock and bring to the boil. Return the chicken to the pan, cover with a tight-fitting lid and cook very gently for about 30 minutes, until the chicken juices run clear when pierced with the point of a knife. Then transfer the chicken to a warm dish, cover and keep warm.

3 Boil the cooking juices hard until they are reduced to about 60ml/4 tbsp. Remove the leaves from the herbs and add to the pan with the watercress leaves and cream. Simmer over a moderate heat until slightly thickened.

4 Return the chicken to the casserole, season to taste with salt and pepper and heat through for a few minutes. Garnish with watercress leaves to serve.

Spatchcocked Devilled Poussin

"Spatchcock" refers to birds that have been split and skewered flat. This shortens the cooking time considerably.

Serves 4
15ml/1 tbsp English mustard powder
15ml/1 tbsp paprika
15ml/1 tbsp ground cumin
20ml/4 tsp tomato ketchup

15ml/1 tbsp lemon juice
65g/2½ oz/5 tbsp butter, melted
4 poussins (about 450g/1lb each)
pinch of salt

1 Mix together the mustard, paprika, cumin, ketchup, lemon juice and salt until smooth, then gradually stir in the butter.

2 Using game shears or strong kitchen scissors, split each poussin along one side of the backbone, then cut down the other side of the backbone to remove it.

3 Open out a poussin, skin-side uppermost, then press down firmly with the heel of your hand. Pass a long skewer through one leg and out through the other to secure the bird open and flat. Repeat with the remaining birds.

4 Spread the mustard mixture evenly over the skin of the birds. Cover loosely and leave in a cool place for at least 2 hours to marinate. Preheat the grill.

5 Place the birds, skin-side uppermost, under the grill and cook for about 12 minutes. Turn the birds over, baste with any juices in the pan, and cook for a further 7 minutes, until the juices run clear when pierced with the point of a knife.

Cook's Tip
For an al fresco meal in the summer, these spatchcocked poussins may be cooked on a barbecue.

Stoved Chicken

"Stoved" is derived from the French *étouffer*, meaning to cook in a covered pot.

Serves 4

1kg/2lb potatoes, cut into
   5mm/¼ in slices
2 large onions, thinly
   sliced
15ml/1 tbsp chopped
   fresh thyme
25g/1oz/2 tbsp butter
15ml/1 tbsp sunflower oil

2 large slices bacon,
   chopped
4 large chicken joints,
   halved
1 bay leaf
600ml/1 pint/2½ cups
   chicken stock
salt and ground black
   pepper

1 Preheat the oven to 150°C/300°F/Gas 2. Make a thick layer of half the potato slices in a large heavy-based casserole, then cover with half the onion. Sprinkle with half of the thyme and the seasoning.

2 Heat the butter and oil in a large frying pan and brown the bacon and chicken. Using a draining spoon, transfer the chicken and bacon to the casserole. Reserve the fat in the pan. Sprinkle the remaining thyme and some seasoning over the chicken. Cover with the remaining onion, followed by a neat layer of overlapping potato slices. Sprinkle with seasoning.

3 Pour the stock into the casserole, brush the potatoes with the reserved fat, then cover with a tight-fitting lid and cook in the oven for about 2 hours, until the chicken is tender.

4 Preheat the grill. Uncover the casserole and place under the grill. Cook until the slices of potatoes are beginning to brown and crisp. Serve hot.

Cook's Tip
Instead of using large chicken joints, use thighs or drumsticks, or a mixture of the two.

Chicken with Red Cabbage

Crushed juniper berries provide a distinctive flavour in this unusual casserole.

Serves 4

50g/oz/4 tbsp butter
4 large chicken joints,
   halved
1 onion, chopped
500g/1¼lb/8¼ cups red
   cabbage, shredded
   finely

4 juniper berries, crushed
12 cooked chestnuts
120ml/4fl oz/½ cup
   full-bodied red wine
salt and ground black
   pepper

1 Heat the butter in a heavy-based flameproof casserole and lightly brown the chicken pieces. Transfer to a plate.

2 Add the onion to the casserole and fry gently until soft and light golden brown. Stir the cabbage and juniper berries into the casserole, season and cook over a moderate heat for about 6–7 minutes, stirring once or twice.

3 Stir the chestnuts into the casserole, then tuck the chicken pieces under the cabbage so they are on the base of the casserole. Pour in the red wine.

4 Cover and cook gently for about 40 minutes until the chicken juices run clear and the cabbage is very tender. Adjust the seasoning to taste and serve immediately.

Italian Chicken

Use chicken legs, breasts or quarters in this colourful dish, and a different type of pasta if you prefer.

Serves 4

25g/1oz/2 tbsp plain
    flour
4 chicken portions
30ml/2 tbsp olive oil
1 onion, chopped
2 garlic cloves, chopped
1 fresh red pepper, seeded
    and chopped
400g/14oz can chopped
    tomatoes
30ml/2 tbsp red pesto
    sauce

4 sun-dried tomatoes in
    oil, chopped
150ml/¼ pint/⅔ cup
    chicken stock
5ml/1 tsp dried oregano
8 black olives, stoned
salt and ground black
    pepper
chopped fresh basil and
    whole basil leaves, to
    garnish
tagliatelle, to serve

1   Place the flour and seasoning in a plastic bag. Add the chicken pieces and shake well until coated. Heat the oil in a flameproof casserole and brown the chicken quickly. Remove with a slotted spoon and set aside.

2   Lower the heat and add the onion, garlic and pepper and cook for 5 minutes. Stir in the remaining ingredients, except the olives, and bring to the boil.

3   Return the sautéed chicken portions to the casserole, season lightly, cover with a tight-fitting lid and simmer for 30–35 minutes, or until the chicken is cooked.

4   Add the black olives and simmer for a further 5 minutes. Transfer to a warmed serving dish, sprinkle with the chopped basil and garnish with basil leaves. Serve with hot tagliatelle.

Cook's Tip
If you do not have red pesto sauce, use green pesto instead. Finely chop then purée two sun-dried tomato pieces in a blender or food processor and add with the other ingredients.

Honey and Orange Glazed Chicken

This dish is popular in the United States and Australia and is ideal for an easy meal served with baked potatoes.

Serves 4

4 x 175g/6oz boneless
    chicken breasts
15ml/1 tbsp sunflower oil
4 spring onions, chopped
1 garlic clove, crushed
45ml/3 tbsp clear honey
60ml/4 tbsp fresh orange
    juice

1 orange, peeled and
    segmented
30ml/2 tbsp soy sauce
fresh lemon balm or flat-
    leaf parsley, to garnish
baked potatoes and mixed
    salad, to serve

1   Preheat the oven to 190°C/375°F/Gas 5. Place the chicken breasts, with skins on, in a single layer in a shallow roasting tin and set aside.

2   Heat the sunflower oil in a small saucepan, and gently fry the spring onions and garlic for about 2 minutes until softened but not browned. Add the honey, orange juice, orange segments and soy sauce to the pan, stirring well, and cook until the honey has completely dissolved.

3   Pour the sauce over the chicken and bake, uncovered, for about 45 minutes, basting once or twice until the chicken is cooked. Check by piercing with the point of a knife; the juices should run clear. Garnish with lemon balm or flat leaf parsley and serve with baked potatoes and a salad.

Cook's Tip
For a slightly spicier version, look out for mustard that has been flavoured with honey to add to this dish instead of the clear honey. Use the same amount.

Cajun Chicken Jambalaya

Wonderfully spicy Cajun cooking was developed by the French-speaking immigrants in Louisiana, USA.

Serves 4

1.2kg/2½lb fresh chicken
1½ onions
1 bay leaf
4 black peppercorns
30ml/2 tbsp vegetable oil
2 garlic cloves, chopped
1 green pepper, seeded
    and chopped
1 celery stick, chopped
225g/8oz/1¼ cups long
    grain rice
115g/4oz chorizo
    sausage, sliced
115g/4oz/1 cup chopped,
    cooked ham

400g/14oz can chopped
    tomatoes
2.5ml/½ tsp hot chilli
    powder
2.5ml/½ tsp cumin seeds
2.5ml/½ tsp ground
    cumin
5ml/1 tsp dried thyme
115g/4oz/1 cup peeled,
    cooked prawns
dash of Tabasco sauce
salt and ground black
    pepper
chopped fresh parsley, to
    garnish

1 Place the chicken in a flameproof casserole and pour over 600ml/1 pint/2½ cups water. Add half an onion, the bay leaf and peppercorns and bring to the boil. Cover and simmer for 1½ hours. Then lift the chicken out of the pan. Skin, bone and chop the meat. Strain the stock and reserve.

2 Chop the remaining whole onion. Heat the oil in a large frying pan and fry the onion, garlic, green pepper and celery for 5 minutes. Stir in the rice. Add the sausage, ham and chicken and fry for 2–3 minutes, stirring frequently.

3 Pour in the tomatoes and 300ml/½ pint/1¼ cups of the reserved stock and add the chilli, cumin and thyme. Bring to the boil, cover and simmer gently for 20 minutes, or until the rice is tender and the liquid absorbed.

4 Stir in the prawns and Tabasco. Cook for 5 minutes more, then season to taste with salt and ground black pepper. Serve hot, garnished with chopped fresh parsley.

Moroccan Chicken Couscous

The combination of sweet and spicy flavours in the sauce and couscous makes this dish irresistible.

Serves 4

15g/½oz/1 tbsp butter
15ml/1 tbsp sunflower oil
4 chicken portions
2 onions, finely chopped
2 garlic cloves, crushed
2.5ml/½ tsp ground
    cinnamon
1.5ml/¼ tsp ground
    ginger
1.5ml/¼ tsp ground
    turmeric
30ml/2 tbsp orange juice
10ml/2 tsp clear honey
pinch of salt
fresh mint sprigs,
    to garnish

For the couscous
350g/12oz/2¼ cups
    couscous
5ml/1 tsp salt
10ml/2 tsp caster sugar
15ml/1 tbsp sunflower oil
2.5ml/½ tsp ground
    cinnamon
pinch of grated nutmeg
15ml/1 tbsp orange
    blossom water
30ml/2 tbsp sultanas
50g/2oz/½ cup chopped
    toasted almonds
45ml/3 tbsp chopped
    pistachios

1 Fry the chicken portions, skin-side down in the butter and oil until golden. Turn them over. Add the onions, garlic, spices, a pinch of salt, the orange juice and 300ml/½ pint/1¼ cups water. Cover and bring to the boil, then simmer for about 30 minutes.

2 Mix the couscous with the salt and 350ml/12fl oz/1½ cups water. Leave for 5 minutes. Add the rest of the ingredients for the couscous.

3 Line a steamer with greaseproof paper and spoon in the couscous. Set over the chicken and steam for 10 minutes.

4 Remove the steamer and keep covered. Stir the honey into the chicken liquid and boil rapidly for 3–4 minutes. Serve the chicken on a bed of couscous with some sauce spooned over. Garnish with fresh mint and serve with the remaining sauce.

Rabbit with Mustard

Rabbit is increasingly available in larger supermarkets, ready prepared and jointed.

Serves 4

15g/½oz/1 tbsp plain flour	10–15ml/2–3 tsp prepared English mustard
15ml/1 tbsp English mustard powder	salt and ground black pepper
4 large rabbit joints	
25g/1oz/2 tbsp butter	**To finish**
30ml/2 tbsp oil	50g/2oz/4 tbsp butter
1 onion, finely chopped	30ml/2 tbsp oil
150ml/¼ pint/⅔ cup beer	50g/2oz/1 cup fresh breadcrumbs
300ml/½ pint/1¼ cups chicken or veal stock	15ml/1 tbsp snipped fresh chives
15ml/1 tbsp tarragon vinegar	15ml/1 tbsp chopped fresh tarragon
25g/1oz/2 tbsp dark brown sugar	

1 Preheat the oven to 160°C/325°F/Gas 3. Mix the flour and mustard powder together, then put on a plate. Dip the rabbit joints in the flour mixture; reserve the excess flour. Heat the butter and oil in a heavy flameproof casserole and brown the rabbit. Transfer to a plate. Stir in the onion and cook until soft.

2 Stir any reserved flour mixture into the casserole, cook for 1 minute, then stir in the beer, stock and vinegar. Bring to the boil and add the sugar and pepper. Simmer for 2 minutes. Return the rabbit and any juices that have collected on the plate to the casserole, cover with a tight-fitting lid and cook in the oven for 1 hour. Stir the mustard and salt to taste into the casserole, cover again and cook for a further 15 minutes.

3 To finish, heat together the butter and oil in a frying pan and fry the breadcrumbs, stirring frequently, until golden, then stir in the herbs. Transfer the rabbit to a warmed serving dish and sprinkle the breadcrumb mixture over the top.

Turkey Hot-pot

Turkey and sausages combine well with kidney beans and other vegetables in this hearty stew.

Serves 4

115g/4oz/scant ½ cup kidney beans, soaked overnight, drained and rinsed	2 carrots, finely chopped
	4 tomatoes, chopped
	10–15ml/2–3 tsp tomato purée
40g/1½oz/3 tbsp butter	bouquet garni
2 herby pork sausages	400ml/14fl oz/1¾ cups chicken stock
450g/1lb turkey casserole meat	salt and ground black pepper
3 leeks, sliced	

1 Cook the kidney beans in unsalted boiling water for 40 minutes, then drain well.

2 Meanwhile, heat the butter in a flameproof casserole, then cook the sausages until browned and the fat runs. Drain on kitchen paper, stir the turkey into the casserole and cook until lightly browned all over, then transfer to a bowl using a slotted spoon. Stir the leeks and carrot into the casserole and brown them lightly, stirring occasionally.

3 Add the chopped tomatoes and tomato purée and simmer gently for about 5 minutes.

4 Chop the sausages and return to the casserole with the beans, turkey, bouquet garni, stock and seasoning. Cover with a tight-fitting lid and cook gently for about 1¼ hours, until the beans are tender and there is very little liquid.

Duck with Cumberland Sauce

Coronation Chicken

A sophisticated dish: the sauce contains both port and brandy, making it very rich.

Serves 4

4 duck portions	60ml/4 tbsp port
grated rind and juice of 1 lemon	pinch of ground mace or ginger
grated rind and juice of 1 large orange	15ml/1 tbsp brandy
60ml/4 tbsp redcurrant jelly	salt and ground black pepper
	orange slices, to garnish

1 Preheat the oven to 190°C/375°F/Gas 5. Place a rack in a roasting tin. Prick the duck portions all over, sprinkle with salt and pepper. Place on the rack and cook in the oven for 45–50 minutes, until the duck skin is crisp and the juices run clear when pricked with the point of a knife.

2 Meanwhile, simmer the lemon and orange rinds and juices together in a saucepan for 5 minutes.

3 Add the redcurrant jelly and stir until melted, then stir in the port. Bring to the boil and add mace or ginger and salt and pepper, to taste.

4 Transfer the duck to a serving plate; keep warm. Pour the fat from the roasting tin, leaving the cooking juices. With the tin over a gentle heat, stir in the brandy, dislodge the sediment and bring to the boil. Stir in the port sauce and serve with the duck, garnished with orange slices.

A cold chicken dish with a mild, curry-flavoured sauce, ideal for summer lunch parties.

Serves 8

½ lemon	15ml/1 tbsp tomato purée
2.25kg/5lb chicken	120ml/4fl oz/½ cup red wine
1 onion, quartered	1 bay leaf
1 carrot, quartered	juice of ½ lemon, or more to taste
large bouquet garni	10–15ml/2–3 tsp apricot jam
8 black peppercorns, crushed	300ml/½ pint/1¼ cups mayonnaise
pinch of salt	120ml/4fl oz/½ cup whipping cream, whipped
fresh watercress sprigs, to garnish	salt and ground black pepper

For the sauce

1 small onion, chopped
15g/½oz/1 tbsp butter
15ml/1 tbsp curry paste

1 Put the lemon half in the chicken cavity, then place the chicken in a saucepan that it just fits. Add the vegetables, bouquet garni, peppercorns and salt.

2 Add sufficient water to come two-thirds of the way up the chicken, bring to the boil, then cover and cook gently for about 1½ hours, until the chicken juices run clear.

3 Transfer the chicken to a large bowl, pour the cooking liquid over and leave to cool. When cool, skin and bone the chicken, then chop.

4 To make the sauce, cook the onion in the butter until soft. Add the curry paste, tomato purée, wine, bay leaf and lemon juice, then cook for 10 minutes. Add the jam; sieve and cool.

5 Beat the sauce mixture into the mayonnaise. Fold in the cream, season to taste with salt and pepper and add the lemon juice, then stir in with the chicken.

Tandoori Chicken Kebabs

This popular dish originates from the Punjab, where it is traditionally cooked in clay ovens known as *tandoors*.

Serves 4

4 boneless chicken breasts (about 175g/6oz each), skinned	1 small onion, cut into wedges and separated into layers
15ml/1 tbsp lemon juice	a little oil, for brushing
45ml/3 tbsp tandoori paste	salt and ground black pepper
45ml/3 tbsp natural yogurt	fresh coriander sprigs, to garnish
1 garlic clove, crushed	pilau rice and naan bread, to serve
30ml/2 tbsp chopped fresh coriander	

1 Chop the chicken breasts into 2.5cm/1in dice, place in a bowl and add the lemon juice, tandoori paste, yogurt, garlic, coriander and seasoning. Cover and leave to marinate in the fridge for 2–3 hours.

2 Preheat the grill. Thread alternate pieces of marinated chicken and onion on to four skewers.

3 Brush the onions with a little oil, lay on a grill rack and cook under a high heat for 10–12 minutes, turning once. Garnish the kebabs with fresh coriander and serve at once with pilau rice and naan bread.

Cook's Tip
If you are using wooden skewers, soak them first in cold water to prevent them catching fire under the grill. For an economical alternative, use chicken thighs instead of breasts.

Chinese Chicken with Cashew Nuts

The cashew nuts give this oriental dish a delightful crunchy texture that contrasts well with the noodles.

Serves 4

4 boneless chicken breasts (about 175g/6oz each), skinned	15ml/1 tbsp sesame oil
3 garlic cloves, crushed	115g/4oz/1 cup roasted cashew nuts
60ml/4 tbsp soy sauce	6 spring onions, cut into 5cm/2in pieces and halved lengthways
30ml/2 tbsp cornflour	spring onion curls and a little chopped fresh red chilli, to garnish
225g/8oz/4 cups dried egg noodles	
45ml/3 tbsp peanut or sunflower oil	

1 Slice the chicken into strips, then combine with the garlic, soy sauce and cornflour. Cover and chill in the fridge for about 30 minutes.

2 Meanwhile, bring a saucepan of water to the boil and add the egg noodles. Turn off the heat and leave to stand for 5 minutes. Drain well and reserve.

3 Heat the oils in a large frying pan or wok and stir-fry the chilled chicken and marinade juices over a high heat for about 3–4 minutes, or until golden brown.

4 Add the cashew nuts and spring onions to the pan or wok and stir-fry for a further 2–3 minutes.

5 Add the drained noodles and stir-fry for 2 minutes more. Toss the noodles well and serve immediately, garnished with the spring onion curls and chopped chilli.

Cook's Tip
For a milder garnish, seed the red chilli before chopping or finely dice some red pepper instead and use with the spring onion curls.

Chinese-style Chicken Salad

For a variation and to add more colour, add some cooked, peeled prawns to this lovely salad.

Serves 4

4 boneless chicken breasts (about 175g/6oz each)	2 carrots, cut into matchsticks
60ml/4 tbsp dark soy sauce	8 spring onions, shredded
pinch of Chinese five-spice powder	75g/3oz/1 cup beansprouts
squeeze of lemon juice	
½ cucumber, peeled and cut into matchsticks	**For the sauce**
5ml/1 tsp salt	60ml/4 tbsp crunchy peanut butter
45ml/3 tbsp sunflower oil	10ml/2 tsp lemon juice
30ml/2 tbsp sesame oil	10ml/2 tsp sesame oil
15ml/1 tbsp sesame seeds	1.5ml/¼ tsp hot chilli powder
30ml/2 tbsp dry sherry	1 spring onion, finely chopped

1 Put the chicken into a saucepan and cover with water. Add 15ml/1 tbsp of the soy sauce, the Chinese five-spice powder and lemon juice. Cover, bring to the boil, then simmer for 20 minutes. Then skin and slice into thin strips.

2 Sprinkle the cucumber matchsticks with salt, leave for 30 minutes, then rinse and pat dry.

3 Fry the sesame seeds in the oils for 30 seconds, then stir in the remaining soy sauce and the sherry. Add the carrots and stir-fry for 2 minutes, then remove from the heat.

4 Mix together the cucumber, spring onions, beansprouts, carrots, pan juices and chicken. Transfer to a shallow dish. Cover and chill for 1 hour.

5 For the sauce, cream the first four ingredients together, then stir in the spring onion. Serve the chicken with the sauce.

Duck, Avocado and Berry Salad

Duck breasts are roasted until crisp with a honey and soy glaze to serve warm with fresh raspberries and avocado.

Serves 4

4 small or 2 large duck breasts, halved if large	salt and ground black pepper
15ml/1 tbsp clear honey	
15ml/1 tbsp dark soy sauce	**For the dressing**
mixed chopped fresh salad leaves such as lamb's lettuce, red chicory or frisée	60ml/4 tbsp olive oil
	15ml/1 tbsp raspberry vinegar
2 avocados, stoned, peeled and cut into chunks	15ml/1 tbsp redcurrant jelly
115g/4oz/1 cup raspberries	salt and ground black pepper

1 Preheat the oven to 200°C/425°F/Gas 7. Prick the skin of each duck breast with a fork. Blend the honey and soy sauce together in a small bowl, then brush all over the skin..

2 Place the duck breasts on a rack set over a roasting tin and season with salt and pepper. Roast in the oven for about 15–20 minutes, until the skins are crisp and the meat cooked.

3 Meanwhile, to make the dressing, put the oil, vinegar, redcurrant jelly and seasoning in a small bowl and whisk well until evenly blended.

4 Slice the duck breasts diagonally and arrange among four individual plates with the salad leaves, avocados and raspberries. Spoon the dressing over the top and serve.

Cook's Tip
Small avocados contain the most flavour and have a good texture. They should be ripe but not too soft, so avoid any whose skins are turning black.

Crumbed Turkey Steaks

The authentic Austrian dish, *wiener schnitzel*, uses veal escalopes, but turkey breasts make a tasty alternative.

Serves 4

4 turkey breast steaks (about 150g/5oz each)	75ml/5 tbsp finely grated Parmesan cheese
40g/1½oz/3 tbsp plain flour, seasoned	25g/1oz/2 tbsp butter
1 egg, lightly beaten	45ml/3 tbsp sunflower oil
75g/3oz/1½ cups fresh breadcrumbs	fresh parsley sprigs, to garnish
	4 lemon wedges, to serve

1 Lay the turkey steaks between two sheets of clear film. Hit each one with a rolling pin until flattened. Snip the edges of the steaks with scissors a few times to prevent them from curling during cooking.

2 Place the seasoned flour on one plate, the egg in a shallow bowl and the breadcrumbs and Parmesan mixed together on another plate.

3 Dip each side of the steaks into the flour and shake off any excess. Next, dip them into the egg and then gently press each side into the breadcrumbs and cheese until evenly coated.

4 Heat the butter and oil in a large frying pan and fry the turkey steaks over a moderate heat for 2–3 minutes on each side, until golden. Garnish with the fresh parsley sprigs and serve with lemon wedges.

Country Cider Hot-pot

Rabbit meat is regaining popularity in Britain and is a healthy, low-fat option, as is all game.

Serves 4

25g/1oz/2 tbsp plain flour	450ml/¾ pint/1¾ cups dry cider
4 boneless rabbit portions	3 carrots, chopped
25g/1oz/2 tbsp butter	2 parsnips, chopped
15ml/1 tbsp vegetable oil	12 ready-to-eat dried prunes, stoned
15 baby onions	1 fresh rosemary sprig
4 rashers streaky bacon, chopped	1 bay leaf
10ml/2 tsp mustard	salt and ground black pepper

1 Preheat the oven to 160°C/325°F/Gas 3. Place the flour and seasoning in a plastic bag, add the rabbit portions and shake until coated. Set aside.

2 Heat the butter and oil in a flameproof casserole and add the onions and bacon. Fry for 4 minutes, until the onions have softened. Remove with a slotted spoon and reserve.

3 Fry the seasoned rabbit portions in the oil left in the flameproof casserole until they are browned all over, then spread a little of the mustard over the top of each portion.

4 Return the onions and bacon to the pan. Pour on the cider and add the carrots, parsnips, prunes, rosemary and bay leaf. Season well. Bring to the boil, then cover with a tight-fitting lid and transfer to the oven. Cook for about 1½ hours until the meat and vegetables are tender.

5 Remove the rosemary sprig and bay leaf and serve the rabbit hot with creamy mashed potatoes, if you wish.

Turkey Pastitsio

A traditional Greek pastitsio is a rich, high fat dish made with beef mince, but this lighter version is just as tasty.

Serves 4–6

450g/1lb lean minced
  turkey
1 large onion, finely
  chopped
60ml/4 tbsp tomato purée
250ml/8fl oz/1 cup red
  wine or stock
5ml/1 tsp ground
  cinnamon
300g/11oz/2½ cups
  macaroni
300ml/½ pint/1¼ cups
  skimmed milk

25g/1oz/2 tbsp sunflower
  margarine
25g/1oz/2 tbsp plain
  flour
5ml/1 tsp grated nutmeg
2 tomatoes, sliced
60ml/4 tbsp wholemeal
  breadcrumbs
salt and ground black
  pepper
green salad, to serve

1 Preheat the oven to 220°C/425°F/Gas 7. Fry the turkey and onion in a non-stick frying pan without fat, stirring until lightly browned.

2 Stir in the tomato purée, red wine or stock and cinnamon. Season with salt and pepper, then cover with a tight-fitting lid and simmer for 5 minutes.

3 Cook the macaroni in boiling salted water until just tender, then drain. Layer with the meat mixture in a wide ovenproof dish.

4 Place the milk, margarine and flour in a saucepan and whisk over a moderate heat until thickened and smooth. Add the nutmeg, and salt and pepper to taste.

5 Pour the sauce evenly over the pasta and meat. Arrange the tomato slices on top and sprinkle lines of breadcrumbs over the surface. Bake for 30–35 minutes, or until golden brown and bubbling. Serve hot with a green salad.

Tuscan Chicken

A simple peasant casserole with all the flavours of Tuscan ingredients. The wine can be replaced by chicken stock.

Serves 4

5ml/1 tsp olive oil
8 chicken thighs, skinned
1 onion, thinly sliced
2 fresh red peppers,
  seeded and sliced
1 garlic clove, crushed
300ml/½ pint/1¼ cups
  passata
150ml/¼ pint/⅔ cup dry
  white wine

large fresh oregano sprig,
  or 5ml/1 tsp dried
  oregano
400g/14oz can cannellini
  beans, drained
45ml/3 tbsp fresh
  breadcrumbs
salt and ground black
  pepper

1 Heat the oil in a non-stick or heavy saucepan and fry the chicken until golden brown. Remove and keep hot. Add the onion and peppers to the pan and gently sauté until softened, but not brown. Stir in the garlic.

2 Add the chicken, passata, wine and oregano. Season well with salt and pepper, bring to the boil, then cover the pan with a tight lid.

3 Lower the heat and simmer gently, stirring occasionally for 30–35 minutes or until the chicken is tender and the juices run clear, not pink, when pierced with the point of a knife.

4 Stir in the cannellini beans and simmer for a further 5 minutes until heated through. Sprinkle with the breadcrumbs and cook under a hot grill until golden brown.

Poussins with Grapes in Vermouth

This sauce could also be served with roast chicken, but poussins have the stronger flavour.

Serves 4

4 oven-ready poussins
　(about 450g/1lb each)
50g/2oz/4 tbsp butter,
　softened
2 shallots, chopped
60ml/4 tbsp chopped
　fresh parsley
225g/8oz/2 cups white
　grapes, preferably
　Muscatel, halved and
　seeded

150ml/¼ pint/⅔ cup
　white vermouth
5ml/1 tsp cornflour
60ml/4 tbsp double cream
30ml/2 tbsp pine nuts,
　toasted
salt and ground black
　pepper
watercress sprigs, to
　garnish

1 Preheat the oven to 200°C/400°F/Gas 6. Wash and dry the poussins. Spread the softened butter all over the poussins and put a hazelnut-sized piece in the cavity of each bird.

2 Mix together the shallots and parsley and place a quarter of the mixture inside each poussin. Put the poussins side by side in a large roasting tin and roast for 40–50 minutes, or until the juices run clear when the thickest part of the flesh is pierced with a skewer. Transfer the poussins to a warmed serving plate. Cover and keep warm.

3 Skim off most of the fat from the roasting tin, then add the grapes and vermouth. Place the tin directly over a low heat for a few minutes to warm and slightly soften the grapes.

4 Lift the grapes out of the tin using a slotted spoon and scatter them around the poussin. Keep covered. Stir the cornflour into the cream, then add to the tin juices. Cook gently for a few minutes, stirring, until the sauce has thickened. Season to taste with salt and pepper. Pour the sauce around the poussins. Sprinkle with the toasted pine nuts and garnish with watercress sprigs.

Chicken Parcels with Herb Butter

These delightful, individual filo pastry parcels contain a wonderfully moist and herby filling.

Serves 4

4 chicken breast fillets,
　skinned
150g/5oz/generous ½ cup
　butter, softened
90ml/6 tbsp mixed
　chopped fresh herbs
　such as thyme,
　parsley, oregano and
　rosemary

5ml/1 tsp lemon juice
5 large sheets filo pastry,
　defrosted if frozen
1 egg, beaten
30ml/2 tbsp freshly
　grated Parmesan
　cheese
salt and ground black
　pepper

1 Season the chicken fillets. Melt 25g/1oz/2 tbsp of the butter in a frying pan and fry the chicken fillets to seal and brown lightly. Allow to cool.

2 Preheat the oven to 190°C/375°F/Gas 5. Put the remaining butter, the herbs, lemon juice and seasoning in a food processor or blender and process until smooth. Melt half of this herb butter.

3 Take one sheet of filo pastry and brush with melted herb butter. Keep the other sheets covered with a damp dish towel. Fold the filo pastry sheet in half and brush again with butter. Place a chicken fillet about 2.5cm/1in from the top end.

4 Dot the chicken with a quarter of the remaining unmelted herb butter. Fold in the sides of the pastry, then roll up to enclose it completely. Place seam-side down on a lightly greased baking sheet. Repeat with the other chicken fillets.

5 Brush the filo parcels with beaten egg. Cut the last sheet of filo into strips, then scrunch and arrange on top. Brush the parcels once again with the egg glaze, then sprinkle with Parmesan cheese. Bake for about 35–50 minutes, until golden brown. Serve hot.

Pot-roast of Venison

The venison is marinated for 24 hours before preparation to give this rich dish an even fuller flavour.

Serves 4–5

1.75kg/4 – 4½lb boned joint of venison	2 onions, finely chopped
75ml/5 tbsp oil	2 carrots, chopped
4 cloves	150g/5oz large mushrooms, sliced
8 black peppercorns, lightly crushed	15g/½oz/1 tbsp plain flour
12 juniper berries, lightly crushed	250ml/8fl oz/1 cup veal stock
250ml/8fl oz/1 cup full-bodied red wine	30ml/2 tbsp redcurrant jelly
115g/4oz lightly smoked streaky bacon, chopped	salt and ground black pepper

1 Put the venison in a bowl, add half the oil, the spices and wine, cover and leave in a cool place for 24 hours, turning the meat occasionally.

2 Preheat the oven to 160°C/325°F/Gas 3. Remove the venison from the bowl and pat dry. Reserve the marinade. Heat the remaining oil in a shallow saucepan, then brown the venison evenly. Transfer to a plate.

3 Stir the bacon, onions, carrots and mushrooms into the pan and cook for about 5 minutes. Stir in the flour and cook for 2 minutes, then remove from the heat and stir in the marinade, stock, redcurrant jelly and seasoning. Return to the heat, bring to the boil, stirring, then simmer for 2–3 minutes.

4 Transfer the venison and sauce to a casserole and cover with a tight-fitting lid. Cook in the oven for about 3 hours, turning the joint from time to time, until tender.

Pheasant with Mushrooms

The wine and mushroom sauce in this recipe is given a lift by the inclusion of anchovy fillets.

Serves 4

1 pheasant, jointed	3 anchovy fillets, soaked for 10 minutes and drained
250ml/8fl oz/1 cup red wine	
45ml/3 tbsp oil	350ml/12fl oz/1½ cups game, veal or chicken stock
60ml/4 tbsp Spanish sherry vinegar	
1 large onion, chopped	bouquet garni
2 rashers smoked bacon	salt and ground black pepper
350g/12oz chestnut mushrooms, sliced	

1 Place the pheasant in a dish, add the wine, half the oil and half the vinegar, and scatter over half the onion. Season with salt and pepper, then cover the dish and leave in a cool place for about 8–12 hours, turning the pheasant occasionally.

2 Preheat the oven to 160°C/325°F/Gas 3. Lift the pheasant from the dish and pat dry with kitchen paper. Reserve the marinade for later.

3 Heat the remaining oil in a flameproof casserole, then brown the pheasant joints. Transfer to a plate.

4 Cut the bacon into strips then add with the remaining onion to the casserole and cook until the onion is soft. Stir in the mushrooms and cook for about 3 minutes.

5 Stir in the anchovies and remaining vinegar and boil until reduced. Add the marinade, cook for 2 minutes, then add the stock and bouquet garni. Return the pheasant to the casserole, cover and bake for about 1½ hours. Transfer the pheasant to a serving dish. Boil the cooking juices to reduce. Discard the bouquet garni. Pour over the pheasant and serve at once.

Minty Yogurt Chicken

Marinated, grilled chicken thighs make a tasty light lunch or supper. Use drumsticks if you prefer.

Serves 4

8 chicken thigh portions	60ml/4 tbsp chopped
15ml/1 tbsp clear honey	fresh mint
30ml/2 tbsp lime juice	salt and ground black
30ml/2 tbsp natural	pepper
yogurt	

1 Skin the chicken thighs and slash the flesh at intervals with a sharp knife. Place in a bowl. Mix together the honey, lime juice, yogurt, seasoning and half the mint.

2 Spoon the marinade over the chicken and leave to marinate for 30 minutes. Line a grill pan with foil and cook the chicken under a moderately hot grill until thoroughly cooked and golden brown, turning occasionally.

3 Sprinkle with remaining mint and serve with potatoes and tomato salad, if you wish.

Mandarin Sesame Duck

The rind, juice and flesh of sweet mandarin oranges are used in this delightful roast dish.

Serves 4

4 duck leg or boned	15ml/1 tbsp sesame seeds
breast portions	4 mandarin oranges
30ml/2 tbsp light soy	5ml/1 tsp cornflour
sauce	salt and ground black
45ml/3 tbsp clear honey	pepper

1 Preheat the oven to 180°C/350°F/Gas 4. Prick the duck skin all over. Slash the breast skin diagonally at intervals. Roast the duck for 1 hour. Mix 15ml/1 tbsp soy sauce with 30ml/2 tbsp honey and brush over the duck. Sprinkle with sesame seeds. Roast for 15 minutes more.

2 Grate the rind from one mandarin and squeeze the juice from two. Mix in the cornflour, remaining soy sauce and honey. Heat, stirring, until thickened and clear. Season. Peel and slice the remaining mandarins. Serve the duck with the mandarin slices and the sauce.

Sticky Ginger Chicken

For a fuller flavour, marinate the chicken drumsticks in the glaze for 30 minutes before cooking.

Serves 4

Mix 30ml/2 tbsp lemon juice, 25g/1oz light muscovado sugar, 5ml/1 tsp grated fresh ginger root, 10ml/2 tsp soy sauce and ground pepper to taste. Using a sharp knife, slash eight chicken drumsticks about three times through the thickest part of the flesh, then toss the chicken in the glaze. Cook it under a hot grill or on a barbecue, turning occasionally and brushing with the glaze, until it is golden and the juices run clear when pierced. Serve on a bed of lettuce, with crusty bread, if you wish.

Oat-crusted Chicken with Sage

Oats make a good, crunchy coating for savoury foods, and offer a good way to add extra fibre.

Serves 4

45ml/3 tbsp milk
10ml/2 tsp English mustard
40g/1½oz/½ cup rolled oats
45ml/3 tbsp chopped fresh sage leaves
8 chicken thighs or drumsticks, skinned

120ml/4fl oz/½ cup fromage frais
5ml/1 tsp wholegrain mustard
salt and ground black pepper
fresh sage leaves, to garnish

1 Preheat the oven to 200°C/400°F/Gas 6. Mix together the milk and English mustard.

2 Mix the oats with 30ml/2 tbsp of the chopped sage and the seasoning on a plate. Brush the chicken with the milk and press into the oats to coat evenly.

3 Place the chicken on a baking sheet and bake for about 40 minutes, or until the juices run clear, not pink, when pierced through the thickest part.

4 Meanwhile, mix together the fromage frais, wholegrain mustard, remaining sage and seasoning, transfer to a serving dish and serve with the chicken. Garnish the chicken with fresh sage leaves.

Cook's Tip
If fresh sage is not available, choose another fresh herb such as thyme or parsley rather than using a dried alternative. These chicken thighs or drumsticks may be served hot or cold.

Chicken in Creamy Orange Sauce

The brandy adds a rich flavour to the sauce, but omit if you prefer and use orange juice alone.

Serves 4

8 chicken thighs or drumsticks, skinned
45ml/3 tbsp brandy
300ml/½ pint/1¼ cups orange juice

3 spring onions, chopped
10ml/2 tsp cornflour
90ml/6 tbsp fromage frais
salt and ground black pepper

1 Fry the chicken pieces without fat in a non-stick or heavy frying pan, turning until evenly browned.

2 Stir in the brandy, orange juice and spring onions. Bring to the boil, then cover and simmer for 15 minutes, or until the chicken is tender and the juices run clear, not pink, when pierced with the point of a sharp knife.

3 Blend the cornflour with a little water, then mix into the fromage frais. Stir this into a small saucepan and cook over a moderate heat until boiling.

4 Adjust the seasoning to taste and serve with boiled rice or pasta and green salad, if you wish.

Cook's Tip
For a healthy version of this dish, suitable for those who are watching their weight, use low-fat fromage frais which is virtually fat-free. The sauce will still be beautifully creamy.

Normandy Roast Chicken

The chicken is turned over halfway through roasting so that it cooks evenly and stays wonderfully moist.

Serves 4

50g/2oz/4 tbsp butter, softened
30ml/2 tbsp chopped fresh tarragon
1 small garlic clove, crushed
1.5kg/3lb fresh chicken
5ml/1 tsp plain flour
150ml/¼ pint/²⁄₃ cup single cream
squeeze of lemon juice
salt and ground black pepper
fresh tarragon and lemon slices, to garnish

1 Preheat the oven to 200°C/400°F/Gas 6. Mix together the butter, 15ml/1 tbsp of the chopped tarragon, the garlic and seasoning in a bowl. Spoon half the butter mixture into the cavity of the chicken.

2 Carefully lift the skin at the neck end of the bird from the breast flesh on each side, then gently push a little of the butter mixture into each pocket and smooth it down over the breasts with your fingers.

3 Season the bird and lay it, breast-side down, in a roasting tin. Roast in the oven for 45 minutes, then turn the chicken over and baste with the juices. Cook for a further 45 minutes.

4 When the chicken is cooked, lift it to drain out any juices from the cavity into the tin, then transfer the bird to a warmed platter and keep warm.

5 Place the roasting tin on the hob and heat until sizzling. Stir in the flour and cook for 1 minute, then stir in the cream, the remaining tarragon, 150ml/¼ pint/²⁄₃ cup water, the lemon juice and seasoning. Boil and stir for 2–3 minutes, until thickened. Garnish the chicken with tarragon and lemon slices and serve with the sauce.

Duck Breasts with Orange Sauce

A simple variation on the classic French whole roast duck, which makes for a more elegant presentation.

Serves 4

4 duck breasts
15ml/1 tbsp sunflower oil
2 oranges
150ml/¼ pint/²⁄₃ cup fresh orange juice
15ml/1 tbsp port
30ml/2 tbsp Seville orange marmalade
15g/½oz/1 tbsp butter
5ml/1 tsp cornflour
salt and ground black pepper

1 Season the duck breast skin. Heat the oil in a frying pan over a moderate heat and add the duck breasts, skin-side down. Cover and cook for 3–4 minutes, until just lightly browned. Turn the breasts over, lower the heat slightly and cook uncovered for 5–6 minutes.

2 Peel the skin and pith from the oranges. Working over a bowl to catch any juice, slice either side of the membranes to release the orange segments, then set aside with the juice.

3 Remove the duck breasts from the pan with a slotted spoon, drain on kitchen paper and keep warm in the oven while making the sauce.

4 Drain off the fat from the frying pan. Add the segmented oranges, all but 30ml/2 tbsp of the orange juice, the port and the orange marmalade. Bring to the boil and then reduce the heat slightly. Whisk small knobs of the butter into the sauce and season with salt and pepper.

5 Blend the cornflour with the reserved orange juice, pour into the pan and stir until slightly thickened. Add the duck breasts and cook gently for about 3 minutes. To serve, arrange the sliced breasts on plates with the sauce.

Pot-roast Poussin

This dish is inspired by the French method of cooking these birds. Pot-roasting keeps them moist and succulent.

Serves 4

15ml/1 tbsp olive oil
1 onion, sliced
1 large garlic clove, sliced
50g/2oz/½ cup diced
  smoked bacon
2 fresh poussins (about
  450g/1lb each)
30ml/2 tbsp melted
  butter
2 baby celery hearts, each
  cut into 4 pieces
8 baby carrots
2 small courgettes, cut
  into chunks
8 small new potatoes

600ml/1 pint/2½ cups
  chicken stock
150ml/¼ pint/⅔ cup dry
  white wine
1 bay leaf
2 fresh thyme sprigs
2 fresh rosemary sprigs
15ml/1 tbsp butter,
  softened
15g/1½oz/1 tbsp plain
  flour
salt and ground black
  pepper
fresh herbs, to garnish

1   Preheat the oven to 190°C/375°F/Gas 5. Heat the olive oil in a large flameproof casserole and sauté the onions, garlic and bacon for 5–6 minutes until the onions have softened. Brush the poussins with half the melted butter and season. Add to the casserole with the vegetables. Pour in the stock and wine and add the herbs. Cover and bake for 20 minutes.

2   Remove the lid and brush the birds with the remaining butter. Bake for 25–30 minutes more until golden. Transfer the poussins to a warmed serving platter and cut each in half with poultry shears or scissors. Remove the vegetables with a slotted spoon and arrange them round the birds. Cover with foil and keep warm.

3   Discard the herbs from the casserole. Mix the butter and flour to a paste. Bring the cooking liquid to the boil then whisk in spoonfuls of paste until thickened. Season and serve with the poussins and vegetables, garnished with herbs.

Coq au Vin

Chicken is flamed in brandy, then braised in red wine with bacon, mushrooms and onions in this classic dish.

Serves 4

50g/2oz/½ cup plain
  flour
1.5kg/3lb chicken, cut
  into 8 joints
15ml/1 tbsp olive oil
65g/2½oz/5 tbsp butter
20 baby onions
75g/3oz rindless streaky
  bacon, diced
about 20 button
  mushrooms

30ml/2 tbsp brandy
75cl bottle red Burgundy
bouquet garni
3 garlic cloves
5ml/1 tsp soft light
  brown sugar
salt and ground black
  pepper
15ml/1 tbsp chopped
  fresh parsley and
  croûtons, to garnish

1   Place 40g/1½oz/3 tbsp of the flour and seasoning in a large plastic bag and coat the chicken joints. Heat the oil and 50g/2oz/4 tbsp of the butter in a large flameproof casserole and sauté the onions and bacon until the onions have browned lightly. Add the mushrooms and fry for 2 minutes more. Remove with a slotted spoon and reserve.

2   Add the chicken pieces to the hot oil and cook for about 5–6 minutes until browned. Add the brandy and, standing well back, light it with a match, then shake the casserole gently until the flames subside.

3   Add the wine, bouquet garni, garlic and sugar, and season. Bring to the boil, cover and simmer for 1 hour, stirring from time to time. Add the onions, bacon and mushrooms, cover and cook for 30 minutes. Transfer the chicken, vegetables and bacon to a warmed dish.

4   Remove the bouquet garni; boil the liquid for 2 minutes. Cream the remaining butter and flour. Whisk in spoonfuls of the mixture to thicken the liquid. Pour the sauce over the chicken and serve garnished with parsley and croûtons.

Moroccan Spiced Roast Poussin

The poussins are stuffed with an aromatic rice mixture and glazed with spiced yogurt in this flavoursome dish.

Serves 4

75g/3oz/1 cup cooked
  long grain rice
1 small onion, chopped
finely grated rind and
  juice of 1 lemon
30ml/2 tbsp chopped
  fresh mint
45ml/3 tbsp chopped
  dried apricots
30ml/2 tbsp natural
  yogurt

10ml/2 tsp ground
  turmeric
10ml/2 tsp ground
  cumin
2 x 450g/1lb poussin
salt and ground black
  pepper
lemon slices and fresh
  mint sprigs, to
  garnish

1 Preheat the oven to 200°C/400°F/Gas 6. Mix together the rice, onion, lemon rind, mint and apricots. Stir in half each of the lemon juice, yogurt, turmeric, cumin, and salt and pepper.

2 Stuff the poussins with the rice mixture at the neck end only. The spare stuffing can be served separately. Place the poussins on a rack in a roasting tin.

3 Mix together the remaining lemon juice, yogurt, turmeric and cumin, then brush this over the poussins. Cover loosely with foil and cook in the oven for 30 minutes.

4 Remove the foil and roast for a further 15 minutes, or until golden brown and the juices run clear, not pink, when the thickest part of the flesh is pierced with a skewer.

5 Cut both the poussins in half with a sharp knife or poultry shears, and serve with the reserved rice. Garnish with slices of lemon and fresh mint sprigs.

Chilli Chicken Couscous

Couscous is a very easy alternative to rice and makes a good base for all kinds of ingredients.

Serves 4

225g/8oz/2 cups
  couscous
1 litre/1¼ pints/4 cups
  boiling water
5ml/1 tsp olive oil
400g/14oz boneless,
  skinless chicken, diced
1 yellow pepper, seeded
  and sliced
2 large courgettes, sliced
  thickly

1 small green chilli,
  thinly sliced, or
  5ml/1 tsp chilli sauce
1 large tomato, diced
425g/15oz can
  chick-peas, drained
salt and ground black
  pepper
fresh coriander or parsley
  sprigs, to garnish

1 Place couscous in a large bowl and pour the boiling water over. Cover and leave to stand for 30 minutes.

2 Heat the oil in a large non-stick frying pan and stir-fry the chicken quickly to seal, then reduce the heat.

3 Stir in the pepper, courgettes and chilli or chilli sauce and cook for 10 minutes, until the vegetables are softened.

4 Stir in the tomato and chick-peas, then add the couscous. Adjust the seasoning and stir over a moderate heat until hot. Serve garnished with sprigs of fresh coriander or parsley.

Cook's Tip
If you prefer, use dried chick-peas in this recipe. Soak them overnight, then drain, place in a saucepan and add water to cover. Bring to the boil, then cook until tender, 45–60 minutes.

Mediterranean Turkey Skewers

These skewers are easy to assemble, and can be cooked under a grill or on a charcoal barbecue.

Serves 4

90ml/6 tbsp olive oil	300g/11oz boned turkey,
45ml/3 tbsp lemon juice	cut into 5cm/2in cubes
1 garlic clove, finely	12–16 pickled onions
chopped	1 red or yellow pepper,
30ml/2 tbsp chopped	cut into 5cm/2in
fresh basil	squares
2 courgettes	salt and ground black
1 long thin aubergine	pepper

1 Mix the oil with the lemon juice, garlic and basil in a small bowl. Season with salt and pepper.

2 Slice the courgettes and aubergine lengthways into strips 5mm/¼in thick. Cut them crossways about two-thirds of the way along their length. Discard the shorter length. Wrap half the turkey pieces with the courgette slices, and the other half with the aubergine slices.

3 Prepare the skewers by alternating the turkey, onions and pepper pieces. If you are using wooden skewers, soak them in water for several minutes. This will prevent them from charring during grilling. Lay the prepared skewers on a platter and sprinkle with the flavoured oil. Then leave them to marinate for at least 30 minutes. Preheat the grill or light the coals to prepare a barbecue.

4 Grill or barbecue for 10 minutes, until the vegetables are tender, turning occasionally. Serve hot.

Duck with Chestnut Sauce

This autumnal dish makes use of the sweet chestnuts that are gathered in Italian woods.

Serves 4–5

1 fresh rosemary sprig	350ml/12fl oz/1½ cups
1 garlic clove, sliced	milk
30ml/2 tbsp olive oil	1 small onion, finely
4 boned duck breasts,	chopped
fat removed	1 carrot, finely chopped
	1 small bay leaf
For the sauce	salt and ground black
450g/1lb/4 cups	pepper
chestnuts	30ml/2 tbsp cream,
5ml/1 tsp oil	warmed

1 Pull the leaves from the sprig of rosemary. Combine them with the garlic and oil in a shallow bowl. Pat the duck breasts dry with kitchen paper. Brush them with the marinade and allow to stand for at least 2 hours before cooking.

2 Preheat the oven to 180°C/350°F/Gas 4. Cut a cross in the flat side of each chestnut with a sharp knife. Place the chestnuts on a baking sheet with the oil and shake the sheet until they are coated with oil. Bake for 20 minutes, then peel.

3 Place the peeled chestnuts in a heavy saucepan with the milk, onion, carrot and bay leaf. Cook slowly for about 10–15 minutes until the chestnuts are tender, then season. Discard the bay leaf. Press the mixture through a sieve.

4 Return the sauce to the pan. Heat gently while the duck breasts are cooking. Just before serving, stir in the cream. If the sauce is too thick, add a little more cream. Preheat the grill, or prepare a barbecue.

5 Grill the duck breasts until medium-rare, for about 6–8 minutes. They should be pink inside. Slice into rounds and arrange on warmed plates. Serve with the heated sauce.

Turkey Spirals

These little spirals may look difficult, but they're so easy to make, and a very good way to pep up plain turkey.

Serves 4

4 thinly sliced turkey
    breast steaks (about
    90g/3½oz each)
20ml/4 tsp tomato purée
15g/½oz large fresh basil
    leaves
1 garlic clove, crushed
15ml/1 tbsp skimmed
    milk

25g/1oz/2 tbsp
    wholemeal flour
salt and ground black
    pepper
passata or fresh tomato
    sauce and pasta with
    fresh basil, to serve

1 Place the turkey steaks on a board. If too thick, flatten them slightly by beating with a rolling pin.

2 Spread each turkey breast steak with tomato purée, then top with a few leaves of basil, a little crushed garlic, and salt and pepper.

3 Roll up firmly around the filling and secure with a cocktail stick. Brush with milk and sprinkle with flour to coat lightly.

4 Place the spirals on a foil-lined grill pan. Cook under a moderately hot grill for 15–20 minutes, turning them occasionally, until thoroughly cooked. Serve hot, sliced with a spoonful or two of passata or fresh tomato sauce and pasta, sprinkled with fresh basil.

Caribbean Chicken Kebabs

These kebabs have a rich, sunshine Caribbean flavour and the marinade keeps them moist without the need for oil.

Serves 4

500g/1¼lb boned chicken
    breasts, skinned
finely grated rind of
    1 lime
30ml/2 tbsp lime juice
15ml/1 tbsp rum or
    sherry

15g/½oz/1 tbsp light
    muscovado sugar
5ml/1 tsp ground
    cinnamon
2 mangoes, peeled and
    diced
rice and salad, to serve

1 Cut the chicken into bite-size chunks and place in a bowl with the lime rind and juice, rum, sugar and cinnamon. Toss well, cover and leave to stand for 1 hour.

2 Save the juices and thread the chicken on to four wooden skewers, alternating with the mango cubes.

3 Cook the skewers under a hot grill or on a barbecue for about 8-10 minutes, turning occasionally and basting with the juices until the chicken is tender and golden brown. Serve at once with rice and salad.

Cook's Tip
These kebabs may be served with a colourful salad and rice. The rum or sherry adds a lovely rich flavour but it is optional, so leave it out if you prefer.

Autumn Pheasant

Pheasant is worth buying as it is low in fat, full of flavour and never dry when cooked in this way.

Serves 4

1 oven-ready pheasant	30ml/2 tbsp
2 small onions, quartered	Worcestershire sauce
3 celery sticks, thickly	pinch of freshly grated
sliced	nutmeg
2 red eating apples,	30ml/2 tbsp toasted
thickly sliced	hazelnuts
120ml/4fl oz/½ cup stock	salt and ground black
15ml/1 tbsp clear honey	pepper

1 Preheat the oven to 180°C/350°F/Gas 4. Fry the pheasant without fat in a non-stick frying pan, turning occasionally until golden. Remove and keep hot.

2 Fry the onions and celery in the pan to brown lightly. Spoon into a casserole and place the pheasant on top. Tuck the apple slices around it.

3 Spoon over the stock, honey and Worcestershire sauce. Sprinkle with nutmeg, salt and pepper, cover with a tight-fitting lid and bake for 1¼–1½ hours or until tender. Sprinkle with nuts and serve hot.

Cook's Tip
Pheasant should be hung by the neck to develop their distinctive flavour for 7–14 days, according to the degree of gaminess preferred. If you are buying the bird ready-prepared, make sure all the tendons have been removed from the legs. This recipe provides an excellent method of cooking older, cock birds which tend to be rather tough and dry if plain roasted.

Chicken Stroganoff

This dish is based on the classic Russian dish, which is made with fillet of beef, and it is just as good.

Serves 4

4 boneless, skinless	300ml/½ pint/1¼ cups
chicken breasts	soured cream
45ml/3 tbsp olive oil	salt and ground black
1 large onion, thinly	pepper
sliced	15ml/1 tbsp chopped
225g/8oz mushrooms,	fresh parsley, to
sliced	garnish

1 Divide the chicken breasts into two natural fillets, place between two sheets of clear film and flatten each to a thickness of 5mm/¼in with a rolling pin.

2 Cut into 2.5cm/1in strips diagonally across the fillets.

3 Heat 30ml/2 tbsp oil in a large frying pan and cook the sliced onion slowly until soft but not coloured.

4 Add the mushrooms and cook until golden brown. Remove and keep warm.

5 Increase the heat, add the remaining oil and fry the chicken very quickly, in small batches, for 3–4 minutes until lightly coloured. Remove and keep warm while frying the rest of the chicken.

6 Return all the chicken, onions and mushrooms to the pan and season with salt and pepper. Stir in the soured cream and bring to the boil. Sprinkle with fresh parsley and serve immediately.

Chicken Tikka

The red food colourings give this dish its traditional bright colour. Serve with lemon wedges and a crisp mixed salad.

Serves 4

175kg/3½ lb chicken
mixed fresh salad leaves
    such as frisée, oakleaf
    lettuce or radiccio,
    to serve

For the marinade
150ml/¼ pint/⅔ cup
    natural low-fat yogurt

5ml/1 tsp ground paprika
10ml/2 tsp grated fresh
    root ginger
1 garlic clove, crushed
10ml/2 tsp garam masala
2.5ml/½ tsp salt
red food colouring
    (optional)
juice of 1 lemon

1 Joint the chicken and cut it into eight even-size pieces, using a sharp knife.

2 Mix all the marinade ingredients in a large dish, add the chicken pieces to coat and chill for 4 hours or overnight to allow the flavours to penetrate the flesh.

3 Preheat the oven to 200°C/400°F/Gas 6. Remove the chicken pieces from the marinade and arrange them in a single layer in a large ovenproof dish. Bake for 30–40 minutes or until tender.

4 Baste with a little of the marinade while cooking. Arrange on a bed of salad leaves and serve hot or cold.

Cook's Tip
This dish would also make an excellent starter. Joint the chicken into smaller pieces and reduce the cooking time slightly, then serve with lemon wedges and just a simple salad garnish.

Simple Chicken Curry

Curry powder can be bought in three different strengths – mild, medium and hot. Use your own preferred type.

Serves 4

8 chicken legs, each piece
    including thigh and
    drumstick
30ml/2 tbsp olive oil
1 onion, thinly sliced
1 garlic clove, crushed
15ml/1 tbsp medium
    curry powder
25g/1oz/1 tbsp plain
    flour

450ml/¾ pint/1¾ cups
    chicken stock
1 beefsteak tomato
15ml/1 tbsp mango
    chutney
15ml/1 tbsp lemon juice
salt and ground black
    pepper
350g/12oz/2½ cups
    boiled rice, to serve

1 Cut the chicken legs in half. Heat the olive oil in a large flameproof casserole and brown the chicken pieces on both sides. Remove and keep warm.

2 Add the onion and garlic clove to the casserole and cook them until tender. Add the curry powder and cook gently for a further 2 minutes.

3 Add the flour and gradually blend in the chicken stock and seasoning.

4 Bring to the boil, replace the chicken pieces, cover and simmer for 20–30 minutes or until tender.

5 Skin the beefsteak tomato by blanching in boiling water for about 15 seconds, then running it under cold water to loosen the skin. Peel and cut into small dice.

6 Add to the chicken with the mango chutney and lemon juice. Heat through gently and adjust the seasoning to taste. Serve with boiled rice and Indian accompaniments.

Chicken Biryani

A *biryani* – from the Urdu – is a dish mixed with rice which resembles a risotto. It provides a one-pan meal.

Serves 4

275g/10oz/1½ cups
  basmati rice, rinsed
2.5ml/½ tsp salt
5 whole cardamom pods
2–3 whole cloves
1 cinnamon stick
45ml/3 tbsp vegetable oil
3 onions, sliced
675g/1½lb boneless,
  skinless, diced chicken
1.5ml/¼ tsp ground
  cloves
5 cardamom pods, seeds
  removed and ground
1.5ml/¼ tsp hot chilli
  powder
5ml/1 tsp ground cumin
5ml/1 tsp ground
  coriander

2.5ml/½ tsp freshly
  ground black pepper
3 garlic cloves, finely
  chopped
5ml/1 tsp finely chopped
  fresh root ginger
juice of 1 lemon
4 tomatoes, sliced
30ml/2 tbsp chopped fresh
  coriander
150ml/¼ pint/⅔ cup
  natural yogurt
2.5ml/½ tsp saffron
  strands soaked in
  10ml/2 tsp hot milk
45ml/3 tbsp toasted flaked
  almonds and fresh
  coriander sprigs, to
  garnish
natural yogurt, to serve

1 Preheat the oven to 190°C/375°F/Gas 5. Boil the rice mixture, salt, cardamom pods, cloves and cinnamon stick for 2 minutes. Then drain, leaving the whole spices in the rice.

2 Brown the onions in the oil. Add the chicken, ground spices, garlic, ginger and lemon juice. Stir-fry for 5 minutes.

3 Transfer to a casserole; top with the tomatoes. In layers, add the coriander, yogurt and rice. Drizzle over the saffron and milk, then 150ml/¼ pint/⅔ cup water.

4 Cover and bake for 1 hour. Transfer to a warmed serving platter and remove the whole spices. Garnish with toasted almonds and coriander and serve with yogurt.

Spatchcock of Poussin

Allow one poussin per person and sharp knives to tackle them. Serve with new potatoes and salad, if wished.

Serves 4

4 poussins
15ml/1 tbsp mixed
  chopped fresh herbs
  such as rosemary and
  parsley, plus extra to
  garnish

15ml/1 tbsp lemon juice
50g/2oz/4 tbsp butter,
  melted
salt and ground black
  pepper
lemon slices, to garnish

1 Remove any trussing strings from the birds, and using a pair of kitchen scissors, cut down on either side of the backbone. Lay the poussins flat and flatten with the help of a rolling pin or mallet, or use the heel of your hand.

2 Thread the legs and wings on to skewers to keep the poussins flat while they are cooking.

3 Brush both sides with melted butter and season with salt and pepper. Sprinkle with lemon juice and herbs.

4 Preheat the grill to moderate heat and cook skin-side first for 6 minutes until golden brown. Turn over, brush with butter and grill for a further 6–8 minutes or until cooked. Garnish with chopped herbs and lemon slices.

Chicken, Leek and Parsley Pie

A filling pie with a two-cheese sauce, this dish is ideal for serving on a cold winter's day.

Serves 4–6

3 boneless chicken breasts
flavourings: carrot,
    onion, peppercorns,
    bouquet garni
shortcrust pastry, made
    with 275g/10oz/
    2½ cups plain flour
50g/2oz/4 tbsp butter
2 leeks, thinly sliced
50g/2oz/½ cup grated
    Cheddar cheese
25g/1 oz/¼ cup grated
    Parmesan cheese

45ml/3 tbsp chopped
    fresh parsley
30ml/2 tbsp wholegrain
    mustard
5ml/1 tsp cornflour
300ml/½ pint/1¼ cups
    double cream
salt and ground black
    pepper
beaten egg, to glaze
mixed fresh green salad
    leaves, to serve

1   Poach the chicken breasts with the flavourings in water to cover, until tender. Cool in the liquid, then cut into strips.

2   Preheat the oven to 200°C/400°F/Gas 6. Divide the pastry into two pieces, one slightly larger than the other. Use the larger piece to line an 18 x 28cm/7 x 11in baking tin. Prick the base, bake for 15 minutes, then leave to cool.

3   Fry the leeks in the butter until soft. Stir in the cheeses and parsley. Spread half the leek mixture over the pastry base, cover with the chicken strips, then top with the remaining leek mixture. Mix the mustard, cornflour and cream. Season and pour into the pie.

4   Moisten the pastry base edges. Use the remaining pastry to cover the pie. Brush with beaten egg and bake for 30–40 minutes until golden and crisp. Serve with salad.

Hampshire Farmhouse Flan

A traditional dish from the south of England, this flan will satisfy the hungriest person.

Serves 4

225g/8oz/2 cups
    wholemeal flour
50g/2oz/4 tbsp butter,
    cubed
50g/2oz/4 tbsp lard
5ml/1 tsp caraway seeds
5ml/1 tbsp oil
1 onion, chopped
1 garlic clove, crushed
225g/8oz/2 cups cooked
    chicken, chopped
75g/3oz watercress
    leaves, chopped

grated rind of ½ lemon
2 eggs, lightly beaten
175ml/6fl oz/¼ cup
    double cream
45ml/3 tbsp natural
    yogurt
large pinch of grated
    nutmeg
45ml/3 tbsp grated
    Caerphilly cheese
beaten egg, to glaze
salt and ground black
    pepper

1   Rub the fats into the flour with a pinch of salt until the mixture resembles breadcrumbs.

2   Stir in the caraway seeds and 45ml/3 tbsp iced water and mix to a firm dough. Knead until smooth, then use to line an 18 x 28cm/7 x 11in loose-based flan tin. Reserve the dough trimmings. Prick the base and chill for 20 minutes. Heat a baking sheet in the oven at 200°C/400°F/Gas 6.

3   Sauté the onion and garlic in the oil until softened. Remove from the heat and cool. Meanwhile, line the pastry case with greaseproof paper and baking beans. Bake for 10 minutes, remove the paper and beans and cook for 5 minutes.

4   Mix the onion, chicken, watercress and lemon rind; spoon into the flan case. Beat the eggs, cream, yogurt, nutmeg, cheese and seasoning; pour over the chicken mixture. Cut the pastry trimmings into 1cm/½ in strips. Brush with egg, then twist and lay in a lattice over the flan. Press on the ends. Bake for 35 minutes, until golden.

Chicken Charter Pie

A light pie with a fresh taste; it is versatile enough to use for light meals or informal dinners.

Serves 4

50g/2oz/4 tbsp butter	20g/¾ oz fresh parsley
4 chicken legs	leaves, finely chopped
1 onion, finely chopped	225g/8oz ready-made
150ml/¼ pint/⅔ cup	puff pastry
milk	120ml/4fl oz/½ cup
150ml/¼ pint/⅔ cup	double cream
soured cream	2 eggs, beaten, plus extra
4 spring onions,	for glazing
quartered	salt and ground black
	pepper

1 Melt the butter in a frying pan and brown the chicken legs. Transfer to a plate. Add the chopped onion to the pan and cook until softened but not browned. Stir the milk, soured cream, spring onions, parsley and seasoning into the pan, bring to the boil, then simmer for 2 minutes.

2 Return the chicken to the pan with any juices, cover and cook gently for 30 minutes. Transfer the chicken mixture to a 1.2 litre/2 pint/5 cup pie dish. Leave to cool.

3 Preheat the oven to 220°C/425°F/Gas 7. Place a narrow strip of pastry on the edge of the pie dish. Moisten the strip, then cover the dish with the pastry. Press the edges together. Make a hole in the centre of the pastry and insert a small funnel of foil. Brush the pastry with beaten egg, then bake for 15–20 minutes.

4 Reduce the oven temperature to 180°C/350°F/Gas 4. Mix the cream and eggs, then pour into the pie through the funnel. Shake the pie to distribute the cream, then return to the oven for 5–10 minutes. Leave the pie in a warm place for about 5–10 minutes before serving, or cool completely.

Chicken and Ham Pie

This is a rich pie flavoured with fresh herbs and lightly spiced with mace – ideal for taking on a picnic.

Serves 8

400g/14oz ready-made	10ml/2 tsp chopped fresh
shortcrust pastry	thyme
800g/1¾ lb chicken	grated rind and juice of
breast	½ large lemon
350g/12oz uncooked	5ml/1 tsp freshly ground
gammon	mace
60ml/4 tbsp double cream	salt and ground black
6 spring onions, finely	pepper
chopped	beaten egg or milk, to
15ml/1 tbsp chopped	glaze
fresh tarragon	

1 Preheat the oven to 190°C/375°F/Gas 5. Roll out one-third of the pastry and use it to line a 20cm/8in pie tin, 5cm/2in deep. Place on a baking sheet.

2 Mince 115g/4oz of the chicken with the gammon, then mix with the cream, spring onions, herbs, lemon rind and 15ml/1 tbsp of the lemon juice; season lightly. Cut the remaining chicken into 1cm/½in pieces and mix with the remaining lemon juice, the mace and seasoning.

3 Make a layer of one-third of the gammon mixture in the pastry base, cover with half the chopped chicken, then add another layer of one-third of the gammon. Add all the remaining chicken followed by the remaining gammon.

4 Dampen the edges of the pastry base and roll out the remaining pastry to make a lid for the pie. Use the trimmings to make a lattice decoration. Make a small hole in the centre of the pie, brush the top with beaten egg or milk, then bake for 20 minutes. Reduce the temperature to 160°C/325°F/Gas 3 and bake for a further 1–1¼ hours. Transfer the pie to a wire rack and leave to cool.

Venison with Cranberry Sauce

Venison steaks are now readily available. Lean and low in fat, they make a healthy choice for a special occasion.

Serves 4

1 orange
1 lemon
75g/3oz/³⁄₄ cup fresh or frozen unthawed cranberries
5ml/1 tsp grated fresh root ginger
1 fresh thyme sprig
5ml/1 tsp Dijon mustard
60ml/4 tbsp redcurrant jelly

150ml/¼ pint/⅔ cup ruby port
30ml/2 tbsp sunflower oil
4 venison steaks
2 shallots, finely chopped
salt and ground black pepper
fresh thyme sprigs, to garnish
mashed potatoes and broccoli, to serve

1 Pare the rind from half the orange and half the lemon using a vegetable peeler, then cut into very fine strips. Blanch the strips in a small saucepan of boiling water for 5 minutes until tender. Drain the strips and refresh under cold water.

2 Squeeze the juice from the citrus fruit and pour into a small pan. Add the cranberries, ginger, thyme, mustard, redcurrant jelly and port. Cook gently until the jelly melts. Bring to the boil, stirring, cover and reduce the heat. Cook for 15 minutes, until the cranberries are just tender.

3 Fry the venison steaks in the oil over a high heat for 2–3 minutes. Turn them over and add the shallots. Cook on the other side for 2–3 minutes, to taste. Just before the end of cooking, pour in the sauce and add the strips of orange and lemon rind. Leave the sauce to bubble for a few seconds to thicken slightly, then remove the thyme sprig and adjust the seasoning to taste.

4 Transfer the venison steaks to warmed plates and spoon over the sauce. Garnish with thyme sprigs and serve accompanied by creamy mashed potatoes and broccoli.

Turkey and Mange-tout Stir-fry

Have all the ingredients prepared before you start cooking this dish, as it will be ready in minutes.

Serves 4

30ml/2 tbsp sesame oil
90ml/6 tbsp lemon juice
1 garlic clove, crushed
1cm/½in piece fresh root ginger, peeled and grated
5ml/1 tsp clear honey
450g/1lb turkey fillets, cut into strips
115g/4oz/1 cup mange-touts, trimmed

30ml/2 tbsp groundnut oil
50g/2oz/½ cup cashew nuts
6 spring onions, cut into strips
225g/8oz can water chestnuts, drained and thinly sliced
pinch of salt
saffron rice, to serve

1 Mix together the sesame oil, lemon juice, garlic, ginger and honey in a shallow non-metallic dish. Add the turkey and mix well. Cover and leave to marinate for 3–4 hours.

2 Blanch the mange-touts in boiling salted water for about 1 minute. Drain and refresh under cold running water.

3 Drain the marinade from the turkey strips and reserve the marinade. Heat the groundnut oil in a wok or large frying pan, add the cashew nuts and stir-fry for about 1–2 minutes until golden brown. Remove the cashew nuts from the wok or frying pan using a slotted spoon and set aside.

4 Add the turkey and stir-fry for 3–4 minutes, until golden brown. Add the spring onions, mange-touts, water chestnuts and the reserved marinade. Cook for a few minutes, until the turkey is tender and the sauce is bubbling and hot. Stir in the cashew nuts and serve with saffron rice.

Cook's Tip
This dish could be served on a bed of medium-width egg noodles for a quick meal.

Farmhouse Venison Pie

A simple and satisfying pie; the venison is cooked in a rich gravy, topped with potato and parsnip mash.

Serves 4

45ml/3 tbsp sunflower oil
1 onion, chopped
1 garlic clove, crushed
3 rashers rindless streaky
  bacon, chopped
675g/1½ lb minced
  venison
115g/4oz button
  mushrooms, chopped
25g/1oz/2 tbsp plain flour
450ml/¾ pint/1¼ cups
  beef stock
150ml/¼ pint/⅔ cup
  ruby port
2 bay leaves

5ml/1 tsp chopped fresh
  thyme
5ml/1 tsp Dijon mustard
15ml/1 tbsp redcurrant
  jelly
675g/1½lb potatoes
450g/1lb parsnips
1 egg yolk
50g/2oz/4 tbsp butter
pinch of freshly grated
  nutmeg
45ml/3 tbsp chopped
  fresh parsley
salt and ground black
  pepper

1 Heat the oil in a large frying pan and fry the onion, garlic and bacon for 5 minutes. Add the venison and mushrooms and cook for a few minutes, stirring, until browned.

2 Stir in the flour and cook for 1–2 minutes, then add the stock, port, herbs, mustard, redcurrant jelly and seasoning. Bring to the boil, cover with a tight-fitting lid and simmer for 30–40 minutes, until tender. Spoon into a large pie dish or four individual ovenproof dishes.

3 While the venison and mushroom mixture is cooking, preheat the oven to 200°C/400°F/Gas 6. Cut the potatoes and parsnips into large chunks. Cook together in boiling salted water for 20 minutes or until tender. Drain and mash, then beat in the egg yolk, butter, nutmeg, parsley and seasoning.

4 Spread the potato and parsnip mixture over the meat and bake for 30–40 minutes, until piping hot and golden brown. Serve at once with a green vegetable, if you wish.

Normandy Pheasant

Calvados, cider, apples and cream – the produce of Normandy – make this a rich and flavoursome dish.

Serves 4

2 oven-ready pheasants
15ml/1 tbsp olive oil
25g/1oz/2 tbsp butter
60ml/4 tbsp Calvados
450ml/¾ pint/1¼ cups
  dry cider
bouquet garni

3 Cox's Pippin apples
150ml/¼ pint/⅔ cup
  double cream
salt and ground black
  pepper
fresh thyme sprigs, to
  garnish

1 Preheat the oven to 160°C/325°F/Gas 3. Joint both the pheasants into four pieces using a large sharp knife. Discard the backbones and knuckles.

2 Heat the oil and butter in a large flameproof casserole. Working in two batches, add the pheasant pieces to the casserole and brown them over a high heat. Return all the pheasant pieces to the casserole.

3 Standing well back, pour over the Calvados and set it alight with a match. Shake the casserole and when the flames have subsided, pour in the cider, then add the bouquet garni and season to taste with salt and pepper. Bring to the boil, cover with a tight-fitting lid and cook for about 50 minutes.

4 Peel, core and thickly slice the apples. Tuck the apple slices around the pheasant. Cover and cook for 5–10 minutes, or until the pheasant is tender. Transfer the pheasant and apples to a warmed serving plate. Keep warm.

5 Remove the bouquet garni, then boil the sauce rapidly to reduce by half to a syrupy consistency. Stir in the double cream and simmer for a further 2–3 minutes until thickened. Taste the sauce and adjust the seasoning if necessary. Spoon the sauce over the pheasant pieces and serve immediately, garnished with fresh thyme sprigs.

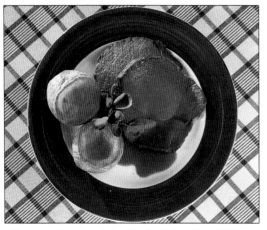

Roast Beef with Yorkshire Pudding

This classic British dish is often served at Sunday lunch, accompanied by potatoes, mustard and horseradish sauce.

Serves 6

1.75kg/4lb joint of beef
30–60ml/2–4 tbsp dripping or oil
300ml/½ pint/1¼ cups vegetable or veal stock, wine or water
salt and ground black pepper

For the puddings
50g/2oz/½ cup plain flour
1 egg, beaten
150ml/¼ pint/⅔ cup water mixed with milk
dripping or oil, for cooking

1 Weigh the beef and calculate the cooking time. Allow 15 minutes per 450g/1lb plus 15 minutes for rare meat, 20 minutes plus 20 minutes for medium, and 25–30 minutes plus 25 minutes for well-done.

2 Preheat the oven to 220°C/425°F/Gas 7. Heat the dripping or oil in a roasting tin in the oven. Place the meat on a rack, fat-side uppermost, then place the rack in the roasting tin. Baste the beef with the dripping or oil, and cook for the required time, basting occasionally.

3 To make the Yorkshire puddings, stir the flour, salt and pepper together in a bowl and form a well in the centre. Pour the egg into the well, then slowly pour in the milk, stirring in the flour to give a smooth batter. Stand for 30 minutes.

4 A few minutes before the meat is ready, spoon a little dripping or oil in each of 12 patty tins and place in the oven until very hot. Remove the meat, season, then cover loosely with foil and keep warm. Quickly divide the batter among the patty tins, then bake for 15–20 minutes, until well risen and brown.

5 Spoon off the fat from the roasting tin. Add the stock, wine or water, stirring, and boil for a few minutes. Season to taste, then serve with the beef and Yorkshire puddings.

Beef Olives

So-called because of their shape, these beef rolls contain a delicious filling made with bacon and mushrooms.

Serves 4

25g/1oz/2 tbsp butter
2 rashers bacon, finely chopped
115g/4oz mushrooms, chopped
15ml/1 tbsp chopped fresh parsley
grated rind and juice of 1 lemon
115g/4oz/2 cups fresh breadcrumbs

675g/1½ lb topside of beef, cut into 8 thin slices
40g/1½ oz/3 tbsp plain flour
45ml/3 tbsp oil
2 onions, sliced
450ml/¾ pint/1¾ cups brown veal stock
salt and ground black pepper

1 Preheat the oven to 160°C/325°F/Gas 3. Melt the butter in a saucepan and fry the bacon and mushrooms for 3 minutes. Mix them with the chopped parsley, lemon rind and juice, breadcrumbs and seasoning.

2 Spread an equal amount of the breadcrumb mixture evenly over the beef slices, leaving a narrow border clear around the edge. Roll up the slices and tie securely with fine string, then dip the beef rolls in the flour to coat lightly, shaking off any excess flour.

3 Heat the oil in a frying pan, then fry the beef rolls until lightly browned. Remove and keep warm. Add the onions and fry until browned. Stir in the remaining flour and cook until lightly browned. Pour in the stock, stirring constantly, bring to the boil, stirring, and simmer for 2–3 minutes.

4 Transfer the rolls to a casserole, pour the sauce over the top, then cover with a tight-fitting lid and cook in the oven for 2 hours. Lift out the "olives" using a slotted spoon and remove the string. Return them to the sauce and serve hot.

Lamb and Spring Vegetable Stew

Known as a *blanquette* in France, this stew may have blanched asparagus spears or French beans added.

Serves 4

65g/2½oz/5 tbsp butter	2 small turnips,
900g/2lb lean boned	quartered
shoulder of lamb, cut	175g/6oz/¾ cup shelled
into 4cm/1¼ in dice	broad beans
600ml/1 pint/2½ cups	15g/½oz/1 tbsp plain
lamb stock or water	flour
150ml/¼ pint/⅔ cup dry	1 egg yolk
white wine	45l/3 tbsp double cream
1 onion, quartered	10ml/2 tsp lemon juice
2 fresh thyme sprigs	salt and ground black
1 bay leaf	pepper
225g/8oz baby onions,	30ml/2 tbsp chopped
halved	fresh parsley, to
225g/8oz young carrots	garnish

1 Sauté the lamb in 25g/1oz/2 tbsp of the butter to seal. Add the stock or water and wine, bring to the boil and skim. Add the quartered onion, thyme and bay leaf. Cover and simmer for 1 hour.

2 Brown the baby onions in 15g/½oz/1 tbsp of the butter. Add to the lamb with the carrots and turnips. Cook for 20 minutes. Add the beans and cook for 10 minutes.

3 Arrange the lamb and vegetables on a serving dish. Cover and keep warm. Discard the onion quarters and herbs. Strain the stock; skim off the fat. Bring to the boil and reduce the stock to 450ml/¾ pint/1¾ cups. Mix the remaining butter and flour to a paste. Whisk into the stock, then simmer briefly.

4 Combine the egg yolk and cream. Add a little hot sauce then stir into the pan. Do not boil. Add the lemon juice, and season. Pour the sauce over the lamb; garnish with parsley.

Beef Paprika with Roasted Peppers

This dish is perfect for family suppers – and roasting the peppers gives an added dimension.

Serves 4

30ml/2 tbsp olive oil	400g/14oz can chopped
675g/1½lb chuck steak,	tomatoes
cut into 4cm/1½in	2 red peppers, seeded and
dice	halved
2 onions, chopped	150ml/¼ pint/⅔ cup
1 garlic clove, crushed	crème fraîche
15g/½oz/1 tbsp plain	salt and ground black
flour	pepper
15ml/1 tbsp paprika, plus	buttered noodles, to serve
extra to garnish	

1 Preheat the oven to 140°C/275°F/Gas 1. Heat the oil in a large flameproof casserole and brown the diced chuck steak in batches. Remove the meat from the casserole using a slotted spoon and set aside.

2 Add the onions and garlic and fry gently until softened but not browned. Stir in the flour and paprika and continue cooking for a further 1–2 minutes, stirring continuously to prevent sticking.

3 Return the meat and any juices that have collected on the plate to the casserole, then add the chopped tomatoes and salt and ground black pepper. Bring to the boil while stirring continuously, then cover with a tight-fitting lid and cook in the oven for 2½ hours.

4 Meanwhile, place the peppers skin-side up on a grill rack and grill until the skins have blistered and charred. Cool, then peel off the skins. Cut the flesh into strips, then add to the casserole and cook for a further 15–30 minutes, or until the meat is tender.

5 Stir in the crème fraîche and sprinkle with a little paprika. Serve hot with buttered noodles.

Beef in Guinness

Guinness gives this stew a deep, rich flavour. Use Beamish or another stout if you prefer.

Serves 6

*900g/2lb chuck steak, cut
    into 4cm/1½ in dice*
plain flour, for coating
45ml/3 tbsp oil
1 large onion, sliced
1 carrot, thinly sliced
*2 celery sticks, thinly
    sliced*
*10ml/2 tsp granulated
    sugar*

*5ml/1 tsp English
    mustard powder*
15ml/1 tbsp tomato purée
*2.5 x 7.5cm/1 x 3in strip
    orange rind*
bouquet garni
*600ml/1 pint/2½ cups
    Guinness*
*salt and ground black
    pepper*

1 Toss the beef in flour to coat. Heat 30ml/2 tbsp of the oil in a large shallow saucepan, then cook the beef in batches until lightly browned. Transfer to a bowl.

2 Add the remaining oil to the pan, then cook the onions until well browned, adding the thinly sliced carrot and celery towards the end.

3 Stir in the sugar, mustard, tomato purée, orange rind, Guinness and seasoning, then add the bouquet garni and bring to the boil. Return the meat, and any juices in the bowl, to the pan; add water, if necessary, so that the meat is covered. Cover the pan with a tight-fitting lid and cook gently for 2–2½ hours, until the meat is very tender.

Cottage Pie

This traditional dish is always a favourite with adults and children alike.

Serves 4

30ml/2 tbsp oil
1 onion, finely chopped
1 carrot, finely chopped
*115g/4oz mushrooms,
    chopped*
*500g/1¼lb lean chuck
    steak, minced*
*300ml/½ pint/1¼ cups
    brown veal stock or
    water*
*15g/½oz/1 tbsp plain
    flour*

1 bay leaf
*10–15ml/2–3 tsp
    Worcestershire sauce*
15ml/1 tbsp tomato purée
*675g/1½lb potatoes,
    boiled*
25g/1oz/2 tbsp butter
45ml/3 tbsp hot milk
*15ml/1 tbsp chopped
    fresh tarragon*
*salt and ground black
    pepper*

1 Heat the oil in a saucepan and cook the onion, carrot and mushrooms, stirring occasionally, until browned. Stir the beef into the pan and cook, stirring to break up the lumps, until lightly browned.

2 Blend a few spoonfuls of the stock or water with the flour, then stir into the pan. Stir in the remaining stock or water and bring to a simmer, stirring. Add the bay leaf, Worcestershire sauce and tomato purée, then cover with a tight-fitting lid and cook very gently for 1 hour, stirring occasionally. Uncover towards the end of cooking to allow any excess liquid to evaporate, if necessary.

3 Preheat the oven to 190°C/375°F/Gas 5. Gently heat the potatoes for a couple of minutes, then mash with the butter, milk and seasoning.

4 Add the tarragon to the mince and season to taste with salt and pepper, then pour into a pie dish. Cover the mince with an even layer of potato and mark the top with the prongs of a fork. Bake for about 25 minutes, until golden brown.

Irish Stew

This wholesome and filling stew is given a slight piquancy by the inclusion of a little anchovy sauce.

Serves 4

4 rashers smoked streaky bacon	300ml/½ pint/1¼ cups brown veal stock
2 celery sticks, chopped	7.5ml/1½ tsp
2 large onions, sliced	Worcestershire sauce
8 middle neck lamb chops (about 1kg/ 2¼lb total weight)	5ml/1 tsp anchovy sauce salt and ground black pepper
1kg/2¼lb potatoes, sliced	fresh parsley, to garnish

1 Preheat the oven to 160°C/325°F/Gas 3. Chop and then fry the bacon for 3–5 minutes until the fat runs, then add the celery and one-third of the onions and continue to cook, stirring occasionally, until browned.

2 Layer the lamb chops, potatoes, vegetables and bacon and remaining onions in a heavy flameproof casserole, seasoning each layer with salt and pepper as you go. Finish with a layer of potatoes.

3 Pour the veal stock, Worcestershire sauce and anchovy sauce into the bacon and vegetable cooking juices in the pan, stir, and bring to the boil. Pour the mixture into the casserole, adding water if necessary so that the liquid comes halfway up the sides of the casserole.

4 Cover the casserole with a tight-fitting lid, then cook in the oven for 3 hours, until the meat and vegetables are tender. Return to the oven for longer if necessary. Serve hot, sprinkled with chopped fresh parsley.

Cook's Tip
This is a good way of cooking cheaper cuts of lamb but for a more elegant dish, use diced lamb or lamb steaks instead of the chops and cook in the oven for 2 hours.

Oatmeal and Herb Rack of Lamb

Ask the butcher to remove the chine bone that runs along the eye of the meat – this will make carving easier.

Serves 6

2 best end necks of lamb (about 900kg/2lb each)	25g/1oz/2 tbsp butter, melted
finely grated rind of 1 lemon	30ml/2 tbsp clear honey salt and ground black
60ml/4 tbsp medium oatmeal	pepper roasted baby vegetables
50g/2oz/1 cup fresh white breadcrumbs	and gravy, to serve fresh herb sprigs, to
60ml/4 tbsp chopped fresh parsley	garnish

1 Preheat the oven to 200°C/400°F/Gas 6. Using a small sharp knife, cut through the skin and meat of both pieces of lamb about 2.5cm/1in from the tips of the bones. Pull off the fatty meat to expose the bones, then scrape around each bone tip until completely clean.

2 Trim all the skin and most of the fat from the meat, then lightly score the remaining fat with a sharp knife. Repeat with the second rack.

3 Mix together the lemon rind, oatmeal, breadcrumbs, the parsley and seasoning, then stir in the melted butter.

4 Brush the fatty side of each rack of lamb with honey, then press the oatmeal mixture evenly over the surface with your fingers until well coated.

5 Place the racks in a roasting tin with the oatmeal sides uppermost. Roast for 40–50 minutes, depending on whether you like rare or medium lamb. Cover loosely with foil if browning too much. To serve, slice each rack into three and accompany with roasted baby vegetables and gravy made with the pan juices. Garnish with herb sprigs.

Beef Wellington

This dish is so-named because of a supposed resemblance of shape and colour to the Duke of Wellington's boot.

Serves 8

1.4kg/3lb fillet of beef
15g/½oz/1 tbsp butter
30ml/2 tbsp oil
½ small onion, finely chopped
175g/6oz mushrooms, chopped
175g/6oz liver pâté
freshly squeezed lemon juice
a few drops of Worcestershire sauce
400g/14oz ready-made puff pastry
salt and ground black pepper
beaten egg, to glaze

1 Preheat the oven to 200°C/425°F/Gas 7. Season the beef with pepper, then tie it at intervals with string.

2 Heat the butter and oil in a roasting tin. Brown the beef over a high heat, then cook in the oven for 20 minutes. Cool and remove the string.

3 Scrape the cooking juices into a pan, add the onion and mushrooms and cook until tender. Cool, then mix with the pâté. Add lemon juice and Worcestershire sauce.

4 Roll out the pastry to a large 5mm/¼in thick rectangle. Spread the pâté mixture on the beef, then place it in the centre of the pastry. Dampen the edges of the pastry, then fold it over the beef to make a neat parcel, tucking in the ends neatly; press to seal.

5 Place the parcel on a baking sheet with the join on the underside and brush with beaten egg. Bake in the oven for 25–45 minutes, depending how well done you like the beef. Serve in generous slices.

Butterflied Cumin and Garlic Lamb

Ground cumin and garlic give the lamb a wonderful Middle-Eastern flavour to this recipe.

Serves 6

1.75kg/4lb leg of lamb
60ml/4 tbsp extra virgin olive oil
30ml/2 tbsp ground cumin
4 – 6 garlic cloves, crushed
salt and ground black pepper
toasted almond and raisin rice, to serve
fresh coriander sprigs and lemon wedges, to garnish

1 To butterfly the lamb, cut away the meat from the bone using a small sharp knife. Remove any excess fat and the thin, parchment-like membrane. Bat out the meat with a rolling pin to an even thickness, then prick the fleshy side of the lamb well with the tip of a knife.

2 In a bowl, mix together the olive oil, cumin and garlic and season with pepper. Spoon the mixture all over the lamb, then rub it well into the crevices. Cover the bowl and leave the lamb to marinate overnight.

3 Preheat the oven to 200°C/400°F/Gas 6. Spread the lamb, skin-side down, on a rack in a roasting tin. Season with salt and roast for 45–60 minutes, until crusty brown on the outside but still pink in the centre.

4 Remove the lamb from the oven and leave it to rest for about 10 minutes. Cut into diagonal slices and serve with the toasted almond and raisin rice. Garnish with the fresh coriander sprigs and lemon wedges.

Cook's Tip
The lamb may be barbecued rather than roasted. Thread it on to two long skewers and barbecue for about 20-25 minutes on each side, until it is cooked to your liking.

Lamb with Mint Sauce

In this flavoursome dish, the classic combination of lamb and mint is given an original twist.

Serves 4

8 lamb noisettes,
  2−2.5cm/³⁄₄−1in
  thick
30ml/2 tbsp oil
45ml/3 tbsp medium-
  bodied dry white wine,
  or vegetable or veal
  stock
salt and ground black
  pepper
fresh mint sprigs, to
  garnish

For the sauce
30ml/2 tbsp boiling
  water
5−10ml/1−2 tsp
  granulated sugar
leaves from a small
  bunch of fresh mint,
  finely chopped
about 30ml/2 tbsp white
  wine vinegar

1 To make the sauce, stir the water and sugar together, then add the mint, vinegar to taste and season with salt and black pepper. Leave for 30 minutes.

2 Season the lamb with pepper. Heat the oil in a large frying pan and fry the lamb, in batches if necessary so that the pan is not crowded, for about 3 minutes on each side for meat that is pink in the middle.

3 Transfer the lamb to a warmed plate and season with salt, then cover and keep warm.

4 Stir the wine or stock into the cooking juices, dislodging the sediment, and bring to the boil. Bubble for a couple of minutes, then pour over the lamb. Garnish the lamb noisettes with small sprigs of mint and serve hot with the mint sauce.

Somerset Pork with Apples

A creamy cider sauce accompanies tender pieces of pork and sliced apples to make a rich supper dish.

Serves 4

25g/1oz/2 tbsp butter
500g/1¼lb pork loin, cut
  into bite-size pieces
12 baby onions, peeled
10ml/2 tsp grated lemon
  rind
300ml/½ pint/1¼ cups
  dry cider
150ml/¼ pint/⅔ cup veal
  stock

2 crisp eating apples such
  as Granny Smith,
  cored and sliced
45ml/3 tbsp chopped
  fresh parsley
100ml/3½fl oz/scant
  ½ cup whipping cream
salt and ground black
  pepper

1 Heat the butter in a large sauté or frying pan and brown the pork in batches. Transfer the pork to a bowl.

2 Add the onions to the pan, brown lightly, then stir in the lemon rind, cider and stock and boil for about 3 minutes. Return all the pork to the pan and cook gently for about 25 minutes, until tender.

3 Add the apples to the pan and continue to cook for a further 5 minutes. Using a slotted spoon, transfer the pork, onions and apples to a warmed serving dish, cover and keep warm. Stir the parsley and cream into the pan and allow to bubble to thicken the sauce slightly. Season, then pour over the pork and serve hot.

Pork with Plums

Plums poached in apple juice are used here to make a delightfully fruity sauce for pork chops.

Serves 4

450g/1lb ripe plums,
  halved and stoned
300ml/½ pint/1¼ cups
  apple juice
40g/1½oz/3 tbsp butter
15ml/1 tbsp oil
4 pork chops (about
  200g/7oz each)

1 onion, finely chopped
pinch of freshly ground
  mace
salt and ground black
  pepper
fresh sage leaves, to
  garnish

1 Simmer the plums in the apple juice until tender. Strain off and reserve the juice, then purée half the plums with a little of the juice.

2 Meanwhile, heat the butter and oil in a large frying pan and fry the chops until brown on both sides, then transfer them to a plate.

3 Add the onion to the pan and cook gently until soft, but not coloured. Return the chops to the pan. Pour over the plum purée and all the juice.

4 Simmer, uncovered, for 10–15 minutes, until the chops are cooked through. Add the remaining plums to the pan, then add the mace and seasoning. Warm the sauce through over a moderate heat and serve garnished with fresh sage leaves.

Lancashire Hot-pot

Browning the lamb and kidneys, plus the extra vegetables and herbs, adds flavour to the traditional basic ingredients.

Serves 4

40g/1½oz/3 tbsp
  dripping, or
45ml/3 tbsp oil
8 medium neck lamb
  chops (about 900g/2lb
  total weight)
175g/6oz lamb's kidneys,
  cut into large pieces
900g/2lb potatoes, thinly
  sliced
3 carrots, thickly sliced
450g/1lb leeks, sliced

3 celery sticks, sliced
15ml/1 tbsp chopped
  fresh thyme
30ml/2 tbsp chopped
  fresh parsley
small fresh rosemary
  sprig
600ml/1 pint/2½ cups
  veal stock
salt and ground black
  pepper

1 Preheat the oven to 170°C/325°F/Gas 3. Heat the dripping or oil in a frying pan and brown the chops and kidneys in batches, then reserve the fat.

2 In a large casserole, make alternate layers of lamb chops, kidneys, three-quarters of the potatoes and the carrots, leeks and celery, sprinkling the herbs and seasoning over each layer as you go. Tuck the rosemary sprig down the side.

3 Arrange the remaining potatoes on top. Pour over the stock, brush with the reserved fat, then cover the casserole with a tight-fitting lid and bake for 2½ hours. Increase the oven temperature to 220°C/425°F/Gas 7. Uncover and cook for a further 30 minutes.

Pork Loin with Celery

Have a change from a plain Sunday roast and try this whole loin of pork in a celery and cream sauce instead.

Serves 4

15ml/1 tbsp oil
50g/2oz/4 tbsp butter
1kg/2¼lb boned, rolled
    loin of pork, rind
    removed and trimmed
1 onion, chopped
bouquet garni
3 fresh dill sprigs
150ml/¼ pint/⅔ cup dry
    white wine
150ml/¼ pint/⅔ cup
    water

sticks from 1 celery head,
    cut into 2.5cm/1in
    lengths
25g/1oz/2 tbsp plain
    flour
150ml/¼ pint/⅔ cup
    double cream
squeeze of lemon juice
salt and ground black
    pepper
chopped fresh dill, to
    garnish

1 Heat the oil and half the butter in a heavy flameproof casserole just large enough to hold the pork and celery, then brown the pork evenly. Transfer the pork to a plate.

2 Add the onion to the casserole and cook until softened but not browned. Place the bouquet garni and the dill sprigs on the onion, then place the pork on top and add any juices from the plate. Pour the wine and water over the pork, season to taste, cover and simmer gently for 30 minutes.

3 Turn the pork, arrange the celery around it, cover again and cook for 40 minutes, until the pork and celery are tender. Transfer the pork and celery to a serving plate, cover and keep warm. Discard the bouquet garni and dill.

4 Cream the remaining butter and flour, then whisk into the cooking liquid while it is barely simmering. Cook for about 2–3 minutes, stirring occasionally. Stir the cream into the casserole, bring to the boil and add a squeeze of lemon juice.

5 Slice the pork, pour some sauce over the slices and garnish with dill. Serve with remaining sauce separately.

Spiced Lamb with Apricots

Inspired by Middle Eastern cooking, this fruity, spicy casserole is simple to make yet looks impressive.

Serves 4

115g/4oz ready-to-eat
    dried apricots
50g/2oz/scant ½ cup
    seedless raisins
2.5ml/½ tsp saffron
    strands
150ml/¼ pint/⅔ cup
    orange juice
15ml/1 tbsp red wine
    vinegar
30–45ml/2–3 tbsp olive
    oil
1.5kg/3lb leg of lamb,
    boned and diced
1 onion, chopped
2 garlic cloves, crushed
10ml/2 tsp ground
    cumin

1.25ml/¼ tsp ground
    cloves
15ml/1 tbsp ground
    coriander
25g/1oz/2 tbsp plain
    flour
600ml/1 pint/2½ cups
    lamb stock
45ml/3 tbsp chopped
    fresh coriander
salt and ground black
    pepper
saffron rice mixed with
    toasted almonds and
    chopped fresh
    coriander, to serve

1 Mix together the dried apricots, raisins, saffron, orange juice and vinegar. Cover and leave to soak for 2–3 hours.

2 Preheat the oven to 160°C/325°F/Gas 3. Heat 30ml/2 tbsp oil in a large flameproof casserole and brown the lamb in batches. Remove and set aside. Add the onion and garlic with a little more of the remaining oil and cook until softened.

3 Stir in the spices and flour and cook for 1–2 minutes more. Return the meat to the casserole. Stir in the stock, fresh coriander and the soaked fruit with its liquid. Season to taste with salt and pepper, then bring to the boil. Cover the casserole with a tight-fitting lid and cook for 1½ hours (adding extra stock if necessary), or until the lamb is tender. Serve with saffron rice mixed with toasted almonds and fresh coriander.

Beef and Mushroom Burgers

It's worth making your own burgers to cut down on fat – in these the meat is extended with mushrooms for extra fibre.

Serves 4

1 small onion, chopped
150g/5oz/2 cups small
  cup mushrooms
450g/1lb lean minced
  beef
50g/2oz/1 cup fresh
  breadcrumbs

5ml/1 tsp dried mixed
  herbs
15ml/1 tbsp tomato purée
flour, for shaping
salt and black pepper

1 Process the onion and mushrooms until finely chopped. Add the beef, breadcrumbs, herbs, tomato purée and seasoning. Process until the mixture binds but still has some texture. Divide into 8–10 pieces and press into burger shapes.

2 Cook the burgers in a non-stick frying pan, or under a hot grill, for 12–15 minutes, turning once, until evenly cooked. Serve with relish and salad, in burger buns or pitta bread.

Ruby Bacon Chops

This dish can be prepared with the minimum of effort, yet would still impress at an informal dinner party.

Serves 4

1 ruby grapefruit
4 lean bacon loin chops

45ml/3 tbsp redcurrant
  jelly
ground black pepper

1 Using a sharp knife, cut away all the peel and pith from the grapefruit. Carefully remove the segments, catching the juice in a bowl.

2 Fry the bacon chops in a non-stick frying pan without fat, turning them once, until golden. Add the reserved grapefruit juice and redcurrant jelly to the pan and stir until melted. Add the grapefruit segments, then season with pepper and serve hot with fresh vegetables.

Beef Strips with Orange and Ginger

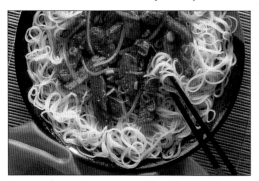

Stir-frying is a good way of cooking with the minimum of fat. It's also one of the quickest ways to cook.

Serves 4

Place 450g/1 lb beef strips in a bowl; sprinkle over the rind and juice of 1 orange. Leave to marinate for at least 30 minutes. Drain the liquid and set aside, then mix the meat with 15ml/1 tbsp soy sauce, 5ml/1 tsp cornflour and 2.5cm/1in root ginger. Heat 10ml/2 tsp sesame oil in a wok or large frying pan and add the beef. Stir-fry for 1 minute, add 1 carrot cut into small strips and stir-fry for a further 2–3 minutes. Stir in 2 sliced spring onions and the reserved liquid, then boil, stirring, until thickened.

Steak, Kidney and Mushroom Pie

If you prefer, omit the kidneys from this pie and substitute more chuck steak in their place.

Serves 4

30ml/2 tbsp sunflower oil
1 onion, chopped
115g/4oz bacon, finely chopped
500g/1¼lb chuck steak, diced
25g/1oz/2 tbsp plain flour
115g/4oz lamb's kidneys
400ml/14fl oz/1¾ cups beef stock
large bouquet garni
115g/4oz button mushrooms
225g/8oz ready-made puff pastry
beaten egg, to glaze
salt and ground black pepper

1 Preheat the oven to 160°C/325°F/Gas 3. Heat the oil in a heavy-based saucepan and cook the bacon and onion until lightly browned.

2 Toss the steak in the flour. Stir the meat into the pan in batches and cook, stirring, until browned. Toss the kidneys in flour; add to the pan with the bouquet garni. Transfer to a casserole dish then pour in the stock, cover with a tight-fitting lid and cook in the oven for 2 hours. Stir in the mushrooms and seasoning and leave to cool.

3 Preheat the oven to 220°C/425°F/Gas 7. Roll out the pastry to 2cm/¾ in larger than the top of a 1.2 litre/2 pint/5 cup pie dish. Cut off a pastry strip and then fit it around the dampened rim of the dish. Brush the pastry strip with water.

4 Tip the meat mixture into the dish. Lay the pastry over the dish, press the edges together to seal, then knock them up with the back of a knife. Make a small slit in the pastry, brush with beaten egg and bake for 20 minutes. Lower the oven temperature to 180°C/350°F/Gas 4 and bake for a further 20 minutes, until the pastry is risen, golden and crisp.

Lamb Pie with Mustard Thatch

This makes a pleasant change from a classic shepherd's pie – and it is a healthier option, as well.

Serves 4

750g/1½lb old potatoes, diced
30ml/2 tbsp skimmed milk
15ml/1 tbsp wholegrain or French mustard
450g/1lb lean minced lamb
1 onion, chopped
2 celery sticks, sliced
2 carrots, diced
150ml/¼ pint/⅔ cup beef stock
60ml/4 tbsp rolled oats
15ml/1 tbsp Worcestershire sauce
30ml/2 tbsp fresh rosemary, chopped, or 10ml/2 tsp dried rosemary
salt and ground black pepper

1 Cook the potatoes in lightly salted boiling water until tender. Drain and mash until smooth, then stir in the milk and mustard. Meanwhile, preheat the oven to 200°C/400°F/Gas 6.

2 Break up the lamb with a fork and fry without any fat in a non-stick pan until lightly browned. Add the onion, celery and carrots to the saucepan and cook for 2–3 minutes, stirring continuously.

3 Stir in the stock and rolled oats. Bring to the boil, then add the Worcestershire sauce and rosemary and season to taste with salt and pepper.

4 Turn the meat mixture into a 1.75 litre/3 pint/7½ cup ovenproof dish and spread the potato topping evenly over the top, swirling with the edge of a knife. Bake for 30–35 minutes, or until golden. Serve hot with fresh vegetables.

Sausage and Bean Ragoût

An economical and nutritious main course that children will love. Serve with garlic and herb bread, if you wish.

Serves 4

350g/12oz/2 cups dried
  flageolet beans, soaked
  overnight
45ml/3 tbsp olive oil
1 onion, finely chopped
2 garlic cloves, crushed
450g/1lb good-quality
  chunky sausages,
  skinned and thickly
  sliced
15ml/1 tbsp tomato purée

30ml/2 tbsp chopped
  fresh parsley
15ml/1 tbsp chopped
  fresh thyme
400g/14oz can chopped
  tomatoes
salt and ground black
  pepper
chopped fresh thyme and
  parsley, to garnish

1 Drain and rinse the soaked beans and place them in a saucepan with enough water to cover. Bring to the boil, cover the pan with a tight-fitting lid and simmer for about 1 hour, or until tender. Drain the beans and set aside.

2 Heat the oil in a frying pan and fry the onion, garlic and sausages until golden.

3 Stir in the tomato purée, tomatoes, chopped parsley and thyme. Season with salt and pepper, then bring to the boil.

4 Add the beans, then cover with a lid and cook gently for about 15 minutes, stirring occasionally, until the sausage slices are cooked through. Garnish with chopped fresh thyme and parsley and serve immediately.

Cook's Tip

For a spicier version, add some skinned, thinly sliced chorizo or kabanos sausage along with the flageolet beans for the last 15 minutes of cooking.

Peppered Steaks with Madeira

A really easy dish for special occasions. Mixed peppercorns have an excellent flavour, though black pepper will do.

Serves 4

15ml/1 tbsp mixed dried
  peppercorns (green,
  pink and black)
4 fillet or sirloin steaks
  (about 175g/6oz each)
15ml/1 tbsp olive oil,
  plus extra oil for
  shallow frying

1 garlic clove, crushed
60ml/4 tbsp Madeira
90ml/6 tbsp fresh beef
  stock
150ml/¼ pint/⅔ cup
  double cream
pinch of salt

1 Finely crush the peppercorns using a coffee grinder or pestle and mortar, then press them evenly on to both sides of the sirloin steaks.

2 Place the steaks in a shallow non-metallic dish, then add the olive oil, garlic and Madeira. Cover the dish and leave to marinate in a cool place for at least 4–6 hours, or preferably overnight for a more intense flavour.

3 Remove the steaks from the dish, reserving the marinade. Brush a little oil over a large heavy-based frying pan and heat until it is hot.

4 Add the steaks and cook over a high heat, according to taste. Allow about 3 minutes' cooking time per side for a medium steak or 2 minutes per side for rare. Remove the steaks from the frying pan and keep them warm.

5 Add the reserved marinade and the fresh beef stock to the pan and bring to the boil, then leave the sauce to bubble until it is well reduced.

6 Add the double cream to the pan, with salt to taste, and stir until it has slightly thickened. Serve the peppered steaks on warmed plates with the sauce.

Pork with Mozzarella and Sage

Here is a variation of the famous dish *saltimbocca alla romana* – the mozzarella adds a delicious creamy flavour.

Serves 2–3
225g/8oz pork tenderloin
1 garlic clove, crushed
75g/3oz mozzarella, cut into 6 slices
6 slices Parma ham
6 large sage leaves
25g/1oz/2 tbsp butter
salt and ground black pepper
potato wedges roasted in olive oil and green beans, to serve

1 Trim any excess fat from the pork, then cut the pork crossways into six pieces about 2.5cm/1in thick.

2 Stand each piece of tenderloin on its end and bat down with a rolling pin to flatten. Rub with garlic and set aside for 30 minutes in a cool place.

3 Place a slice of mozzarella on top of each pork steak and season with salt and pepper. Lay a slice of Parma ham on top of each, crinkling it a little to fit.

4 Press a sage leaf on to each and secure with a cocktail stick. Melt the butter in a large heavy-based frying pan and cook the pork for about 2 minutes on each side until you see the mozzarella melting. Remove the cocktail sticks and serve immediately with roasted potatoes and green beans.

Five-spice Lamb

This aromatic lamb casserole is a perfect dish to serve at an informal supper party.

Serves 4
30–45ml/2–3 tbsp oil
1.5kg/3–3½lb leg of lamb, boned and diced
1 onion, chopped
10ml/2 tsp grated fresh root ginger
1 garlic clove, crushed
5ml/1 tsp five-spice powder
30ml/2 tbsp hoi-sin sauce
15ml/1 tbsp soy sauce
300ml/½ pint/1¼ cups passata
250ml/8fl oz/1 cup lamb stock
1 red pepper, seeded and diced
1 yellow pepper, seeded and diced
30ml/2 tbsp chopped fresh coriander
15ml/1 tbsp sesame seeds, toasted
salt and ground black pepper

1 Preheat the oven to 160°C/325°F/Gas 3. In a large, flameproof casserole, heat 30ml/2 tbsp of the oil and then brown the diced lamb in batches over a high heat. Remove to a plate and set aside.

2 Add the onion, ginger and garlic to the casserole with a little more of the oil, if necessary, and cook for 5 minutes, or until softened.

3 Return the lamb to the casserole. Stir in the five-spice powder, hoi-sin sauce, soy sauce, passata and stock, and season to taste with salt and pepper Bring to the boil, then cover with a tight-fitting lid and cook in the oven for about 1¼ hours.

4 Remove the casserole from the oven, stir in the peppers, then cover and return to the oven for a further 15 minutes, or until the lamb is very tender.

5 Sprinkle with the chopped fresh coriander and toasted sesame seeds. Serve hot accompanied by rice, if you wish.

Rich Beef Casserole

Use a full-bodied red wine such as a Burgundy to create the flavoursome sauce in this casserole.

Serves 4–6

900g/2lb chuck steak, cut
    into dice
2 onions, roughly chopped
1 bouquet garni
6 black peppercorns
15ml/1 tbsp red wine
    vinegar
1 bottle red wine
45–60ml/3–4 tbsp
    olive oil
3 celery sticks, thickly
    sliced

50g/2oz/½ cup plain flour
300ml/½ pint/1¼ cups
    beef stock
30ml/2 tbsp tomato purée
2 garlic cloves, crushed
175g/6oz chestnut
    mushrooms, halved
400g/14oz can artichoke
    hearts, drained
    and halved
chopped fresh parsley and
    thyme, to garnish

1 Combine the meat, onions, bouquet garni, peppercorns, vinegar and wine. Cover and leave to marinate overnight.

2 The next day, preheat the oven to 160°C/325°F/Gas 3. Strain the meat, reserving the marinade, and pat dry. Heat the oil in a large flameproof casserole and fry the meat and onions in batches, adding a little more oil if necessary. Remove and set aside. Add the celery and fry until browned, then remove this also and set it aside with the meat.

3 Sprinkle the flour into the casserole and cook for 1 minute. Gradually add the reserved marinade and the stock, and bring to the boil, stirring continuously. Return the meat, onions and celery to the casserole, then stir in the tomato purée and crushed garlic.

4 Cover the casserole with a tight-fitting lid and cook in the oven for about 2¼ hours. Stir in the mushrooms and artichokes, cover again and cook for a further 15 minutes, until the meat is tender. Garnish with parsley and thyme, and serve hot with creamy mashed potatoes, if you wish.

Pork Steaks with Gremolata

Gremolata is a popular Italian dressing of garlic, lemon and parsley – it adds a hint of sharpness to the pork.

Serves 4

30ml/2 tbsp olive oil
4 pork shoulder steaks
1 onion, chopped
2 garlic cloves, crushed
400g/14oz can tomatoes
30ml/2 tbsp tomato purée
150ml/¼ pint/⅔ cup dry
    white wine
bouquet garni
3 anchovy fillets, drained
    and chopped

salt and ground black
    pepper
salad leaves, to serve

For the gremolata
45ml/3 tbsp chopped
    fresh parsley
grated rind of ½ lemon
grated rind of 1 lime
1 garlic clove, chopped

1 Heat the oil in a large flameproof casserole and brown the pork steaks on both sides. Remove and set aside.

2 Add the onions to the casserole and cook until soft. Add the garlic and cook for 1–2 minutes. Chop the tomatoes and add with the tomato purée and wine. Add the bouquet garni, then boil rapidly for 3–4 minutes to reduce and thicken the sauce slightly. Return the pork to the casserole, then cover with a tight-fitting lid and cook for about 30 minutes. Stir in the chopped anchovies. Cover the casserole and cook for a further 15 minutes, or until the pork is tender.

3 Meanwhile, to make the gremolata, mix together the parsley, lemon and lime rinds and garlic.

4 Remove the pork steaks and discard the bouquet garni. Reduce the sauce over a high heat, if it is not already thick. Taste and adjust the seasoning if necessary.

5 Return the pork to the casserole, then sprinkle with the gremolata. Cover and cook for a further 5 minutes, then serve hot with salad leaves.

Beef Casserole and Dumplings

A traditional English recipe, this delicious casserole is topped with light herby dumplings for a filling meal.

Serves 4
15ml/1 tbsp oil	salt and ground black
450g/1lb minced beef	pepper
16 button onions	
2 carrots, thickly	**For the dumplings**
sliced	115g/4oz/1 cup shredded
2 celery sticks, thickly	vegetable suet
sliced	50g/2oz/4 tbsp plain
25g/1oz/2 tbsp plain	flour
flour	15ml/1 tbsp chopped
600ml/1 pint/2½ cups	fresh parsley
beef stock	

1   Preheat the oven to 180°C/350°F/Gas 4. Heat the oil in a flameproof casserole and fry the minced beef for 5 minutes until brown and sealed.

2   Add the onions; fry over a moderate heat for 5 minutes, stirring all the time.

3   Stir in the sliced carrots, the celery and the flour, then cook for a further 1 minute.

4   Add the beef stock and season to taste with salt and ground black pepper. Bring to the boil. Cover and cook in the oven for 1¼ hours.

5   For the dumplings, mix together the suet, flour and fresh parsley. Add sufficient cold water to form a smooth dough.

6   Roll the dumpling mixture into eight equal-size balls and place them around the top of the casserole. Return the casserole, uncovered, to the oven for another 20 minutes. Serve with broccoli florets, if liked.

Stilton Burgers

This tasty recipe contains a delicious surprise. The lightly melted Stilton cheese is encased in the crunchy burger.

Serves 4
450g/1lb minced beef	50g/2oz/½ cup crumbled
1 onion, finely chopped	Stilton cheese
1 celery stick, chopped	4 burger buns
5ml/1 tsp mixed	salt and ground black
dried herbs	pepper
5ml/1 tsp mustard	

1   Place the minced beef in a bowl with the chopped onion and celery. Mix together, then season with salt and pepper.

2   Stir in the herbs and mustard, bringing them together to form a firm mixture.

3   Divide the mixture into eight equal portions. Place four on a chopping board and flatten each one slightly.

4   Place the crumbled cheese in the centre of each.

5   Flatten the remaining mixture and place on top. Mould the mixture together, encasing the crumbled cheese, and shape into four burgers.

6   Grill under a moderate heat for 10 minutes, turning once, or until cooked through. Split the burger buns and place a burger inside each. Serve with a freshly made salad and some mustard pickle.

Cook's Tip
These burgers could be made with minced lamb or pork for a variation, but make sure they are thoroughly cooked and not pink inside.

Indian Curried Lamb Samosas

Authentic samosa pastry is rather difficult to make but these samosas work equally well using puff pastry.

Serves 4

15ml/1 tbsp oil
1 garlic clove, crushed
175g/6oz minced lamb
4 spring onions, finely chopped
10ml/2 tsp medium-hot curry paste
4 ready-to-eat dried apricots, chopped
1 small potato, diced
10ml/2 tsp apricot chutney
30ml/2 tbsp frozen peas
squeeze of lemon juice

15ml/1 tbsp chopped fresh coriander
225g/8oz ready-made puff pastry
beaten egg, to glaze
5ml/1 tsp cumin seeds
salt and ground black pepper
45ml/3 tbsp natural yogurt with chopped fresh mint, to serve
fresh mint sprigs, to garnish

1 Preheat the oven to 220°C/425°F/Gas 7 and dampen a large non-stick baking sheet. Fry the garlic in the oil for 30 seconds, then add the lamb. Fry for about 5 minutes, stirring, until the meat is well browned.

2 Stir in the spring onion, curry paste, apricots and potato, and cook for 2–3 minutes. Then add the chutney, peas and 60ml/4 tbsp water. Cover and simmer for 10 minutes, stirring occasionally. Stir in the lemon juice and coriander, season to taste, remove and leave to cool.

3 Roll out the pastry and cut into four 15cm/6in squares. Place a quarter of the curry mixture in the centre of each square and brush the edges with beaten egg. Fold over to make a triangle and seal the edges. Knock up the edges with the back of a knife and make a small slit in the top of each.

4 Brush each samosa with beaten egg and sprinkle over the cumin seeds. Place on the damp baking sheet and bake for about 20 minutes. Serve garnished with mint sprigs and with the minty yogurt handed round separately.

Breton Pork and Bean Casserole

This is a traditional French dish, called *cassoulet*. There are many variations in the different regions of France.

Serves 4

30ml/2 tbsp olive oil
1 onion, chopped
2 garlic cloves, chopped
450g/1lb lean shoulder of pork, diced
350g/12oz lean lamb (preferably leg), diced
225g/8oz coarse pork and garlic sausage, cut into chunks
400g/14oz can chopped tomatoes

30ml/2 tbsp red wine
15ml/1 tbsp tomato purée
bouquet garni
400g/14oz can cannellini beans, drained and rinsed
50g/2oz/1 cup brown breadcrumbs
salt and ground black pepper
green salad and French bread, to serve

1 Preheat the oven to 160°C/325°F/Gas 3. Heat the oil in a large flameproof casserole and fry the onions and garlic until softened. Remove with a slotted spoon and reserve.

2 Add the pork, lamb and sausage chunks to the casserole and fry over a high heat until browned on all sides. Add the onions and garlic to the meat.

3 Stir in the chopped tomatoes, wine and tomato purée and add 300ml/½ pint/1¼ cups water. Season to taste with salt and pepper and add the bouquet garni. Cover and bring to the boil, then transfer the casserole to the preheated oven and cook for 1½ hours.

4 Remove the bouquet garni, stir in the beans and sprinkle the breadcrumbs over the top. Return to the oven, uncovered, for a further 30 minutes, until the top is golden brown. Serve hot with a green salad and French bread to mop up the juices.

Cook's Tip
Replace the lamb with duck breast, but be sure to drain off any fat before adding the breadcrumbs.

Pan-fried Mediterranean Lamb

The warm, summery flavours of the Mediterranean are combined for a simple weekday meal.

Serves 4

8 lean lamb cutlets	45ml/3 tbsp chopped
1 onion, thinly sliced	fresh basil leaves
2 red peppers, seeded and	30ml/2 tbsp chopped
sliced	black olives
400g/14oz can plum	salt and ground black
tomatoes	pepper
1 garlic clove, crushed	

1 Trim any excess fat from the lamb, then fry without fat in a non-stick frying pan until golden brown.

2 Add the onion and red peppers to the pan. Cook, stirring, for a few minutes to soften, then add the plum tomatoes, garlic and fresh basil leaves.

3 Cover and simmer for 20 minutes or until the lamb is tender. Stir in the olives, season to taste with salt and pepper and serve hot, with pasta if you wish.

Cook's Tip
The red peppers give this dish a slightly sweet taste. If you prefer, use green peppers for a more savoury stew.

Greek Lamb Pie

Ready-made filo pastry is so easy to use and gives a most professional look to this lamb and spinach pie.

Serves 4

sunflower oil, for	5ml/1 tsp grated nutmeg
brushing	350g/12oz young spinach
450g/1lb minced lamb	leaves
1 onion, sliced	275g/10oz packet
1 garlic clove, crushed	ready-made filo pastry
400g/14oz can plum	5ml/1 tsp sesame seeds
tomatoes	salt and ground black
30ml/2 tbsp chopped	pepper
fresh mint	

1 Preheat the oven to 200°C/400°F/Gas 6. Lightly oil a 22cm/8½in round springform tin.

2 Fry the mince and onion without fat in a non-stick pan until golden. Add the garlic, tomatoes, mint and nutmeg and season with salt and pepper. Bring to the boil, stirring from time to time. Simmer, stirring occasionally, until most of the liquid has evaporated.

3 Wash the spinach and remove any tough stalks, then cook in only the water clinging to the leaves for about 2 minutes, until just wilted.

4 Lightly brush each sheet of filo pastry with oil and lay in overlapping layers in the tin, leaving enough overhanging to wrap over the top.

5 Spoon in the meat and spinach, then wrap the pastry over to enclose, scrunching it slightly. Sprinkle with sesame seeds and bake for about 25–30 minutes, or until golden and crisp. Serve hot, with salad or vegetables, as you wish.

Cheesy Pasta Bolognese

If you like lasagne, you will love this dish. It is especially popular with children too.

Serves 4

30ml/2 tbsp olive oil	sprig of fresh thyme
1 onion, chopped	225g/8oz/2 cups dried
1 garlic clove, crushed	penne pasta
1 carrot, diced	300ml/½ pint/1¼ cups
2 celery sticks, chopped	milk
2 rashers streaky bacon,	25g/1oz/2 tbsp butter
finely chopped	25g/1oz/2 tbsp plain flour
5 button mushrooms,	150g/5oz/1 cup diced
chopped	mozzarella cheese
450g/1lb lean minced beef	60ml/4 tbsp grated
120ml/4fl oz/½ cup red	Parmesan cheese
wine	salt and ground black
15ml/1 tbsp tomato purée	pepper
200g/7oz can chopped	fresh basil sprigs, to
tomatoes	garnish

1 Fry the onion, garlic, carrot and celery in the olive oil until softened. Add the bacon and fry for 3–4 minutes. Add the mushrooms, fry for 2 minutes, then fry the beef until brown.

2 Add the wine, tomato purée, 45ml/3 tbsp water, tomatoes and the sprig of fresh thyme. Bring to the boil, cover, and simmer for 30 minutes.

3 Preheat the oven to 200°C/400°F/Gas 6. Cook the pasta. Meanwhile, place the milk, butter and flour in a saucepan, heat gently, whisking until thickened. Stir in the mozzarella and half of the Parmesan cheeses, and season.

4 Drain the pasta and stir into the cheese sauce. Uncover the Bolognese sauce and boil rapidly for 2 minutes. Spoon the sauce into an ovenproof dish, top with the pasta mixture and sprinkle with the remaining Parmesan. Bake for 25 minutes, or until golden. Garnish with basil and serve hot.

Corned Beef and Egg Hash

This classic American hash is a popular brunch dish and should be served with chilli sauce for an authentic touch.

Serves 4

30ml/2 tbsp vegetable oil	1.5ml/¼ tsp grated
25g/1oz/2 tbsp butter	nutmeg
1 onion, finely chopped	1.5ml/¼ tsp paprika
1 small green pepper,	4 eggs
seeded and diced	salt and ground black
2 large boiled potatoes,	pepper
diced	chopped fresh parsley, to
350g/12oz can corned	garnish
beef, diced	chilli sauce, to serve

1 Heat the oil and butter together in a large frying pan and fry the onion for 5–6 minutes until softened. In a bowl, mix together the pepper, potatoes, corned beef, nutmeg and paprika; season to taste with salt and pepper. Add to the pan and toss gently to distribute the cooked onion. Press down lightly; fry over a moderate heat for 3–4 minutes, until a golden brown crust has formed on the bottom.

2 Stir the mixture through to distribute the crust, then repeat the frying twice, until the mixture is well browned.

3 Make four wells in the hash and crack an egg into each one. Cover and cook gently for about 4–5 minutes, until the egg whites are just set.

4 Sprinkle with chopped parsley and cut the hash into quarters. Serve hot with chilli sauce.

Cook's Tip

Put the can of corned beef in the fridge for about 30 minutes before using. It will firm up and you will be able to cut it into cubes more easily than if it is used at room temperature.

Best-ever American Burgers

These meaty quarter-pounders are far superior in taste and texture to anything you can buy ready-made.

Makes 4 burgers
15ml/1 tbsp vegetable oil
1 small onion, chopped
450g/1lb minced beef
1 large garlic clove, crushed
5ml/1 tsp ground cumin
10ml/2 tsp ground coriander
30ml/2 tbsp tomato purée or ketchup
5ml/1 tsp wholegrain mustard
dash of Worcestershire sauce

30ml/2 tbsp mixed chopped fresh herbs such as parsley, thyme and oregano or marjoram
15ml/1 tbsp lightly beaten egg
salt and ground black pepper
flour, for shaping
oil, for frying (optional)
mixed salad, chips and relish, to serve

1 Heat the oil in a frying pan, add the onion and cook for 5 minutes, until softened. Remove from the pan, drain on kitchen paper and leave to cool.

2 Mix together the beef, garlic, spices, tomato purée or ketchup, mustard, Worcestershire sauce, herbs, beaten egg and seasoning in a bowl. Stir in the cooled onions.

3 Sprinkle a board with flour and shape the mixture into four burgers with floured hands and a palette knife. Cover and chill in the fridge for 15 minutes.

4 Heat a little oil in a pan and fry the burgers over a moderate heat for about 5 minutes each side, depending on how rare you like them. Alternatively, cook under a moderate grill for the same time. Serve with salad, chips and relish.

Cook's Tip
If you prefer, make eight smaller burgers to serve in buns, with melted cheese and tomato slices.

Bacon and Sausage Sauerkraut

Juniper berries and crushed coriander seeds flavour this traditional dish from Alsace.

Serves 4
30ml/2 tbsp oil
1 large onion, thinly sliced
1 garlic clove, crushed
450g/1lb bottled sauerkraut, rinsed and drained
1 eating apple, cored and chopped
5 juniper berries
5 coriander seeds, crushed

450g/1lb piece of lightly smoked bacon loin roast
225g/8oz whole smoked pork sausage, pricked
175ml/6fl oz/¾ cup unsweetened apple juice
150ml/¼ pint/⅔ cup chicken stock
1 bay leaf
8 small salad potatoes

1 Preheat the oven to 180°C/350°F/Gas 4. Heat the oil in a flameproof casserole and fry the onion and garlic for about 3–4 minutes, until softened. Stir in the sauerkraut, apple, juniper berries and coriander seeds.

2 Lay the piece of bacon loin and the sausage on top of the sauerkraut, pour on the apple juice and stock, and add the bay leaf. Cover and bake in the oven for about 1 hour.

3 Remove from the oven and pop the potatoes into the casserole. Add a little more stock if necessary, cover and bake for a further 30 minutes, or until the potatoes are tender.

4 Just before serving, lift out the bacon and sausages on to a board and slice. Spoon the sauerkraut on to a warmed platter, top with the meat and surround with the potatoes.

Ginger Pork with Black Bean Sauce

Preserved black beans provide a unique flavour in this dish. Look for them in specialist Chinese food stores.

Serves 4

350g/12oz pork fillet
1 garlic clove, crushed
15ml/1 tbsp grated fresh
  root ginger
90ml/6 tbsp chicken stock
30ml/2 tbsp dry sherry
15ml/1 tbsp light soy
  sauce
5ml/1 tsp sugar
10ml/2 tsp cornflour
45ml/3 tbsp groundnut
  oil
2 yellow peppers, seeded
  and cut into strips
2 red peppers, seeded and
  cut into strips
1 bunch spring onions,
  sliced diagonally
45ml/3 tbsp preserved
  black beans, coarsely
  chopped
fresh coriander sprigs, to
  garnish

1 Cut the pork into thin slices across the grain of the meat. Put the slices into a dish and mix them with the garlic and ginger. Leave to marinate at room temperature for 15 minutes.

2 Blend together the stock, sherry, soy sauce, sugar and cornflour in a small bowl, then set the sauce mixture aside.

3 Heat the oil in a wok or large frying pan and stir-fry the marinated pork for 2–3 minutes. Add the peppers and spring onions and continue to stir-fry for a further 2 minutes.

4 Add the beans and sauce mixture and cook, stirring, until thick. Serve hot, garnished with the fresh coriander sprigs.

Cook's Tip
If you cannot find preserved black beans, use the same amount of black bean sauce instead.

Golden Pork and Apricot Casserole

The rich golden colour and warm spicy flavour of this simple casserole make it ideal for a chilly winter's day.

Serves 4

4 lean pork loin chops
1 onion, thinly sliced
2 yellow peppers, seeded
  and sliced
10ml/2 tsp medium
  curry powder
15g/½oz/1 tbsp plain
  flour
250ml/8fl oz/1 cup
  chicken stock
115g/4oz ready-to-eat
  dried apricots
30ml/2 tbsp wholegrain
  mustard
salt and ground black
  pepper

1 Trim the excess fat from the pork and fry without fat in a large heavy or non-stick saucepan until lightly browned.

2 Add the onion and yellow peppers to the pan and stir over a moderate heat for 5 minutes. Then stir in the curry powder and the flour.

3 Add the stock, stirring, then add the apricots and mustard. Cover with a tight-fitting lid and simmer for 25–30 minutes, until tender. Adjust the seasoning to taste and serve hot, with rice or new potatoes, if you wish.

Sukiyaki-style Beef

This dish incorporates all the traditional Japanese elements – meat, vegetables, noodles and beancurd.

Serves 4

450g/1lb thick rump
   steak
200g/7oz/3½ cups
   Japanese rice noodles
15ml/1 tbsp shredded
   suet
200g/7oz hard beancurd,
   cut into dice
8 shiitake mushrooms,
   trimmed
2 leeks, sliced into
   2.5cm/1in lengths

90g/3½oz/scant 1 cup
   baby spinach, to serve

For the stock
15g/½oz/1 tbsp caster
   sugar
90ml/6 tbsp rice wine
45ml/3 tbsp dark soy
   sauce
120ml/4fl oz/½ cup
   water

1   Cut the beef into thin even-size slices.

2   Blanch the rice noodles in boiling water for 2 minutes, then strain well.

3   Mix together all the stock ingredients in a bowl.

4   Heat a wok, then add the suet. When the suet is melted, stir-fry the beef for 2–3 minutes until it is cooked, but still pink in colour.

5   Pour the stock over the beef.

6   Add the remaining ingredients and cook for 4 minutes, until the leeks are tender. Serve a selection of the different ingredients, with a few baby spinach leaves, to each person.

Cook's Tip
Add a touch of authenticity and serve this complete meal with chopsticks and a porcelain spoon to collect the stock juices.

Stir-fried Pork with Mustard

Fry the apples for this dish very carefully, because they will disintegrate if they are overcooked.

Serves 4

500g/1¼lb pork fillet
1 tart apple, such as
   Granny Smith
40g/1½oz/3 tbsp
   unsalted butter
15g/½oz/1 tbsp caster
   sugar
1 small onion, finely
   chopped
30ml/2 tbsp Calvados or
   brandy

15ml/1 tbsp Meaux or
   coarse grain mustard
15ml/¼ pint/⅔ cup
   double cream
30ml/2 tbsp chopped
   fresh parsley
salt and ground black
   pepper
fresh flat leaf parsley
   sprigs, to garnish

1   Cut the pork fillet into thin even size slices.

2   Peel and core the apple. Cut into thick slices.

3   Heat a wok, then add half the butter. When the butter is hot, add the apple slices, sprinkle over the sugar, and stir-fry for 2–3 minutes. Remove the apple and set aside. Wipe out the wok with kitchen paper.

4   Reheat the wok, then add the remaining butter and stir-fry the pork fillet and onion together for 2–3 minutes, until the pork is golden and the onion has begun to soften.

5   Stir in the Calvados or brandy and boil until it is reduced by half. Stir in the mustard.

6   Add the cream and simmer for about 1 minute, then stir in the parsley. Serve garnished with sprigs of flat leaf parsley.

Cook's Tip
If you haven't got a wok, use a large frying pan, preferably with deep, sloping sides.

Hungarian Beef Goulash

Spicy beef stew served with caraway flavoured dumplings will satisfy even the largest appetites.

Serves 4

30ml/2 tbsp vegetable oil
1 kg/2lb braising steak,
   diced
2 onions, chopped
1 garlic clove, crushed
15g/½oz/1 tbsp plain
   flour
10ml/2 tsp paprika
5ml/1 tsp caraway seeds
400g/14oz can chopped
   tomatoes
300ml/½ pint/1¼ cups
   beef stock
1 large carrot, chopped
1 red pepper, seeded and
   chopped

soured cream, to serve
pinch of paprika, to
   garnish

For the dumplings
115g/4oz/1 cup
   self-raising flour
40g/2oz/½ cup shredded
   suet
15ml/1 tbsp chopped
   fresh parsley
2.5ml/½ tsp caraway
   seeds
salt and ground black
   pepper

1 Heat the oil in a flameproof casserole and fry the meat for 5 minutes over a high heat, stirring, until browned. Remove with a slotted spoon. Add the onions and garlic and fry gently for 5 minutes, until softened. Add the flour, paprika and caraway seeds, stir and cook for 2 minutes.

2 Return the meat to the casserole; stir in the tomatoes and stock. Bring to the boil, cover, simmer for 2 hours.

3 To make the dumplings, sift the flour and seasoning into a bowl, add the suet, parsley, caraway seeds and about 45–60ml/3–4 tbsp water and mix to a soft dough. Divide into eight pieces and roll into balls. Cover and reserve.

4 After 2 hours, stir the carrot and red pepper into the goulash, and season. Drop the dumplings into the goulash, cover and simmer for 25 minutes. Serve in bowls topped with a spoonful of soured cream sprinkled with paprika.

Pork Satay with Peanut Sauce

These delightful little satay sticks from Thailand make a good light meal or a drinks party snack.

Makes 8

½ small onion, chopped
2 garlic cloves, crushed
30ml/2 tbsp lemon juice
15ml/1 tbsp soy sauce
5ml/1 tsp ground
   coriander
2.5ml/½ tsp ground
   cumin
5ml/1 tsp ground turmeric
30ml/2 tbsp vegetable oil
450g/1lb pork tenderloin
fresh coriander sprigs, to
   garnish
boiled rice, to serve

For the sauce
50g/2oz creamed coconut,
   chopped
60ml/4 tbsp crunchy
   peanut butter
15ml/1 tbsp lemon juice

2.5ml/½ tsp ground
   cumin
2.5ml/½ tsp ground
   coriander
5ml/1 tsp soft brown
   sugar
15ml/1 tbsp soy sauce
1–2 dried red chillies,
   seeded and chopped
15ml/1 tbsp chopped fresh
   coriander

For the salad
½ small cucumber, peeled
   and diced
15ml/1 tbsp white wine
   vinegar
15ml/1 tbsp chopped fresh
   coriander
salt and ground black
   pepper

1 Process the first eight ingredients until smooth. Cut the pork into strips, mix with the marinade, and chill. Preheat the grill to hot. Thread two or three pork pieces on to each of eight soaked skewers and grill for 2–3 minutes each side, basting with the marinade.

2 To make the sauce, dissolve the creamed coconut in 150ml/¼ pint/⅔ cup boiling water. Put the remaining ingredients into a saucepan, stir in the coconut, bring to the boil, stirring, and simmer for 5 minutes.

3 Mix together all the salad ingredients. Arrange the satay sticks on a platter, garnish with coriander sprigs and season.

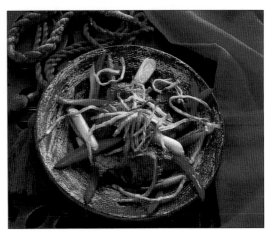

Stir-fried Pork with Lychees

No extra oil or fat is needed to cook this dish, as the pork produces enough on its own.

Serves 4
450g/1lb fatty pork, such as belly pork, with the skin on or off
30ml/2 tbsp hoi-sin sauce
4 spring onions, sliced diagonally

175g/6oz lychees, peeled, stoned and cut into slivers
salt and ground black pepper
fresh lychees and parsley sprigs, to garnish

1 Cut the pork into bite-size pieces.

2 Pour the hoi-sin sauce over the pork and leave to marinate for at least 30 minutes.

3 Heat a wok, then add the pork and stir-fry for 5 minutes until crisp and golden. Add the spring onions and stir-fry for a further 2 minutes.

4 Scatter the lychee slivers over the pork, and season well with salt and pepper. Garnish with fresh lychees and fresh parsley sprigs, to serve.

Cook's Tip
Lychees have a very pretty pink skin which, when peeled, reveals a soft fleshy berry with a hard shiny stone. If you cannot buy fresh lychees, this dish can be made with drained canned lychees.

Sizzling Beef with Celeriac Straw

The crisp celeriac matchsticks look like fine pieces of straw when cooked and have a mild celery-like flavour.

Serves 4
450g/1lb celeriac
150ml/¼ pint/⅔ cup vegetable oil
1 red pepper
6 spring onions
450g/1lb rump steak
60ml/4 tbsp beef stock

30ml/2 tbsp sherry vinegar
10ml/2 tsp Worcestershire sauce
10ml/2 tsp tomato purée
salt and ground black pepper

1 Peel the celeriac and then cut it into fine matchsticks, using a cleaver if you have one, or a large sharp knife.

2 Heat the wok, then add two-thirds of the oil. When the oil is hot, fry the celeriac matchsticks in batches until golden brown and crispy. Drain well on kitchen paper.

3 Chop the red pepper and the spring onions into 2.5cm/1in lengths, using diagonal cuts.

4 Chop the beef into strips, across the grain of the meat.

5 Heat a wok, then add the remaining oil. When the oil is hot, stir-fry the chopped spring onions and red pepper for about 2–3 minutes.

6 Add the beef strips and stir-fry for a further 3–4 minutes until well browned. Add the stock, vinegar, Worcestershire sauce and tomato purée. Season well with salt and pepper and serve with the celeriac "straw".

Cook's Tip
The Chinese use a large cleaver for preparing most vegetables. With a little practice, you will discover that it is the ideal kitchen utensil for cutting fine vegetable matchsticks and chopping thin strips of meat.

Turkish Lamb and Apricot Stew

Almond and parsley–flavoured couscous accompanies this rich stew of lamb, apricots and chick-peas.

Serves 4

1 large aubergine, diced
30ml/2 tbsp sunflower oil
1 onion, chopped
1 garlic clove, crushed
5ml/1 tsp ground cinnamon
3 whole cloves
450g/1lb boned leg of lamb, diced
400g/14oz can chopped tomatoes
115g/4oz ready-to-eat dried apricots
115g/4oz/1 cup canned chick-peas, drained
5ml/1 tsp clear honey
salt and ground black pepper
couscous, to serve
30ml/2 tbsp olive oil
30ml/2 tbsp chopped almonds, fried in a little oil
chopped fresh parsley, to garnish

1 Place the diced aubergine in a colander, sprinkle with salt and leave for about 30 minutes. Heat the oil in a large flameproof casserole and fry the onion and garlic for about 5 minutes, until softened but not browned.

2 Stir in the ground cinnamon and whole cloves and fry for a further 1 minute. Add the lamb and cook for 5–6 minutes more, stirring occasionally to brown the pieces evenly.

3 Rinse, drain and pat dry the aubergine with kitchen paper, add to the casserole and cook for 3 minutes, stirring well. Add the chopped tomatoes, 300ml/½ pint/1¼ cups water and the apricots, and season to taste with salt and pepper. Bring to the boil, then cover and simmer gently for about 45 minutes.

4 Stir the chick-peas and honey into the stew, then cook for a final 15–20 minutes, or until the lamb is tender. Serve the dish accompanied by couscous with the olive oil, fried almonds and chopped parsley stirred into it.

Curried Lamb and Lentils

This colourful curry is packed with protein and low in fat, and makes a flavoursome yet healthy meal.

Serves 4

8 lean boned lamb leg steaks (about 500g/ 1¼ lb total weight)
1 onion, chopped
2 carrots, diced
1 celery stick, chopped
15ml/1 tbsp hot curry paste
30ml/2 tbsp tomato purée
475ml/16fl oz/2 cups stock
175g/6oz/1 cup green lentils
salt and ground black pepper
fresh coriander leaves, to garnish
boiled rice, to serve

1 In a large non-stick saucepan, fry the lamb steaks without fat until browned, turning once.

2 Add the vegetables and cook for 2 minutes, then stir in the curry paste, tomato purée, stock and lentils.

3 Bring to the boil, cover with a tight-fitting lid and simmer gently for 30 minutes until tender. Add some extra stock, if necessary. Season to taste and serve garnished with coriander and accompanied by rice.

Cook's Tip
Pick over the lentils carefully before adding them to the saucepan. They sometimes contain small stones which are unpleasant to find while eating a meal.

Middle-Eastern Lamb Kebabs

Skewered, grilled meats are a staple of Middle Eastern cooking. Here, marinated lamb is grilled with vegetables.

Makes 4

450g/1lb boned leg of
  lamb, diced
75ml/5 tbsp olive oil
15ml/1 tbsp chopped
  fresh oregano or
  thyme, or 10ml/2 tsp
  dried oregano
15ml/1 tbsp chopped
  fresh parsley
juice of ½ lemon

½ small aubergine,
  thickly sliced and
  quartered
4 baby onions, halved
2 tomatoes, quartered
4 fresh bay leaves
salt and ground black
  pepper
pitta bread and natural
  yogurt, to serve

1 Place the lamb in a bowl. Mix together the olive oil, oregano or thyme, parsley, lemon juice, salt and pepper. Pour over the lamb; mix well. Cover and marinate for about 1 hour.

2 Preheat the grill. Thread the marinated lamb, aubergine, onions, tomatoes and bay leaves alternately on to four large skewers. (If using wooden skewers, soak them first.)

3 Place the kebabs on a grill rack and brush the vegetables liberally with the leftover marinade. Cook the kebabs under a medium heat for about 8–10 minutes on each side, basting once or twice with the juices that have collected in the bottom of the grill pan. Serve the kebabs hot, accompanied by hot pitta bread and natural yogurt.

Cook's Tip
For a more piquant marinade, add one or two cloves of garlic, peeled and crushed.

Mexican Spiced Roast Leg of Lamb

Make sure you push the garlic slices deeply into the meat or they will burn and develop a bitter flavour.

Serves 4

1 small leg or half leg of
  lamb (about
  1.25kg/2½ lb)
15ml/1 tbsp dried
  oregano
5ml/1 tsp ground cumin
5ml/1 tsp hot chilli
  powder

2 garlic cloves
45ml/3 tbsp olive oil
30ml/2 tbsp red wine
  vinegar
salt and ground black
  pepper
fresh oregano sprigs, to
  garnish

1 Preheat the oven to 220°C/425°F/Gas 7. Place the leg of lamb on a large chopping board.

2 Place the oregano, cumin, chilli powder and one of the garlic cloves, crushed, into a bowl. Pour on half of the olive oil and mix well to form a paste. Set the paste aside.

3 Using a sharp knife, make a criss-cross pattern of fairly deep slits going through the skin and just into the meat of the leg of lamb. Press the spice paste into the meat slits with the back of a round-bladed knife. Peel and slice the remaining garlic clove thinly and cut each slice in half again. Push the pieces of garlic deeply into the slits made in the meat.

4 Mix the vinegar and remaining oil, pour over the joint and season with salt and pepper.

5 Bake for about 15 minutes at the higher temperature, then reduce the heat to 180°C/350°F/Gas 4 and cook for a further 1¼ hours (or a little longer if you like your meat well done). Serve the lamb with a delicious gravy made with the spicy pan juices and garnish with fresh oregano sprigs.

Boeuf Bourguignon

This French classic is named after the region it comes from, Burgundy, where the local red wine is used to flavour it.

Serves 4

30ml/2 tbsp olive oil
225g/8oz piece streaky
   bacon, diced
12 whole baby onions
900g/2lb braising steak,
   cut into 5cm/2in
   squares
1 large onion, thickly
   sliced
15g/½ oz/1 tbsp plain
   flour

about 450ml/¾ pint/1¾
   cups red Burgundy
   wine
bouquet garni
1 garlic clove
225g/8oz button
   mushrooms, halved
salt and ground black
   pepper
chopped fresh parsley, to
   garnish

1 Heat the oil in a flameproof casserole and fry the bacon and baby onions for 7–8 minutes, until the onions have browned and the bacon fat is transparent. Remove with a slotted spoon and reserve.

2 Add the beef to the casserole and fry quickly on all sides until evenly browned. Add the sliced onion and continue cooking for 4–5 minutes.

3 Sprinkle over the flour and stir well. Pour over the wine and add the bouquet garni and garlic. Cover with a tightly fitting lid and simmer gently for about 2 hours. Stir in the reserved sautéed onions and bacon and add a little extra wine, if necessary.

4 Add the mushrooms. Cover again and cook for a further 30 minutes. Remove the bouquet garni and garlic and garnish with chopped fresh parsley.

Spiced Lamb Bake

A quite delicious South African shepherd's pie. The recipe was originally poached from the Afrikaners' Malay slaves.

Serves 4

15ml/1 tbsp vegetable oil
1 onion, chopped
675g/1½lb minced lamb
30ml/2 tbsp medium
   curry paste
30ml/2 tbsp mango
   chutney
30ml/2 tbsp freshly
   squeezed lemon juice

60ml/4 tbsp chopped,
   blanched almonds
30ml/2 tbsp sultanas
75g/3oz creamed
   coconut, crumbled
2 eggs
2 bay leaves
salt and ground black
   pepper

1 Preheat the oven to 180°C/350°F/Gas 4. Heat the oil in a frying pan and cook the chopped onion for 5–6 minutes, until softened but not browned.

2 Add the lamb and cook over a moderate heat, turning frequently, until browned all over. Stir in the curry paste, chutney, lemon juice, almonds and sultanas, season well with salt and pepper and cook for about 5 minutes.

3 Transfer the mixture to an ovenproof dish and cook in the oven, uncovered, for 10 minutes.

4 Meanwhile, dissolve the crumbled creamed coconut in 200ml/7fl oz/scant 1 cup boiling water and cool slightly. Beat in the eggs and a little seasoning.

5 Remove the dish from the oven and pour the coconut custard over the meat mixture. Lay the bay leaves on the top and return the dish to the oven for 30–35 minutes, or until the top is set and golden. Serve hot.

Greek Pasta Bake

Another excellent main meal (called *pastitsio* in Greece), this recipe is both economical and filling.

Serves 4

15ml/1 tbsp oil	2 large tomatoes
450g/1lb minced lamb	115g/4oz cup pasta
1 onion, chopped	shapes
2 garlic cloves, crushed	450g/1lb tub Greek-style
30ml/2 tbsp tomato purée	yogurt
25g/1oz/2 tbsp plain	2 eggs
flour	salt and ground black
300ml/½ pint/1¼ cups	pepper
lamb stock	green salad, to serve

1 Preheat the oven to 190°C/375°F/Gas 5. Heat the oil in a large saucepan and fry the lamb for 5 minutes. Add the onion and garlic and continue to fry for a further 5 minutes.

2 Stir in the tomato purée and flour. Cook for 1 minute.

3 Stir in the lamb stock and season to taste with salt and pepper. Bring to the boil and cook for 20 minutes.

4 Slice the tomatoes, place the meat in an ovenproof dish and arrange the tomatoes on top.

5 Bring a pan of salted water to the boil and cook the pasta shapes for 8–10 minutes until *al dente*. Drain well.

6 Mix together the pasta, yogurt and eggs. Spoon on top of the tomatoes and cook in the preheated oven for 1 hour. Serve hot with a crisp green salad.

Cook's Tip
Choose open pasta shapes for this dish rather than tubes so the sauce coats the pasta all over. Try shells, spirals or farfalle.

Bacon Koftas

These easy koftas are good for barbecues and summer grills, served with lots of salad.

Serves 4

225g/8oz lean smoked	finely grated rind of
back bacon, roughly	1 lemon
chopped	1 egg white
75g/3oz/1½ cups fresh	ground black pepper
wholemeal	pinch of paprika
breadcrumbs	lemon rind and fresh
2 spring onions, chopped	parsley leaves, to
15ml/1 tbsp chopped	garnish
fresh parsley	

1 Place the bacon in a food processor with the breadcrumbs, spring onions, parsley, lemon rind, egg white and pepper. Process the mixture until it is finely chopped and begins to bind together. Alternatively, use a mincer.

2 Divide the bacon mixture into eight even-size pieces and shape into long ovals around eight previously soaked wooden or bamboo skewers.

3 Sprinkle the koftas with paprika and cook under a hot grill or on a barbecue for about 8–10 minutes, turning them occasionally, until browned and cooked through. Garnish with lemon rind and parsley leaves, then serve hot with lemon rice and salad.

Cook's Tip
This is a good way to spread a little meat a long way as each portion requires only 50g/2oz bacon. Use good quality bacon, preferably dry cured, for this recipe.

Peking Beef and Pepper Stir-fry

Once the steak has marinated, this colourful dish can be prepared in just a few minutes.

Serves 4

350g/12oz rump or sirloin steak, sliced into strips
30ml/2 tbsp soy sauce
30ml/2 tbsp medium sherry
15ml/1 tbsp cornflour
5ml/1 tsp brown sugar
15ml/1 tbsp sunflower oil
15ml/1 tbsp sesame oil
1 garlic clove, finely chopped
15ml/1 tbsp grated fresh root ginger
1 red pepper, seeded and sliced
1 yellow pepper, seeded and sliced
115g/4oz/1 cup sugar snap peas
4 spring onions, cut into 5cm/2in pieces
30ml/2 tbsp Chinese oyster sauce
hot noodles, to serve

1 In a bowl, mix together the steak strips, soy sauce, sherry, cornflour and brown sugar. Cover and leave to marinate for 30 minutes.

2 Heat the oils in a wok or large frying pan and stir-fry the garlic and ginger quickly for about 30 seconds. Add the peppers, sugar snap peas and spring onions and stir-fry over a high heat for 3 minutes.

3 Add the beef with the marinade juices to the wok or frying pan and stir-fry for a further 3–4 minutes.

4 Finally, pour in the oyster sauce and 60ml/4 tbsp water and stir until the sauce has thickened slightly. Serve immediately with hot noodles.

Texan Barbecued Ribs

This barbecue or oven-roast dish of pork spare ribs cooked in a sweet and sour sauce is a favourite in the United States.

Serves 4

1.5kg/3lb (about 16) lean pork spare ribs
1 onion, finely chopped
1 large garlic clove, crushed
120ml/4fl oz/½ cup tomato purée
30ml/2 tbsp orange juice
30ml/2 tbsp red wine vinegar
5ml/1 tsp mustard
10ml/2 tsp clear honey
25g/1oz/2 tbsp soft light brown sugar
dash of Worcestershire sauce
30ml/2 tbsp vegetable oil
salt and ground black pepper
chopped fresh parsley, to garnish

1 Preheat the oven to 200°C/400°F/Gas 6. Place the pork spare ribs in a large shallow roasting tin; bake for 20 minutes.

2 Meanwhile, in a saucepan mix together the onion, garlic, tomato purée, orange juice, wine vinegar, mustard, clear honey, brown sugar, Worcestershire sauce, oil and seasoning. Bring to the boil and simmer for about 5 minutes.

3 Remove the ribs from the oven and then reduce the oven temperature to 180°C/350°F/Gas 4. Spoon over half the sauce, covering the ribs well and bake for 20 minutes. Turn them over, baste with the remaining sauce and cook for about a further 25 minutes.

4 Sprinkle the spare ribs with parsley before serving and allow three or four ribs per person. Provide finger bowls for washing sticky fingers.

Skewers of Lamb with Mint

For a more substantial meal, serve these skewers on a bed
of flavoured rice or couscous.

Serves 4

300ml/½ pint/1¼ cups Greek-style yogurt	1 aubergine, cut into 2.5cm/1in dice
½ garlic clove, crushed	2 small red onions, quartered
generous pinch of saffron powder	salt and ground black pepper
30ml/2 tbsp chopped fresh mint	small fresh mint leaves, to garnish
30ml/2 tbsp clear honey	mixed salad and hot pitta bread, to serve
45ml/3 tbsp olive oil	
3 lamb neck fillets (about 675g/1½lb total)	

1 Mix the yogurt, garlic, saffron, mint, honey, oil and pepper
together in a shallow dish.

2 Trim the lamb and cut into 2.5cm/1in cubes. Add to the
marinade and stir until well coated. Cover and leave to
marinate for at least 4 hours, or preferably overnight.

3 Blanch the diced aubergine in a saucepan of boiling salted
water for about 1–2 minutes. Drain well and then pat dry on
kitchen paper.

4 Remove the diced lamb from the marinade. Thread the
lamb, aubergine and onion pieces alternately on to skewers. If
you are using wooden skewers, soak them in water first. This
will prevent them from charring during grilling. Grill for
10–12 minutes, turning and basting occasionally with the
marinade, until the lamb is tender.

5 Serve the skewers garnished with mint leaves and
accompanied by a mixed salad and hot pitta bread.

Beef Stew with Red Wine

A slow-cooked casserole of tender beef in a red wine and
tomato sauce, with black olives and red pepper.

Serves 6

75ml/5 tbsp olive oil	250ml/8fl oz/1 cup red wine
1.1kg/2½lb boned beef chuck, cut into 3cm/1½in dice	400g/14oz can plum tomatoes, chopped, with their juice
1 onion, very finely sliced	120ml/4fl oz/½ cup beef or chicken stock
2 carrots, chopped	about 15 black olives, stoned and halved
45ml/3 tbsp finely chopped fresh parsley	salt and ground black pepper
1 garlic clove, chopped	1 large red pepper, cut into strips
1 bay leaf	
a few fresh thyme sprigs	
pinch of freshly ground nutmeg	

1 Preheat the oven to 180°C/350°F/Gas 4. Brown the meat,
in batches, in 45ml/3 tbsp of the oil in a large heavy-based
flameproof casserole. Remove to a side plate as the meat is
browned, and set aside until needed.

2 Add the remaining oil, the onion and carrots to the
casserole. Cook over a low heat until the onion softens. Add
the parsley and garlic, and cook for a further 3–4 minutes.

3 Return the meat to the casserole, raise the heat, and stir
well to mix the vegetables with the meat. Stir in the bay leaf,
thyme and nutmeg. Add the wine, bring to the boil and cook,
stirring, for 4–5 minutes. Stir in the tomatoes, stock and
olives, and mix well. Season to taste with salt and pepper.
Cover the casserole with a tight-fitting lid and place in the
centre of the preheated oven. Bake for 1½ hours.

4 Remove the casserole from the oven. Stir in the strips of
pepper. Return the casserole to the oven and cook, uncovered,
for 30 minutes more, or until the beef is tender.

Grilled Mixed Peppers

Soft smoky grilled peppers make a lovely combination with the slightly tart salsa.

Serves 4

4 medium peppers in
   different colours
45ml/3 tbsp chopped
   fresh flat-leaf parsley
45ml/3 tbsp chopped
   fresh dill
45ml/3 tbsp chopped
   fresh mint
1 small red onion, finely
   chopped
15ml/1 tbsp capers,
   coarsely chopped
50g/2oz/¼ cup Greek
   olives, pitted and
   sliced

1 fresh green chilli,
   seeded and finely
   chopped
60g/4 tbsp pistachios,
   chopped
75ml/5 tbsp extra-virgin
   olive oil
45ml/3 tbsp fresh lime
   juice
115g/4oz/½ cup
   medium-fat feta
   cheese, crumbled
25g/1oz gherkins, finely
   chopped

1 Preheat the grill. Place the whole peppers on a tray and grill until charred and blistered.

2 Place the peppers in a plastic bag and leave to cool.

3 Peel, seed and cut the peppers into even strips.

4 To make the salsa, mix all the remaining ingredients together, and stir in the pepper strips.

Vegetable and Tofu Kebabs

A colourful mixture of vegetables and tofu, skewered, glazed and grilled until tender.

Serves 4

1 yellow pepper
2 small courgettes
225g/8oz piece of
   firm tofu
8 cherry tomatoes
6 button mushrooms
15ml/1 tbsp wholegrain
   mustard

15ml/1 tbsp clear honey
30ml/2 tbsp olive oil
salt and ground black
   pepper
cooked mixed rice and
   wild rice, to serve
lime wedges and flat-leaf
   parsley, to garnish

1 Cut the pepper in half and remove the seeds. Cut each half into quarters and cut each quarter in half.

2 Top and tail the courgettes. Cut each courgette into seven or eight chunks.

3 Cut the tofu into 4cm/1½in pieces.

4 Thread the pepper pieces, courgette chunks, tofu, cherry tomatoes and mushrooms alternately on to four metal or bamboo skewers. If you are using bamboo skewers, soak them in a bowl of cold water first. This will prevent them from charring during grilling.

5 Whisk the mustard, honey and olive oil in a small bowl. Season to taste with salt and pepper.

6 Put the kebabs on to a baking sheet. Brush them with the mustard and honey glaze. Cook under the grill for 8 minutes, turning once or twice during cooking. Serve with a mixture of long grain and wild rice, and garnish with lime wedges and flat leaf parsley.

Soufflé Omelette

This delectable soufflé omelette is light and delicate enough to melt in the mouth.

Serves 1
2 eggs, separated
30ml/2 tbsp cold water
15ml/1 tbsp chopped
    fresh coriander
7.5ml/½ tbsp olive oil

30ml/2 tbsp mango
    chutney
25g/1oz/¼ cup grated
    Jarlsberg cheese
salt and ground black
    pepper

1 Beat the egg yolks together with the cold water, coriander and salt and pepper.

2 Whisk the egg whites until stiff peaks form and gently fold into the egg yolk mixture.

3 Heat the oil in a frying pan, pour in the egg mixture and reduce the heat. Do not stir. Cook until the omelette becomes puffy and golden brown on the underside (carefully lift one edge with a palette knife to check).

4 Spoon on the chutney and sprinkle on the Jarlsberg. Fold over and slide on to a warm plate. Eat immediately. (If preferred, before adding the chutney and cheese, place the pan under a hot grill to set the top.)

Cook's Tip
A light hand is essential to the success of this dish. Do not overmix the egg whites into the egg yolks or the mixture will be heavy.

Cheesy Bubble and Squeak

This London breakfast dish was originally made on Mondays with leftover vegetables from the Sunday lunch.

Serves 4
about 450g/1lb/3 cups
    mashed potato
about 225g/8oz/4 cups
    shredded cooked
    cabbage or kale
1 egg, beaten
115g/4oz/1 cup grated
    Cheddar cheese

pinch of freshly grated
    nutmeg
salt and ground black
    pepper
plain flour, for coating
oil, for frying

1 Mix the potatoes with the cabbage or kale, egg, cheese, nutmeg and seasoning. Divide and shape into eight patties.

2 Chill in the fridge for an hour or so, if possible, as this enables the mixture to become firm and makes it easier to fry. Toss the patties in the flour. Heat about 1cm/½in oil in a frying pan until it is quite hot.

3 Carefully slide the patties into the oil and fry on each side for about 3 minutes until golden and crisp. Drain on kitchen paper and serve hot and crisp.

Aubergine and Red Pepper Pâté

This simple pâté of baked aubergine, pink peppercorns and red peppers has more than a hint of garlic.

Serves 4

3 aubergines
2 fresh large red
   peppers
5 garlic cloves,
   unpeeled

7.5ml/1½ tsp pink
   peppercorns in brine,
   drained and crushed
30ml/2 tbsp chopped
   fresh coriander

1 Preheat the oven to 200°C/400°F/Gas 6. Arrange the whole aubergines, peppers and garlic cloves on a baking sheet and place in the oven. After 10 minutes remove the garlic cloves and turn over the aubergines and peppers.

2 Peel the garlic cloves and place in the bowl of a blender or food processor.

3 After a further 20 minutes remove the blistered and charred peppers from the oven and place in a plastic bag. Leave to cool.

4 After a further 10 minutes take out the aubergines. Split in half and scoop the flesh into a sieve placed over a bowl. Press the flesh with a spoon to remove the bitter juices.

5 Add the mixture to the garlic and process until smooth. Place in a large mixing bowl.

6 Peel and chop the red peppers and stir into the aubergine mixture. Mix in the pink peppercorns and chopped fresh coriander and serve at once.

Cook's Tip
Serve the pâté with Melba toast, if you like. Simply grill some slices of crustless white bread on both sides, being careful to remove any loose crumbs, then slice the crispy golden toasts horizontally.

Red Pepper Watercress Parcels

The peppery watercress flavour combines well with sweet red pepper in these crisp little filo pastry parcels.

Makes 8

3 red peppers
175g/6oz watercress
225g/8oz 1 cup ricotta
   cheese
50g/2oz/¼ cup toasted,
   chopped almonds

8 sheets filo pastry,
   thawed if frozen
30ml/2 tbsp olive oil
salt and ground black
   pepper

1 Preheat the oven to 190°C/375°F/Gas 5. Place the peppers under a hot grill until blistered and charred. Place in a plastic bag. When cool enough to handle, peel, seed and pat dry on kitchen paper.

2 Place the peppers and watercress in a food processor and pulse until coarsely chopped. Spoon into a bowl.

3 Mix in the ricotta and almonds, and season to taste with salt and pepper.

4 Working with one sheet of filo pastry at a time, cut out two 18cm/7in and two 5cm/2in squares from each sheet. Brush one large square with a little olive oil and place a second large square at an angle of 45 degrees to form a star shape.

5 Place one of the small squares in the centre of the star shape, brush lightly with olive oil and top with a second small square.

6 Top with one-eighth of the red pepper mixture. Bring the edges together to form a purse shape and twist to seal. Place on a lightly greased baking sheet and cook for 25–30 minutes until golden. Serve immediately.

Nutty Cheese Balls

An extremely quick and simple recipe. Try making a small version to serve as canapés at a drinks party.

Serves 4

225g/8oz/1 cup low-fat
    soft cheese such as
    Quark
50g/2oz/½ cup dolcelatte
    cheese
15ml/1 tbsp finely
    chopped onion
15ml/1 tbsp finely
    chopped celery stick
15ml/1 tbsp finely
    chopped fresh parsley

15ml/1 tbsp finely
    chopped gherkin
5ml/1 tsp brandy or port
    (optional)
pinch of paprika
50g/2oz/½ cup walnuts,
    roughly chopped
90ml/6 tbsp snipped
    fresh chives
salt and ground black
    pepper

1 Beat the soft cheese and dolcelatte together using a spoon, until quite smooth.

2 Mix in all the remaining ingredients, except the snipped chives, stirring well to combine.

3 Divide the mixture into 12 pieces and roll into balls.

4 Roll each ball gently in the snipped chives. Leave to chill in the fridge for about an hour before serving.

Cook's Tip
For an alternative look, mix the chives with the rest of the ingredients but omit the walnuts. Instead, chop the walnuts finely and use to roll on to the cheese balls.

Fried Tomatoes with Polenta Crust

This recipe works well with green tomatoes freshy picked from the garden or greenhouse.

Serves 4

4 large firm under-ripe
    tomatoes
115g/4oz/1 cup polenta
    or coarse cornmeal
5ml/1 tsp dried oregano
    or marjoram

2.5ml/½ tsp garlic
    powder
plain flour, for dredging
1 egg, beaten with
    seasoning
oil, for deep-frying

1 Cut the tomatoes into thick slices. Mix the polenta or cornmeal with the oregano or marjoram and garlic powder.

2 Put the flour, egg and polenta into different bowls. Dip the tomato slices into the flour, then into the egg and finally into the polenta or cornmeal.

3 Fill a shallow frying pan one-third full of oil and heat steadily until quite hot.

4 Slip the tomato slices into the oil carefully, a few at a time, and fry on each side until crisp. Remove and drain. Repeat with the remaining tomatoes, reheating the oil in between each batch. Serve with salad.

Cannellini Bean Purée

The slightly bitter radicchio and chicory make a wonderful marriage with the creamy citrus bean purée.

Serves 4

400g/14oz can cannellini beans	15ml/1 tbsp finely chopped fresh rosemary
45ml/3 tbsp low-fat fromage blanc	4 heads of chicory
finely grated rind and juice of 1 large orange	2 radicchio
	15ml/1 tbsp walnut oil

1 Drain the beans, rinse, and drain again. Purée the beans in a food processor or blender with the fromage blanc, half the orange rind, orange juice and rosemary. Set aside.

2 Cut the heads of chicory in half lengthways.

3 Cut each radicchio into eight wedges.

4 Lay out the chicory and radicchio on a baking sheet and brush with walnut oil. Grill for 2–3 minutes. Serve with the purée and scatter over the remaining orange rind.

Cook's Tip
Substitute different beans for the cannellini beans, if you like. Try haricot, mung or broad beans instead.

Broccoli and Chestnut Terrine

Served hot or cold, this versatile terrine is just as suitable for a dinner party as for a picnic.

Serves 4–6

450g/1lb/4 cups broccoli florets	60ml/4 tbsp low-fat natural yogurt
225g/8oz/2 cups cooked chestnuts, roughly chopped	30ml/2 tbsp finely grated Parmesan cheese
50g/2oz/1 cup fresh wholemeal breadcrumbs	2 eggs, beaten
	salt, freshly grated nutmeg and ground black pepper

1 Preheat the oven to 180°C/350°F/Gas 4. Base-line a 900g/2lb loaf tin with non-stick baking paper.

2 Blanch or steam the broccoli for 3–4 minutes until just tender. Drain well. Reserve a quarter of the smallest florets and chop the rest finely.

3 Mix together the chestnuts, breadcrumbs, yogurt and Parmesan, and season to taste with salt and pepper.

4 Fold in the chopped broccoli, reserved florets and the beaten eggs.

5 Spoon the broccoli mixture into the prepared tin.

6 Place in a roasting tin and pour in boiling water to come halfway up the sides of the loaf tin. Bake for 20–25 minutes. Remove from the oven and tip out on to a plate or tray. Serve cut into even slices.

Cook's Tip
If you do not have a non-stick loaf tin, grease it lightly with olive or sunflower oil after base-lining.

Baked Squash with Parmesan

Spaghetti squash is an unusual vegetable – when baked, the flesh separates into long strands.

Serves 2

1 spaghetti squash	1 shallot, chopped
115g/4oz/½ cup butter	5ml/1 tsp lemon juice
45ml/3 tbsp mixed	50g/2oz/scant ¾ cup
chopped fresh herbs	freshly grated
such as parsley, chives	Parmesan cheese
and oregano	salt and ground black
1 garlic clove, crushed	pepper

1 Preheat the oven to 180°C/350°F/Gas 4. Cut the squash in half lengthways. Place the halves, cut-side down, in a roasting tin. Pour a little water around them, then bake for about 40 minutes, until tender.

2 Meanwhile, put the butter, herbs, garlic, shallot and lemon juice in a food processor or blender and process until thoroughly blended and creamy in consistency. Season to taste with salt and pepper.

3 When the squash is tender, scrape out any seeds and cut a thin slice from the base of each half, so that they will sit level. Place the squash halves on warmed serving plates.

4 Using a fork, pull out a few of the spaghetti-like strands in the centre of each. Add a dollop of herb butter, then sprinkle with a little of the grated Parmesan. Serve the remaining herb butter and Parmesan separately, adding them as you pull out more strands.

Asparagus Rolls with Herb Sauce

For a taste sensation, try tender asparagus spears wrapped in crisp filo pastry served with a buttery herb sauce.

Serves 2

50g/2oz/4 tbsp butter	175g/6oz/¾ cup butter,
5 sheets filo pastry	softened
10 asparagus spears	15ml/1 tbsp chopped
	fresh herbs
For the sauce	salt and ground black
2 shallots, finely chopped	pepper
1 bay leaf	snipped fresh chives, to
150ml/¼ pint/⅔ cup dry	garnish
white wine	

1 Preheat the oven to 200°C/400°F/Gas 6. Melt the butter. Cut the filo pastry sheets in half. Brush a half sheet with melted butter. Fold one corner of the sheet down to the bottom edge to give a wedge shape.

2 Trim the asparagus, then lay a spear on top at the longest pastry edge and roll up towards the shortest edge. Make nine more rolls in the same way.

3 Lay the rolls on a greased baking sheet. Brush with the remaining melted butter. Bake in the preheated oven for about 8 minutes until golden.

4 Meanwhile, put the shallots, bay leaf and wine into a saucepan. Cover with a tight-fitting lid and cook over a high heat until the wine is reduced to 45–60ml/3–4 tbsp.

5 Strain the wine mixture into a bowl. Whisk in the butter, a little at a time, until the sauce is smooth and glossy.

6 Stir in the herbs and season to taste with salt and pepper. Return to the pan and keep the sauce warm. Serve the rolls on individual plates with a salad garnish, if liked. Serve the butter sauce separately, sprinkled with a few snipped chives.

Multi-mushroom Stroganoff

A pan-fry of sliced mushrooms swirled with soured cream makes a delicious accompaniment to pasta or rice.

Serves 3–4
45ml/3 tbsp olive oil
450g/1lb fresh mixed
    wild and cultivated
    mushrooms such as
    ceps, shiitakes or
    oysters, sliced
3 spring onions, sliced
2 garlic cloves, crushed
30ml/2 tbsp dry sherry or
    vermouth

300ml/½ pint/1¼ cups
    soured cream or crème
    fraîche
15ml/1 tbsp chopped
    fresh marjoram or
    thyme leaves
chopped fresh parsley, to
    garnish

1 Heat the oil in a large frying pan and fry the mushrooms gently, stirring them from time to time until they are softened and just cooked.

2 Add the spring onions, garlic and sherry or vermouth and cook for 1 minute more. Season well with salt and pepper.

3 Stir in the soured cream or crème fraîche and heat to just below boiling. Stir in the marjoram or thyme, then scatter over the parsley. Serve with rice, pasta or boiled new potatoes.

Cook's Tip
To create the most interesting flavour in this dish, use at least three different varieties of mushroom, preferably incorporating some woodland or wild mushrooms.

Ratatouille with Cheese Croûtons

Crunchy croûtons and creamy Camembert provide a tasty topping on hot, bought or home-made ratatouille.

Serves 2
3 thick slices white bread
225g/8oz firm
    Camembert cheese
60ml/4 tbsp olive oil

1 garlic clove, chopped
400g/14oz can ratatouille
fresh parsley sprigs, to
    garnish

1 Trim the crusts from the bread slices and discard. Cut the bread into 2.5cm/1in squares. Cut the Camembert cheese into 2.5cm/1in cubes.

2 Heat 45ml/3 tbsp of the oil in a frying pan and cook the bread over a high heat for 5 minutes, stirring constantly, until golden all over. Reduce the heat, add the garlic and cook for 1 minute more. Remove the croûtons with a slotted spoon.

3 Tip the ratatouille into a saucepan and place over a moderate heat, stirring occasionally, until hot.

4 Heat the remaining oil in the frying pan. Add the cheese cubes and sear over a high heat for 1 minute. Divide the hot ratatouille between two serving bowls, spoon the croûtons and cheese on top, garnish with parsley and serve at once.

Tofu and Crunchy Vegetables

High protein tofu is nicest if marinated lightly before it is cooked. If you use the smoked tofu, it's even tastier.

Serves 4

2 x 225g/8oz packets smoked tofu, diced
45ml/3 tbsp soy sauce
30ml/2 tbsp dry sherry or vermouth
15ml/1 tbsp sesame oil
45ml/3 tbsp groundnut or sunflower oil
2 leeks, thinly sliced
2 carrots, cut into sticks

1 large courgette, thinly sliced
115g/4oz baby corn, halved
115g/4oz button or shiitake mushrooms, sliced
15ml/1 tbsp sesame seeds
1 packet egg noodles, cooked

1 Marinate the tofu in the soy sauce, sherry or vermouth and sesame oil for at least 30 minutes. Drain and reserve the marinade for later.

2 Heat the groundnut or sunflower oil in a wok and stir-fry the tofu cubes until browned all over. Remove and reserve.

3 Stir-fry the leeks, carrots, courgette and baby corn, stirring and tossing for about 2 minutes. Add the mushrooms and cook for a further 1 minute.

4 Return the tofu to the wok and pour in the marinade. Heat until bubbling, then scatter over the sesame seeds.

5 Serve as soon as possible with the hot cooked noodles, dressed in a little sesame oil, if you wish.

Cook's Tip
The actual cooking of this dish takes just a few minutes, so have all the ingredients prepared before you start.

Sprouting Beans and Pak Choi

Supermarkets are becoming more cosmopolitan and many stock fresh ethnic vegetables.

Serves 4

45ml/3 tbsp groundnut oil
3 spring onions, sliced
2 garlic cloves, cut into slivers
2.5cm/1in piece fresh root ginger, cut into slivers
1 carrot, cut into thick sticks
150g/5oz/scant 1 cup sprouting beans (lentils, mung beans, chick-peas)
200g/7oz pak choi cabbage, shredded

50g/2oz/½ cup unsalted cashew nuts or halved almonds

For the sauce

45ml/3 tbsp light soy sauce
30ml/2 tbsp dry sherry
15ml/1 tbsp sesame oil
150ml/¼ pint/⅔ cup cold water
5ml/1 tsp cornflour
5ml/1 tsp clear honey
salt and ground black pepper

1 Heat the groundnut oil in a large wok and stir-fry the onions, garlic, ginger and carrot for 2 minutes. Add the sprouting beans and fry for another 2 minutes, stirring and tossing all the ingredients together.

2 Add the pak choi and cashew nuts or almonds and stir-fry until the cabbage leaves are just wilting. Quickly mix all the sauce ingredients together in a jug and pour them, stirring all the time, into the wok.

3 The vegetables will be coated in a thin glossy sauce. Season with salt and pepper and serve as soon as possible.

Cook's Tip
If you cannot find pak choi, use Chinese cabbage instead and prepare and cook in the same way.

Tomato Omelette Envelopes

These delicious chive omelettes are folded and filled with tomato and melting Camembert cheese.

Serves 2

1 small onion	115g/4oz Camembert
4 tomatoes	cheese, rinded and
30ml/2 tbsp vegetable oil	diced
4 eggs	salt and ground black
30ml/2 tbsp snipped	pepper
fresh chives	

1 Cut the onion in half. Cut each half into thin wedges. Cut the tomatoes into wedges of similar size.

2 Heat 15ml/1 tbsp of the oil in a frying pan and cook the onion for 2 minutes over a moderate heat, then raise the heat and add the tomatoes. Cook for a further 2 minutes, then remove the pan from the heat.

3 Beat the eggs with the chives in a bowl. Season to taste with salt and pepper. Heat the remaining oil in an omelette pan. Add half the egg mixture and tilt the pan to spread thinly. Cook for 1 minute.

4 Flip the omelette over and cook for 1 minute more. Remove from the pan and keep hot. Make a second omelette with the remaining egg mixture.

5 Return the tomato mixture to a high heat. Add the cheese and toss the mixture over the heat for 1 minute.

6 Divide the mixture between the omelettes and fold them over. Serve at once. Add crisp lettuce leaves and chunks of granary bread, if you wish.

Cook's Tip
Add a few sliced mushrooms to the filling, if you wish, or use them in place of the tomatoes for a change.

Curried Eggs

Hard-boiled eggs are served on a mild creamy sauce base with just a hint of curry.

Serves 2

4 eggs	10ml/2 tsp tandoori paste
15ml/1 tbsp sunflower oil	10ml/2 tsp freshly
1 small onion, chopped	squeezed lemon juice
2.5cm/1in piece of fresh	50ml/2fl oz/¼ cup single
root ginger, peeled and	cream
grated	15ml/1 tbsp finely
2.5ml/½ tsp ground	chopped fresh
cumin	coriander
2.5ml/½ tsp garam	salt and ground black
masala	pepper
22.5ml/1½ tbsp tomato	fresh coriander sprigs, to
purée	garnish

1 Put the eggs in a saucepan of water. Bring to the boil, lower the heat and simmer for 10 minutes.

2 Meanwhile, heat the oil in a frying pan and cook the onion for 2–3 minutes. Add the fresh root ginger and cook for a further 1 minute.

3 Stir in the ground cumin, garam masala, tomato purée, tandoori paste, lemon juice and cream. Cook for 1–2 minutes more, then stir in the coriander. Season with salt and pepper.

4 Drain the eggs, remove the shells and cut each egg in half. Spoon the sauce into a serving bowl, top with the eggs and garnish with fresh coriander. Serve at once.

Cook's Tip
If you store your eggs in the fridge, make sure you allow them to come to room temperature before you boil them. This way, they are less likely to crack.

Potatoes with Blue Cheese

We are so used to eating potatoes as a side dish, we tend to forget they can make a good main meal too, as here.

Serves 4

450g/1lb small new
  potatoes
small head of celery,
  sliced
small red onion, thinly
  sliced
115g/4oz blue cheese,
  mashed

150ml/¼ pint/⅔ cup
  single cream
salt and ground black
  pepper
90g/3½oz/scant 1 cup
  walnut pieces
30ml/2 tbsp chopped
  fresh parsley

1 Cover the potatoes with water and then boil for about 15 minutes, adding the sliced celery and onion to the pan for the last 5 minutes or so.

2 Drain the vegetables and put them into a shallow serving dish, making sure they are evenly distributed.

3 In a small saucepan slowly melt the cheese in the cream, stirring occasionally. Do not allow the mixture to boil but heat it until it scalds.

4 Season the sauce to taste. Pour it over the vegetables and scatter the walnuts and parsley over the top. Serve hot.

Cook's Tip
Choose any blue cheese you like, such as Stilton, Danish blue, blue vinney or blue brie.

Greek Spinach and Cheese Pies

These individual spinach, feta and Parmesan cheese pies are easy to make using ready-made filo pastry.

Makes 4

15ml/1 tbsp olive oil
1 small onion, finely
  chopped
275g/10oz/2½ cups fresh
  spinach, stalks
  removed
50g/2oz/4 tbsp butter,
  melted
4 sheets filo pastry

1 egg
large pinch of freshly
  grated nutmeg
75g/3oz/¾ cup crumbled
  feta cheese
15ml/1 tbsp grated
  Parmesan cheese
salt and ground black
  pepper

1 Preheat the oven to 190°C/375°F/Gas 5. Fry the onion in the oil for 5–6 minutes, until softened. Add the spinach leaves and cook, stirring, until the spinach has wilted and some of the liquid evaporated. Leave to cool.

2 Brush four 10cm/4in diameter loose-based tartlet tins with melted butter. Cut two sheets of filo into eight 14cm/4½in squares each. Cover the remaining sheets with a dish towel.

3 Brush four squares at a time with melted butter. Line the first tartlet tin with one square, gently easing it into the base and up the sides. Leave the edges overhanging. Lay the remaining squares on top of the first, turning them so the corners form a star shape. Repeat for the remaining tins.

4 Beat the egg with the nutmeg and seasoning, then stir in the cheeses and spinach. Divide the mixture between the tins and smooth level. Fold the overhanging over the filling.

5 Cut the third pastry sheet into eight 10cm/4in rounds. Brush with butter and place two on top of each tartlet. Press around the edges to seal. Brush the last pastry sheet with butter and cut into strips. Gently twist each strip and lay them on top of the tartlets. Bake for about 30–35 minutes, until golden. Serve hot or cold.

Chilli Beans with Basmati Rice

Red kidney beans, chopped tomatoes and hot chilli make a great combination in this colourful, flavoursome dish.

Serves 4

350g/12oz/2 cups
 basmati rice
30ml/2 tbsp olive oil
1 large onion, chopped
1 garlic clove, crushed
15ml/12 tbsp hot chilli
 powder
15g/½oz/1 tbsp plain
 flour
15ml/1 tbsp tomato purée

400g/14oz can chopped
 tomatoes
400g/14oz can red kidney
 beans, drained
150ml/¼ pint/⅔ cup hot
 vegetable stock
chopped fresh parsley, to
 garnish
salt and ground black
 pepper

1 Wash the rice several times under cold running water. Drain well. Bring a large saucepan of water to the boil. Add the rice and cook for 10–12 minutes, until tender. Meanwhile, heat the oil in a frying pan and cook the chopped onion and garlic for about 2 minutes.

2 Stir the chilli powder and flour into the onion and garlic mixture. Cook for 2 minutes more, stirring frequently.

3 Stir in the tomato purée and chopped tomatoes. Rinse and drain the kidney beans well and add to the pan with the hot vegetable stock. Cover and cook for a final 12 minutes, stirring from time to time.

4 Season the chilli sauce to taste with salt and pepper. Drain the rice and serve at once with the chilli beans, garnished with a little chopped fresh parsley.

Cook's Tip
Serve the chilli beans with a pasta of your choice or hot pitta bread, if you prefer.

Lentil Stir-fry

Mushrooms, artichoke hearts, sugar snap peas and green lentils make a satisfying stir-fry supper.

Serves 2–3

115g/4oz/1 cup
 sugar snap peas
25g/1oz/2 tbsp butter
1 small onion, chopped
115g/4oz cup brown cap
 mushrooms, sliced
400g/14oz can artichoke
 hearts, drained and
 halved

400g/14oz can green
 lentils, drained
60ml/4 tbsp single cream
25g/1oz/¼ cup flaked
 almonds, toasted
salt and ground black
 pepper
French bread, to serve

1 Bring a saucepan of salted water to the boil, add the sugar snap peas and cook for about 4 minutes until just tender. Drain, refresh under cold running water, then drain again. Pat the peas dry with kitchen paper and set aside.

2 Melt the butter in a frying pan and cook the chopped onion for 2–3 minutes, stirring occasionally.

3 Add the sliced mushrooms to the onions. Stir until well combined, then cook for 2–3 minutes until just tender. Add the artichoke hearts, sugar snap peas and lentils to the pan. Stir-fry for 2 minutes.

4 Stir in the cream and almonds and cook for 1 minute. Season to taste with salt and pepper. Serve at once, with chunks of French bread.

Cook's Tip
Use dried green lentils if you prefer. Cook them according to the manufacturer's instructions first and then add them to the stir-fry with the artichokes and sugar snap peas.

Arabian Spinach

Stir-fry spinach with onions and spices, then mix in a can of chick-peas and you have a quick, delicious main meal.

Serves 4

30ml/2 tbsp olive or
    sunflower oil
1 onion, sliced
2 garlic cloves, crushed
400g/14oz/3½ cups
    spinach, washed and
    shredded

5ml/1 tsp cumin seeds
425g/15oz can
    chick-peas, drained
knob of butter
salt and ground black
    pepper

1 Heat the oil in a large frying pan or wok and fry the onion for about 5 minutes until softened. Add the garlic and cumin seeds, then fry for another minute.

2 Add the spinach, in stages, stirring until the leaves begin to wilt. Fresh spinach leaves condense down dramatically on cooking and they will all fit into the pan.

3 Stir in the chick-peas, butter and season with salt and pepper. Reheat until just bubbling, then serve hot. Drain off any pan juices, if you wish, but this dish is rather good served with a little sauce.

Courgettes en Papillote

An impressive dinner party accompaniment, these puffed paper parcels should be broken open at the table.

Serves 4

2 courgettes
1 leek
225g/8oz young
    asparagus, trimmed
4 tarragon sprigs

4 garlic cloves, unpeeled
1 egg, beaten
salt and ground black
    pepper

1 Preheat the oven to 200°C/400°F/Gas 6. Using a potato peeler, slice the courgettes lengthways into thin strips.

2 Cut the leek into very fine julienne strips and cut the asparagus evenly into 5cm/2in lengths.

3 Cut out four sheets of greaseproof paper measuring about 30 x 38cm/12 x 15in and fold in half. Draw a large curve to make a heart shape when unfolded. Cut along the inside of the line and open out.

4 Divide the courgettes, asparagus and leek evenly between each paper heart, positioning the filling on one side of the fold line, and topping each with a sprig of fresh tarragon and an unpeeled garlic clove. Season to taste with salt and pepper.

5 Brush the edges lightly with the beaten egg and fold over.

6 Pleat the edges together so that each parcel is completely sealed. Lay the parcels on a baking sheet and cook for about 10 minutes. Serve immediately.

Cook's Tip
Experiment with other vegetables and herbs such as sugar snap peas and mint, or baby carrots and rosemary. The possibilities are endless.

Green Lentil and Cabbage Salad

This warm crunchy salad makes a satisfying meal if served with crusty French bread or wholemeal rolls.

Serves 4–6

*225g/8oz/1 cup Puy
   lentils
1.3 litres/2¼ pints/6 cups
   cold water
1 garlic clove
1 bay leaf
1 small onion, peeled and
   studded with 2 cloves
15ml/1 tbsp olive oil
1 red onion, finely sliced*

*2 garlic cloves, crushed
15ml/1 tbsp thyme leaves
350g/12oz/6 cups finely
   shredded cabbage
finely grated rind and
   juice of 1 lemon
15ml/1 tbsp raspberry
   vinegar
salt and ground black
   pepper*

1 Rinse the lentils in cold water and place in a large saucepan with the water, peeled garlic clove, bay leaf and clove-studded onion. Bring to the boil and cook for about 10 minutes. Reduce the heat, cover the pan with a tight-fitting lid and simmer gently for 15–20 minutes. Drain and remove the onion, garlic and bay leaf.

2 Heat the oil in a large pan and cook the red onion, garlic and thyme for 5 minutes until softened.

3 Add the shredded cabbage and cook for 3–5 minutes until just cooked but still crunchy.

4 Stir in the cooked lentils, grated lemon rind and juice and the raspberry vinegar. Season with salt and pepper and serve.

Cook's Tip
Vary the type of cabbage you use in this recipe, if you like. Choose a white cabbage or a Savoy, or try fresh spring greens instead.

Tomato and Basil Tart

You could make individual tartlets instead of one large tart if you prefer, but reduce the baking time slightly.

Serves 6–8

*175g/6oz/1½ cups flour
2.5ml/½ tsp salt
115g/4oz/½ cup butter or
   margarine, chilled
45–75ml/3–5 tbsp water
30ml/2 tbsp extra virgin
   olive oil*

For the filling
*175g/6oz mozzarella
   cheese, thinly sliced*

*12 fresh basil leaves,
   6 roughly torn
4–5 tomatoes, cut into
   5mm/¼ in slices
salt and ground black
   pepper
60ml/4 tbsp freshly
   grated Parmesan
   cheese*

1 Place the flour and salt in a bowl, then rub in the butter until the mixture resembles breadcrumbs. Add 45ml/3 tbsp water and combine with a fork until the dough holds together. Mix in more water if needed. Gather the dough into a ball, wrap in greaseproof paper and chill for 40 minutes. Preheat the oven to 190°C/375°F/Gas 5.

2 Roll out the pastry to a thickness of 5mm/¼in and use to line a 28cm/11in fluted loose-bottomed flan tin. Prick the base and chill for 20 minutes in the fridge.

3 Line the pastry with a sheet of baking parchment. Fill with dried beans. Place the flan tin on a baking sheet; bake blind for 15 minutes. Remove from the oven. Leave the oven on.

4 Remove the beans and paper. Brush the pastry with oil. Line with the mozzarella. Sprinkle the torn basil over the top.

5 Arrange the tomato slices over the cheese. Dot with the whole basil leaves. Season with salt and pepper, Parmesan and oil. Bake for 35 minutes. If the cheese exudes a lot of liquid during baking, tilt the tin and spoon it off to keep the pastry crisp. Serve hot or at room temperature.

Spinach and Potato Galette

Creamy layers of potato, spinach and fresh herbs make a warming and filling supper dish.

Serves 6

900g/2lb large potatoes
450g/1lb/4 cups fresh
  spinach
400g/14oz/1¾ cups low-
  fat cream cheese
15ml/1 tbsp grainy
  mustard

2 eggs
50g/2oz mixed chopped
  fresh herbs such as
  chives, parsley, chervil
  or sorrel
salt and ground black
  pepper

1 Preheat the oven to 180°C/350°F/Gas 4. Base-line a deep 23cm/9in round cake tin with non-stick baking paper. Place the potatoes in a large saucepan and cover with cold water. Bring to the boil and cook for 10 minutes. Drain well and allow to cool slightly before slicing thinly.

2 Wash the spinach and place in a large pan with only the water that is clinging to the leaves. Cover and cook, stirring once, until the spinach has just wilted. Drain well in a sieve and squeeze out the excess moisture with the back of a spoon. Chop the spinach finely.

3 Beat together the cream cheese, mustard and eggs, then stir in the chopped spinach and fresh herbs.

4 Place a layer of the sliced potatoes in the lined tin, arranging them in concentric circles. Top with a spoonful of the cream cheese mixture and spread out. Continue layering, seasoning with salt and pepper as you go, until all the potatoes and the cream cheese mixture are used up.

5 Cover the tin with a piece of foil, scrunched around the edge, and place in a roasting tin.

6 Half-fill the roasting tin with boiling water and cook the galette in the oven for 45–50 minutes. Turn out on to a plate and serve hot or cold.

Cowboy Hot-pot

A great dish to serve as a children's main meal, which adults will enjoy too – if they are allowed to join the posse.

Serves 4–6

45ml/3 tbsp sunflower oil
1 onion, sliced
1 fresh red pepper, sliced
1 sweet potato or
  2 carrots, chopped
115g/4oz/scant ½ cup
  chopped green beans
400g/14oz can baked
  beans
200g/7oz can sweetcorn
15ml/1 tbsp tomato purée

5ml/1 tsp barbecue spice
  seasoning
115g/4oz cheese
  (preferably smoked),
  diced
450g/1lb potatoes, thinly
  sliced
25g/1oz/2 tbsp butter,
  melted
salt and ground black
  pepper

1 Preheat the oven to 190°C/375°F/Gas 5. Heat the oil in a frying pan and gently fry the onion, pepper and sweet potato or carrots until softened but not browned.

2 Add the green beans, baked beans, sweetcorn (and liquid), tomato purée and barbecue spice seasoning. Bring to the boil, then simmer for 5 minutes.

3 Cover the vegetable and cheese mixture with the sliced potato, brush with butter, season with salt and pepper and bake for 30–40 minutes until golden brown on top and the potato is cooked.

Cook's Tip
Use any vegetable mixture you like in this versatile hot-pot, according to what you have to hand.

Quorn with Ginger, Chilli and Leeks

Quorn easily absorbs different flavours and retains a good firm texture, making it ideal for stir-frying.

Serves 4

225g/8oz packet Quorn, diced
45ml/3 tbsp dark soy sauce
30ml/2 tbsp dry sherry or vermouth
10ml/2 tsp honey
150ml/¼ pint/⅔ cup vegetable stock
10ml/2 tsp cornflour

45ml/3 tbsp sunflower or groundnut oil
3 leeks, thinly sliced
1 red chilli, seeded and sliced
2.5cm/1in piece fresh root ginger, peeled and shredded
salt and ground black pepper

1 Toss the Quorn in the soy sauce and sherry or vermouth until well coated and leave to marinate for about 30 minutes.

2 Strain the Quorn from the marinade and reserve the juices in a jug. Mix the marinade with the honey, vegetable stock and cornflour to make a paste.

3 Heat the oil in a wok or large frying pan and, when hot, stir-fry the Quorn until it is crisp on the outside. Remove the Quorn and set aside.

4 Reheat the oil and stir-fry the leeks, chilli and ginger for about 2 minutes until they are just soft. Season to taste with salt and pepper.

5 Return the Quorn to the pan, together with the marinade, and stir well until the liquid is thick and glossy. Serve hot with rice or egg noodles.

Cook's Tip
Quorn is a versatile, microprotein food, now available in most supermarkets. If you cannot find it, you could use tofu instead.

Chinese Potatoes with Chilli Beans

This oriental-inspired dish gains particular appeal by way of its tasty sauce.

Serves 4

4 potatoes, cut into thick chunks
3 spring onions, sliced
1 large fresh chilli, seeded and sliced
30ml/2 tbsp sunflower or groundnut oil
2 garlic cloves, crushed
400g/14oz can red kidney beans

30ml/2 tbsp dark soy sauce
15ml/1 tbsp sesame oil
salt and ground black pepper
15ml/1 tbsp sesame seeds, to sprinkle
chopped fresh coriander or parsley, to garnish

1 Boil the potatoes until they are just tender. Take care not to overcook them. Drain and reserve.

2 In a large frying pan or wok, stir-fry the spring onions and chilli in the oil for about 1 minute, then add the garlic and fry for a few seconds longer.

3 Rinse and drain the kidney beans, then add them to the pan with the potatoes, stirring well. Finally add the soy sauce and sesame oil.

4 Season to taste with salt and pepper and cook the vegetables until they are well heated through. Sprinkle with the sesame seeds and the chopped fresh coriander or parsley.

Sweetcorn and Bean Tamale Pie

This is a hearty dish with a cheesy polenta topping which covers sweetcorn and kidney beans in a rich hot sauce.

Serves 4
2 corn on the cob
30ml/2 tbsp vegetable oil
1 onion, chopped
2 garlic cloves, crushed
1 red pepper, seeded and chopped
2 green chillies, seeded and chopped
10ml/2 tbsp ground cumin
450g/1lb ripe tomatoes, peeled, seeded and chopped
15ml/1 tbsp tomato purée
425g/15oz can red kidney beans, drained and rinsed

15ml/1 tbsp chopped fresh oregano
oregano leaves, to garnish

For the topping
115g/4oz/1 cup polenta
15g/½oz/1 tbsp plain flour
2.5ml/½ tsp salt
10ml/2 tsp baking powder
1 egg, lightly beaten
120ml/4fl oz/½ cup milk
15g/½oz/1 tbsp butter, melted
50g/2oz/½ cup grated smoked Cheddar cheese

1 Preheat the oven to 220°C/425°F/Gas 7. Husk the corn on the cob, then par-boil for 8 minutes. Drain, leave to cool slightly, then remove the kernels with a sharp knife.

2 Fry the onion, garlic and pepper in the oil for 5 minutes, until softened. Add the chillies and cumin; fry for 1 minute. Stir in the tomatoes, tomato purée, beans, corn kernels and oregano. Season to taste. Simmer, uncovered, for 10 minutes.

3 To make the topping, mix the polenta, flour, salt, baking powder, egg, milk and butter to form a thick batter.

4 Transfer the bean mixture to an ovenproof dish, spoon the polenta mixture over and spread evenly. Bake for 30 minutes. Remove from the oven, sprinkle the cheese over the top, then bake for a further 5–10 minutes, until golden.

Pepper and Potato Tortilla

Traditionally a Spanish dish, tortilla is best eaten cold in chunky wedges and makes an ideal picnic food.

Serves 4
2 potatoes
45ml/3 tbsp olive oil
1 large onion, thinly sliced
2 garlic cloves, crushed
1 green pepper, thinly sliced

1 red pepper, thinly sliced
6 eggs, beaten
115g/4oz/1 cup grated mature Cheddar or Mahón cheese
salt and ground black pepper

1 Do not peel the potatoes, but wash them well. Par-boil them for about 10 minutes, then drain and, when they are cool enough to handle, slice them thickly. Switch on the grill so that it warms up while you prepare the rest of the dish.

2 In a large non-stick or well seasoned frying pan, heat the oil and fry the onion, garlic and pepper over a moderate heat for 5 minutes until softened.

3 Add the potatoes and continue frying, stirring from time to time until the potatoes are completely cooked and the vegetables are soft. Add a little extra oil if the pan seems rather too dry.

4 Pour in half the beaten eggs, then sprinkle over half the grated Cheddar or Mahón cheese, then the rest of the egg. Season with salt and pepper and finish with a layer of cheese.

5 Continue to cook over a low heat, without stirring, half covering the pan with a lid to help set the eggs.

6 When the mixture is firm, flash the pan under the hot grill to seal the top just lightly. Leave the tortilla in the pan to cool. This helps it firm up further and makes it easier to turn out. Cut into generous wedges to serve.

Chick-pea Stew

This hearty chick-pea and vegetable stew is delicious served with garlic-flavoured mashed potato.

Serves 4

30ml/2 tbsp olive oil
1 small onion, finely chopped
225g/8oz carrots, halved lengthways and thinly sliced
2.5ml/½ tsp ground cumin
5ml/1 tsp ground coriander
25g/1oz/2 tbsp plain flour
225g/8oz courgettes, sliced
200g/7oz can sweetcorn, drained
400g/14oz can chick-peas, drained
30ml/2 tbsp tomato purée
200ml/7fl oz/scant 1 cup hot vegetable stock
salt and ground black pepper
mashed potato, to serve

1 Heat the oil in a frying pan. Add the onion and carrots. Toss the vegetables to coat them in the oil, then cook over a moderate heat for 4 minutes.

2 Add the ground cumin, coriander and flour. Stir and cook for 1 minute more.

3 Cut the courgette slices in half. Add them to the pan with the sweetcorn, chick-peas, tomato purée and vegetable stock. Stir well. Cook for 10 minutes, stirring frequently.

4 Taste the stew and season to taste with salt and pepper. Serve at once with mashed potato.

Cook's Tip
To make garlic-flavoured mashed potato, peel and crush a garlic clove, fry it lightly in butter, then stir into the mashed potato until well combined.

Potato and Broccoli Stir-fry

This wonderful stir-fry combines potato, broccoli and red pepper with just a hint of fresh ginger.

Serves 2

450g/1lb potatoes
45ml/3 tbsp groundnut oil
50g/2oz/4 tbsp butter
1 small onion, chopped
1 red pepper, seeded and chopped
225g/8oz broccoli, broken into florets
2.5cm/1in piece of fresh root ginger, peeled and grated
salt and ground black pepper

1 Peel the potatoes and cut them into 1cm/½in dice.

2 Heat the oil in a large frying pan and cook the potatoes for 8 minutes over a high heat, stirring and tossing occasionally, until browned and just tender.

3 Drain off the oil. Add the butter to the potatoes in the pan. As soon as it melts, add the chopped onion and red pepper. Stir-fry for 2 minutes.

4 Add the broccoli florets and ginger to the pan. Stir-fry for 2–3 minutes more, taking care not to break up the potatoes. Season to taste with salt and pepper and serve at once.

Vegetables with Lentil Bolognese

Instead of a cheese sauce, it makes a pleasant change to top lightly steamed vegetables with a delicious lentil sauce.

Serves 6

1 small cauliflower
  broken into florets
225g/8oz/2 cups broccoli
  florets
2 leeks, thickly sliced
225g/8oz Brussels
  sprouts, halved if large

For the lentil Bolognese sauce
1 onion, chopped
2 garlic cloves, crushed
2 carrots, coarsely grated
2 celery sticks, chopped

45ml/3 tbsp olive oil
115g/4oz/½ cup red
  lentils
400g/14oz can chopped
  tomatoes
30ml/2 tbsp tomato purée
450ml/¾ pint/2 cups
  stock
15ml/1 tbsp fresh
  marjoram, chopped,
  or 5ml/1 tsp dried
  marjoram
salt and ground black
  pepper

1 In a large saucepan, gently fry the onion, garlic, carrots and celery in the oil for about 5 minutes, until they are soft. Add the lentils, tomatoes, tomato purée, stock, marjoram and seasoning. Bring the mixture to the boil, then partially cover with a lid and simmer for 20 minutes until thick and soft.

2 Place all the vegetables in a steamer over a pan of boiling water and cook for 8–10 minutes until just tender.

3 Drain and place in a shallow serving dish. Spoon the sauce on top, stirring slightly to mix. Serve hot.

Black Bean and Vegetable Stir-fry

This colourful and very flavoursome vegetable mixture is coated in a classic Chinese sauce.

Serves 4

8 spring onions
225g/8oz button
  mushrooms
1 red pepper
1 green pepper
2 large carrots
60ml/4 tbsp sesame oil
2 garlic cloves, crushed

60ml/4 tbsp black bean
  sauce
90ml/6 tbsp warm water
225g/8oz/scant 3 cups
  beansprouts
salt and ground black
  pepper

1 Thinly slice the spring onions and button mushrooms. Set aside in separate bowls.

2 Cut both the peppers in half, remove the seeds and slice the flesh into thin strips.

3 Cut the carrots in half. Cut each half into thin strips lengthways. Stack the slices and cut through them to make very fine strips.

4 Heat the oil in a large wok or frying pan until very hot and stir-fry the spring onions and garlic for 30 seconds.

5 Add the mushrooms, peppers and carrots. Stir-fry for a further 5–6 minutes over a high heat until the vegetables are just beginning to soften.

6 Mix the black bean sauce with the water. Add to the wok or pan and cook for another 3–4 minutes. Stir in the beansprouts and stir-fry for a final 1 minute until all the vegetables are coated in the sauce. Season to taste with salt and pepper. Serve at once.

Tomato and Okra Stew

Okra is an unusual and delicious vegetable. It releases a sticky sap when cooked, which helps to thicken the stew.

Serves 4

15ml/1 tbsp olive oil	275g/10oz okra
1 onion, chopped	30ml/2 tbsp chopped
400g/14oz can pimientos,	fresh parsley
drained	salt and ground black
2 x 400g/14oz cans	pepper
chopped tomatoes	

1 Heat the oil in a saucepan and cook the chopped onion for about 2–3 minutes.

2 Roughly chop the pimientos and add to the onion. Add the chopped tomatoes and mix well.

3 Cut the tops off the okra and cut into halves or quarters if large. Add to the tomato sauce in the pan. Season to taste with plenty of salt and pepper.

4 Bring the vegetable stew to the boil, then lower the heat, cover the pan with a tight-fitting lid and simmer for 12 minutes until the vegetables are tender and the sauce has thickened. Stir in the chopped parsley and serve at once.

Cook's Tip
Okra is now available all year round. Do not buy them any longer than 7.5–10cm/3–4in and look for clean, dark green pods – a brown tinge indicates staleness. When preparing, if the ridges look tough or damaged, scrape them with a sharp knife.

Chunky Vegetable Paella

This Spanish rice dish is now enjoyed the world over. This version includes aubergine and chick-peas.

Serves 6

large pinch of saffron	225g/8oz/1¼ cups
strands	risotto rice
1 aubergine, cut into	600ml/1 pint/2½ cups
thick chunks	stock
90ml/6 tbsp olive oil	450g/1lb fresh tomatoes,
1 large onion, thickly	skinned and chopped
sliced	115g/4oz sliced
3 garlic cloves, crushed	mushrooms
1 yellow pepper, sliced	115g/4oz/scant ½ cup cut
1 red pepper, sliced	green beans
10ml/2 tsp paprika	400g/14oz can chick-peas

1 Steep the saffron in 45ml/3 tbsp hot water. Sprinkle the aubergine with salt, leave to drain in a colander for 30 minutes, then rinse and dry.

2 In a large paella or frying pan, heat the oil and fry the onion, garlic, peppers and aubergine for about 5 minutes, stirring occasionally. Sprinkle in the paprika and stir again.

3 Mix in the rice, then pour in the stock, tomatoes, saffron and seasoning. Bring to the boil, then simmer the mixture for about 15 minutes, uncovered, shaking the pan frequently and stirring from time to time.

4 Stir in the mushrooms, green beans and chick-peas (with their liquid). Continue cooking for a further 10 minutes, then serve hot, direct from the pan.

Onion and Gruyère Tart

The secret of this tart is to cook the onions very slowly until they almost caramelize.

Serves 4

175g/6oz/1½ cups plain
  flour
pinch of salt
75g/3oz/6 tbsp butter,
  diced
1 egg yolk

15–30ml/1–2 tbsp
  wholegrain mustard
2 eggs, plus 1 egg yolk
300ml/½ pint/1 cup
  double cream
75g/3oz/generous ½ cup
  grated Gruyère cheese
pinch of freshly grated
  nutmeg
salt and ground black
  pepper

For the filling

50g/2oz/4 tbsp butter
450g/1lb onions, thinly
  sliced

1 To make the pastry, sift the flour and salt into a bowl. Add the butter and rub into the flour with your fingertips until the mixture resembles fine breadcrumbs. Add the egg yolk and 15ml/1 tbsp cold water and mix to a firm dough. Chill in the fridge for 30 minutes.

2 Preheat the oven to 200°C/400°F/Gas 6. Knead the pastry, then roll it out on a lightly floured work surface and use to line a 23cm/9in loose-based flan tin. Prick the base all over with a fork, line the pastry case with greaseproof paper and fill with baking beans.

3 Bake the pastry case blind for 15 minutes. Remove the paper and beans and bake for a further 10–15 minutes, until the pastry case is crisp. Meanwhile, melt the butter in a saucepan, add the onions, cover with a tight-fitting lid and cook for 20 minutes, stirring occasionally, until golden.

4 Reduce the oven temperature to 180°C/350°F/Gas 4. Spread the pastry case with mustard and top with the onions. Mix together the eggs, egg yolk, cream, cheese, nutmeg and seasoning. Pour over the onions. Bake for 30–35 minutes, until golden. Serve warm.

Potato and Spinach Gratin

Pine nuts add a satisfying crunch to this gratin of wafer-thin potato slices and spinach in a creamy cheese sauce.

Serves 2

450g/1lb potatoes
1 garlic clove, crushed
3 spring onions, thinly
  sliced
150ml/¼ pint/⅔ cup
  single cream
250ml/8fl oz/1 cup milk
225g/8oz frozen chopped
  spinach, thawed

115g/4oz/1 cup grated
  mature Cheddar
  cheese
25g/1oz/¼ cup pine nuts
salt and ground black
  pepper
lettuce and tomato salad,
  to serve

1 Peel the potatoes and cut them carefully into wafer-thin slices. Spread them out in a large, heavy-based, non-stick frying pan.

2 Scatter the crushed garlic and sliced spring onions evenly over the potatoes.

3 Pour the cream and milk over the potatoes. Place the pan over a gentle heat, cover and cook for 8 minutes or until the potatoes are tender.

4 Using both hands, squeeze the spinach dry. Add the spinach to the potatoes, mixing lightly. Cover the pan with a tight-fitting lid and cook for 2 minutes more.

5 Season to taste with salt and pepper, then spoon the mixture into a gratin dish. Preheat the grill.

6 Sprinkle the grated cheese and pine nuts over the spinach mixture. Lightly toast under the grill for 2–3 minutes until the topping is golden. A simple lettuce and tomato salad makes an excellent accompaniment to this dish.

Stuffed Peppers

Sweet peppers can be stuffed and baked with a variety of fillings, from cooked vegetables to rice or pasta.

Serves 6

6 peppers, any colour
200g/7oz/generous 1 cup rice
60ml/4 tbsp olive oil
1 large onion, chopped
3 anchovy fillets, chopped
2 garlic cloves, finely chopped
3 tomatoes, peeled and cut into small dice

60ml/4 tbsp white wine
45ml/3 tbsp finely chopped fresh parsley
114g/4oz/scant ½ cup mozzarella
90ml/6 tbsp freshly grated Parmesan cheese
salt and ground black pepper

1 Cut the tops off the peppers. Scoop out the seeds and the fibrous insides. Blanch the peppers and their tops in a large saucepan of boiling water for 3–4 minutes. Remove, and stand upside down on wire racks to drain.

2 Boil the rice according to the packet instructions, but drain and rinse it in cold water 3 minutes before the recommended cooking time has elapsed. Drain again.

3 Sauté the onion in the oil until soft. Mash in the anchovies and garlic. Add the tomatoes and wine; cook for 5 minutes.

4 Preheat the oven to 190°C/375°F/Gas 5. Remove the tomato mixture from the heat. Stir in the rice, parsley, the mozzarella and 60ml/4 tbsp of the Parmesan cheese. Season to taste with salt and pepper.

5 Pat the insides of the peppers dry with kitchen paper. Sprinkle with salt and pepper. Stuff the peppers. Sprinkle the tops with the remaining Parmesan and a little oil. Arrange the peppers in a shallow baking dish. Pour in enough water to come 1cm/½in up the sides of the peppers. Bake for 25 minutes. Serve at once.

Broccoli and Ricotta Cannelloni

When piping the filling into the cannelloni tubes, hold them upright on the work surface.

Serves 4

12 dried cannelloni tubes, 7.5cm/3in long
450g/1lb/4 cups broccoli florets
75g/3oz/1½ cups fresh breadcrumbs
150ml/¼ pint/⅔ cup milk
60ml/4 tbsp olive oil, plus extra for brushing
225g/8oz/1 cup ricotta cheese
pinch of grated nutmeg
90ml/6 tbsp freshly grated Parmesan or Pecorino cheese

salt and ground black pepper
30ml/2 tbsp pine nuts, for sprinkling

For the tomato sauce
30ml/2 tbsp olive oil
1 onion, finely chopped
1 garlic clove, crushed
2 x 400g/14oz cans chopped tomatoes
15ml/1 tbsp tomato purée
4 black olives, stoned and chopped
5ml/1 tsp dried thyme

1 Preheat the oven to 190°C/375°F/Gas 5 and grease an ovenproof dish. Bring a saucepan of water to the boil, add a little olive oil and simmer the pasta, uncovered, until nearly cooked. Boil the broccoli until tender. Drain the pasta and rinse under cold water. Drain the broccoli, then process in a food processor or blender until smooth.

2 Mix together the breadcrumbs, milk and oil. Add the ricotta, broccoli purée, nutmeg, 60ml/4 tbsp Parmesan cheese and seasoning.

3 For the sauce, fry the onions and garlic in the oil for 5 minutes. Stir in the tomatoes, tomato purée, olives and thyme, and season. Boil for 2 minutes; pour in the dish.

4 Open the pasta tubes. Pipe in the filling using a 1cm/½in nozzle pipe. Arrange in the dish. Brush with olive oil, then sprinkle over the remaining cheese and pine nuts. Bake for 30 minutes, or until golden on top.

Pasta with Spring Vegetables

If you are not fond of fennel, use a small onion instead. Prepare in the same way.

Serves 4

115g/4oz/1 cup broccoli
  florets
115g/4oz baby leeks
225g/8oz asparagus
1 small fennel bulb
115g/4oz/1 cup fresh or
  frozen peas
40g/1½oz/3 tbsp butter
1 shallot, chopped
300ml/½ pint/1¼ cups
  double cream

45ml/3 tbsp mixed
  chopped fresh herbs,
  such as parsley, thyme
  and sage
350g/12oz/3 cups dried
  penne pasta
salt and ground black
  pepper
freshly grated Parmesan
  cheese, to serve

1 Divide the broccoli florets into tiny sprigs. Cut the leeks and asparagus diagonally into 5cm/2in lengths. Trim the fennel bulb and remove any tough outer leaves. Cut into wedges, leaving the layers attached at the root ends so the pieces stay intact.

2 Cook each vegetable separately in boiling salted water until just tender – use the same water for each vegetable. Drain well and keep warm.

3 Melt the butter in a separate saucepan, and cook the chopped shallot, stirring occasionally, until softened but not browned. Stir in the herbs and cream and cook for a few minutes, until slightly thickened.

4 Meanwhile, cook the pasta in boiling salted water for 10 minutes or according to the instructions on the packet. Drain well and add to the sauce with all the vegetables. Toss gently to combine and season to taste with plenty of pepper.

5 Serve the pasta hot, with plenty of freshly grated Parmesan cheese.

Pasta Carbonara

A classic Roman dish traditionally made with spaghetti, which is equally delicious with fresh egg tagliatelle.

Serves 4

350–450g/12oz–1lb
  fresh tagliatelle
15ml/1 tbsp olive oil
225g/8oz piece of ham,
  bacon or pancetta, cut
  into 2.5cm/1in sticks
115g/4oz button
  mushrooms, sliced

4 eggs, lightly beaten
75ml/5 tbsp single cream
salt and ground black
  pepper
30ml/2 tbsp finely grated
  Parmesan cheese
fresh basil sprigs, to
  garnish

1 Cook the pasta in a pan of boiling salted water, with a little oil added, for 6–8 minutes or until *al dente*.

2 Meanwhile, heat the oil in a frying pan and fry the ham for 3–4 minutes, then add the mushrooms and fry for a further 3–4 minutes. Turn off the heat and reserve. Lightly beat the eggs and cream together in a bowl and season well with salt and pepper.

3 When the pasta is cooked, drain it well and return to the pan. Add the ham, mushrooms and any pan juices and stir into the pasta.

4 Pour in the eggs, cream and half the Parmesan cheese. Stir well and as you do this the eggs will cook in the heat of the pasta. Pile on to warmed serving plates, sprinkle with the remaining Parmesan and garnish with basil.

Spinach and Hazelnut Lasagne

Use frozen spinach in this hearty and satisfying dish if you are short of time.

Serves 4

900g/2lb/8 cups fresh
 spinach
300ml/½ pint/1¼ cups
 vegetable stock
1 onion, finely chopped
1 garlic clove, crushed
75g/3oz/¾ cup hazelnuts
30ml/2 tbsp chopped
 fresh basil

6 sheets lasagne
400g/14oz can chopped
 tomatoes
250ml/8fl oz/1 cup
 low-fat fromage frais
salt and ground black
 pepper
flaked hazelnuts and
 chopped fresh parsley

1 Preheat the oven to 200°C/400°F/Gas 6. Wash the spinach; cook with no extra water over a high heat for 2 minutes until wilted. Drain well. Simmer the onion and garlic in 30ml/ 2 tbsp stock until soft. Stir in the spinach, hazelnuts and basil.

2 In a large ovenproof dish, layer the spinach, lasagne and tomatoes; season as you go. Pour in the remaining stock. Spread the fromage frais over the top. Bake for 45 minutes. Serve hot, sprinkled with hazelnuts and chopped parsley.

Tagliatelle with Hazelnut Pesto

Hazelnuts are used instead of pine nuts in the pesto sauce, providing a healthier, lower-fat option.

Serves 4

2 garlic cloves, crushed
25g/1oz fresh basil leaves
25g/1oz/¼ cup chopped
 hazelnuts

200g/7oz/scant 1 cup soft
 cheese
225g/8oz tagliatelle
ground black pepper

1 Place the garlic, basil, hazelnuts and cheese in a food processor or blender and process to a thick paste.

2 Cook the tagliatelle in lightly salted boiling water until just tender, then drain well.

3 Spoon the sauce into the hot pasta, tossing until melted. Sprinkle with pepper and serve hot.

Cook's Tip
If fresh tuna is available, use 450g/1lb, cut into small chunks and add after step 2. Simmer for 6–8 minutes, then add the chilli, olives and pasta.

Spaghetti with Tuna Sauce

Use 450g/1lb fresh spaghetti in place of the dried pasta in this piquant dish, if you prefer.

Serves 4

Cook 225g/8oz spaghetti, drain and keep hot. Boil 1 garlic clove and 400g/14oz can chopped tomatoes and simmer for 2–3 minutes. Add 425g/15oz canned tuna and 2.5ml/½ tsp chilli sauce (optional), 4 black olives and the spaghetti. Heat well and season to taste.

Penne with Broccoli and Chilli

For a milder sauce you could omit the chilli, but it does give
this dish a great kick.

Serves 4
*450g/1lb/4 cups small
  broccoli florets
30ml/2 tbsp stock
1 garlic clove, crushed
1 small red chilli, finely
  sliced, or 2.5ml/½ tsp
  chilli sauce*

*60ml/4 tbsp natural
  low-fat yogurt
30ml/2 tbsp toasted pine
  nuts or cashew nuts
350g/12oz/3¼ cups
  penne
salt and ground black
  pepper*

1 Add the pasta to a large pan of lightly salted boiling water
and return to the boil. Place the broccoli in a steamer basket
over the top. Cover and cook for 8–10 minutes until both are
just tender. Drain.

2 Heat the stock and add the crushed garlic and chilli or
chilli sauce. Stir over a low heat for 2–3 minutes.

3 Stir in the broccoli, pasta and yogurt. Adjust the seasoning,
sprinkle with nuts and serve hot.

Linguine with Pesto Sauce

Pesto originates in Liguria, where the sea breezes are said
to give the local basil a particularly fine flavour.

Serves 5–6
*65g/2½oz fresh basil
  leaves
3–4 garlic cloves, peeled
45ml/3 tbsp pine nuts
2.5ml/½ tsp salt
75ml/5 tbsp extra virgin
  olive oil*

*50g/2oz/scant ¾ cup
  freshly grated
  Parmesan cheese
60ml/4 tbsp freshly
  grated Pecorino cheese
salt and ground black
  pepper
500g/1¼lb linguine*

1 Place the basil, garlic, pine nuts, salt and olive oil in a food
processor or blender and process until smooth. Remove to a
bowl. (If desired, the sauce may be frozen at this point, before
the cheeses are added.)

2 Add the cheeses and stir to combine thoroughly. Season to
taste with salt and pepper.

3 Cook the pasta in a large saucepan of rapidly boiling
salted water until it is *al dente*. Just before draining it, take
about 60ml/4 tbsp of the cooking water and stir it into the
pesto sauce.

4 Drain the pasta and toss with the sauce. Serve at once,
with extra cheese if wished.

Cook's Tip
*Pecorino cheese is not as widely available as Parmesan.
If you cannot find it, use all Parmesan instead.*

Spaghetti with Herb Sauce

Fresh herbs make a wonderful aromatic sauce – the heat from the pasta releases their flavour to delicious effect.

Serves 4

50g/2oz chopped mixed fresh herbs such as parsley, basil and thyme
2 garlic cloves, crushed
60ml/4 tbsp pine nuts, toasted
150ml/¼ pint/⅔ cup olive oil
350g/12oz dried spaghetti
60ml/4 tbsp freshly grated Parmesan cheese
salt and ground black pepper
fresh basil leaves, to garnish

1 Put the herbs, garlic and half the pine nuts into a food processor or blender. With the machine running slowly, add the oil and process to form a thick purée.

2 Cook the spaghetti in plenty of boiling salted water for about 8 minutes, until *al dente*. Drain thoroughly.

3 Transfer the herb purée to a large warm bowl, then add the spaghetti and Parmesan. Toss well to coat the pasta with the sauce. Season with salt and peppper, sprinkle the remaining pine nuts and the basil leaves on top and serve hot.

Tagliatelle with Saffron Mussels

Tagliatelle is served with mussels in a saffron and cream sauce in this recipe, but use other pasta if you prefer.

Serves 4

1.75kg/4–4½lb live mussels in the shell
150ml/¼ pint/⅔ cup dry white wine
2 shallots, finely chopped
350g/12oz dried tagliatelle
25g/1oz/2 tbsp butter
2 garlic cloves, crushed
250ml/8fl oz/1 cup double cream
large pinch of saffron strands
1 egg yolk
salt and ground black pepper
30ml/2 tbsp chopped fresh parsley, to garnish

1 Scrub the mussels well under cold running water. Remove the beards and discard any mussels that are open. Place the mussels in a large saucepan with the wine and shallots. Cover with a tight-fitting lid and cook over a high heat, shaking the pan occasionally, for 5–8 minutes until the mussels have opened. Drain the mussels, reserving the liquid. Discard any that remain closed. Shell all but a few of the mussels and keep warm. Bring the reserved cooking liquid to the boil, then reduce by half. Strain into a jug.

2 Cook the pasta in a large pan of boiling salted water for 10 minutes or according to the instructions on the packet.

3 Meanwhile, melt the butter in a frying pan and fry the garlic for 1 minute. Pour in the mussel liquid, cream and saffron strands. Heat gently until the sauce thickens slightly. Remove the pan from the heat and stir in the egg yolk and shelled mussels, and season to taste with salt and pepper.

4 Drain the tagliatelle and transfer to warmed serving bowls. Spoon the sauce over and sprinkle with chopped parsley. Garnish with the mussels in shells and serve at once.

Pasta Rapido with Parsley Pesto

Here's a fresh, lively sauce that will stir the appetite and pep up any pasta supper.

Serves 4

450g/1lb/4 cups dried pasta	**For the sauce**
75g/3oz/¾ cup whole almonds	*40g/1½oz fresh flat leaf parsley*
50g/2oz/½ cup flaked almonds toasted	*2 garlic cloves, crushed*
25g/1oz/generous ¼ cup freshly grated Parmesan cheese	*45ml/3 tbsp olive oil*
45ml/3 tbsp lemon juice	*5ml/1 tsp sugar*
pinch of salt	*250ml/8fl oz/1 cup boiling water*

1 Bring a large saucepan of salted water to the boil and cook the pasta according to the instructions on the packet. Toast the whole and flaked almonds separately under a moderate grill until golden brown. Set the flaked almonds aside.

2 To make the sauce, chop the parsley finely in a food processor. Add the whole almonds and reduce to a fine consistency. Add the garlic, olive oil, lemon juice, sugar and water. Combine to make a sauce.

3 Drain the pasta and combine with half of the sauce. (The remainder of the sauce will keep in a screw-top jar in the fridge for up to ten days.) Top with freshly grated Parmesan cheese and the flaked almonds.

Macaroni Cheese with Mushrooms

This macaroni cheese is served in a light creamy sauce with mushrooms and topped with pine nuts.

Serves 4

450g/1lb quick-cooking elbow macaroni	*2.5ml/½ tsp celery salt*
45ml/3 tbsp olive oil	*5ml/1 tsp Dijon mustard*
225g/8oz button mushrooms, sliced	*175g/6oz/1½ cups grated Cheddar*
2 fresh thyme sprigs	*25g/1oz/generous ¼ cup freshly grated Parmesan cheese*
50g/2oz/4 tbsp plain flour	*25g/1oz/¼ cup pine nuts*
1 vegetable stock cube	*salt and ground black pepper*
600ml/1 pint/2½ cups milk	

1 Bring a saucepan of salted water to the boil and cook the macaroni according to the instructions on the packet.

2 Heat the oil in a heavy saucepan and cover and cook the mushrooms and thyme over a gentle heat for 2–3 minutes. Stir in the flour and draw from the heat, add the stock cube and stir continuously until evenly blended. Add the milk a little at a time, stirring after each addition. Add the celery salt, mustard and Cheddar cheese and season to taste with salt and pepper. Stir and simmer for about 1–2 minutes, until the sauce has thickened.

3 Preheat a moderate grill. Drain the macaroni well, toss into the sauce and turn out into four individual dishes or one large flameproof gratin dish. Scatter with grated Parmesan cheese and pine nuts, then grill until brown and bubbly.

Pasta with Roasted Pepper Sauce

Add other vegetables such as French beans or courgettes or even chick-peas to make this sauce more substantial.

Serves 4

2 fresh red peppers
2 yellow peppers
45ml/3 tbsp olive oil
1 onion, sliced
2 garlic cloves, crushed
400g/14oz can chopped
    plum tomatoes

2.5ml/½ tsp mild chilli
    powder
450g/1lb/4 cups dried
    pasta shells or spirals
salt and ground black
    pepper
freshly grated Parmesan
    cheese, to serve

1 Preheat the oven to 200°C/400°F/Gas 6. Place the peppers on a baking sheet and bake for about 20 minutes or until they are beginning to char. Alternatively, grill the peppers, turning them from time to time.

2 Rub the skins off the peppers under cold water. Halve, remove the seeds and roughly chop the flesh.

3 Heat the oil in a saucepan and cook the onion and garlic gently for 5 minutes until soft and golden.

4 Stir in the chilli powder, cook for 2 minutes, then add the tomatoes and peppers. Bring to the boil and simmer for about 10–15 minutes until slightly thickened and reduced. Season with salt and pepper to taste.

5 Bring a pan of salted water to the boil and cook the pasta according to the instructions on the packet. Drain well and toss with the sauce. Serve piping hot with lots of freshly grated Parmesan cheese.

Stir-fried Vegetables with Pasta

This is a colourful oriental-style dish, easily prepared using pasta instead of Chinese noodles.

Serves 4

1 carrot
175g/6oz small
    courgettes
175g/6oz runner or other
    green beans
175g/6oz baby corn cobs
450g/1lb ribbon pasta
    such as tagliatelle
pinch of salt
30ml/2 tbsp corn oil, plus
    extra for tossing the
    pasta

1cm/½in piece fresh root
    ginger, peeled and
    finely chopped
2 garlic cloves, finely
    chopped
90ml/6 tbsp yellow bean
    sauce
6 spring onions, sliced
    into 2.5cm/1in lengths
30ml/2 tbsp dry sherry
5ml/1 tsp sesame seeds

1 Slice the carrot and courgettes diagonally into chunks. Slice the beans diagonally, then cut the baby corn cobs diagonally in half.

2 Cook the pasta in plenty of boiling salted water according to the instructions on the packet. Drain, then rinse under hot water. Toss in a little oil.

3 Heat 30ml/2 tbsp oil until smoking in a wok or frying pan and add the ginger and garlic. Stir-fry for 30 seconds, then add the carrots, beans and courgettes.

4 Stir-fry for 3–4 minutes then stir in the yellow bean sauce. Stir-fry for 2 minutes, add the spring onions, sherry and pasta and stir-fry for a further 1 minute until piping hot. Sprinkle with sesame seeds and serve immediately.

Tagliatelle with Gorgonzola Sauce

Gorgonzola is a creamy Italian blue cheese. You could use Danish Blue or Pipo Crème instead.

Serves 4

25g/1oz/2 tbsp butter, plus extra for tossing the pasta
225g/8oz Gorgonzola cheese
150ml/¼ pint/⅔ cup double or whipping cream
30ml/2 tbsp dry vermouth
5ml/1 tsp cornflour
30ml/1 tbsp chopped fresh sage
450g/1lb tagliatelle
salt and ground black pepper

1 Melt 25g/1oz/2 tbsp butter in a heavy saucepan (it needs to be thick-based to prevent the cheese from burning). Stir in 175g/6oz/1½ cups crumbled Gorgonzola cheese and stir over a very gentle heat for 2–3 minutes until the cheese is melted.

2 Pour in the cream, vermouth and cornflour, whisking well to amalgamate. Stir in the chopped sage, then season to taste with salt and pepper. Cook, whisking all the time, until the sauce boils and thickens. Set aside.

3 Boil the pasta in plenty of salted water according to the instructions on the packet. Drain well and toss with a little butter to coat evenly.

4 Reheat the sauce gently, whisking well. Divide the pasta among four serving bowls, top with the sauce and sprinkle over the remaining cheese. Serve immediately.

Cook's Tip
If you do not have vermouth, use a good quality dry sherry in its place.

Rigatoni with Garlic Crumbs

A hot and spicy dish – halve the quantity of chilli if you would prefer a milder flavour.

Serves 4–6

45ml/3 tbsp olive oil
2 shallots, chopped
8 rashers streaky bacon, chopped
10ml/2 tsp crushed dried chillies
400g/14oz can chopped tomatoes with herbs
6 slices white bread, crusts removed
115g/4oz/½ cup butter
2 garlic cloves, chopped
450g/1lb/4 cups rigatoni
salt and ground black pepper

1 Heat the oil in a saucepan and fry the shallots and bacon gently for 6–8 minutes until golden. Add the dried chillies and chopped tomatoes, half-cover with a lid and simmer for about 20 minutes.

2 Meanwhile, place the bread in a blender or food processor and process to fine crumbs.

3 Heat the butter in a frying pan and stir-fry the garlic and breadcrumbs until golden and crisp. (Be careful not to let the crumbs catch and burn.)

4 Bring a pan of lightly salted water to the boil and cook the pasta according to the instructions on the packet. Drain well.

5 Toss the pasta with the tomato sauce and divide among four serving bowls.

6 Sprinkle with the crumbs and serve immediately.

Cook's Tip
If you are preparing this dish for vegetarians leave out the bacon, or replace it with sliced mushrooms.

Pasta with Tomatoes and Rocket

This pretty-coloured pasta dish relies for its success on the slightly peppery taste of the rocket.

Serves 4

450g/1lb/4 cups pasta
   shells
450g/1lb ripe cherry
   tomatoes
45ml/3 tbsp olive oil

75g/3oz fresh rocket
salt and ground black
   pepper
Parmesan cheese
   shavings, to serve

1 Bring a saucepan of water to the boil and cook the pasta according to the instructions on the packet. Drain well.

2 Halve the tomatoes. Trim, wash and dry the rocket.

3 Heat the oil in a large saucepan and gently cook the tomatoes for barely 1 minute. The tomatoes should only just be heated through and not be allowed to disintegrate.

4 Add the pasta to the pan, then the rocket. (Roughly tear any rocket leaves that are over-large.) Carefully stir to mix and heat through. Season to taste with salt and pepper. Serve hot, with plenty of shaved Parmesan cheese.

Cook's Tip
Rocket is increasingly available in supermarkets. However, if you cannot find it, it is easy to grow in the garden or in a window-box.

Pasta Spirals with Pepperoni

A warming supper dish, this pepperoni and tomato sauce could be served on any type of pasta.

Serves 4

1 onion
1 red pepper
1 green pepper
30ml/2 tbsp olive oil,
   plus extra for tossing
   the pasta
800g/1¾lb canned
   chopped tomatoes
30ml/2 tbsp tomato purée

10ml/2 tsp paprika
175g/6oz pepperoni or
   chorizo
45ml/3 tbsp chopped
   fresh parsley
450g/1lb/4 cups green
   pasta spirals
salt and ground black
   pepper

1 Chop the onion. Halve and seed the peppers, removing the cores, then cut the flesh into dice.

2 Heat the oil in a saucepan and cook the onion for about 2 minutes, until beginning to colour. Stir in the peppers, tomatoes, tomato purée and paprika, bring to the boil and simmer uncovered for 15–20 minutes until the sauce is reduced and thickened.

3 Slice the sausage and stir into the sauce with about half the chopped parsley. Season to taste with salt and pepper.

4 While the sauce is simmering, cook the pasta in plenty of boiling salted water according to the instructions on the packet. Drain well. Toss the pasta with the remaining parsley in a little extra olive oil. Divide among warmed bowls and top with the sauce.

Cook's Tip
All types of sausages are suitable to include in this dish. If using raw sausages, add them with the onion and cook thoroughly.

Pasta with Tuna and Capers

Pasta shapes are tossed in a flavoursome sauce made with tuna, capers, anchovies and fresh basil.

Serves 4

400g/14oz can tuna fish
   in oil
30ml/2 tbsp olive oil
2 garlic cloves, crushed
800g/1¾ lb canned
   chopped tomatoes
6 canned anchovy fillets,
   drained
30ml/2 tbsp capers in
   vinegar, drained

30ml/2 tbsp chopped
   fresh basil
salt and ground black
   pepper
450g/1lb/4 cups
   garganelle, penne or
   rigatoni
fresh basil sprigs, to
   garnish

1 Drain the oil from the tuna into a saucepan, add the olive oil and heat gently until it stops spitting.

2 Add the garlic and fry until golden. Stir in the tomatoes and simmer for 25 minutes until thickened.

3 Flake the tuna and cut the anchovies in half. Stir into the sauce with the capers and chopped basil. Season to taste with salt and pepper.

4 Cook the pasta in plenty of boiling salted water according to the instructions on the packet. Drain well and toss with the sauce. Garnish with fresh basil sprigs.

Cook's Tip
This piquant sauce could be made without the addition of tomatoes – just heat the oil, add the other ingredients and heat through gently before tossing with the pasta.

Pasta Bows with Smoked Salmon

In Italy, pasta cooked with smoked salmon is becoming very fashionable. This is a quick and luxurious sauce.

Serves 4

6 spring onions, sliced
50g/2oz/4 tbsp butter
90ml/6 tbsp dry white
   wine or vermouth
450ml/¾ pint/1¾ cups
   double cream
pinch of freshly grated
   nutmeg
225g/8oz smoked salmon

30ml/2 tbsp chopped
   fresh dill or 15ml/
   1 tbsp dried dill
freshly squeezed lemon
   juice
450g/1lb/4 cups pasta
   bows
salt and ground black
   pepper

1 Slice the spring onions finely. Melt the butter in a saucepan and fry the spring onions for about 1 minute until they begin to soften.

2 Add the wine or vermouth and boil hard to reduce to about 30ml/2 tbsp. Stir in the cream and add salt, pepper and nutmeg to taste. Bring to the boil and simmer for about 2–3 minutes until slightly thickened.

3 Cut the smoked salmon into 2.5cm/1in squares and stir into the sauce with the dill. Taste and add a little lemon juice. Keep the sauce warm.

4 Cook the pasta in plenty of boiling salted water according to the instructions on the packet. Drain well. Toss the pasta with the sauce and serve immediately.

Cook's Tip
This dish could also be prepared with canned salmon, broken into bite-size pieces, if you prefer.

Pasta with Prawns and Feta Cheese

This dish contains a delicious combination of fresh prawns and sharp-tasting feta cheese.

Serves 4

450g/1lb/4 cups medium raw prawns	small bunch fresh chives
6 spring onions	450g/1lb/4 cups penne, garganelle or rigatoni
50g/2oz/4 tbsp butter	salt and ground black
225g/8oz feta cheese	pepper

1 Remove the heads from the prawns by twisting and pulling off. Peel the prawns and discard the shells. Chop the spring onions.

2 Melt the butter in a frying pan and cook the prawns. When they turn pink, add the spring onions and cook gently for 1 minute more.

3 Cut the feta cheese into 1cm/½in dice. Stir the dice into the prawn mixture and season to taste with pepper.

4 Cut the chives into 2.5cm/1in lengths and stir half into the prawn mixture.

5 Bring a saucepan of salted water to the boil and cook the pasta according to the instructions on the packet. Drain well, pile into a warmed serving dish and top with the sauce. Scatter with the remaining chives and serve.

Cook's Tip
Substitute goat's cheese for the feta cheese if you like; prepare the dish in the same way.

Tagliatelle with Prosciutto

This is a simple dish, prepared in minutes from the best ingredients, with a thick covering of Parmesan cheese.

Serves 4

115g/4oz prosciutto	salt and ground black
450g/1lb tagliatelle	pepper
75g/3oz/6 tbsp butter	a few fresh sage leaves, to
50g/2oz/½ cup grated Parmesan cheese	garnish

1 Cut the prosciutto into strips of the same width as the tagliatelle. Cook the pasta in plenty of boiling salted water according to the instructions on the packet.

2 Meanwhile, melt the butter gently in a saucepan and heat the prosciutto strips through, but do not fry.

3 Drain the tagliatelle well and pile into a warm serving dish. Sprinkle all the Parmesan cheese over the top.

4 Pour the buttery prosciutto over the top of the tagliatelle and Parmesan. Season well with pepper and garnish with the sage leaves.

Cook's Tip
Buy Parmesan cheese in a block and grate it yourself. The flavour is far superior to that of ready-grated Parmesan cheese.

Cannelloni al Forno

This recipe provides a lighter, healthier alternative to the usual beef-filled, béchamel-coated version.

Serves 4–6

450g/1lb boned chicken
    breast, skinned and
    cooked
225g/8oz mushrooms
2 garlic cloves, crushed
30ml/2 tbsp chopped
    fresh parsley
15ml/1 tbsp chopped
    fresh tarragon
1 egg, beaten

squeeze of lemon juice
12–18 cannelloni tubes
1 jar of passata
50g/2oz/scant ¾ cup
    freshly grated
    Parmesan cheese
salt and ground black
    pepper
fresh parsley sprig, to
    garnish

1 Preheat the oven to 200°C/400°F/Gas 6. Place the chicken in a food processor and blend until finely minced. Transfer to a bowl and set aside.

2 Place the mushrooms, garlic, parsley and tarragon in the food processor and blend until finely minced. Beat the mushroom mixture into the chicken with the egg, salt and pepper and lemon juice to taste.

3 Bring a saucepan of salted water to the boil and cook the cannelloni according to the instructions on the packet. Drain well on a clean dish towel.

4 Place the filling in a piping bag fitted with a large plain nozzle. Use this to fill each tube of cannelloni.

5 Lay the filled cannelloni tightly together in a single layer in a buttered shallow ovenproof dish. Spoon over the passata and sprinkle with Parmesan cheese. Bake in the oven for 30 minutes or until brown and bubbling. Serve garnished with a sprig of parsley.

Fettuccine all'Alfredo

A classic from Rome, this dish is simply pasta tossed with double cream, butter and freshly grated Parmesan cheese.

Serves 4

25g/1oz/2 tbsp butter
150ml/¼ pint/⅔ cup
    double cream, plus
    60ml/4 tbsp extra
450g/1lb fettuccine
pinch of freshly grated
    nutmeg

salt and ground black
    pepper
50g/2oz/scant ¾ cup
    freshly grated
    Parmesan cheese, plus
    extra to serve

1 Place the butter and 150ml/¼ pint/⅔ cup cream in a heavy saucepan, bring to the boil and simmer for 1 minute until slightly thickened.

2 Bring a saucepan of salted water to the boil and cook the fettuccine according to the instructions on the packet, but for about 2 minutes' less time. The pasta should still be a little firm or *al dente*.

3 Drain the pasta very thoroughly and turn into the pan with the cream sauce.

4 Place the pan on the heat and turn the pasta in the sauce to coat it evenly.

5 Add the remaining cream, the cheese, salt and pepper to taste and a little grated nutmeg. Toss until well coated and heated through. Serve immediately with some extra grated Parmesan cheese.

Cook's Tip
Popular additions to this recipe are fresh or frozen peas, and thin strips of ham if you are not catering for vegetarians.

Onion and Gorgonzola Pizzettes

Serves 4

1 quantity Basic Pizza
   Dough (see below)
30ml/2 tbsp garlic oil
2 small red onions
150g/5oz Gorgonzola

2 garlic cloves
10ml/2 tsp chopped fresh
   sage
pinch of black pepper

Preheat the oven to 220°C/425°F/Gas 7. Divide the dough
into eight pieces and roll out each one on a lightly floured
surface to a small oval about 5mm/¼in thick. Place well apart
on two greased baking sheets and prick with a fork. Brush the
bases well with 15ml/1 tbsp of the garlic oil. Halve, then slice
the onions into thin wedges. Scatter over the pizza bases.
Remove the rind from the Gorgonzola. Cut the cheese into
small cubes, then scatter it over the onions. Cut the garlic
lengthways into thin strips and sprinkle over, along with the
sage. Drizzle the remaining oil on top and grind over plenty
of pepper. Bake for 10–15 minutes until crisp and golden.
Serve immediately.

Basic Pizza Dough

Makes one 25–30cm/10–12in round pizza base

175g/6oz/1½ cups strong
   white flour
1.25ml/¼ tsp salt
5ml/1 tsp easy-blend
   dried yeast

120–150ml/4–5fl oz/
   ½–¾ cup lukewarm
   water
15ml/1 tbsp olive oil

Sift the flour and salt into a large mixing bowl and stir in the
yeast. Make a well in the centre; pour in the water and oil.
Mix to a soft dough. Knead the dough on a lightly floured
board for 10 minutes until smooth and elastic. Place in a
greased bowl, cover with clear film and leave to double in
size for about 1 hour. Turn out on to a lightly floured surface,
knead gently for 2–3 minutes and use as required.

Feta and Roasted Garlic Pizza

This is a pizza for garlic lovers. Mash down the cloves as
you eat – they should be soft and sweet-tasting.

Serves 4

1 garlic bulb, unpeeled
45ml/3 tbsp olive oil
1 red pepper, seeded and
   quartered
1 yellow pepper, seeded
   and quartered
2 plum tomatoes

1 quantity Basic Pizza
   Dough (see below left)
175g/6oz/1½ cups feta,
   crumbled
pinch of black pepper
15–30ml/1–2 tbsp
   chopped fresh oregano,
   to garnish

1 Preheat the oven to 220°C/425°F/Gas 7. Break the garlic
into cloves, discarding the outer papery layers. Toss in 15ml/
1 tbsp of the olive oil.

2 Place the peppers skin-side up on a baking sheet and grill,
turning them until the skins are evenly charred. Place in a
covered bowl for 10 minutes, then peel off the skins. Cut the
flesh into strips.

3 Make a slash in the skin of each tomato, then put them in a
bowl and pour over boiling water. Leave for 30 seconds, then
plunge into cold water. Peel, seed and roughly chop the flesh.
Divide the pizza dough into four pieces and roll out each one
on a lightly floured surface to an equal-sized circle of about
13cm/5in diameter.

4 Place the dough circles well apart on two greased baking
sheets, then push up the dough edges to form a thin rim
around the edges of the sheets. Brush the dough circles with
half the remaining oil and scatter over the chopped tomatoes.
Top with the peppers, crumbled feta cheese and garlic cloves.
Drizzle over the remaining oil and season to taste with
pepper. Bake in the oven for 15–20 minutes until crisp and
golden. Garnish with chopped oregano; serve immediately.

Mussel and Leek Pizzettes

Serve these subtly flavoured seafood pizzettes with a crisp green salad for a light lunch.

Serves 4
450g/1lb live mussels
120ml/4fl oz/½ cup dry
  white wine
1 quantity Basic Pizza
  Dough
15ml/1 tbsp olive oil
50g/2oz Gruyère cheese
50g/2oz mozzarella
2 small leeks
salt and ground black
  pepper

1 Preheat the oven to 220°C/425°F/Gas 7. Place the mussels in a bowl of cold water to soak, and scrub well. Remove the beards and discard any mussels that are open.

2 Place the mussels in a saucepan. Pour over the dry white wine, cover with a tight-fitting lid and cook over a high heat, shaking the pan occasionally, for 5–10 minutes until the mussels have opened.

3 Drain off the cooking liquid. Remove the mussels from their shells, discarding any that remain closed. Leave to cool.

4 Divide the dough into four pieces and roll out each one on a lightly floured surface to a 13cm/5in circle. Place well apart on two greased baking sheets, then push up the dough edges to form a thin trim. Brush the pizza bases with the oil. Grate the cheeses and sprinkle half evenly over the bases.

5 Thinly slice the leeks, then scatter over the cheese. Bake for 10 minutes, then remove from the oven.

6 Arrange the mussels on top. Season with salt and pepper and sprinkle over the remaining cheese. Bake for a further 5–10 minutes until crisp and golden. Serve immediately.

Cook's Tip
Frozen or canned mussels can also be used but will give a different flavour and texture to these pizzettes.

Wild Mushroom Pizzettes

Fresh wild mushrooms add a distinctive flavour to these pizzettes, which make an ideal starter.

Serves 4
45ml/3 tbsp olive oil
350g/12oz fresh mixed
  wild mushrooms,
  washed and sliced
2 shallots, chopped
2 garlic cloves, finely
  chopped
30ml/2 tbsp chopped
  fresh mixed thyme and
  flat leaf parsley
1 quantity Basic Pizza
  Dough
40g/1½oz/generous
  ¼ cup grated Gruyère
  cheese
30ml/2 tbsp freshly
  grated Parmesan
salt and ground black
  pepper

1 Preheat the oven to 220°C/425°F/Gas 7. Heat 30ml/2 tbsp of the oil in a frying pan and fry the mushrooms, shallots and garlic over a moderate heat, stirring occasionally, until all the juices have evaporated.

2 Stir in half the herbs and seasoning, then set aside to cool.

3 Divide the dough into four pieces and roll out each one on a lightly floured surface to a 13cm/5in circle. Place well apart on two greased baking sheets, then push up the dough edges to form a thin rim. Brush the pizza bases with the remaining oil and top with the wild mushroom mixture.

4 Mix together the Gruyère and Parmesan, then sprinkle over. Bake for 15–20 minutes until crisp and golden. Remove from the oven and scatter over the remaining herbs to serve.

Cook's Tip
If you cannot find wild mushrooms, a mixture of cultivated mushrooms, such as shiitake, oyster and chestnut, would do just as well.

Ham, Pepper and Mozzarella Pizzas

Succulent roasted peppers, salty Parma ham and creamy mozzarella make a delicious topping for these pizzas.

Serves 2

4 thick slices ciabatta bread	4 slices Parma ham, cut into thick strips
1 red pepper, roasted and peeled	75g/3oz mozzarella
	pinch of black pepper
1 yellow pepper, roasted and peeled	tiny fresh basil leaves, to garnish

1 Lightly toast the slices of ciabatta bread on both sides until they are golden.

2 Cut the roast peppers into thick strips and arrange on the toasted bread with the Parma ham.

3 Thinly slice the mozzarella and arrange on top. Grind over plenty of pepper. Place under a hot grill for 2–3 minutes until the cheese is bubbling.

4 Arrange the basil leaves on top and serve immediately.

Fruity French Bread Pizza

This recipe uses French bread as a base instead of the more usual pizza dough, for a change.

Serves 4

2 small baguettes	½ small green pepper, seeded and cut into thin strips
1 jar ready-made tomato sauce or pizza topping	
75g/3oz sliced cooked ham	75g/3oz mature Cheddar cheese
4 rings canned pineapple, drained and chopped	salt and ground black pepper

1 Preheat the oven to 200°C/400°F/Gas 6. Cut the baguettes in half lengthways and toast the outsides under a grill until crisp and golden.

2 Spread the tomato sauce or pizza topping over the toasted baguette halves.

3 Cut the ham into strips and arrange on the baguettes with the pineapple and pepper. Season with salt and pepper.

4 Grate the Cheddar and sprinkle over the top. Bake or grill for 15–20 minutes until crisp and golden. Serve immediately.

Cook's Tip
These pizzas may be grilled instead of baked in the oven. Cook them for the same length of time under a moderate heat but check that they do not burn.

Marinara Pizza

The combination of garlic, good quality olive oil and oregano gives this pizza an unmistakably Italian flavour.

Serves 2–3
60ml/4 tbsp olive oil
675g/1½ lb plum
   tomatoes, peeled,
   seeded and chopped
1 pizza base, 25–30cm/
   10–12in diameter

4 garlic cloves, cut into
   slivers
15ml/1 tbsp chopped
   fresh oregano
salt and ground black
   pepper

1 Preheat the oven to 220°C/425°F/Gas 7. In a saucepan, heat 30ml/2 tbsp of the oil. Add the tomatoes and cook, stirring frequently for about 5 minutes until soft.

2 Place the tomatoes in a metal sieve and leave them to drain for about 5 minutes.

3 Transfer the tomatoes to a food processor or blender and purée until smooth.

4 Brush the pizza base with half the remaining oil. Spoon over the tomatoes and sprinkle with garlic and oregano. Drizzle over the remaining oil and season to taste. Bake for 15–20 minutes until crisp and golden. Serve at once.

Cook's Tip
Ready-made pizza bases are available from most supermarkets and come in a range of sizes. It is useful to keep a few in the freezer.

Quattro Formaggi

Rich and cheesy, these individual pizzas are quick to make, and the aroma of melting cheese is irresistible.

Serves 4
1 quantity Basic Pizza
   Dough
15ml/1 tbsp garlic oil
½ small red onion, very
   thinly sliced
50g/2oz dolcelatte
50g/2oz mozzarella

50g/2oz/½ cup grated
   Gruyère
30ml/2 tbsp freshly
   grated Parmesan
15ml/1 tbsp chopped
   fresh thyme
pinch of black pepper

1 Preheat the oven to 220°C/425°F/Gas 7. Divide the dough into four pieces and roll out each one on a lightly floured surface into a 13cm/5in circle. Place well apart on two greased baking sheets, then push up the dough edges to make a thin rim. Brush with garlic oil and top with the red onion.

2 Cut the dolcelatte and mozzarella into dice and scatter over the bases. Mix together the Gruyère, Parmesan and thyme and sprinkle over.

3 Grind over plenty of pepper. Bake for 15–20 minutes until crisp and golden and the cheeses are bubbling. Serve hot.

Pizza with Fresh Vegetables

This pizza can be made with any vegetable combination.
Blanch or sauté before baking in the oven.

Serves 4

400g/14oz peeled plum
  tomatoes, weighed
  whole (or canned
  without their juice)
2 broccoli spears
225g/8oz fresh asparagus
2 small courgettes
75ml/5 tbsp olive oil
50g/2oz/½ cup shelled
  peas, fresh or frozen
4 spring onions, sliced

1 quantity Basic Pizza
  Dough
75g/3oz/generous ½ cup
  diced mozzarella
  cheese
10 fresh basil leaves, torn
  into pieces
2 garlic cloves, finely
  chopped
salt and ground black
  pepper

1 Preheat the oven to 240°C/475°F/Gas 9 for at least
20 minutes before baking the pizza. Strain the tomatoes
through the medium holes of a food mill placed over a bowl,
scraping in all the pulp.

2 Peel the broccoli stems and asparagus, and blanch with the
courgettes in a large saucepan of boiling unsalted water for
4–5 minutes. Drain and cut into bite-size pieces.

3 Heat 30ml/2 tbsp of the olive oil in a small saucepan. Stir
in the peas and spring onions, and cook for 5–6 minutes,
stirring frequently. Remove from the heat.

4 Roll out the pizza dough to a 25cm/10in circle and place
on a greased baking sheet. Spread the puréed tomatoes on to
the dough, leaving the rim uncovered. Add all the other
vegetables, spreading them evenly over the tomatoes.

5 Sprinkle with the mozzarella, basil, garlic, salt and pepper
and remaining olive oil. Immediately place the pizza in the
oven. Bake for about 20 minutes, or until the crust is golden
brown and the cheese has melted.

Four Seasons Pizza

The topping on this pizza is divided into four quarters, one
for each "season", creating a colourful effect.

Serves 4

450g/1lb peeled plum
  tomatoes, weighed
  whole (or canned
  without their juice)
75ml/5 tbsp olive oil
115g/4oz mushrooms,
  thinly sliced
1 garlic clove, finely
  chopped
1 quantity Basic Pizza
  Dough
350g/12oz/scant 2½ cups
  diced mozzarella

4 thin slices of ham, cut
  into 5cm/2in squares
32 black olives, stoned
  and halved
8 artichoke hearts,
  preserved in oil,
  drained and cut in
  half
5ml/1 tsp oregano leaves,
  fresh or dried
salt and ground black
  pepper

1 Preheat the oven to 240°C/475°F/Gas 9 for at least
20 minutes before baking the pizza. Strain the tomatoes
through the medium holes of a food mill placed over a bowl,
scraping in all the pulp.

2 Heat 30ml/2 tbsp of the oil in a saucepan and lightly sauté
the mushrooms. Stir in the garlic and set aside.

3 Roll out the pizza dough to a 25cm/10in circle and place
on a greased baking sheet. Spread the puréed tomatoes on the
prepared pizza dough, leaving the rim uncovered. Sprinkle
evenly with the mozzarella. Spread the mushrooms over one
quarter of the pizza.

4 Arrange the ham on another quarter, and the olives and
artichoke hearts on the two remaining quarters. Sprinkle with
oregano, salt and pepper, and the remaining olive oil.
Immediately place the pizza in the oven. Bake for about
15–20 minutes, or until the crust is golden brown and the
topping is bubbling.

Fiorentina Pizza

Spinach is the star ingredient of this pizza. A grating of nutmeg heightens its flavour.

Serves 2–3

175g/6oz/1½ cups fresh spinach
45ml/3 tbsp olive oil
1 small red onion, thinly sliced
1 pizza base, 25–30cm/ 10–12in diameter
1 jar ready-made tomato sauce or pizza topping
pinch of freshly grated nutmeg
150g/5oz mozzarella
1 egg
25g/1oz/¼ cup grated Gruyère cheese

1 Preheat the oven to 220°C/425°F/Gas 7. Remove the stalks from the spinach and wash the leaves in plenty of cold water. Drain well and pat dry with kitchen paper.

2 Heat 15ml/1 tbsp of the oil in a large frying pan and fry the onion until softened. Add the spinach and continue to fry until just wilted. Drain off any excess liquid.

3 Brush the pizza base with half the remaining oil. Spread over the tomato sauce or pizza topping, then top with the spinach mixture. Grate over some nutmeg.

4 Thinly slice the mozzarella and arrange over the spinach. Drizzle over the remaining oil. Bake for 10 minutes, then remove from the oven.

5 Make a small well in the centre of the pizza and drop the egg into the hole.

6 Sprinkle over the Gruyère and return to the oven for a further 5–10 minutes until crisp and golden.

Chilli Beef Pizza

Minced beef and red kidney beans combined with oregano, cumin and chillies give this pizza a Mexican character.

Serves 4

30ml/2 tbsp olive oil
1 red onion, finely chopped
1 garlic clove, crushed
½ red pepper, seeded and finely chopped
175g/6oz lean minced beef
2.5ml/½ tsp ground cumin
2 fresh red chillies, seeded and chopped
115g/4oz/scant ½ cup (drained weight) canned red kidney beans, rinsed
1 jar ready-made tomato sauce or pizza topping
15ml/1 tbsp chopped fresh oregano
50g/2oz/½ cup grated mozzarella
75g/3oz/¾ cup grated oak-smoked Cheddar
1 pizza base, 25-30cm/ 10-12in diameter
salt and ground black pepper

1 Preheat the oven to 220°C/425°F/Gas 7. Heat 15ml/1 tbsp of the oil in a frying pan and gently fry the onion, garlic and pepper until soft. Increase the heat, add the beef, and brown well, stirring constantly.

2 Add the cumin and chillies and continue to cook, stirring, for about 5 minutes. Add the beans and seasoning.

3 Spread the tomato sauce over the pizza base.

4 Spoon over the beef mixture, then scatter over the oregano.

Tuna, Anchovy and Caper Pizza

This pizza makes a substantial supper dish for two to three people when accompanied by a simple salad.

Serves 2–3
For the pizza dough
115g/4oz/1 cup
  self- raising flour
115g/4oz/1 cup
  self-raising wholemeal
  flour
pinch of salt
50g/2oz/4 tbsp butter,
  diced
about 150ml/¼ pint/
  ⅔ cup milk

For the topping
30ml/2 tbsp olive oil

1 jar ready-made tomato
  sauce or pizza topping
1 small red onion
200g/7oz can tuna,
  drained
15ml/1 tbsp capers
12 black olives, stoned
45ml/3 tbsp freshly
  grated Parmesan
  cheese
50g/2oz can anchovy
  fillets, drained and
  halved lengthways
ground black pepper

1 Place the flour and salt in a bowl and rub in the butter until the mixture resembles fine breadcrumbs. Add the milk and mix to a soft dough with a wooden spoon. Knead on a lightly floured surface until smooth.

2 Preheat the oven to 220°C/425°F/Gas 7. Roll out the dough on a lightly floured surface to a 25cm/10in circle. Place on a greased baking sheet and brush with 15ml/4 tbsp of the oil. Spread the tomato sauce or pizza topping evenly over the dough, leaving the edge uncovered.

3 Cut the onion into thin wedges and arrange on top. Roughly flake the tuna with a fork and scatter over the onion. Sprinkle over the capers, black olives and Parmesan cheese. Place the anchovy fillets over the top of the pizza in a criss-cross pattern. Drizzle over the remaining oil, then grind over plenty of pepper. Bake for 15–20 minutes until crisp and golden. Serve immediately.

Salmon and Avocado Pizza

Smoked and fresh salmon make a delicious pizza topping when mixed with avocado.

Serves 3–4
150g/5oz salmon fillet
120ml/4fl oz/½ cup dry
  white wine
1 pizza base, 25–30cm/
  10–12in diameter
15ml/1 tbsp olive oil
400g/14oz can chopped
  tomatoes, drained well
115g/4oz/scant 1 cup
  grated mozzarella
1 small avocado

10ml/2 tsp lemon juice
30ml/2 tbsp crème
  fraîche
75g/3oz smoked salmon,
  cut into strips
15ml/1 tbsp capers
30ml/2 tbsp snipped
  fresh chives, to
  garnish
ground black pepper

1 Preheat the oven to 220°C/425°F/Gas 7. Place the salmon fillet in a frying pan, pour over the wine and season with pepper. Bring slowly to the boil over a gentle heat, remove from the heat, cover with a tight-fitting lid and cool. (The fish will cook in the cooling liquid.) Skin and flake the salmon into small pieces, removing any bones.

2 Brush the pizza base with the oil and spread the drained tomatoes over the top. Sprinkle over 50g/2oz/scant ½ cup of mozzarella. Bake for 10 minutes, then remove from the oven.

3 Meanwhile, halve, stone and peel the avocado. Cut the flesh into small dice and toss carefully in the lemon juice.

4 Dot teaspoonfuls of the crème fraîche over the pizza base.

5 Arrange the fresh and smoked salmon, avocado, capers and remaining mozzarella on top. Season to taste with pepper. Bake for 5–10 minutes until crisp and golden.

6 Sprinkle over the chives and serve immediately.

Mushroom and Pancetta Pizzas

Use any type and combination of mushrooms you like for these simple yet tasty individual pizzas.

Serves 4

1 quantity Basic Pizza
  Dough
60ml/4 tbsp olive oil
2 garlic cloves, crushed
225g/8oz fresh mixed
  ceps and chestnut
  mushrooms, roughly
  chopped

75g/3oz pancetta,
  roughly chopped
15ml/1 tbsp chopped
  fresh oregano
45ml/3 tbsp freshly
  grated Parmesan
  cheese
salt and ground black
  pepper

1 Preheat the oven to 220°C/425°F/Gas 7. Divide the dough into four pieces and roll out each one on a lightly floured surface to a 13cm/5in circle. Place well apart on two greased baking sheets.

2 Heat 30ml/2 tbsp of the olive oil in a frying pan and fry the garlic and mushrooms gently until the mushrooms are tender and the juices have evaporated. Season to taste with salt and pepper, then cool.

3 Brush the pizza bases with 15ml/1 tbsp oil, then spoon over the mushrooms. Scatter over the pancetta and oregano. Sprinkle with Parmesan and drizzle over the remaining oil. Bake for 10–15 minutes, until crisp. Serve immediately.

Cook's Tip
Pancetta is available in larger supermarkets and Italian delicatessens. If you cannot find it, use thickly sliced fried bacon instead.

Pepperoni Pizza

Mixed peppers, mozzarella cheese and pepperoni make a delicious topping for this luxurious pizza.

Serves 4
For the sauce
30ml/2 tbsp olive oil
1 onion, finely chopped
1 garlic clove, crushed
400g/14oz can chopped
  tomatoes with herbs
15ml/1 tbsp tomato purée

For the pizza base
275g/10oz/2½ cups plain
  flour
2.5ml/½ tsp salt
5ml/1 tsp easy-blend
  dried yeast
30ml/2 tbsp olive oil

For the topping
½ each red, yellow and
  green pepper, sliced
  into rings
150g/5oz mozzarella
  cheese, sliced
75g/3oz pepperoni
  sausage, thinly sliced
8 black olives, stoned
3 sun-dried tomatoes,
  chopped
2.5ml/½ tsp dried
  oregano
olive oil, for drizzling

1 For the sauce, fry the onions and garlic in the oil until softened. Add the tomatoes and tomato purée. Boil rapidly for 5 minutes until reduced slightly. Leave to cool.

2 To make the pizza base, sift the flour and salt into a bowl. Sprinkle over the yeast and make a well in the centre. Pour in 175ml/6fl oz/¾ cup warm water and the olive oil. Mix to a soft dough. Knead the dough on a lightly floured surface for about 5–10 minutes, until smooth. Roll out to a 25cm/10in round, press up the edges slightly and place on a greased baking sheet.

3 Spread over the tomato sauce and top with the peppers, mozzarella, pepperoni, olives and tomatoes. Sprinkle over the oregano and drizzle with olive oil. Cover loosely and leave in a warm place for 30 minutes. Meanwhile, preheat the oven to 220°C/425°F/ Gas 7. Bake for 25–30 minutes then serve.

Farmhouse Pizza

This is the ultimate party pizza. Served cut into fingers, it is ideal for a large and hungry gathering.

Serves 8

90ml/6 tbsp olive oil
225g/8oz button
   mushrooms, sliced
2 quantities Basic Pizza
   Dough
1 jar ready-made tomato
   sauce or pizza topping
300g/10oz mozzarella
   cheese, thinly sliced
115g/4oz wafer thin
   smoked ham slices

6 bottled artichoke hearts
   in oil, drained and
   sliced
50g/2oz can anchovy
   fillets, drained and
   halved lengthways
10 black olives, stoned
   and halved
30ml/2 tbsp chopped
   fresh oregano
15ml/3 tbsp grated
   Parmesan cheese
ground black pepper

1 Preheat the oven to 220°C/425°F/Gas 7. In a large frying pan, heat 30ml/2 tbsp of the oil. Gently fry the mushrooms for 5 minutes until all the juices have evaporated. Remove from the heat and leave to cool.

2 Roll out the dough on a lightly floured surface to make a 30 x 25cm/12 x 10in rectangle. Transfer to a greased baking sheet, then push up the dough edges to form a thin rim. Brush with 30ml/2 tbsp of the oil.

3 Spread the tomato sauce or pizza topping over the dough, then arrange the sliced mozzarella over the sauce.

4 Scrunch up the ham and arrange on top with the artichoke hearts, mushrooms and anchovies.

5 Dot with the olives, then sprinkle over the oregano and Parmesan. Drizzle over the remaining oil and season to taste with pepper. Bake for about 25 minutes until crisp and golden. Serve immediately.

Crab and Parmesan Calzonelli

These miniature calzone owe their popularity to their impressive presentation.

Makes 10–12

1 quantity Basic Pizza
   Dough
115g/4oz mixed prepared
   crab meat, defrosted if
   frozen
15ml/1 tbsp double cream
30ml/2 tbsp freshly
   grated Parmesan

30ml/2 tbsp chopped
   fresh parsley
1 garlic clove, crushed
salt and ground black
   pepper
fresh parsley sprigs, to
   garnish

1 Preheat the oven to 200°C/400°F/Gas 6. Roll out the pizza dough on a lightly floured surface to 3mm/⅛ in thick. Using a 7.5cm/3in plain round pastry cutter, stamp out ten to twelve circles of dough.

2 In a bowl, mix together the crab meat, cream, Parmesan, parsley and garlic, and season to taste with salt and pepper.

3 Spoon a little of the filling on to one half of each circle. Dampen the edges of the dough with water and fold over to enclose the filling.

4 Seal the edges by pressing with a fork. Place well apart on two greased baking sheets. Bake for 10–15 minutes until golden. Garnish with parsley sprigs.

Cook's Tip
If you prefer, use prawns instead of crab meat. If frozen, make sure they are fully thawed first.

Ham and Mozzarella Calzone

A calzone is a kind of "inside-out" pizza – the dough is on the outside and the filling on the inside.

Serves 2

1 quantity Basic Pizza
  Dough
115g/4oz/½ cup ricotta
  cheese
30ml/2 tbsp freshly
  grated Parmesan
1 egg yolk
30ml/2 tbsp chopped
  fresh basil

75g/3oz cooked ham,
  finely chopped
75g/3oz mozzarella, cut
  into small dice
olive oil, for brushing
salt and ground black
  pepper

1 Preheat the oven to 220°C/425°F/Gas 7. Divide the dough in half and roll out each piece on a lightly floured surface to an 18cm/7in circle.

2 In a bowl, mix together the ricotta and Parmesan cheeses, egg yolk, basil and seasoning.

3 Spread the mixture over half of each circle, leaving a 2.5cm/1in border, then scatter the ham and mozzarella on top. Dampen the edges with water, then fold over the other half of dough to enclose the filling.

4 Press the edges firmly together to seal. Place on two greased baking sheets. Brush with oil and make a small hole in the top of each to allow the steam to escape. Bake for 15–20 minutes until golden. Serve immediately.

Cook's Tip
For a vegetarian version, replace the ham with fried mushrooms or chopped cooked spinach.

Aubergine and Shallot Calzone

Aubergines, shallots and sun-dried tomatoes make an unusual filling for calzone.

Serves 2

45ml/3 tbsp olive oil
3 shallots, chopped
4 baby aubergines
1 garlic clove, chopped
50g/2oz (drained weight)
  sun-dried tomatoes in
  oil, chopped
1.5ml/¼ tsp dried red
  chilli flakes
10ml/2 tsp chopped fresh
  thyme

1 quantity Basic Pizza
  Dough
75g/3oz/generous ½ cup
  dried mozzarella
salt and ground black
  pepper
15–30ml/1–2 tbsp
  freshly grated
  Parmesan cheese, to
  serve

1 Preheat the oven to 220°C/425°F/Gas 7. Trim the baby aubergines, then cut into small dice.

2 Fry the shallots in some oil until soft. Add the aubergines, garlic, sun-dried tomatoes, red chilli flakes, thyme and season to taste. Cook for 4–5 minutes, stirring frequently, until the aubergine is beginning to soften.

3 Divide the dough in half and roll out each piece on a lightly floured surface to an 18cm/7in circle. Spread the aubergine mixture over half of each circle, leaving a 2.5cm/1in border, then scatter the mozzarella over.

4 Dampen the edges with water, then fold the other half of dough over to enclose the filling. Press the edges firmly together to seal. Place on two greased baking sheets.

5 Brush with half the remaining oil and make a small hole in the top of each to allow the steam to escape. Bake for about 15–20 minutes until golden. Remove from the oven and brush with the remaining oil. Sprinkle over the Parmesan and serve the calzone immediately.

Root Vegetable Couscous

Harissa is a very fiery Tunisian chilli sauce which can be bought ready-made from Middle-Eastern shops.

Serves 4

350g/12oz/2¼ cups
  couscous
45ml/3 tbsp olive oil
4 baby onions, halved
675g/1½lb fresh mixed
  root vegetables such as
  carrots, swede, turnip,
  celeriac and sweet
  potatoes, cubed
2 garlic cloves, crushed
pinch of saffron strands
2.5ml/½ tsp each ground
  cinnamon and ginger
2.5ml/½ tsp ground
  turmeric
5ml/1 tsp each ground
  cumin and coriander
15ml/1 tbsp tomato purée
450ml/¾ pint/1¾cups
  hot vegetable stock

1 small fennel bulb,
  quartered
115g/4oz/1 cup cooked or
  canned chick-peas
50g/2oz/½ cup seedless
  raisins
30ml/2 tbsp chopped
  fresh coriander
30ml/2 tbsp chopped
  fresh flat leaf parsley
salt and ground black
  pepper

For the spiced sauce

15ml/1 tbsp olive oil
15ml/1 tbsp lemon juice
15ml/1 tbsp chopped
  fresh coriander
2.5–5ml/½–1 tsp
  harissa

1 Put the couscous in a bowl, cover with hot water; drain. Gently fry the onions for 3 minutes, then add the root vegetables and fry for 5 minutes. Add the garlic and spices and cook for 1 minute, stirring. Transfer the vegetable mixture to a large deep saucepan. Stir in the tomato purée, stock, fennel, chick-peas, raisins, chopped coriander and flat leaf parsley. Bring to the boil. Put the couscous into a muslin-lined steamer and place this over the vegetable mixture. Cover and simmer for 20 minutes, or until the vegetables are tender.

2 To make the sauce, mix all the ingredients into 250ml/8fl oz/1 cup of the vegetable liquid. Spoon the couscous on to a plate and pile the vegetables on top. Serve at once, handing round the sauce separately.

Risotto with Mushrooms

The addition of wild mushrooms gives a lovely woodland flavour to this risotto.

Serves 3–4

25g/1oz dried wild
  mushrooms, preferably
  porcini
175g/6oz fresh cultivated
  mushrooms
juice of ½ lemon
75g/3oz/6 tbsp butter
30ml/2 tbsp finely
  chopped fresh parsley
900ml/1½ pints/3¾cups
  meat or chicken stock,
  preferably home-made
30ml/2 tbsp olive oil

1 small onion, finely
  chopped
275g/10oz/1½ cups
  medium grain risotto
  rice, such as arborio
120ml/4fl oz/½ cup dry
  white wine
salt and ground black
  pepper
45ml/3 tbsp freshly
  grated Parmesan
  cheese

1 Place the dried mushrooms in a small bowl with about 350ml/12fl oz/1½ cups warm water. Leave to soak for at least 40 minutes. Rinse the mushrooms. Filter the soaking water through a strainer lined with kitchen paper, and reserve. Place in a pan with the stock; simmer until needed.

2 Slice the mushrooms. Toss with the lemon juice. Melt a third of the butter in a large frying pan. Stir in the mushrooms and cook until they begin to brown. Stir in the parsley, cook for 30 seconds more, and remove to a side dish.

3 Heat another third of the butter with the olive oil in the mushroom pan. Cook the onion until golden. Add the rice and stir for 1–2 minutes. Add all the mushrooms. Pour in the wine, cook until it evaporates. Add the stock until it evaporates; cook the rice until al dente, about 20–35 minutes.

4 Remove the risotto pan from the heat. Stir in the remaining butter and the Parmesan. Grind in a little pepper, and taste again for salt; adjust if necessary. Allow the risotto to rest for 3–4 minutes before serving.

Tomato Risotto

Use plum tomatoes in this dish, if possible, for their fresh vibrant flavour and meaty texture.

Serves 4

675g/1½lb firm ripe
   tomatoes
50g/2oz/4 tbsp butter
1 onion, finely chopped
1.2 litres/2 pints/5 cups
   vegetable stock
275g/10oz/1¼ cups
   arborio rice
400g/14oz can cannellini
   beans

50g/2oz/½ cup finely
   grated Parmesan
   cheese
salt and ground black
   pepper
10 – 12 fresh basil leaves,
   shredded, and freshly
   grated Parmesan
   cheese, to serve

1 Halve the tomatoes and scoop out the seeds into a sieve placed over a bowl. Press the seeds with a spoon to extract all the juice. Set aside.

2 Grill the tomatoes skin-side up until the skins are evenly blackened and blistered. Rub off the skins and dice the flesh.

3 Melt the butter in a large frying pan and cook the onion for 5 minutes until beginning to soften. Add the tomatoes, the reserved juice and seasoning, then cook, stirring occasionally, for about 10 minutes. Meanwhile, bring the vegetable stock to the boil in another pan.

4 Add the rice to the tomatoes and stir to coat, then add a ladleful of the stock and stir gently until absorbed. Repeat, adding a ladleful of stock at a time, until all the stock is absorbed and the rice is tender and creamy.

5 Stir in the cannellini beans and grated Parmesan and heat through for a few minutes. Just before serving the risotto, sprinkle each portion with shredded basil leaves and shavings of Parmesan.

Grilled Polenta with Peppers

Grilled slices of herby polenta are topped with yellow and red pepper strips for a delicious, colourful dish.

Serves 4

115g/4oz/scant 1 cup
   polenta
25g/1oz/2 tbsp butter
15 – 30ml/1 – 2 tbsp
   mixed chopped herbs
   such as parsley, thyme
   and sage
melted butter, for
   brushing
60ml/4 tbsp olive oil
1 – 2 garlic cloves, cut
   into slivers

2 roasted red peppers,
   peeled and cut into
   strips
2 roasted yellow peppers,
   peeled and cut into
   strips
15ml/1 tbsp balsamic
   vinegar
salt and ground black
   pepper
fresh herb sprigs, to
   garnish

1 Bring 600ml/1 pint/2½ cups salted water to the boil in a heavy saucepan. Trickle in the polenta, beating continuously, then cook gently for 15–20 minutes, stirring occasionally, until the mixture is no longer grainy and comes away from the sides of the pan.

2 Remove the pan from the heat and beat in the butter, herbs and plenty of pepper.

3 Pour the polenta into a small pudding basin, smooth the surface and leave until cold and firm.

4 Turn out the polenta on to a board and cut into thick slices. Brush the polenta slices with melted butter and grill each side for about 4–5 minutes, until golden brown.

5 Meanwhile, heat the olive oil in a frying pan, add the garlic and peppers and stir-fry for 1–2 minutes. Stir in the balsamic vinegar and seasoning.

6 Spoon the pepper mixture over the polenta slices and garnish with fresh herb sprigs. Serve hot.

Okra Fried Rice

This spicy rich dish is given a creamy consistency by the natural juices of the sliced okra.

Serves 3–4

30ml/2 tbsp vegetable oil
15g/½oz/1 tbsp butter or margarine
1 garlic clove, crushed
½ red onion, finely chopped
115g/4oz okra, topped and tailed
30ml/2 tbsp diced green and red peppers
2.5ml/½ tsp dried thyme
2 green chillies, finely chopped
2.5ml/½ tsp five-spice powder
1 vegetable stock cube
30ml/2 tbsp soy sauce
15ml/1 tbsp chopped fresh coriander
225g/8oz/2½ cups cooked rice
salt and ground black pepper
fresh coriander sprigs, to garnish

1 Heat the oil and butter or margarine in a frying pan or wok and cook the garlic and onion over a moderate heat for 5 minutes until soft.

2 Thinly slice the okra, add to the pan or wok and sauté gently for 6–7 minutes.

3 Add the green and red peppers, thyme, chillies and five-spice powder and cook for 3 minutes, then crumble in the stock cube.

4 Add the soy sauce, coriander and rice and heat through, stirring well. Season to taste with salt and pepper. Serve hot, garnished with coriander sprigs.

Cook's Tip
Reduce the amount of chopped green chilli you include in this dish, if you wish.

Asparagus and Cheese Risotto

Arborio rice is *the* risotto rice and gives this authentic Italian dish a unique creamy texture.

Serves 4

1.5ml/¼ tsp saffron strands
750ml/1¼ pints/3⅓ cups hot chicken stock
25g/1oz/2 tbsp butter
30ml/2 tbsp olive oil
1 large onion, finely chopped
2 garlic cloves, finely chopped
225g/8oz/1¼ cups arborio rice
300ml/½ pint/1¼ cups dry white wine
225g/8oz asparagus tips (or asparagus cut into 5cm/2in lengths), cooked
75g/3oz/1 cup finely grated Parmesan cheese
salt and ground black pepper
fresh Parmesan cheese shavings and fresh basil sprigs, to garnish
ciabatta bread rolls and green salad, to serve

1 Sprinkle the saffron over the stock and leave to infuse for 5 minutes. Heat the butter and oil in a frying pan and fry the onion and garlic for about 6 minutes until softened.

2 Add the rice and stir-fry for 1–2 minutes to coat the grains with the butter and oil. Pour on 300ml/½ pint/1¼ cups of the stock and saffron. Cook gently, stirring frequently, until it is absorbed. Repeat with another 300ml/½ pint/1¼ cups stock. When that is absorbed, add the wine and carry on cooking and stirring until the rice has a creamy consistency.

3 Add the asparagus and remaining stock, and stir until the liquid is absorbed and the rice is tender. Stir in the Parmesan cheese and season to taste with salt and pepper.

4 Spoon the risotto on to warmed plates and garnish with the Parmesan cheese shavings and fresh basil. Serve with hot ciabatta rolls and a crisp green salad, if you wish.

Louisiana Rice

Minced pork and chicken livers with mixed vegetables make a tasty dish that is a meal in itself.

Serves 4

60ml/4 tbsp vegetable oil	5ml/1 tsp dried thyme
1 small aubergine, diced	2.5ml/½ tsp dried
225g/8oz minced pork	oregano
1 green pepper, seeded	475ml/16fl oz/2 cups
and chopped	chicken stock
2 celery sticks, chopped	225g/8oz chicken livers,
1 onion, chopped	minced
1 garlic clove, crushed	150g/5oz/¼ cup long
5ml/1 tsp cayenne pepper	grain rice
5ml/1 tsp paprika	1 bay leaf
5ml/1 tsp ground black	45ml/3 tbsp chopped
pepper	fresh parsley
2.5ml/½ tsp salt	celery leaves, to garnish

1 Heat the oil in a frying pan until really hot, then stir-fry the aubergine for about 5 minutes. Add the pork and cook for about 6–8 minutes, until browned, using a wooden spoon to break up any lumps.

2 Add the pepper, celery, onion, garlic, cayenne pepper, paprika, pepper, salt, thyme and oregano. Cover and cook over a high heat for 5–6 minutes, stirring frequently from the bottom to scrape up and distribute the crispy bits of pork.

3 Pour on the chicken stock and stir to clean the bottom of the pan. Cover and cook for 6 minutes over a moderate heat. Stir in the chicken livers, cook for a further 2 minutes, then stir in the rice and add the bay leaf.

4 Reduce the heat, cover and simmer for about 6–7 minutes more. Turn off the heat and leave to stand for a further 10–15 minutes until the rice is tender. Remove the bay leaf and stir in the chopped parsley. Serve the rice hot, garnished with the celery leaves.

Indian Pilau Rice

Basmati rice is the most popular choice for Indian dishes, but you could use long grain rice instead.

Serves 4

225g/8oz/1¼ cups	1.5ml/¼ tsp salt
basmati rice, rinsed	2 whole cloves
well	4 cardamom pods, lightly
1 small onion, finely	crushed
chopped	5 black peppercorns
1 garlic clove, crushed	450ml/¾ pint/1¾ cups
30ml/2 tbsp vegetable oil	chicken stock
5ml/1 tsp fennel seeds	15ml/1 tbsp ground
15ml/1 tbsp sesame seeds	almonds
2.5ml/½ tsp ground	fresh coriander sprigs,
turmeric	to garnish
5ml/1 tsp ground cumin	

1 Soak the rice in water for 30 minutes. Heat the oil in a saucepan, add the onions and garlic, then fry them gently for 5–6 minutes, until softened.

2 Stir in the fennel and sesame seeds, the turmeric, cumin, salt, cloves, cardamom pods and peppercorns and fry for about 1 minute. Drain the rice well, add to the pan and stir-fry for a further 3 minutes.

3 Pour on the chicken stock. Bring to the boil, then cover with a tight-fitting lid, reduce the heat to very low and then simmer gently for 20 minutes, without removing the lid, until all the liquid has been absorbed.

4 Remove from the heat and leave to stand for 2–3 minutes. Fluff up the rice with a fork and stir in the ground almonds. Garnish with coriander sprigs.

Cook's Tip
Soak the rice for 30 minutes in cold water before cooking, if you have time.

Chinese Special Fried Rice

This staple of Chinese cuisine consists of a mixture of chicken, shrimps and vegetables with fried rice.

Serves 4

175g/6oz/1 cup long grain white rice
45ml/3 tbsp groundnut oil
1 garlic clove, crushed
4 spring onions, finely chopped
115g/4oz/1 cup diced cooked chicken
115g/4oz/1 cup peeled, cooked shrimps
50g/2oz/½ cup frozen peas

1 egg, beaten with a pinch of salt
50g/2oz lettuce, finely shredded
30ml/2 tbsp light soy sauce
pinch of caster sugar
salt and ground black pepper
15ml/1 tbsp chopped, roasted cashew nuts, to garnish

1 Rinse the rice in two to three changes of warm water to wash away some of the starch. Drain well.

2 Put the rice in a saucepan and add 15ml/1 tbsp of the oil and 350ml/12fl oz/1½ cups water. Cover and bring to the boil, stir once, then cover and simmer for 12–15 minutes, until nearly all the water has been absorbed. Turn off the heat and leave, covered, to stand for 10 minutes. Fluff up with a fork and leave to cool.

3 Heat the remaining oil in a wok or frying pan and stir-fry the garlic and spring onions for 30 seconds.

4 Add the chicken, shrimps and peas and stir-fry for about 1–2 minutes, then add the cooked rice and stir-fry for a further 2 minutes. Pour in the egg and stir-fry until just set. Stir in the lettuce, soy sauce, sugar and seasoning.

5 Transfer to a warmed serving bowl, sprinkle with the chopped cashew nuts and serve immediately.

Lemony Bulgur Wheat Salad

This Middle-Eastern salad, called *tabbouleh*, is delicious as an accompaniment to grilled meats or fish, or on its own.

Serves 4

225g/8oz/1½ cups bulgur wheat
4 spring onions, finely chopped
75ml/5 tbsp each chopped fresh mint and parsley
15ml/1 tbsp chopped fresh coriander

2 tomatoes, skinned and chopped
juice of 1 lemon
75ml/5 tbsp olive oil
salt and ground black pepper
fresh mint sprigs, to garnish

1 Place the bulgur wheat in a bowl, pour on enough boiling water to cover and leave to soak for 20 minutes.

2 After soaking, place the bulgur wheat in a large sieve and drain thoroughly. Transfer to a bowl.

3 Stir in the spring onions, herbs, tomatoes, lemon juice, olive oil and seasoning. Mix well and chill in the fridge for about an hour. Garnish with mint.

Cook's Tip

Add some stoned, halved black olives to the salad just before serving, if you wish.

Tanzanian Vegetable Rice

Serve this tasty rice with baked chicken, or a fish dish and a delicious fresh relish – *kachumbali.*

Serves 4

350g/12oz/2 cups basmati rice	2 garlic cloves, crushed
45ml/3 tbsp vegetable oil	115g/4oz/1 cup sweetcorn
1 onion, chopped	½ fresh red or green pepper, chopped
750ml/1¼ pints/3 cups vegetable stock or water	1 large carrot, grated

1 Wash the rice in a sieve under cold water, then leave to drain for about 15 minutes.

2 Heat the oil in a large saucepan and fry the onion for a few minutes over a moderate heat until just soft.

3 Add the rice and stir-fry for about 10 minutes, taking care to keep stirring all the time so that the rice doesn't stick to the base of the pan.

4 Add the stock or water and the garlic and stir well. Bring to the boil and cook over a high heat for 5 minutes, then reduce the heat, cover with a tight-fitting lid and cook the rice for 20 minutes.

5 Scatter the corn over the rice, then spread the pepper on top and lastly sprinkle over the grated carrot.

6 Cover tightly and steam over a low heat until the rice is cooked, then mix together with a fork and serve immediately.

Rice with Seeds and Spices

A change from plain boiled rice, this spicy dish makes a colourful accompaniment for curries or grilled meats.

Serves 4

5ml/1 tsp sunflower oil	400ml/14fl oz/1⅔cups stock
2.5ml/½ tsp ground turmeric	120ml/4fl oz/½ cup natural yogurt
6 cardamom pods, lightly crushed	15ml/1 tbsp each toasted sunflower seeds and toasted sesame seeds
5ml/1 tsp coriander seeds, lightly crushed	salt and ground black pepper
1 garlic clove, crushed	fresh coriander leaves, to garnish
200g/7oz/1 cup basmati rice	

1 Heat the oil in a non-stick frying pan and fry the spices and garlic for about 1 minute, stirring all the time.

2 Add the rice and stock, bring to the boil, then cover and simmer for 15 minutes or until just tender.

3 Stir in the yogurt and the toasted sunflower and sesame seeds. Adjust the seasoning and serve hot, garnished with coriander leaves.

Cook's Tip
Although basmati rice gives the best texture and flavour, you could substitute ordinary long grain rice if you prefer.

Lemon and Herb Risotto Cake

This unusual rice dish can be served as a main course with salad, or as a satisfying side dish.

Serves 4

1 small leek, thinly sliced
600ml/1 pint/2½ cups
    chicken stock
225g/8oz/1¼ cups
    arborio rice
finely grated rind of
    1 lemon
30ml/2 tbsp chopped
    fresh chives

30ml/2 tbsp chopped
    fresh parsley
75g/3oz/generous ½ cup
    grated mozzarella
    cheese
salt and ground black
    pepper
fresh parsley and lemon
    wedges, to garnish

1 Preheat the oven to 200°C/400°F/Gas 6. Lightly oil a 22cm/8½in round loose-bottomed cake tin.

2 Cook the leek in a large saucepan with 45ml/3 tbsp stock, stirring over a moderate heat, to soften. Add the rice and the remaining stock.

3 Bring to the boil. Cover the pan with a tight-fitting lid and simmer gently, stirring occasionally, for about 20 minutes, or until all the liquid is absorbed.

4 Stir in the lemon rind, herbs, cheese and seasoning. Spoon into the tin, cover with foil and bake for 30–35 minutes or until lightly browned. Turn out and serve in slices, garnished with parsley and lemon wedges.

Cook's Tip
This risotto cake is equally delicious served cold, so makes ideal picnic food.

Bulgur and Lentil Pilaff

Bulgur wheat is very easy to cook and can be used in almost any way you would normally use rice, hot or cold.

Serves 4

5ml/1 tsp olive oil
1 large onion, thinly
    sliced
2 garlic cloves, crushed
5ml/1 tsp ground
    coriander
5ml/1 tsp ground cumin
5ml/1 tsp ground
    turmeric
2.5ml/½ tsp ground
    allspice

225g/8oz/1¼ cups bulgur
    wheat
about 750ml/1¼ pints/
    3⅓ cups stock or water
115g/4oz button
    mushrooms, sliced
115g/4oz/⅔ cup green
    lentils
salt, ground black pepper
    and cayenne pepper

1 Heat the oil in a non-stick saucepan and fry the onion, garlic and spices for 1 minute, stirring.

2 Stir in the bulgur wheat and cook, stirring, for about 2 minutes, until lightly browned. Add the stock or water, mushrooms and lentils.

3 Simmer over a very gentle heat for about 25–30 minutes, until the bulgur wheat and lentils are tender and all the liquid is absorbed. Add more stock or water, if necessary.

4 Season well with salt, black pepper and cayenne pepper and serve hot.

Cook's Tip
Green lentils can be cooked without presoaking, as they cook quite quickly and keep their shape. However, if you have time, soaking them first will shorten the cooking time slightly.

Minted Couscous Castles

Couscous, flavoured with mint and then moulded, makes an unusual accompaniment to a meal.

Serves 6

225g/8oz/1¼ cups couscous
475ml/16fl oz/2 cups boiling stock
15ml/1 tbsp freshly squeezed lemon juice
2 tomatoes, diced
30ml/2 tbsp chopped fresh mint
oil, for brushing
salt and ground black pepper
fresh mint sprigs, to garnish

1 Place the couscous in a bowl and pour over the boiling stock. Cover the bowl and leave to stand for 30 minutes, until all the stock is absorbed and the grains are tender.

2 Stir in the lemon juice with the tomatoes and chopped mint. Adjust the seasoning with salt and pepper.

3 Brush the insides of four cups or individual moulds with oil. Spoon in the couscous mixture and pack down firmly. Chill in the fridge for several hours.

4 Turn out and serve cold, or alternatively, cover and heat gently in a low oven or microwave, then turn out and serve hot, garnished with mint.

Cook's Tip
Most couscous is sold ready-cooked so can be prepared as above. However, some types require steaming first, so check the instructions on the packet.

Creole Jambalaya

This version of jambalaya is made with chicken instead of the more traditional ham.

Serves 6

4 chicken thighs, boned, skinned and diced
about 300ml/½ pint/ 1¼ cups chicken stock
1 large green pepper, seeded and sliced
3 celery sticks, sliced
4 spring onions, sliced
400g/14oz can tomatoes
5ml/1 tsp ground cumin
5ml/1 tsp ground allspice
2.5ml/½ tsp cayenne pepper
5ml/1 tsp dried thyme
300g/10oz/1½ cups long grain rice
200g/7oz/scant 2 cups peeled, cooked prawns
salt and ground black pepper

1 Fry the chicken in a non-stick saucepan without fat, turning occasionally, until golden brown.

2 Add 15ml/1 tbsp stock with the pepper, celery and onions. Cook for a few minutes to soften, then add the tomatoes, spices and thyme.

3 Stir in the rice and remaining stock. Cover closely and cook for about 20 minutes, stirring occasionally, until the rice is tender. Add more stock if necessary.

4 Add the peeled prawns and heat well. Season to taste and serve with a crisp salad, if you wish.

Red Fried Rice

This vibrant rice dish owes its appeal to the bright colours of red onion, red pepper and cherry tomatoes.

Serves 2

115g/4oz/⅔ cup rice
30ml/2 tbsp groundnut oil
1 small red onion, chopped
1 red pepper, seeded and chopped

225g/8oz cherry tomatoes, halved
2 eggs, beaten
salt and ground black pepper

1 Wash the rice several times under cold running water. Drain well. Bring a large saucepan of water to the boil, add the rice and cook for 10–12 minutes.

2 Meanwhile, heat the oil in a wok until very hot and stir-fry the onion and red pepper for 2–3 minutes. Add the cherry tomatoes and stir-fry for a further 2 minutes.

3 Pour in the beaten eggs all at once. Cook for 30 seconds without stirring, then stir to break up the eggs as they set.

4 Drain the cooked rice thoroughly, add to the wok and toss it over the heat with the vegetable and egg mixture for 3 minutes. Season the fried rice with salt and pepper to taste.

Cook's Tip
Use basmati rice for this dish, if possible. Its slightly crunchy texture complements the softness of the egg.

Kedgeree

Popular for breakfast in Victorian times, kedgeree has its origins in *khichri*, an Indian rice and lentil dish.

Serves 4

500g/1¼lb smoked haddock
115g/4oz/scant ½ cup long grain rice
30ml/2 tbsp lemon juice
150ml/¼ pint/⅔ cup single or soured cream
pinch of freshly grated nutmeg
pinch of cayenne pepper

2 hard-boiled eggs, peeled and cut into wedges
50g/2oz/4 tbsp butter, diced
30ml/2 tbsp chopped fresh parsley
salt and ground black pepper
fresh parsley sprigs, to garnish

1 Poach the haddock, just covered by water, for about 10 minutes, until the flesh flakes easily. Lift the fish from the cooking liquid with a draining spoon, then remove any skin and bones. Flake the flesh.

2 Pour the rice into a measuring jug and note the volume, then tip out, pour the fish cooking liquid into the jug and top up with water, until it measures twice the volume of the rice.

3 Bring the fish cooking liquid to the boil, add the rice, stir, then cover with a tight-fitting lid and simmer for about 15 minutes, until the rice is tender and the liquid absorbed. While the rice is cooking, preheat the oven to 180°C/350°F/Gas 4, and butter a baking dish.

4 Remove the rice from the heat and stir in the lemon juice, cream, flaked fish, nutmeg and cayenne. Add the egg wedges to the rice mixture and stir in gently.

5 Tip the rice mixture into the baking dish, dot with butter and bake for about 25 minutes.

6 Stir the chopped parsley into the kedgeree, adjust the seasoning to taste and garnish with fresh parsley sprigs.

Nut Pilaff with Omelette Rolls

This pilaff combines a wonderful mixture of textures – soft fluffy rice with crunchy nuts and omelette rolls.

Serves 2

175g/6oz/1 cup basmati
  rice
15ml/1 tbsp sunflower oil
1 small onion, chopped
1 red pepper, finely diced
350ml/12fl oz/1½ cups
  hot vegetable stock
2 eggs

25g/1oz/¼ cup salted
  peanuts
15ml/1 tbsp soy sauce
salt and ground black
  pepper
fresh parsley sprigs, to
  garnish

1 Wash the rice several times under cold running water. Drain thoroughly. Heat half the oil in a large frying pan and fry the onion and red pepper for 2–3 minutes, then stir in the rice and stock. Bring to the boil and cook for 10 minutes until the rice is tender.

2 Meanwhile, beat the eggs lightly and season to taste with salt and pepper. Heat the remaining oil in a second large frying pan. Pour in the eggs and tilt the pan to cover the base thinly. Cook the omelette for 1 minute, then flip it over and cook the other side for 1 minute.

3 Slide the omelette on to a clean board and roll it up tightly. Cut the omelette roll into eight slices.

4 Stir the peanuts and the soy sauce into the pilaff and add pepper to taste. Turn the pilaff into a serving dish, then arrange the omelette rolls on top and garnish with the parsley. Serve at once.

Cook's Tip
Try salted cashew nuts or toasted flaked almonds in this dish for a change.

Aubergine Pilaff

This hearty dish is made with bulgur wheat, aubergine and pine nuts, subtly flavoured with fresh mint.

Serves 2

2 aubergines
60–90ml/4–6 tbsp
  sunflower oil
1 small onion, finely
  chopped
175g/6oz/1 cup bulgur
  wheat
450ml/¾ pint/1¾ cups
  vegetable stock

30ml/2 tbsp pine nuts,
  toasted
15ml/1 tbsp chopped
  fresh mint
salt and ground black
  pepper
lime and lemon wedges
  and fresh mint sprigs,
  to garnish

1 Top and tail the aubergines. Using a sharp knife, cut them into neat sticks and then into 1cm/½in dice.

2 Heat 60ml/4 tbsp of the oil in a large frying pan and sauté the onion for 1 minute.

3 Add the diced aubergine. Cook over a high heat, stirring frequently, for about 4 minutes until just tender. Add the remaining oil if needed.

4 Stir in the bulgur wheat, mixing well, then pour in the vegetable stock. Bring to the boil, then lower the heat and simmer for 10 minutes or until all the liquid has evaporated. Season with salt and pepper to taste.

5 Add the pine nuts, stir gently with a wooden spoon, then stir in the mint.

6 Spoon the pilaff on to individual plates and garnish each portion with lime and lemon wedges. Sprinkle with torn mint leaves for extra colour.

Cabbage with Bacon

In this dish, smoked bacon enhances the flavour of cabbage, making it a delicious vegetable accompaniment.

Serves 2–4

30ml/2 tbsp oil	500g/1¼ lb cabbage,
1 onion, finely chopped	shredded
115g/4oz smoked bacon,	salt and ground black
finely chopped	pepper

1 Heat the oil in a large saucepan and cook the onion and bacon for about 7 minutes, stirring occasionally.

2 Add the cabbage and season with salt and pepper. Stir for a few minutes over a moderately high heat until the cabbage begins to lose volume.

3 Continue to cook the cabbage, stirring it frequently for 8–10 minutes until tender, but still crisp. (For softer cabbage, cover the pan for part of the cooking.) Serve immediately.

Cook's Tip
This dish is equally delicious if prepared using spring greens instead of cabbage. To make a more substantial dish to serve for lunch or supper, add some chopped button mushrooms and some skinned, seeded and chopped tomatoes.

Braised Red Cabbage

Lightly spiced with a sharp, sweet flavour, this dish goes well with roast pork, duck and game dishes.

Serves 4–6

1kg/2lb red cabbage	15g/½oz/1 tbsp dark
2 onions, chopped	brown sugar
2 cooking apples, peeled,	45ml/3 tbsp red wine
cored and grated	vinegar
5ml/1 tsp freshly grated	25g/1oz/2 tbsp butter or
nutmeg	margarine, cut into
1.5ml/¼ tsp ground	dice
cloves	salt and ground black
1.5ml/¼ tsp ground	pepper
cinnamon	

1 Preheat the oven to 160°C/325°F/Gas 3. Cut away and discard the large white ribs from the outer cabbage leaves using a large sharp knife, then finely shred the cabbage.

2 Layer the shredded cabbage in a large ovenproof dish with the onions, apples, spices, sugar and seasoning. Pour over the vinegar and add the diced butter or margarine.

3 Cover the ovenproof dish and cook in the oven for about 1½ hours, stirring a couple of times, until the cabbage is very tender. Serve hot.

Cook's Tip
This recipe can be cooked in advance. Bake the cabbage for 1½ hours, then leave to cool. To complete the cooking, bake in the oven at the same temperature for about 30 minutes, stirring occasionally.

Lemony Carrots

The carrots are cooked until just tender in lemony stock which is then thickened to make a light tangy sauce.

Serves 4

600ml/1 pint/2½ cups
water
450g/1lb carrots, thinly
sliced
bouquet garni
15ml/1 tbsp freshly
squeezed lemon juice

pinch of freshly grated
nutmeg
20g/¾ oz/1½ tbsp butter
15ml/½oz/1 tbsp plain
flour
salt and ground black
pepper

1 Bring the water to the boil in a large saucepan, then add the carrots, bouquet garni, lemon juice, nutmeg and seasoning and simmer until the carrots are tender. Remove the carrots using a slotted spoon, then keep warm.

2 Boil the cooking liquid hard until it has reduced to about 300ml/½ pint/1¼ cups. Discard the bouquet garni.

3 Mash 15g/½ oz/1 tbsp of the butter and all of the flour together, then gradually whisk into the simmering reduced cooking liquid, whisking well after each addition, then simmer for about 3 minutes, until the sauce has thickened.

4 Return the carrots to the pan, heat through in the sauce, then remove from the heat. Stir in the remaining butter and serve immediately.

Ratatouille

Ratatouille may be served hot or cold, as a starter, side dish or vegetarian main course.

Serves 4

2 large aubergines,
roughly chopped
4 courgettes, roughly
chopped
150ml/¼ pint/⅔ cup
olive oil
2 onions, sliced
2 garlic cloves, chopped
1 large red pepper, seeded
and roughly chopped
2 large yellow peppers,
seeded and roughly
chopped

1 fresh rosemary sprig
1 fresh thyme sprig
5ml/1 tsp coriander
seeds, crushed
3 plum tomatoes,
skinned, seeded and
chopped
8 basil leaves, roughly
torn
salt and ground black
pepper
fresh parsley or basil
sprigs, to garnish

1 Place the aubergines in a colander, sprinkle with salt and place a plate with a weight on top to extract the bitter juices. Leave for 30 minutes.

2 Heat the olive oil in a large saucepan and gently fry the onions for about 6–7 minutes until just softened. Add the garlic and cook for a further 2 minutes.

3 Rinse, drain and pat dry the aubergines with kitchen paper. Add to the pan with the peppers, increase the heat and sauté until the peppers are just turning brown.

4 Add the herbs and coriander seeds, then cover the pan and cook gently for about 40 minutes.

5 Add the tomatoes and season to taste with salt and pepper. Cook gently for a further 10 minutes, until the vegetables are soft but not too mushy. Remove the sprigs of herbs. Stir in the torn basil leaves and check the seasoning. Leave to cool slightly and serve warm or cold, garnished with sprigs of parsley or basil.

Parsnips with Almonds

Parsnips have an affinity with most nuts, so you could use walnuts or hazelnuts instead of the almonds.

Serves 4

450g/1lb small parsnips
35g/1¼oz/scant 3 tbsp
   butter
25g/1oz/¼ cup flaked
   almonds
15g/½oz/1 tbsp soft light
   brown sugar

pinch of ground mixed
   spice
15ml/1 tbsp lemon juice
salt and ground black
   pepper
chopped fresh chervil or
   parsley, to garnish

1 Cook the parsnips in boiling salted water until almost tender. Drain well. When the parsnips are cool enough to handle, cut each in half across its width, then quarter these halves lengthways.

2 Heat the butter in a frying pan and cook the parsnips and almonds gently, stirring and turning carefully until they are lightly flecked with brown.

3 Mix together the sugar and mixed spice, sprinkle over the parsnips and stir to mix, then trickle over the lemon juice. Season to taste with salt and pepper and heat for 1 minute. Serve sprinkled with chopped fresh chervil or parsley.

Turnips with Orange

Sprinkle toasted nuts such as flaked almonds or chopped walnuts over the turnips to add contrast.

Serves 4

50g/2oz/4 tbsp butter
15ml/1 tbsp oil
1 small shallot, finely
   chopped
450g/1lb small turnips,
   quartered

300ml/½ pint/1¼ cups
   freshly squeezed
   orange juice
salt and ground black
   pepper

1 Heat the butter and oil in a saucepan and cook the shallot gently, stirring occasionally, until soft but not coloured.

2 Add the turnips to the shallot and heat. Shake the pan frequently until the turnips start to absorb the butter and oil.

3 Pour the orange juice on to the turnips, then simmer gently for about 30 minutes, until the turnips are tender and the orange juice is reduced to a buttery sauce. Season with salt and pepper, if required, and serve hot.

Red Cabbage with Pears and Nuts

A sweet and sour, spicy red cabbage dish, with the added crunch of pears and walnuts.

Serves 6

15ml/1 tbsp walnut oil
1 onion, sliced
2 whole star anise
5ml/1 tsp ground
   cinnamon
pinch of ground cloves
450g/1lb red cabbage,
   finely shredded
25g/1oz/2 tbsp dark
   brown sugar
45ml/3 tbsp red wine
   vinegar

300ml/½ pint/1¼ cup
   red wine
150ml/¼ pint/scant
   ¾ cup port
2 pears, cut into
   1cm/½in cubes
115g/4oz/½ cup raisins
salt and ground black
   pepper
115g/4oz/½ cup walnut
   halves

1 Heat the oil in a large pan. Add the onion and cook gently for about 5 minutes until softened.

2 Add the star anise, cinnamon, cloves and cabbage and cook for about 3 minutes more.

3 Stir in the sugar, vinegar, red wine and port. Cover the pan and simmer gently for 10 minutes, stirring occasionally.

4 Stir in the cubed pears and raisins and cook for a further 10 minutes or until the cabbage is tender. Season to taste. Mix in the walnut halves and serve.

Swiss Soufflé Potatoes

Baked potatoes are great for cold weather eating, and are both economical and satisfying.

Serves 4

4 baking potatoes
115g/4oz/scant 1 cup
   grated Gruyère cheese
115g/4oz/½ cup herb-
   flavoured butter

60ml/4 tbsp double cream
2 eggs, separated
salt and ground black
   pepper

1 Preheat the oven to 220°C/425°F/Gas 7. Scrub the potatoes, then prick them all over with a fork. Bake for about 1–1½ hours until tender. Remove them from the oven and reduce the temperature to 180°C/350°F/Gas 4.

2 Cut each potato in half and scoop out the flesh into a bowl. Return the potato shells to the oven to crisp them up while making the filling.

3 Mash the potato flesh using a fork then add the Gruyère, herb-flavoured butter, cream and egg yolks, and season to taste with salt and pepper. Beat well until smooth.

4 Whisk the egg whites in a separate bowl until stiff peaks form, then fold into the potato mixture.

5 Pile the mixture back into the potato shells and bake for 20–25 minutes, until risen and golden brown.

Cook's Tip
Choose a floury variety of potato for this dish for the best results.

Thai Vegetables with Noodles

This dish makes a delicious vegetarian supper on its own, or it could be served as an accompaniment.

Serves 4

225g/8oz/4 cups egg
  noodles
15ml/1 tbsp sesame oil
45ml/3 tbsp groundnut
  oil
2 garlic cloves, thinly
  sliced
2.5cm/1in piece fresh root
  ginger, finely chopped
2 fresh red chillies, seeded
  and sliced
115g/4oz/1 cup broccoli
  florets
115g/4oz baby sweetcorn

175g/6oz shiitake or
  oyster mushrooms,
  sliced
1 bunch spring onions,
  sliced
115g/4oz pak choi or
  Chinese leaves,
  shredded
115g/4oz/generous 1 cup
  beansprouts
15–30ml/1–2 tbsp dark
  soy sauce
salt and ground black
  pepper

1 Bring a saucepan of salted water to the boil and cook the egg noodles according to the instructions on the packet. Drain well and toss in the sesame oil. Set aside.

2 Heat the groundnut oil in a wok or large frying pan and stir-fry the garlic and ginger for 1 minute. Add the chillies, broccoli, baby sweetcorn and mushrooms and stir-fry for a further 2 minutes.

3 Add the spring onions, shredded pak choi or Chinese leaves and beansprouts and stir-fry for another 2 minutes.

4 Toss in the drained noodles with the soy sauce and pepper.

5 Continue to cook over a high heat, stirring, for a further 2–3 minutes, until the ingredients are well mixed and warmed through. Serve at once.

Cauliflower with Three Cheeses

The mingled flavours of three cheeses give a new twist to cauliflower cheese.

Serves 4

4 baby cauliflowers
250ml/8fl oz/1 cup single
  cream
75g/3oz dolcelatte cheese,
  diced
75g/3oz mozzarella
  cheese, diced

45ml/3 tbsp freshly
  grated Parmesan
  cheese
pinch of freshly grated
  nutmeg
ground black pepper
toasted breadcrumbs, to
  garnish

1 Cook the cauliflowers in a large saucepan of boiling salted water for 8–10 minutes, until just tender.

2 Meanwhile, put the cream into a small pan with the cheeses. Heat gently until the cheeses have melted, stirring occasionally. Season to taste with nutmeg and pepper.

3 When the cauliflowers are cooked, drain them thoroughly and place one on each of four warmed plates.

4 Spoon a little of the cheese sauce over each cauliflower and sprinkle each with a few of the toasted breadcrumbs. Serve at once.

Cook's Tip
For a more economical dish or if baby cauliflowers are not available, use one large cauliflower instead. Cut it into quarters with a large sharp knife and remove the central core.

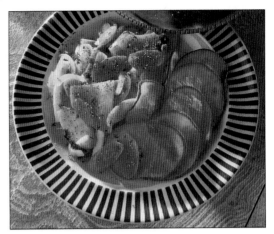

Potato Gnocchi with Sauce

These delicate potato dumplings are dressed with a tasty creamy hazelnut sauce.

Serves 4

675g/1½ lb large potatoes
115g/4oz/1 cup plain
  flour

For the hazelnut sauce
115g/4oz/½ cup
  hazelnuts, roasted
1 garlic clove, roughly
  chopped

½ tsp grated lemon rind
½ tsp lemon juice
30ml/2 tbsp sunflower oil
150g/5oz/¾ cup low-fat
  fromage blanc
salt and ground black
  pepper

1 Place 65g/2½ oz of the hazelnuts in a blender with the garlic, grated lemon rind and juice. Blend until coarsely chopped. Gradually add the oil and blend until smooth. Spoon into a bowl and mix in the fromage blanc. Season.

2 Place the potatoes in a pan of cold water. Bring to the boil and cook for 20–25 minutes. Drain well in a colander. While still warm, peel and purée the potatoes by passing them through a food mill into a bowl.

3 Add the flour a little at a time (you may not need all of the flour, as potatoes vary in texture). Stop adding flour when the mixture is smooth and slightly sticky. Add salt to taste.

4 Roll the mixture out on to a floured board to form a sausage 1cm/½in in diameter. Cut into 2cm/¾in lengths.

5 Take one piece at a time and press it on to a floured fork. Roll each piece slightly while pressing it along the prongs and off the fork. Flip on to a floured plate or tray. Continue with the rest of the mixture. Cook the gnocchi in a large pan of boiling water for about 3–4 minutes. When cooked, they will rise to the surface. Drain and serve with the hazelnut sauce.

Winter Vegetable Hot-pot

Use whatever vegetables you have to hand in this richly flavoured and substantial one-pot meal.

Serves 4

2 onions, sliced
4 carrots, sliced
1 small swede, sliced
2 parsnips, sliced
3 small turnips, sliced
½ celeriac, cut into
  matchsticks
2 leeks, thinly sliced
30ml/2 tbsp mixed
  chopped fresh herbs
  such as parsley and
  thyme

1 garlic clove, chopped
1 bay leaf, crumbled
300ml/½ pint/1¼ cups
  vegetable stock
15g/½oz/1 tbsp plain
  flour
675g/1½lb red-skinned
  potatoes, scrubbed and
  thinly sliced
50g/2oz/4 tbsp butter
salt and ground black
  pepper

1 Preheat the oven to 190°C/375°F/Gas 5. Arrange all the vegetables, except the potatoes, in layers in a large casserole with a tight-fitting lid, seasoning them lightly with salt and pepper and sprinkling them with chopped herbs, garlic and crumbled bay leaf as you go.

2 Blend the vegetable stock into the flour and pour over the vegetables. Arrange the potatoes in overlapping layers on top. Dot with butter and cover tightly.

3 Cook in the oven for 1¼ hours, or until the vegetables are tender. Remove the lid from the casserole and cook for a further 15–20 minutes until the top layer of potatoes is golden and crisp at the edges. Serve hot.

Cook's Tip
Make sure the root vegetables are cut into even-size slices so they cook uniformly.

Beans with Tomatoes

Young runner beans should not have "strings" down the sides, but older ones will. Remove them before cooking.

Serves 4

675g/1½lb/2 cups sliced runner beans	salt and ground black pepper
40g/1½oz/3 tbsp butter	chopped fresh tarragon, to garnish
4 ripe tomatoes, peeled and chopped	

1 Bring a saucepan of water to the boil, add the beans, return to the boil and cook for 3 minutes. Drain well.

2 Heat the butter in a pan, add the tomatoes and beans and season with salt and pepper. Cover the pan with a tight-fitting lid and simmer gently for about 10–15 minutes, until the beans are tender.

3 Tip the beans and tomatoes into a warm serving dish and sprinkle over the chopped tarragon to garnish. Serve hot as an accompaniment to grilled meats, poultry or fish.

Rosemary Roasties

The potatoes are roasted with their skins on, giving them far more flavour than traditional roast potatoes.

Serves 4

1kg/2lb small red potatoes	30ml/2 tbsp fresh rosemary leaves
10ml/2 tsp walnut or sunflower oil	salt and paprika

1 Preheat the oven to 240°C/475°F/Gas 9. Leave the potatoes whole with the skins on, or if large, cut in half. Place the potatoes in a large saucepan of cold water and bring to the boil, then drain immediately.

2 Return the potatoes to the saucepan and drizzle the walnut or sunflower oil over them. Shake the pan to coat the potatoes evenly in the oil.

3 Tip the potatoes into a shallow roasting tin. Sprinkle with rosemary, salt and paprika. Roast for 30 minutes or until crisp. Served hot, these potatoes are good with roast lamb.

Vegetable Ribbons

This mixed vegetable side dish looks impressive and will delight dinner party guests.

Serves 4

Using a vegetable peeler or sharp knife, cut 3 medium carrots and 3 medium courgettes into thin ribbons. Bring 120ml/4 fl oz/½ cup chicken stock to the boil, add the carrots. Return the stock to the boil; add the courgettes. Boil rapidly for 2–3 minutes, or until the vegetable ribbons are just tender. Stir in 30ml/2 tbsp chopped fresh parsley, season lightly with salt and ground black pepper, and serve hot.

Courgette and Tomato Bake

A *tian* is a heavy earthenware dish in which many French vegetable dishes are cooked. This is one example.

Serves 4
45ml/3 tbsp olive oil	10ml/2 tsp chopped fresh
1 onion, chopped	thyme
1 garlic clove, crushed	15ml/1 tbsp chopped
3 rashers lean bacon,	fresh parsley
chopped	60ml/4 tbsp grated
4 courgettes, grated	Parmesan cheese
2 tomatoes, skinned,	2 eggs, lightly beaten
seeded and chopped	15ml/1 tbsp fromage frais
115g/4oz/scant ¾ cup	salt and ground black
cooked long grain rice	pepper

1 Preheat the oven to 180°C/350°F/Gas 4. Grease a shallow ovenproof dish with a little olive oil.

2 Heat the oil in a frying pan and fry the onion and garlic for 5 minutes until softened.

3 Add the bacon and fry for 2 minutes, then stir in the courgettes and fry for a further 8 minutes, stirring from time to time and letting some of the liquid evaporate. Remove the pan from the heat.

4 Add the tomatoes, cooked rice, herbs, 30ml/2 tbsp of the Parmesan cheese, the eggs and fromage frais, and season to taste with salt and pepper. Mix together well.

5 Spoon the courgette mixture into the dish and sprinkle over the remaining Parmesan cheese. Bake for 45 minutes, until set and golden. Serve hot.

Cook's Tip
For a dinner party, divide the mixture among four lightly greased individual gratin dishes and bake for about 25 minutes until set and golden.

Spanish Green Beans with Ham

Judias verdes con jamón are green beans cooked with the Spanish raw-cured Serrano ham.

Serves 4
450g/1lb French beans	75g/3oz Serrano ham,
45ml/3 tbsp olive oil	chopped
1 onion, thinly sliced	salt and ground black
2 garlic cloves, finely	pepper
chopped	

1 Cook the beans, left whole, in boiling salted water for about 5–6 minutes, until they are just tender but still with a little bit of bite.

2 Meanwhile, heat the oil in a saucepan and fry the onions for 5 minutes, until softened and translucent. Add the garlic and ham and cook for a further 1–2 minutes.

3 Drain the beans, then add them to the pan and cook, stirring occasionally, for 2–3 minutes. Season well with salt and pepper and serve hot.

Cook's Tip
Serrano ham is increasingly available in large supermarkets and has the advantage of being cheaper than Parma ham. However, if you cannot find it, use Parma ham or bacon instead.

Sweet Potatoes with Bacon

This sweet potato dish is often served for Thanksgiving in North America to celebrate the settlers' first harvest.

Serves 4

2 large sweet potatoes
(450g/1lb each),
washed
50g/2oz/½ cup soft light
brown sugar
30ml/2 tbsp lemon juice
40g/1½ oz/3 tbsp butter

4 rashers smoked streaky
bacon, cut into thin
strips
salt and ground black
pepper
sprig of flat leaf parsley,
to garnish

1 Preheat the oven to 190°C/375°F/Gas 5 and lightly butter a shallow ovenproof dish. Cut the unpeeled sweet potatoes crossways into four and place the pieces in a pan of boiling water. Cover with a tight-fitting lid and cook until just tender, about 25 minutes.

2 Drain the potatoes and, when cool enough to handle, peel and slice quite thickly. Arrange in a single layer, overlapping, in the prepared dish.

3 Sprinkle over the sugar and lemon juice and dot with butter. Top with the bacon and season with salt and pepper.

4 Bake uncovered for 35–40 minutes, basting once or twice, until the potatoes are tender.

5 Preheat the grill to a high heat. Grill the potatoes for about 2–3 minutes, until they are browned and the bacon crispy. Serve hot, garnished with parsley.

Potatoes Baked with Tomatoes

This simple hearty dish from the south of Italy is best made with fresh tomatoes but canned plum tomatoes will do.

Serves 6

2 large red or yellow
onions, thinly sliced
900g/2¼ lb potatoes,
peeled and thinly
sliced
450g/1lb fresh tomatoes
(or canned, with their
juice), sliced
90ml/6 tbsp olive oil

115g/4oz/1 cup freshly
grated Parmesan or
mature Cheddar
cheese
salt and ground black
pepper
50ml/2fl oz/¼ cup water
a few fresh basil leaves, to
garnish (optional)

1 Preheat the oven to 180°C/350°F/Gas 4. Brush a large baking dish generously with oil.

2 Arrange a layer of onions in the dish, followed by layers of potatoes and tomatoes. Pour on a little of the oil, and sprinkle with the cheese. Season with salt and pepper.

3 Repeat until the vegetables are used up, ending with an overlapping layer of potatoes and tomatoes. Tear the basil leaves into pieces, and add them here and there among the vegetables. Sprinkle the top with cheese and a little oil.

4 Pour on the water. Bake for 1 hour, or until tender.

5 If the top begins to brown too much, place a sheet of foil or a flat baking sheet on top of the dish. Serve hot, garnished with basil leaves, if you wish.

Aubergine Baked with Cheeses

This famous dish, with its rich tomato sauce, is a speciality of Italy's southern regions.

Serves 4–6

900g/2lb aubergines	**For the tomato sauce**
flour, for coating	60ml/4 tbsp olive oil
oil, for frying	1 onion, very finely
40g/1½oz/½ cup freshly	chopped
grated Parmesan	1 garlic clove, chopped
cheese	450g/1lb fresh tomatoes,
400g/14oz mozzarella	or canned, chopped,
cheese, sliced very	with their juice
thinly	a few fresh basil leaves or
salt and ground black	parsley sprigs
pepper	

1 Cut the aubergines into 1cm/½in rounds, sprinkle with salt, and leave to drain for about 1 hour.

2 For the tomato sauce, cook the onion in the oil until translucent. Stir in the garlic and the tomatoes (if using fresh tomatoes, add 45ml/3 tbsp water). Season to taste; add the basil or parsley. Cook for 30 minutes. Purée in a food mill.

3 Pat the aubergine slices dry, coat them lightly in flour. Heat a little oil in a large non-stick frying pan. Add one layer of aubergines, and cook over low to moderate heat with the pan covered until they soften. Turn, and cook on the other side. Remove from the pan, repeat with the remaining slices.

4 Preheat the oven to 180°C/350°F/Gas 4. Grease a wide shallow baking dish or tin. Spread a little tomato sauce in the base. Cover with a layer of aubergine. Sprinkle with a few teaspoons of Parmesan, season to taste with salt and pepper, and cover with a layer of mozzarella. Spoon on some tomato sauce. Repeat until all the ingredients are used up, ending with a covering of the tomato sauce and a sprinkling of Parmesan. Sprinkle with a little olive oil, and bake for about 45 minutes, until golden and bubbling.

Stuffed Onions

These savoury onions make a good light lunch or supper. Small onions could be stuffed and served as a side dish.

Serves 6

6 large onions	pinch of freshly grated
75g/3oz/scant ½ cup	nutmeg
ham, cut into small	75g/3oz/¾ cup freshly
dice	grated cheese such as
1 egg	Parmesan or mature
50g/2oz/1 cup dried	Cheddar
breadcrumbs	90ml/6 tbsp olive oil
45ml/3 tbsp finely	salt and ground black
chopped fresh parsley	pepper
1 garlic clove, chopped	

1 Peel the onions without cutting through the bases. Cook them in a large pan of boiling water for about 20 minutes. Drain, and refresh in plenty of cold water.

2 Using a small sharp knife, cut around and scoop out each central section. Remove about half the inside (save it for soup). Lightly salt the empty cavities, and leave the onions to drain upside down.

3 Preheat the oven to 200°C/400°F/Gas 6. Beat the ham into the egg in a small bowl. Stir in the breadcrumbs, parsley, garlic, nutmeg and all but 45ml/3 tbsp of the grated cheese. Add 45ml/3 tbsp of the oil, and season with salt and pepper.

4 Pat the insides of the onions dry with kitchen paper. Stuff them using a small spoon. Arrange the onions in one layer in an oiled baking dish.

5 Sprinkle the tops with the remaining cheese and then with oil. Bake for 45 minutes, or until the onions are tender and golden on top.

Baked Fennel with Parmesan Cheese

Fennel is widely eaten in Italy, both raw and cooked. It is delicious married with the sharpness of Parmesan.

Serves 4–6
200g/2lb fennel bulbs, washed and cut in half
50g/2oz/4 tbsp butter
40g/1½oz/½ cup freshly grated Parmesan cheese

1 Cook the fennel bulbs in a large saucepan of boiling water until softened but not mushy. Drain well. Preheat the oven to 200°C/400°F/Gas 6.

2 Cut the fennel bulbs lengthways into four or six pieces. Place them in a buttered baking dish.

3 Dot with butter. Sprinkle with the grated Parmesan. Bake in the hot oven until the cheese is golden brown, about 20 minutes. Serve at once.

Cook's Tip
For a more substantial version of this dish, finely chop 75g/3oz ham and scatter it over the fennel before topping with the Parmesan cheese.

Courgettes with Sun-dried Tomatoes

Sun-dried tomatoes have a concentrated sweet flavour that goes well with courgettes.

Serves 6
10 sun-dried tomatoes, dry or preserved in oil and drained
175ml/6fl oz/¾ cup warm water
75ml/5 tbsp olive oil
1 large onion, finely sliced
2 garlic cloves, finely chopped
900g/2lb courgettes, cut into thin strips
salt and ground black pepper

1 Slice the tomatoes into thin strips. Place in a bowl with the warm water. Allow to stand for 20 minutes.

2 Heat the oil in a large frying pan or saucepan and then cook the onion over low to moderate heat until it softens but does not brown.

3 Stir in the garlic and the courgettes. Cook for about 5 minutes, continuing to stir the mixture.

4 Stir in the tomatoes and their soaking liquid. Season to taste with salt and pepper. Raise the heat slightly and cook until the courgettes are just tender. Serve hot or cold.

Broccoli Cauliflower Gratin

Broccoli and cauliflower combine well, and this dish is much lighter than a classic cauliflower cheese.

Serves 4

*1 small cauliflower
  (about 250g/9oz)
1 head broccoli (about
  250g/9oz)
120ml/4fl oz/½ cup
  natural low-fat yogurt
75g/3oz/¼ cup grated
  reduced-fat Cheddar
  cheese*

*5ml/1 tsp wholegrain
  mustard
30ml/2 tbsp wholemeal
  breadcrumbs
salt and ground black
  pepper*

1 Break the cauliflower and broccoli into florets and cook in lightly salted boiling water for 8–10 minutes, until just tender. Drain well and transfer to a flameproof dish.

2 Mix together the yogurt, grated cheese and mustard, then season the mixture with pepper and spoon over the cauliflower and broccoli.

3 Sprinkle the breadcrumbs over the top and place under a moderately hot grill until golden brown. Serve hot.

Cook's Tip
When preparing the cauliflower and broccoli, discard the tougher parts of the stalks, then break the florets into even-size pieces so they will cook evenly.

Tex-Mex Baked Potatoes with Chilli

A spicy chilli bean sauce tops baked potatoes and is served with a dollop of soured cream.

Serves 4

*2 large potatoes
15ml/1 tbsp oil
1 garlic clove, crushed
1 small onion, chopped
½ small red pepper,
  seeded and chopped
225g/8oz lean minced
  beef
½ small fresh red chilli,
  seeded and chopped
5ml/1 tsp ground cumin
pinch of cayenne pepper
200g/7oz can chopped
  tomatoes
30ml/2 tbsp tomato purée*

*2.5ml/½ tsp dried
  oregano
2.5ml/½ tsp dried
  marjoram
200g/7oz can red kidney
  beans, drained and
  rinsed
15ml/1 tbsp chopped
  fresh coriander
salt and ground black
  pepper
60ml/4 tbsp soured
  cream
chopped fresh parsley, to
  garnish*

1 Preheat the oven to 220°C/425°F/Gas 7. Rub the potatoes with a little oil and pierce with skewers. Bake them on the top shelf for 30 minutes before beginning to cook the chilli.

2 Heat the oil in a pan and fry the garlic, onion and pepper gently for 4–5 minutes, until softened.

3 Add the beef and fry until browned all over, then stir in the chilli, cumin, cayenne pepper, tomatoes, tomato purée, 60ml/4 tbsp water and the herbs. Cover with a tight-fitting lid and simmer for about 25 minutes, stirring occasionally.

4 Remove the lid, stir in the kidney beans and cook for 5 minutes. Turn off the heat and stir in the chopped fresh coriander. Season to taste and set aside.

5 Cut the baked potatoes in half and place them in serving bowls. Top with the chilli mixture and a dollop of soured cream, then garnish with chopped fresh parsley.

Bombay Spiced Potatoes

This Indian potato dish uses a delicately aromatic mixture of whole and ground spices.

Serves 4

4 large potatoes (Maris Piper or King Edward), diced
60ml/4 tbsp sunflower oil
1 garlic clove, finely chopped
10ml/2 tsp brown mustard seeds
5ml/1 tsp black onion seeds (optional)
5ml/1 tsp ground turmeric
5ml/1 tsp ground cumin
5ml/1 tsp ground coriander
5ml/1 tsp fennel seeds
salt and ground black pepper
generous squeeze of lemon juice
chopped fresh coriander and lemon wedges, to garnish

1 Bring a saucepan of salted water to the boil, add the potatoes and simmer for about 4 minutes, until just tender. Drain well.

2 Heat the oil in a large frying pan and add the garlic along with all the whole and ground spices. Stir-fry gently for 1–2 minutes, until the mustard seeds start to pop.

3 Add the potatoes and stir-fry over a moderate heat for about 5 minutes, until heated through and well coated with the spicy oil.

4 Season well and sprinkle over the lemon juice. Garnish with chopped fresh coriander and lemon wedges. Serve as an accompaniment to curries or strongly flavoured meat dishes.

Cook's Tip
Look out for black onion seeds – kalonji – in Indian or Pakistani food stores.

Spanish Chilli Potatoes

The Spanish name for this dish, *patatas bravas*, means fierce, hot potatoes. Reduce the amount of chilli if you wish.

Serves 4

900g/2lb new or salad potatoes
60ml/4 tbsp olive oil
1 onion, finely chopped
2 garlic cloves, crushed
15ml/1 tbsp tomato purée
200g/7oz can chopped tomatoes
15ml/1 tbsp red wine vinegar
2–3 small dried red chillies, seeded and chopped finely, or 5–10ml/1–2 tsp hot chilli powder
5ml/1 tsp paprika
salt and ground black pepper
fresh flat leaf parsley sprig, to garnish

1 Boil the potatoes in their skins for 10–12 minutes or until just tender. Drain them well and leave to cool, then cut in half and set aside.

2 Heat the oil in a large saucepan and fry the onions and garlic for 5–6 minutes, until just softened. Stir in the tomato purée, tomatoes, vinegar, chilli and paprika and simmer for about 5 minutes.

3 Add the potatoes and mix into the sauce mixture until well coated. Cover with a tight-fitting lid and simmer gently for about 8–10 minutes, or until the potatoes are tender. Season well and transfer to a warmed serving dish. Serve garnished with a sprig of flat leaf parsley.

Spicy Jacket Potatoes

These lightly spiced potatoes make a glorious snack, light lunch or accompaniment to a meal.

Serves 2–4

2 large baking potatoes
5ml/1 tsp sunflower oil
1 small onion, chopped
2.5cm/1in piece fresh
    ginger root, grated
5ml/1 tsp ground cumin
5ml/1 tsp ground
    coriander

2.5ml/½ tsp ground
    turmeric
generous pinch of garlic
    salt
natural yogurt and fresh
    coriander sprigs, to
    serve

1 Preheat the oven to 190°C/375°F/Gas 5. Prick the potatoes with a fork. Bake for 40 minutes, or until soft.

2 Cut the potatoes in half and scoop out the flesh. Heat the oil in a non-stick frying pan; fry the onion for a few minutes to soften. Stir in the ginger, cumin, coriander and turmeric.

3 Stir over a gentle heat for about 2 minutes, then add the potato flesh, and garlic salt to taste.

4 Cook the potato mixture for a further 2 minutes, stirring occasionally. Spoon the mixture back into the potato shells and top each with a spoonful of natural yogurt and a sprig or two of fresh coriander. Serve hot.

Two Beans Provençal

A tasty side dish, these beans would complement a simple main course of grilled meat, poultry or fish.

Serves 4

5ml/1 tsp olive oil
1 small onion, finely
    chopped
1 garlic clove, crushed
225g/8oz/scant 1 cup
    French beans

225g/8oz/scant 1 cup
    runner beans
2 tomatoes, skinned and
    chopped
salt and ground black
    pepper

1 Heat the oil in a heavy-based or non-stick frying pan and sauté the chopped onion over a moderate heat until softened but not browned.

2 Add the garlic, the French and runner beans and the tomatoes, then season well and cover tightly.

3 Cook over a fairly gentle heat, shaking the pan from time to time, for about 30 minutes, or until the beans are tender. Serve hot.

Cook's Tip
For a dry version of this dish, omit the tomatoes. Simply fry the onion and garlic until softened, boil the beans in lightly salted water until tender, then stir into the rich mixture and combine well.

Chinese Crispy Seaweed

In northern China they use a special kind of seaweed for this dish, but spring greens make a good alternative.

Serves 4

225g/8oz spring greens
groundnut or sunflower
  oil, for deep-frying
1.5ml/¼ tsp salt

10ml/2 tsp soft light
  brown sugar
30–45ml/2–3 tbsp
  toasted, flaked
  almonds

1 Cut out and discard any tough stalks from the spring greens. Place about six leaves on top of each other and roll up into a tight roll.

2 Using a sharp knife, slice across into thin shreds. Lay on a tray and leave to dry for about 2 hours.

3 Heat about 5–7.5cm/2–3in of oil in a wok or pan to 190°C/375°F. Carefully place a handful of the leaves into the oil – it will bubble and spit for the first 10 seconds and then die down. Deep fry for about 45 seconds, or until a slightly darker green – do not let the leaves burn.

4 Remove with a slotted spoon, drain on kitchen paper and transfer to a serving dish. Keep warm in the oven while frying the remainder.

5 When you have fried all the shredded leaves, sprinkle with the salt and sugar and toss lightly. Garnish with the toasted almonds.

Cook's Tip
Make sure that your deep frying pan is deep enough to allow the oil to bubble up during cooking. The pan should be less than half full.

Leek and Parsnip Purée

Vegetable purées are popular in Britain and France served with meat, chicken or fish dishes.

Serves 4

2 large leeks, sliced
3 parsnips, sliced
knob of butter
45ml/3 tbsp top of the
  milk or single
  cream
30ml/2 tbsp fromage frais

generous squeeze of
  lemon juice
salt and ground black
  pepper
large pinch of freshly
  grated nutmeg, to
  garnish

1 Steam or boil the leeks and parsnips together for about 15 minutes, until tender. Drain well, then place in a food processor or blender.

2 Add the remaining ingredients to the processor or blender. Combine them all until really smooth, then check the seasoning. Transfer to a warmed bowl and garnish with a sprinkling of nutmeg.

Middle-Eastern Vegetable Stew

This spiced dish of mixed vegetables can be served as a side dish or as a vegetarian main course.

Serves 4–6

45ml/3 tbsp vegetable or
   chicken stock
1 green pepper, seeded
   and sliced
2 courgettes, sliced
2 carrots, sliced
2 celery sticks, sliced
2 potatoes, diced
400g/14oz can chopped
   tomatoes
5ml/1 tsp chilli powder

30ml/2 tbsp chopped
   fresh mint
15ml/1 tbsp ground
   cumin
400g/14oz can
   chick-peas, drained
salt and ground black
   pepper
fresh mint sprigs,
   to garnish

1 Heat the vegetable or chicken stock in a large flameproof casserole until boiling, then add the sliced pepper, courgettes, carrot and celery. Stir over a high heat for 2–3 minutes, until the vegetables are just beginning to soften.

2 Add the potatoes, tomatoes, chilli powder, mint and cumin. Add the chick-peas and bring to the boil.

3 Reduce the heat, cover the casserole with a tight-fitting lid and simmer for 30 minutes, or until all the vegetables are tender. Season to taste with salt and pepper and serve hot, garnished with mint leaves.

Summer Vegetable Braise

Tender young vegetables are ideal for quick cooking in a minimum of liquid. Use any vegetable mixture you like.

Serves 4

175g/6oz baby carrots
175g/6oz/1½ cups sugar
   snap peas or
   mange-touts
115g/4oz baby corn cobs
90ml/6 tbsp vegetable
   stock

10ml/2 tsp lime juice
salt and ground black
   pepper
chopped fresh parsley and
   snipped fresh chives,
   to garnish

1 Place the carrots, peas and baby corn cobs in a large heavy-based saucepan with the vegetable stock and lime juice. Bring to the boil.

2 Cover the pan and reduce the heat, then simmer for about 6–8 minutes, shaking the pan occasionally, until the vegetables are just tender.

3 Season the vegetables to taste with salt and pepper, then stir in the chopped fresh parsley and snipped chives. Cook the vegetables for a few seconds more, stirring them once or twice until the herbs are well mixed, then serve at once with grilled lamb chops or roast chicken.

Cook's Tip
You can cook a winter version of this dish using seasonal root vegetables. Cut them into even slice chunks and cook for slightly longer.

Straw Potato Cake

These potatoes are so–named in France because of their resemblance to a woven straw doormat.

Serves 4

450g/1lb baking potatoes
22.5ml/1½ tbsp melted butter

15ml/1 tbsp vegetable oil
salt and ground black pepper

1 Peel the potatoes and grate them coarsely, then immediately toss them with the melted butter and season with salt and pepper.

2 Heat the oil in a large frying pan. Add the potato mixture and press down to form an even layer that covers the pan. Cook over a moderate heat for 7–10 minutes until the base is well browned.

3 Loosen the potato cake by shaking the pan or running a thin palette knife under it.

4 To turn it over, invert a large baking sheet over the frying pan and, holding it tightly against the pan, turn them both over together. Lift off the frying pan, return it to the heat and add a little more oil if it looks dry. Slide the potato cake into the frying pan and continue cooking until it is crisp and browned on the second side. Serve hot.

Cook's Tip
Make several small potato cakes instead of one large one, if you prefer. Simply adjust the cooking time.

Sautéed Wild Mushrooms

This is a quick dish to prepare and makes an ideal side dish for all kinds of grilled and roast meats.

Serves 6

900g/2lb fresh mixed wild and cultivated mushrooms such as morels, porcini, chanterelles, oyster or shiitake
30ml/2 tbsp olive oil
25g/1oz/2 tbsp unsalted butter
2 garlic cloves, chopped

3 or 4 shallots, finely chopped
45–60ml/3–4 tbsp chopped fresh parsley, or a mixture of different chopped fresh herbs
salt and ground black pepper

1 Wash and carefully dry the mushrooms. Trim the stems and cut the mushrooms into quarters, or slice if they are very large.

2 Heat the oil in a large frying pan over a moderately high heat. Add the butter and swirl to melt, then stir in the prepared mushrooms and cook for 4–5 minutes until beginning to brown.

3 Add the garlic and shallots to the pan and cook for a further 4–5 minutes until the mushrooms are tender and any liquid given off has evaporated. Season to taste with salt and pepper and stir in the parsley or mixed herbs and serve hot.

Cook's Tip
Use as many different varieties of cultivated and wild mushrooms as you can find to create a tasty and attractive dish.

Celeriac Purée

Many chefs add potato to celeriac purée, but this recipe
highlights the pure flavour of the vegetable.

Serves 4

1 large celeriac (about   *pinch of grated nutmeg*
750g/1¾ lb), peeled   *salt and ground black*
15g/½oz/1 tbsp butter   *pepper*

1 Cut the celeriac into large dice, put in a saucepan with
enough cold water to cover and add a little salt. Bring to the
boil over a moderately high heat and cook gently for about
10–15 minutes until tender.

2 Drain the celeriac, reserving a little of the cooking liquid,
and place in a food processor fitted with a metal blade or a
blender. Process until smooth, adding a little of the cooking
liquid if it needs thinning.

3 Stir in the butter and season to taste with salt, pepper and
nutmeg. Reheat, if necessary, before serving.

Creamy Spinach Purée

Crème fraîche or béchamel sauce usually gives this dish its
creamy richness. Here is a quick light alternative.

Serves 4

675g/1½lb/4½ cups leaf   *milk (if required)*
spinach, stems   *pinch of freshly grated*
removed   *nutmeg*
115g/4oz/½ cup full or   *salt and ground black*
medium-fat soft cheese   *pepper*

1 Rinse the spinach, shake lightly and place in a deep
frying pan or wok. Cook over a moderate heat for about
3–4 minutes until wilted. Drain in a colander, pressing with
the back of a spoon. The spinach does not need to be
completely dry.

2 Purée the spinach and soft cheese in a food processor
fitted with a metal blade or a blender until well blended, then
transfer to a bowl. If the purée is too thick to fall easily from a
spoon, add a little milk, spoonful by spoonful. Season to taste
with salt, pepper and nutmeg. Transfer to a heavy-based
saucepan and reheat gently before serving.

Cannellini Bean Purée

This inexpensive dip is a healthy multi-purpose option;
use low-fat fromage frais to lower its calorie content.

Serves 4

Drain 400g/14 oz can cannellini beans, rinse, drain again.
Purée in a blender or food processor with 45ml/3 tbsp
fromage blanc, grated zest, rind and juice of 1 large orange
and 15ml/1 tbsp finely chopped fresh rosemary. Set aside.
Cut 4 heads of chicory in half lengthwise and cut 2
medium radicchio into 8 wedges. Lay them on a baking
tray and brush with 15ml/1 tbsp walnut oil. Grill for 2–3
minutes. Serve with the purée; scatter over the orange rind.

New Potato and Chive Salad

The secret of a good potato salad is to mix the potatoes with the dressing while they are still hot so that they absorb it.

Serves 4– 6

675g/1½lb new potatoes
4 spring onions
45ml/3 tbsp olive oil
15ml/1 tbsp white wine
vinegar
4ml/¾ tsp Dijon mustard

175ml/6fl oz/¾ cup good
quality mayonnaise
45ml/3 tbsp snipped
fresh chives
salt and ground black
pepper

1 Cook the potatoes, unpeeled, in boiling salted water until tender. Meanwhile, finely chop the white parts of the spring onions along with a little of the green parts.

2 Whisk together the oil, vinegar and mustard. Drain the potatoes well, then immediately toss lightly with the vinegar mixture and spring onions and leave to cool. Stir the mayonnaise and chives into the potatoes and chill in the fridge until ready to serve with grilled pork, lamb chops or roast chicken.

Watercress Potato Salad Bowl

New potatoes are good hot or cold, and this colourful and nutritious salad makes the most of them.

Serves 4

450g/1lb small new
potatoes, unpeeled
1 bunch watercress
200g/7oz cherry
tomatoes, halved
30ml/2 tbsp pumpkin
seeds

45ml/3 tbsp low-fat
fromage frais
15ml/1 tbsp cider vinegar
5ml/1 tsp soft light
brown sugar
salt and paprika

1 Cook the potatoes in lightly salted boiling water until just tender, then drain and leave to cool.

2 Toss together the potatoes, watercress, tomatoes and pumpkin seeds. Place the fromage frais, vinegar, sugar, salt and paprika in a screw-top jar and shake well to mix. Pour over the salad just before serving.

Frankfurter Salad

A last minute salad you can throw together using store-cupboard ingredients.

Serves 4

Boil 700g/1½lb new potatoes in salted water for 20 minutes. Drain, cover and keep warm. Hard-boil 2 eggs for 12 minutes, shell and quarter. Score the skins of 350g/12oz frankfurters cork-screw fashion, cover with boiling water and simmer for 5 minutes. Drain, cover and keep warm. Distribute the leaves of 1 butterhead lettuce and 225g/8 oz young spinach among 4 plates, moisten the potatoes and frankfurters with dressing and scatter over the salad. Finish with the eggs, season and serve.

Salad Niçoise

Serve this rich and filling salad as a main course, simply with crusty bread.

Serves 4

90ml/6 tbsp olive oil
30ml/2 tbsp tarragon
  vinegar
5ml/1 tsp tarragon or
  Dijon mustard
1 small garlic clove,
  crushed
115g/4oz/1 cup French
  beans
12 small new potatoes
3–4 Little Gem lettuces,
  roughly chopped
200g/7oz can tuna in oil,
  drained

6 anchovy fillets, halved
  lengthways
12 black olives, stoned
4 tomatoes, chopped
4 spring onions, finely
  chopped
10ml/2 tsp capers
30ml/2 tbsp pine nuts
2 hard-boiled eggs,
  chopped
salt and ground black
  pepper
crusty bread, to serve

1 Mix the oil, vinegar, mustard, garlic and seasoning with a wooden spoon in the base of a large salad bowl.

2 Cook the French beans and potatoes in separate saucepans of boiling salted water until just tender. Drain and add to the bowl with the lettuce, tuna, anchovies, olives, tomatoes, spring onions and capers.

3 Just before serving, toast the pine nuts in a small frying pan until lightly browned.

4 Sprinkle over the salad while still hot, add the eggs and toss all the ingredients together well. Serve with chunks of hot crusty bread.

Cook's Tip
Look out for salad potatoes, such as Charlotte, Belle de Fontenay or Pink Fir Apple, to use in this recipe.

Caesar Salad

Any crisp lettuce will do in this delicious salad, which was created by Caesar Cardini in the 1920s.

Serves 4

1 large cos lettuce
4 thick slices white or
  granary bread,
  without crusts
45ml/3 tbsp olive oil
1 garlic clove, crushed

For the dressing
1 egg
1 garlic clove, chopped

30ml/2 tbsp lemon juice
dash of Worcestershire
  sauce
3 anchovy fillets, chopped
120ml/4fl oz/½ cup olive
  oil
75ml/5 tbsp grated
  Parmesan cheese
salt and ground black
  pepper

1 Preheat the oven to 220°C/425°F/Gas 7. Separate, rinse and dry the lettuce leaves. Tear the outer leaves roughly and chop the heart. Arrange the lettuce in a large salad bowl.

2 Dice the bread and mix with the olive oil and garlic in a separate bowl until the bread has soaked up the oil. Lay the bread dices on a baking sheet and place in the oven for about 6–8 minutes (keeping an eye on them) until golden. Remove and leave to cool.

3 To make the dressing, break the egg into the bowl of a food processor or blender and add the garlic, lemon juice, Worcestershire sauce and one of the anchovy fillets. Process until smooth.

4 With the motor running, pour in the olive oil in a thin stream until the dressing has the consistency of single cream. Season to taste with salt and pepper, if needed.

5 Pour the dressing over the salad leaves and toss well, then toss in the garlic croûtons, Parmesan cheese and finally the remaining anchovies and serve immediately.

Tuna and Bean Salad

This substantial salad makes a good light meal, and can be very quickly assembled from canned ingredients.

Serves 4–6

2 x 400g/14oz cans
  cannellini or borlotti
  beans
2 x 200g/7oz cans tuna
  fish, drained
60ml/4 tbsp extra virgin
  olive oil

30ml/2 tbsp lemon juice
salt and ground black
  pepper
15ml/1 tbsp chopped
  fresh parsley
3 spring onions, thinly
  sliced

1 Pour the beans into a large strainer and rinse under cold water. Drain well. Place in a serving dish.

2 Break the tuna into fairly large flakes with a fork and arrange over the beans.

3 Make the dressing by combining the oil with the lemon juice in a small bowl. Season with salt and pepper, and stir in the parsley. Mix well. Pour over the beans and tuna.

4 Sprinkle the spring onions over the salad and toss well before serving.

Cook's Tip
If you prefer a milder onion flavour, gently sauté the spring onions in a little oil until softened, but not browned, before adding them to the salad.

Grilled Pepper Salad

This colourful salad is a southern Italian creation; all the ingredients thrive in the Mediterranean sun.

Serves 6

4 large peppers, red or
  yellow or a
  combination of both
30ml/2 tbsp capers in
  salt, vinegar or brine,
  rinsed
18–20 black or green
  olives

For the dressing
90ml/6 tbsp extra virgin
  olive oil
2 garlic cloves, chopped
30ml/2 tbsp balsamic or
  wine vinegar
salt and ground black
  pepper

1 Place the peppers under a hot grill and turn occasionally until they are black and blistered on all sides. Remove from the heat and place in a paper bag. Leave for 5 minutes.

2 Peel the peppers, then cut them into quarters. Remove the stems and seeds.

3 Cut the peppers into strips, and arrange them in a serving dish. Distribute the capers and olives evenly over them.

4 To make the dressing, mix the oil and garlic together in a small bowl, crushing the garlic with a spoon to release as much flavour as possible. Mix in the vinegar, and season to taste with salt and pepper. Pour over the salad, mix well, and allow to stand for at least 30 minutes before serving.

Cook's Tip
Skinning the peppers brings out their delicious sweet flavour and is well worth the extra effort.

Chicken Liver and Tomato Salad

Warm salads are especially welcome during the autumn months when the evenings are growing shorter and cooler.

Serves 4

225g/½lb young
  spinach, stems
  removed
1 frisée lettuce
105ml/7 tbsp groundnut
  or sunflower oil
175g/6oz rindless bacon,
  cut into strips

3 slices day-old bread,
  without crusts, cut
  into short fingers
450g/1lb chicken livers
115g/4oz cherry tomatoes
salt and ground black
  pepper

1 Wash and spin the salad leaves. Place in a salad bowl. Heat 60ml/4 tbsp of the oil in a large frying pan and cook the bacon for 3–4 minutes until crisp and brown. Remove the bacon with a slotted spoon and leave to drain on a piece of kitchen paper.

2 To make the croûtons, fry the bread in the bacon-flavoured oil, tossing until crisp and golden. Drain on kitchen paper.

3 Heat the remaining 45ml/3 tbsp of oil in the frying pan and fry the chicken livers briskly for 2–3 minutes. Transfer the livers to the salad leaves, add the bacon, croûtons and tomatoes. Season with salt and pepper, toss and serve.

Cook's Tip
Although fresh chicken livers are preferable, frozen ones could be used in this salad. It is important to make sure they are completely thawed before cooking.

Maryland Salad

Chicken, sweetcorn, bacon, banana and watercress are combined here in a sensational main-course salad.

Serves 4

4 free-range chicken
  breasts, boned
225g/8oz rindless
  unsmoked bacon
4 baby sweetcorn
40g/1½oz/3 tbsp soft
  butter, softened
4 ripe bananas, peeled
  and halved
4 firm tomatoes, halved
4 escarole or butterhead
  lettuces

1 bunch watercress
  (about 115g/4oz)
salt and ground black
  pepper

For the dressing
75ml/5 tbsp groundnut
  oil
15ml/1 tbsp white wine
  vinegar
10ml/1 tsp maple syrup
10ml/2 tsp mild mustard

1 Season the chicken breasts, brush with oil and barbecue or grill for 15 minutes, turning once. Barbecue or grill the bacon for 8–10 minutes or until crisp.

2 Bring a large saucepan of salted water to the boil. Trim the baby sweetcorn or leave the husks on if you prefer. Boil for 20 minutes. For extra flavour, brush with butter and brown over the barbecue or under the grill. Barbecue or grill the bananas and tomatoes for 6–8 minutes. You can brush these with butter too if you wish.

3 To make the dressing, combine the oil, vinegar, maple syrup and mustard with 15ml/1 tbsp water in a screw-top jar and shake well.

4 Wash, spin thoroughly and dress the escarole or butterhead lettuce and the watercress.

5 Distribute the salad leaves among four large plates. Slice the chicken and arrange over the leaves with the bacon, banana, sweetcorn and tomatoes.

Leeks with Mustard Dressing

Pour the dressing over the leeks while they are still warm so that they absorb the mustardy flavours.

Serves 4
8 slim leeks (each about 13cm/5in long)
5–10ml/1–2 tsp Dijon mustard
10ml/2 tsp white wine vinegar
1 hard-boiled egg, halved lengthways
75ml/5 tbsp light olive oil
10ml/2 tsp chopped fresh parsley
salt and ground black pepper

1 Steam the leeks over a saucepan of boiling water until they are just tender.

2 Meanwhile, stir together the mustard and vinegar in a bowl. Scoop the egg yolk into the bowl and mash thoroughly into the vinegar mixture using a fork.

3 Gradually work in the oil to make a smooth sauce, then season to taste with salt and pepper.

4 Lift the leeks out of the steamer and place on several layers of kitchen paper, then cover the leeks with several more layers of kitchen paper and pat dry.

5 Transfer the leeks to a serving dish while still warm, spoon the dressing over them and leave to cool. Finely chop the egg white using a large sharp knife, then mix with the chopped fresh parsley and scatter over the leeks. Chill in the fridge until ready to serve.

Cook's Tip
Pencil-slim baby leeks are increasingly available nowadays, and are beautifully tender. Use three or four of these smaller leeks per serving.

Lettuce and Herb Salad

For a really quick salad, look out for pre-packed bags of mixed baby lettuce leaves in the supermarket.

Serves 4
½ cucumber
mixed lettuce leaves
1 bunch watercress (about 115g/4oz)
1 chicory head, sliced
45ml/3 tbsp mixed chopped fresh herbs such as parsley, thyme, tarragon, chives and chervil

For the dressing
15ml/1 tbsp white wine vinegar
5ml/1 tsp prepared mustard
75ml/5 tbsp olive oil
salt and ground black pepper

1 Peel the cucumber, if you wish, then cut it in half lengthways and scoop out the seeds. Thinly slice the flesh. Tear the lettuce leaves into bite-size pieces.

2 Toss the cucumber, lettuce, watercress, chicory and herbs together in a bowl, or arrange them in the bowl in layers, if you prefer.

3 To make the dressing, mix the vinegar and mustard together, then whisk in the oil and seasoning.

4 Stir the dressing, then pour over the salad, toss lightly to coat the salad vegetables and leaves. Serve at once.

Cook's Tip
Do not dress the salad until just before serving, otherwise the lettuce leaves will wilt.

Goat's Cheese Salad

The robust flavours of the goat's cheese and buckwheat combine especially well with figs and walnuts in this salad.

Serves 4

175g/6oz/1 cup couscous
30ml/2 tbsp toasted
    buckwheat
1 hard-boiled egg
30ml/2 tbsp chopped
    fresh parsley
60ml/4 tbsp olive oil,
    preferably Sicilian
45ml/3 tbsp walnut oil
115g/4oz rocket

½ frisée lettuce
175g/6oz crumbly white
    goat's cheese
50g/2oz/½ cup broken
    walnuts, toasted
4 ripe figs, trimmed and
    almost cut into four
    (leaving the pieces
    joined at the base)

1 Place the couscous and buckwheat in a bowl, cover with boiling water and leave to soak for 15 minutes. Place in a sieve if necessary to drain off any remaining water, then spread out on a metal tray and allow to cool.

2 Shell the hard-boiled egg and pass it through a fine grater.

3 Toss the egg, parsley and couscous in a bowl. Combine the two oils and use half to moisten the couscous mixture.

4 Wash and spin the salad leaves, dress with the remaining oil and distribute among four large plates.

5 Pile the couscous in the centre of the leaves, crumble on the goat's cheese, scatter with toasted walnuts, and add the trimmed figs.

Cook's Tip
Serve this strongly flavoured salad with a gutsy red wine from the Rhône or South of France.

Waldorf Ham Salad

Waldorf salad originally consisted of apples, celery and mayonnaise. This ham version is a meal in itself.

Serves 4

3 apples, peeled
15ml/1 tbsp lemon juice
2 slices cooked ham
    (about 175g/6oz each)
3 celery sticks
150ml/¼ pint/⅔ cup
    mayonnaise
1 escarole or Batavia
    lettuce

1 small radicchio, finely
    shredded
½ bunch watercress
45ml/3 tbsp walnut oil or
    olive oil
2oz/50g/½ cup walnut
    pieces, toasted
salt and ground black
    pepper

1 Core, slice and shred the apples finely. Moisten with lemon juice to keep them white. Cut the cooked ham into 5cm/2in strips, then cut the celery into similar-size pieces, and combine in a bowl.

2 Add the mayonnaise to the apples, ham and celery and stir to combine well.

3 Wash and spin the salad leaves. Shred the leaves finely, then toss with the walnut or olive oil. Distribute the leaves among four plates. Pile the mayonnaise mixture in the centre, scatter with toasted walnuts, season to taste with salt and pepper, and serve at once.

Baby Leaf Salad with Croûtons

Crispy ciabatta croutons give a lovely crunch to this mixed leaf and avocado salad.

Serves 4

15ml/1 tbsp olive oil
1 garlic clove, crushed
15ml/1 tbsp freshly
    grated Parmesan
    cheese
15ml/1 tbsp chopped
    fresh parsley
4 slices ciabatta bread,
    crusts removed, cut
    into small dice
1 large bunch watercress
large handful of rocket

1 bag mixed baby salad
    leaves, including oak
    leaf and cos lettuce
1 ripe avocado

For the dressing
45ml/3 tbsp olive oil
15ml/1 tbsp walnut oil
juice of ½ lemon
2.5ml/½ tsp Dijon
    mustard
salt and ground black
    pepper

1 Preheat the oven to 190°C/375°F/Gas 5. Put the oil, garlic, Parmesan, parsley and bread in a bowl and toss to coat well. Spread out the diced bread on a baking sheet and bake for about 8 minutes until crisp. Leave to cool.

2 Remove any coarse or discoloured stalks or leaves from the watercress and place in a serving bowl with the rocket and baby salad leaves.

3 Halve the avocado and remove the stone. Peel and cut into chunks, then add it to the salad bowl.

4 To make the dressing, mix together the oils, lemon juice, mustard and seasoning in a small bowl or screw-top jar until evenly blended. Pour over the salad and toss well. Sprinkle over the croûtons and serve at once.

Wild Rice with Grilled Vegetables

Grilling brings out the delicious and varied flavour of these summer vegetables.

Serves 4

225g/8oz/1¼ cups wild
    and long grain rice
    mixture
1 large aubergine, thickly
    sliced
1 red, 1 yellow and 1
    green pepper, seeded
    and cut into quarters
2 red onions, sliced
225g/8oz brown cap or
    shiitake mushrooms
2 small courgettes, cut in
    half lengthways

olive oil, for brushing
30ml/2 tbsp chopped
    fresh thyme

For the dressing
90ml/6 tbsp extra virgin
    olive oil
30ml/2 tbsp balsamic
    vinegar
2 garlic cloves, crushed
salt and ground black
    pepper

1 Put the rice mixture in a saucepan of cold salted water. Bring to the boil, reduce the heat, cover with a tight-fitting lid and cook gently for 30–40 minutes or according to the packet instructions, until all the grains are tender.

2 To make the dressing, mix together the olive oil, vinegar, garlic and seasoning in a small bowl or screw-topped jar until well blended. Set aside while you grill the vegetables.

3 Arrange the vegetables on a grill rack. Brush with olive oil and grill for 8–10 minutes, until tender and well browned, turning them occasionally and brushing again with oil.

4 Drain the rice and toss in half the dressing. Tip into a serving dish and arrange the grilled vegetables on top. Pour over the remaining dressing and scatter over the chopped fresh thyme.

Russian Salad

Russian salad became fashionable in the hotel dining rooms of Europe in the 1920s and 1930s.

Serves 4

115g/4oz large button
  mushrooms
120ml/4fl oz/½ cup
  mayonnaise
15ml/1 tbsp freshly
  squeezed lemon juice
350g/12oz peeled, cooked
  prawns
1 large dill pickle,
  finely chopped, or
  30ml/2 tbsp capers
115g/4oz broad beans
115g/4oz small new
  potatoes, scrubbed or
  scraped

115g/4oz young carrots,
  trimmed and peeled
115g/4oz baby sweetcorn
115g/4oz baby turnips,
  trimmed
15ml/1 tbsp olive oil,
  preferably French or
  Italian
4 eggs, hard-boiled and
  shelled
pinch of salt, pepper and
  paprika
25g/1oz canned
  anchovies, cut into
  fine strips, to garnish

1 Slice the mushrooms thinly, then cut into matchsticks. Combine the mayonnaise and lemon juice. Fold the mayonnaise into the mushrooms and prawns, add the dill pickle or capers, then season to taste with salt and pepper.

2 Bring a large saucepan of salted water to the boil, add the broad beans, and cook for 3 minutes. Drain and cool under running water, then pinch the beans between thumb and forefinger to release them from their tough skins. Boil the potatoes for 20 minutes and the remaining vegetables for 6 minutes. Drain and cool under running water.

3 Toss the vegetables with oil and divide among four shallow bowls. Spoon on the dressed prawns and place a hard-boiled egg in the centre. Garnish the egg with strips of anchovy and sprinkle with paprika.

Crunchy Coleslaw

Home-made coleslaw is quite quick and easy to make – and it tastes fresh, crunchy and wonderful.

Serves 4–6

¼ firm white cabbage
1 small onion, finely
  chopped
2 celery sticks, thinly
  sliced
2 carrots, coarsely grated
5–10ml/1–2 tsp
  caraway seeds
  (optional)
1 eating apple, cored and
  chopped (optional)

50g/2oz/½ cup walnuts,
  chopped (optional)
salt and ground black
  pepper

For the dressing

45ml/3 tbsp mayonnaise
30ml/2 tbsp single cream
  or natural yogurt
5ml/1 tsp grated lemon
  rind

1 Cut and discard the core from the cabbage quarter, then shred the leaves finely. Place them in a large bowl.

2 Toss the onion, celery and carrot into the cabbage, plus the caraway seeds, apple and walnuts, if using. Season well with salt and pepper.

3 Mix the dressing ingredients together in a small bowl, then stir into the vegetables. Cover the salad with clear film and allow to stand for 2 hours, stirring occasionally, then chill lightly in the fridge before serving.

Pear and Roquefort Salad

Choose ripe but firm Comice or Williams' pears for this attractive and deeply flavoursome salad.

Serves 4

3 ripe pears
lemon juice
about 175g/6oz mixed
    fresh salad leaves
175g/6oz Roquefort
    cheese
50g/2oz/½ cup hazelnuts,
    toasted and chopped

For the dressing
30ml/2 tbsp hazelnut oil
45ml/3 tbsp olive oil
15ml/1 tbsp cider vinegar
5ml/1 tsp Dijon mustard
salt and ground black
    pepper

1 To make the dressing, mix together the oils, vinegar and mustard in a bowl or screw-top jar. Season to taste with salt and pepper.

2 Peel, core and slice the pears and toss them in lemon juice.

3 Divide the salad leaves among four serving plates, then place the pears on top. Crumble the cheese and scatter over the salad along with the toasted hazelnuts. Spoon over the dressing and serve at once.

Mediterranean Mixed Pepper Salad

Serve this colourful salad either as a tasty starter or as an accompaniment to cold meats for lunch or supper.

Serves 4

2 red peppers, halved and
    seeded
2 yellow peppers, halved
    and seeded
150ml/¼ pint/⅔ cup
    olive oil

1 onion, thinly sliced
2 garlic cloves, crushed
generous squeeze of
    lemon juice
chopped fresh parsley, to
    garnish

1 Grill the pepper halves for about 5 minutes, until the skin has blistered and blackened. Pop them into a polythene bag, seal and leave for 5 minutes.

2 Meanwhile, heat 30ml/2 tbsp of the olive oil in a frying pan and fry the onion for about 5–6 minutes, until softened and translucent. Remove from the heat and reserve.

3 Take the peppers out of the bag and peel off the skins. Discard the pepper skins and slice each pepper half into fairly thin strips.

4 Place the peppers, cooked onions and any oil from the pan into a bowl. Add the crushed garlic, pour in the remaining olive oil, add a generous squeeze of lemon juice and season to taste. Mix well, cover and marinate for 2–3 hours, stirring the mixture once or twice.

5 Just before serving, garnish the pepper salad with chopped fresh parsley.

Californian Salad

Full of vitality and vitamins, this is a lovely light and healthy salad for sunny summer days.

Serves 4

1 small crisp lettuce, torn into pieces
225g/8oz/2 cups young spinach leaves
2 carrots, coarsely grated
115g/4oz cherry tomatoes, halved
2 celery sticks, thinly sliced
75g/3oz/1⁄2 cup raisins
50g/2oz/1⁄2 cup blanched almonds or unsalted cashew nuts, halved
30ml/2 tbsp sunflower seeds
30ml/2 tbsp sesame seeds, lightly toasted

For the dressing

45ml/3 tbsp extra virgin olive oil
30ml/2 tbsp cider vinegar
10ml/2 tsp clear honey
juice of 1 small orange
salt and ground black pepper

1 Put the salad vegetables, raisins, almonds or cashew nuts and seeds into a large bowl.

2 Put all the dressing ingredients into a screw-top jar, shake them up well and pour over the salad.

3 Toss the salad thoroughly and divide it among four small salad bowls. Serve chilled, sprinkled with salt and pepper.

Scandinavian Cucumber and Dill

This unusual salad is particularly complementary to hot and spicy food.

Serves 4

2 cucumbers
30ml/2 tbsp snipped fresh chives
30ml/2 tbsp chopped fresh dill
150ml/1⁄4 pint/2⁄3 cup soured cream or fromage frais
salt and ground black pepper

1 Slice the cucumbers as thinly as possible, preferably in a food processor or with a slicer.

2 Place the slices in layers in a colander set over a plate to catch the juices. Sprinkle each layer evenly, but not too heavily, with salt.

3 Leave the cucumber to drain for up to 2 hours, then lay out the slices on a clean dish towel and pat them dry.

4 Mix the cucumber with the herbs, cream or fromage frais and plenty of pepper. Serve as soon as possible.

Cook's Tip

The juices in this salad continue forming after salting, so only dress it when you are ready to serve.

Chicory, Fruit and Nut Salad

Mildly bitter chicory is wonderful with sweet fruit, and is delicious when complemented by a creamy curry sauce.

Serves 4

45ml/3 tbsp mayonnaise	2 heads of chicory
15ml/1 tbsp Greek-style yogurt	50g/2oz/1 cup flaked coconut
15ml/1 tbsp mild curry paste	50g/2oz/½ cup cashew nuts
90ml/6 tbsp single cream	2 red eating apples
½ iceberg lettuce	75g/3oz/½ cup currants

1 Mix together the mayonnaise, Greek-style yogurt, curry paste and single cream in a small bowl. Cover and chill in the fridge until required.

2 Tear the iceberg lettuce into even-size pieces and put into a salad bowl.

3 Cut the root end off each head of chicory and discard. Slice the chicory and add it to the salad bowl. Preheat the grill.

4 Spread out the coconut flakes on a baking sheet. Grill for 1 minute until golden. Tip into a bowl and set aside. Toast the cashew nuts for 2 minutes until golden.

5 Quarter the apples and cut out the cores. Slice the apple quarters and add to the lettuce with the toasted coconut, cashew nuts and currants.

6 Spoon the dressing over the salad, toss lightly and serve.

Cook's Tip
Choose a sweet, well-flavoured variety of red apple for this salad, such as Braeburn or Royal Gala.

Tzatziki

This Greek salad is typically served with grilled lamb and chicken, but is also good with salmon and trout.

Serves 4

1 cucumber	1 clove garlic, crushed
5ml/1 tsp salt	5ml/1 tsp caster sugar
45ml/3 tbsp finely chopped fresh mint, plus a few springs to garnish	200ml/7 fl oz strained Greek-style yogurt
	paprika, to garnish (optional)

1 Peel the cucumber. Reserve a little to use as a garnish if you wish and cut the rest in half lengthways. Remove the seeds with a teaspoon and discard. Slice the cucumber thinly and combine with salt. Leave for about 15-20 minutes. Salt will soften the cucumber and draw out any bitter juices.

2 Combine the mint, garlic, sugar and yogurt in a bowl, reserving a few sprigs of mint as decoration.

3 Rinse the cucumber in a sieve under cold running water to flush away the salt. Drain well and combine with the yogurt. Decorate with cucumber and mint. Serve cold, garnished with paprika if you wish.

Cook's Tip
If preparing tzatziki in a hurry, leave out the method for salting the cucumber at the end of step 1. The cucumber will have a more crunchy texture, and will be slightly less sweet.

Tomato and Bread Salad

This salad is a traditional peasant dish from Tuscany which was created to use up bread that was several days old.

Serves 4

400g/14oz stale white or
  brown bread or rolls
4 large tomatoes
1 large red onion, or
  6 spring onions
a few fresh basil leaves,
  to garnish

For the dressing
60ml/4 tbsp extra virgin
  olive oil
30ml/2 tbsp white wine
  vinegar
salt and ground black
  pepper

1 Cut the bread or rolls into thick slices. Place in a shallow bowl and soak with cold water. Leave for at least 30 minutes.

2 Cut the tomatoes into chunks. Place in a serving bowl. Finely slice the onion or spring onions, and add them to the tomatoes. Squeeze as much water out of the bread as possible, and add it to the vegetables.

3 Mix together the dressing ingredients. Season to taste with salt and pepper. Pour it over the salad and mix well. Decorate with the basil leaves. Allow to stand in a cool place for at least 2 hours before serving.

Fennel and Orange Salad

This salad originated in Sicily, following the seventeenth-century custom of serving fennel at a meal's end.

Serves 4

2 large fennel bulbs
  (about 675g/1½ lb
  total)
2 sweet oranges
2 spring onions,
  to garnish

For the dressing
60ml/4 tbsp extra virgin
  olive oil
30ml/2 tbsp fresh lemon
  juice
salt and ground black
  pepper

1 Wash the fennel bulbs and remove any brown or stringy outer leaves. Slice the bulbs and stems into thin pieces. Place in a shallow serving bowl.

2 Peel the oranges with a sharp knife, cutting away the white pith. Slice thinly. Cut each slice into thirds. Arrange over the fennel, adding any juice from the oranges.

3 To make the dressing, mix the oil and lemon juice together. Season with salt and pepper. Pour the dressing over the salad and mix well.

4 Slice the white and green sections of the spring onions thinly. Sprinkle over the salad.

Parmesan and Poached Egg Salad

Soft poached eggs, hot garlic croûtons and cool crisp salad leaves make an unforgettable combination.

Serves 2

½ small loaf white bread
75ml/5 tbsp extra virgin
olive oil
2 eggs
115g/4oz mixed salad
leaves

2 garlic cloves, crushed
2.5ml/½ tbsp white wine
vinegar
30ml/2 tbsp freshly
shaved Parmesan
cheese
black pepper

1 Remove the crust from the bread. Cut the bread into 2.5cm/1in cubes.

2 Heat 30ml/2 tbsp of the oil in a frying pan and cook the bread for about 5 minutes, tossing the cubes occasionally, until they are golden brown.

3 Meanwhile, bring a saucepan of water to the boil. Slide in the eggs carefully, one at a time. Gently poach the eggs for 4 minutes until lightly cooked.

4 Divide the salad leaves between two plates. Remove the croûtons from the pan and arrange them over the leaves. Wipe the pan clean with kitchen paper.

5 Heat the remaining oil in the pan and cook the garlic and vinegar over a high heat for about 1 minute. Pour the warm dressing over the salad leaves and croûtons.

6 Place a poached egg on each salad. Scatter with shavings of Parmesan cheese and a little freshly ground black pepper.

Cook's Tip
Add a dash of vinegar to the water before poaching the eggs. This helps to keep the whites together. To ensure that a poached egg has a good shape, swirl the water with a spoon before sliding in the egg.

Classic Greek Salad

If you have ever visited Greece you'll know that a Greek salad with a chunk of bread makes a delicious filling meal.

Serves 4

1 cos lettuce
½ cucumber, halved
lengthways
4 tomatoes
8 spring onions
75g/3oz Greek black
olives

115g/4oz feta cheese
90ml/6 tbsp white wine
vinegar
150ml/¼ pint/⅔ cup
extra virgin olive oil
salt and ground black
pepper

1 Tear the lettuce leaves into pieces and place them in a large serving bowl. Slice the cucumber and add to the bowl.

2 Cut the tomatoes into wedges and put them into the bowl.

3 Slice the spring onions. Add them to the bowl along with the olives and toss well.

4 Cut the feta cheese into dice and add to the salad.

5 Put the vinegar and olive oil into a small bowl and season to taste with salt and pepper. Whisk well. Pour the dressing over the salad and toss to combine. Serve at once with extra olives and chunks of bread, if you wish.

Cook's Tip
This salad can be assembled in advance, but should only be dressed just before serving. Keep the dressing at room temperature as chilling deadens its flavours.

Potato Salad with Egg and Lemon

Potato salads are a popular addition to any salad spread and are enjoyed with an assortment of cold meats and fish.

Serves 4
900g/2lb new potatoes,
*   scrubbed or scraped*
1 onion, finely chopped
1 hard-boiled egg
300ml/½ pint/1¼ cups
*   mayonnaise*
1 garlic clove, crushed

finely grated juice and
*   zest of 1 lemon*
60ml/4 tbsp chopped
*   fresh parsley*
salt and ground black
*   pepper*

1 Bring the potatoes to the boil in a saucepan of salted water. Simmer for 20 minutes. Drain and allow to cool. Cut the potatoes into large dice, season with salt and pepper to taste, and combine with the onion.

2 Shell the hard-boiled egg and grate into a mixing bowl, then add the mayonnaise. Combine the garlic and lemon rind and juice in a small bowl and stir into the mayonnaise.

Cook's Tip
Use an early season variety of potato for this salad or look out for baby salad potatoes. They will not disintegrate when boiled and have a sweet flavour.

Sweet Turnip Salad

The robust flavoured turnip partners well with the taste of horseradish and caraway seeds in this delicious salad.

Serves 4
350g/12oz turnips
2 spring onions, white
*   part only, chopped*
15g/½oz/1 tbsp caster
*   sugar*

pinch of salt
30ml/2 tbsp creamed
*   horseradish*
10ml/2 tsp caraway seeds

1 Peel, slice and shred the turnips – or you could grate them if you wish.

2 Add the spring onions, sugar and salt, then rub together with your hands to soften the turnip.

3 Fold in the creamed horseradish and caraway seeds and serve the salad immediately.

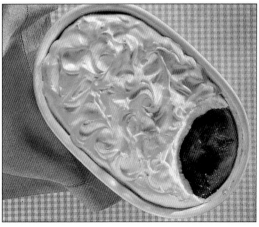

Queen of Puddings

This pudding was developed from a seventeenth-century recipe by Queen Victoria's chefs at Buckingham Palace.

Serves 4

75g/3oz/1½ cups fresh
   breadcrumbs
50g/2oz/4 tbsp caster
   sugar, plus
5ml/1 tsp grated rind
   of 1 lemon

600ml/1 pint/2½ cups
   milk
4 eggs
45ml/3 tbsp raspberry
   jam, warmed

1 Stir the breadcrumbs, 25g/1oz/2 tbsp of the sugar and the lemon rind together in a heatproof bowl. Bring the milk to the boil in a saucepan, then stir into the breadcrumbs.

2 Separate three of the eggs and beat the yolks with the whole egg. Stir into the breadcrumb mixture, pour into a buttered baking dish and leave to stand for 30 minutes. Meanwhile, preheat the oven to 160°C/325°F/Gas 3. Bake the pudding for 50–60 minutes, until set.

3 Whisk the egg whites in a large clean bowl until stiff but not dry, then gradually whisk in just under 25g/1oz/2tbsp caster sugar until the mixture is thick and glossy, taking care not to overwhip.

4 Spread the jam over the pudding, then spoon over the meringue to cover the top completely. Evenly sprinkle about 5ml/1tsp sugar over the meringue, then bake for a further 15 minutes, until the meringue is beginning to turn a light golden colour.

Pear and Blackberry Brown Betty

All this delicious fruity pudding needs to go with it is some hot home-made custard, pouring cream or ice cream.

Serves 4–6

75g/3oz/6 tbsp butter,
   diced
175g/6oz/3 cups
   breadcrumbs
450g/1lb ripe pears
450g/1lb/4 cups
   blackberries

grated rind and juice of 1
   small orange
115g/4oz/½ cup
   demerara sugar
extra demerara sugar, for
   sprinkling

1 Preheat the oven to 180°C/350°F/Gas 4. Heat the butter in a heavy-based frying pan over a moderate heat and add the breadcrumbs. Stir until golden.

2 Peel and core the pears, then cut them into thick slices and mix with the blackberries, orange rind and juice.

3 Mix the demerara sugar with the breadcrumbs, then layer with the fruit in a 900ml/1½ pint/3 cup buttered baking dish, beginning and ending with a layer of sugared breadcrumbs.

4 Sprinkle the extra demerara sugar over the top. Cover the baking dish, then bake the pudding for 20 minutes. Uncover the pudding, then bake for a further 30–35 minutes, until the fruit is cooked and the top is brown and crisp.

Baked Stuffed Apples

When apples are plentiful, this traditional pudding is a popular and easy choice.

Serves 4

75g/3oz/scant 1 cup
   ground almonds
25g/1oz/2 tbsp butter,
   softened
5ml/1 tsp clear honey

1 egg yolk
50g/2oz dried apricots,
   chopped
4 cooking apples,
   preferably Bramleys

1 Preheat the oven to 200°C/400°F/Gas 6. Beat together the almonds, butter, honey, egg yolk and apricots.

2 Stamp out the cores from the cooking apples using a large apple corer, then score a line with the point of a sharp knife around the circumference of each apple.

3 Lightly grease a shallow baking dish, then arrange the cooking apples in the dish.

4 Divide the apricot mixture among the cavities in the apples, then bake in the oven for 45–60 minutes, until the apples are fluffy.

Kentish Cherry Batter Pudding

Kent, known as the "Garden of England", is particularly well known for cherries and the dishes made from them.

Serves 4

45ml/3 tbsp Kirsch
   (optional)
450g/1lb dark cherries,
   stoned
50g/2oz/½ cup plain
   flour
50g/2oz/4 tbsp caster
   sugar

2 eggs, separated
300ml/½ pint/¼ cup
   milk
75g/3oz/6 tbsp butter,
   melted
caster sugar, for
   sprinkling

1 Sprinkle the Kirsch, if using, over the cherries in a small bowl and leave them to soak for about 30 minutes.

2 Mix the flour and sugar together, then slowly stir in the egg yolks and milk to make a smooth batter. Stir in half the butter and leave for 30 minutes.

3 Preheat the oven to 220°C/425°F/Gas 7, then pour the remaining butter into a 600ml/1 pint/2½ cup baking dish and put in the oven to heat.

4 Whisk the egg whites until stiff peaks form, then fold into the batter with the cherries and Kirsch, if using. Pour into the dish and bake for 15 minutes.

5 Reduce the oven temperature to 180°C/350°F/Gas 4 and bake for 20 minutes, or until golden and set in the centre. Serve sprinkled with sugar.

Sticky Toffee Pudding

If you prefer, use pecan nuts instead of walnuts in this delightfully gooey pudding.

Serves 6

115g/4oz/1 cup toasted walnuts, chopped	60ml/4 tbsp double cream
175g/6oz/³⁄₄ cup butter	30ml/2 tbsp lemon juice
175g/6oz/1½ cups soft brown sugar	2 eggs, beaten
	115g/4oz/1 cup self-raising flour

1 Grease a 900ml/1½ pint/3¾ cup pudding basin and add half the nuts.

2 Heat 50g/2oz/4 tbsp of the butter with 50g/2oz/4 tbsp of the sugar, the cream and 15ml/1 tbsp of the lemon juice in a small saucepan, stirring until smooth. Pour half into the pudding basin, then swirl to coat it a little way up the sides.

3 Beat the remaining butter and sugar until light and fluffy, then gradually beat in the eggs. Fold in the flour and the remaining nuts and lemon juice and spoon into the basin.

4 Cover the basin with greaseproof paper with a pleat folded in the centre, then tie securely with string.

5 Steam the pudding for 1¼ hours, or until it is completely set in the centre.

6 Just before serving, gently warm the remaining sauce. Unmould the pudding on to a warm plate and pour over the warm sauce.

Easy Chocolate and Orange Soufflé

The base in this soufflé is a simple semolina mixture, rather than the thick white sauce of most soufflés.

Serve 4

50g/2oz/scant ½ cup semolina	90ml/6 tbsp fresh orange juice
50g/2oz/scant ½ cup soft brown sugar	3 eggs, separated
600ml/1 pint/2½ cups milk	65g/2½oz plain chocolate, grated
grated rind of 1 orange	icing sugar, for sprinkling

1 Preheat the oven to 200°C/400°F/Gas 6. Butter a shallow 1.75 litre/3 pint/7½ cup ovenproof dish.

2 Pour the milk into a heavy-based saucepan, sprinkle over the semolina and brown sugar, then heat, stirring the mixture all the time, until boiling and thickened.

3 Remove the pan from the heat; beat in the orange rind and juice, egg yolks and all but 15ml/1 tbsp of the chocolate.

4 Whisk the egg whites until stiff but not dry, then lightly fold into the semolina mixture in three batches. Spoon the mixture into the dish and bake for about 30 minutes until just set in the centre and risen. Sprinkle the top with the reserved chocolate and the icing sugar, then serve immediately.

Plum and Walnut Crumble

Walnuts add a lovely crunch to the fruit layer in this rich crumble – almonds would be equally good.

Serves 4–6

*75g/3oz/³⁄₄ cup walnut
   pieces
900g/2lb plums
75g/6oz/1½ cups
   demerara sugar*

*75g/3oz/6 tbsp butter or
   hard margarine, cut
   into dice
75g/6oz/1½ cups plain
   flour*

1 Preheat the oven to 180°C/350°F/Gas 4. Spread the nuts on a baking sheet and place in the oven for 8–10 minutes, until evenly coloured.

2 Butter a 1.2 litre/2 pint/5 cup baking dish. Halve and stone the plums, then put them into the dish and stir in the nuts and half of the demerara sugar.

3 Rub the butter or margarine into the flour until the mixture resembles coarse crumbs. (Alternatively, use a food processor.) Stir in the remaining sugar and continue to rub in until fine crumbs are formed.

4 Cover the fruit with the crumb mixture and press it down lightly. Bake the pudding for about 45 minutes, until the top is golden brown and the fruit tender.

Cook's Tip

*To make an oat and cinnamon crumble, substitute
rolled oats for half the flour in the crumble mixture and
add 2.5–5ml/½ –1 tsp ground cinnamon, to taste.*

Baked Rice Pudding

Canned rice pudding simply cannot compare with this creamy home-made version, especially if you like the skin.

Serves 4

*50g/2oz/¼ cup pudding
   rice
25g/1oz/2 tbsp soft light
   brown sugar
50g/2oz/4 tbsp butter
900ml/1½ pints/3¾ cups
   milk*

*small strip of lemon rind
pinch of freshly grated
   nutmeg
fresh mint sprigs, to
   decorate
raspberries, to serve*

1 Preheat the oven to 150°C/300°F/Gas 2, then butter a 1.2 litre/2 pint/5 cup shallow baking dish.

2 Put the rice, sugar and butter into the dish, stir in the milk and lemon rind and sprinkle a little nutmeg over the surface.

3 Bake the rice pudding in the oven for about 2½ hours, stirring after 30 minutes and another couple of times during the next 2 hours until the rice is tender and the pudding has a thick and creamy consistency.

4 If you like skin on top, leave the rice pudding undisturbed for the final 30 minutes of cooking (otherwise, stir it again). Serve hot, decorated with fresh mint sprigs and raspberries.

Cook's Tip

*Baked rice pudding is even more delicious with fruit.
Add some sultanas, raisins or chopped ready-to-eat
dried apricots to the pudding, or serve it alongside
sliced fresh peaches or nectarines, fresh raspberries or
fresh strawberries.*

Floating Islands in Plum Sauce

This unusual, low-fat pudding is simpler to make than it looks, and is quite delicious.

Serves 4

450g/1lb red plums
300ml/½ pint/1¼ cups apple juice
2 egg whites
30ml/2 tbsp concentrated apple juice syrup
pinch of freshly grated nutmeg

1 Halve the plums and remove the stones. Place them in a wide saucepan with the apple juice.

2 Bring to the boil, then cover with a tight-fitting lid and leave to simmer gently until the plums are tender.

3 Meanwhile, place the egg whites in a clean, dry bowl and whisk until stiff peaks form.

4 Gradually whisk in the apple juice syrup, whisking until the meringue holds fairly firm peaks.

5 Using a tablespoon, scoop the meringue mixture into the gently simmering plum sauce. (You may need to cook the "islands" in two batches.)

6 Cover again and allow to simmer gently for 2–3 minutes, until the meringues are just set. Serve straight away, sprinkled with a little freshly grated nutmeg.

Cook's Tip
For ease of preparation when you are entertaining, the plum sauce can be made in advance and reheated just before you cook the meringues.

Souffléed Rice Pudding

The inclusion of fluffy egg whites in this rice pudding makes it unusually light.

Serves 4

65g/2½oz/¼ cup short grain pudding rice
45ml/3 tbsp clear honey
750ml/1¼ pints/3⅓ cups semi-skimmed milk
1 vanilla pod or 2.5ml/ ½ tsp vanilla essence
2 egg whites
5ml/1 tsp finely grated nutmeg

1 Place the pudding rice, clear honey and the milk in a heavy-based or non-stick saucepan and bring to the boil. Add the vanilla pod, if using.

2 Reduce the heat and cover with a tight-fitting lid. Leave to simmer gently for about 1–1¼ hours, stirring occasionally to prevent sticking, until most of the liquid has been absorbed.

3 Remove the vanilla pod from the saucepan, or if using vanilla essence, add this to the rice mixture now. Preheat the oven to 220°C/425°F/Gas 7.

4 Place the egg whites in a clean dry bowl and whisk until stiff peaks form.

5 Using a metal spoon or spatula, fold the egg whites evenly into the rice mixture and tip into a 1 litre/1¾ pint/4 cup ovenproof dish.

6 Sprinkle with grated nutmeg and bake for 15–20 minutes, until the pudding is well risen and golden brown. Serve hot.

Cabinet Pudding

Dried and glacé fruit, sponge cake and ratafias, spiked with brandy if you wish, make a rich pudding.

Serves 4

25g/1oz/2½ tbsp raisins, chopped
30ml/2 tbsp brandy (optional)
25g/1oz glacé cherries, halved
25g/1oz angelica, chopped
2 trifle sponge cakes

50g/2oz ratafias
2 eggs
2 egg yolks
25g/1oz/2 tbsp sugar
450ml/¾ pint/1¾ cups single cream or milk
few drops of vanilla essence

1 Soak the raisins in the brandy, if using, for several hours.

2 Butter a 750ml/1¼ pint/3⅔ cup charlotte mould and arrange some of the cherries and angelica in the base.

3 Dice the sponge cakes and crush the ratafias. Mix with the remaining cherries and angelica, raisins and brandy, if using, and spoon into the mould.

4 Lightly whisk together the eggs, egg yolks and sugar. Bring the cream or milk just to the boil, then stir into the egg mixture with the vanilla essence.

5 Strain the egg mixture into the mould, then set aside for 15–30 minutes.

6 Preheat the oven to 160°C/325°F/Gas 3. Place the mould in a roasting tin, cover with baking paper and pour in boiling water. Bake for 1 hour, or until set. Leave for 2–3 minutes, then turn out on to a warm plate.

Eve's Pudding

The tempting apples beneath the sponge topping are the reason for this pudding's name.

Serves 4–6

115g/4oz/½ cup butter, softened
115g/4oz/½ cup caster sugar
2 eggs, beaten
grated rind and juice of 1 lemon
90g/3½oz/scant 1 cup self-raising flour

40g/1½oz/generous ¼ cup ground almonds
115g/4oz/½ cup soft brown sugar
500-675g/1½lb cooking apples, cored and thinly sliced
25g/1oz/¼ cup flaked almonds

1 Beat together the butter and caster sugar in a large mixing bowl until the mixture is very light and fluffy.

2 Gradually beat the eggs into the butter mixture, beating well after each addition, then fold in the lemon rind, flour and ground almonds.

3 Mix the brown sugar, apples and lemon juice, tip into the dish, add the sponge mixture, then the almonds. Bake for 40–45 minutes, until golden.

Surprise Lemon Pudding

The surprise is a delicious tangy lemon sauce that forms beneath the light topping in this pudding.

Serves 4

75g/3oz/6 tbsp butter, softened
175g/6oz/1½ cups soft brown sugar
4 eggs, separated

grated rind and juice of 4 lemons
50g/2oz/½ cup self-raising flour
120ml/4fl oz/½ cup milk

1 Preheat the oven to 180°C/350°F/Gas 4, then butter an 18cm/7in soufflé dish or cake tin and stand it in a roasting tin.

2 Beat the butter and sugar together in a large bowl until pale and very fluffy. Beat in one egg yolk at a time, beating well after each addition and gradually beating in the lemon rind and juice until well mixed; do not worry if the mixture curdles a little at this stage.

3 Sift the flour and stir into the lemon mixture until well mixed, then gradually stir in the milk.

4 Whisk the egg whites in a separate bowl until stiff peaks form but the whites are not dry, then lightly, but thoroughly, fold into the lemon mixture in three batches. Carefully pour the mixture into the soufflé dish or cake tin, then pour boiling water into the roasting tin to come halfway up the sides.

5 Bake the pudding in the centre of the oven for about 45 minutes, or until risen, just firm to the touch and golden brown on top. Serve at once.

Castle Puddings with Custard

These attractive puddings may be baked in ramekin dishes if you do not have dariole moulds.

Serves 4

about 45ml/3 tbsp blackcurrant, strawberry or raspberry jam
115g/4oz/½ cup butter, softened
115g/4oz/½ cup caster sugar
2 eggs, beaten
few drops of vanilla essence

130g/4½oz/generous 1 cup self-raising flour

For the custard
450ml/¾ pint/1 scant cup milk
4 eggs
15–25g/½–1oz/1–2 tbsp sugar
few drops of vanilla essence

1 Preheat the oven to 180°C/350°F/Gas 4. Butter eight dariole moulds. Put about 10ml/2 tsp of your chosen jam in the base of each mould.

2 Beat the butter and sugar together until light and fluffy, then gradually beat in the eggs, beating well after each addition, and add the vanilla essence towards the end. Lightly fold in the flour, then divide the mixture among the moulds. Bake the puddings for about 20 minutes until well risen and a light golden colour.

3 To make the sauce, whisk the eggs and sugar together. Bring the milk to the boil in a heavy, preferably non-stick, saucepan, then slowly pour on to the sweetened egg mixture, stirring constantly.

4 Return the milk to the pan and heat very gently, stirring, until the mixture thickens enough to coat the back of a spoon; do not allow to boil. Cover the pan and remove from the heat.

5 Remove the moulds from the oven, leave to stand for a few minutes, then turn the puddings on to warmed plates and serve with the custard.

Bread and Butter Pudding

An unusual version of a classic recipe, this pudding is made with French bread and mixed dried fruit.

Serves 4–6

4 ready-to-eat dried
   apricots, finely
   chopped
15ml/1 tbsp raisins
30ml/2 tbsp sultanas
15ml/1 tbsp chopped
   mixed peel
1 French loaf (about
   200g/7oz), thinly
   sliced
50g/2oz/4 tbsp butter,
   melted
450ml/¾ pint/1¾ cups
   milk
150ml/¼ pint/⅔ cup
   double cream

115g/4oz/½ cup caster
   sugar
3 eggs
2.5ml/½ tsp vanilla
   essence
30ml/2 tbsp whisky

For the cream
150ml/¼ pint/⅔ cup
   double cream
30ml/2 tbsp Greek-style
   yogurt
15–30ml/1–2 tbsp
   whisky
15g/½ oz/1 tbsp caster
   sugar

1 Preheat the oven to 180°C/350°F/Gas 4. Butter a deep 1.5 litre/2½ pint/6¼ cup ovenproof dish. Mix together the dried fruits. Brush the bread on both sides with butter. Fill the dish with alternate layers of bread and dried fruit starting with fruit and finishing with bread. Heat the milk and cream in a saucepan until just boiling. Whisk together the sugar, eggs and vanilla essence.

2 Whisk the milk mixture into the eggs, then strain into the dish. Sprinkle the whisky over the top. Press the bread down, cover with foil and leave to stand for 20 minutes.

3 Place the dish in a roasting tin half filled with water and bake for 1 hour, or until the custard is just set. Remove the foil and cook for 10 minutes more, until golden. Just before serving, heat all the cream ingredients in a small pan, stirring. Serve with the hot pudding.

Chocolate Amaretti Peaches

This dessert is quick and easy to prepare, yet sophisticated enough to serve at the most elegant dinner party.

Serves 4

115g/4oz amaretti
   biscuits, crushed
50g/2oz plain chocolate,
   chopped
grated rind of ½ orange
15ml/1 tbsp clear honey
1.5ml/¼ tsp ground
   cinnamon

1 egg white, lightly
   beaten
4 firm ripe peaches
150ml/¼ pint/⅔ cup
   white wine
15g/½oz/1 tbsp caster
   sugar
whipped cream, to serve

1 Preheat the oven to 190°C/375°F/Gas 5. Mix together the crushed amaretti biscuits, chocolate, orange rind, honey and cinnamon in a bowl. Add the beaten egg white and mix to bind the mixture together.

2 Halve and stone the peaches and fill the cavities with the chocolate mixture, mounding it up slightly.

3 Arrange the stuffed peaches in a lightly buttered shallow ovenproof dish which will just hold the fruit comfortably. Pour the wine into a measuring jug and stir in the sugar.

4 Pour the wine mixture around the peaches. Bake for 30–40 minutes, until the peaches are tender. Serve at once with a little of the cooking juices spooned over and the whipped cream.

Cook's Tip
Prepare this dessert using fresh nectarines or apricots instead of peaches, if you wish.

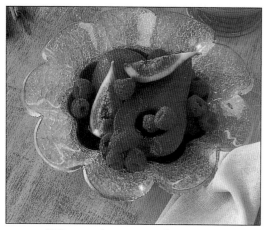

Warm Autumn Compote

This is a simple yet quite sophisticated dessert featuring succulent ripe autumnal fruits.

Serves 4

75g/3oz/generous ¼ cup
   caster sugar
1 bottle red wine
1 vanilla pod, split
1 strip pared lemon rind

4 pears
2 purple figs, quartered
225g/8oz/2 cups
   raspberries
lemon juice, to taste

1 Put the caster sugar and red wine in a large saucepan and heat gently until the sugar has completely dissolved. Add the vanilla pod and lemon rind and bring to the boil. Reduce the heat and simmer for 5 minutes.

2 Peel and halve the pears, then scoop out the cores, using a melon baller or teaspoon. Add the pears to the syrup and poach for about 15 minutes, turning them several times so they colour evenly.

3 Add the quartered figs and poach for a further 5 minutes, until the fruits are tender.

4 Transfer the poached pears and figs to a serving bowl using a slotted spoon, then scatter over the raspberries.

5 Return the syrup to the heat and boil rapidly to reduce slightly and concentrate the flavour. Add a little lemon juice to taste. Strain the syrup over the fruits and serve warm.

Apple Soufflé Omelette

Apples sautéed until they are slightly caramelized make a delicious autumn filling for this sweet omelette.

Serves 2

4 eggs, separated
30ml/2 tbsp single cream
15g/½oz/1 tbsp caster
   sugar
15g/½oz/1 tbsp butter
sifted icing sugar, for
   dredging

For the filling
1 eating apple, peeled,
   cored and sliced
25g/1oz/2 tbsp butter
25g/1oz/2 tbsp soft light
   brown sugar
45ml/3 tbsp single cream

1 To make the filling, sauté the apple slices in the butter and sugar until just tender. Stir in the cream and keep warm, while making the omelette.

2 Place the egg yolks in a bowl with the cream and sugar and beat well. Whisk the egg whites until stiff peaks form, then fold into the yolk mixture.

3 Melt the butter in a large heavy-based frying pan, pour in the soufflé mixture and spread evenly. Cook for 1 minute until golden underneath, then place under a hot grill to brown the top.

4 Slide the omelette on to a plate, spoon the apple mixture on to one side, then fold over. Dredge the icing sugar over thickly, then quickly mark in a criss-cross pattern with a hot metal skewer. Serve the omelette immediately.

Cook's Tip
In the summer months, make the filling for the omelette using fresh raspberries or strawberries.

Warm Lemon and Syrup Cake

This simple cake is made special by the lemony syrup which is poured over it when baked.

Serves 8

3 eggs
175g/6oz/³⁄₄ cup butter, softened
175g/6oz/³⁄₄ cup caster sugar
175g/6oz/1½ cups self-raising flour
50g/2oz/½ cup ground almonds
1.5ml/¼ tsp freshly grated nutmeg

50g/2oz candied lemon peel, finely chopped
grated rind of 1 lemon
30ml/2 tbsp freshly squeezed lemon juice
poached pears, to serve

For the syrup

175g/6oz/¼ cup caster sugar
juice of 3 lemons

1 Preheat the oven to 180°C/350°F/Gas 4. Lightly grease and base-line a deep round 20cm/8in cake tin.

2 Place all the cake ingredients in a large bowl and beat well for 2–3 minutes, until light and fluffy.

3 Tip the mixture into the prepared tin, spread level and bake for 1 hour, or until golden and firm to the touch.

4 To make the syrup, put the caster sugar, lemon juice and 75ml/5 tbsp water in a saucepan. Heat gently, stirring until the sugar has completely dissolved, then boil, without stirring, for 1–2 minutes.

5 Turn out the cake on to a plate with a rim. Prick the surface of the cake all over with a fork, then pour over the hot syrup. Leave to soak for about 30 minutes. Serve the cake warm with thin wedges of poached pears.

Papaya and Pineapple Crumble

Crumbles are always popular with children and adults, but you can ring the changes with this exotic variation.

Serves 4–6

For the topping
175g/6oz/1½ cups plain flour
75g/3oz/6 tbsp butter, diced
75g/3oz/generous ¼ cup caster sugar
75g/3oz/½ cup mixed chopped nuts

For the filling
1 medium-ripe pineapple
1 large ripe papaya
15g/½oz/1 tbsp caster sugar
5ml/1 tsp mixed spice
grated rind of 1 lime
natural yogurt, to serve

1 Preheat the oven to 180°C/350°F/Gas 4. To make the topping, sift the flour into a bowl and rub in the butter until the mixture resembles breadcrumbs. Stir in the caster sugar and mixed chopped nuts.

2 Peel the pineapple, remove the eyes, then cut in half. Cut away the core and cut the flesh into bite-size chunks. Halve the papaya and scoop out the seeds using a spoon. Peel, then cut the flesh into similar size pieces.

3 Put the pineapple and papaya chunks into a large pie dish. Sprinkle over the sugar, mixed spice and lime rind and toss gently to mix.

4 Spoon the crumble topping over the fruit and spread out evenly with a fork, but don't press it down. Bake in the oven for 45–50 minutes, until golden brown. Serve the crumble hot or warm with natural yogurt.

Zabaglione

A much-loved simple Italian pudding traditionally made with Marsala, an Italian fortified wine.

Serves 4

4 egg yolks
50g/2oz/4 tbsp caster sugar
60ml/4 tbsp Marsala
amaretti biscuits, to serve

1 Place the egg yolks and caster sugar in a large heatproof bowl and whisk with an electric whisk until the mixture is pale and thick.

2 Gradually add the Marsala, about 15ml/1 tbsp at a time, whisking well after each addition (at this stage the mixture will be quite runny).

3 Place the bowl over a saucepan of gently simmering water and continue to whisk for at least 5–7 minutes, until the mixture becomes thick and mousse-like; when the beaters are lifted they should leave a thick trail on the surface of the mixture. (If you don't beat the mixture for long enough, the zabaglione will be too runny and will probably separate.)

4 Pour into four warmed stemmed glasses and serve immediately with the amaretti biscuits for dipping.

Cook's Tip
If you don't have any Marsala, substitute Madeira, a medium-sweet sherry or a dessert wine.

Thai-fried Bananas

This is a very simple and quick Thai pudding – bananas are simply fried in butter, brown sugar and lime juice.

Serves 4

40g/1½oz/3 tbsp unsalted butter
4 large slightly under-ripe bananas
15ml/1 tbsp desiccated coconut
50g/2oz/4 tbsp soft light brown sugar
60ml/4 tbsp lime juice
2 lime slices, to decorate
thick and creamy natural yogurt, to serve

1 Heat the butter in a large frying pan or wok and fry the bananas for 1–2 minutes on each side, or until they are lightly golden in colour.

2 Meanwhile, dry fry the coconut in a small frying pan until lightly browned and reserve.

3 Sprinkle the sugar into the pan with the bananas, add the lime juice and cook, stirring, until dissolved. Sprinkle the coconut over the bananas, decorate with lime slices and serve with the thick and creamy yogurt.

Crêpes Suzette

This dish is a classic of French cuisine and still enjoys worldwide popularity as a dessert or a daytime treat.

Makes 8

115g/4oz/1 cup plain flour
pinch of salt
1 egg
1 egg yolk
300ml/½ pint/1¼ cups
    semi-skimmed milk
15g/½oz/1 tbsp butter,
    melted, plus extra, for
    shallow frying

For the sauce
2 large oranges
50g/2oz/4 tbsp butter
50g/2oz/½ cup soft light
    brown sugar
15ml/1 tbsp Grand
    Marnier
15ml/1 tbsp brandy

1 Sift the flour and salt into a bowl and make a well in the centre. Crack the egg and extra yolk into the well. Stir the eggs to incorporate all the flour. When the mixture thickens, gradually pour in the milk, beating well after each addition, until a smooth batter is formed. Stir in the butter, transfer to a jug, cover and chill for 30 minutes. Heat a shallow frying pan, add a little butter and heat until sizzling. Pour in a little batter, tilting the pan to cover the base. Cook over a moderate heat for 1–2 minutes until lightly browned underneath, then flip and cook for a further minute. Make eight crêpes and stack them on a plate.

2 Pare the rind from one of the oranges and reserve about 5ml/1 tsp. Squeeze the juice from both oranges.

3 To make the sauce, melt the butter in a large frying pan and heat the sugar with the rind and juice until dissolved and gently bubbling. Fold each crêpe in quarters. Add to the pan one at a time, coat in the sauce and fold in half again. Move to the side of the pan to make room for the others.

4 Pour on the Grand Marnier and brandy and cook gently for 2–3 minutes, until the sauce has slightly caramelized. Sprinkle with the reserved orange rind and serve at once.

Bananas with Rum and Raisins

Choose almost-ripe bananas with evenly coloured skins, all yellow or just green at the tips for this dessert.

Serves 4

40g/1½oz/scant ¼ cup
    seedless raisins
75ml/5 tbsp dark rum
50g/2oz/4 tbsp unsalted
    butter
50g/2oz/½ cup soft light
    brown sugar
4 bananas, peeled and
    halved lengthways

1.5ml/¼ tsp grated
    nutmeg
1.5ml/¼ tsp ground
    cinnamon
30ml/2 tbsp slivered
    almonds, toasted
chilled cream or vanilla
    ice cream, to serve
    (optional)

1 Put the raisins in a bowl with the rum. Leave them to soak for about 30 minutes to plump up.

2 Melt the butter in a frying pan, add the sugar and stir until completely dissolved. Add the bananas and cook for a few minutes until tender.

3 Sprinkle the spices over the bananas, then pour over the rum and raisins. Carefully set alight using a long taper and stir gently to mix.

4 Scatter over the slivered almonds and serve immediately with chilled cream or vanilla ice cream, if you wish.

Cook's Tip
Stand well back when you set the rum alight and shake the pan gently until the flames subside.

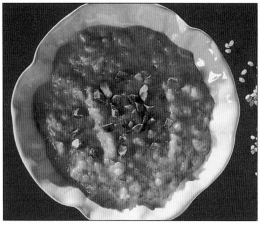

Orange Rice Pudding

In Spain, Greece, Italy and Morocco rice puddings are a favourite dish, especially when sweetened with honey.

Serves 4

50g/2oz/¼ cup short
  grain pudding rice
600ml/1 pint/2½ cups
  milk
30–45ml/2–3 tbsp clear
  honey, to taste

finely grated rind of
  ½ small orange
150ml/¼ pint/⅔ cup
  double cream
15ml/1 tbsp chopped
  pistachios, toasted

1 Mix the rice with the milk, honey and orange rind in a saucepan and bring to the boil, then reduce the heat, cover with a tight-fitting lid and simmer very gently for about 1¼ hours, stirring regularly.

2 Remove the lid and continue cooking and stirring for about 15–20 minutes, until the rice is creamy.

3 Pour in the cream and simmer for 5–8 minutes longer. Serve the rice sprinkled with the chopped toasted pistachios in individual warmed bowls.

Apple and Blackberry Nut Crumble

This much-loved dish of Bramley apples and blackberries is topped with a golden, sweet crumble.

Serves 4

900g/2lb (about
  4 medium) Bramley
  apples, peeled, cored
  and sliced
115g/4oz/½ cup butter,
  cubed
115g/4oz/½ cup soft light
  brown sugar
175g/6oz/1½ cups
  blackberries

75g/3oz/¾ cup
  wholemeal flour
75g/3oz/¾ cup plain
  flour
2.5ml/½ tsp ground
  cinnamon
45ml/3 tbsp chopped
  mixed nuts, toasted
custard, cream or ice
  cream, to serve

1 Preheat the oven to 180°C/350°F/Gas 4. Lightly butter a 1.2 litre/2 pint/5 cup ovenproof dish.

2 Place the apples in a saucepan with 25g/1oz/2 tbsp of the butter, 25g/1oz/2 tbsp of the sugar and 15ml/1 tbsp water. Cover with a tight-fitting lid and cook gently for about 10 minutes, until just tender but still holding their shape.

3 Remove from the heat and gently stir in the blackberries. Spoon the mixture into the ovenproof dish and set aside while you make the topping.

4 To make the crumble topping, sift the flours and cinnamon into a bowl (tip in any of the bran left in the sieve). Add the remaining 75g/3oz/6 tbsp butter and rub into the flour with your fingertips until the mixture resembles fine breadcrumbs (or you can use a food processor).

5 Stir in the remaining 75g/3oz/generous ¼ cup sugar and the nuts and mix well. Sprinkle the crumble topping over the fruit. Bake for 35–40 minutes, until the top is golden brown. Serve hot with custard, cream or ice cream.

Apple Couscous Pudding

This unusual couscous mixture makes a delicious family pudding with a rich fruity flavour.

Serves 4

600ml/2 pints/2½ cups
  apple juice
115g/4oz/ ⅔ cup couscous
40g/1½oz/¼ cup sultanas
2.5ml/½ tsp mixed spice
1 large Bramley cooking
  apple, peeled, cored
  and sliced

2 tbsp demerara sugar
natural low fat yogurt,
  to serve

1 Preheat the oven to 200°C/400°F/Gas 6. Place the apple juice, couscous, sultanas and spice in a pan and bring to the boil, stirring. Cover and simmer for 10–12 minutes, until all the free liquid is absorbed.

2 Spoon half the couscous mixture into a 1.2 litre/2 pint/5 cup ovenproof dish and top with half the apple slices. Top with the remaining couscous.

3 Arrange the remaining apple slices overlapping over the top and sprinkle with demerara sugar. Bake for 25–30 minutes, or until golden brown. Serve hot with yogurt.

Banana, Maple and Lime Crêpes

Crêpes are a treat any day of the week, and they can be made in advance and stored in the freezer for convenience.

Serves 4

115g/4oz/1 cup plain
  flour
1 egg white
250ml/8fl oz/1 cup
  skimmed milk
50ml/2 fl oz/¼ cup cold
  water
sunflower oil, for frying

For the filling
4 bananas, sliced
45ml/3 tbsp maple or
  golden syrup
30ml/2 tbsp freshly
  squeezed lime juice
strips of lime rind, to
  decorate

1 Beat together the flour, egg white, milk and water until smooth and bubbly. Chill in the fridge until needed.

2 Heat a small amount of oil in a non-stick frying pan and pour in enough batter just to coat the base. Swirl it around the pan to coat evenly.

3 Cook until golden, then toss or turn and cook the other side. Place on a plate, cover with foil and keep hot while making the remaining pancakes.

4 To make the filling, place the bananas, syrup and lime juice in a saucepan and simmer gently for 1 minute. Spoon into the pancakes and fold into quarters. Sprinkle with shreds of lime rind to decorate. Serve hot, with yogurt or fromage frais, if you wish.

Cook's Tip
To freeze the crêpes, interleaf them with non-stick baking paper and seal in a plastic bag. They should be used within 3 months.

Spiced Pears in Cider

Any variety of pear can be used for cooking, but choose a firm variety such as Conference for this recipe.

Serves 4

4 medium-firm pears
250ml/8fl oz/1 cup dry
   cider
thinly pared strip of
   lemon rind
1 cinnamon stick

25g/1oz/2 tbsp light
   muscovado sugar
5ml/1 tsp arrowroot
ground cinnamon, to
   sprinkle

1 Peel the pears thinly, leaving them whole with the stalks on. Place in a saucepan with the cider, lemon rind and cinnamon. Cover and simmer gently, turning the pears occasionally for 15–20 minutes, or until tender.

2 Lift out the pears. Boil the syrup, uncovered, to reduce by about half. Remove the lemon rind and cinnamon stick, then stir in the sugar.

3 Mix the arrowroot with 15ml/1 tbsp cold water in a small bowl until smooth, then stir into the syrup. Bring to the boil and stir over the heat until thickened and clear.

4 Pour the sauce over the pears and sprinkle with ground cinnamon. Leave to cool slightly, then serve warm with fromage frais, if you wish.

Cook's Tip
Whole pears look impressive but if you prefer they can be halved and cored before cooking. This will shorten the cooking time slightly.

Fruity Bread Pudding

A delicious old-fashioned family favourite is given a lighter, healthier touch in this version.

Serves 4

75g/3oz/⅓ cup mixed
   dried fruit
150ml/¼ pint/⅔ cup
   apple juice
115g/4oz stale brown or
   white bread, diced
5ml/1 tsp mixed spice

1 large banana, sliced
150ml/¼ pint/⅔ cup
   skimmed milk
15g/½oz/1 tbsp
   demerara sugar
natural yogurt, to serve

1 Preheat the oven to 200°C/400°F/Gas 6. Place the mixed dried fruit in a small saucepan with the apple juice and bring to the boil.

2 Remove the pan from the heat and stir in the diced bread, mixed spice and banana. Spoon the mixture into a shallow 1.2 litre/2 pint/5 cup ovenproof dish; pour over the milk.

3 Sprinkle with demerara sugar and bake for about 25–30 minutes, until firm and golden brown. Serve hot or cold with natural yogurt.

Cook's Tip
Different types of bread will absorb varying amounts of liquid, so you may need to adjust the amount of milk used to allow for this.

Crunchy Gooseberry Crumble

Gooseberries are perfect for traditional family puddings such as this extra special crumble.

Serves 4

500g/1¼lb/4¼ cups gooseberries
50g/2oz/4 tbsp caster sugar
75g/3oz/1 cup rolled oats
75g/3oz/¼ cup wholemeal flour
60ml/4 tbsp sunflower oil
50g/2oz/4 tbsp demerara sugar
30ml/2 tbsp chopped walnuts
natural yogurt or custard, to serve

1 Preheat the oven to 200°C/400°F/Gas 6. Place the gooseberries in a saucepan with the caster sugar. Cover the pan and cook over a low heat for 10 minutes, until the gooseberries are just tender. Tip into an ovenproof dish.

2 To make the crumble, place the oats, flour and oil in a bowl and stir with a fork until evenly mixed.

3 Stir in the demerara sugar and walnuts, then spread evenly over the gooseberries. Bake for 25–30 minutes, or until golden and bubbling. Serve hot with yogurt or custard.

Cook's Tip
When gooseberries are out of season substitute other fruits, such as apples, plums or rhubarb.

Gingerbread Upside-down Pudding

A proper pudding goes down well on a cold winter's day. This one is quite quick to make and looks very impressive.

Serves 4–6

sunflower oil, for brushing
15g/½oz/1 tbsp soft brown sugar
4 peaches, halved and stoned, or canned peach halves, drained
8 walnut halves

For the base
130g/4½oz/½ cup wholemeal flour
2.5ml/½ tsp bicarbonate of soda
7.5ml/1½ tsp ground ginger
5ml/1 tsp ground cinnamon
115g/4oz/½ cup molasses sugar
1 egg
120ml/4fl oz/½ cup skimmed milk
50ml/2fl oz/¼ cup sunflower oil

1 Preheat the oven to 180°C/350°F/Gas 4. Brush the base and sides of a 23cm/9in round springform cake tin with oil. Sprinkle the soft brown sugar evenly over the base.

2 Arrange the peaches, cut-side down, in the tin with a walnut half in each.

3 To make the base, sift together the flour, bicarbonate of soda, ginger and cinnamon, then stir in the sugar. Beat together the egg, milk and oil, then mix into the dry ingredients until smooth.

4 Pour the mixture evenly over the peaches and bake for 35–40 minutes, until firm to the touch. Turn out on to a serving plate. Serve hot with yogurt or custard, if liked.

Cook's Tip
The soft brown sugar caramelizes during baking, creating a delightfully sticky topping.

Cherry Clafoutis

When fresh cherries are in season this makes a deliciously simple dessert for any occasion. Serve warm with a little pouring cream.

Serves 6

675g/1½lb fresh cherries
50g/2oz/½ cup plain
    flour
pinch of salt
4 eggs, plus 2 egg yolks
115g/4oz/½ cup caster
    sugar

600ml/1 pint/2½ cups
    milk
50g/2oz/¼ cup melted
    butter
caster sugar, for dusting
    (optional)

1 Preheat the oven to 190°C/375°F/Gas 5. Lightly butter the base and sides of a shallow ovenproof dish. Stone the cherries and place in the dish.

2 Sift the flour and salt into a bowl. Add the eggs, egg yolks, sugar and a little of the milk and whisk to a smooth batter.

3 Gradually whisk in the rest of the milk and the butter, then strain the batter over the cherries. Bake for 40–50 minutes until golden and just set. Serve warm, dusted with caster sugar, if you like.

Cook's Tip
Use 2 x 425g/15oz cans stoned black cherries, thoroughly drained, if fresh cherries are not available. For a special dessert, add 45ml/3 tbsp kirsch to the batter.

Apple and Orange Pie

A simple but tasty two-fruit pie: make sure you choose really juicy oranges or even blood oranges.

Serves 4

400g/14oz ready-made
    shortcrust pastry
3 oranges, peeled
900g/2lb cooking apples,
    cored and thickly
    sliced

25g/1oz/2 tbsp demerara
    sugar
beaten egg, to glaze
caster sugar, for
    sprinkling

1 Roll out the pastry on a lightly floured surface to about 2cm/¾in larger than the top of a 1.2 litre/2 pint/5 cup pie dish. Cut off a narrow strip around the edge of the pastry and fit on the rim of the pie dish.

2 Preheat the oven to 190°C/375°F/Gas 5. Hold one orange at a time over a bowl to catch the juice; cut down between the membranes to remove the segments.

3 Mix the segments and juice, the apples and sugar in the pie dish. Place a pie funnel in the centre of the dish.

4 Dampen the pastry strip. Cover the dish with the rolled out pastry and press the edges to the pastry strip. Brush the top with beaten egg, then bake for 35–40 minutes, until lightly browned. Sprinkle with caster sugar before serving.

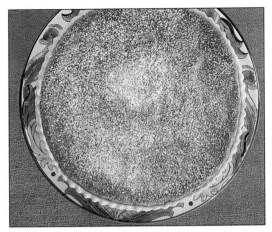

Bakewell Tart

Although the pastry base technically makes this a tart, the original recipe calls it a pudding.

Serves 4

225g/8oz ready-made
    puff pastry
30ml/2 tbsp raspberry or
    apricot jam
2 eggs
2 egg yolks
115g/4oz/½ cup caster
    sugar

115g/4oz/½ cup butter,
    melted
50g/2oz/⅔ cup ground
    almonds
few drops of almond
    essence
sifted icing sugar, for
    dredging

1 Preheat the oven to 200°C/400°F/Gas 6. Roll out the pastry on a lightly floured surface and use it to line an 18cm/7in pie plate or fluted loose-based flan tin. Spread the jam over the base of the pastry case.

2 Whisk the eggs, egg yolks and sugar together in a large bowl until thick and pale.

3 Gently stir the butter, ground almonds and almond essence into the mixture.

4 Pour the mixture into the pastry case and bake for about 30 minutes, until the filling is just set and browned. Dredge with icing sugar before eating hot, warm or cold.

Cook's Tip
Since the pastry case isn't baked blind first, place a baking sheet in the oven while it preheats, then place the pie dish or flan tin on the hot sheet. This will ensure that the base of the pastry case cooks through.

Yorkshire Curd Tart

The distinguishing characteristic of this tart is the allspice, or "clove pepper" as it was once known locally.

Serves 8

225g/8oz/2 cups plain
    flour
115g/4oz/½ cup butter,
    cubed
1 egg yolk

For the filling
large pinch of allspice
90g/3½oz/1 scant cup
    soft light brown sugar

3 eggs, beaten
grated rind and juice of
    1 lemon
40g/1½oz/3 tbsp butter,
    melted
450g/1lb/2 cups curd
    cheese
75g/3oz/½ cup raisins or
    sultanas

1 Place the flour in a bowl. Add the butter and rub it into the flour with your fingertips until the mixture resembles breadcrumbs. (Alternatively, you can use a food processor.) Stir the egg yolk into the flour mixture with a little water to bind the dough together.

2 Turn the dough on to a lightly floured surface, knead lightly and briefly, then form into a ball. Roll out the pastry thinly and use to line a 20cm/8in fluted loose-based flan tin. Chill for 15 minutes in the fridge.

3 Preheat the oven to 190°C/375°F/Gas 5. To make the filling, mix the allspice with the sugar, then stir in the eggs, lemon rind and juice, melted butter, curd cheese and the raisins or sultanas.

4 Pour the filling into the pastry case, then bake for about 40 minutes until the pastry is cooked and the filling is lightly set and golden brown. Serve still slightly warm, cut into wedges, with cream, if you wish.

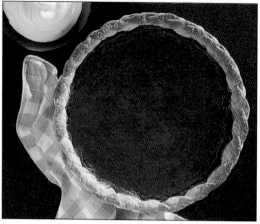

American Spiced Pumpkin Pie

This traditional pie is served in the United States and Canada at Thanksgiving, when pumpkins are plentiful.

Serves 4–6

175g/6oz/1½ cups plain flour
pinch of salt
75g/3oz/6 tbsp unsalted butter
15g/½oz/1 tbsp caster sugar
450g/1lb peeled fresh pumpkin, diced, or 400g/14oz canned pumpkin, drained

115g/4oz/1 cup soft light brown sugar
1.5ml/¼ tsp salt
1.5ml/¼ tsp ground allspice
2.5ml/½ tsp ground cinnamon
2.5ml/½ tsp ground ginger
2 eggs, lightly beaten
120ml/4fl oz/½ cup double cream
whipped cream, to serve

1 Place the flour in a bowl with a pinch of salt. Rub in the butter until the mixture resembles breadcrumbs. Add the sugar and 30–45ml/2–3 tbsp water. Mix to a soft dough. Knead briefly, flatten into a round, wrap and chill for 1 hour.

2 Preheat the oven to 200°C/400°F/Gas 6 with a baking sheet inside. If using fresh pumpkin, steam for 15 minutes, then cool. Purée in a food processor or blender until smooth.

3 Line a 23.5cm/9½in x 2.5cm/1in deep pie tin with the pastry. Prick the base. Cut out leaf shapes from the excess pastry and mark veins with the back of a knife. Brush the edges with water and stick on the leaves. Chill.

4 Mix together the pumpkin purée, sugar, salt, spices, eggs and cream and pour into the pastry case. Place on the preheated baking sheet and bake for 15 minutes. Then reduce the temperature to 180°C/350°F/Gas 4 and cook for a further 30 minutes, or until the filling is set and the pastry golden. Serve warm with whipped cream.

Pear and Blueberry Pie

A variation on plain blueberry pie, this pudding is just as delicious served cold as it is warm.

Serves 4

225g/8oz/2 cups plain flour
pinch of salt
50g/2oz/4 tbsp lard, diced
50g/2oz/4 tbsp butter, diced
675g/1½lb/4½ cups blueberries
25g/1oz/2 tbsp caster sugar

15ml/1 tbsp arrowroot
2 ripe but firm pears, peeled, cored and sliced
2.5ml/½ tsp ground cinnamon
grated rind of ½ lemon
beaten egg, to glaze
caster sugar, for sprinkling

1 Sift the flour and salt into a bowl. Rub in the fats until the mixture resembles fine breadcrumbs. Mix to a dough with 45ml/3 tbsp cold water. Chill for 30 minutes.

2 Place 225g/8oz/2 cups of the blueberries in a saucepan with the sugar. Cover with a lid and cook gently until the blueberries have softened. Press through a nylon sieve. Blend the arrowroot with 30ml/2 tbsp cold water and add to the blueberries. Bring to the boil, stirring until thickened. Allow to cool slightly.

3 Preheat the oven to 190°C/375°F/Gas 5 with a baking sheet inside. Roll out just over half the pastry on a lightly floured surface and use to line a 20cm/8in shallow pie dish.

4 Mix together the remaining blueberries, the pears, ground cinnamon and lemon rind and spoon into the dish. Pour over the blueberry purée.

5 Use the remaining pastry to cover the pie. Make a slit in the centre. Brush with egg and sprinkle with caster sugar. Bake on the baking sheet for 40–45 minutes, until golden. Serve warm, with crème fraîche, if you wish.

Mississippi Pecan Pie

For a truly authentic touch of the Deep South, use maple
syrup instead of golden syrup in this rich dessert.

Serves 4–6

For the pastry
115g/4oz/1 cup plain
  flour
50g/2oz/4 tbsp butter
25g/1oz/2 tbsp caster
  sugar
1 egg yolk

For the filling
175g/6oz/5 tbsp golden
  syrup

50g/2oz/⅓ cup dark
  muscovado sugar
50g/2oz/4 tbsp butter
3 eggs, lightly beaten
2.5ml/½ tsp vanilla
  essence
150g/5oz/1¼ cups pecan
  nuts
fresh cream or ice cream,
  to serve

1 Place the flour in a bowl. Dice the butter, then rub it into
the flour with your fingertips until the mixture resembles
breadcrumbs. (Alternatively use a food processor.) Stir in the
sugar, egg yolk and about 30ml/2 tbsp cold water. Mix to a
dough and knead on a lightly floured surface until smooth.

2 Roll out the pastry and use it to line a 20cm/8in fluted
loose-based flan tin. Prick the base, then line with greaseproof
paper and fill with baking beans. Chill for 30 minutes in the
fridge. Preheat the oven to 200°C/400°F/Gas 6.

3 Bake the pastry case blind for 10 minutes. Remove the
paper and beans and continue to bake for 5 more minutes.
Reduce the oven temperature to 180°C/350°F/Gas 4.

4 To make the filling, heat the syrup, sugar and butter in a
saucepan until the sugar dissolves. Remove from the heat and
cool slightly. Whisk in the eggs and vanilla essence and stir in
the pecan nuts.

5 Pour into the pastry case and bake for 35–40 minutes,
until the filling is set. Serve with cream or ice cream.

Upside-down Apple Tart

Cox's Pippin apples are perfect to use in this tart because
they hold their shape so well.

Serves 4

For the pastry
50g/2oz/4 tbsp butter,
  softened
40g/1½oz/3 tbsp caster
  sugar
1 egg
115g/4oz/1 cup plain
  flour
pinch of salt

For the apple layer
75g/3oz/generous ¼ cup
  butter, softened
75g/3oz/scant ½ cup soft
  light brown sugar
10 Cox's Pippin apples,
  peeled, cored and
  thickly sliced
whipped cream, to serve

1 For the pastry, cream the butter and sugar until pale and
creamy. Beat in the egg, sift in the flour and salt and mix to a
soft dough. Knead, wrap and chill for 1 hour.

2 For the apple layer, grease a 23cm/9in cake tin, then add
50g/2oz/4 tbsp of the butter. Place on the hob and melt the
butter. Remove from the heat and sprinkle over 50g/2oz/
4 tbsp of the sugar. Arrange the apple slices on top, sprinkle
with the remaining sugar and dot with the remaining butter.

3 Preheat the oven to 230°C/450°F/Gas 8. Place the cake tin
on the hob again over a low to moderate heat for about
15 minutes, until a light golden caramel forms on the base.

4 Roll out the pastry on a lightly floured surface to around
the same size as the tin and lay it on top of the apples. Tuck
the pastry edges down around the sides of the apples.

5 Bake for about 20–25 minutes, until the pastry is golden.
Remove from the oven and leave to stand for 5 minutes.

6 Place an upturned plate on top of the tin and, holding the
two together with a dish towel, turn the apple tart out on to
the plate. Serve while still warm with whipped cream.

Mango and Coconut Stir-fry

Choose a ripe mango for this recipe. If you buy one that is a little under-ripe, leave it in a warm place for a day or two before using.

Serves 4

¼ coconut
1 large, ripe mango
juice of 2 limes
rind of 2 limes, finely grated

15ml/1 tbsp sunflower oil
15g/½oz/1 tbsp butter
30ml/1½ tbsp clear honey
crème fraîche, to serve

1 Prepare the coconut flakes by draining the milk from the coconut and peeling the flesh with a vegetable peeler.

2 Peel the mango. Cut the stone out of the middle of the fruit. Cut each half of the mango into slices.

3 Place the mango slices in a bowl and pour over the lime juice and rind, to marinate them.

4 Meanwhile, heat a wok, then add 10ml/2 tsp of the oil. When the oil is hot, add the butter. When the butter has melted, stir in the coconut flakes and stir-fry for 1–2 minutes until the coconut is golden brown. Remove and drain on kitchen towels. Wipe out the wok. Strain the mango slices, reserving the juice.

5 Heat the wok and add the remaining oil. When the oil is hot, add the mango and stir-fry for 1–2 minutes, then add the juice and allow to bubble and reduce for 1 minute. Stir in the honey, sprinkle on the coconut flakes and serve with crème fraîche.

Cook's Tip
Because of the delicate taste of desserts, always make sure your wok has been scrupulously cleaned so there is no transference of flavours.

Peach and Raspberry Crumble

A quick and easy tasty dessert, this crumble is good served hot on its own or with low fat custard.

Serves 4

75g/3oz/⅔ cup plain wholemeal flour
75g/3oz/¾ cup medium oatmeal
75g/3oz/6 tbsp butter
50g/2oz/¼ cup light soft brown sugar

2.5ml/½ tsp ground cinnamon
400g/14oz can peach slices in fruit juice
225g/8oz/1⅓ cups raspberries
30ml/2 tbsp clear honey

1 Preheat the oven to 180°C/350°F/Gas 4. Put the flour and oatmeal in a bowl and mix together.

2 Rub in the butter until the mixture resembles breadcrumbs, then stir in the sugar and cinnamon.

3 Drain the peach slices, reserving the juice.

4 Roughly chop the peaches and put them in an ovenproof dish, then scatter over the raspberries.

5 Mix together the reserved peach juice and honey, pour over the fruit and stir.

6 Spoon the crumble mixture over the fruit, pressing it down lightly. Bake for about 45 minutes, until golden brown on top. Serve hot.

Cook's Tip
Use other combinations of fruit such as apples and blueberries for a tasty change.

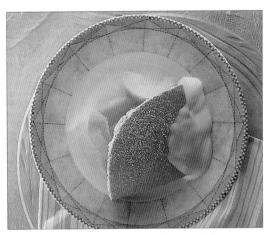

Pineapple and Peach Pudding

A tasty combination of pineapple and peaches, serve this old favourite with custard or ice cream.

Serves 6

75ml/5 tbsp golden syrup
227g/8oz can pineapple cubes in fruit juice
175g/6oz/⅔ cup ready-to-eat dried peaches, chopped
115g/4oz/⅔ cup caster sugar
115g/4oz/8 tbsp butter
175g/6oz/1 ½ cups self-raising wholemeal flour
5 ml/1 tsp baking powder
2 eggs

1 Preheat the oven to 180°C/350 °F/Gas 4. Lightly grease an 18cm/7in loose-bottomed round cake tin and line the base with non-stick baking paper.

2 Heat the golden syrup gently in a saucepan and pour over the bottom of the tin.

3 Strain the pineapple, reserving 45ml/3 tbsp of the juice.

4 Mix together the pineapple and peaches and scatter them over the syrup layer.

5 Put the caster sugar, butter, flour, baking powder, eggs and reserved pineapple juice in a bowl and beat together until smooth.

6 Spread the cake mixture evenly over the fruit and level the surface. Bake for about 45 minutes until risen and golden brown. Turn out carefully on to a serving plate and serve hot in slices.

Cook's Tip
Other combinations of canned and dried fruit work just as well as, such as apricots and pears, or peaches and figs.

Feather-light Peach Pudding

On chilly days, try this hot fruit pudding with its tantalizing sponge topping.

Serves 4

400g/14oz can peach slices
50g/2oz/4 tbsp butter
40g/1½oz/¼ cup soft light brown sugar
1 egg, beaten
65g/2½oz/½ cup plain flour
5ml/1 tsp baking powder
2.5ml/½ tsp ground cinnamon
60ml/4 tbsp milk
2.5ml/½ tsp vanilla essence
10ml/2 tsp icing sugar, for dusting
custard, to serve

1 Preheat the oven to 180°C/350°F/Gas 4. Drain the peaches and put into a l litre/1 pint/4 cup pie dish with 30ml/2 tbsp of the juice.

2 Put all the remaining ingredients, except the icing sugar and custard into a mixing bowl. Beat for 3–4 minutes, until thoroughly combined.

3 Spoon the sponge mixture over the peaches and level the top evenly. Cook in the oven for 35–40 minutes, or until springy to the touch.

4 Lightly dust the top with icing sugar before serving hot with the custard.

Cook's Tip
For a simple sauce, blend 5ml/1 tsp arrowroot with 15ml/1 tbsp peach juice in a small saucepan. Stir in the remaining peach juice from the can and bring to the boil. Simmer for 1 minute until thickened and clear.

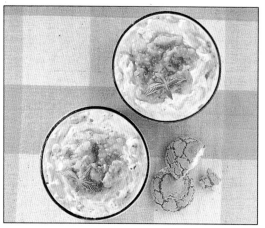

Gooseberry and Elderflower Cream

When elderflowers are in season, instead of using the cordial, cook two to three elderflower heads with the gooseberries.

Serves 4

500g/1¼ lb/4¼ cups
  gooseberries
300ml/½ pint/1¼ cups
  double cream
about 115g/4oz/1 cup
  sifted icing sugar, to
  taste

30ml/2 tbsp elderflower
  cordial or orange
  flower water
  (optional)
fresh mint sprigs, to
  decorate
almond biscuits, to serve

1 Place the gooseberries in a heavy saucepan, cover and cook over a low heat, shaking the pan occasionally, until the gooseberries are tender. Tip the gooseberries into a bowl, crush them, then leave to cool completely.

2 Beat the cream until soft peaks form, then fold in half of the crushed gooseberries. Sweeten with icing sugar and add the elderflower cordial, or orange flower water to taste, if using. Sweeten the remaining gooseberries.

3 Layer the cream mixture and the crushed gooseberries in four dessert dishes or tall glasses, then cover and chill. Decorate the dessert with the fresh mint sprigs and serve with almond biscuits.

Cook's Tip
If preferred, the cooked gooseberries can be puréed and sieved instead of crushed.

Eton Mess

This dish forms part of the picnic meals enjoyed by parents and pupils at Eton school.

Serves 4

500g/1¼ lb/4¼ cups
  strawberries, roughly
  chopped
45–50ml/3–4 tbsp
  Kirsch

300ml/½ pint/1¼ cups
  double cream
6 small white meringues
fresh mint sprigs, to
  decorate

1 Put the strawberries in a bowl, sprinkle over the Kirsch, then cover and chill in the fridge for 2–3 hours.

2 Whip the cream until soft peaks form, then gently fold in the strawberries with their juices.

3 Crush the meringues into rough chunks, then scatter over the strawberry mixture and fold in gently.

4 Spoon the strawberry mixture into a glass serving bowl, decorate with the fresh mint sprigs and serve immediately.

Cook's Tip
If you would prefer to make a less rich version of this dessert, use Greek-style or thick and creamy natural yogurt instead of part or all of the cream. Simply beat the yogurt gently before adding the strawberries.

Cranachan

Crunchy toasted oatmeal and soft raspberries combine to give this dessert a lovely texture.

Serves 4
60ml/4 tbsp clear honey
45ml/3 tbsp whisky
50g/2oz/¾ cup medium
   oatmeal
300ml/½ pint/1¼ cups
   double cream

350g/12oz/3 cups
   raspberries
fresh mint sprigs, to
   decorate

1 Gently warm the honey in the whisky, then leave to cool.

2 Preheat the grill. Spread the oatmeal in a very shallow layer in the grill pan and toast, stirring occasionally, until browned. Leave to cool.

3 Whip the cream in a large bowl until soft peaks form, then gently stir in the oats, honey and whisky until well combined.

4 Reserve a few raspberries for decoration, then layer the remainder with the oat mixture in four tall glasses. Cover and chill in the fridge for 2 hours.

5 About 30 minutes before serving, transfer the glasses to room temperature. Decorate with the reserved raspberries and mint sprigs.

Old English Trifle

If you are making this pudding for children, replace the sherry and brandy with orange juice.

Serves 6
75g/3oz day-old sponge
   cake, broken into
   bite-size pieces
8 ratafias, broken into
   halves
100ml/3½fl oz/⅓ cup
   medium sherry
30ml/2 tbsp brandy
350g/12oz/3 cups
   prepared fruit such as
   raspberries, peaches or
   strawberries
300ml/½ pint/1¼ cups
   double cream

40g/1½oz/scant ½ cup
   toasted flaked
   almonds, to decorate
strawberries, to decorate

For the custard
4 egg yolks
25g/1oz/2 tbsp caster
   sugar
450ml/¾ pint/1¼ cups
   single or whipping
   cream
few drops of vanilla
   essence

1 Put the sponge cake and ratafias in a glass serving dish, then sprinkle over the sherry and brandy and leave until they have been absorbed.

2 To make the custard, whisk the egg yolks and caster sugar together. Bring the cream to the boil in a heavy saucepan, then pour on to the egg yolk mixture, stirring constantly.

3 Return the mixture to the pan and heat very gently, stirring all the time with a wooden spoon, until the custard thickens enough to coat the back of the spoon; do not allow to boil. Leave to cool, stirring occasionally.

4 Put the fruit in an even layer over the sponge cake and ratafias in the serving dish, then strain the custard over the fruit and leave to set. Lightly whip the cream, spread it over the custard, then chill the trifle well. Decorate with flaked almonds and strawberries just before serving.

Cherry Syllabub

This recipe follows the style of the earliest syllabubs and produces a frothy creamy layer over a liquid one.

Serves 4

225g/8oz/2 cups ripe dark cherries, stoned and chopped
30ml/2 tbsp Kirsch
2 egg whites
30ml/2 tbsp lemon juice

150ml/¼ pint/⅔ cup sweet white wine
75g/3oz/generous ¼ cup caster sugar
300ml/½ pint/1¼ cups double cream

1 Divide the chopped cherries among six tall dessert glasses and sprinkle over the Kirsch.

2 In a clean bowl, whisk the egg whites until stiff peaks form. Gently fold in the lemon juice, wine and sugar.

3 In a separate bowl (but using the same whisk), lightly beat the cream, then fold into the egg white mixture. Spoon the cream mixture over the cherries, then chill overnight in the fridge.

Damask Cream

It is important not to move this simple, light, yet elegant dessert while it is setting, otherwise it will separate.

Serves 4

600ml/1 pint/2½ cups milk
40g/1½oz/3 tbsp caster sugar
several drops of triple-strength rose water

10ml/2 tsp rennet
60ml/4 tbsp double cream
sugared rose petals, to decorate (optional)

1 Gently heat the milk and 25g/1oz/2 tbsp of the sugar, stirring, until the sugar has melted and the temperature of the mixture feels neither hot nor cold. Stir rose water to taste into the milk, then remove the saucepan from the heat and stir in the rennet.

2 Pour the milk into a serving dish and leave undisturbed for 2–3 hours, until set. Stir the remaining sugar into the cream, then carefully spoon over the junket. Decorate with sugared rose petals, if you wish.

Mandarins in Orange-flower Syrup

Mandarins, tangerines, clementines, mineolas: any of these lovely citrus fruits are suitable to use in this recipe.

Serves 4

Pare some rind from one mandarin and cut it into fine shreds for decoration. Squeeze the juice from two mandarins and reserve it. Peel eight further mandarins, removing the white pith. Arrange the whole fruit in a wide dish. Mix the reserved juice, 1 tbsp confectioner's sugar and 2 tsp orange-flower water and pour it over the fruit. Cover and chill. Blanch the rind in boiling water for 30 seconds. Drain, cool and sprinkle over the mandarins, with pistachio nuts, to serve.

Chocolate Blancmange

For a special dinner party, flavour the blancmange with peppermint essence, crème de menthe or orange liqueur.

Serves 4

60ml/4 tbsp cornflour
600ml/1 pint/2½ cups
milk
40g/1½ oz/3 tbsp caster
sugar

50–115g/2–4oz plain
chocolate, chopped
vanilla essence, to taste
chocolate curls, to
decorate

1 Rinse a 750ml/1¼ pint/3⅓ cup fluted mould with cold water and leave it upside down to drain. Blend the cornflour to a smooth paste with a little of the milk.

2 Bring the remaining milk to the boil, preferably in a non-stick saucepan, then pour on to the blended mixture, stirring all the time.

3 Pour all the milk back into the saucepan and bring slowly to the boil over a low heat, stirring all the time until the mixture boils and thickens. Remove the pan from the heat, then add the sugar, chopped chocolate and a few drops of vanilla essence. Stir until the chocolate has melted.

4 Pour the chocolate mixture into the mould and leave in a cool place for several hours to set.

5 To unmould the blancmange, place on a large serving plate, then holding the plate and mould firmly together, invert them. Give both plate and mould a gentle but firm shake to loosen the blancmange, then lift off the mould. Scatter white and plain chocolate curls over the top of the blancmange to decorate and serve at once.

Cook's Tip

If you prefer, set the blancmange in four or six individual moulds.

Honeycomb Mould

These honeycomb moulds have a fresh lemon flavour. The layered mixture looks most attractive.

Serves 4

30ml/2 tbsp cold water
15g/½ oz gelatine
2 eggs, separated
75g/3oz/generous ¼ cup
caster sugar

475ml/16fl oz/2 cups
milk
grated rind of 1 small
lemon
60ml/4 tbsp lemon juice

1 Chill four individual moulds or, if you prefer, use a 1.2 litre/2 pint/5 cup jelly mould. Mix together the water and the gelatine and leave to soften for 5 minutes. Place the bowl over a small saucepan of hot water and stir from time to time until dissolved.

2 Meanwhile, whisk the egg yolks and sugar together until pale, thick and fluffy.

3 Bring the milk to the boil in a heavy, preferably non-stick, saucepan, then slowly pour on to the egg yolk mixture, stirring all the time.

4 Return the milk mixture to the pan, then heat gently, stirring continuously until thickened. Do not allow to boil or it will curdle. Remove from the heat and stir in the grated lemon rind and juice.

5 Stir 2 or 3 spoonfuls of the lemon mixture into the gelatine, and then stir this back into the saucepan. In a clean dry bowl, whisk the egg whites until they are stiff but not too dry, then gently fold into the mixture in the saucepan in three batches, being careful to retain the oil.

6 Rinse the moulds or mould with cold water and drain well, then pour in the lemon mixture. Leave to cool, then cover and chill in the fridge until set. To serve, invert on to four individual or one serving plate.

Peach Melba

The original dish created for the opera singer Dame Nelli Melba had peaches and ice cream served upon an ice swan.

Serves 4

300g/11oz/scant 2 cups
   raspberries
squeeze of lemon juice
icing sugar, to taste

2 large ripe peaches or
   425g/15oz can sliced
   peaches
8 scoops vanilla ice cream

1 Press the raspberries through a non-metallic sieve.

2 Add a little lemon juice to the raspberry purée and sweeten to taste with icing sugar.

3 Dip fresh peaches in boiling water for 4–5 seconds, then slip off the skins, halve along the indented line, then slice; or tip canned peaches into a sieve and drain them.

4 Place two scoops of ice cream in each individual glass dish, top with peach slices, then pour over the raspberry purée. Serve immediately.

Summer Pudding

You may use any seasonal berries you wish in this unique and ever-popular dessert.

Serves 4

about 8 thin slices day-
   old white bread, crusts
   removed

800g/1¼lb/4½ cups
   mixed summer fruits
about 25g/1oz/2 tbsp
   sugar

1 Cut a round from one slice of bread to fit in the base of a 1.2 litre/2 pint/5 cup pudding basin, then cut strips of bread about 5cm/2in wide to line the basin, overlapping the strips.

2 Gently heat the fruit, sugar and 30ml/2 tbsp water in a large heavy-based saucepan, shaking the pan occasionally, until the juices begin to run.

3 Reserve about 45ml/3 tbsp fruit juice, then spoon the fruit and remaining juice into the basin, taking care not to dislodge the bread.

4 Cut the remaining bread to fit entirely over the fruit. Stand the basin on a plate and cover with a saucer or small plate that will just fit inside the top of the basin. Place a heavy weight on top. Chill the pudding and the reserved fruit juice overnight in the fridge.

5 Run a knife carefully around the inside of the basin rim, then invert the pudding on to a cold serving plate. Pour over the reserved juice and serve.

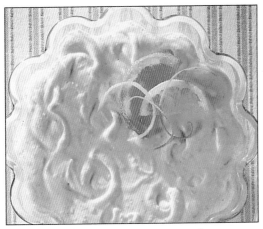

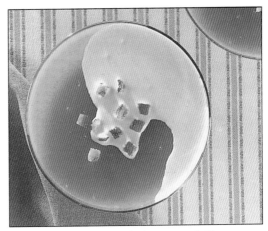

Boodles Orange Fool

This fruit fool has become the speciality of Boodles Club, a gentlemen's club in London's St James's area.

Serves 4

4 trifle sponge cakes, cubed

300ml/½ pint/1¼ cups double cream

25–50g/1–2oz/2–4 tbsp caster sugar

grated rind and juice of 2 oranges

grated rind and juice of 1 lemon

orange and lemon slices and rind, to decorate

1 Line the bottom and halfway up the sides of a large glass serving bowl or china dish with the cubed trifle sponge cakes.

2 Whip the cream with the sugar until it starts to thicken, then gradually whip in the fruit juices, adding the fruit rinds towards the end.

3 Carefully pour the cream mixture into the bowl or dish, taking care not to dislodge the sponge. Cover and chill for about 3–4 hours. Serve the fool decorated with orange and lemon slices and rind.

Apricot and Orange Jelly

You could also make this light dessert using nectarines or peaches instead of apricots.

Serves 4

350g/12oz well-flavoured fresh ripe apricots, stoned

50–75g/2–3oz/about ⅓ cup sugar

about 300ml/½ pint/ 1¼ cups freshly squeezed orange juice

15ml/1 tbsp gelatine

single cream, to serve

finely chopped candied orange peel, to decorate

1 Heat the apricots, sugar and 120ml/4fl oz/ ½ cup of the orange juice, stirring until the sugar has dissolved. Simmer gently until the apricots are tender.

2 Press the apricot mixture through a nylon sieve into a small measuring jug.

3 Pour 45ml/3 tbsp orange juice into a small heatproof bowl, sprinkle over the gelatine and leave for about 5 minutes, until softened.

4 Place the bowl over a saucepan of hot water and heat until the gelatine has dissolved. Pour into the apricot mixture slowly, stirring all the time. Make up to 600ml/1 pint/ 2½ cups with the orange juice.

5 Pour the apricot mixture into four individual dishes and chill in the fridge until set. Pour a thin layer of cream over the surface of the jellies before serving, decorated with candied orange peel.

Summer Berry Medley

Make the most of seasonal fruits in this refreshing dessert.
The sauce is also good swirled into plain fromage frais.

Serves 4 – 6

175g/6oz/1½ cups
    redcurrants, stripped
    from their stalks
175g/6oz/1½ cups
    raspberries
50g/2oz/¼ cup caster
    sugar
30 – 45ml/2 – 3 tbsp
    crème de framboise

450 – 675g/1 – 1½lb/
    4½ cups fresh mixed
    soft summer fruits
    such as strawberries,
    raspberries,
    blueberries,
    redcurrants and
    blackcurrants
vanilla ice cream, to
    serve

1 Place the redcurrants in a bowl with the raspberries, caster
sugar and crème de framboise. Cover and leave to macerate
for 1–2 hours.

2 Put the macerated fruit with its juices in a saucepan and
cook gently for 5–6 minutes, stirring occasionally, until the
fruit is just tender.

3 Pour the fruit into a blender or food processor and process
until smooth. Press through a nylon sieve to remove any pips.
Leave to cool, then chill in the fridge.

4 Divide the mixed soft fruit among four individual glass
serving dishes and pour over the sauce. Serve with scoops of
vanilla ice cream.

Brown Bread Ice Cream

This delicious textured ice cream is best served with a
blackcurrant sauce spiked with crème de cassis.

Serves 6

50g/2oz/½ cup roasted
    and chopped
    hazelnuts, ground
75g/3oz/1½ cups
    wholemeal
    breadcrumbs
50g/2oz/½ cup demerara
    sugar
3 egg whites
115g/4oz/½ cup caster
    sugar
300ml/½ pint/1¼ cups
    double cream

few drops of vanilla
    essence

For the sauce
225g/8oz/2 cups
    blackcurrants
75g/3oz/generous ¼ cup
    caster sugar
15ml/1 tbsp crème de
    cassis
fresh mint sprigs, to
    decorate

1 Combine the hazelnuts and breadcrumbs on a baking
sheet, then sprinkle over the demerara sugar. Place under a
moderate grill and cook until crisp and browned.

2 Whisk the egg whites in a bowl until stiff, then gradually
whisk in the caster sugar until thick and glossy. Whip the
cream until soft peaks form and fold into the meringue with
the breadcrumb mixture and vanilla essence.

3 Spoon the mixture into a 1.2 litre/2 pint/5 cup loaf tin.
Smooth the top level, then cover and freeze until firm.

4 To make the sauce, put the blackcurrants in a small bowl
with the sugar. Toss gently to mix and leave for about
30 minutes. Purée the blackcurrants in a food processor or
blender, then press through a nylon sieve until smooth. Add
the crème de cassis and chill in the fridge.

5 To serve, arrange a slice of ice cream on a plate, spoon over
a little sauce and decorate with fresh mint sprigs.

Muscat Grape Frappé

The flavour and perfume of the Muscat grape is rarely more enticing than when captured in this icy-cool salad. Because of its alcohol content this dish is not suitable for young children.

Serves 4

½ bottle Muscat wine, Beaumes de Venise, Frontignan or Rivsaltes

450g/1lb Muscat grapes

1 Pour the wine into a stainless steel or enamel tray, add 150ml/5fl oz/⅔ cup water and freeze for 3 hours or until completely solid.

2 Remove the seeds from the grapes with a pair of tweezers. If you have time, peel the grapes.

3 Scrape the frozen wine with a tablespoon to make a fine ice. Combine the grapes with the ice and spoon into 4 shallow glasses and serve.

Iced Chocolate and Nut Gâteau

Autumn hazelnuts add crunchiness to this popular iced dinner-party dessert.

Serves 6–8

75g/3oz/¾ cup shelled hazelnuts
about 32 sponge fingers
150ml/¼ pint/⅔ cup cold strong black coffee
30ml/2 tbsp Cognac or other brandy

450ml/¾ pint/1¾ cups double cream
75g/3oz/scant 1 cup icing sugar, sifted
150g/5oz plain chocolate
icing sugar and cocoa powder, for dusting

1 Preheat the oven to 200°C/400°F/Gas 6. Spread out the hazelnuts on a baking sheet and toast them in the oven for 5 minutes until golden. Transfer the nuts to a clean dish towel and rub off the skins. Cool, then chop finely.

2 Line a 1.2 litre/2 pint/5 cup loaf tin with clear film and cut the sponge fingers to fit the base and sides. Reserve the remaining biscuits.

3 Mix the coffee with the Cognac or other brandy in a shallow dish. Dip the sponge fingers briefly into the coffee mixture and return to the tin, sugary-side down.

4 Whip the cream with the icing sugar until it holds soft peaks. Roughly chop 75g/3oz of the chocolate, and fold into the cream with the hazelnuts.

5 Melt the remaining chocolate in a heatproof bowl set over a saucepan of barely simmering water. Cool, then fold into the cream mixture. Spoon into the tin.

6 Moisten the remaining biscuits in the coffee mixture and lay over the filling. Wrap and freeze until firm.

7 Remove the gâteau from the freezer 30 minutes before serving. Turn out on to a serving plate and dust with icing sugar and cocoa powder.

Blackberry Brown Sugar Meringue

A rich pudding which is elegant enough in presentation to be served at an autumnal dinner party.

Serves 6

For the meringue
175g/6oz/1½ cups soft
    light brown sugar
3 egg whites
5ml/1 tsp distilled malt
    vinegar
2.5ml/½ tsp vanilla
    essence

For the filling
350–450g/12oz–1lb/
    3–4 cups blackberries
30ml/2 tbsp crème de
    cassis
300ml/½ pint/1¼ cups
    double cream
15ml/1 tbsp icing sugar,
    sifted
small blackberry leaves,
    to decorate (optional)

1 Preheat the oven to 160°C/325°F/Gas 3. Draw a 20cm/8in circle on a sheet of non-stick baking paper, turn over and place on a baking sheet. Spread the brown sugar out on a baking sheet, dry in the oven for 8–10 minutes, then sieve.

2 Whisk the egg whites in a bowl until stiff. Add half the dried brown sugar, 15g/½oz/1 tbsp at a time, whisking well after each addition. Add the vinegar and vanilla essence, then fold in the remaining sugar.

3 Spoon the meringue on to the drawn circle on the paper, making a hollow in the centre. Bake for 45 minutes, then turn off the oven and leave the meringue in the oven with the door slightly open, until cold. Meanwhile, place the blackberries in a bowl, sprinkle over the crème de cassis and leave to macerate for 30 minutes.

4 When the meringue is cold, carefully peel off the non-stick baking paper and transfer the meringue to a serving plate. Lightly whip the cream with the icing sugar and spoon into the centre. Top with the blackberries and decorate with small blackberry leaves, if liked. Serve at once.

Clementines in Cinnamon Caramel

The combination of sweet, yet sharp clementines and caramel sauce with a hint of spice is divine.

Serves 4–6

8–12 clementines
225g/8oz/1 cup
    granulated sugar
300ml/½ pint/1¼ cups
    hand-hot water

2 cinnamon sticks
30ml/2 tbsp orange-
    flavoured liqueur
25g/1oz/¼ cup shelled
    pistachio nuts

1 Pare the rind from two clementines using a vegetable peeler and cut it into fine strips. Set aside.

2 Peel the clementines, removing all the pith but keeping them intact. Put the fruits in a serving bowl.

3 Gently heat the sugar in a pan until it dissolves and turns a rich golden brown. Immediately turn off the heat.

4 Pour the water into the pan, protecting your hand with a dish towel (the mixture will bubble and splutter). Bring slowly to the boil, stirring until the caramel dissolves. Add the shredded peel and cinnamon sticks, then simmer for 5 minutes. Stir in the liqueur.

5 Leave the syrup to cool for about 10 minutes, then pour over the clementines. Cover the bowl and chill for several hours or overnight.

6 Blanch the pistachio nuts in boiling water. Drain, cool and remove the dark outer skins. Scatter over the clementines and serve at once.

Chocolate Chestnut Roulade

Don't worry if this moist sponge cracks as you roll it – this is the sign of a good roulade.

Serves 8

175g/6oz plain chocolate
30ml/2 tbsp strong black coffee
5 eggs, separated
175g/6oz/1 cup caster sugar
250ml/18fl oz/1 cup double cream

225g/8oz unsweetened chestnut purée
45–60ml/3–4 tbsp icing sugar, plus extra for dusting
single cream, to serve

1 Preheat the oven to 180°C/350°F/Gas 4, then line and oil a 33 x 23cm/13 x 9in Swiss roll tin; use non-stick baking paper. Melt the chocolate in a bowl, then stir in the coffee. Leave to cool slightly.

2 Whisk the egg yolks and sugar together until thick and light, then stir in the cooled chocolate mixture. Whisk the egg whites in another bowl until stiff. Stir a spoonful into the chocolate mixture to lighten it, then gently fold in the rest.

3 Pour the mixture into the prepared tin, and spread level. Bake for 20 minutes. Remove from the oven, cover with a dish towel and leave to cool in the tin for several hours.

4 Whip the cream until soft peaks form. Mix together the chestnut purée and icing sugar; fold into the whipped cream.

5 Dust a sheet of greaseproof paper with icing sugar. Turn out the roulade on to this paper and peel off the lining paper. Trim the sides. Gently spread the chestnut cream evenly over the roulade to within 2.5cm/1in of the edges. Using the greaseproof paper to help you, carefully roll up the roulade as tightly and evenly as possible. Chill the roulade for about 2 hours, then dust liberally with icing sugar. Cut into thick slices. Serve with a little single cream poured over each slice.

Pasta Timbales with Apricot Sauce

If orzo cannot be found, other small soup pastas can be used for this dessert, which is made like a rice pudding.

Serves 4

100g/4oz/1 cup orzo
75g/3oz/⅓ cup caster sugar
pinch of salt
25g/1oz/2 tbsp butter
1 vanilla pod, split
750ml/1¼ pints/3⅓ cups milk
300ml/10fl oz/1¼ cups ready-made custard

45ml/3 tbsp Kirsch
15ml/1 tbsp powdered gelatine
oil, for greasing
400g/14oz canned apricots in juice
lemon juice
fresh flowers, to decorate (optional)

1 Place the pasta, sugar, pinch of salt, butter, vanilla pod and milk into a heavy saucepan and bring to the boil. Turn down the heat and simmer for 25 minutes until the pasta is tender and most of the liquid is absorbed. Stir frequently to prevent it from sticking.

2 Remove the vanilla pod and transfer the pasta to a bowl to cool. Stir in the custard and add 30ml/2 tbsp of the Kirsch.

3 Sprinkle the gelatine over 45ml/2 tbsp water in a small bowl set in a pan of barely simmering water. Allow to become spongy and heat gently to dissolve. Stir into the pasta.

4 Lightly oil 4 timbale moulds and spoon in the pasta. Chill for 2 hours until set.

5 Meanwhile, liquidize the apricots, pass through a sieve and add lemon juice and Kirsch to taste. Dilute with a little water if too thick. Loosen the timbales from their moulds and turn out on to individual plates. Serve with apricot sauce, decorated with fresh flowers if you wish.

Coffee Jellies with Amaretti Cream

This impressive dessert is very easy to prepare. For the best results, use a high–roasted Arabica bean for the coffee.

Serves 4

*75g/3oz/generous ¼ cup
  caster sugar
450ml/¾ pint/1¾ cups
  hot strong coffee
30–45ml/2–3 tbsp dark
  rum or coffee liqueur
20ml/4 tsp gelatine*

For the amaretti cream
*150ml/¼ pint/⅔ cup
  double cream*

*15ml/1 tbsp icing sugar,
  sifted
10–15ml/2–3 tsp
  instant coffee
  granules dissolved
  in 15ml/4 tbsp hot
  water
6 large amaretti biscuits,
  crushed*

1 Put the sugar in a saucepan with 75ml/5 tbsp water and stir over a gentle heat until dissolved. Increase the heat and allow the syrup to boil steadily, without stirring, for about 3–4 minutes.

2 Stir the hot coffee and rum or coffee liqueur into the syrup, then sprinkle the gelatine over the top and stir the mixture until it is completely dissolved.

3 Carefully pour the coffee jelly mixture into four wetted 150ml/ ¼ pint/⅔ cup moulds, allow to cool and then leave in the fridge for several hours until set.

4 To make the amaretti cream, lightly whip the cream with the icing sugar until the mixture holds stiff peaks. Stir in the coffee, then gently fold in all but 30ml/2 tbsp of the crushed amaretti biscuits.

5 Unmould the jellies on to four individual serving plates and spoon a little of the amaretti cream to one side. Dust over the reserved amaretti crumbs and serve at once.

Chocolate Date Torte

A stunning cake that tastes wonderful. Rich and gooey – it's a chocoholic's delight!

Serves 8

*4 egg whites
115g/4oz/½ cup caster
  sugar
200g/7oz plain chocolate
175g/6oz Medjool dates,
  stoned and chopped
175g/6oz/1½ cups
  walnuts or pecan
  nuts, chopped*

*5ml/2 tsp vanilla essence,
  plus a few extra drops*

For the frosting
*200g/7oz/scant 1 cup
  fromage frais
200g/7oz/scant 1 cup
  mascarpone
icing sugar, to taste*

1 Preheat the oven to 180°C/350°F/Gas 4. Lightly grease and base-line a 20cm/8in springform cake tin.

2 To make the frosting, mix together the fromage frais and mascarpone, and a few drops of vanilla essence and icing sugar to taste, then set aside.

3 Whisk the egg whites in a bowl until stiff peaks form. Whisk in 30ml/2 tbsp of the caster sugar until the meringue is thick and glossy, then fold in the remainder.

4 Chop 175g/6oz of the chocolate. Carefully fold into the meringue with the dates, nuts and 5ml/1 tsp of the vanilla essence. Pour into the prepared tin, spread level and bake for about 45 minutes, until risen around the edges.

5 Allow to cool in the tin for about 10 minutes, then turn out on to a wire rack. Peel off the lining paper and leave until completely cold. When cool, swirl the frosting over the top of the torte.

6 Melt the remaining chocolate in a bowl over hot water. Spoon into a small paper piping bag, snip off the top and drizzle the chocolate over the torte. Chill in the fridge before serving, cut into wedges.

Crème Caramel

This creamy, caramel-flavoured custard from France enjoys worldwide popularity.

Serves 4–6

115g/4oz/½ cup granulated sugar	6 eggs
300ml/½ pint/1¼ cups milk	75g/3oz/generous ¼ cup caster sugar
300ml/½ pint/1¼ cups single cream	2.5ml/½ tsp vanilla essence

1 Preheat the oven to 150°C/300°F/Gas 2 and half-fill a large roasting tin with water. Place the granulated sugar in a saucepan with 60ml/4 tbsp water and heat gently, swirling the pan occasionally, until the sugar has dissolved. Increase the heat and boil for a good caramel colour. Immediately pour the caramel into an ovenproof soufflé dish. Place in the roasting tin and set aside.

2 To make the egg custard, heat the milk and cream together in a pan until almost boiling. Meanwhile, beat the eggs, caster sugar and vanilla essence together in a bowl using a large balloon whisk.

3 Whisk the hot milk into the eggs and sugar, then strain the liquid through a sieve into the soufflé dish, on top of the cooled caramel base.

4 Transfer the tin to the centre of the oven and bake for about 1½–2 hours (topping up the water level after 1 hour), or until the custard has set in the centre. Lift the dish carefully out of the water and leave to cool, then cover and chill overnight in the fridge.

5 Loosen the sides of the chilled custard with a knife and then place an inverted plate (large enough to hold the caramel sauce that will flow out as well) on top of the dish. Holding the dish and plate together, turn upside down and give the whole thing a quick shake to release the crème caramel.

Australian Hazelnut Pavlova

A hazelnut meringue base is topped with orange cream, nectarines and raspberries in this lovely dessert.

Serves 4–6

3 egg whites	15ml/1 tbsp orange juice
175g/6oz/1 cup caster sugar	30ml/2 tbsp natural thick and creamy yogurt
5ml/1 tsp cornflour	2 ripe nectarines, stoned and sliced
5ml/1 tsp white wine vinegar	225g/8oz/2 cups raspberries, halved
40g/1½oz/generous ¼ cup chopped roasted hazelnuts	15–30ml/1–2 tbsp redcurrant jelly, warmed
250ml/8fl oz/1 cup double cream	

1 Preheat the oven to 140°C/275°F/Gas 1. Lightly grease a baking sheet. Draw a 20cm/8in circle on a sheet of baking parchment. Place pencil-side down on the baking sheet.

2 Place the egg whites in a clean, dry, grease-free bowl and whisk with an electric mixer until stiff peaks form. Whisk in the caster sugar 15g/½oz/1 tbsp at a time, whisking well after each addition.

3 Add the cornflour, vinegar and hazelnuts and fold in carefully with a large metal spoon.

4 Spoon the meringue on to the marked circle and spread out to the edges, making a dip in the centre.

5 Bake for about 1¼–1½hours, until crisp. Leave to cool completely and transfer to a serving platter.

6 Whip the double cream and orange juice until the mixture is just thick, stir in the yogurt and spoon on to the meringue. Top with the prepared fruit and drizzle over the warmed redcurrant jelly. Serve immediately.

Chinese Fruit Salad

For an unusual fruit salad with an oriental flavour, try this mixture of fruits in a tangy lime and lychee syrup.

Serves 4

115g/4oz/½ cup caster
  sugar
thinly pared rind and
  juice of 1 lime
400g/14oz can lychees in
  syrup
1 ripe mango, stoned and
  sliced

1 eating apple, cored and
  sliced
2 bananas, chopped
1 star fruit, sliced
  (optional)
5ml/1 tsp sesame seeds,
  toasted

1 Place the caster sugar in a small saucepan with the lime rind and 300ml/ ½ pint/1¼ cups water. Heat gently until the sugar dissolves completely, then increase the heat and boil gently for about 7–8 minutes. Remove the saucepan from the heat and leave on one side to cool the syrup.

2 Drain the lychees into a jug and pour the juice into the cooled lime syrup with the lime juice. Place all the prepared fruit in a bowl and pour over the lime and lychee syrup. Chill in the fridge for about 1 hour. Just before serving, sprinkle with toasted sesame seeds.

Cook's Tip
Try different combinations of fruit in this salad. You might like to include pawpaw, kiwi fruit or pineapple for a change.

Apricot and Almond Jalousie

Jalousie means "shutter", and the slatted pastry topping of this pie looks exactly like French window shutters.

Serves 4

225g/8oz ready-made
  puff pastry
a little beaten egg
90ml/6 tbsp apricot
  conserve

25g/1oz/2 tbsp caster
  sugar
30ml/2 tbsp flaked
  almonds
cream, to serve

1 Preheat the oven to 220°C/425°F/Gas 7. Roll out the pastry on a lightly floured surface and cut into a square measuring 30cm/12in. Cut in half to make two rectangles.

2 Place one piece of pastry on a wetted baking sheet and brush all round the edges with beaten egg. Spread over the apricot conserve.

3 Fold the remaining rectangle in half lengthways and cut about eight diagonal slits from the centre fold to within about 1cm/½in from the edge all the way along.

4 Unfold the cut pastry and lay it on top of the pastry on the baking sheet. Press the pastry edges together well to seal and knock them up with the back of a knife.

5 Brush the slashed pastry with water and sprinkle over the caster sugar and flaked almonds.

6 Bake in the oven for 25–30 minutes, until well risen and golden brown. Remove the jalousie from the oven and leave to cool. Serve sliced, with cream or natural yogurt.

Cook's Tip
Make smaller individual jalousies and serve them with morning coffee, if you like. Use other flavours of fruit conserve for a change.

Baked American Cheesecake

The lemon-flavoured cream cheese provides a subtle filling for this classic dessert.

Makes 9 squares
For the base
175g/6oz/1½ cups
   crushed digestive
   biscuits
40g/1½oz/3 tbsp butter,
   melted

For the topping
450g/1lb/2½ cups curd
   cheese or full-fat soft
   cheese
115g/4oz/½ cup caster
   sugar

3 eggs
finely grated rind of
   1 lemon
15ml/1 tbsp lemon juice
2.5ml/½ tsp vanilla
   essence
15ml/1 tbsp cornflour
30ml/2 tbsp soured
   cream
150ml/¼ pint/⅔ cup
   soured cream and
   1.5ml/¼ tsp ground
   cinnamon, to decorate

1 Preheat the oven to 170°C/325°F/Gas 3. Lightly grease and line an 18cm/7in square loose-based cake tin.

2 Place the crushed biscuits and butter in a bowl and mix well. Tip into the base of the prepared cake tin and press down firmly with a potato masher.

3 Place the cheese in a bowl, add the sugar and beat well until smooth. Add the eggs one at a time, beating well after each addition and then stir in the lemon rind and juice, the vanilla essence, cornflour and soured cream. Beat until the mixture is completely smooth.

4 Pour the mixture on to the biscuit base and smooth the top level. Bake for 1¼ hours, or until the cheesecake has set in the centre. Turn off the oven but leave the cheesecake inside until completely cold.

5 Remove the cheesecake from the tin, top with the soured cream and swirl with the back of a spoon. Sprinkle with cinnamon and cut into squares.

Mango Ice Cream

Canned mangoes are used to make this deliciously rich and creamy ice cream, which has an oriental flavour.

Serves 4–6
2 x 425g/15oz cans sliced
   mango, drained
50g/2oz/¼ cup caster
   sugar
30ml/2 tbsp lime juice
15ml/1 tbsp gelatine

350ml/12fl oz/1½ cups
   double cream, lightly
   whipped
fresh mint sprigs, to
   decorate

1 Reserve four slices of mango for decoration and chop the remainder. Place the mango pieces in a bowl with the caster sugar and lime juice.

2 Put 45ml/3 tbsp hot water in a small heatproof bowl and sprinkle over the gelatine. Place over a saucepan of gently simmering water and stir until dissolved. Pour on to the mango mixture and mix well.

3 Add the lightly whipped cream and fold into the mango mixture. Pour the mixture into a plastic freezer container and freeze until half frozen.

4 Place the half-frozen ice cream in a food processor or blender and process until smooth. Spoon back into the container and return to the freezer to freeze completely.

5 Remove from the freezer 10 minutes before serving and place in the fridge. Serve scoops of ice cream decorated with pieces of the reserved sliced mango and fresh mint sprigs.

Rippled Chocolate Ice Cream

Rich, smooth and packed with chocolate, this heavenly ice cream is an all-round-the-world chocoholics' favourite.

Serves 4

60ml/4 tbsp chocolate
  and hazelnut spread
450ml/³⁄₄ pint/1³⁄₄ cups
  double cream
15ml/1 tbsp icing sugar

50g/2oz plain chocolate,
  chopped
plain chocolate curls, to
  decorate

1 Mix together the chocolate and hazelnut spread and 75ml/5 tbsp of the double cream in a bowl.

2 Place the remaining cream in a second bowl, sift in the icing sugar and beat until softly whipped.

3 Lightly fold in the chocolate and hazelnut mixture with the chopped chocolate until the mixture is rippled. Transfer to a plastic freezer container and freeze for 3–4 hours, until firm.

4 Remove the ice cream from the freezer about 10 minutes before serving to allow it to soften slightly. Spoon or scoop into dessert dishes or glasses and top each serving with a few plain chocolate curls.

Fruited Rice Ring

This pudding ring looks beautiful but you could stir the fruit in and serve in individual dishes instead.

Serves 4

65g/2½oz/¼ cup short
  grain pudding rice
900ml/1½ pints/3¾ cups
  semi-skimmed milk
1 cinnamon stick
175g/6oz dried fruit
  salad

175ml/6fl oz/³⁄₄ cup
  orange juice
40g/1½oz/3 tbsp caster
  sugar
finely grated rind of
  1 small orange

1 Place the rice, milk and cinnamon stick in a large saucepan and bring to the boil. Cover and simmer, stirring occasionally, for about 1½ hours, until all the liquid is absorbed.

2 Meanwhile, place the fruit and orange juice in a pan and bring to the boil. Cover and simmer very gently for about 1 hour, until tender and all the liquid is absorbed.

3 Remove the cinnamon stick from the rice and discard. Stir in the caster sugar and orange rind.

4 Tip the cooked fruit salad into the base of a lightly oiled 1.5 litre/2½ pint/6 cup ring mould. Spoon the rice over, smoothing it down firmly. Chill in the fridge.

5 Run a knife around the edge of the mould and turn out the rice carefully on to a serving plate.

Apricot Mousse

This light fluffy dessert can be made with any dried fruits instead of apricots – try dried peaches, prunes or apples.

Serves 4

300g/10oz ready-to-eat dried apricots
300ml/½ pint/1¼ cups fresh orange juice
200g/7oz/¾ cup low-fat fromage frais
2 egg whites
fresh mint, to decorate

1 Place the apricots in a saucepan with the orange juice and heat gently until boiling. Cover the pan and simmer gently for 3 minutes.

2 Cool slightly, then place in a food processor or blender and process until smooth. Stir in the fromage frais.

3 Whisk the egg whites until stiff enough to hold soft peaks, then fold gently into the apricot mixture.

4 Spoon the mousse into four stemmed glasses or one large serving dish. Chill in the fridge before serving. Decorate with sprigs of fresh mint.

Cook's Tip
To make a speedier, fool-type dessert, omit the egg whites and simply swirl together the apricot mixture and the fromage frais.

Apple Foam with Blackberries

Any seasonal soft fruit can be used for this lovely dessert if blackberries are not available.

Serves 4

225g/8oz/2 cups blackberries
150ml/¼ pint/generous ½ cup apple juice
5ml/1 tsp powdered gelatine
15ml/1 tbsp clear honey
2 egg whites

1 Place the blackberries in a saucepan with 60ml/4 tbsp of the apple juice and heat gently until the fruit is soft. Remove from the heat, cool, then chill in the fridge.

2 Sprinkle the gelatine over the remaining apple juice in a small pan and stir over a gentle heat until dissolved. Stir in the honey.

3 Whisk the egg whites until stiff peaks form. Continue whisking hard and gradually pour in the hot gelatine mixture until well mixed.

4 Quickly spoon the foam into rough mounds on individual plates. Chill. To serve, spoon the blackberries and juice around the foam rounds.

Cook's Tip
Make sure you dissolve the gelatine over a very low heat. It must not boil, or it will lose its setting ability.

Raspberry Passion Fruit Swirls

If passion fruit is not available, this simple dessert can be made with raspberries alone.

Serves 4

300g/11oz/generous
  2½ cups raspberries
2 passion fruit
350ml/12fl oz/1⅓ cups
  low-fat fromage frais

25g/1oz/2 tbsp caster
  sugar
raspberries and sprigs of
  fresh mint, to decorate

1 Mash the raspberries in a small bowl with a fork until the juice runs. Scoop out the passion fruit pulp into a separate bowl with the fromage frais and sugar and mix well.

2 Spoon alternate spoonfuls of the raspberry pulp and the fromage frais mixture into stemmed glasses or one large serving dish, stirring lightly to create a swirled effect.

3 Decorate the desserts with whole raspberries and sprigs of fresh mint. Serve chilled.

Creamy Mango Cheesecake

This low-fat cheesecake is as creamy as any other, but makes a healthier dessert option.

Serves 4

115g/4oz/1¼ cups
  rolled oats
40g/1½oz/3 tbsp
  sunflower margarine
30ml/2 tbsp clear honey
1 large ripe mango
300g/10oz/1¼ cups low-
  fat soft cheese

150ml/¼ pint/⅔ cup
  low-fat natural yogurt
finely grated rind of
  1 small lime
45ml/3 tbsp apple juice
20ml/4 tsp gelatine
fresh mango and lime
  slices, to decorate

1 Preheat the oven to 200°C/400°F/Gas 6. Mix together the oats, margarine and honey; press into the base of a 20cm/8in loose-bottomed cake tin. Bake for 12–15 minutes. Cool.

2 Peel, stone and roughly chop the mango. Process with the cheese, yogurt and lime rind until smooth. Heat the apple juice until boiling, sprinkle the gelatine over it, stir to dissolve, then stir into the cheese mixture. Pour into the tin and chill until set. Turn out and decorate with mango and lime slices.

Frudités with Honey Dip

This dish is shared and would be ideal to serve at an informal lunch or supper party.

Serves 4

Place 225g/8oz/1 cup Greek-style yogurt in a dish, beat until smooth, then stir in 45ml/3 tbsp clear honey, leaving a marbled effect. Cut a selection of fruits into wedges or bite-size pieces or leave whole, depending on your choice. Arrange on a platter with the bowl of dip in the centre. Serve chilled.

Boston Banoffee Pie

This dessert's rich, creamy, toffee-style filling just can't be
resisted – but who cares!

Serves 4–6

150g/5oz/1¼ cups plain
  flour
225g/8oz/1 cup butter
50g/2oz/¼ cup caster
  sugar
½ x 400g/14oz can
  skimmed, sweetened
  condensed milk

115g/4oz/⅔ cup soft
  light brown sugar
30ml/2 tbsp golden syrup
2 small bananas, sliced
a little lemon juice
whipped cream and
  grated plain chocolate

1 Preheat the oven to 160°C/325°F/Gas 3. Place the flour
and 115g/4oz/ ½ cup of the butter in a bowl, then stir in the
caster sugar. Squeeze the mixture together with your hands
until it forms a dough. Press into the base of a 20cm/8in
loose-based fluted flan tin. Bake blind for 25–30 minutes,
until the pastry is lightly browned.

2 Place the remaining butter with the condensed milk,
brown sugar and golden syrup into a non-stick saucepan and
heat gently, stirring, until the butter has melted and the sugar
has completely dissolved.

3 Bring to a gentle boil and cook for 7 minutes, stirring all
the time (to prevent burning), until the mixture thickens and
turns a light caramel colour. Pour on to the cooked pastry
base and leave until cold.

4 Sprinkle the bananas with lemon juice and arrange in
overlapping circles on top of the caramel filling, leaving a gap
in the centre. Pipe a swirl of whipped cream in the centre and
sprinkle with the grated chocolate.

Cook's Tip
*Do not peel and slice the bananas until you are ready to
serve or they will become slimy.*

Strawberry and Blueberry Tart

This tart works equally well using either autumn or winter
fruits as long as there is a riot of colour.

Serves 6–8

225g/8oz/2 cups plain
  flour
pinch of salt
75g/3oz/scant ¾ cup
  icing sugar
150g/5oz/generous ½ cup
  unsalted butter
1 egg yolk

For the filling
350g/12oz/1¼ cups
  mascarpone

30ml/2 tbsp icing sugar
few drops of vanilla
  essence
finely grated rind of
  1 orange
450–675g/1–1½lb/
  4½ cups fresh mixed
  strawberries and
  blueberries
90ml/6 tbsp redcurrant
  jelly
30ml/2 tbsp orange juice

1 Sift the flour, salt and sugar in a bowl. Dice the butter and
rub it in until the mixture resembles coarse breadcrumbs. Mix
in the egg yolk and 10ml/2 tsp cold water. Gather the dough
together, knead lightly, wrap and chill for 1 hour.

2 Preheat the oven to 190°C/375°F/Gas 5. Roll out the
pastry and use to line a 25cm/10in fluted flan tin. Prick the
base and chill for 15 minutes in the fridge.

3 Line the chilled pastry case with greaseproof paper and
baking beans, then bake blind for 15 minutes. Remove the
paper and beans and bake for a further 15 minutes, until crisp
and golden. Leave to cool in the tin.

4 Beat together the mascarpone, sugar, vanilla essence and
orange rind in a mixing bowl until smooth.

5 Remove the pastry case from the tin, then spoon in the
filling and pile the fruits on top. Heat the redcurrant jelly with
the orange juice until runny, sieve, then brush over the fruit to
form a glaze.

Strawberries in Spiced Grape Jelly

This light dessert would be ideal to serve after a rich and filling main course.

Serves 4

450ml/¾ pint/1¾ cups red grape juice	225g/8oz/2 cups strawberries, chopped
1 cinnamon stick	strawberries and
1 small orange	shredded orange rind,
15ml/1 tbsp gelatine	to decorate

1 Place the grape juice in a saucepan with the cinnamon and thinly pared orange rind. Infuse over a gentle heat for 10 minutes, then remove the cinnamon and orange rind. Sprinkle the squeezed orange juice over the gelatine. Stir into the grape juice to dissolve. Allow to cool until just beginning to set.

2 Stir in the strawberries and then quickly tip the mixture into a 1 litre/1¾ pint/4 cup mould or serving dish. Chill in the fridge until it has set. Dip the mould quickly into hot water and invert on to a serving plate. Decorate with fresh strawberries and shreds of orange rind.

Plum and Port Sorbet

Rather a grown-up sorbet, this one, but you could use fresh still red grape juice in place of the port or wine.

Serves 4

900g/2lb ripe red plums, stoned and halved	45ml/3 tbsp ruby port or red wine
75g/3oz/generous ¼ cup caster sugar	crisp sweet biscuits, to serve
45ml/3 tbsp water	

1 Place the plums in a saucepan with the sugar and water. Stir over a gentle heat until the sugar is melted, then cover and simmer gently for about 5 minutes, until the fruit is soft.

2 Turn into a food processor or blender and purée until smooth, then stir in the port or red wine. Cool completely, then tip into a plastic freezer container and freeze until the sorbet is firm around the edges. Process until smooth. Spoon back into the freezer container and freeze until solid.

3 Allow to soften slightly at room temperature for about 15–20 minutes before serving in scoops, with sweet biscuits.

Quick Apricot Blender Whip

This is one of the quickest desserts you could make – and also one of the prettiest.

Serves 4

Drain the juice from 400g/14oz can apricot halves in juice and place the fruit in a blender or food processor with 1 tbsp Grand Marnier or brandy. Process until smooth. Spoon the fruit purée and ¾ cup plain strained yogurt in alternate spoonfuls into four tall glasses or glass dishes, swirling them together slightly to give a marbled effect. Lightly toast 2 tbsp slivered almonds until they are golden. Let them cool slightly and then sprinkle them on top.

Tofu Berry Brulée

This is a lighter variation of a classic dessert. Use any soft fruits that are in season.

Serves 4

225g/8oz/2 cups red
  berry fruits such as
  strawberries,
  raspberries and
  redcurrants

300g/11oz packet silken
  tofu
45ml/3 tbsp icing sugar
65g/2½oz/¼ cup
  demerara sugar

1 Halve or quarter any large strawberries, but leave the smaller ones whole. Mix with the other chosen berries.

2 Place the tofu and icing sugar in a food processor or blender and process until smooth.

3 Stir in the fruits and spoon into a flameproof dish with a 900ml/1½ pint/3¾ cup capacity. Sprinkle the top with enough demerara sugar to cover evenly.

4 Place under a very hot grill until the sugar melts and caramelizes. Chill in the fridge before serving.

Cook's Tip
Choose silken tofu rather than firm tofu as it gives a smoother texture in this type of dish. Firm tofu is better for cooking in chunks.

Emerald Fruit Salad

This vibrant green fruit salad contains a hint of lime and is sweetened with honey.

Serves 4

30ml/2 tbsp lime juice
30ml/2 tbsp clear honey
2 green eating apples,
  cored and sliced
1 ripe Ogen melon, diced

2 kiwi fruit, sliced
1 star fruit, sliced
fresh mint sprigs, to
  decorate

1 Mix together the lime juice and honey in a large bowl, then toss in the apple slices.

2 Stir in the melon, kiwi fruit and star fruit. Place in a glass serving dish and chill in the fridge before serving.

3 Decorate with mint sprigs and serve with yogurt or fromage frais, if you wish.

Cook's Tip
Colour-themed fruit salads are fun to create and easy, given the wide availability of exotic fruits. You could try an orange-coloured salad using cantaloupe melon, apricots, peaches or nectarines, oranges or satsumas, and mango or pawpaw.

Peach and Ginger Pashka

This simpler adaptation of a Russian Easter favourite is made with lighter ingredients than the traditional version.

Serves 4–6

350g/12oz/1½ cups low-fat cottage cheese
2 ripe peaches
120ml/4fl oz/½ cup low-fat natural yogurt
2 pieces stem ginger in syrup, drained and chopped

30ml/2 tbsp stem ginger syrup
2.5ml/½ tsp vanilla essence
peach slices and toasted flaked almonds, to decorate

1 Drain the cottage cheese and rub through a sieve into a bowl. Stone and roughly chop the peaches.

2 Mix together the chopped peaches, cottage cheese, yogurt, ginger, syrup and vanilla essence.

3 Line a new clean flowerpot or a sieve with a piece of clean fine cloth such as muslin.

4 Tip in the cheese mixture, then wrap over the cloth and place a weight on top. Leave over a bowl in a cool place to drain overnight. To serve, unwrap the cloth and invert the pashka on to a plate. Decorate with peach slices and almonds.

Chilled Chocolate Slice

This is a very rich family pudding, but it is also designed to use up the occasional leftover.

Serves 6–8

115g/4oz/½ cup butter, melted
225g/8oz ginger biscuits, finely crushed
50g/2oz stale sponge cake crumbs
60–75ml/4–5 tbsp orange juice
115g/4oz stoned dates

25g/1oz/¼ cup finely chopped nuts
175g/6oz bitter chocolate
300ml/½ pint/1¼ cups whipping cream
grated chocolate and icing sugar, to decorate

1 Mix together the butter and ginger biscuit crumbs, then pack around the sides and base of an 18cm/7in loose-based flan tin. Chill in the fridge while making the filling.

2 Put the cake crumbs into a large bowl with the orange juice and leave to soak. Warm the dates thoroughly, then mash and blend into the cake crumbs along with the nuts.

3 Melt the chocolate with 45–60ml/3–4 tbsp of the cream. Softly whip the rest of the cream, then fold in the melted chocolate mixture.

4 Stir the cream and chocolate mixture into the crumbs and mix well. Pour into the biscuit case, mark into portions and leave to set. Scatter over the grated chocolate and dust with icing sugar. Serve cut in wedges.

Tangerine Trifle

An unusual variation on a traditional trifle – of course, you can add a little alcohol if you wish.

Serves 4

5 trifle sponges, halved
   lengthways
30ml/2 tbsp apricot jam
15–20 ratafia biscuits
142g/4 3/4oz packet
   tangerine jelly
300g/11oz can mandarin
   oranges, drained,
   reserving juice

600ml/1 pint/2½ cups
   ready-made
   (or home-made)
   custard
whipped cream and
   shreds of orange rind,
   to decorate
caster sugar, for
   sprinkling

1 Spread the halved sponge cakes with apricot conserve and arrange in the base of a deep serving bowl or glass dish. Sprinkle the ratafias over the top.

2 Break up the jelly into a heatproof measuring jug, add the juice from the canned mandarins and dissolve in a saucepan of hot water or in the microwave. Stir until the liquid clears.

3 Make up to 600ml/1 pint/2½ cups with ice cold water, stir well and leave to cool for up to 30 minutes. Scatter the mandarin oranges over the cake and ratafias.

4 Pour the jelly over the mandarin oranges, cake and ratafias and chill in the fridge for 1 hour, or more.

5 When the jelly has set, pour the custard over the top and chill again in the fridge.

6 When ready to serve, pipe the whipped cream over the custard. Wash the orange rind shreds, sprinkle them with caster sugar and use to decorate the trifle.

Blackberry and Apple Romanoff

Rich yet fruity, this dessert is popular with most people and very quick and easy to make.

Serves 6–8

350g/12oz sharp eating
   apples, peeled, cored
   and chopped
40g/1½oz/3 tbsp caster
   sugar
250ml/8fl oz/1 cup
   whipping cream
5ml/1 tsp grated lemon
   rind
90ml/6 tbsp Greek-style
   yogurt

50g/2oz (about 4–6)
   crisp meringues,
   roughly crumbled
225g/8oz/2 cups
   blackberries (fresh
   or frozen)
whipped cream, a few
   blackberries and
   fresh mint leaves,
   to decorate

1 Line a 900ml–1.2 litre/1½–2 pint/4–5 cup pudding basin with clear film. Toss the chopped apples into a saucepan with 1oz/2 tbsp sugar and cook for 2–3 minutes, or until softening. Mash with a fork and leave to cool.

2 Whip the cream and fold in the lemon rind, yogurt, the remaining sugar, apples and meringues.

3 Gently stir in the blackberries, then tip the mixture into the pudding basin and freeze for 1–3 hours.

4 Turn out on to a plate and remove the clear film. Decorate with whirls of whipped cream, blackberries and mint leaves.

Apple and Hazelnut Shortcake

This is a variation on the classic strawberry shortcake and is equally delicious.

Serves 8–10

150g/5oz/generous 1 cup
  plain wholemeal flour
50g/2oz/½ cup ground
  hazelnuts
50g/2oz/6 tbsp icing
  sugar, sifted
150g/5oz/generous 1 cup
  unsalted butter
3 sharp eating apples
5ml/1 tsp lemon juice
15–25g/½–1oz/1–2
  tbsp caster sugar

15ml/1 tbsp chopped
  fresh mint, or 5ml/
  1 tsp dried mint
250ml/8fl oz/1 cup
  whipping cream
a few drops of vanilla
  essence
a few fresh mint leaves
  and whole hazelnuts,
  to decorate

1 Process the flour, ground hazelnuts and icing sugar with the butter in a food processor in short bursts, until they come together. Bring the dough together, adding a very little iced water if needed. Knead briefly, wrap and chill for 30 minutes.

2 Preheat the oven to 160°C/325°F/Gas 3. Cut the dough in half and roll out each half to an 18cm/7in round. Place on greaseproof paper on baking sheets. Bake for 40 minutes, or until crisp. Allow to cool.

3 Peel, core and chop the apples into a saucepan with the lemon juice. Add sugar to taste; cook for 2–3 minutes, until just soft. Mash the apple gently with the mint; leave to cool.

4 Whip the cream with the vanilla essence. Place one shortbread base on a serving plate. Spread half the apple and half the cream on top.

5 Place the second shortcake on top, then spread over the remaining apple and cream, swirling the top layer of cream gently. Decorate the top with mint leaves and a few whole hazelnuts, then serve at once.

Lemon Cheesecake

A lovely light cream cheese filling is sandwiched between brandy snaps in this tasty dessert.

Serves 8

½ x 142g/4¾ oz packet
  lemon jelly
450g/1lb/2 cups low-fat
  cream cheese
10ml/2 tsp grated lemon
  rind
75–115g/3–4oz/about ½
  cup caster sugar

a few drops of vanilla
  essence
150ml/¼ pint/½ cup
  Greek-style yogurt
8 brandy snaps
a few fresh mint leaves
  and icing sugar, to
  decorate

1 Dissolve the jelly in 45–60ml/3–4 tbsp boiling water in a heatproof measuring jug and, when clear, add sufficient cold water to make up to 150ml/¼ pint/⅔ cup. Chill in the fridge until beginning to thicken. Meanwhile, line a 450g/1lb loaf tin with clear film.

2 Cream the cheese with the lemon rind, sugar and vanilla and beat until light and smooth. Then fold in the thickening lemon jelly and the yogurt. Spoon into the prepared tin and chill until set. Preheat the oven to 160°C/325°F/Gas 3.

3 Place two or three brandy snaps at a time on a baking sheet. Place in the oven for no more than 1 minute, until soft enough to unroll and flatten out completely. Leave on a cold plate or tray to harden again. Repeat with the remaining brandy snaps.

4 To serve, turn the cheesecake out on to a board with the help of the clear film. Cut into eight slices and place one slice on each brandy snap base. Decorate with mint leaves and dust with icing sugar.

Frozen Strawberry Mousse Cake

Children love this cake because it is pink and pretty, and it is just like an ice cream treat.

Serves 4–6

*425g/15oz can
  strawberries in syrup
15ml/1 tbsp powdered
  gelatine
6 trifle sponge cakes
45ml/3 tbsp strawberry
  conserve*

*200ml/7fl oz/scant 1 cup
  crème fraîche
200ml/7fl oz/scant 1 cup
  whipped cream, to
  decorate*

1 Strain the syrup from the strawberries into a large heatproof jug. Sprinkle over the gelatine and stir well. Stand the jug in a saucepan of hot water and stir until the gelatine has dissolved.

2 Leave to cool, then chill in the fridge for just under 1 hour, until beginning to set. Meanwhile, cut the sponge cake in half lengthways and then spread the cut surfaces evenly with the strawberry conserve.

3 Slowly whisk the crème fraîche into the strawberry jelly, then whisk in the canned strawberries. Line a deep 20cm/8in loose-based cake tin with non-stick baking paper.

4 Pour half the strawberry mousse mixture into the tin, arrange the sponge cakes over the surface and then spoon over the remaining mousse mixture, pushing down any sponge cakes which rise up.

5 Freeze for 1–2 hours until firm. Unmould the cake and carefully remove the lining paper. Transfer to a serving plate. Decorate with whirls of cream, a few strawberry leaves and a fresh strawberry, if you have them.

Lemon and Blackberry Soufflé

This tangy dessert is complemented wonderfully by a rich blackberry sauce.

Serves 6

*grated rind of 1 lemon
  and juice of 2 lemons
15ml/1 tbsp powdered
  gelatine
5 size 4 eggs, separated
150g/4oz/1¼ cups caster
  sugar
a few drops of vanilla
  essence
400ml/14fl oz/1²⁄₃cups
  whipping cream*

For the sauce
*175g/6oz/1½ cups
  blackberries (fresh or
  frozen)
25–40g/1–1½oz/2–3
  tbsp caster sugar
a few fresh blackberries
  and blackberry leaves,
  to decorate*

1 Place the lemon juice in a small saucepan and heat through. Sprinkle on the gelatine and leave to dissolve, or heat further until clear. Allow to cool. Put the lemon rind, egg yolks, sugar and vanilla into a large bowl and whisk until the mixture is very thick, pale and really creamy.

2 Whisk the egg whites until almost stiff. Whip the cream until stiff. Stir the gelatine mixture into the yolks, then fold in the whipped cream and lastly the egg whites. When lightly but thoroughly blended, turn into a 1.5 litre/2½ pint/6 cup soufflé dish and freeze for about 2 hours.

3 To make the sauce, place the blackberries in a pan with the sugar and cook for 4–6 minutes until the juices begin to run and all the sugar has dissolved. Pass through a nylon sieve to remove the seeds, then chill until ready to serve.

4 When the soufflé is almost frozen, scoop or spoon out on to individual plates and serve with the blackberry sauce.

Apricot and Banana Compote

This compote is delicious served on its own or with custard or ice cream. Served for breakfast, it makes a tasty start to the day.

Serves 4

225g/8oz /1 cup
   ready-to-eat dried
   apricots
300ml/½ pint/1¼ cups
   orange juice
150ml/¼ pint/⅔ cup apple
   juice

5ml/ 1 tsp ground ginger
3 medium bananas, sliced
25g/1oz/¾ cup toasted
   flaked almonds,
   to serve

1 Put the apricots in a saucepan with the fruit juices and ginger and stir. Cover, bring to the boil and simmer gently for 10 minutes, stirring occasionally.

2 Set aside to cool, leaving the lid on. Once cool, stir in the sliced bananas.

3 Spoon the fruit and juices into a serving dish.

4 Serve immediately, or cover and chill for several hours before serving. Sprinkle with flaked almonds just before serving.

Cook's Tip
Use other combinations of dried and fresh fruit such as prunes or figs and apples or peaches.

Iced Pineapple Crush

The sweet tropical flavours of pineapple and lychees combine well with richly scented strawberries to make this a most refreshing salad.

Serves 4

2 small pineapples
450g/1lb strawberries
400g/14 oz can lychees

45ml/3 tbsp kirsch or
   white rum
30ml/2 tbsp icing sugar

1 Remove the crown from both pineapples by cutting around the top and twisting sharply. Reserve the leaves for decoration.

2 Cut the pineapple in half diagonally with a large serrated knife.

3 Cut around the flesh inside the skin with a small serrated knife, keeping the skin intact. Remove the core from the pineapples.

4 Chop the pineapples and combine with the strawberries and lychees, taking care not to damage the fruit.

5 Combine the kirsch or rum with the icing sugar, pour over the fruit and freeze for 45 minutes.

6 Tip the fruit out into the pineapple skins and decorate with pineapple leaves.

Cook's Tip
A ripe pineapple will resist pressure when squeezed and will have a sweet, fragrant smell. In winter, freezing conditions can cause the flesh to blacken.

Winter Fruit Salad

A colourful, refreshing and nutritious fruit salad that is ideal served with cream or Greek-style yogurt.

Serves 6

227g/8oz can pineapple cubes in fruit juice
200ml/7fl oz/ scant 1 cup freshly squeezed orange juice
200ml/7fl oz/ scant 1 cup apple juice
30ml/2 tbsp orange or apple liqueur
30ml/2 tbsp clear honey (optional)
2 oranges, peeled

2 green-skinned eating apples, chopped
2 pears, chopped
4 plums, stoned and chopped
12 fresh dates, stoned and chopped
115g/4oz/2 cups ready-to-eat dried apricots
fresh mint sprigs, to decorate

1 Drain the pineapple, reserving the juice. Put the pineapple juice, orange juice, apple juice, liqueur and honey, if using, in a large serving bowl and stir.

2 Segment the oranges, catching any juice in the bowl, and put the orange segments and pineapple in the fruit juice mixture.

3 Add the apples and pears to the bowl.

4 Stir in the plums, dates and apricots, cover and chill for several hours. Decorate with fresh mint sprigs to serve.

Cook's Tip
Use other unsweetened fruit juices such as pink grapefruit and pineapple juice in place of the orange and apple juice.

Fresh Figs in Honey and Wine

Any variety of figs can be used in this recipe, their ripeness determining the cooking time. Choose ones that are plump and firm, and use quickly as they don't store well.

Serves 6

450ml/¾ pint/1⅞ cups dry white wine
75g/3oz/⅓ cup clear honey
50g/2oz/¼ cup caster sugar
1 small orange
8 whole cloves
450g/1lb fresh figs
1 cinnamon stick

mint sprigs or bay leaves, to decorate

For the cream
300ml/½pint/1¼ cups double cream
1 vanilla pod
5ml/1 tsp caster sugar

1 Put the wine, honey and sugar in a heavy-based saucepan and heat gently until the sugar dissolves.

2 Stud the orange with the cloves and add to the syrup with the figs and cinnamon. Cover and simmer very gently for 5–10 minutes until the figs are softened. Transfer to a serving dish and leave to cool.

3 Put 150ml/¼ pint/⅔ cup of the cream in a small saucepan with the vanilla pod. Bring almost to the boil, then leave to cool and infuse for 30 minutes. Remove the vanilla pod and mix with the remaining cream and sugar in a bowl. Whip lightly. Transfer to a serving dish. Decorate the figs with the mint sprigs or bay leaves, then serve with the cream.

Farmhouse Biscuits

Delightfully wholesome, these farmhouse biscuits are ideal to serve with morning coffee.

Makes 18

115g/4oz/¹/₂ cup butter or margarine, at room temperature
90g/3¹/₂oz/7 tbsp light brown sugar
65g/2¹/₂oz/5 tbsp crunchy peanut butter
1 egg
50g/2oz/¹/₂ cup plain flour

2.5ml/¹/₂ tsp baking powder
2.5ml/¹/₂ tsp ground cinnamon
1.5ml/¹/₄ tsp salt
175g/6oz/1¹/₂ cups muesli
50g/2oz/¹/₂ cup raisins
50g/2oz/¹/₂ cup chopped walnuts

1 Preheat the oven to 180°C/350°F/Gas 4. Grease a baking sheet.

2 Cream the butter or margarine and sugar until light and fluffy. Beat in the peanut butter and then beat in the egg.

3 Sift the flour, baking powder, cinnamon and salt over the peanut butter mixture and stir to blend. Stir in the muesli, raisins and walnuts. Taste the mixture to see if it needs more sugar, as the sugar content of muesli varies.

4 Drop rounded tablespoonfuls of the mixture on to the prepared baking sheet about 2.5cm/1in apart. Press gently with the back of a spoon to spread each mound into a circle.

5 Bake until lightly coloured, about 15 minutes. With a palette knife, transfer to a wire rack to cool. Store in an airtight container.

Crunchy Oatmeal Biscuits

For nutty oatmeal biscuits, substitute an equal quantity of chopped walnuts or pecan nuts for the cereal.

Makes 14

175g/6oz/³/₄ cup butter or margarine, at room temperature
175g/6oz/³/₄ cup caster sugar
1 egg yolk
175g/6oz/1¹/₂ cups plain flour

5ml/1 tsp bicarbonate of soda
2.5ml/¹/₂ tsp salt
50g/2oz/²/₃ cup rolled oats
50g/2oz/²/₃ cup small crunchy nugget cereal

1 Cream the butter or margarine and sugar together until light and fluffy. Mix in the egg yolk.

2 Sift over the flour, bicarbonate of soda and salt, then stir into the butter mixture. Add the oats and cereal and stir to blend. Chill for at least 20 minutes.

3 Preheat the oven to 190°C/375°F/Gas 5. Grease a baking sheet.

4 Roll the mixture into balls. Place them on the baking sheet and flatten with the base of a floured glass.

5 Bake until golden, about 10–12 minutes. Then with a palette knife, transfer to a wire rack to cool. Store in an airtight container.

Apricot Yogurt Cookies

These cookies do not keep well, so it is best to eat them within two days, or to freeze them.

Makes 16

*175g/6oz/1¹/₂ cups plain
  flour
5ml/1 tsp baking powder
5ml/1 tsp ground
  cinnamon
75g/3oz/scant 1 cup
  rolled oats
75g/3oz/¹/₂ cup light
  muscovado sugar
115g/4oz/¹/₂ cup chopped
  ready-to-eat dried
  apricots*

*15ml/1 tbsp flaked
  hazelnuts or almonds
150g/5oz/scant ²/₃ cup
  natural yogurt
45ml/3 tbsp sunflower oil
demerara sugar, to
  sprinkle*

1 Preheat the oven to 190°C/375°F/Gas 5. Lightly oil a large baking sheet.

2 Sift together the flour, baking powder and cinnamon. Stir in the oats, sugar, apricots and nuts.

3 Beat together the yogurt and oil, then stir evenly into the mixture to make a firm dough. If necessary, add a little more yogurt.

4 Use your hands to roll the mixture into about 16 small balls, place on the baking sheet and flatten with a fork.

5 Sprinkle with demerara sugar. Bake for 15–20 minutes, or until firm and golden brown. Transfer to a wire rack to cool. Store in an airtight container.

Oat and Apricot Clusters

You can change the ingredients according to what's in your cupboard – try peanuts, pecan nuts, raisins or dates.

Makes 12

*50g/2oz/4 tbsp butter or
  margarine
50g/2oz/4 tbsp clear
  honey
50g/2oz/¹/₂ cup medium
  oatmeal
50g/2oz/¹/₄ cup chopped
  ready-to-eat dried
  apricots*

*15ml/1 tbsp banana chips
15ml/1 tbsp dried
  coconut shreds
50–75g/2–3oz/
  2–3 cups cornflakes
  or crispy cereal*

1 Place the butter or margarine and honey in a small pan and warm over a low heat, stirring until well blended.

2 Add the oatmeal, apricots, banana chips, coconut and cornflakes or crispy cereal and mix well.

3 Spoon the mixture into 12 paper cases, piling it up roughly. Transfer to a baking sheet and chill until set and firm.

Oaty Coconut Biscuits

The coconut gives these biscuits both a wonderful texture and a great taste.

Makes 48

175g/6oz/2 cups
 quick-cooking oats
75g/3oz/1¹/₂ cups
 desiccated coconut
225g/8oz/1 cup butter
115g/4oz/¹/₂ cup caster
 sugar
50g/2oz/¹/₄ cup dark
 brown sugar
2 eggs

60ml/4 tbsp milk
7.5ml/1¹/₂ tsp vanilla
 essence
115g/4oz/1 cup
 plain flour, sifted
2.5ml/¹/₂ tsp bicarbonate
 of soda
2.5ml/¹/₂ tsp salt
5ml/1 tsp ground
 cinnamon

1 Preheat the oven to 200°C/400°F/Gas 6. Spread the oats and coconut on a baking sheet. Bake for 8–10 minutes.

2 Cream the butter and sugars. Beat in the eggs, milk and vanilla. Fold in the dry ingredients. Add the oats and coconut. Drop spoonfuls of mixture on two greased baking sheets. Bake for 8–10 minutes. Cool on a wire rack.

Crunchy Jumbles

For even crunchier biscuits, add 50g/2oz/¹/₂ cup walnuts, coarsely chopped, with the cereal and chocolate chips.

Makes 36

115g/4oz/¹/₂ cup butter
 or margarine, at room
 temperature
225g/8oz/1 cup caster
 sugar
1 egg
5ml/1 tsp vanilla essence
150g/5oz/1¹/₄ cups plain
 flour, sifted

2.5ml/¹/₂ tsp bicarbonate
 of soda
1.5ml/¹/₄ tsp salt
50g/2oz/2¹/₄ cups crisped
 rice cereal
175g/6oz/1 cup chocolate
 chips

1 Preheat the oven to 180°C/350°F/Gas 4. Grease two baking sheets. Cream the butter or margarine and sugar until fluffy. Add the egg and vanilla essence. Add the flour and bicarbonate of soda and the salt and fold in.

2 Add the cereal and chocolate chips and mix thoroughly. Drop spoonfuls 5cm/2in apart onto baking sheets and bake for 10–12 minutes. Transfer to a wire rack to cool.

Cinnamon-coated Cookies

Walnut cookies are rolled in a cinnamon and sugar mixture to give a delicate spicy flavour.

Makes 30

Preheat the oven to 190°C/375°F/Gas 5. Grease two baking sheets. Cream 115g/4oz/¹/₂ cup butter, 225g/8oz/1 cup sugar and 5ml/1 tsp vanilla essence. Beat in 2 eggs and 50ml/2fl oz/¹/₄ cup milk. Sift over 350g/12oz/3 cups plain flour and 5ml/1 tsp bicarbonate of soda. Stir in 50g/2oz/¹/₂ cup chopped walnuts. Chill for 15 minutes then roll into balls. Roll the balls in a sugar and cinnamon mixture. Bake for 10 minutes, then cool on a wire rack.

Ginger Biscuits

So much tastier than shop-bought varieties, these ginger biscuits will disappear quickly, so make a large batch!

Makes 60

275g/10oz/2¹/₂ cups plain flour
5ml/1 tsp bicarbonate of soda
7.5ml/1¹/₂ tsp ground ginger
1.5ml/¹/₄ tsp ground cinnamon
1.5ml/¹/₄ tsp ground cloves

115g/4oz/¹/₂ cup butter or margarine, at room temperature
350g/12oz/1³/₄ cups caster sugar
1 egg, beaten
60ml/4 tbsp treacle
5ml/1 tsp fresh lemon juice

1 Preheat the oven to 160°C/325°F/Gas 3. Lightly grease three to four baking sheets.

2 Sift the flour, bicarbonate of soda and spices into a small bowl. Set aside.

3 Cream the butter or margarine and two-thirds of the sugar together. Stir in the egg, treacle and lemon juice. Add the flour mixture and mix in thoroughly with a wooden spoon to make a soft dough.

4 Shape the dough into 2cm/¾ in balls. Roll the balls in the remaining sugar and place about 5cm/2in apart on the baking sheets.

5 Bake until the biscuits are just firm to the touch, about 12 minutes. With a palette knife, transfer the biscuits to a wire rack and leave to cool.

Cream Cheese Spirals

These biscuits look so impressive and melt in the mouth, yet they are surprisingly easy to make.

Makes 32

225g/8oz/1 cup butter, at room temperature
225g/8oz/1 cup cream cheese
10ml/2 tsp caster sugar
225g/8oz/2 cups plain flour
1 egg white, beaten with 15ml/1 tbsp water, for glazing

caster sugar, for sprinkling

For the filling

115g/4oz/1 cup finely chopped walnuts
115g/4oz/³/₄ cup light brown sugar
5ml/1 tsp ground cinnamon

1 Cream the butter, cream cheese and sugar until soft. Sift over the flour and mix until combined. Gather into a ball and divide in half. Flatten each half, wrap in greaseproof paper and chill for 30 minutes. Meanwhile, mix all the filling ingredients together and set aside.

2 Preheat the oven to 190°C/375°F/Gas 5. Grease two baking sheets. Working with one half of the dough at a time, roll out thinly into a 28cm/11in circle. Using a dinner plate as a guide, trim the edges with a knife.

3 Brush the surface with the egg white glaze, and then sprinkle evenly with half the filling.

4 Cut the circle into 16 segments. Starting from the base of the triangles, roll up to form spirals.

5 Place on the baking sheets and brush with the remaining glaze. Sprinkle with caster sugar. Bake until golden, about 15–20 minutes. Cool on a wire rack.

Italian Almond Biscotti

Serve biscotti after a meal, for dunking in sweet white wine, such as an Italian Vin Santo or a French Muscat.

Makes 48

200g/7oz/1¾ cups whole unblanched almonds	pinch of salt
	pinch of saffron powder
	2.5ml/½ tsp bicarbonate of soda
215g/7½ oz/scant 2 cups plain flour	2 eggs
90g/3½ oz/½ cup sugar	1 egg white, lightly beaten

1 Preheat the oven to 190°C/375°F/Gas 5. Grease and flour two baking sheets.

2 Spread the almonds on an ungreased baking sheet and bake until lightly browned, about 15 minutes. When cool, grind 50g/2oz/⅓ cup of the almonds in a food processor, blender, or coffee grinder until pulverized. Coarsely chop the remaining almonds in two or three pieces each. Set aside.

3 Combine the flour, sugar, salt, saffron powder, bicarbonate of soda and ground almonds in a bowl and mix to blend. Make a well in the centre and add the eggs. Stir to form a rough dough. Transfer to a floured surface and knead until well blended. Knead in the chopped almonds.

4 Divide the dough into three equal parts. Roll into logs about 2.5cm/1in diameter. Place on one of the prepared sheets, brush with the egg white and bake for 20 minutes. Remove from the oven. Lower the oven temperature to 140°C/275°F/Gas 1.

5 With a very sharp knife, cut into each log at an angle making 1cm/½ in slices. Return the slices on the baking sheets to the oven and bake for 25 minutes. Transfer to a wire rack to cool.

Orange Biscuits

These classic citrus-flavoured biscuits are ideal for a tasty treat at any time of the day.

Makes 30

115g/4oz/½ cup butter, at room temperature	200g/7oz/1¾ cups plain flour
200g/7oz/1 cup sugar	15ml/1 tbsp cornflour
2 egg yolks	2.5ml/½ tsp salt
15ml/1 tbsp fresh orange juice	5ml/1 tsp baking powder
grated rind of 1 large orange	

1 Cream the butter and sugar until light and fluffy. Add the yolks, orange juice and rind, and continue beating to blend.

2 In another bowl, sift together the flour, cornflour, salt and baking powder. Add to the butter mixture and stir until it forms a dough. Wrap the dough in greaseproof paper and chill for 2 hours.

3 Preheat the oven to 190°C/375°F/Gas 5. Grease two baking sheets. Roll spoonfuls of the dough into balls and place 2.5–5cm/1–2in apart on the baking sheets.

4 Press down with a fork to flatten. Bake until golden brown, about 8–10 minutes. Using a palette knife, transfer to a wire rack to cool.

Raspberry Sandwich Biscuits

These biscuits may be stored in an airtight container with sheets of greaseproof paper between the layers.

Makes 32

175g/6oz/1 cup blanched
    almonds
175g/6oz/1½ cups plain
    flour
175g/6oz/¾ cup butter,
    at room temperature
115g/4oz/½ cup caster
    sugar
grated rind of 1 lemon

5ml/1 tsp vanilla essence
1 egg white
1.5ml/¼ tsp salt
25g/1oz/¼ cup flaked
    almonds
250ml/8fl oz/1 cup
    raspberry jam
15ml/1 tbsp fresh lemon
    juice

1 Process the blanched almonds and 45ml/3 tbsp flour in a food processor or blender until finely ground. Cream the butter and sugar together until light and fluffy. Stir in the lemon rind and vanilla. Add the ground almonds and remaining flour and mix well. Gather into a ball, wrap in greaseproof paper, and chill for 1 hour.

2 Preheat the oven to 160°C/325°F/Gas 3. Line two baking sheets wih greaseproof paper. Divide the biscuit mixture into four equal parts. Working with one section at a time, roll out to a thickness of 3mm/⅛ in on a lightly floured surface. With a 6cm/2½in fluted pastry cutter, stamp out circles. Using a 2cm/¾in piping nozzle or pastry cutter, stamp out the centres from half the circles. Place the rings and circles 2.5cm/1in apart on the baking sheets.

3 Whisk the egg white with the salt until just frothy. Chop the flaked almonds. Brush the biscuit rings with the egg white, then sprinkle over the almonds. Bake until lightly browned, about 12–15 minutes. Cool for a few minutes on the baking sheets then transfer to a wire rack.

4 In a saucepan, melt the jam with the lemon juice until it comes to a simmer. Brush the jam over the biscuit circles and sandwich together with the rings.

Christmas Cookies

Decorate these delicious cookies with festive decorations or make them at any time of year.

Makes 30

175g/6oz/¾ cup
    unsalted butter, at
    room temperature
285g/10oz/1½ cups
    caster sugar
1 egg
1 egg yolk
5ml/1 tsp vanilla
    essence

grated rind of 1 lemon
1.5ml/¼ tsp salt
285g/10oz/2½ cups
    plain flour

**For decorating
(optional)**
coloured icing and
    small decorations

1 Preheat the oven to 180°C/350°F/Gas 4. With an electric mixer, cream the butter until soft. Add the sugar gradually and continue beating until light and fluffy. Using a wooden spoon, slowly mix in the whole egg and the egg yolk. Add the vanilla essence, lemon rind and salt. Stir to mix well. Add the flour and stir until blended. Gather the mixture into a ball, wrap in greaseproof paper, and chill for 30 minutes.

2 On a floured surface, roll out the mixture about 3mm/⅛in thick. Stamp out shapes or rounds with biscuit cutters. Bake until lightly coloured, about 8 minutes. Transfer to a wire rack and leave to cool completely before icing and decorating, if wished.

Apricot Specials

Try other dried fruit, such as peaches or prunes, to vary the flavour of these special bars.

Makes 12

*90g/3¹/₂oz/generous
¹/₂ cup light brown
sugar
75g/3oz/³/₄ cup plain
flour
75g/3oz/6 tbsp cold
unsalted butter, cut
in pieces*

For the topping
*150g/5oz/generous
¹/₂ cup dried apricots
250ml/8fl oz/1 cup water
grated rind of 1 lemon
65g/2¹/₂oz/generous ¹/₄
cup caster sugar
10ml/2 tsp cornflour
50g/2oz/¹/₂ cup chopped
walnuts*

1 Preheat the oven to 180°C/350°F/Gas 4. In a mixing bowl, combine the brown sugar and flour. With a pastry blender, cut in the butter until the mixture resembles coarse breadcrumbs.

2 Transfer to a 20cm/8in square baking tin and press level. Bake for 15 minutes. Remove from the oven but leave the oven on.

3 Meanwhile, for the topping, combine the apricots and water in a saucepan and simmer until soft; about 10 minutes. Strain the liquid and reserve. Chop the apricots.

4 Return the apricots to the saucepan and add the lemon rind, caster sugar, cornflour and 60ml/4 tbsp of the soaking liquid. Cook for 1 minute.

5 Cool slightly before spreading the topping over the base. Sprinkle over the walnuts and bake for 20 minutes more. Cool in the tin before cutting into bars.

Brandy Snaps

You could serve these brandy snaps without the cream filling to eat with rich vanilla ice cream.

Makes 18

*50g/2oz/4 tbsp butter, at
room temperature
150g/5oz/generous
¹/₂ cup caster sugar
20ml/1 rounded tbsp
golden syrup
40g/1¹/₂oz/¹/₃ cup plain
flour*

*2.5ml/¹/₂ tsp ground
ginger*

For the filling
*250ml/8fl oz/1 cup
whipping cream
30ml/2 tbsp brandy*

1 Cream together the butter and sugar until light and fluffy, then beat in the golden syrup. Sift over the flour and ginger and mix together. Transfer the mixture to a work surface and knead until smooth. Cover and chill for 30 minutes.

2 Preheat the oven to 190°C/375°F/Gas 5. Grease a baking sheet. Working in batches of four, shape the mixture into walnut-size balls. Place well apart on the baking sheet and flatten slightly. Bake until golden and bubbling, about 10 minutes.

3 Remove from the oven and leave to cool for a few moments. Working quickly, slide a palette knife under each one, turn over, and wrap around the handle of a wooden spoon (have four spoons ready). If they firm up too quickly, reheat for a few seconds to soften. When firm, slide the brandy snaps off and place on a wire rack to cool.

4 When all the brandy snaps are cool, prepare the filling. Whip the cream and brandy until soft peaks form. Pipe into each end of the brandy snaps just before serving.

Chocolate Pretzels

Pretzels come in many flavours – here is a chocolate version to bake and enjoy.

Makes 28

*150g/5oz/1¼ cups plain
  flour
1.5ml/¼ tsp salt
20g/¾ oz/6 tbsp
  unsweetened cocoa
  powder
115g/4oz/½ cup butter,
  at room temperature*

*130g/4½oz/scant ⅔ cup
  sugar
1 egg
1 egg white, lightly
  beaten, for glazing
sugar crystals, for
  sprinkling*

1 Sift together the flour, salt and cocoa powder. Set aside. Lightly grease two baking sheets. Cream the butter until light. Add the sugar and continue beating until light and fluffy. Beat in the egg. Add the dry ingredients and stir to blend. Gather the dough into a ball, wrap in clear film and chill for 1 hour.

2 Roll the dough into 28 small balls. Chill the balls until needed. Preheat the oven to 190°C/375°F/Gas 5. Roll each ball into a rope about 25cm/10in long. With each rope, form a loop with the two ends facing you. Twist the ends and fold back on to the circle, pressing in to make a pretzel shape. Place on the baking sheets.

3 Brush the pretzels with the egg white. Sprinkle sugar crystals over the tops and bake in the oven until firm, about 10–12 minutes. Transfer to a wire rack to cool.

Ginger Cookies

If your children enjoy cooking with you, mixing and rolling the dough, or cutting out different shapes, this is the ideal recipe to let them practise on.

Makes 16

*115g/4oz/8 tbsp soft
  brown sugar
115g/4oz/½ cup soft
  margarine
pinch of salt
few drops vanilla essence
175g/6oz/1½ cup
  wholemeal flour*

*15g/½oz/1 tbsp cocoa,
  sifted
10ml/2 tsp ground ginger
a little milk
glacé icing and glacé
  cherries, to decorate*

1 Preheat the oven to 190°C/375°F/Gas 5. Cream the sugar, margarine, salt and vanilla essence together until very soft and light.

2 Work in the flour, cocoa and ginger, adding a little milk, if necessary, to bind the mixture. Knead lightly on a floured surface until smooth.

3 Roll out the dough on a lightly floured surface to about 5mm/1¼in thick. Stamp out shapes using biscuit cutters and place on baking sheets.

4 Bake the cookies for 10–15 minutes, leave to cool on the baking sheets until firm, then transfer to a wire rack to cool completely. Decorate with the glacé icing and glacé cherries.

Chocolate Macaroons

Roll one side of the macaroons in chopped nuts and bake nut-side up for a crunchier variation.

Makes 24

50g/2oz plain chocolate, melted
175g/6oz/1¹/₂ cups blanched almonds
225g/8oz/1 cup caster sugar
3 egg whites
2.5ml/¹/₂ tsp vanilla essence
1.5ml/¹/₄ tsp almond essence
icing sugar, for dusting

1 Preheat the oven to 160°C/325°F/Gas 3. Line two baking sheets with greaseproof paper then grease. Grind the almonds in a food processor or blender. Transfer to a bowl, then blend in the sugar, egg whites, vanilla and almond essence. Stir in the chocolate. The mixture should just hold its shape; if too soft, chill for 15 minutes.

2 Shape the mixture into walnut-size balls. Place on the baking sheets and flatten slightly. Brush with a little water; dust with icing sugar. Bake until just firm, 10–12 minutes. With a palette knife, transfer to a wire rack to cool.

Chocolate-orange Sponge Drops

Light and crispy, with a marmalade filling, these sponge drops are truly decadent.

Makes 14–15

2 eggs
50g/2oz/¹/₄ cup caster sugar
2.5ml/¹/₂ tsp grated orange rind
50g/2oz/¹/₂ cup plain flour
60ml/4 tbsp fine shred orange marmalade
40g/1¹/₂oz plain chocolate, cut into small pieces

1 Preheat the oven to 200°C/400°F/Gas 6. Line three baking sheets with baking paper. Put the eggs and sugar in a bowl over a pan of simmering water. Whisk until thick and pale. Remove from the pan and whisk until cool. Whisk in the orange rind. Sift the flour over and fold it in gently.

2 Put 28–30 dessertspoonfuls of the mixture on the baking sheets. Bake for 8 minutes, until golden. Cool slightly, then transfer to a wire rack. Sandwich pairs together with marmalade. Melt the chocolate and drizzle over the drops.

Coconut Macaroons

Have a change from after-dinner mints, and serve these delicious coconut macaroons with coffee instead.

Makes 24

Preheat the oven to 180°C/350°F/Gas 4. Grease two baking sheets. Sift 40g/1½ oz/⅓ cup plain flour and 1.5ml/1¼ tsp salt into a bowl, then stir in 225g/8oz/4 cups desiccated coconut. Pour in 170ml/5½fl oz/scant ¾ cup sweetened condensed milk. Add 5ml/1 tsp vanilla essence; stir from the centre to a thick mixture. Drop tablespoonfuls of the mixture 2.5cm/1in apart on the baking sheets. Bake until golden brown, about 20 minutes. Cool on a wire rack.

Peanut Butter Biscuits

For added crunchiness, stir in 75g/3oz/½ cup peanuts, coarsely chopped, with the peanut butter.

Makes 24

150g/5oz/1¼ cups plain flour	*170g/5¾ oz/scant 1 cup light brown sugar*
2.5ml/½ tsp bicarbonate of soda	*1 egg*
2.5ml/½ tsp salt	*5ml/1 tsp vanilla essence*
115g/4oz/½ cup butter, at room temperature	*260g/9½oz/scant 1¼ cups crunchy peanut butter*

1 Sift together the flour, bicarbonate of soda and salt and set aside. In another bowl, cream the butter and sugar together until light and fluffy.

2 In a third bowl, mix the egg and vanilla, then gradually beat into the butter mixture. Stir in the peanut butter and the chopped peanuts, if using, and blend thoroughly. Stir in the dry ingredients. Chill for 30 minutes, or until firm.

3 Preheat the oven to 180°C/350°F/Gas 4. Grease two baking sheets. Spoon out rounded teaspoonfuls of the dough and roll into balls.

4 Place the balls on the baking sheets and press flat with a fork into circles about 6cm/2½in in diameter, making a criss-cross pattern. Bake in the oven until lightly coloured, about 12–15 minutes. Transfer to a wire rack to cool.

Chocolate-chip Cookies

A perennial favourite with all the family, these cookies contain walnuts as well as chocolate chips.

Makes 24

115g/4oz/½ cup butter or margarine, at room temperature	*175g/6oz/1½ cups plain flour*
45g/1¾ oz/scant ¼ cup caster sugar	*2.5ml/½ tsp bicarbonate of soda*
100g/3¾ oz/generous ½ cup dark brown sugar	*1.5ml/¼ tsp salt*
1 egg	*175g/6oz/1 cup chocolate chips*
2.5ml/½ tsp vanilla essence	*50g/2oz/½ cup walnuts, chopped*

1 Preheat the oven to 180°C/350°F/Gas 4. Lightly grease two large baking sheets. With an electric mixer, cream the butter or margarine and both the sugars together until light and fluffy.

2 In another bowl, mix the egg and the vanilla essence, then gradually beat into the butter mixture. Sift over the flour, bicarbonate of soda and salt and stir. Add the chocolate chips and walnuts, and mix to combine well.

4 Place heaped teaspoonfuls of the dough 5cm/2in apart on the baking sheets. Bake in the oven until lightly coloured, about 10–15 minutes. Transfer to a wire rack to cool.

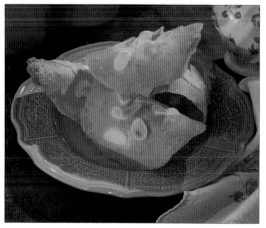

Almond Tile Biscuits

These biscuits are named after the French roof tiles they so closely resemble.

Makes about 24

65g/2¹/₂oz/scant ¹/₂ cup whole blanched almonds, lightly toasted
65g/2¹/₂oz/¹/₃ cup caster sugar
40g/1¹/₂oz/3 tbsp unsalted butter, softened

2 egg whites
2.5ml/¹/₂ tsp almond essence
40g/1¹/₂oz/¹/₃ cup plain flour, sifted
50g/2oz/¹/₂ cup flaked almonds

1 Preheat the oven to 200°C/400°F/Gas 6. Grease well two baking sheets. Place the almonds and 30ml/2 tbsp of the sugar in a blender or food processor and process until finely ground, but not pasty.

2 Beat the butter until creamy, add the remaining sugar and beat until light and fluffy. Gradually beat in the egg whites until the mixture is well blended, then beat in the almond essence. Sift the flour over the butter mixture and fold in, then fold in the almond mixture.

3 Drop tablespoonfuls of the mixture on to the baking sheets 15cm/6in apart. With the back of a wet spoon, spread each mound into a paper-thin 7.5cm/3in circle. Sprinkle with the flaked almonds.

4 Bake the biscuits, one sheet at a time, for 5–6 minutes until the edges are golden and the centres still pale. Remove the baking sheet to a wire rack and, working quickly, use a palette knife to loosen the edges of a biscuit. Lift the biscuit on the palette knife and place over a rolling pin, then press down the sides of the biscuit to curve it. Repeat with the remaining biscuits, and leave to cool.

Brittany Butter Biscuits

These little biscuits are similar to shortbread, but richer in taste and texture.

Makes 18–20

6 egg yolks, lightly beaten
15ml/1 tbsp milk
250g/9oz/2 cups plain flour
175g/6oz/generous ³/₄ cup caster sugar

200g/7oz/scant 1 cup lightly salted butter at room temperature, cut into small pieces

1 Preheat the oven to 180°C/350°F/Gas 4. Lightly butter a large baking sheet. Mix 15ml/1 tbsp of the egg yolks with the milk for a glaze. Set aside.

2 Sift the flour into a large bowl and make a central well. Add the egg yolks, sugar and butter and, using your fingertips, work them together until smooth and creamy. Gradually blend in the flour to form a smooth but slightly sticky dough.

3 Using floured hands, pat out the dough to 8mm/⅛in thick and cut out circles using a 7.5cm/3in biscuit cutter. Transfer the circles to the baking sheet, brush with egg glaze, then score to create a lattice pattern.

4 Bake for 12–15 minutes until golden. Cool in the tin on a wire rack for 15 minutes, then transfer to the wire rack to cool completely.

Ginger Florentines

These colourful, chewy biscuits are delicious served with vanilla or other flavoured ice cream.

Makes 30

50g/2oz/4 tbsp butter
115g/4oz/¹/₂ cup
　caster sugar
50g/2oz/¹/₄ cup mixed
　glacé cherries, chopped
25g/1oz/generous 1 tbsp
　candied orange peel,
　chopped
50g/2oz/¹/₂ cup flaked
　almonds
50g/2oz/¹/₂ cup chopped
　walnuts

25g/1oz/1 tbsp glacé
　ginger, chopped
30ml/2 tbsp plain flour
2.5ml/¹/₂ tsp ground
　ginger

To finish
50g/2oz plain chocolate,
　melted
50g/2oz white chocolate,
　melted

1 Preheat the oven to 180°C/350°F/Gas 4. Beat the butter and sugar together until light and fluffy. Thoroughly mix in all the remaining ingredients, except the melted plain and white chocolate.

2 Line some baking sheets with non-stick baking paper. Put four small spoonfuls of the mixture on to each sheet, spacing them well apart to allow for spreading. Flatten the biscuits and bake for 5 minutes.

3 Remove the biscuits from the oven and flatten with a wet fork, shaping them into neat rounds. Return to the oven for about 3–4 minutes, until they are golden brown. Work in batches if necessary.

4 Let them cool on the baking sheets for 2 minutes to firm up, and then transfer them to a wire rack. When they are cold and firm, spread plain chocolate on the undersides of half the biscuits and white chocolate on the undersides of the rest.

Christmas Biscuits

These are great fun for children to make as presents, and any shape of biscuit cutter can be used.

Makes about 12

75g/3oz/6 tbsp butter
50g/2oz/generous ¹/₂ cup
　icing sugar
finely grated rind of
　1 small lemon
1 egg yolk
175g/6oz/1¹/₂ cups plain
　flour

pinch of salt

To decorate
2 egg yolks
red and green edible food
　colouring

1 Beat the butter, sugar and lemon rind together until pale and fluffy. Beat in the egg yolk, and then sift in the flour and the salt. Knead together to form a smooth dough. Wrap and chill for 30 minutes.

2 Preheat the oven to 190°C/375°F/Gas 5. On a lightly floured surface, roll out the dough to 3mm/¹/₈in thick. Using a 6cm/2¹/₂in fluted cutter, stamp out as many biscuits as you can, with the cutter dipped in flour to prevent it from sticking to the dough.

3 Transfer the biscuits on to lightly greased baking sheets. Mark the tops lightly with a 2.5cm/1in holly leaf cutter and use a 5mm/¹/₄in plain piping nozzle for the berries. Chill for 10 minutes, until firm.

4 Meanwhile, put each egg yolk into a small cup. Mix red food colouring into one and green food colouring into the other. Using a small, clean paintbrush, carefully paint the colours on to the biscuits. Bake for 10–12 minutes, or until they begin to colour around the edges. Let them cool slightly on the baking sheets, then transfer to a wire rack.

Traditional Sugar Biscuits

These lovely old-fashioned biscuits would be ideal to serve at an elegant tea party.

Makes 36

350g/12oz/3 cups plain
 flour
5ml/1 tsp bicarbonate
 of soda
10ml/2 tsp baking
 powder
1.5ml/¼ tsp grated
 nutmeg
115g/4oz/½ cup butter
 or margarine, at room
 temperature

225g/8oz/generous 1 cup
 caster sugar
2.5ml/½ tsp vanilla
 essence
1 egg
120ml/4fl oz/½ cup milk
coloured or demerara
 sugar, for sprinkling

1 Sift the flour, bicarbonate of soda, baking powder and nutmeg into a small bowl. Set aside. Cream the butter or margarine, caster sugar and vanilla essence together until the mixture is light and fluffy. Add the egg and beat to mix well.

2 Add the flour mixture alternately with the milk, stirring with a wooden spoon to make a soft dough. Wrap the dough in clear film and chill for 30 minutes.

3 Preheat the oven to 180°C/350°F/Gas 4. Roll out the dough on a lightly floured surface to a 3mm/⅛in thickness. Cut into circles with a biscuit cutter.

4 Transfer the biscuits to ungreased baking sheets. Sprinkle each one with sugar. Bake until golden, 10–12 minutes. With a palette knife, transfer the biscuits to a wire rack to cool.

Spicy Pepper Biscuits

Despite the warm, complex flavour added by the spices, these light biscuits are simple to make.

Makes 48

200g/7oz/¾ cup plain
 flour
50g/2oz/¼ cup cornflour
10ml/2 tsp baking
 powder
2.5ml/½ tsp ground
 cardamom
2.5ml/½ tsp ground
 cinnamon
2.5ml/½ tsp grated
 nutmeg
2.5ml/½ tsp ground
 ginger
2.5ml/½ tsp ground
 allspice
2.5ml/½ tsp salt

2.5ml/½ tsp freshly
 ground black pepper
225g/8oz butter or
 margarine, at room
 temperature
90g/3½ oz/½ cup light
 brown sugar
2.5ml/½ tsp vanilla
 essence
5ml/1 tsp finely grated
 lemon rind
50ml/2fl oz/¼ cups
 whipping cream
75g/3oz/¾ cup finely
 ground almonds
50ml/2 tbsp icing sugar

1 Preheat the oven to 180°C/350°F/Gas 4. Sift the flour, cornflour, baking powder, spices, salt and pepper into a bowl.

2 Cream the butter or margarine and brown sugar until light and fluffy. Beat in the vanilla essence and lemon rind.

3 With the mixer on low speed, add the flour mixture alternately with the cream, beginning and ending with flour. Stir in the ground almonds.

4 Shape the dough into 2cm/¾in balls. Place them on ungreased baking sheets about 2.5cm/1in apart. Bake until golden brown underneath, about 15–20 minutes.

5 Leave to cool on the baking sheets for about 1 minute before transferring to a wire rack to cool completely. Before serving, sprinkle lightly with icing sugar.

Sultana Cornmeal Biscuits

These little yellow biscuits come from the Veneto region
of Italy, and Marsala wine enhances their regional appeal.

Makes about 48

65g/2½oz/½ cup sultanas	*pinch of salt*
50g/2oz/½ cup finely	*225g/8oz/1 cup butter*
ground yellow	*200g/7oz/1 cup*
cornmeal	*granulated sugar*
175g/6oz/1½ cups plain	*2 eggs*
flour	*15ml/1 tbsp Marsala or*
7.5ml/1½ tsp baking	*5ml/1 tsp vanilla*
powder	*essence*

1 Soak the sultanas in a small bowl of warm water for
15 minutes. Drain. Preheat the oven to 180°C/350°F/Gas 4.
Sift the cornmeal and flour, the baking powder and the salt
together into a bowl.

2 Cream the butter and sugar together until light and fluffy.
Beat in the eggs, one at a time. Beat in the Marsala or vanilla
essence. Add the dry ingredients to the batter, beating until
well blended. Stir in the sultanas.

3 Drop heaped teaspoonfuls of batter on to a greased baking
sheet in rows about 2in apart. Bake for 7–8 minutes, or until
the biscuits are golden brown at the edges. Remove to a wire
rack to cool.

Mexican Cinnamon Biscuits

Pastelitos are traditional sweet shortbreads at weddings in
Mexico, dusted in icing sugar to match the bride's dress.

Makes 20

115g/4oz/¹/₂ cup butter	*1.5ml/¹/₄ tsp ground*
25g/1oz/2 tbsp caster	*cinnamon*
sugar	*30ml/2 tbsp chopped*
115g/4oz/1 cup plain	*mixed nuts*
flour	*25g/1oz/¹/₄ cup icing*
50g/2oz/¹/₄ cup cornflour	*sugar, sifted*

1 Preheat the oven to 160°C/325°F/Gas 3. Lightly grease a
baking sheet. Place the butter and sugar in a bowl and beat
until pale and creamy.

2 Sift in the plain flour, cornflour and cinnamon and
gradually work in with a wooden spoon until the mixture
comes together. Knead lightly until completely smooth.

3 Take tablespoonfuls of the mixture, roll into 20 small balls
and arrange on the baking sheet. Press a few chopped nuts
into the top of each one and then flatten slightly.

4 Bake the biscuits for about 30–35 minutes, until pale
golden. Remove from the oven and, while they are still warm,
toss them in the sifted icing sugar. Leave the biscuits to cool
on a wire rack before serving.

Toasted Oat Meringues

Meringues needn't be plain. Try these oaty ones for a lovely crunchy change.

Makes 12

50g/2oz/generous ¹/₂ cup rolled oats	7.5ml/1¹/₂ tsp cornflour
2 egg whites	175g/6oz/³/₄ cup caster sugar
1.5ml/¹/₄ tsp salt	

1 Preheat the oven to 140°C/275°F/Gas 1. Spread the oats on a baking sheet and toast in the oven until golden, for about 10 minutes. Lower the heat to 120°C/250°F/Gas ½. Grease and flour a baking sheet.

2 Beat the egg whites and salt until they start to form soft peaks. Sift over the cornflour and continue beating until the whites hold stiff peaks. Add half the sugar; whisk until glossy. Add the remaining sugar and fold in, then fold in the oats.

3 Place tablespoonfuls of the mixture on to the baking sheet and bake for 2 hours, then turn off the oven. Turn over the meringues, and leave in the oven until cool.

Meringues

Make these classic meringues as large or small as you like. Serve as a tea-time treat or as an elegant dessert.

Makes about 24

4 egg whites	2.5ml/¹/₂ tsp vanilla or almond essence (optional)
1.5ml/¹/₄ tsp salt	
275g/10oz/1¹/₄ cups caster sugar	250ml/8fl oz/1 cup whipping cream

1 Preheat the oven to 110°C/225°F/Gas ¼. Grease and flour two large baking sheets. Beat the egg whites and salt in a metal bowl. When they start to form soft peaks, add half the sugar and continue beating until the mixture holds stiff peaks.

2 With a large metal spoon, fold in the remaining sugar and vanilla or almond essence, if using. Pipe or spoon the meringue mixture on to the baking sheets. Bake for 2 hours, turn off the oven. Loosen the meringues, invert, and set in another place on the sheets to prevent sticking. Leave in the oven until cool. Whip the cream and use to fill the meringues.

Chewy Chocolate Biscuits

If you have a weakness for chocolate, add 75g/3oz/¹/₂ cup chocolate chips to the mixture with the nuts.

Makes 18

Preheat the oven to 180°C/350°F/Gas 4. Line two baking sheets with greaseproof paper and grease. Using an electric mixer, beat 4 egg whites until frothy. Sift over 275g/10oz/2 cups icing sugar and 5ml/1 tsp coffee. Add 15ml/1 tbsp water, beat on low speed to blend, then on high until thick. Fold in 115g/4oz/1 cup chopped walnuts. Place generous spoonfuls of the mixture 2.5cm/1in apart on the sheets. Bake for 12–15 minutes. Transfer to a wire rack to cool.

Lavender Cookies

Instead of lavender you can use other flavourings, such as cinnamon, lemon, orange or mint.

Makes about 30

150g/5oz/⅔ cup butter
115g/4oz/½ cup
  granulated sugar
1 egg, beaten
15ml/1 tbsp dried
  lavender flowers

175g/6oz/1½ cups
  self-raising flour
leaves and flowers,
  to decorate

1 Preheat the oven to 180°C/350°F/Gas 4. Grease two baking sheets. Cream the butter and sugar together, then stir in the egg. Mix in the lavender flowers and the flour.

2 Drop spoonfuls of the mixture on to the baking sheets. Bake for about 15–20 minutes, until the biscuits are golden. Serve with some fresh leaves and flowers to decorate.

Chocolate Amaretti

As an alternative decoration, lightly press a few coffee sugar crystals on top of each cookie before baking.

Makes 24

150g/5oz/scant 1 cup
  blanched, toasted
  whole almonds
115g/4oz/¹/₂ cup caster
  sugar
15ml/1 tbsp unsweetened
  cocoa powder

30ml/2 tbsp icing sugar
2 egg whites
pinch of cream of tartar
5ml/1 tsp almond essence
flaked almonds,
  to decorate

1 Preheat the oven to 160°C/325°F/Gas 3. Line a large baking sheet with non-stick baking paper or foil. In a food processor fitted with a metal blade, process the toasted almonds with half the sugar until they are finely ground but not oily. Transfer to a bowl and sift in the cocoa and icing sugar; stir to blend. Set aside.

2 Beat the egg whites and cream of tartar until stiff peaks form. Sprinkle in the remaining sugar 15ml/1 tbsp at a time, beating well after each addition, and continue beating until the whites are glossy and stiff. Beat in the almond essence.

3 Sprinkle over the almond mixture and gently fold into the egg whites until just blended. Spoon the mixture into a large piping bag fitted with a plain 1cm/½in nozzle. Pipe 4cm/1½in rounds, 2.5cm/1in apart, on the baking sheet. Press a flaked almond into the centre of each.

4 Bake the cookies for 12–15 minutes or until they appear crisp. Remove the baking sheet to a wire rack to cool for 10 minutes. With a metal palette knife, remove the cookies to the wire rack to cool completely.

Melting Moments

These biscuits are very crisp and light – and they really do melt in your mouth.

Makes 16–20

40g/1¹/₂oz/3 tbsp butter
   or margarine
65g/2¹/₂oz/5 tbsp lard
75g/3oz/scant ¹/₂ cup
   caster sugar
¹/₂ egg, beaten
a few drops of vanilla or
   almond essence

150g/5oz/1¹/₄ cups
   self-raising flour
rolled oats, for coating
4–5 glacé cherries,
   quartered, to decorate

1 Preheat the oven to 180°C/350°F/Gas 4. Beat together the butter or margarine, lard and sugar, then gradually beat in the egg and vanilla or almond essence.

2 Stir the flour into the beaten mixture, with floured hands, then roll into 16–20 small balls. Spread the rolled oats on a sheet of greaseproof paper and toss the balls in them to coat evenly.

3 Place the balls, spaced slightly apart, on two baking sheets, place a piece of cherry on top of each and bake for about 15–20 minutes, until lightly browned. Allow the biscuits to cool on the sheets for 5 minutes before transferring to a wire rack to cool completely.

Easter Biscuits

This is a seasonal recipe, but these biscuits can be enjoyed at any time of the year.

Makes 16–18

115g/4oz/¹/₂ cup butter
   or margarine
75g/3oz/scant ¹/₂ cup
   caster sugar, plus
   extra for sprinkling
1 egg, separated
200g/7oz/1¾ cups plain
   flour

2.5ml/¹/₂ tsp mixed spice
2.5ml/¹/₂ tsp ground
   cinnamon
50g/2oz/4 tbsp currants
15ml/1 tbsp chopped
   mixed peel
15–30ml/1–2 tbsp milk

1 Preheat the oven to 200°C/400°F/Gas 6. Lightly grease two baking sheets. Cream together the butter or margarine and sugar until light and fluffy, then beat in the egg yolk.

2 Sift the flour and spices over the egg mixture, then fold in with the currants and peel, adding sufficient milk to make a fairly soft dough.

3 Turn the dough on to a floured surface, knead lightly until just smooth, then roll out using a floured rolling pin, to about a 5mm/¹/₄in thickness. Cut the dough into circles using a 5cm/2in fluted biscuit cutter. Transfer the circles to the baking sheets and bake for 10 minutes.

4 Beat the egg white, then brush over the biscuits. Sprinkle with caster sugar and return to the oven for a further 10 minutes, until golden. Transfer to a wire rack to cool.

Shortbread

Once you have tasted this shortbread, you'll never buy a packet from a shop again.

Makes 8

150g/5oz/generous ½ cup unsalted butter, at room temperature
115g/4oz/½ cup caster sugar
150g/5oz/1¼ cups plain flour
65g/2½oz/½ cup rice flour
1.5ml/¼ tsp baking powder
1.5ml/¼ tsp salt

1 Preheat the oven to 160°C/325°F/Gas 3. Lightly grease a 20cm/8in shallow round cake tin. Cream the butter and sugar together until light and fluffy. Sift over the flours, baking powder and salt, and mix well.

2 Press the mixture neatly into the prepared tin, smoothing the surface with the back of a spoon. Prick all over with a fork, then score into eight equal wedges.

3 Bake until golden, about 40–45 minutes. Leave in the tin until cool enough to handle, then unmould and recut the wedges while still hot. Store in an airtight container.

Flapjacks

For a spicier version, add 5ml/1 tsp ground ginger to the melted butter.

Makes 8

50g/2oz/¼ cup butter
20ml/1 rounded tbsp golden syrup
65g/2½oz/scant ½ cup dark brown sugar
115g/4oz/generous 1 cup quick-cooking oats
1.5ml/¼ tsp salt

1 Preheat the oven to 180°C/350°F/Gas 4. Line and grease a 20cm/8in shallow round cake tin. Place the butter, golden syrup and sugar in a pan over a low heat. Cook, stirring, until melted and combined.

2 Remove from the heat and add the oats and salt. Stir the mixture to blend. Spoon the mixture into the prepared tin and smooth the surface. Place in the centre of the oven and bake until golden brown, 20–25 minutes. Leave in the tin until cool enough to handle, then unmould and cut into wedges while still hot. Store in an airtight container.

Chocolate Delights

This method of making biscuits ensures they are all of a uniform size.

Makes 50

25g/1oz plain chocolate
25g/1oz bitter cooking
   chocolate
225g/8oz/2 cups plain
   flour
2.5ml/¹⁄₂ tsp salt
225g/8oz/1 cup unsalted
   butter, at room
   temperature

225g/8oz/generous 1 cup
   caster sugar
2 eggs
5ml/1 tsp vanilla essence
115g/4oz/1 cup finely
   chopped walnuts

1 Melt the chocolate in the top of a double boiler, or in a heatproof bowl set over a pan of gently simmering water. Set aside. In a bowl, sift together the flour and salt. Set aside.

2 Cream the butter until soft. Add the sugar and continue beating until the mixture is light and fluffy. Mix the eggs and vanilla essence, then gradually stir into the butter mixture. Stir in the chocolate, then the flour. Finally, stir in the nuts.

3 Divide the mixture into four equal parts, and roll each into a 5cm/2in diameter log. Wrap tightly in foil and chill or freeze until firm.

4 Preheat the oven to 190°C/375°F/Gas 5. Grease two baking sheets. With a sharp knife, cut the logs into 5mm/¼in slices. Place the circles on the baking sheets and bake until lightly coloured, about 10 minutes. Using a palette knife, transfer to a wire rack to cool.

Cinnamon Treats

Place these biscuits in a heart-shaped basket, as here, and serve them up with love.

Makes 50

250g/9oz/generous
   2 cups plain flour
2.5ml/¹⁄₂ tsp salt
10ml/2 tsp ground
   cinnamon

225g/8oz/1 cup unsalted
   butter, at room
   temperature
225g/8oz/generous 1 cup
   caster sugar
2 eggs
5ml/1 tsp vanilla essence

1 Sift together the flour, salt and cinnamon together into a bowl. Set aside.

2 Cream the butter until soft. Add the sugar and continue beating until the mixture is light and fluffy. Beat the eggs and vanilla essence together, then gradually stir into the butter mixture. Stir in the dry ingredients.

3 Divide the mixture into four equal parts, then roll each into a 5cm/2in diameter log. Wrap tightly in foil and chill or freeze until firm.

4 Preheat the oven to 190°C/375°F/Gas 5. Grease two baking sheets. With a sharp knife, cut the logs into 5mm/¼in slices. Place the rounds on the baking sheets and bake until lightly coloured, about 10 minutes. Using a palette knife, transfer to a wire rack to cool.

Chunky Chocolate Drops

Do not allow these cookies to cool completely on the baking sheet or they will break when you try to lift them.

Makes 18

175g/6oz plain chocolate
115g/4oz/1/2 cup unsalted
    butter
2 eggs
90g/31/2oz/1/2 cup
    granulated sugar
50g/2oz/1/4 cup (packed)
    light brown sugar
40g/11/2oz/1/3 cup plain
    flour
25g/1oz/1/4 cup
    unsweetened cocoa
    powder
5ml/1 tsp baking powder
10ml/2 tsp vanilla
    essence

pinch of salt
115g/4oz/1 cup pecan
    nuts, toasted and
    coarsely chopped
175g/6oz/1 cup plain
    chocolate chips
115g/4oz fine quality
    white chocolate,
    chopped into 5mm/
    1/4in pieces
115g/4oz fine quality
    milk chocolate,
    chopped into 5mm/
    1/4in pieces

1 Preheat the oven to 160°C/325°F/Gas 3. Grease two large baking sheets. In a medium saucepan over a low heat, melt the plain chocolate and butter until smooth, stirring frequently. Remove from the heat to cool slightly.

2 Beat the eggs and sugars for 2–3 minutes until pale and creamy. Gradually beat in the melted chocolate mixture. Beat in the flour, cocoa, baking powder, vanilla and salt, just to blend. Add the nuts, chocolate chips and chocolate pieces.

3 Drop 4–6 heaped tablespoonfuls of the mixture on to each baking sheet 10cm/4in apart and flatten each to a round about 7.5cm/3in. Bake for 8–10 minutes until the tops are shiny and cracked and the edges look crisp.

4 Remove the baking sheets to a wire rack to cool for about 2 minutes, until the cookies are just set, then remove them to the wire rack to cool completely. Continue to bake in batches.

Chocolate Crackle-tops

These cookies are best eaten on the day they are baked, as they dry slightly on storage.

Makes 38

200g/7oz plain chocolate,
    chopped
90g/31/2oz/7 tbsp
    unsalted butter
115g/4oz/1/2 cup caster
    sugar
3 eggs
5ml/1 tsp vanilla essence
215g/71/2oz/scant 2 cups
    plain flour

25g/1oz/1/4 cup
    unsweetened cocoa
    powder
2.5ml/1/2 tsp baking
    powder
pinch of salt
175g/6oz/11/2 cups icing
    sugar, for coating

1 Heat the chocolate and butter over a low heat until smooth, stirring frequently. Remove from the heat. Stir in the sugar, and continue stirring until dissolved. Add the eggs, one at a time, beating well after each addition; stir in the vanilla. In a separate bowl, sift together the flour, cocoa, baking powder and salt. Gradually stir into the chocolate mixture until just blended. Cover and chill for at least 1 hour.

2 Preheat the oven to 160°C/325°F/Gas 3. Grease two or three large baking sheets. Place the icing sugar in a small, deep bowl. Using a teaspoon, scoop the dough into small balls and roll in your hands into 4cm/11/2in balls.

3 Drop the balls, one at a time, into the icing sugar and roll until heavily coated. Remove each ball with a slotted spoon and tap against the bowl to remove any excess sugar. Place on the baking sheets 4cm/11/2in apart.

4 Bake the cookies for 10–15 minutes or until the tops feel slightly firm when touched with your fingertip. Remove the baking sheets to a wire rack for 2–3 minutes, then with a palette knife remove the cookies to the wire rack to cool.

Chocolate-chip Oat Biscuits

Oat biscuits are given a delicious lift by the inclusion of chocolate chips. Try caramel chips for a change, if you like.

Makes 60

115g/4oz/1 cup plain
   flour
2.5ml/¹/₂ tsp bicarbonate
   of soda
1.5ml/¹/₄ tsp baking
   powder
1.5ml/¹/₄ tsp salt
115g/4oz/¹/₂ cup butter
   or margarine, at room
   temperature
115g/4oz/generous ¹/₂ cup
   caster sugar

90g/3¹/₂oz/generous
   ¹/₂ cup light brown
   sugar
1 egg
2.5ml/¹/₂ tsp vanilla
   essence
75g/3oz/scant ¹/₂ cup
   rolled oats
175g/6oz/1 cup plain
   chocolate chips

1 Preheat the oven to 180°C/350°F/Gas 4. Grease three or four baking sheets. Sift the flour, bicarbonate of soda, baking powder and salt into a mixing bowl. Set aside.

2 With an electric mixer, cream the butter or margarine and the sugars together. Add the egg and vanilla, and beat until light and fluffy. Add the flour mixture and beat on low speed until thoroughly blended. Stir in the rolled oats and plain chocolate chips, mixing well with a wooden spoon. The dough should be crumbly.

3 Drop heaped teaspoonfuls on to the baking sheets, about 2.5cm/1in apart. Bake until just firm around the edges but still soft in the centres, about 15 minutes. With a palette knife, transfer the biscuits to a wire rack to cool.

Chocolate and Coconut Slices

These tasty family favourites are easier to slice if they are allowed to cool overnight.

Makes 24

175g/6oz/2 cups crushed
   digestive biscuits
50g/2oz/¹/₄ cup caster
   sugar
pinch of salt
115g/4oz/¹/₂ cup butter
   or margarine,
   melted

75g/3oz/1¹/₂ cups
   desiccated coconut
250g/9oz plain chocolate
   chips
250ml/8fl oz/1 cup
   sweetened condensed
   milk
115g/4oz/1 cup chopped
   walnuts

1 Preheat the oven to 180°C/350°F/Gas 4. In a bowl, combine the crushed biscuits, sugar, salt and butter or margarine. Press the mixture evenly over the base of an ungreased 33 x 23cm/13 x 9in baking dish.

2 Sprinkle the coconut over the biscuit base, then scatter over the chocolate chips. Pour the condensed milk evenly over the chocolate. Sprinkle the walnuts on top. Bake in the oven for 30 minutes. Unmould on to a wire rack and leave to cool.

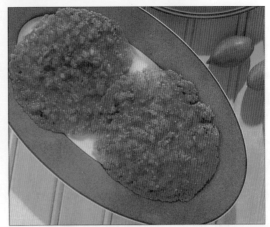

Nut Lace Wafers

To create a different taste, add some finely grated orange peel to these delicate biscuits.

Makes 18

65g/2¹/₂oz/scant ¹/₂ cup
blanched almonds
50g/2oz/¹/₄ cup butter
40g/1¹/₂oz/¹/₃ cup plain
flour

90g/3¹/₂oz/¹/₂ cup caster
sugar
30ml/2 tbsp double cream
2.5ml/¹/₂ tsp vanilla
essence

1 Preheat the oven to 190°C/375°F/Gas 5. Lightly grease two baking sheets.

2 With a sharp knife, chop the almonds as finely as possible. Alternatively, use a food processor or blender to chop the nuts very finely.

3 Melt the butter in a saucepan over a low heat. Remove from the heat and stir in the remaining ingredients and the finely chopped almonds.

4 Drop teaspoonfuls 6cm/2½in apart on the prepared sheets. Bake until golden, about 5 minutes. Cool on the baking sheets briefly, just until the wafers are stiff enough to remove. With a palette knife, transfer to a wire rack to cool.

Oatmeal Lace Rounds

These rich, nutty biscuits are very quick and simple to make and will be enjoyed by everyone.

Makes 36

165g/5¹/₂oz/²/₃ cup butter
or margarine
130g/4¹/₂oz/1¹/₄ cups
quick-cooking
porridge oats
170g/5³/₄ oz/³/₄ cup dark
brown sugar
155g/5¹/₄oz/²/₃ cup caster
sugar

40g/1¹/₂oz/¹/₃ cup plain
flour
1.5ml/¹/₄ tsp salt
1 egg, lightly beaten
5ml/1 tsp vanilla essence
65g/2¹/₂oz/ generous
¹/₂ cup pecan nuts or
walnuts, finely
chopped

1 Preheat the oven to 180°C/350°F/Gas 4. Lightly grease two baking sheets.

2 Melt the butter or margarine in a saucepan over a low heat. Set aside. In a mixing bowl, combine the oats, brown sugar, caster sugar, flour and salt. Make a well in the centre and add the butter or margarine, egg and vanilla. Mix until blended, then stir in the chopped nuts.

3 Drop rounded teaspoonfuls of the mixture about 5cm/2in apart on the prepared baking sheets. Bake in the oven until lightly browned on the edges and bubbling all over, about 5–8 minutes. Cool on the baking sheets for 2 minutes, then transfer to a wire rack to cool completely.

Nutty Chocolate Squares

These delicious squares are incredibly rich, so cut them smaller if you wish.

Makes 16

2 eggs
10ml/2 tsp vanilla
  essence
1.5ml/¹/₄ tsp salt
175g/6oz/1¹/₂ cups pecan
  nuts, coarsely chopped
50g/2oz/¹/₂ cup plain
  flour
50g/2oz/¹/₄ cup caster
  sugar

120ml/4fl oz/¹/₂ cup
  golden syrup
75g/3oz plain chocolate,
  finely chopped
40g/1¹/₂oz/3 tbsp butter
16 pecan nut halves, to
  decorate

1 Preheat the oven to 160°C/325°F/Gas 3. Line the base and sides of a 20cm/8in square baking tin with greaseproof paper and lightly grease the paper.

2 Whisk together the eggs, vanilla and salt. In another bowl, mix together the chopped pecan nuts and flour. Set both aside until needed.

3 In a saucepan, bring the sugar and golden syrup to the boil. Remove from the heat, stir in the chocolate and butter, and blend thoroughly with a wooden spoon. Mix in the beaten egg mixture, then fold in the pecan nut mixture.

4 Pour the mixture into the baking tin and bake until set, about 35 minutes. Cool in the tin for 10 minutes before unmoulding. Cut into 5cm/2in squares and press pecan nut halves into the tops while warm. Cool on a wi   k.

Raisin Brownies

Cover these brownies with a light chocolate frosting for a truly decadent treat, if you wish.

Makes 16

115g/4oz/¹/₂ cup butter
  or margarine
50g/2oz/¹/₂ cup cocoa
  powder
2 eggs
225g/8oz/generous 1 cup
  caster sugar

5ml/1 tsp vanilla essence
40g/1¹/₂oz/¹/₃ cup plain
  flour
75g/3oz/³/₄ cup chopped
  walnuts
75g/3oz/generous ¹/₂ cup
  raisins

1 Preheat the oven to 180°C/350°F/Gas 4. Line the base and sides of a 20cm/8in square baking tin with greaseproof paper and grease the paper.

2 Gently melt the butter or margarine in a small saucepan. Remove from the heat and stir in the cocoa powder. With an electric mixer, beat the eggs, sugar and vanilla together until light. Add the cocoa mixture and stir to blend.

3 Sift the flour over the cocoa mixture and gently fold in. Add the walnuts and raisins and scrape the mixture into the prepared baking tin.

4 Bake in the centre of the oven for 30 minutes. Leave in the tin to cool before cutting into 5cm/2in squares and removing. The brownies should be soft and moist.

Chocolate-chip Brownies

A double dose of chocolate is incorporated into these melt-in-the-mouth brownies.

Makes 24

115g/4oz plain chocolate	pinch of salt
115g/4oz/½ cup butter	150g/5oz/1¼ cups plain
3 eggs	flour
200g/7oz/1 cup sugar	175g/6oz/1 cup chocolate
2.5ml/½ tsp vanilla	chips
essence	

1 Preheat the oven to 180°C/350°F/Gas 4. Then line a 33 x 23cm/13 x 9in baking tin with greaseproof paper and grease the paper.

2 Melt the chocolate and butter together in the top of a double boiler, or in a heatproof bowl set over a pan of gently simmering water.

3 Beat together the eggs, sugar, vanilla and salt. Stir in the chocolate mixture. Sift over the flour and fold in. Add the chocolate chips.

4 Pour the mixture into the baking tin and spread evenly. Bake until just set, about 30 minutes. The brownies should be slightly moist inside. Leave to cool in the tin.

5 To turn out, run a knife all around the edge and invert on to a baking sheet. Remove the paper. Place another sheet on top and invert again. Cut into bars for serving.

Marbled Brownies

Flavoursome and impressive in appearance, these fancy brownies are also great fun to make.

Makes 24

225g/8oz plain chocolate	**For the plain mixture**
75g/3oz/⅓ cup butter	50g/2oz/4 tbsp butter, at
4 eggs	room temperature
300g/11oz/1½ cups sugar	175g/6oz/¾ cup cream
150g/5oz/1¼ cups plain	cheese
flour	90g/3½ oz/1½ cups
2.5ml/½ tsp salt	sugar
5ml/1 tsp baking powder	2 eggs
10ml/2 tsp vanilla	25g/1oz/4 tbsp plain
essence	flour
115g/4oz/1 cup walnuts,	5ml/1 tsp vanilla essence
chopped	

1 Preheat the oven to 180°C/350°F/Gas 4 . Then line a 33 x 23cm/13 x 9in baking tin with greaseproof paper and grease.

2 Melt the chocolate and butter over a very low heat, stirring. Set aside to cool. Meanwhile, beat the eggs until light and fluffy. Gradually beat in the sugar. Sift over the flour, salt and baking powder and fold to combine.

3 Stir in the cooled chocolate mixture. Add the vanilla and walnuts. Measure and set aside 475ml/16fl oz/2 cups of the chocolate mixture. For the plain mixture, cream the butter and cream with an electric mixer. Add the sugar and continue beating until blended. Beat in the eggs, flour and vanilla.

4 Spread the unmeasured chocolate mixture in the tin. Pour over the plain mixture. Drop spoonfuls of the reserved chocolate mixture on top.

5 With a palette knife, swirl the mixtures to marble. Do not blend completely. Bake until just set, 35–40 minutes. Turn out when cool and cut into squares for serving.

Oatmeal and Date Brownies

These brownies are marvellous as a break-time treat. The
secret of chewy, moist brownies is not to overcook them.

Makes 16

150g/5oz plain chocolate
50g/2oz/4 tbsp butter
75g/3oz/scant 1 cup
  quick-cooking
  porridge oats
25g/1oz/3 tbsp
  wheatgerm
25g/1oz/¹⁄₃ cup milk
  powder
2.5ml/¹⁄₂ tsp baking
  powder

2.5ml/¹⁄₂ tsp salt
50g/2oz/¹⁄₂ cup chopped
  walnuts
50g/2oz/¹⁄₃ cup dates,
  chopped
50g/2oz/¹⁄₄ cup molasses
  sugar
5ml/1 tsp vanilla essence
2 eggs, beaten

1 Break the chocolate into a heatproof bowl and add the
butter. Place over a pan of simmering water and stir until
completely melted.

2 Cool the chocolate, stirring occasionally. Preheat the oven
to 180°C/350°F/Gas 4. Grease and line a 20cm/8in square
cake tin.

3 Combine all the dry ingredients together in a bowl, then
beat in the melted chocolate, vanilla and eggs. Pour the
mixture into the cake tin, level the surface and bake in the
oven for 20–25 minutes until firm around the edges yet still
soft in the centre.

4 Cool the brownies in the tin, then chill in the fridge.
When they are more solid, turn them out of the tin and cut
into 16 squares.

Banana Chocolate Brownies

Nuts traditionally give brownies their chewy texture. Here
oat bran is used instead, creating a wonderful alternative.

Makes 9

75ml/5 tbsp cocoa
  powder
15ml/1 tbsp caster sugar
75ml/5 tbsp milk
3 large bananas, mashed
215g/7¹⁄₂oz/1 cup soft
  light brown sugar

5ml/1 tsp vanilla essence
5 egg whites
75g/3oz/³⁄₄ cup self-
  raising flour
75g/3oz/²⁄₃ cup oat bran
icing sugar, for dusting

1 Preheat the oven to 180°C/350°F/Gas 4. Line a 20cm/8in
square cake tin with non-stick baking paper.

2 Blend the cocoa and caster sugar with the milk. Add the
bananas, soft brown sugar and vanilla essence. Lightly beat
the egg whites with a fork. Add the chocolate mixture and
continue to beat well. Sift the flour over the mixture and fold
in with the oat bran. Pour into the prepared tin.

3 Cook in the oven for 40 minutes, or until firm. Cool in the
tin for 10 minutes, then turn out on to a wire rack. Cut into
squares and lightly dust with icing sugar before serving.

White Chocolate Brownies

If you wish, hazelnuts can be substituted for the macadamia nuts in the topping.

Serves 12

150g/5oz/1 cup plain
    flour
2.5ml/½ tsp baking
    powder
pinch of salt
175g/6oz fine quality
    white chocolate,
    chopped
90g/3½ oz/½ cup caster
    sugar
115g/4oz/½ cup unsalted
    butter, cut into pieces

2 eggs, lightly beaten
5ml/1 tsp vanilla essence
175g/6oz semi-sweet
    chocolate chips

For the topping
200g/7oz milk chocolate,
    chopped
215g/7½ oz/1 cup
    unsalted macadamia
    nuts, chopped

1 Preheat the oven to 180°C/350°F/Gas 4. Grease a 23cm/9in springform tin. Sift together the flour, baking powder and salt, and set aside.

2 In a medium saucepan over a moderate heat, melt the white chocolate, sugar and butter until smooth, stirring frequently. Cool slightly, then beat in the eggs and vanilla. Stir in the chocolate chips. Spread evenly in the prepared tin, smoothing the top.

3 Bake for 20–25 minutes until a toothpick inserted 5cm/2in from the side of the tin comes out clean. Remove from the oven to a heatproof surface, sprinkle chopped milk chocolate over the surface (avoid touching the side of tin) and return to oven for 1 minute.

4 Remove from the oven and, using the back of a spoon, gently spread out the softened chocolate. Sprinkle with the macadamia nuts and gently press into the chocolate. Cool on a wire rack for 30 minutes; chill for 1 hour. Run a sharp knife around the side of the tin to loosen; then unclip and remove. Cut into thin wedges to serve.

Maple-Pecan Nut Brownies

This recipe provides a delicious adaptation of the classic American chocolate brownie.

Makes 12

115g/4oz/½ cup butter,
    melted
75g/3oz/½ cup light soft
    brown sugar
90ml/6 tbsp maple syrup
2 eggs
115g/4oz/1 cup
    self-raising flour

75g/3oz/¾ cup pecan
    nuts, chopped
115g/4oz/⅔ cup plain
    chocolate chips
50g/2oz/¼ cup unsalted
    butter
12 pecan nut halves, to
    decorate

1 Preheat the oven to 180°C/350°F/Gas 4. Line and grease a 25 x 18cm/10 x 7in cake tin.

2 Beat together the melted butter, sugar, 60ml/4 tbsp of the maple syrup, eggs and flour for 1 minute, or until smooth. Stir in the nuts and transfer to the cake tin. Smooth the surface and bake for 30 minutes, until risen and firm to the touch. Cool in the tin for 10 minutes, then transfer to a wire rack to cool completely.

3 Melt the chocolate chips, butter and remaining syrup over a low heat. Cool slightly, then spread over the cake. Press in the pecan nut halves, leave to set for about 5 minutes, then cut into bars.

American Chocolate Fudge Brownies

This is the classic American recipe, but omit the frosting if you find it too rich.

Makes 12

175g/6oz/³/₄ cup butter
40g/1¹/₂oz/6 tbsp cocoa powder
2 eggs, lightly beaten
175g/6oz/1 cup soft light brown sugar
2.5ml/¹/₂ tsp vanilla essence
115g/4oz/1 cup chopped pecan nuts

50g/2oz/¹/₂ cup self-raising flour

For the frosting
115g/4oz plain chocolate
25g/1oz/2 tbsp butter
15ml/1 tbsp soured cream

1 Preheat the oven to 180°C/350°F/Gas 4. Grease then line a 20cm/8in square shallow cake tin with greaseproof paper. Melt the butter in a pan and stir in the cocoa powder. Set aside to cool.

2 Beat together the eggs, sugar and vanilla essence in a bowl, then stir in the cooled cocoa mixture with the nuts. Sift over the flour and fold into the mixture with a metal spoon.

3 Pour the mixture into the cake tin and bake in the oven for 30–35 minutes, until risen. Remove from the oven (the mixture will still be quite soft and wet, but it cooks further while cooling) and leave to cool in the tin.

4 To make the frosting, melt the chocolate and butter together in a pan and remove from the heat. Beat in the soured cream until smooth and glossy. Leave to cool slightly, and then spread over the top of the brownies. When set, cut into 12 pieces.

Fudge-glazed Chocolate Brownies

These brownies are just about irresistible, so hide them from friends – or make lots!

Makes 16

250g/9oz bittersweet chocolate, chopped
25g/1oz unsweetened chocolate, chopped
115g/4oz/¹/₂ cup unsalted butter, cut into pieces
90g/3¹/₂ oz/¹/₂ cup light brown sugar
50g/2oz/¹/₄ cup granulated sugar
2 eggs
15ml/1 tbsp vanilla essence
65g/2¹/₂ oz/¹/₂ cup plain flour
115g/4oz/1 cup pecans or walnuts, toasted and chopped

150g/5oz white chocolate, chopped
pecan halves, to decorate (optional)

Fudgy Chocolate Glaze
175g/6oz bittersweet chocolate, chopped
50g/2oz/4 tbsp unsalted butter, cut into pieces
30ml/2 tbsp corn or golden syrup
10ml/2 tsp vanilla essence
5ml/1 tsp instant coffee

1 Preheat oven to 180°C/350°F/Gas 4. Line a 20cm/8in square baking tin with foil then grease the foil.

2 In a saucepan over a low heat, melt the dark chocolates and butter. Off the heat, add the sugars and stir for 2 minutes. Beat in the eggs and vanilla; blend in the flour. Stir in the nuts and white chocolate. Pour into the tin. Bake for 20–25 minutes. Cool in the tin for 30 minutes then lift, using the foil, on to a wire rack to cool for 2 hours.

3 For the glaze, melt all the ingredients in a pan until smooth, stirring. Chill for 1 hour then spread over the brownies. Chill until set then cut into squares.

Chocolate Raspberry Macaroon Bars

Any seedless preserve, such as strawberry or apricot, can be substituted for the raspberry in this recipe.

Makes 16–18

115g/4oz/¹/₂ cup unsalted butter, softened
50g/2oz/¹/₂ cup icing sugar
25g/1oz/¹/₄ cup unsweetened cocoa powder
pinch of salt
5ml/1 tsp almond essence
120g/4oz/1¹/₄ cups plain flour

15ml/1 tbsp raspberry flavour liqueur
175g/6oz/1 cup milk chocolate chips
175g/6oz/1¹/₂ cups finely ground almonds
4 egg whites
pinch of salt
200g/7oz/1 cup caster sugar
2.5ml/¹/₂ tsp almond essence
50g/2oz/¹/₂ cup flaked almonds

For the topping

150g/5oz/¹/₂ cup seedless raspberry preserve

1 Preheat the oven to 160°C/325°F/Gas 3. Then line a 23 x 33cm/9 x 13in baking tin with foil and grease. Beat together the butter, sugar, cocoa and salt until blended. Beat in the almond essence and flour to make a crumbly dough.

2 Turn the dough into the tin and smooth the surface. Prick with a fork. Bake for 20 minutes until just set. Remove from the oven and increase the temperature to 190°C/375°F/Gas 5. Combine the raspberry preserve and liqueur. Spread over the cooked crust, then sprinkle with the chocolate chips.

3 In a food processor fitted with a metal blade, process the almonds, egg whites, salt, sugar and almond essence. Pour over the jam layer, spreading evenly. Sprinkle with almonds.

4 Bake for 20–25 minutes until the top is golden and puffed. Cool in the tin for 20 minutes. Carefully remove from the tin and cool completely. Peel off the foil and cut into bars.

Chewy Fruit Muesli Slice

The apricots give these slices a wonderful chewy texture and the apple keeps them moist.

Makes 8

75g/3oz/scant ¹/₂ cup ready-to-eat dried apricots, chopped
1 eating apple, cored and grated
150g/5oz/1¹/₄ cups Swiss-style muesli

150ml/¹/₄ pint/²/₃ cup apple juice
15g/¹/₂oz/1 tbsp sunflower margarine

1 Preheat the oven to 190°C/375°F/Gas 5. Place all the ingredients in a large bowl and mix well.

2 Press the mixture into a 20cm/8in round non-stick sandwich tin and bake for 35–40 minutes, or until lightly browned and firm. Mark the muesli slice into wedges and leave to cool in the tin.

Blueberry Streusel Slice

If you are short of time, use ready-made pastry for this delightful streusel.

Makes 30

225g/8oz shortcrust pastry
50g/2oz/½ cup plain flour
1.5ml/¼ tsp baking powder
40g/1½oz/3 tbsp butter or margarine
25g/1oz/2 tbsp fresh white breadcrumbs

50g/2oz/⅓ cup soft light brown sugar
1.5ml/¼ tsp salt
50g/2oz/4 tbsp flaked or chopped almonds
30ml/4 tbsp blackberry or bramble jelly
115g/4oz/1 cup blueberries, fresh or frozen

1 Preheat the oven to 180°C/350°F/Gas 4. Roll out the pastry on a lightly floured surface and line an 18 x 28cm/7 x 11in Swiss roll tin. Prick the base evenly with a fork.

2 Rub together the plain flour, baking powder, butter or margarine, breadcrumbs, sugar and salt until really crumbly, then mix in the almonds.

3 Spread the pastry with the jelly, sprinkle with the blueberries, then cover evenly with the streusel topping, pressing down lightly. Bake for 30–40 minutes, reducing the temperature after 20 minutes to 160°C/325°F/Gas 3.

4 Remove from the oven when golden on the top and the pastry is cooked through. Cut into slices while still hot, then allow to cool.

Sticky Date and Apple Bars

If possible allow this mixture to mature for 1–2 days before cutting – it will get stickier and even more delicious!

Makes 16

115g/4oz/½ cup margarine
50g/2oz/⅓ cup soft dark brown sugar
50g/2oz/4 tbsp golden syrup
115g/4oz/¾ cup chopped dates
115g/4oz/generous 1 cup rolled oats

115g/4oz/1 cup wholemeal self-raising flour
225g/8oz/2 eating apples, peeled, cored and grated
5–10ml/1–2 tsp lemon juice
20–25 walnut halves

1 Preheat the oven to 190°C/375°F/Gas 5. Then line an 18–20cm/7–8in square or rectangular loose-based cake tin. In a large pan, heat the margarine, sugar, syrup and dates, stirring until the dates soften completely.

2 Gradually work in the oats, flour, apples and lemon juice until well mixed. Spoon into the tin and spread out evenly. Top with the walnut halves.

3 Bake for 30 minutes, then reduce the temperature to 160°C/325°F/Gas 3 and bake for 10–20 minutes more, until firm to the touch and golden. Cut into squares or bars while still warm, or wrap in foil when nearly cold and keep for 1–2 days before eating.

Figgy Bars

Make sure you have napkins handy when you serve these deliciously sticky bars.

Makes 48

350g/12oz/1¹/₂ cups
 dried figs
3 eggs
175g/6oz/³/₄ cup caster
 sugar
75g/3oz/³/₄ cup plain
 flour
5ml/1 tsp baking powder
2.5ml/¹/₂ tsp ground
 cinnamon
1.5ml/¹/₄ tsp ground
 cloves

1.5ml/¹/₄ tsp grated
 nutmeg
1.5ml/¹/₄ tsp salt
75g/3oz/³/₄ cup finely
 chopped walnuts
30ml/2 tbsp brandy or
 cognac
icing sugar, for dusting

1 Preheat the oven to 160°C/325°F/Gas 3. Then line a 30 x 20 x 3cm/12 x 8 x 1½in baking tin with greaseproof paper and grease the paper.

2 With a sharp knife, chop the figs roughly. Set aside. In a bowl, whisk the eggs and sugar until well blended. In another bowl, sift together the dry ingredients, then fold into the egg mixture in several batches.

3 Scrape the mixture into the baking tin and bake until the top is firm and brown, about 35–40 minutes. It should still be soft underneath.

4 Leave to cool in the tin for 5 minutes, then unmould and transfer to a sheet of greaseproof paper lightly sprinkled with icing sugar. Cut into bars.

Lemon Bars

A surprising amount of lemon juice goes into these bars, but you will appreciate why when you taste them.

Makes 36

50g/2oz/¹/₂ cup icing
 sugar
175g/6oz/1¹/₂ cups plain
 flour
2.5ml/¹/₂ tsp salt
175g/6oz/³/₄ cup butter,
 cut in small pieces

For the topping
4 eggs
350g/12oz/1¹/₂ cups
 caster sugar
grated rind of 1 lemon
120ml/4fl oz/¹/₂ cup fresh
 lemon juice
175ml/6fl oz/³/₄ cup
 whipping cream
icing sugar, for dusting

1 Preheat the oven to 160°C/325°F/Gas 3. Grease a 33 x 23cm/13 x 9in baking tin.

2 Sift the sugar, flour and salt into a bowl. With a pastry blender, cut in the butter until the mixture resembles coarse breadcrumbs. Press the mixture into the base of the tin. Bake until golden brown, about 20 minutes.

3 Meanwhile, for the topping, whisk the eggs and sugar together until blended. Add the lemon rind and juice, and mix well.

4 Lightly whip the cream and fold into the egg mixture. Pour over the still warm base, return to the oven, and bake until set, about 40 minutes. Cool completely before cutting into bars. Dust with icing sugar.

Spiced Raisin Bars

**If you like raisins, these gloriously spicy bars are for you.
Omit the walnuts if you prefer.**

Makes 30

100g/3³/₄ oz/scant 1 cup plain flour	*215g/7¹/₂oz/1¹/₂ cups raisins*
7.5ml/1¹/₂ tsp baking powder	*115g/4oz/¹/₂ cup butter or margarine, at room*
5ml/1 tsp ground cinnamon	*temperature*
2.5ml/¹/₂ tsp grated nutmeg	*90g/3¹/₂oz/¹/₂ cup sugar*
1.5ml/¹/₄ tsp ground cloves	*2 eggs*
1.5ml/¹/₄ tsp mixed spice	*170g/5³/₄ oz/scant ¹/₂ cup black treacle*
	50g/2oz/¹/₂ cup walnuts, chopped

1 Preheat the oven to 180°C/350°F/Gas 4. Then line a
33 x 23cm/13 x 9in baking tin with greaseproof paper and
grease the paper.

2 Sift together the flour, baking powder and spices. Place the
raisins in another bowl and toss with a few tablespoons of the
flour mixture.

3 With an electric mixer, cream the butter or margarine and
sugar together until light and fluffy. Beat in the eggs, one at a
time, then the black treacle. Stir in the flour mixture, raisins
and walnuts.

4 Spread evenly in the baking tin. Bake until just set, about
15–18 minutes. Cool in the tin before cutting into bars.

Toffee Meringue Bars

**Two delicious layers complement each other beautifully in
these easy-to-make bars.**

Makes 12

	For the topping
50g/2oz/4 tbsp butter	*1 egg white*
215g/7¹/₂oz/scant 1¹/₄ cups dark brown sugar	*1.5ml/¹/₄ tsp salt*
1 egg	*15ml/1 tbsp golden syrup*
2.5ml/¹/₂ tsp vanilla essence	*90g/3¹/₂oz/¹/₂ cup caster sugar*
65g/2¹/₂oz/9 tbsp plain flour	*50g/2oz/¹/₂ cup walnuts, finely chopped*
2.5ml/¹/₂ tsp salt	
1.5ml/¹/₄ tsp grated nutmeg	

1 Combine the butter and brown sugar in a saucepan and
heat until bubbling. Set aside to cool.

2 Preheat the oven to 180°C/350°F/Gas 4. Line the base and
sides of a 20cm/8in square cake tin with greaseproof paper
and grease the paper.

3 Beat the egg and vanilla into the cooled sugar mixture. Sift
over the flour, salt and nutmeg and fold in. Spread in the base
of the cake tin.

4 For the topping, beat the egg white with the salt until it
holds soft peaks. Beat in the golden syrup, then the sugar, and
continue beating until the mixture holds stiff peaks. Fold in
the nuts and spread on top. Bake for 30 minutes. Cut into bars
when completely cool.

Chocolate Walnut Bars

These double-decker bars should be stored in the fridge in an airtight container.

Makes 24

50g/2oz/²/₃ cup walnuts
55g/2¹/₄oz/generous
  ¹/₄ cup caster sugar
100g/3³/₄ oz/scant 1 cup
  plain flour, sifted
90g/3¹/₂ oz/6 tbsp cold
  unsalted butter, cut
  into pieces

For the topping
25g/1oz/2 tbsp unsalted
  butter

90ml/6 tbsp water
25g/1oz/¹/₄ cup
  unsweetened cocoa
  powder
90g/3¹/₂oz/¹/₂ cup caster
  sugar
5ml/1 tsp vanilla essence
1.5ml/¹/₄ tsp salt
2 eggs
icing sugar, for dusting

1 Preheat the oven to 180°C/350°F/Gas 4. Grease the base and sides of a 20cm/8in square baking tin.

2 Grind the walnuts with a few tablespoons of the sugar in a food processor or blender. In a bowl, combine the ground walnuts, remaining sugar and flour. Rub in the butter until the mixture resembles coarse breadcrumbs. Alternatively, use a food processor. Pat the walnut mixture evenly into the base of the baking tin. Bake for 25 minutes.

3 Meanwhile, for the topping, melt the butter with the water. Whisk in the cocoa powder and sugar. Remove from the heat, stir in the vanilla essence and salt, then cool for 5 minutes. Whisk in the eggs until blended. Pour the topping over the baked crust.

4 Return to the oven and bake until set, about 20 minutes. Set the tin on a wire rack to cool, then cut into bars and dust with icing sugar.

Hazelnut Squares

These crunchy, nutty squares are made in a single bowl. What could be simpler?

Makes 9

50g/2oz plain chocolate
65g/2¹/₂oz/5 tbsp butter
  or margarine
225g/8oz/generous 1 cup
  caster sugar
50g/2oz/¹/₂ cup plain
  flour
2.5ml/¹/₂ tsp baking
  powder

2 eggs, beaten
2.5ml/¹/₂ tsp vanilla
  essence
115g/4oz/1 cup skinned
  hazelnuts, roughly
  chopped

1 Preheat the oven to 180°C/350°F/Gas 4. Grease a 20cm/8in square baking tin.

2 In a heatproof bowl set over a pan of barely simmering water, melt the chocolate and butter or margarine. Remove the bowl from the heat.

3 Add the sugar, flour, baking powder, eggs, vanilla and half of the hazelnuts to the melted mixture and stir well with a wooden spoon.

4 Pour the mixture into the prepared tin. Bake in the oven for 10 minutes, then sprinkle the reserved hazelnuts over the top. Return to the oven and continue baking until firm to the touch, about 25 minutes.

5 Cool in the tin, set on a wire rack for 10 minutes, then unmould on to the rack and cool completely. Cut into squares before serving.

Fruity Tea Bread

Serve this bread thinly sliced, toasted or plain, with butter or cream cheese and jam.

Makes one 23 x 13cm/9 x 5in loaf

225g/8oz/2 cups plain
    flour
115g/4oz/generous ¹/₂ cup
    caster sugar
15ml/1 tbsp baking
    powder
2.5ml/¹/₂ tsp salt
grated rind of 1 large
    orange
160ml/5¹/₂fl oz/generous
    ²/₃ cup fresh orange
    juice

2 eggs, lightly beaten
75g/3oz/6 tbsp butter or
    margarine, melted
115g/4oz/1 cup fresh
    cranberries or
    bilberries
50g/2oz/¹/₂ cup chopped
    walnuts

1 Preheat the oven to 180°C/350°F/Gas 4. Then line a 23 x 13cm/9 x 5in loaf tin with greaseproof paper and grease the paper.

2 Sift the flour, sugar, baking powder and salt into a mixing bowl. Then stir in the orange rind. Make a well in the centre and add the fresh orange juice, eggs and melted butter or margarine. Stir from the centre until the ingredients are blended; do not overmix. Add the berries and walnuts and stir until blended.

3 Transfer the mixture to the prepared tin and bake until a skewer inserted in the centre of the loaf comes out clean, about 45–50 minutes. Leave to cool in the tin for 10 minutes before transferring to a wire rack to cool completely.

Date and Pecan Loaf

Walnuts may be used instead of pecan nuts to make this luxurious tea bread.

Makes one 23 x 13cm/9 x 5in loaf

175g/6oz/1 cup chopped
    stoned dates
175ml/6fl oz/³/₄ cup
    boiling water
50g/2oz/4 tbsp unsalted
    butter, at room
    temperature
50g/2oz/¹/₃ cup dark
    brown sugar
50g/2oz/¹/₄ cup caster
    sugar
1 egg, at room
    temperature

30ml/2 tbsp brandy
165g/5¹/₂oz/generous
    ¹/₄ cup plain flour
10ml/2 tsp baking
    powder
2.5ml/¹/₂ tsp salt
4ml/³/₄ tsp freshly grated
    nutmeg
75g/3oz/³/₄ cup coarsely
    chopped pecan nuts

1 Place the dates in a bowl and pour over the boiling water. Set aside to cool. Preheat the oven to 180°C/350°F/Gas 4. Line a 23 x 13cm/9 x 5in loaf tin with greaseproof paper and then grease the paper.

2 With an electric mixer, cream the butter and sugars until light and fluffy. Beat in the egg and brandy, then set aside.

3 Sift the flour, baking powder, salt and nutmeg together, at least three times. Fold the dry ingredients into the sugar mixture in three batches, alternating with the dates and water. Fold in the nuts.

4 Pour the mixture into the prepared tin and bake until a skewer inserted in the centre comes out clean, about 45–50 minutes. Leave the loaf to cool in the tin for 10 minutes before transferring to a wire rack to cool completely.

Wholemeal Banana Nut Loaf

A hearty and filling loaf, this would be ideal as a winter
tea-time treat.

Makes one 23 x 13cm/9 x 5in loaf

115g/4oz/½ cup butter,
  at room temperature
115g/4oz/generous ½ cup
  caster sugar
2 eggs, at room
  temperature
115g/4oz/1 cup plain
  flour
5ml/1 tsp bicarbonate of
  soda

1.5ml/¼ tsp salt
5ml/1 tsp ground
  cinnamon
50g/2oz/½ cup
  wholemeal flour
3 large ripe bananas
5ml/1 tsp vanilla essence
50g/2oz/½ cup chopped
  walnuts

1 Preheat the oven to 180°C/350°F/Gas 4. Line the base and
sides of a 23 x 13cm/9 x 5in loaf tin with greaseproof paper
and grease the paper.

2 With an electric mixer, cream the butter and sugar together
until light and fluffy. Add the eggs, one at a time, beating well
after each addition.

3 Sift the plain flour, bicarbonate of soda, salt and cinnamon
over the butter mixture and stir to blend. Then stir in the
wholemeal flour.

4 With a fork, mash the bananas to a purée, then stir into the
mixture. Stir in the vanilla and nuts.

5 Pour the mixture into the prepared tin and spread level.
Bake until a skewer inserted in the centre comes out clean,
about 50–60 minutes. Leave to stand for 10 minutes before
transferring to a wire rack to cool completely.

Apricot Nut Loaf

Apricots, raisins and walnuts combine to make a lovely
light tea bread.

Makes one 23 x 13cm/9 x 5in loaf

115g/4oz/½ cup dried
  apricots
1 large orange
75g/3oz/generous ½ cup
  raisins
150g/5oz/⅔ cup caster
  sugar
85ml/5½ tbsp/⅓ cup oil
2 eggs, lightly beaten

250g/9oz/generous
  2 cups plain flour
10ml/2 tsp baking
  powder
2.5ml/½ tsp salt
5ml/1 tsp bicarbonate of
  soda
50g/2oz/½ cup chopped
  walnuts

1 Place the apricots in a bowl, cover with lukewarm water
and leave to stand for 30 minutes. Preheat the oven to
180°C/350°F/Gas 4. Line a 23 x 13cm/9 x 5in loaf tin with
greaseproof paper and grease the paper.

2 With a vegetable peeler, remove the orange rind, leaving
the pith. Chop the strips finely.

3 Drain the apricots and chop coarsely. Place in a bowl with
the orange rind and raisins. Squeeze the peeled orange.
Measure the juice and add enough hot water to obtain
175ml/6fl oz/¾ cup liquid. Add the orange juice mixture to
the apricot mixture. Stir in the sugar, oil and eggs. Set aside.

4 In another bowl, sift together the flour, baking powder, salt
and bicarbonate of soda. Fold the flour mixture into the
apricot mixture in three batches, then stir in the walnuts.

5 Spoon the mixture into the prepared tin and bake until a
skewer inserted in the centre of the loaf comes out clean,
about 55–60 minutes. If the loaf browns too quickly, protect
the top with a sheet of foil. Cool in the tin for 10 minutes, then
transfer to a wire rack to cool completely.

Bilberry Tea Bread

A lovely crumbly topping makes this tea bread extra special.

Makes 8 pieces

50g/2oz/4tbsp butter or margarine, at room temperature
175g/6oz/¾ cup caster sugar
1 egg, at room temperature
120ml/4fl oz/½ cup milk
225g/8oz/2 cups plain flour
10ml/2 tsp baking powder
2.5ml/½ tsp salt

275g/10oz/¾ cup fresh bilberries, or blueberries

For the topping

115g/4oz/½ cup sugar
40g/1½oz/⅓ cup plain flour
2.5ml/½ tsp ground cinnamon
50g/2oz/4 tbsp butter, cut into pieces

1 Preheat the oven to 190°C/375°F/Gas 5. Grease a 23cm/9in baking dish.

2 With an electric mixer, cream the butter or margarine with the sugar until light and fluffy. Add the egg, beat to combine, then mix in the milk until well blended.

3 Sift over the flour, baking powder and salt and stir just enough to blend the ingredients. Add the berries and stir. Transfer to the baking dish.

4 For the topping, place the sugar, flour, cinnamon and butter in a mixing bowl. Cut in with a pastry blender until the mixture resembles coarse breadcrumbs. Sprinkle the topping over the mixture in the baking dish. Bake until a skewer inserted in the centre comes out clean, about 45 minutes. Serve warm or cold.

Dried Fruit Loaf

Use any combination of dried fruit you like in this delicious tea bread.

Makes one 23 x 13cm/9 x 5in loaf

450g/1lb/2¾ cups mixed dried fruit, such as currants, raisins, chopped dried apricots and dried cherries
300ml/½ pint/1¼ cups cold strong tea
200g/7oz/generous 1 cup dark brown sugar
grated rind and juice of 1 small orange

grated rind and juice of 1 lemon
1 egg, lightly beaten
200g/7oz/1¾ cups plain flour
15ml/1 tbsp baking powder
1.5ml/¼ tsp salt

1 In a bowl, mix the dried fruit with the cold tea and leave to soak overnight.

2 Preheat the oven to 180°C/350°F/Gas 4. Line the base and sides of a 23 x 13cm/9 x 5in loaf tin with greaseproof paper and grease the paper.

3 Strain the fruit, reserving the liquid. In a bowl, combine the sugar, orange and lemon rind, and fruit. Pour the orange and lemon juice into a measuring jug; if the quantity is less than 250ml/8fl oz/1 cup, then top up with the soaking liquid. Stir the citrus juices and egg into the dried fruit mixture.

4 Sift the flour, baking powder and salt together into another bowl. Stir into the fruit mixture until blended.

5 Transfer to the tin and bake until a skewer inserted in the centre comes out clean; about 1¼ hours. Leave in the tin for 10 minutes before unmoulding.

Corn Bread

Serve this bread as an accompaniment to a meal, with soup, or take it on a picnic.

Makes one 23 x 13cm/9 x 5in loaf

115g/4oz/1 cup plain flour	*350ml/12fl oz/1¹/₂ cups milk*
65g/2¹/₂oz/generous ¹/₄ cup caster sugar	*2 eggs*
5ml/1 tsp salt	*75g/3oz/6 tbsp butter, melted*
15ml/1 tbsp baking powder	*115g/4oz/¹/₂ cup margarine, melted*
175g/6oz/scant 1¹/₂ cups cornmeal or polenta	

1 Preheat the oven to 200°C/400°F/Gas 6. Then line a 23 x 13cm/9 x 5in loaf tin with greaseproof paper and grease the paper.

2 Sift the flour, sugar, salt and baking powder into a mixing bowl. Add the cornmeal or polenta and stir to blend. Make a well in the centre. Whisk together the milk, eggs, melted butter and margarine. Pour the mixture into the well. Stir until just blended; do not overmix.

3 Pour into the tin and bake until a skewer inserted in the centre comes out clean, about 45 minutes. Serve hot or at room temperature.

Spicy Sweetcorn Bread

An interesting variation on basic corn bread; adjust the number of chillies used according to taste.

Makes 9 squares

3–4 whole canned chillies, drained	*5ml/1 tsp bicarbonate of soda*
2 eggs	*10ml/2 tsp salt*
475ml/16fl oz/2 cups buttermilk	*175g/6oz/scant 1¹/₂ cups cornmeal or polenta*
50g/2oz/4 tbsp butter, melted	*350g/12oz/2 cups canned sweetcorn or frozen sweetcorn, thawed*
50g/2oz/¹/₂ cup plain flour	

1 Preheat the oven to 200°C/400°F/Gas 6. Line the base and sides of a 23cm/9in square cake tin with greaseproof paper and lightly grease the paper.

2 With a sharp knife, finely chop the canned chillies and set aside until needed.

3 In a large bowl, whisk the eggs until frothy, then whisk in the buttermilk. Add the melted butter.

4 Sift the flour, bicarbonate of soda and salt together into another large bowl. Fold into the buttermilk mixture in three batches, then fold in the cornmeal or polenta in three batches. Finally, fold in the chillies and sweetcorn.

5 Pour the mixture into the tin and bake until a skewer inserted in the centre comes out clean; about 25–30 minutes. Leave in the tin for 2–3 minutes before unmoulding. Cut into squares and serve warm.

Sweet Sesame Loaf

Lemon and sesame seeds make a great partnership in this light tea bread.

Makes one 23 x 13cm/9 x 5in loaf

75g/3oz/6 tbsp sesame
    seeds
275g/10oz/2¹/₂ cups plain
    flour
12.5ml/2¹/₂ tsp baking
    powder
5ml/1 tsp salt
50g/2oz/4 tbsp butter or
    margarine, at room
    temperature

130g/4¹/₂oz/scant ²/₃ cup
    sugar
2 eggs, at room
    temperature
grated rind of 1 lemon
350ml/12fl oz/1¹/₂ cups
    milk

1 Preheat the oven to 180°C/350°F/Gas 4. Carefully line a 23 x 13cm/9 x 5in loaf tin with greaseproof paper and then grease the paper.

2 Reserve 25g/1oz/2 tbsp of the sesame seeds. Spread the rest on a baking sheet and bake in the oven until lightly toasted, about 10 minutes.

3 Sift the flour, baking powder and salt into a bowl. Stir in the toasted sesame seeds and set aside.

4 Cream the butter or margarine and sugar together until light and fluffy. Beat in the eggs, then stir in the lemon rind and milk. Pour the milk mixture over the dry ingredients and fold in with a large metal spoon until just blended.

5 Pour into the tin and sprinkle over the reserved sesame seeds. Bake until a skewer inserted in the centre comes out clean, about 1 hour. Cool in the tin for 10 minutes. Turn out on to a wire rack to cool completely.

Cardamom and Saffron Tea Loaf

An aromatic sweet bread ideal for afternoon tea, or lightly toasted for breakfast.

Makes one 900g/2lb loaf

generous pinch of saffron
    strands
750ml/1¹/₄ pints/3 cups
    lukewarm milk
25g/1oz/2 tbsp butter
1kg/2¹/₄ lb/8 cups strong
    plain flour
2 sachets easy-blend
    dried yeast

40g/1¹/₂ oz/3 tbsp caster
    sugar
6 cardamom pods, split
    open and seeds
    extracted
115g/4oz/scant ³/₄ cup
    raisins
30ml/2 tbsp clear honey
1 egg, beaten

1 Crush the saffron straight into a cup containing a little of the warm milk and leave to infuse for 5 minutes. Rub the butter into the flour, then mix in the yeast, sugar, cardamom seeds and raisins.

2 Beat the remaining milk with the honey and egg, then mix this into the flour, along with the saffron milk and strands, to form a firm dough. Turn out the dough and knead it on a lightly floured surface for 5 minutes.

3 Return the dough to the mixing bowl, cover with oiled clear film and leave in a warm place until doubled in size.

4 Preheat the oven to 200°C/400°F/Gas 6. Grease a 900g/2lb loaf tin. Turn the dough out on to a floured surface, punch down, knead for 3 minutes, then shape into a fat roll and fit into the tin. Cover with a sheet of lightly oiled clear film and stand in a warm place until the dough begins to rise again.

5 Bake the loaf for 25 minutes until golden brown and firm on top. Turn out on to a wire rack and as it cools brush the top with clear honey.

Courgette Tea Bread

Like carrots, courgettes are a vegetable that work well in baking, adding moistness and lightness to the bread.

Makes one 23 x 13cm/9 x 5in loaf

50g/2oz/4 tbsp butter	5ml/1 tsp baking powder
3 eggs	5ml/1 tsp salt
250ml/8fl oz/1 cup vegetable oil	5ml/1 tsp ground cinnamon
285g/10¹/₂oz/1¹/₂ cups sugar	5ml/1 tsp grated nutmeg
2 unpeeled courgettes, grated	1.5ml/¹/₄ tsp ground cloves
275g/10oz/2¹/₂ cups plain flour	115g/4oz/1 cup chopped walnuts
10ml/2 tsp bicarbonate of soda	

1 Preheat the oven to 180°C/350°F/Gas 4. Line the base and sides of a 23 x 13cm/9 x 5in loaf tin with greaseproof paper and grease the paper.

2 In a saucepan, melt the butter over a low heat. Set aside until needed.

3 With an electric mixer, beat the eggs and oil together until thick. Beat in the sugar, then stir in the melted butter and the courgettes. Set aside.

4 In another bowl, sift all the dry ingredients together three times. Carefully fold into the courgette mixture. Fold in the chopped walnuts.

5 Pour into the tin and bake until a skewer inserted in the centre comes out clean, about 60–70 minutes. Leave to stand for 10 minutes before turning out on to a wire rack to cool.

Mango Tea Bread

A delicious tea bread with an exotic slant – baked with juicy ripe mango.

Makes two 23 x 13cm/9 x 5in loaves

275g/10oz/2¹/₂ cups plain flour	285g/10¹/₂oz/1¹/₂ cups sugar
10ml/2 tsp bicarbonate of soda	120ml/4fl oz/¹/₂ cup vegetable oil
10ml/2 tsp ground cinnamon	1 large ripe mango, peeled and chopped
2.5ml/¹/₂ tsp salt	85g/3¹/₄oz/generous
115g/4oz/¹/₂ cup margarine, at room temperature	1¹/₂ cups desiccated coconut
3 eggs, at room temperature	65g/2¹/₂oz/¹/₂ cup raisins

1 Preheat the oven to 180°C/350°F/Gas 4. Line the base and sides of two 23 x 13cm/9 x 5in loaf tins with greaseproof paper and grease the paper.

2 Sift together the flour, bicarbonate of soda, cinnamon and salt. Set aside until needed.

3 Cream the margarine until soft. Beat in the eggs and sugar until light and fluffy. Beat in the oil.

4 Fold the dry ingredients into the creamed ingredients in three batches, then fold in the mango, two-thirds of the coconut and the raisins.

5 Spoon the batter into the tins. Sprinkle over the remaining coconut. Bake until a skewer inserted in the centre comes out clean, about 50–60 minutes. Leave to stand for 10 minutes before turning out on to a wire rack to cool completely.

American-style Corn Sticks

If you don't have a corn-stick mould, use éclair tins or a bun tray and reduce the cooking time by 10 minutes.

Makes 6

1 egg
120ml/4fl oz/^{1}/$_2$ cup milk
15ml/1 tbsp vegetable oil
115g/4oz/scant 1 cup cornmeal or polenta

50g/2oz/^{1}/$_2$ cup plain flour
10ml/2 tsp baking powder
45ml/3 tbsp caster sugar

1 Preheat the oven to 190°C/375°F/Gas 5. Grease a cast-iron corn-stick mould.

2 Beat the egg in a small bowl. Stir in the milk and vegetable oil, and set aside.

3 In a mixing bowl, stir together the cornmeal or polenta, flour, baking powder and sugar. Pour in the egg mixture and stir with a wooden spoon to combine.

4 Spoon the mixture into the prepared mould. Bake until a skewer inserted in the centre of a corn stick comes out clean, about 25 minutes. Cool in the mould on a wire rack for 10 minutes before unmoulding.

Savoury Sweetcorn Bread

For a spicy bread, stir 30ml/2 tbsp chopped fresh chillies into the mixture with the cheese and sweetcorn.

Makes 9

2 eggs, lightly beaten
250ml/8fl oz/1 cup buttermilk
115g/4oz/1 cup plain flour
115g/4oz/scant 1 cup cornmeal or polenta
10ml/2 tsp baking powder

2.5ml/^{1}/$_2$ tsp salt
15ml/1 tbsp caster sugar
115g/4oz/1 cup Cheddar cheese, grated
225g/8oz/1^1/$_3$ cups sweetcorn, fresh or frozen and thawed

1 Preheat the oven to 200°C/400°F/Gas 6. Then grease a 23cm/9in square baking tin.

2 Combine the eggs and buttermilk in a small bowl and whisk until well mixed. Set aside.

3 In another bowl, stir together the flour, cornmeal or polenta, baking powder, salt and sugar. Add the egg mixture and stir with a wooden spoon to combine. Stir in the cheese and sweetcorn.

4 Pour the mixture into the baking tin. Bake until a skewer inserted in the centre comes out clean, about 25 minutes. Unmould the bread on to a wire rack and leave to cool. Cut into squares before serving.

Herb Popovers

Popovers are delicious flavoured with herbs, and served as a snack or starter.

Makes 12

3 eggs
250ml/8fl oz/1 cup milk
25g/1oz/2 tbsp butter,
    melted
75g/3oz/³/₄ cup plain
    flour

1.5ml/¹/₄ tsp salt
1 small sprig each mixed
    fresh herbs, such as
    chives, tarragon, dill
    and parsley

1 Preheat the oven to 220°C/425°F/Gas 7. Grease 12 small ramekins or individual baking cups.

2 With an electric mixer, beat the eggs until blended. Beat in the milk and melted butter. Sift together the flour and salt, then beat into the egg mixture to combine thoroughly.

3 Strip the herb leaves from the stems and chop finely. Mix together and measure out 30ml/2 tbsp. Stir the measured herbs into the batter.

4 Half-fill the prepared ramekins or baking cups. Bake until golden; 25–30 minutes. Do not open the oven door during baking time or the popovers may collapse. For drier popovers, pierce each one with a knife after 30 minutes baking time and then bake for a further 5 minutes. Serve the herb popovers hot.

Cheese Popovers

Serve these popovers simply as an accompaniment to a meal, or make a filling and serve them as a starter.

Makes 12

3 eggs
250ml/8fl oz/1 cup milk
25g/1oz/2 tbsp butter,
    melted
75g/3oz/³/₄ cup plain
    flour

1.5ml/¹/₄ tsp salt
1.5ml/¹/₄ tsp paprika
25g/1oz/¹/₃ cup freshly
    grated Parmesan
    cheese

1 Preheat the oven to 220°C/425°F/Gas 7. Grease 12 small ramekins or individual baking cups.

2 With an electric mixer, beat the eggs until blended. Beat in the milk and melted butter. Sift together the flour, salt and paprika, then beat into the egg mixture. Add the Parmesan cheese and stir in.

3 Half-fill the prepared cups and bake until golden, about 25–30 minutes. Do not open the oven door or the popovers may collapse. For drier popovers, pierce each one with a knife after about 30 minutes baking time and then bake for another 5 minutes. Serve hot.

Sweet Potato and Raisin Bread

Serve buttered slices of this subtly-spiced loaf at coffee or tea time.

Makes one 900g/2lb loaf

350g/12oz/3 cups flour
10ml/2tsp baking powder
2.5ml/½ tsp salt
5ml/1 tsp ground
  cinnamon
2.5ml/½ tsp grated
  nutmeg
450g/1lb mashed cooked
  sweet potatoes

90g/3½ oz light brown
  sugar
115g/4oz/½ cup butter or
  margarine, melted and
  cooled
3 eggs, beaten
75g/3oz/generous ½ cup
  raisins

1 Preheat the oven to 180°C/350°F/Gas 4. Grease a 900g/2lb loaf dish or tin.

2 Sift the flour, baking powder, salt, cinnamon, and nutmeg into a small bowl. Set aside.

3 With an electric mixer, beat the mashed sweet potatoes with the brown sugar, butter or margarine, and eggs until well mixed.

4 Add the flour mixture and the raisins. Stir with a wooden spoon until the flour is just mixed in.

5 Transfer the batter to the prepared dish or tin. Bake until a skewer inserted in the centre of the loaf comes out clean, about 1–1¼ hours.

6 Let the bread cool in the pan on a wire rack for 15 minutes, then unmould from the dish or tin on to the wire rack and leave to cool completely.

Lemon and Walnut Tea Bread

Beaten egg whites give this citrus-flavour loaf a lovely light and crumbly texture.

Makes one 23 x 13cm/9 x 5in loaf

115g/4oz/½ cup butter
  or margarine, at room
  temperature
90g/3½oz/½ cup sugar
2 eggs, at room
  temperature, separated
grated rind of 2 lemons
30ml/2 tbsp lemon juice

215g/7½oz/scant 2 cups
  plain flour
10ml/2 tsp baking
  powder
120ml/4fl oz/½ cup milk
50g/2oz/½ cup chopped
  walnuts
1.5ml/¼ teaspoon salt

1 Preheat the oven to 180°C/350°F/Gas 4. Then line a 23 x 13cm/9 x 5in loaf tin with greaseproof paper and grease the paper.

2 Cream the butter or margarine with the sugar until light and fluffy. Beat in the egg yolks. Add the lemon rind and juice and stir until blended. Set aside.

3 In another bowl, sift together the flour and baking powder three times. Fold into the butter mixture in three batches, alternating with the milk. Fold in the walnuts. Set aside.

4 Beat the egg whites and salt until stiff peaks form. Fold a large spoonful of the egg whites into the walnut mixture to lighten it. Fold in the remaining egg whites carefully until the mixture is just blended.

5 Pour the batter into the prepared tin and bake until a skewer inserted in the centre of the loaf comes out clean, about 45–50 minutes. Cool in the tin for 5 minutes before turning out on to a wire rack to cool completely.

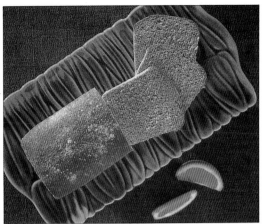

Date and Nut Maltloaf

Choose any type of nut you like to include in this very rich and fruit-packed tea bread.

Makes two 450g/1lb loaves

300g/11oz/2 cups strong plain flour
275g/10oz/2 cups strong plain wholemeal flour
5ml/1 tsp salt
75g/3oz/6 tbsp soft brown sugar
1 sachet easy-blend dried yeast
50g/2oz/4 tbsp butter or margarine
15ml/1 tbsp black treacle
60ml/4 tbsp malt extract

scant 250ml/8fl oz/1 cup lukewarm milk
115g/4oz/¹⁄₂ cup chopped dates
50g/2oz/¹⁄₂ cup chopped nuts
75g/3oz/generous ¹⁄₂ cup sultanas
75g/3oz/generous ¹⁄₂ cup raisins
30ml/2 tbsp clear honey, to glaze

1 Sift the flours and salt into a large bowl, then tip in the wheat flakes from the sieve. Stir in the sugar and yeast.

2 Put the butter or margarine in a small pan with the treacle and malt extract. Stir over a low heat until melted. Leave to cool, then combine with the milk.

3 Stir the milk mixture into the dry ingredients and knead thoroughly for 15 minutes until the dough is elastic.

4 Knead in the fruits and nuts. Transfer the dough to an oiled bowl, cover with clear film and leave in a warm place for about 1¹⁄₂ hours, until the dough has doubled in size.

5 Grease two 450g/1lb loaf tins. Knock back the dough and knead lightly. Divide in half, form into loaves and place in the tins. Cover and leave in a warm place for 30 minutes, until risen. Meanwhile, preheat the oven to 190°C/375°F/Gas 5.

6 Bake for 35–40 minutes, until well risen. Cool on a wire rack. Brush with honey while warm.

Orange Wheatloaf

Perfect just with butter as a breakfast tea bread and lovely for banana sandwiches.

Makes one 450g/1lb loaf

275g/10oz/2¹⁄₄ cups wholemeal plain flour
2.5ml/¹⁄₂ tsp salt
25g/1oz/2 tbsp butter
25g/1oz/2 tbsp soft light brown sugar

¹⁄₂ sachet easy-blend dried yeast
grated rind and juice of ¹⁄₂ orange

1 Sift the flour into a large bowl and return any wheat flakes from the sieve. Add the salt and rub in the butter lightly with your fingertips.

2 Stir in the sugar, yeast and orange rind. Pour the orange juice into a measuring jug and use hot water to make up to 200ml/7fl oz/scant 1 cup (the liquid should not be more than hand hot).

3 Stir the liquid into the flour and mix to a soft ball of dough. Knead gently on a lightly floured surface until quite smooth and elastic.

4 Place the dough in a greased 450g/1lb loaf tin and leave in a warm place until nearly doubled in size. Preheat the oven to 220°C/425°F/Gas 7.

5 Bake the bread for 30–35 minutes, or until it sounds hollow when tapped underneath. Tip out of the tin and cool on a wire rack.

Orange and Honey Tea Bread

Honey gives a special flavour to this tea bread. Serve just with a scraping of butter.

Makes one 23 x 13cm/9 x 5in loaf

385g/13¹/₂oz/scant
   3¹/₂cups plain flour
12.5ml/2¹/₂ tsp baking
   powder
2.5ml/¹/₂ tsp bicarbonate
   of soda
2.5ml/¹/₂ tsp salt
25g/1oz/2 tbsp margarine
250ml/8fl oz/1 cup clear
   honey

1 egg, at room
   temperature, lightly
   beaten
25ml/1¹/₂ tbsp grated
   orange rind
175ml/6fl oz/³/₄ cup
   freshly squeezed
   orange juice
115g/4oz/1 cup chopped
   walnuts

1 Preheat the oven to 160°C/325°F/Gas 3. Line the base and sides of a 23 x 13cm/9 x 5in loaf tin with greaseproof paper and grease the paper.

2 Sift the flour, baking powder, bicarbonate of soda and salt together in a bowl.

3 Cream the margarine until soft. Stir in the honey until blended, then stir in the egg. Add the orange rind and stir to combine thoroughly.

4 Fold the flour mixture into the honey and egg mixture in three batches, alternating with the orange juice. Stir in the chopped walnuts.

5 Pour into the prepared tin and bake in the oven until a skewer inserted in the centre comes out clean, about 60–70 minutes. Leave for 10 minutes before turning out on to a wire rack to cool completely.

Apple Loaf

Ring the changes with this loaf by using different nuts and dried fruit.

Makes one 23 x 13cm/9 x 5in loaf

1 egg
250ml/8fl oz/1 cup
   bottled or home-made
   apple sauce
50g/2oz/4 tbsp butter or
   margarine, melted
100g/3³/₄oz/scant ³/₄ cup
   dark brown sugar
45g/1³/₄oz/scant ¹/₄ cup
   caster sugar
275g/10oz/2¹/₂ cups plain
   flour
10ml/2 tsp baking
   powder

2.5ml/¹/₂ tsp bicarbonate
   of soda
2.5ml/¹/₂ tsp salt
5ml/1 tsp ground
   cinnamon
2.5ml/¹/₂ tsp grated
   nutmeg
65g/2¹/₂oz/¹/₂ cup
   currants or raisins
50g/2oz/¹/₂ cup pecan
   nuts or walnuts,
   chopped

1 Preheat the oven to 180°C/350°F/Gas 4. Line the base and sides of a 23 x 13cm/9 x 5in loaf tin with greaseproof paper and grease the paper.

2 Break the egg into a bowl and beat lightly. Stir in the apple sauce, butter or margarine and both sugars. Set aside.

3 In another bowl, sift together the flour, baking powder, bicarbonate of soda, salt, cinnamon and nutmeg. Fold the dry ingredients, including the currants or raisins and the nuts, into the apple sauce mixture in three batches.

4 Pour into the prepared tin and bake in the oven until a skewer inserted in the centre of the loaf comes out clean, about 1 hour. Leave to stand in the tin for 10 minutes, then turn out on to a wire rack to cool completely.

Fruit and Brazil Nut Tea Bread

Mashed bananas are a classic ingredient in tea breads, and help to create a moist texture.

Makes one 23 x 13cm/9 x 5in loaf

225g/8oz/2 cups plain flour	2 bananas, peeled and mashed
10ml/2 tsp baking powder	115g/4oz/½ cup dried figs, chopped
5ml/1 tsp mixed spice	50g/2oz/½ cup brazil nuts, chopped
115g/4oz/½ cup butter, diced	
115g/4oz/¾ cup light soft brown sugar	**To decorate**
2 eggs, lightly beaten	8 whole brazil nuts
30ml/2 tbsp milk	4 whole dried figs, halved
30ml/2 tbsp dark rum	30ml/2 tbsp apricot jam
	5ml/1 tsp dark rum

1 Preheat the oven to 180°C/350°F/Gas 4. Grease and base-line a 23 x 13cm/9 x 5in loaf tin. Sift the flour, baking powder and mixed spice into a bowl. Rub in the butter until the mixture resembles fine breadcrumbs. Stir in the sugar.

2 Make a well in the centre and work in the eggs, milk and rum until combined. Stir in the remaining ingredients and transfer to the loaf tin.

3 Press the whole brazil nuts and halved figs gently into the mixture, to form an attractive pattern. Bake for 1¼ hours, or until a skewer inserted in the centre comes out clean. Cool in the tin for 10 minutes, then transfer to a wire rack.

4 Heat the jam and rum together in a small saucepan. Increase the heat and boil for 1 minute. Remove from the heat and pass through a fine sieve. Cool the glaze slightly, brush over the warm cake, and leave to cool completely.

Glazed Banana Spiced Loaf

The lemony glaze perfectly sets off the flavours in this banana tea bread.

Makes one 23 x 13cm/9 x 5in loaf

115g/4oz/½ cup butter, at room temperature	1.5ml/¼ tsp ground cloves
165g/5½oz/generous ⅔ cup caster sugar	175ml/6fl oz/¾ cup soured cream
2 eggs, at room temperature	1 large ripe banana, mashed
215g/7½oz/scant 2 cups plain flour	5ml/1 tsp vanilla essence
5ml/1 tsp salt	
5ml/1 tsp bicarbonate of soda	**For the glaze**
2.5ml/½ tsp grated nutmeg	115g/4oz/1 cup icing sugar
1.5ml/¼ tsp mixed spice	15–30ml/1–2 tbsp lemon juice

1 Preheat the oven to 180°C/350°F/Gas 4. Line a 23 x 13cm/9 x 5in loaf tin with greaseproof paper and grease the paper.

2 Cream the butter and sugar until light and fluffy. Add the eggs, one at a time, beating well after each addition.

3 Sift together the flour, salt, bicarbonate of soda, nutmeg, mixed spice and cloves. Add to the butter mixture and stir to combine well. Add the soured cream, banana and vanilla and mix to just blend. Pour into the prepared tin.

4 Bake until the top springs back when touched lightly, about 45–50 minutes. Cool in the tin for 10 minutes. Turn out on to a wire rack.

5 For the glaze, combine the icing sugar and lemon juice, then stir until smooth. Place the cooled loaf on a rack set over a baking sheet. Pour the glaze over the loaf and allow to set.

Banana Bread

For a change, add 50–75g/2–3oz/½–¾ cup chopped walnuts with the dry ingredients or pecan nuts.

Makes one 21 x 11cm/8½ x 4½in loaf

200g/7oz/1¾ cups plain
   flour
11.5ml/2¼ tsp baking
   powder
2.5ml/½ tsp salt
4ml/¾ tsp ground
   cinnamon (optional)
60ml/4 tbsp wheatgerm

65g/2½oz/5 tbsp butter,
   at room temperature
115g/4oz/generous ½ cup
   caster sugar
4ml/¾ tsp grated lemon
   rind
3 ripe bananas, mashed
2 eggs, beaten

1 Preheat the oven to 180°C/350°F/Gas 4. Grease and flour a 21 x 11cm/8½ x 4½in loaf tin.

2 Sift the flour, baking powder, salt and cinnamon, if using, into a bowl. Stir in the wheatgerm.

3 In another bowl, combine the butter with the caster sugar and grated lemon rind. Beat thoroughly until the mixture is light and fluffy.

4 Add the mashed bananas and eggs, and mix well. Add the dry ingredients and blend quickly and evenly.

5 Spoon into the loaf tin. Bake for 50–60 minutes or until a wooden skewer inserted in the centre comes out clean. Cool in the tin for 5 minutes, then turn out on to a wire rack to cool completely.

Banana Orange Loaf

For the best banana flavour and a really good, moist texture, make sure the bananas are ripe for this cake.

Makes one 23 x 13cm/9 x 5in loaf

90g/3½oz/generous
   ⅔ cup wholemeal
   plain flour
90g/3½oz/generous
   ¾ cup plain flour
5ml/1 tsp baking powder
5ml/1 tsp ground mixed
   spice
45ml/3 tbsp flaked
   hazelnuts, toasted

2 large ripe bananas
1 egg
30ml/2 tbsp sunflower oil
30ml/2 tbsp clear honey
finely grated rind and
   juice of 1 small orange
4 orange slices, halved
10ml/2 tsp icing sugar

1 Preheat the oven to 180°C/350°F/Gas 4. Brush a 23 x 13cm/9 x 5in loaf tin with sunflower oil and line the base with non-stick baking paper.

2 Sift the flours with the baking powder and spice into a large bowl, adding any bran that is caught in the sieve. Stir the hazelnuts into the dry ingredients.

3 Peel and mash the bananas. Beat in the egg, oil, honey and the orange rind and juice. Stir evenly into the dry ingredients.

4 Spoon into the prepared tin and smooth the top. Bake for 40–45 minutes, or until firm and golden brown. Turn out on to a wire rack to cool.

5 Sprinkle the orange slices with the icing sugar and grill until golden. Use to decorate the cake.

Marmalade Tea Bread

If you prefer, leave the top of the loaf plain and serve sliced and lightly buttered instead.

Makes one 22 x 11cm/8½ x 4½in loaf

200g/7oz/1¾ cups plain flour
5ml/1 tsp baking powder
6.5ml/1¼ tsp ground cinnamon
90g/3½oz/7 tbsp butter or margarine
50g/2oz/⅓ cup soft light brown sugar
60ml/4 tbsp chunky orange marmalade
1 egg, beaten
about 45ml/3 tbsp milk
60ml/4 tbsp glacé icing and shreds of orange and lemon rind, to decorate

1 Preheat the oven to 160°C/325°F/Gas 3. Lightly butter a 22 x 11cm/8½ x 4½in loaf tin, then line the base with greaseproof paper and grease the paper.

2 Sift the flour, baking powder and cinnamon together, toss in the butter, then rub in until the mixture resembles coarse breadcrumbs. Stir in the sugar.

3 In a separate bowl, mix together the marmalade, egg and most of the milk, then stir into the flour mixture to make a soft dropping consistency, adding more milk if necessary.

4 Transfer the mixture to the tin and bake for 1¼ hours, or until firm to the touch. Leave the cake to cool for 5 minutes, then turn on to a wire rack, peel off the lining paper, and leave to cool completely.

5 Drizzle the glacé icing over the top of the cake and decorate with the orange and lemon rind.

Cherry Marmalade Muffins

Purists say you should never serve a muffin cold, so enjoy these fresh from the oven.

Makes 12

225g/8oz/2 cups self-raising flour
5ml/1 tsp ground mixed spice
75g/3oz/scant ½ cup caster sugar
115g/4oz/½ cup glacé cherries, quartered
30ml/2 tbsp orange marmalade
150ml/¼ pint/⅔ cup milk
50g/2oz/4 tbsp sunflower margarine
marmalade, to glaze

1 Preheat the oven to 200°C/400°F/Gas 6. Lightly grease 12 deep muffin cups with oil.

2 Sift together the flour and spice, then stir in the sugar and glacé cherries.

3 Mix the marmalade with the milk and beat into the dry ingredients with the margarine. Spoon into the greased cups. Bake for 20–25 minutes, until golden brown and firm. Turn out on to a wire rack and brush the tops of the muffins, with warmed marmalade.

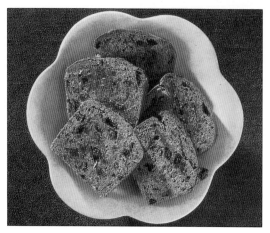

Spiced Date and Walnut Cake

Nuts and dates are a classic flavour combination. Use pecan nuts instead of walnuts, if you wish.

Makes one 900g/2lb cake

300g/11 oz/2¾ cups
 wholemeal self-raising
 flour
10ml/2 tsp mixed spice
150g/5oz/generous ¾ cup
 chopped dates
50g/2oz/½ cup chopped
 walnuts

60ml/4 tbsp sunflower oil
115g/4oz/⅔ cup dark
 muscovado sugar
300ml/½ pint/1¼ cups
 milk
walnut halves, to
 decorate

1 Preheat the oven to 180°C/350°F/Gas 4. Line a 900g/2lb loaf tin with greaseproof paper and grease the paper.

2 Sift together the flour and spice, adding back any bran from the sieve. Stir in the dates and walnuts.

3 Mix the oil, sugar and milk, then stir evenly into the dry ingredients. Spoon into the loaf tin and arrange the walnut halves on top.

4 Bake the cake in the oven for about 45–50 minutes, or until golden brown and firm. Turn out the cake, remove the lining paper, and leave to cool on a wire rack.

Prune and Peel Rock Buns

The fruit content of these scones gives them plenty of flavour – and they're a low-fat option too!

Makes 12

225g/8oz/2 cups plain
 flour
10ml/2 tsp baking
 powder
75g/3oz/½ cup demerara
 sugar
50g/2oz/½ cup chopped
 ready-to-eat dried
 prunes

50g/2oz/⅓ cup chopped
 mixed peel
finely grated rind of
 1 lemon
50ml/2fl oz/¼ cup
 sunflower oil
75ml/5 tbsp skimmed
 milk

1 Preheat the oven to 200°C/400°F/Gas 6. Lightly oil a large baking sheet. Sift together the flour and baking powder, then stir in the sugar, prunes, peel and lemon rind.

2 Mix the oil and milk, then stir into the mixture, to make a dough which just binds together.

3 Spoon into rocky heaps on the baking sheet and bake for 20 minutes, until golden. Leave to cool on a wire rack.

Raisin Bran Buns

Serve these buns warm or at room temperature, on their own, with butter, or with cream cheese.

Makes 15

50g/2oz/4 tbsp butter or margarine
40g/1½oz/⅓ cup plain flour
50g/2oz/½ cup wholemeal flour
7.5ml/1½ tsp bicarbonate of soda
1.5ml/¼ tsp salt
5ml/1 tsp ground cinnamon
25g/1oz/generous 1 cup bran

75g/3oz/generous ½ cup raisins
65g/2½oz/scant ½ cup dark brown sugar
50g/2oz/¼ cup caster sugar
1 egg
250ml/8fl oz/1 cup buttermilk
juice of ½ lemon

1 Preheat the oven to 200°C/400°F/Gas 6. Lightly grease 15 bun-tray cups. Put the butter or margarine in a saucepan and melt over a gentle heat. Set aside.

2 In a mixing bowl, sift together the flours, bicarbonate of soda, salt and cinnamon. Add the bran, raisins and sugars and stir until blended.

3 In another bowl, mix together the egg, buttermilk, lemon juice and melted butter. Add the buttermilk mixture to the dry ingredients and stir in lightly and quickly until just moistened. Do not mix until smooth.

4 Spoon the mixture into the prepared bun-tray cups, filling them almost to the top. Half-fill any empty cups with water. Bake until golden, about 15–20 minutes. Remove to a wire rack to cool slightly or serve immediately.

Raspberry Crumble Buns

The crumble topping adds an unusual twist to these lovely fruit buns.

Makes 12

175g/6oz/1½ cups plain flour
50g/2oz/¼ cup caster sugar
45g/1¾ oz/scant ⅓ cup light brown sugar
10ml/2 tsp baking powder
1.5ml/¼ tsp salt
5ml/1 tsp ground cinnamon
115g/4oz/½ cup butter, melted
1 egg
120ml/4fl oz/½ cup milk
150g/5oz/¾ cup fresh raspberries

grated rind of 1 lemon

For the crumble topping

25g/1oz/¼ cup finely chopped pecan nuts or walnuts
50g/2oz/⅓ cup dark brown sugar
45ml/3 tbsp plain flour
5ml/1 tsp ground cinnamon
45ml/3 tbsp butter, melted

1 Preheat the oven to 180°C/350°F/Gas 4. Lightly grease 12 bun-tray cups or use 12 paper cases. Sift the flour into a bowl. Add the sugars, baking powder, salt and cinnamon, and stir to blend.

2 Make a well in the centre. Place the butter, egg and milk in the well and mix until just combined. Stir in the raspberries and lemon rind. Spoon the mixture into the prepared bun tray, filling the cups almost to the top.

3 For the crumble topping, mix the nuts, dark brown sugar, flour and cinnamon in a bowl. Add the melted butter and stir to blend.

4 Spoon some of the crumble over each bun. Bake until browned, about 25 minutes. Transfer to a wire rack to cool slightly. Serve warm.

Banana and Pecan Muffins

As a variation on this recipe, substitute an equal quantity of walnuts for the pecan nuts.

Makes 8

150g/5oz/1¼ cups plain flour
7.5ml/1½ tsp baking powder
50g/2oz/4 tbsp butter or margarine, at room temperature
150g/5oz caster sugar
1 egg
5ml/1tsp teaspoon vanilla essence
3 bananas, mashed
50g/2oz/½ cup pecan nuts, chopped
75ml/5tbsp milk

1 Preheat the oven to 190°C/375°F/Gas 5. Lightly grease 8 deep muffin cups. Sift the flour and baking powder into a small bowl. Set aside.

2 With an electric mixer, cream the butter or margarine and sugar together. Add the egg and vanilla and beat until fluffy. Mix in the banana.

3 Add the pecan nuts. With the mixer on low speed, beat in the flour mixture alternately with the milk.

4 Spoon the mixture into the prepared muffin cups, filling them two-thirds full. Bake until golden brown and a skewer inserted into the centre of a muffin comes out clean, about 20–25 minutes.

5 Let the muffins cool in the cups on a wire rack for about 10 minutes. To loosen, run a knife gently around each muffin and unmould on to the wire rack. Leave to cool 10 minutes longer before serving.

Blueberry and Cinnamon Muffins

These moist and "moreish" muffins appeal equally to adults and children.

Makes 8

115g/4oz/1 cup plain flour
15ml/1tbsp baking powder
pinch of salt
65g/2½ oz/¼ cup light brown sugar
1 egg
175ml/6fl oz/¾ cup milk
45ml/3tbsp vegetable oil
10ml/2tsp ground cinnamon
115g/4oz/⅔ cup fresh or thawed frozen blueberries

1 Preheat the oven to 190°C/375°F/Gas 5. Lightly grease 8 deep muffin cups.

2 With an electric mixer, beat the first eight ingredients together until smooth. Fold in the blueberries.

3 Spoon the mixture into the muffin cups, filling them two-thirds full. Bake until a skewer inserted in the centre of a muffin comes out clean, about 25 minutes.

4 Let the muffins cool in the cups on a wire rack for about 10 minutes, then unmould them on to the wire rack and allow to cool completely, to serve slightly warm.

Carrot Buns

Carrots give these buns a lovely moist consistency, and a delightful taste too.

Makes 12

175g/6oz/³/₄ cup margarine, at room temperature
90g/3¹/₂oz/generous ¹/₂ cup dark brown sugar
1 egg, at room temperature
15ml/1 tbsp water
225g/8oz/1¹/₂ cups grated carrots
150g/5oz/1¹/₄ cups plain flour
5ml/1 tsp baking powder
2.5ml/¹/₂ tsp bicarbonate of soda
5ml/1 tsp ground cinnamon
1.5ml/¹/₄ tsp grated nutmeg
2.5ml/¹/₂ tsp salt

1 Preheat the oven to 180°C/350°F/Gas 4. Grease a 12-cup bun tray or use paper cases.

2 With an electric mixer, cream the margarine and sugar until light and fluffy. Beat in the egg and water, then stir in the carrots.

3 Sift over the flour, baking powder, bicarbonate of soda, cinnamon, nutmeg and salt. Stir to blend.

4 Spoon the mixture into the prepared bun tray, filling the cups almost to the top. Bake until the tops spring back when touched lightly, about 35 minutes. Leave to stand for about 10 minutes in the bun tray before transferring to a wire rack to cool completely.

Dried Cherry Buns

Dried cherries have a wonderful tart flavour, quite unlike glacé cherries.

Makes 16

250ml/8fl oz/1 cup plain yogurt
175g/6oz/³/₄ cup dried cherries
115g/4oz/¹/₂ cup butter, at room temperature
175g/6oz/generous ³/₄ cup caster sugar
2 eggs, at room temperature
5ml/1 tsp vanilla essence
200g/7oz/generous 1³/₄ cups plain flour
10ml/2 tsp baking powder
5ml/1 tsp bicarbonate of soda
1.5ml/¹/₄ tsp salt

1 In a mixing bowl, combine the yogurt and cherries. Cover and leave to stand for 30 minutes. Preheat the oven to 180°C/350°F/Gas 4. Grease 16 bun-tray cups or use paper cases.

2 With an electric mixer, cream the butter and sugar together until light and fluffy. Add the eggs, one at a time, beating well after each addition. Add the vanilla and the cherry mixture and stir to blend. Set aside.

3 In another bowl, sift together the flour, baking powder, bicarbonate of soda and salt. Fold into the cherry mixture in three batches.

4 Fill the prepared cups two-thirds full. For even baking, half-fill any empty cups with water. Bake until the tops spring back when touched lightly, about 20 minutes. Transfer to a wire rack to cool completely.

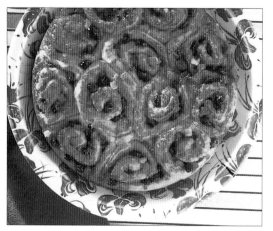

Chelsea Buns

A traditional English recipe, Chelsea buns enjoy wide popularity elsewhere in the world.

Makes 12

225g/8oz/2 cups strong
  white flour
2.5ml/¹/₂ tsp salt
40g/1¹/₂oz/3 tbsp
  unsalted butter
7.5ml/1¹/₂ tsp easy-blend
  dried yeast
120ml/4fl oz/¹/₂ cup milk

1 egg, beaten
75g/3oz/¹/₂ cup mixed
  dried fruit
25g/1oz/2¹/₂ tbsp chopped
  mixed peel
50g/2oz/¹/₃ cup soft light
  brown sugar
clear honey, to glaze

1 Preheat the oven to 190°C/375°F/Gas 5. Grease a 18cm/7in square tin. Sift together the flour and salt; rub in 25g/1oz/2 tbsp of the butter.

2 Stir in the yeast and make a central well. Slowly add the milk and egg, stirring, then beat until the dough leaves the sides of the bowl clean.

3 Knead the dough until smooth. Place in an oiled bowl, cover and set aside until doubled in size. Transfer to a floured surface and roll it out to a rectangle 30 x 23cm/12 x 9in.

4 Mix the dried fruits peel and sugar. Melt the remaining butter and brush over the dough. Scatter over the fruit mixture, leaving a 2.5cm/1in border. Roll up the dough from a long side. Seal the edges, then cut into 12 slices.

5 Place the slices, cut-sides up, in the greased tin. Cover and set aside until doubled in size. Bake for 30 minutes, until a rich golden brown. Brush with honey and leave to cool slightly in the tin before turning out.

Sticky Nut Buns

These buns will be popular, so save time by making double the recipe and freezing half for another occasion.

Makes 12

160ml/5¹/₂ fl oz/generous
  ²/₃ cup lukewarm milk
15ml/1 tbsp easy-blend
  dried yeast
30ml/2 tbsp caster sugar
450g/1lb/4 cups strong
  white flour
5ml/1 tsp salt
115g/4oz/¹/₂ cup cold
  butter, cut into small
  pieces
2 eggs, lightly beaten
finely grated rind of 1
  lemon

For the topping and filling

275g/10oz/1³/₄ cups dark
  brown sugar
65g/2¹/₂oz/5 tbsp butter
120ml/4fl oz/¹/₂ cup
  water
75g/3oz/³/₄ cup chopped
  pecan nuts or walnuts
45ml/3 tbsp caster sugar
10ml/2 tsp ground
  cinnamon
165g/5¹/₂oz/generous
  1 cup raisins

1 Preheat the oven to 180°C/350°F/Gas 4. Mix the milk, yeast and sugar and leave until frothy. Combine the flour and salt, and rub in the butter. Add the yeast mixture, eggs and lemon rind. Stir to a rough dough. Knead until smooth, then return to the bowl, cover and leave until doubled in size.

2 Cook the brown sugar, butter and water in a heavy saucepan until syrupy, about 10 minutes. Place 15ml/1 tbsp syrup in the base of twelve 4cm/¹/₂in muffin cups. Sprinkle a thin layer of nuts in each, reserving the remainder.

3 Punch down the dough; roll out to a 45 x 30cm/18 x 12in rectangle. Combine the caster sugar, cinnamon, raisins and reserved nuts. Sprinkle over the dough. Roll up tightly from a long edge and cut into 2.5cm/1in rounds. Place in the muffin cups, cut-sides up. Leave to rise for 30 minutes.

4 Bake until golden, about 25 minutes. Invert the tins on to a baking sheet, leave for 5 minutes, then remove the tins. Cool on a wire rack, sticky-sides up.

Oatmeal Buttermilk Muffins

These easy-to-make muffins make a healthy treat for breakfast, or a snack at any time.

Makes 12

75g/3oz/1 cup rolled oats
250ml/3fl oz/1 cup buttermilk
115g/4oz/¹/₂ cup butter, at room temperature
75g/3oz/¹/₂ cup dark brown sugar, firmly packed

1 egg, at room temperature
115g/4oz/1 cup flour
5ml/1 tsp baking powder
1.5m/¹/₄ tsp baking soda
25g/1oz/¹/₄ cup rains

1 In a bowl, combine the oats and buttermilk and leave to soak for 1 hour.

2 Grease a 12-cup muffin pan or use paper cases.

3 Preheat the oven to 200°C/400°F/Gas 6. With an electric mixer, cream the butter and sugar until light and fluffy. Beat in the egg.

4 In another bowl, sift together the flour, baking powder, bicarbonate of soda, and salt. Stir into the butter mixture, alternating with the oat mixture. Fold in the raisins. Do not overmix.

5 Fill the prepared cups two-thirds full. Bake until a cake tester inserted in the centre comes out clean, 20–25 minutes. Transfer to a rack to cool.

Pumpkin Muffins

Molasses adds a delicious flavour to these spicy muffins. For a change, add dried apricots instead of currants.

Makes 14

150g/5oz/²/₃ cup butter or margarine, at room temperature
175g/6oz/³/₄ cup dark brown sugar, firmly packed
115g/4oz/¹/₃ cup molasses
1 egg, at room temperature, beaten
225g/8oz/1 cup cooked or canned pumpkin

200g/7oz/1³/₄ cups flour
1.5ml/¹/₄ tsp salt
5ml/1 tsp bicarbonate of soda
10ml/1 tsp ground cinnamon
5ml/1 tsp grated nutmeg
50g/2oz/¹/₄ cup currants or raisins

1 Preheat the oven to 200°C/400°F/Gas 6. Grease 14 muffin cups or use paper cases.

2 With an electric mixer, cream the butter or margarine. Add the sugar and molasses and beat until light and fluffy.

3 Add the egg and pumpkin and stir until well blended.

4 Sift over the flour, salt, bicarbonate of soda, cinnamon, and nutmeg. Fold just enough to blend; do not overmix.

5 Fold in the currants or raisins.

6 Spoon the batter into the prepared muffin cups, filling them three-quarters full.

7 Bake for 12–15 minutes until the tops spring back when touched lightly. Serve warm or cold.

Blueberry Muffins

Hot blueberry muffins with a hint of vanilla are an American favourite for breakfast, brunch or tea.

Makes 12

350g/12oz/3 cups plain flour
10ml/2 tsp baking powder
1.5ml/¼ tsp salt
115g/4oz/½ cup caster sugar
2 eggs, beaten

300ml/½ pint/1¼ cups milk
115g/4oz/½ cup butter, melted
5ml/1 tsp vanilla essence
175g/6oz/1½ cups blueberries

1 Preheat the oven to 200°C/400°F/Gas 6. Grease a 12-cup muffin tin.

2 Sift the flour, baking powder and salt into a large mixing bowl and stir in the sugar.

3 Place the eggs, milk, butter and vanilla essence in a separate bowl and whisk together well.

4 Fold the egg mixture into the dry ingredients with a metal spoon, then gently stir in the blueberries.

5 Spoon the mixture into the muffin cups, filling them to just below the top. Place the muffin tin on the top shelf of the oven and bake for 20–25 minutes, until the muffins are well risen and lightly browned. Leave the muffins in the tin for about 5 minutes, and then turn them out on to a wire rack to cool. Serve warm or cold.

Apple and Cranberry Muffins

Not too sweet but good and spicy, these muffins will be a favourite with family and friends.

Makes 12

50g/2oz/4 tbsp butter
1 egg
90g/3½oz/½ cup caster sugar
grated rind of 1 orange
120ml/4fl oz/½ cup fresh orange juice
150g/5oz/1¼ cups plain flour
5ml/1 tsp baking powder
2.5ml/½ tsp bicarbonate of soda
5ml/1 tsp ground cinnamon

2.5ml/½ tsp grated nutmeg
2.5ml/½ tsp mixed spice
1.5ml/¼ tsp ground ginger
1.5ml/¼ tsp salt
1–2 eating apples
175g/6oz/1½ cups cranberries
50g/2oz/½ cup chopped walnuts
icing sugar, for dusting (optional)

1 Preheat the oven to 180°C/350°F/Gas 4. Grease a 12-cup muffin tin or use paper cases. Melt the butter over a gentle heat. Set aside to cool.

2 Place the egg in a mixing bowl and whisk lightly. Add the melted butter and whisk to combine, then add the sugar, orange rind and juice. Whisk to blend.

3 In a large bowl, sift together the flour, baking powder, bicarbonate of soda, spices and salt. Quarter, core and peel the apples. With a sharp knife, chop coarsely.

4 Make a well in the dry ingredients and pour in the egg mixture. With a spoon, stir until just blended. Add the apples, cranberries and walnuts and stir to blend.

5 Fill the cups three-quarters full and bake until the the tops spring back when touched lightly, about 25–30 minutes. Transfer to a wire rack to cool. Dust with icing sugar before serving, if desired.

Yogurt and Honey Muffins

For a more substantial texture, fold in 50g/2oz/½ cup chopped walnuts with the flour.

Makes 12

50g/2oz/4 tbsp butter
75ml/5 tbsp clear honey
250ml/8fl oz/1 cup plain yogurt
1 large egg, at room temperature
grated rind of 1 lemon
50ml/2fl oz/¼ cup lemon juice
150g/5oz/¼ cup plain flour
175g/6oz/½ cup wholemeal flour
7.5ml/1½ tsp bicarbonate of soda
1.5ml/¼ tsp grated nutmeg

1 Preheat the oven to 190°C/375°F/Gas 5. Grease a 12-cup muffin tin or use paper cases.

2 In a saucepan, melt the butter and honey. Remove from the heat and set aside to cool slightly.

3 In a bowl, whisk together the yogurt, egg, lemon rind and juice. Add the butter and honey mixture. Set aside.

4 In another bowl, sift together the dry ingredients. Fold them into the yogurt mixture to blend.

5 Fill the prepared cup two-thirds full. Bake until the tops spring back when touched lightly, about 20–25 minutes. Cool in the tin for 5 minutes before turning out. Serve warm or at room temperature.

Prune Muffins

Prunes bring a delightful moisture to these tasty and wholesome muffins.

Makes 12

1 egg
250ml/8fl oz/1 cup milk
120ml/4fl oz/½ cup vegetable oil
45g/1¾ oz/scant ¼ cup caster sugar
25g/1oz/2 tbsp dark brown sugar
275g/10oz/2½ cups plain flour
10ml/2 tsp baking powder
2.5ml/½ tsp salt
1.5ml/¼ tsp grated nutmeg
115g/4oz/½ cup cooked stoned prunes, chopped

1 Preheat the oven to 200°C/400°F/Gas 6. Grease a 12-cup muffin tin or use paper cases.

2 Break the egg into a mixing bowl and beat with a fork. Beat in the milk and oil. Stir in the sugars and set aside.

3 Sift the flour, baking powder, salt and nutmeg into a mixing bowl. Make a well in the centre, pour in the egg mixture and stir until moistened. Do not overmix; the batter should be slightly lumpy. Finally, fold in the prunes.

4 Fill the prepared cups two-thirds full. Bake until golden brown, about 20 minutes. Leave to stand for 10 minutes before turning out. Serve warm or at room temperature.

Crunchy Muesli Muffins

The muesli in these muffins gives them an unusual texture
and makes them ideal to serve for breakfast.

Makes 10

150g/5oz/1¼ cups plain
  flour
12.5ml/2½ tsp baking
  powder
30ml/2 tbsp caster sugar
200g/7oz/1½ cups
  toasted oat cereal with
  raisins

250ml/8fl oz/1 cup milk
50g/2oz/4tbsp butter,
  melted, or corn oil
1 egg, beaten

1 Preheat the oven to 200°C/400°F/Gas 6. Grease 10 cups of
a muffin tin or use paper cases.

2 Sift the flour, baking powder and sugar together into a
large bowl. Add the oat cereal and stir to blend.

3 In a separate bowl, combine the milk, melted butter or
corn oil and the beaten egg. Add to the dry ingredients. Stir
until moistened, but do not overmix.

4 Spoon the mixture into the cups, leaving room for the
muffins to rise. Half-fill any empty cups with water. Bake in
the oven for 20 minutes, or until golden brown. Transfer to a
wire rack to cool.

Raspberry Muffins

If you are using frozen raspberries, work quickly as the
cold berries make the mixture solidify.

Makes 12

115g/4oz/1 cup
  self-raising flour
115g/4oz/1 cup
  wholemeal self-raising
  flour
45ml/3 tbsp caster sugar
2.5ml/½ tsp salt
2 eggs, beaten

200ml/7fl oz/scant 1 cup
  milk
50g/2oz/4 tbsp butter,
  melted
175g/6oz/1 cup
  raspberries, fresh or
  frozen (defrosted for
  less than 30 minutes)

1 Preheat the oven to 190°C/375°F/Gas 5. Lightly grease a
12-cup muffin tin, or use paper cases. Sift the dry ingredients
together, then tip in any wheat flakes left in the sieve.

2 Beat the eggs, milk and melted butter together and stir
into the dry ingredients to make a thick batter.

3 Stir the raspberries in gently. If you mix too much the
raspberries begin to disintegrate and colour the dough. Spoon
into the cups or paper cases.

4 Bake for 30 minutes, until well risen and just firm. Leave
to cool in the tin placed on a wire rack. Serve warm or cool.

Scones

Traditionally, scones should be served with butter, clotted or whipped cream and jam.

Makes 10–12

225g/8oz/2 cups plain
  flour
15ml/1 tbsp baking
  powder
50g/2oz/4 tbsp butter,
  diced

1 egg, beaten
75ml/5 tbsp milk
1 beaten egg, to glaze

1 Preheat the oven to 220°C/425°F/Gas 7. Lightly butter a baking sheet. Sift the flour and baking powder together, then rub in the butter.

2 Make a well in the centre of the flour mixture, add the egg and milk and mix to a soft dough using a round-bladed knife.

3 Turn out the scone dough on to a floured surface, and knead very lightly until smooth.

4 Roll out the dough to about a 2cm/¾ in thickness and cut into 10 or 12 circles using a 5cm/2in plain or fluted cutter dipped in flour.

5 Transfer to the baking sheet, brush with egg, then bake for about 8 minutes, until risen and golden. Cool slightly on a wire rack before serving.

Drop Scones

If you place the cooked scones in a folded dish towel they will stay soft and moist.

Makes 8–10

115g/4oz/1 cup plain
  flour
5ml/1 tsp bicarbonate of
  soda
5ml/1 tsp cream of tartar

25g/1oz/2 tbsp butter,
  diced
1 egg, beaten
150ml/¼ pint/
  ²⁄₃ cup milk

1 Lightly grease a griddle or heavy-based frying pan, then preheat it.

2 Sift the flour, bicarbonate of soda and cream of tartar together, then rub in the butter until the mixture resembles breadcrumbs. Make a well in the centre, then stir in the egg and sufficient milk to give the consistency of double cream.

3 Drop spoonfuls of the mixture, spaced slightly apart, on to the griddle or frying pan. Cook over a steady heat for 2–3 minutes, until bubbles rise to the surface and burst.

4 Turn the scones over and cook for a further 2–3 minutes, until golden underneath. Serve warm with butter and honey.

Wholemeal Scones

Split these wholesome scones in two with a fork while still warm and spread with butter and jam, if you wish.

Makes 16

175g/6oz/¾ cup cold
  butter
350g/12oz/3 cups
  wholemeal flour
150g/5oz/1¼ cups plain
  flour
30ml/2 tbsp sugar

2.5ml/½ tsp salt
12.5ml/2½ tsp
  bicarbonate of soda
2 eggs
175g/6fl oz/3¾ cup
  buttermilk
35g/1¼oz/¼ cup raisins

1 Preheat the oven to 200°C/400°F/Gas 6. Grease and flour a large baking sheet.

2 Cut the butter into small pieces. Combine all the dry ingredients in a bowl. Add the butter and rub in until the mixture resembles coarse breadcrumbs. Set aside.

3 In another bowl, whisk together the eggs and buttermilk. Set aside 30ml/2 tbsp for glazing, then stir the remaining egg mixture into the dry ingredients until it just holds together. Stir in the raisins.

4 Roll out the dough to about 2cm/¾in thickness. Stamp out circles with a biscuit cutter. Place on the baking sheet and brush with the glaze.

5 Bake until golden, about 12–15 minutes. Allow to cool slightly before serving.

Orange and Raisin Scones

Split these scones when cool and toast them under a preheated grill. Butter them while still hot.

Makes 16

275g/10oz/2½ cups plain
  flour
25ml/1½ tsp baking
  powder
60g/2¼oz/generous/
  ¼ cup sugar
2.5ml/½ tsp salt
65g/2½oz/5 tbsp butter,
  diced

65g/2½oz/5 tbsp
  margarine, diced
grated rind of 1 large
  orange
50g/2oz/scant ½ cup
  raisins
120ml/4fl oz/½ cup
  buttermilk
milk, to glaze

1 Preheat the oven to 220°C/425°F/Gas 7. Grease and flour a large baking sheet.

2 Combine the dry ingredients in a large bowl. Add the butter and margarine and rub in until the mixture resembles coarse breadcrumbs.

3 Add the orange rind and raisins. Gradually stir in the buttermilk to form a soft dough. Roll out the dough to about a 2cm/¾in thickness. Stamp out circles with a biscuit cutter. Place on the baking sheet and brush the tops with milk.

4 Bake until golden, about 12–15 minutes. Serve hot or warm, with butter, or whipped or clotted cream and jam.

Cheese and Chive Scones

Feta cheese makes an excellent substitute for butter in these tangy savoury scones.

Makes 9

115g/4oz/1 cup
  self-raising flour
150g/5oz/1 cup
  wholemeal self-raising
  flour
2.5ml/½ tsp salt
75g/3oz feta cheese

15ml/1 tbsp chopped
  fresh chives
150ml/¼ pint/⅔ cup
  milk, plus extra to
  glaze
1.5ml/¼ tsp cayenne
  pepper

1 Preheat the oven to 200°C/400°F/Gas 6. Sift the flours and salt into a mixing bowl. Add any bran left in the sieve.

2 Crumble the feta cheese and rub into the dry ingredients. Stir in the chives, then add the milk and mix to a soft dough.

3 Turn out on to a floured surface and lightly knead until smooth. Roll out to a 2cm/¾ in thickness and stamp out scones with a 6cm/2½in biscuit cutter.

4 Transfer the scones to a non-stick baking sheet. Brush with milk, then sprinkle over the cayenne pepper. Bake in the oven for 15 minutes, or until golden brown. Serve warm or cold.

Sunflower Sultana Scones

Sunflower seeds give these wholesome fruit scones an interesting flavour and appealing texture.

Makes 10–12

225g/8oz/2 cups
  self-raising flour
5ml/1 tsp baking powder
25g/1oz/2 tbsp soft
  sunflower margarine
30ml/2 tbsp golden caster
  sugar
50g/2oz/scant ½ cup
  sultanas

30ml/2 tbsp sunflower
  seeds
150g/5oz/⅔ cup natural
  yogurt
about 30–45ml/
  2–3 tbsp skimmed
  milk

1 Preheat the oven to 230°C/450°F/Gas 8. Lightly oil a baking sheet. Sift the flour and baking powder into a bowl and rub in the margarine evenly.

2 Stir in the sugar, sultanas and half the sunflower seeds, then mix in the yogurt, with just enough milk to make a fairly soft, but not sticky, dough.

3 Roll out on a lightly floured surface to about a 2cm/¾ in thickness. Cut into 6cm/2½ in flower shapes or rounds with a biscuit cutter and lift on to the baking sheet.

4 Brush with milk and sprinkle with the reserved sunflower seeds, then bake for 10–12 minutes, until well risen and golden brown. Cool the scones on a wire rack. Serve split and spread with jam or low-fat spread.

Buttermilk Scones

If time is short, drop heaped tablespoonfuls of the mixture on to the baking sheet.

Makes 10
225g/8oz/2 cups plain
    flour
5ml/1 tsp baking powder
2.5ml/½ tsp bicarbonate
    of soda

5ml/1 tsp salt
50g/2oz/4 tbsp butter or
    margarine, chilled
175ml/6fl oz/¾ cup
    buttermilk

1 Preheat the oven to 220°C/425°F/Gas 7. Sift the flour, baking powder, bicarbonate of soda and salt into a mixing bowl. Cut in the butter or margarine with a fork until the mixture resembles coarse breadcrumbs.

2 Add the buttermilk and mix until well combined to form a soft dough. Turn the dough on to a lightly floured surface and knead for about 30 seconds.

3 Roll out the dough to a 1cm/½in thickness. Use a floured 6cm/2½in pastry cutter to cut out rounds. Transfer the rounds to a baking sheet and bake until golden brown, about 10–12 minutes. Serve hot with butter and honey.

Date Oven Scones

To ensure light, well-risen scones, don't handle the dough too much or roll it out too thinly.

Makes 12
225g/8oz/2 cups
    self-raising flour
pinch of salt
50g/2oz/4 tbsp butter
50g/2oz/¼ cup caster
    sugar

50g/2oz/⅓ cup chopped
    dates
150ml/¼ pint/⅔ cup milk
1 beaten egg, to glaze

1 Preheat the oven to 230°C/450°F/Gas 8. Sift the flour and salt into a bowl and, using a pastry blender or your fingers, rub in the butter until the mixture resembles fine breadcrumbs. Add the sugar and chopped dates, and stir to blend.

2 Make a well in the centre of the dry ingredients and add the milk. Stir with a fork until the mixture comes together in a fairly soft dough.

3 Turn the dough out on to a lightly floured surface and knead gently for 30 seconds. Roll it out to a 2cm/¾in thickness. Cut out circles with a biscuit cutter. Arrange them, not touching, on an ungreased baking sheet, then glaze with the beaten egg.

4 Bake in the oven for 8–10 minutes, or until well risen and golden brown. Using a palette knife, transfer the scones to a wire rack to cool completely.

Cheese and Marjoram Scones

A great success for a hearty tea. With savoury toppings, these scones can make a good basis for a light lunch.

Makes 18

115g/4oz/1 cup
    wholemeal flour
115g/4oz/1 cup
    self-raising flour
pinch of salt
45ml/1½oz/3 tbsp butter
1.5ml/¼ tsp dry mustard
10ml/2 tsp dried
    marjoram

50–75g/2–3oz/
    ½–¾ cup finely grated
    Cheddar cheese
120ml/4fl oz/½ cup milk,
    or as required
50g/2oz/½ cup pecan
    nuts or walnuts,
    chopped

1 Gently sift the two flours into a bowl and add the salt. Cut the butter into small pieces, and rub into the flour until the mixture resembles fine breadcrumbs.

2 Add the mustard, marjoram and grated cheese, and mix in sufficient milk to make a soft dough. Knead the dough lightly.

3 Preheat the oven to 220°C/425°F/Gas 7. Lightly grease two or three baking sheets. Roll out the dough on a floured surface to about a 2cm/¾in thickness and cut it out with a 5cm/2in square biscuit cutter. Place the scones, slightly apart, on the baking sheets.

4 Brush the scones with a little milk and then sprinkle the chopped pecan nuts or walnuts over the top. Bake for about 12 minutes. Serve warm, spread with butter.

Dill and Potato Cakes

The inclusion of dill in these potato cakes makes them quite irresistible.

Makes 10

225g/8oz/2 cups
    self-raising flour
40g/1½oz/3 tbsp butter,
    softened
pinch of salt
15ml/1 tbsp finely
    chopped fresh dill

175g/6oz/scant 1 cup
    mashed potato,
    freshly made
30–45ml/2–3 tbsp milk

1 Preheat the oven to 230°C/450°F/Gas 8. Grease a baking sheet. Sift the flour into a bowl and add the butter, salt and dill. Mix in the mashed potato and enough milk to make a soft, pliable dough.

2 Roll out the dough on a well-floured surface until fairly thin. Cut into circles with a 7.5cm/3in biscuit cutter.

3 Place the potato cakes on the baking sheet, and bake for 20–25 minutes until risen and golden.

White Bread

There is nothing quite like the smell and taste of home-baked bread, eaten while still warm.

Makes two 23 x 13cm/9 x 5in loaves

50ml/2fl oz/¼ cup lukewarm water	*25g/1oz/2 tbsp butter or margarine, at room temperature*
15ml/1 tbsp active dried yeast	*10ml/2 tsp salt*
30ml/2 tbsp sugar	*about 900g/2lb/8 cups strong flour*
475ml/16fl oz/2 cups lukewarm milk	

1 Combine the water, yeast and 15ml/1 tbsp of the sugar in a measuring jug and leave for 15 minutes until frothy.

2 Pour the milk into a large bowl. Add the remaining sugar, the butter or margarine, and salt. Stir in the yeast mixture, then stir in the flour, 150g/5oz/1¼ cups at a time, until a stiff dough is obtained.

3 Transfer the dough to a floured surface. Knead the dough until it is smooth and elastic, then place it in a large greased bowl, cover with a plastic bag, and leave to rise in a warm place until doubled in volume, about 2–3 hours.

4 Grease two 23 x 13cm/9 x 5in loaf tins. Punch down the dough and divide in half. Form into loaf shapes and place in the tins, seam-sides down. Cover and leave to rise again until almost doubled in volume, about 45 minutes. Meanwhile, preheat the oven to 190°C/375°F/Gas 5.

5 Bake until firm and brown, about 45–50 minutes. Turn out and tap the base of a loaf: if it sounds hollow the loaf is done. If necessary, return to the oven and bake for a few minutes longer. Turn out and cool on a wire rack.

Multigrain Bread

Try different flours, such as rye, cornmeal, buckwheat or barley to replace the wheatgerm and the soya flour.

Makes two 22 x 11cm/8½ x 4½in loaves

15ml/1 tbsp active dried yeast	*30ml/2 tbsp honey*
50ml/2fl oz/¼ cup lukewarm water	*2 eggs, lightly beaten*
65g/2½oz/¾ cup rolled oats	*25g/1oz wheatgerm*
475ml/16fl oz/2 cups milk	*175g/6oz/1½ cups soya flour*
10ml/2 tsp salt	*350g/12oz/scant 2½ cups wholemeal flour*
50ml/2fl oz/¼ cup oil	*about 450g/1lb/4 cups strong flour*
50g/2oz/⅓ cup light brown sugar	

1 Combine the yeast and water, stir, and leave for about 15 minutes to dissolve. Place the oats in a large bowl. Scald the milk, then pour over the rolled oats. Stir in the salt, oil, sugar and honey. Leave until lukewarm.

2 Stir in the yeast mixture, eggs, wheatgerm, soya and wholemeal flours. Gradually stir in enough strong flour to obtain a rough dough. Transfer the dough to a floured surface and knead, adding flour if necessary, until smooth and elastic. Return to a clean bowl, cover and leave to rise in a warm place until doubled in volume, about 2½ hours.

3 Grease two 22 x 11cm/8½ x 4½in loaf tins. Punch down the risen dough and knead briefly. Then divide the dough into quarters. Roll each quarter into a cylinder 4cm/1½in thick. Twist together two cylinders and place in a tin; repeat for the remaining cylinders. Cover and leave to rise until doubled in volume again, about 1 hour. Meanwhile, preheat the oven to 190°C/375°F/Gas 5.

4 Bake until the bases sound hollow when tapped lightly, about 45–50 minutes. Turn out and cool on a wire rack.

Plaited Loaf

It doesn't take much effort to turn an ordinary dough mix into this work of art.

Makes one loaf

15ml/1 tbsp active dried yeast
5ml/1 tsp honey
250ml/8fl oz/1 cup lukewarm milk
50g/2oz/4 tbsp butter, melted

425g/15oz/3¾ cups strong flour
5ml/1 tsp salt
1 egg, lightly beaten
1 egg yolk, beaten with 5ml/1 tsp milk, to glaze

1 Combine the yeast, honey, milk and butter. Stir and leave for 15 minutes to dissolve.

2 In a large bowl, mix together the flour and salt. Make a central well; add the yeast mixture and egg. With a wooden spoon, stir from the centre, gradually incorporating the flour, to obtain a rough dough.

3 Transfer to a floured surface and knead until smooth and elastic. Place in a clean bowl, cover and leave to rise in a warm place until doubled in volume, about 1½ hours.

4 Grease a baking sheet. Punch down the dough and divide into three equal pieces. Roll each piece into a long thin strip. Begin plaiting with the centre strip, tucking in the ends. Cover loosely and leave to rise in a warm place for 30 minutes. Meanwhile, preheat the oven to 190°C/375°F/Gas 5. Brush the bread with the egg and milk glaze and bake until golden, about 40–45 minutes. Turn out on to a wire rack to cool.

Oatmeal Bread

A healthy, rustic-looking bread made with rolled oats as well as flour.

Makes two loaves

475ml/16fl oz/2 cups milk
25g/1oz/2 tbsp butter
50g/2oz/4 tbsp cup dark brown sugar
10ml/2 tsp salt
15ml/1 tbsp active dried yeast

50ml/2fl oz/¼ cup lukewarm water
400g/14oz/4 cups rolled oats
675–900g/1½–2lb/ 6–8 cups strong white flour

1 Scald the milk. Remove from the heat and stir in the butter, brown sugar and salt. Leave until lukewarm.

2 Combine the yeast and warm water in a large bowl and leave until frothy. Stir in the milk mixture. Add 275g/10oz/ 3 cups of the oats and enough flour to obtain a soft dough.

3 Transfer to a floured surface and knead until smooth and elastic. Place in a greased bowl, cover with a plastic bag, and leave until doubled in volume, about 2–3 hours.

4 Grease a large baking sheet. Transfer the dough to a lightly floured surface and divide in half. Shape into rounds. Place on the baking sheet, cover with a dish towel and leave to rise until doubled in volume, about 1 hour.

5 Preheat the oven to 200°C/400°F/Gas 6. Score the tops and sprinkle with the remaining oats. Bake until the bases sound hollow when tapped, about 45–50 minutes. Turn out on to wire racks to cool.

Country Bread

A filling bread made with a mixture of wholemeal and white flour.

Makes two loaves

350g/12oz/scant 2½ cups
  wholemeal flour
350g/12oz/3 cups plain
  flour
150g/5oz/1¼ cups strong
  plain flour
20ml/4 tsp salt
50g/2oz/4 tbsp butter, at
  room temperature
475ml/16fl oz/2 cups
  lukewarm milk

For the starter

15ml/1 tbsp active dried
  yeast
250ml/8fl oz/1 cup
  lukewarm water
150g/5oz/1¼ cups plain
  flour
1.5ml/¼ tsp caster sugar

1 Combine all the starter ingredients in a bowl. Cover and leave in a warm place for 2–3 hours.

2 Place the flours, salt and butter in a food processor and process just until blended, about 1–2 minutes. Stir together the milk and starter, then slowly pour into the processor, with the motor running, until the mixture forms a dough. Knead until smooth.

3 Place in an ungreased bowl, cover with a plastic bag, and leave to rise in a warm place until doubled in size, about 1½ hours. Knead again then return to the bowl and leave until tripled in size, about 1½ hours.

4 Grease a baking sheet. Divide the dough in half. Cut off one-third of the dough from each half and shape into four balls. Top each large ball with a small ball and press the centre with the handle of a wooden spoon to secure. Cover with a plastic bag, slash the top, and leave to rise.

5 Preheat the oven to 200°C/400°F/Gas 6. Dust the loaves with flour and bake until browned and the bases sound hollow when tapped, 45–50 minutes. Cool on a wire rack.

Wholemeal Rolls

To add interest when serving, make these individual rolls into different shapes if you wish.

Makes 12

15ml/2 tbsp active dried
  yeast
50ml/2fl oz/¼ cup
  lukewarm water
5ml/1 tsp caster sugar
175ml/6fl oz/¾ cup
  lukewarm buttermilk
1.5ml/¼ tsp bicarbonate
  of soda

5ml/1 tsp salt
40g/1½oz/3 tbsp butter,
  at room temperature
200g/7oz/scant 1½ cups
  wholemeal flour
150g/5oz/1¼ cups plain
  flour
1 beaten egg, to glaze

1 In a large bowl, combine the yeast, water and sugar. Stir, and leave for 15 minutes to dissolve.

2 Add the buttermilk, bicarbonate of soda, salt and butter and stir to blend. Stir in the wholemeal flour. Add just enough of the plain flour to obtain a rough dough.

3 Knead on a floured surface until smooth. Divide into three equal parts. Roll each into a cylinder, then cut in four.

4 Grease a baking sheet. Form the pieces into torpedo shapes, place on the baking sheet, cover and leave in a warm place until doubled in size.

5 Preheat the oven to 200°C/400°F/Gas 6. Brush the rolls with the egg. Bake until firm, about 15–20 minutes. Leave to cool on a wire rack.

Wholemeal Bread

A simple wholesome bread to be enjoyed by the whole family at any time.

Makes one 23 x 13cm/9 x 5in loaf

525g/1lb 5oz/generous 4 cups wholemeal flour
10ml/2 tsp salt
20ml/4 tsp active dried yeast
450ml/¾ pint/1¾ cups lukewarm water
30ml/2 tbsp honey
30ml/2 tbsp oil
40g/1½oz wheatgerm
milk, to glaze

1 Warm the flour and salt in a bowl in the oven at its lowest setting for 10 minutes. Meanwhile, combine the yeast with half of the water and leave to dissolve.

2 Make a central well in the flour. Pour in the yeast mixture, the remaining water, honey, oil and wheatgerm. Stir from the centre until smooth.

3 Grease a 23 x 13cm/9 x 5in loaf tin. Knead the dough just enough to shape into a loaf. Put it in the tin and cover with a plastic bag. Leave in a warm place until the dough is about 2.5cm/1in higher than the tin rim, about 1 hour.

4 Preheat the oven to 200°C/400°F/Gas 6. Brush the loaf with milk, and bake until the base sounds hollow when tapped, about 35–40 minutes. Cool on a wire rack.

Two-tone Bread

A tasty, malty bread that, when cut, reveals an attractive swirled interior.

Makes two 350g/12oz loaves

25ml/1½ tbsp active dried yeast
120ml/4fl oz/½ cup warm water
55g/2¼oz/generous ¼ cup caster sugar
675g/1½lb/6 cups strong plain flour
7.5ml/½ tbsp salt
600ml/1 pint/2½ cups warm milk
65g/2½oz/5 tbsp butter or margarine, melted and cooled
45ml/3 tbsp black treacle
275g/10oz/2 cups strong wholemeal plain flour

1 Dissolve the yeast in the water with 5ml/1 tsp of the sugar. Sift 350g/12oz/3 cups of the white flour, the salt and remaining sugar. Make a well and add the yeast, milk and butter. Mix in gradually to form a smooth soft batter.

2 Divide the batter into two bowls. To one bowl, add 275g/10oz/2½ cups of the strong white flour and mix together to a soft dough. Knead until smooth. Shape into a ball, put into a greased bowl and rotate to grease all over. Cover with clear film.

3 Mix the treacle and wholemeal flour into the second bowl. Add enough of the remaining white flour to make a soft dough. Knead until smooth. Shape into a ball, put in a greased bowl and cover. Leave the doughs to rise in a warm place for about 1 hour until doubled in size. Grease two 22 x 11cm/8½ x 4½in loaf tins.

4 Preheat the oven to 220°C/425°F/Gas 7. Punch down the dough and divide each ball in half. Roll out half of the light dough to a 30 x 20cm/12 x 8in rectangle. Roll out half of the dark dough to the same size. Set the dark dough rectangle on the light one. Roll up tightly from a short side. Set in a loaf tin. Repeat. Cover the tins and leave the dough to rise until doubled in size. Bake for 30–35 minutes.

Pleated Rolls

Fancy home-made rolls show that every care has been taken to ensure a welcoming dinner party.

Makes 48 rolls

15ml/1tbsp active dried yeast	10ml/2tsp salt
475ml/16fl oz/2 cups lukewarm milk	2 eggs
115g/4oz/½ cup margarine	985g–1.2kg/2lb 3oz–2½lb/ scant 7–8 cups strong flour
50g/2oz/4tbsp sugar	50g/2oz/4tbsp butter

1 Combine the yeast and 120ml/4fl oz/½ cup milk in a large bowl. Stir and leave for 15 minutes to dissolve. Scald the remaining milk, leave to cool for 5 minutes, then beat in the margarine, sugar, salt and eggs. Leave until lukewarm.

2 Pour the milk mixture into the yeast mixture. Stir in half the flour with a wooden spoon. Add the remaining flour, 190g/5oz/1¼ cups at a time, to obtain a rough dough.

3 Transfer the dough to a floured surface, knead until elastic. Place in a clean bowl, cover with a plastic bag and leave to rise in a warm place until doubled in volume.

4 In a saucepan, melt the butter and set aside. Lightly grease two baking sheets. Punch down the dough and divide into four equal pieces. Roll each piece into a 30 x 20cm/12 x 8in rectangle, about 5mm/¼ in thick. Cut each of the rectangles into four long strips, then cut each strip into three 10 x 5cm/ 4 x 2in rectangles. Brush each rectangle with melted butter, then fold the rectangles in half, so that the top extends about 1cm/½ in over the bottom. Place the rectangles slightly overlapping on the baking sheet, with the longer sides facing up.

5 Cover and chill for 30 minutes. Preheat the oven to 180°C/350°F/Gas 4. Bake until golden, 18–20 minutes. Cool slightly before serving.

Cheese Bread

This flavoured bread is ideal to serve with hot soup for a hearty snack lunch.

Makes one 23 x 13cm/9 x 5in loaf

15ml/1 tbsp active dried yeast	10ml/2 tsp salt
250ml/8fl oz/1 cup lukewarm milk	90g/3½ oz/scant 1 cup grated mature Cheddar cheese
25g/1oz/2 tbsp butter	
425g/15oz/3¾ cups strong white flour	

1 Combine the yeast and milk. Stir and leave for 15 minutes to dissolve. Meanwhile, melt the butter, leave to cool, then add to the yeast mixture.

2 Mix the flour and salt together in a large bowl. Make a central well and pour in the yeast mixture. With a wooden spoon, stir from the centre to obtain a rough dough. If the dough seems too dry, add 30–45ml/2–3 tbsp water.

3 Transfer to a floured surface and knead until smooth and elastic. Return to the bowl, cover and leave to rise in a warm place until doubled in volume, about 2–3 hours.

4 Grease a 23 x 13cm/9 x 5in loaf tin. Punch down the dough and knead in the cheese to distribute it evenly. Twist the dough, form into a loaf shape and place in the tin, tucking the ends under. Leave in a warm place until the dough rises above the rim of the tin.

5 Preheat the oven to 200°C/400°F/Gas 6. Bake for 15 minutes, then lower the heat to 190°C/375°F/Gas 5 and bake until the base sounds hollow when tapped, about a further 30 minutes.

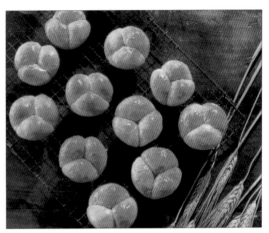

Poppyseed Knots

The poppyseeds look attractive and add a slightly nutty flavour to these rolls.

Makes 12

300ml/½ pint/1¼ cups
 lukewarm milk
50g/2oz/4tbsp butter, at
 room temperature
5ml/1 tsp caster sugar
10ml/2 tsp active dry
 yeast
1 egg yolk

10ml/2 tsp salt
500–575g/1lb 2oz/
 4–4½ cup 4oz plain
 flour
1 egg beaten with 10ml/2
 tsp of water, to glaze
poppyseeds, for
 sprinkling

1 In a large bowl, stir together the milk, butter, sugar and yeast. Leave for 15 minutes to dissolve. Stir in the egg yolk, salt and 275g/10oz/2½ cups of the flour. Add half the remaining flour and stir to obtain a soft dough.

2 Transfer to a floured surface and knead, adding flour if necessary, until smooth and elastic. Place in a bowl, cover and leave in a warm place until the dough doubles in volume, about 1½–2 hours.

3 Grease a baking sheet. Punch down the dough with your fist and cut into 12 pieces the size of golf balls. Roll each piece into a rope, twist to form a knot and place 2.5cm/1in apart on the sheet. Cover loosely and leave to rise in a warm place until doubled in volume, about 1–1½ hours.

4 Preheat the oven to 180°C/350°F/Gas 4. Brush the knots with the egg glaze and sprinkle over the poppyseeds. Bake until the tops are lightly browned, about 30 minutes. Cool slightly on a wire rack before serving.

Clover Leaf Rolls

For a witty touch, make one "lucky four-leaf clover" in the batch.

Makes 24

300ml/½ pint/1¼ cups
 milk
30ml/2 tbsp caster sugar
50g/2oz/4 tbsp butter, at
 room temperature
10ml/2 tsp active dried
 yeast

1 egg
10ml/2 tsp salt
450–500g/1–1¼lb/
 4–5 cups plain flour
melted butter, to glaze

1 Heat the milk to lukewarm, pour into a large bowl and stir in the sugar, butter and yeast. Leave for 15 minutes. Stir in the egg and salt. Gradually stir in 475g/1lb 2oz/4½ cups of the flour. Add just enough extra to obtain a rough dough. Knead until smooth. Place in a greased bowl, cover and leave in a warm place until doubled in size, about 1½ hours.

2 Grease two 12-cup bun trays. Punch down the dough, and make 72 equal-size balls.

3 Place three balls, in one layer, in each bun cup. Cover loosely and leave to rise in a warm place until doubled in size, about 1½ hours.

4 Preheat the oven to 200°C/400°F/Gas 6. Brush the rolls with glaze. Bake until lightly browned, about 20 minutes. Cool slightly on a wire rack before serving.

French Bread

For truly authentic bread you should use flour grown and milled in France.

Makes 2 loaves

15ml/1 tbsp active dried yeast
475ml/16fl oz/2 cups lukewarm water
15ml/1 tbsp salt
850 – 900g/1lb 14oz – 2lb/ 3½–4 cups plain flour
semolina or flour, for sprinkling

1 In a large bowl, combine the yeast and water, stir, and leave for 15 minutes. Stir in the salt.

2 Add the flour, 150g/5oz/1¼ cups at a time, to obtain a smooth dough. Knead for 5 minutes.

3 Shape into a ball, place in a greased bowl and cover with a plastic bag. Leave to rise in a warm place until doubled in size, about 2 – 4 hours.

4 On a lightly floured surface shape into two long loaves. Place on a baking sheet sprinkled with semolina or flour and leave to rise for 5 minutes.

5 Score the tops diagonally with a sharp knife. Brush with water and place in a cold oven. Place a pan of boiling water on the base of the oven and set the oven to 200°C/400°F/ Gas 6. Bake until crusty and golden, about 40 minutes. Cool on a wire rack.

Croissants

Enjoy breakfast Continental-style with these melt-in-your-mouth croissants.

Makes 18

15ml/1 tbsp active dried yeast
325ml/11fl oz/1⅓ cups lukewarm milk
10ml/2 tsp caster sugar
12.5ml/1½ tsp salt
450g/1lb/4 cups plain flour
225g/8oz/1 cup cold unsalted butter
1 egg, beaten with 10ml/2 tsp water, to glaze

1 In an electric mixer bowl, stir together the yeast and milk. Leave for about 15 minutes. Stir in the sugar, salt and about 150g/5oz/1¼ cups of the flour.

2 Using a dough hook, slowly add the remaining flour. Beat on a high speed until the dough pulls away from the sides of the bowl. Cover and leave to rise in a warm place until doubled in size, about 1½ hours. Knead until smooth, wrap in greaseproof paper and chill for 15 minutes.

3 Roll out the butter between two sheets of greaseproof paper to make two 15 x 10cm/6 x 4in rectangles. Roll out the dough to 30 x 20cm/12 x 8in. Interleave the butter with the dough. With a short side facing you, roll it out again to 30 x 20cm/12 x 8in. Fold in thirds again, wrap and chill for 30 minutes. Repeat procedure twice, then chill for 2 hours.

4 Roll out the dough to a rectangle about 3mm/⅛ in thick. Trim the sides. Cut into 18 equal-size triangles. Roll up from base to point. Place point-down on baking sheets and form crescents. Cover and leave to rise in a warm place until more than doubled in size, about 1 – 1½ hours.

5 Preheat the oven to 240°C/475°F/Gas 9. Brush with egg. Bake for 2 minutes. Lower the heat to 190°C/375°F/Gas 5 and bake until golden, about 10 – 12 minutes. Serve warm.

Individual Brioches

These buttery rolls with their distinctive topknots are delicious served with jam at coffee time.

Makes 8

15ml/1 tbsp active dried yeast	2.5ml/½ tsp salt
15ml/1 tbsp caster sugar	75g/3oz/6 tbsp butter, cut into six pieces, at room temperature
30ml/2 tbsp warm milk	
2 eggs	1 egg yolk, beaten with 10ml/2 tsp water, to glaze
about 200g/7oz/1¾ cups plain flour	

1 Butter eight individual brioche or muffin tins. Put the yeast and sugar in a small bowl, add the milk and stir until dissolved. Leave to stand for 5 minutes, then beat in the eggs.

2 Put the flour and salt into a food processor, then, with the machine running, slowly pour in the yeast mixture. Scrape down the sides and process until the dough forms a ball. Add the butter and pulse to blend.

3 Transfer the dough to a buttered bowl and cover with a dish towel. Leave to rise in a warm place for 1 hour, then punch down.

4 Shape three-quarters of the dough into eight balls and put into the tins. Shape the last quarter into eight small balls, make a depression in the top of each large ball and set a small ball into it.

5 Leave to rise in a warm place for 30 minutes. Preheat the oven to 200°C/400°F/Gas 6.

6 Brush the brioches with the egg glaze. Bake for about 15–18 minutes, until golden brown. Transfer to a wire rack and leave to cool completely.

Dinner Milk Rolls

Making bread especially for your dinner guests is not only a wonderful gesture, it is also quite easy to do.

Makes 12–16

750g/1½lb/6 cups strong plain flour	cold milk, to glaze
10ml/2 tsp salt	poppy, sesame and sunflower seeds, or sea salt flakes, for sprinkling
25g/1oz/2 tbsp butter	
1 sachet easy-blend dried yeast	
450ml/¾ pint/1¾ cups lukewarm milk	

1 Sift together the flour and salt into a large bowl. Rub in the butter, then stir in the yeast. Mix to a firm dough with the milk (you may not need it all).

2 Knead the dough for 5 minutes, then return to the bowl, cover with oiled clear film and leave to rise until doubled in volume.

3 Grease a baking sheet. Punch down the dough and knead again, then divide into 12–16 pieces and make into shapes of your choice. Place on the baking sheet, glaze the tops with milk, and sprinkle over your chosen seeds or sea salt flakes.

4 Leave to start rising again. Meanwhile, preheat the oven to 230°C/450°F/Gas 8. Bake the rolls for 12 minutes or until golden brown and cooked. Cool on a wire rack. Eat the same day as they will not keep.

Dill Bread

Tasty herb breads such as this are expensive to buy ready-made – if they can be found at all.

Makes two loaves

20ml/4 tsp active dried yeast	60ml/4 tbsp oil
475ml/16fl oz/2 cups lukewarm water	1 large bunch of dill, finely chopped
30ml/2 tbsp sugar	2 eggs, lightly beaten
1.05kg/2lb 5½ oz/scant 9½ cups strong flour	150g/5½ oz/⅔ cup cottage cheese
½ onion, chopped	20ml/4 tsp salt
	milk, to glaze

1 Mix together the yeast, water and sugar in a large bowl and leave for 15 minutes to dissolve. Stir in about half of the flour. Cover and leave to rise in a warm place for 45 minutes.

2 In a frying pan, cook the onion in 15ml/1 tbsp of the oil until soft. Set aside to cool, then stir into the yeast mixture. Stir the dill, eggs, cottage cheese, salt and the remaining oil into the yeast. Gradually add the remaining flour until the dough is too stiff to stir.

3 Transfer to a floured surface and knead until smooth and elastic. Place in a bowl, cover and leave to rise until doubled in volume, about 1–1½ hours.

4 Grease a large baking sheet. Cut the dough in half and shape into two rounds. Place on the sheet and leave to rise in a warm place for 30 minutes.

5 Preheat the oven to 190°C/375°F/Gas 5. Score the tops, brush with the milk to glaze and bake until browned, about 50 minutes. Transfer to a wire rack to cool.

Spiral Herb Bread

When you slice this unusual loaf, its herbal secret is revealed inside.

Makes two 23 x 13cm/9 x 5in loaves

30ml/2 tbsp active dried yeast	1 large bunch of parsley, finely chopped
600ml/1 pint/2½ cups lukewarm water	1 bunch of spring onions, chopped
425g/15oz/3¾ cups strong white flour	1 garlic clove, finely chopped
500g/1lb 2oz/generous 3½ cups wholemeal flour	salt and ground black pepper
15ml/1 tbsp salt	1 egg, lightly beaten
25g/1oz/2 tbsp butter	milk, for glazing

1 Combine the yeast and 50ml/2fl oz/¼ cup of the water, stir and leave for 15 minutes to dissolve.

2 Combine the flours and salt in a large bowl. Make a central well and pour in the yeast mixture and the remaining water. With a wooden spoon, stir to a rough dough. Transfer to a floured surface; knead until smooth. Return to the bowl, cover with a plastic bag, and leave until doubled in size.

3 Meanwhile, combine the butter, parsley, spring onions and garlic in a large frying pan. Cook over a low heat, stirring, until softened. Season and set aside.

4 Grease two 23 x 13cm/9 x 5in loaf tins. When the dough has risen, cut in half and roll each half into a rectangle 35 x 23cm/14 x 9in. Brush with the beaten egg; spread with the herb mixture. Roll up to enclose the filling, pinch the short ends to seal. Place in the tins, seam-sides down. Cover, leave in a warm place until the dough rises above the tin rims.

5 Preheat the oven to 190°C/375°F/Gas 5. Brush the loaves with milk and bake until the bases sound hollow when tapped, about 55 minutes• Cool on a wire rack.

Sesame Seed Bread

This delicious bread breaks into individual rolls. It is ideal for entertaining.

Makes one 23cm/9in loaf

*10ml/2 tsp active dried
  yeast
300ml/½ pint/1¼ cups
  lukewarm water
200g/7oz/1¾ cups plain
  flour
200g/7oz/scant 1½ cups
  wholemeal flour*

*10ml/2 tsp salt
65g/2½oz/5 tbsp toasted
  sesame seeds
milk, to glaze
30ml/2 tbsp sesame
  seeds, for sprinkling*

1 Combine the yeast and 75ml/5 tbsp of the water and leave to dissolve. Mix the flours and salt in a large bowl. Make a central well and pour in the yeast and water. Stir from the centre to obtain a rough dough.

2 Transfer to a floured surface and knead until smooth and elastic. Return to the bowl and cover with a plastic bag. Leave in a warm place until the dough has doubled in size, about 1½–2 hours.

3 Grease a 23cm/9in round cake tin. Punch down the dough and knead in the sesame seeds. Divide the dough into 16 balls and place in the tin. Cover with a plastic bag and leave in a warm place until risen above the rim.

4 Preheat the oven to 220°C/425°F/Gas 7. Brush the loaf with milk and sprinkle with the sesame seeds. Bake for 15 minutes. Lower the heat to 190°C/375°F/Gas 5 and bake until the base sounds hollow when tapped, about 30 minutes. Cool on a wire rack.

Rye Bread

To bring out the flavour of the caraway seeds, toast them lightly in the oven first.

Makes one loaf

*200g/7oz/scant 1½ cups
  rye flour
475ml/16fl oz/2 cups
  boiling water
120ml/4fl oz/½ cup black
  treacle
65g/2½oz/5 tbsp butter,
  cut into pieces
15ml/1 tbsp salt
30ml/2 tbsp caraway
  seeds*

*15ml/1 tbsp active dried
  yeast
120ml/4fl oz/½ cup
  lukewarm water
about 850g/1lb 14oz/
  7½ cups plain flour
semolina or flour, for
  dusting*

1 Mix the rye flour, boiling water, treacle, butter, salt and caraway seeds in a large bowl. Leave to cool.

2 In another bowl, mix the yeast and lukewarm water and leave to dissolve. Stir into the rye flour mixture. Stir in just enough plain flour to obtain a stiff dough. If it becomes too stiff, stir with your hands. Transfer to a floured surface and knead thoroughly until the dough is no longer sticky and is smooth and shiny.

3 Place in a greased bowl, cover with a plastic bag, and leave in a warm place until doubled in volume. Punch down the dough, cover, and leave to rise again for 30 minutes.

4 Preheat the oven to 180°C/350°F/Gas 4. Dust a baking sheet with semolina or flour.

5 Shape the dough into a ball. Place on the sheet and score several times across the top. Bake until the base sounds hollow when tapped, about 40 minutes. Cool on a wire rack.

Rosemary Focaccia

Italian flat bread is easy to make using a packet mix. Additions include olives and sun-dried tomatoes.

Makes two loaves

450g/1lb packet white
  bread mix
60ml/4 tbsp extra virgin
  olive oil
10ml/2 tsp dried
  rosemary, crushed
8 sun-dried tomatoes,
  chopped

12 black olives, stoned
  and chopped
200ml/7fl oz/scant 1 cup
  lukewarm water
sea salt flakes, for
  sprinkling

1 Combine the bread mix with half the oil, the rosemary, tomatoes, olives and water to form a firm dough.

2 Knead the dough on a lightly floured surface for about 5 minutes. Return to the mixing bowl and cover with a piece of oiled clear film. Leave the dough to rise in a warm place until doubled in size. Meanwhile, lightly grease two baking sheets and preheat the oven to 220°C/425°F/Gas 7.

3 Punch down the dough and knead again. Divide into two and shape into flat rounds. Place on the baking sheet, and make indentations with your fingertips. Trickle over the remaining olive oil and sprinkle with sea salt flakes.

4 Bake the focaccia for 12–15 minutes until golden brown and cooked. Turn out on to wire racks to cool. This bread is best eaten slightly warm.

Saffron Focaccia

A dazzling yellow bread that is both light in texture and distinctive in flavour.

Makes one loaf

pinch of saffron strands
150ml/¼ pint/⅔ cup
  boiling water
225g/8oz/2 cups plain
  flour
2.5ml/½ tsp salt
5ml/1 tsp easy-blend
  dried yeast
15ml/1 tbsp olive oil

For the topping

2 garlic cloves, sliced
1 red onion, cut into thin
  wedges
rosemary sprigs
12 black olives, stoned
  and coarsely chopped
15ml/1 tbsp olive oil

1 Place the saffron in a heatproof jug and pour in the boiling water. Leave to infuse until lukewarm.

2 Place the flour, salt, yeast and olive oil in a food processor. Turn on and gradually add the saffron and its liquid. Process until the dough forms a ball.

3 Turn on to a floured surface; knead for 10–15 minutes. Place in a bowl, cover and leave to rise until doubled in size, about 30–40 minutes.

4 Punch down the dough and roll into an oval shape about 1cm/½in thick. Place on a lightly greased baking sheet and leave to rise for 30 minutes.

5 Preheat the oven to 200°C/400°F/Gas 6. With your fingers, press indentations over the surface of the bread.

6 Cover with the topping ingredients, brush lightly with olive oil, and bake for 25 minutes or until the loaf sounds hollow when tapped on the base. Leave to cool on a wire rack.

Rosemary Bread

Sliced thinly, this herb bread is delicious with cheese or soup for a light meal.

Makes one 23 x 13cm/9 x 5in loaf

1 sachet easy-blend dried yeast	*15ml/1 tbsp sugar*
175g/6oz/1¼ cups wholemeal flour	*5ml/1 tsp salt*
	15ml/1 tbsp sesame seeds
175g/6oz/1½ cups self-raising flour	*15ml/1 tbsp dried chopped onion*
25g/1oz/2 tbsp butter	*15ml/1 tbsp fresh rosemary leaves*
50ml/2fl oz/¼ cup warm water	*115g/4oz/1 cup cubed Cheddar cheese*
250ml/8fl oz/1 cup milk, at room temperature	*rosemary leaves and coarse salt, to decorate*

1 Mix the yeast with the flours in a large mixing bowl. Melt the butter. Then stir the warm water, milk, sugar, butter, salt, sesame seeds, onion and rosemary into the flour. Knead thoroughly until quite smooth.

2 Flatten the dough, then add the cheese cubes. Knead them in until they are well combined.

3 Place the dough into a clean bowl greased with a little melted butter. Cover with a dish towel and put in a warm place for 1½ hours, or until the dough has doubled in size.

4 Grease a 23 x 13cm/9 x 5in loaf tin with butter. Punch down the dough and shape into a loaf. Place in the tin, cover with the dish towel and leave for about 1 hour until doubled in size. Preheat the oven to 190°C/375°F/Gas 5.

5 Bake for 30 minutes. Cover the loaf with foil for the last 5–10 minutes of baking. Turn the bread out on to a wire rack to cool. Garnish with some rosemary leaves and coarse salt scattered on top.

Potato Bread

Don't add butter or milk to the potatoes when you mash them, or the dough will be too sticky.

Makes two 23 x 13cm/9 x 5in loaves

20ml/4 tsp active dried yeast	*30ml/2 tbsp oil*
	20ml/4 tsp salt
250ml/8fl oz/1 cup lukewarm milk	*850–900g/1lb 4oz–2lb/3½–4 cups plain flour*
225g/8oz potatoes, boiled (reserve 250ml/ 8fl oz/1 cup of the cooking liquid)	

1 Combine the yeast and milk in a large bowl and leave to dissolve, about 15 minutes. Meanwhile, mash the potatoes.

2 Add the potatoes, oil and salt to the yeast mixture and mix well. Stir in the reserved cooking water, then stir in the flour, in six separate batches, to form a stiff dough. Knead until smooth, return to the bowl, cover, and leave in a warm place until doubled in size, about 1–1½ hours. Punch down, then leave to rise again for 40 minutes.

3 Grease two 23 x 13cm/9 x 5in loaf tins. Roll the dough into 20 small balls. Place two rows of balls in each tin. Leave until the dough has risen above the rims of the tins.

4 Preheat the oven to 200°C/400°F/Gas 6. Bake the dough for 10 minutes, then lower the heat to 190°C/375°F/Gas 5. Bake until the bases of the loaves sound hollow when tapped, about 40 minutes. Cool on a wire rack.

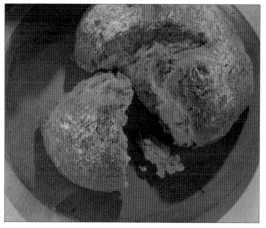

Irish Soda Bread

Easy to make, this distinctive bread goes well with soup, cheese and traditional, rustic-style dishes.

Makes one loaf

275g/10oz/2½ cups plain flour
150g/5oz/1 cup wholemeal flour
5ml/1 tsp bicarbonate of soda
5ml/1 tsp salt

25g/1oz/2 tbsp butter or margarine, at room temperature
300ml/½ pint/1¼ cups buttermilk
15ml/1 tbsp plain flour, for dusting

1 Preheat the oven to 200°C/400°F/Gas 6. Grease a baking sheet. Sift together the flours, bicarbonate of soda and salt. Make a central well and add the butter or margarine and buttermilk. Working from the centre, stir to combine the ingredients until a soft dough is formed.

2 With floured hands, gather the dough into a ball. Knead for 3 minutes. Shape the dough into a large round.

3 Place on the baking sheet. Cut a cross in the top with a sharp knife and dust with the flour. Bake until brown, about 40–50 minutes. Transfer to a wire rack to cool.

Sage Soda Bread

This wonderful loaf, quite unlike bread made with yeast, has a velvety texture and a powerful sage aroma.

Makes one loaf

225g/8oz/⅔ cups wholemeal flour
115g/4oz/1 cup strong white flour
2.5ml/½ tsp salt
5ml/1 tsp bicarbonate of soda

30ml/2 tbsp shredded fresh sage
300–450ml/½– ¾ pint/1¼–1¾ cups buttermilk

1 Preheat the oven to 220°C/425°F/Gas 7. Sift the dry ingredients into a bowl. Stir in the sage and add enough buttermilk to make a soft dough.

2 Shape the dough into a round loaf and place on a lightly greased baking sheet.

3 Cut a deep cross in the top. Bake in the oven for about 40 minutes, or until the loaf is well risen and sounds hollow when tapped on the base. Leave to cool on a wire rack.

Breadsticks

If preferred, use other seeds, such as poppy or caraway, in these sticks.

Makes 18–20
15ml/1 tbsp active dried yeast
300ml/½ pint/1¼ cups lukewarm water
425g/15oz/scant 4 cups plain flour
10ml/2 tsp salt
5ml/1 tsp caster sugar
30ml/2 tbsp olive oil
1 egg, beaten, to glaze
150g/5oz/10 tbsp sesame seeds, toasted
coarse salt, for sprinkling

1 Combine the yeast and water, stir and leave for about 15 minutes. Place the flour, salt, sugar and olive oil in a food processor. With the motor running, slowly pour in the yeast mixture and process until the dough forms a ball.

2 Knead until smooth. Place in a bowl, cover and leave to rise in a warm place for 45 minutes. Grease two baking sheets.

3 Roll the dough into 18–20 30cm/12in sticks. Place on the baking sheets, brush with egg then sprinkle with sesame seeds and coarse salt. Leave to rise, uncovered, for 20 minutes.

4 Preheat the oven to 200°C/400°F/Gas 6. Bake until golden, about 15 minutes. Turn off the heat but leave in the oven for a further 5 minutes. Serve warm or cool.

Tomato Breadsticks

Once you've tried this simple recipe you'll never buy manufactured breadsticks again.

Makes 16
225g/8oz/2 cups plain flour
2.5ml/½ tsp salt
7.5ml/½ tbsp easy-blend dried yeast
5ml/1 tsp honey
5ml/1 tsp olive oil
150ml/¼ pint/⅔ cup warm water
6 halves sun-dried tomatoes in olive oil, drained and chopped
15ml/1 tbsp milk
10ml/2 tsp poppyseeds

1 Place the flour, salt and yeast in a food processor. Add the honey and olive oil and, with the machine running, gradually pour in the water until the dough starts to cling together (you may not need all the water). Process for a further 1 minute.

2 Turn out the dough on to a floured surface and knead for 3–4 minutes, until springy and smooth. Knead in the sun-dried tomatoes. Form into a ball and place in a lightly oiled bowl. Leave to rise for 5 minutes.

3 Preheat the oven to 150°C/300°F/Gas 2. Divide the dough into 16 pieces and roll each piece into a 28 x 1cm/11 x ½in stick. Place on a lightly greased baking sheet and leave to rise in a warm place for 15 minutes.

4 Brush the sticks with milk and sprinkle with poppy seeds. Bake for 30 minutes. Leave to cool on a wire rack.

Walnut Bread

This rich bread could be served at a dinner party with the cheese course, or with a rustic ploughman's lunch.

Makes one loaf

420g/15oz/3 cups
   wholemeal flour
140g/5oz/1¼ cups strong
   flour
12.5ml/2½ tsp salt
500ml/18fl oz/2¼ cups
   lukewarm water

15ml/1tbsp clear honey
15ml/1tbsp active dried
   yeast
140g/5oz/1 cup walnut
   pieces, plus more to
   decorate
1 beaten egg, to glaze

1 Combine the flours and salt in a large bowl. Make a well in the centre and add 250ml/8fl oz/1 cup of the water, the honey and the yeast. Set aside until the mixture is frothy.

2 Add the remaining water. With a wooden spoon, stir from the centre, incorporating flour with each turn, to obtain a smooth dough. Add more flour if the dough is too sticky and use your hands if the dough becomes too stiff to stir.

3 Transfer to a floured board and knead, adding flour if necessary, until the dough is smooth and elastic. Place in a greased bowl and roll the dough around in the bowl to coat thoroughly on all sides. Cover with a plastic bag and leave in a warm place until doubled in volume. Punch down the dough and knead in the walnuts evenly.

4 Grease a baking sheet. Shape the dough into a round loaf and place on the baking sheet. Press in walnut pieces to decorate the top. Cover loosely with a damp cloth and leave to rise in a warm place until doubled in size, 25–30 minutes.

5 Preheat the oven to 220°C/425°F/Gas 7. With a sharp knife, score the top. Brush with the beaten egg. Bake for 15 minutes. Lower the heat to 190°C/375°F/Gas 5 and bake until the base sounds hollow when tapped, about 40 minutes. Cool on a rack.

Pecan Nut Rye Bread

A tasty homespun loaf that recalls the old folk cooking of the United States.

Makes two 21.5 x 11.5cm/8½ x 4½in loaves

25ml/1½ tbsp active
   dried yeast
700ml/22fl oz/2¾ cups
   lukewarm water
675g/1½lb/6 cups strong
   flour
500g/1¼lb/5 cups rye
   flour

30ml/2tbsp salt
15ml/1tbsp clear honey
10ml/2tsp caraway seeds,
   (optional)
115g/4oz/8tbsp butter, at
   room temperature
225g/8oz pecan nuts,
   chopped

1 Combine the yeast and 120ml/4fl oz/½ cup of the water. Stir and leave for 15 minutes to dissolve. In the bowl of an electric mixer, combine the flours, salt, honey, caraway seeds and butter. With the dough hook, mix on low speed until well blended.

2 Add the yeast mixture and the remaining water and mix on medium speed until the dough forms a ball. Transfer to a floured surface and knead in the pecan nuts.

3 Return the dough to a bowl, cover with a plastic bag and leave in a warm place until doubled, about 2 hours. Grease two 21.5 x 11.5cm/8½ x 4½ in loaf tins. Punch down the risen dough.

4 Divide the dough in half and form into loaves. Place in the tins, seam-sides down. Dust the tops with flour. Cover with plastic bags and leave to rise in a warm place until doubled in volume, about 1 hour.

5 Preheat the oven to 190°C/375°F/Gas 5. Bake until the bases sound hollow when tapped, 45–50 minutes. Transfer to wire racks to cool completely.

Prune Bread

Makes 1 loaf

225g/8oz/1 cup
  dried prunes
15ml/1 tbsp easy-blend
  dried yeast
75g/3oz/⅔ cup
  wholemeal flour
385–420g/13½
  –15oz/3–4cups
  strong flour
2.5ml/½ tsp bicarbonate

of soda
5ml/1 tsp salt
5ml/1 tsp pepper
30g/1oz butter, at room
  temperature
175ml/6fl oz/⅔ cup
  buttermilk
55g/2oz/½ cup
  walnuts, chopped
milk, for glazing

1 Simmer the prunes in water to cover until soft, or soak overnight. Drain, reserving 60ml/4 tbsp of the soaking liquid. Stone and chop the prunes.

2 Combine the yeast and the reserved prune liquid, stir and leave for 15 minutes to dissolve.

3 In a large bowl, stir together the flours, bicarbonate of soda, salt and pepper. Make a well in the centre.

4 Add the prunes, butter, and buttermilk. Pour in the yeast mixture. With a wooden spoon, stir from the centre, folding in more flour with each turn, to obtain a rough dough.

5 Transfer to a floured surface and knead until smooth and elastic. Return to the bowl, cover with a plastic bag and leave to rise in a warm place until doubled in volume, for about 1½ hours. Grease a baking sheet.

6 Punch down the dough with your fist, then knead in the walnuts. Shape the dough into a long, cylindrical loaf. Place on the baking sheet, cover loosely, and leave to rise in a warm place for 45 minutes. Preheat the oven to 220°C/425°F/Gas 7.

7 With a sharp knife, score the top. Brush with milk and bake for 15 minutes. Lower to 190°C/375°F/Gas 5 and bake for 35 minutes more, until the bottom sounds hollow. Cool.

Courgette Crown Bread

Adding grated courgettes and cheese to a loaf mixture will keep it tasting fresher for longer.

Serves 8

450g/1lb/3 cups coarsely
  grated courgettes
salt
500g/1¼ lb/5 cups plain
  flour
2 sachets easy-blend
  dried yeast

60ml/4 tbsp freshly
  grated Parmesan
  cheese
ground black pepper
30ml/2 tbsp olive oil
lukewarm water, to mix
milk, to glaze
sesame seeds, to garnish

1 Spoon the courgettes into a colander, sprinkling them lightly with salt. Leave to drain for 30 minutes, then pat dry with kitchen paper.

2 Mix the flour, yeast and Parmesan together and season with black pepper. Stir in the oil and courgettes, and add enough lukewarm water to make a firm dough.

3 Knead the dough on a lightly floured surface until smooth, then return to the mixing bowl, cover it with oiled clear film and leave it to rise in a warm place, until doubled in size. Meanwhile, grease and line a 23cm/9in round sandwich tin. Preheat the oven to 200°C/400°F/Gas 6.

4 Punch down the dough, and knead it lightly. Break into 8 balls, roll each one and arrange them, touching, in the tin. Brush the tops with milk and sprinkle over the sesame seeds.

5 Allow to rise again, then bake for 25 minutes or until golden brown. Cool slightly in the tin, then turn out on to a wire rack.

Raisin Bread

Makes 2 loaves

15ml/1 tbsp easy-blend
    dried yeast
450ml/¾ pint/1¾ cups
    lukewarm milk
150g/5oz raisins
65g/2½ oz4 tbsp currants
15ml/1 tbsp sherry or
    brandy
2.5/½ tsp grated nutmeg

grated rind of 1 large
    orange
60g/2¼ oz/7 tbsp sugar
15ml/1 tbsp salt
115g/4oz/8 tbsp
    butter, melted
700 – 850g/1lb 8oz – 1lb
    14oz strong flour
1 egg beaten with 15ml/
    1 tbsp cream

1 Stir the yeast with 120ml/4fl oz/½ cup of the milk and leave to stand for 15 minutes to dissolve. Mix the raisins, currants, sherry or brandy, nutmeg and orange rind together.

2 In another bowl, mix the remaining milk, sugar, salt and half the butter. Add the yeast mixture. With a wooden spoon, stir in half the flour, 150g/5oz at a time, until blended. Add the remaining flour as needed for a stiff dough.

3 Transfer to a floured surface and knead until smooth and elastic. Place in a greased bowl, cover and leave to rise in a warm place until doubled in volume, about 2½ hours.

4 Punch down the dough, return to the bowl, cover and leave to rise in a warm place for 30 minutes. Grease two 21.5 x 11.5cm/8½ x 4½ in bread tins. Divide the dough in half and roll each half into a 50 x 18cm/20 x 7in rectangle.

5 Brush the rectangles with the remaining melted butter. Sprinkle over the raisin mixture, then roll up tightly, tucking in the ends slightly as you roll. Place in the prepared tins, cover, and leave to rise until almost doubled in volume.

6 Preheat the oven to 200℃/400℉/Gas 6. Brush the loaves with the egg and milk. Bake for 20 minutes. Lower to 180℃/350℉/Gas 4 and bake until golden, 25 – 30 minutes more. Cool on racks.

Coconut Bread

This bread is delicious served with a cup of hot chocolate or a glass of fruit punch.

Makes 1 loaf

175g/6oz/¾ cup butter
115g/4oz/⅔ cup
    demerara sugar
225g/8oz/2 cups self-
    raising flour
200g/7oz/scant 2 cups
    plain flour
115g/4oz desiccated
    coconut
5ml/1 tsp mixed spice

10ml/2 tsp vanilla
    essence
15ml/1 tbsp rum
2 eggs
about 150ml/¼ pint/
    ⅔ cup milk
15ml/1 tbsp caster sugar,
    blended with 30ml/
    2 tbsp water, to glaze

1 Preheat the oven to 180℃/350℉/Gas 4. Grease two 450g/1lb loaf tins.

2 Place the butter and sugar in a large bowl and sift in the flour. Rub in the ingredients together with your fingertips until the mixture resembles fine breadcrumbs.

3 Add the coconut, mixed spice, vanilla essence, rum, eggs and milk and mix together well with your hands. If the mixture is too dry, moisten with milk. Knead on a floured board until firm and pliable.

4 Halve the mixture and place in the prepared loaf tins. Glaze with sugared water and bake for 1 hour until the loaves are cooked. Test with a skewer, the loaves are ready when the skewer comes out clean.

Danish Wreath

Serves 10–12

5ml/1 tsp easy-blend
   dried yeast
175ml/6fl oz/¾ cup milk
50g/2oz/4 tbsp sugar
450g/1lb/4 cups strong
   white flour
2.5ml/½ tsp salt
2.5ml/½ tsp vanilla
   essence
1 egg, beaten
2 x 115g/4oz/½ cup
   blocks unsalted butter

1 egg yolk beaten with
   10ml/2 tsp water
115g/4oz/1 cup icing
   sugar

For the filling

200g/7oz/generous 1 cup
   dark brown sugar
5ml/1 tsp ground
   cinnamon
50g/2oz/½ cup walnuts
   or pecans, plus extra

1 Mix the yeast, milk and 2.5ml/½ tsp of the sugar. Leave for 15 minutes to dissolve. Mix the flour, sugar and salt. Make a well; add the yeast, vanilla and egg to make a rough dough. Knead until smooth, wrap and chill.

2 Roll the butter to form two 15 x 10cm/6 x 4in rectangles. Roll the dough to a 30 x 20cm/12 x 8in rectangle. Place one butter rectangle in the centre. Fold the bottom third of dough over and seal the edge. Place the other butter rectangle on top and cover with the top third of the dough.

3 Roll the dough into a 30 x 20cm/12 x 8in rectangle. Fold into thirds. Wrap and chill for 30 minutes. Repeat twice more. After the third fold, chill for 1–2 hours. Grease a baking sheet.

4 Roll out the dough to a 63 x 15cm/25 x 6in strip. Mix the filling ingredients and spread over, leaving a 1cm/½in edge. Roll the dough into a cylinder, place on the sheet in a circle and seal the edges. Cover and leave to rise for 45 minutes.

5 Preheat the oven to 200°C/400°F/Gas 6. Slash the top every 5cm/2in, cutting 1cm/½in deep. Brush with the egg and milk. Bake for 35–40 minutes until golden. Cool. To serve, mix the icing sugar with some water, then drizzle over the wreath. Sprinkle with some nuts.

Kugelhopf

A traditional round moulded bread from Germany, flavoured with Kirsch or brandy.

Makes one ring loaf

100g/3¾ oz/¾ cup raisins
15ml/1 tbsp Kirsch or
   brandy
15ml/1 tbsp easy-blend
   dried yeast
120ml/4fl oz/½ cup
   lukewarm water
115g/4oz/½ cup unsalted
   butter, at room
   temperature
90g/3½oz/½ cup sugar
3 eggs, at room
   temperature

grated rind of 1 lemon
5ml/1 tsp salt
2.5ml/½ tsp vanilla
   essence
425g/15oz/3¾ cups
   strong white flour
120ml/4fl oz/½ cup milk
25g/1oz/¼ cup flaked
   almonds
80g/3¼oz/generous
   ½ cup whole blanched
   almonds, chopped
icing sugar, for dusting

1 In a bowl, combine the raisins and Kirsch or brandy. Combine the yeast and water, stir and leave for 15 minutes.

2 Cream the butter and sugar until thick and fluffy. Beat in the eggs, one at a time. Add the lemon rind, salt and vanilla. Stir in the yeast mixture. Add the flour, alternating with the milk, until well blended. Cover and leave to rise in a warm place until doubled in volume, about 2 hours.

3 Grease a 2.75 litre/4½ pint/11¼ cup kugelhopf mould, then sprinkle the flaked almonds evenly over the base. Work the raisins and chopped almonds into the dough, then spoon into the mould. Cover with a polythene bag, and leave to rise in a warm place until the dough almost reaches the top of the tin, about 1 hour.

4 Preheat the oven to 180°C/350°F/Gas 4. Bake until golden brown, about 45 minutes. If the top browns too quickly, cover with foil. Cool in the tin for 15 minutes, then turn out on to a wire rack. Dust the top lightly with icing sugar.

Open Apple Pie

If using eating apples for this pie, make sure they are firm-fleshed rather than soft.

Serves 8

1.5kg/3 – 3½lb tart eating
  or cooking apples
45g/1¾oz/scant ¼ cup
  sugar
10ml/2 tsp ground
  cinnamon
grated rind and juice of
  1 lemon
25g/1oz/2 tbsp butter,
  diced
30 – 45ml/2 – 3 tbsp
  honey, to glaze

For the pastry
275g/10oz/2½ cups plain
  flour
2.5ml/½ tsp salt
115g/4oz/½ cup butter,
  cut into pieces
60g/2¼oz/4½ tbsp
  vegetable fat or lard,
  cut into pieces
75 – 90ml/5 – 6 tbsp iced
  water

1 For the pastry, sift the flour and salt into a bowl. Add the butter and fat and rub in until the mixture resembles coarse breadcrumbs. Stir in just enough water to bind the dough. Gather into a ball, wrap and chill for at least 20 minutes.

2 Preheat the oven to 200°C/400°F/Gas 6. Place a baking sheet in the oven.

3 Peel, core and slice the apples. Combine with the sugar, cinnamon, lemon rind and juice.

4 Roll out the pastry to a 30cm/12in circle. Use to line a 23cm/9in pie dish, leaving an overhanging edge. Fill with the apples. Fold in the edges and crimp loosely. Dot the apples with diced butter.

5 Bake on the hot baking sheet until the pastry is golden and the apples are tender, about 45 minutes.

6 Melt the honey in a saucepan and brush over the apples to glaze. Serve warm or at room temperature.

Apple and Cranberry Lattice Pie

Serves 8

grated rind of 1 orange
45ml/3 tbsp orange juice
2 large cooking apples
170g/6oz/1⅓ cups
  cranberries
70g/2½oz/½ cup raisins
25g/1oz/4 tbsp walnuts,
  chopped
215g/7½oz/generous 1
  cup caster sugar
115g/4oz/½ cup dark
  brown sugar
15g/½oz/2 tbsp plain
  flour

For the crust
285g/10oz/2½ cups plain
  flour
2.5ml/½ tsp salt
85g/3oz/6 tbsp cold
  butter, cut into pieces
85g/3oz/½ cup cold
  vegetable fat or lard,
  cut into pieces
65 – 125ml/2 – 4fl oz iced
  water

1 For the crust, sift the flour and salt, add the butter and fat and rub in well. Stir in enough water to bind the dough. Form into two equal balls, wrap and chill for at least 20 minutes.

2 Put the orange rind and juice into a bowl. Peel and core the apples and grate into the bowl. Stir in the cranberries, raisins, walnuts, all except 1 tbsp of the caster sugar, the brown sugar and flour. Place a baking sheet in the oven and preheat to 200°C/400°F/Gas 6.

3 Roll out one ball of dough about 3mm/⅛in thick. Transfer to a 23cm/9in pie plate and trim. Spoon the cranberry and apple mixture into the shell.

4 Roll out the remaining dough to a circle about 28cm/11in in diameter. With a serrated pastry wheel, cut the dough into 10 strips, 2cm/¾in wide. Place five strips horizontally across the top of the tart at 2.5cm/1in intervals. Weave in five vertical strips and trim. Sprinkle the top with sugar.

5 Bake for 20 minutes. Reduce heat to 180°C/350°F/Gas 4 and bake until the crust is golden and the filling is bubbling, about 15 minutes more.

Peach Leaf Pie

Serves 8

1.1kg/2½lb ripe peaches
juice of 1 lemon
90g/3½oz/½ cup sugar
45ml/3 tbsp cornflour
1.5ml/¼ tsp grated
  nutmeg
2.5ml/½ tsp ground
  cinnamon
25g/1oz/2 tbsp butter,
  diced

For the pastry

275g/10oz/2½ cups plain
  flour
4ml/¾ tsp salt
115g/4oz/½ cup cold
  butter, cut into pieces
60g/2¼oz/4½ tbsp cold
  vegetable fat or lard,
  cut into pieces
75–90ml/5–6 tbsp iced
  water
1 egg beaten with 15ml/
  1 tbsp water

1 Make the pastry as described for Open Apple Pie on page 86. Gather into two balls, one slightly larger than the other. Wrap and chill for at least 20 minutes. Place a baking sheet in the oven and preheat to 220°C/425°F/Gas 7.

2 Drop the peaches into boiling water for 20 seconds, then transfer to a bowl of cold water. When cool, peel off the skins. Slice the flesh and combine with the lemon juice, sugar, cornflour and spices. Set aside.

3 Roll out the larger dough ball to 3mm/⅛in thick. Use to line a 23cm/9in pie tin. Chill. Roll out the remaining dough to 5mm/¼in thick. Cut out leaves 8cm/3in long. Mark veins. With the scraps, roll a few balls.

4 Brush the pastry base with egg glaze. Add the peaches and dot with the butter. To assemble, start from the outside edge and cover the peaches with a ring of leaves. Place a second, staggered ring above. Continue until covered. Place the balls in the centre. Brush with glaze. Bake on the hot baking sheet for 10 minutes. Lower the heat to 180°C/350°F/Gas 4 and bake for 35–40 minutes more.

Walnut and Pear Lattice Pie

For the lattice top, either weave strips of pastry or use a special pastry cutter to create a lattice effect.

Serves 6–8

450g/1lb shortcrust
  pastry
450g/2lb pears, peeled,
  cored and thinly sliced
50g/2oz/4 tbsp caster
  sugar
25g/1oz/2 tbsp plain
  flour
2.5ml/½ tsp grated
  lemon rind
25g/1oz/scant ¼ cup
  raisins or sultanas

25g/1oz/4 tbsp chopped
  walnuts
2.5ml/½ tsp ground
  cinnamon
50g/2oz/½ cup icing
  sugar
15ml/1 tbsp lemon juice
about 10ml/2 tsp cold
  water

1 Preheat the oven to 190°C/375°F/Gas 5. Roll out half of the pastry and use it to line a 23cm/9in tin that is about 5cm/2in deep.

2 Combine the pears, caster sugar, flour and lemon rind. Toss to coat the fruit. Mix in the raisins, nuts and cinnamon. Put the filling into the pastry case and spread it evenly.

3 Roll out the remaining pastry and use to make a lattice top. Bake the pie for 55 minutes or until the pastry is golden brown on top.

4 Combine the icing sugar, lemon juice and water in a bowl and stir until smooth. Remove the pie from the oven. Drizzle the glaze evenly over the top, on the pastry and filling. Leave the pie to cool in its tin on a wire rack.

Lemon Meringue Pie

A classic dish whose popularity never seems to wane.

Serves 8

225g/8oz shortcrust
   pastry
grated rind and juice of 1
   large lemon
250ml/8fl oz/1 cup plus
   15ml/1 tbsp cold
   water
115g/4oz/generous
   ½ cup caster sugar
   plus 90ml/6 tbsp extra

25g/1oz/2 tbsp butter
45ml/3 tbsp cornflour
3 eggs, separated
pinch of salt
pinch of cream of tartar

1 Line a 23cm/9in pie dish with the pastry, folding under a 1cm/½in overhang. Crimp the edge and chill for 20 minutes.

2 Preheat the oven to 200°C/400°F/Gas 6. Prick the pastry case base, line with greaseproof paper and fill with baking beans. Bake for 12 minutes. Remove the paper and beans and bake until golden, 6–8 minutes more.

3 In a saucepan, combine the lemon rind and juice with 250ml/8fl oz/1 cup of the water, 115g/4oz/generous ½ cup of the sugar, and the butter. Bring to the boil.

4 Meanwhile, dissolve the cornflour in the remaining water. Add the egg yolks. Beat into the lemon mixture, return to the boil and whisk until thick, about 5 minutes. Cover the surface with greaseproof paper and leave to cool.

5 For the meringue, beat the egg whites with the salt and cream of tartar until stiffly peaking. Add the remaining sugar and beat until glossy.

6 Spoon the lemon mixture into the pastry case. Spoon the meringue on top, sealing it with the pastry rim. Bake until golden, 12–15 minutes.

Blueberry Pie

Serve this tangy blueberry pie with crème fraîche or double cream.

Serves 6–8

450g/1lb shortcrust
   pastry
500g/1¼lb/5 cups
   blueberries
165g/5½oz/generous
   ⅔ cup caster sugar
45ml/3 tbsp plain flour

5ml/1 tsp grated orange
   rind
1.5ml/¼ tsp grated
   nutmeg
30ml/2 tbsp orange juice
5ml/1 tsp lemon juice

1 Preheat the oven to 190°C/375°F/Gas 5. On a lightly floured surface, roll out half of the pastry and use it to line a 23cm/9in pie tin that is 5cm/2in deep.

2 Combine the blueberries, 150g/5oz/¾cup of the sugar, the flour, orange rind and nutmeg. Toss the mixture gently to coat all the fruit.

3 Pour the blueberry mixture into the pastry case and spread evenly. Sprinkle over the citrus juices.

4 Roll out the remaining pastry and cover the pie. Cut out small decorative shapes from the top. Use to decorate the pastry, and finish the edge.

5 Brush the top with water and sprinkle with the remaining caster sugar. Bake for 45 minutes, or until the pastry is golden brown. Serve warm or at room temperature.

Creamy Banana Pie

Do not prepare the topping for this pie too soon before serving or the banana slices will discolour.

Serves 6

200g/7oz/2¼ cups ginger biscuits, finely crushed
65g/2½oz/5 tbsp butter or margarine, melted
2.5ml/½ tsp grated nutmeg or ground cinnamon
175g/6oz/1 ripe banana, mashed
350g/12oz/1½ cups cream cheese, at room temperature

50ml/generous 3 tbsp thick natural yogurt or soured cream
45ml/3 tbsp dark rum or 5ml/1 tsp vanilla essence

For the topping
250ml/8fl oz/1 cup whipping cream
3–4 bananas

1 Preheat the oven to 190°C/375°F/Gas 5. For the crust, combine the crushed biscuits, butter or margarine and spice. Mix thoroughly with a wooden spoon.

2 Press the biscuit mixture into a 23cm/9in pie dish, building up thick sides with a neat edge. Bake for 5 minutes, then leave to cool.

3 Beat the mashed bananas with the cream cheese. Fold in the yogurt or soured cream and rum or vanilla. Spread the filling in the biscuit case. Chill for at least 4 hours or preferably overnight.

4 For the topping, whip the cream until soft peaks form. Spread on the pie filling. Slice the bananas and arrange on top in a decorative pattern.

Red Berry Sponge Tart

When soft berry fruits are in season, serve this delicious tart warm with scoops of vanilla ice cream.

Serves 4

450g/1lb/4 cups soft berry fruits, such as raspberries, black-berries, blackcurrants, redcurrants, strawberries and blueberries
2 eggs

50g/2oz/¼ cup caster sugar, plus extra to taste (optional)
15ml/1 tbsp flour
75g/3oz/¾ cup ground almonds
vanilla ice cream, to serve

1 Preheat the oven to 190°C/375°F/Gas 5. Grease and line a 23cm/9in pie tin with greaseproof paper. Scatter the fruit in the base of the tin with a little sugar if the fruits are tart.

2 Beat the eggs and sugar together for about 3–4 minutes, or until they leave a thick trail across the surface. Combine the flour and almonds, then fold into the egg mixture with a palette knife, retaining as much air as possible.

3 Spread the mixture on top of the fruit base, bake in the preheated oven for 15 minutes, then turn out on to a serving plate .

De Luxe Mincemeat Tart

Serves 8

225g/8oz/2 cups plain
  flour
10ml/2 tsp ground
  cinnamon
50g/2oz/½ cup walnuts,
  finely ground
115g/4oz/½ cup butter
50g/2oz/4 tbsp caster
  sugar, plus extra for
  dusting
1 egg
2 drops vanilla essence
15ml/1 tbsp cold water

For the mincemeat

2 eating apples, peeled,
  cored and grated
225g/8oz/generous
  1½ cups raisins

115g/4oz/½ cup dried
  apricots, chopped
115g/4oz/½ cup ready-
  to-eat dried figs or
  prunes, chopped
225g/8oz green grapes,
  halved and seeded
50g/2oz/½ cup chopped
  almonds
finely grated rind of
  1 lemon
30ml/2 tbsp lemon juice
30ml/2 tbsp brandy or
  port
1.5ml/¼ tsp mixed spice
115g/4oz/generous ½ cup
  soft light brown sugar
25g/1oz/2 tbsp butter,
  melted

1 Process the flour, cinnamon, nuts and butter in a food
processor or blender to make fine crumbs. Turn into a bowl
and stir in the sugar. Beat the egg with the vanilla and water
and stir into the dry ingredients. Form a soft dough, knead
until smooth, wrap and chill for 30 minutes.

2 Mix the mincemeat ingredients together. Use two-thirds of
the pastry to line a 23cm/9in, loose-based flan tin. Push the
pastry well into the edges, then trim. Fill with the mincemeat.

3 Roll out the remaining pastry and cut into 1cm/½in strips.
Arrange the strips in a lattice over the top of the pastry, wet
the joins and press them together. Chill for 30 minutes.

4 Preheat a baking sheet in the oven at 190°C/375°F/Gas 5.
Brush the pastry with water and dust with caster sugar. Bake
the tart on the baking sheet for 30–40 minutes. Cool in the tin
on a wire rack for 15 minutes. Then remove the tin.

Crunchy Apple and Almond Flan

Don't put sugar with the apples as this produces too much
liquid. The sweetness is in the pastry and topping.

Serves 8

75g/3oz/6 tbsp butter
175g/6oz/1½ cups plain
  flour
25g/1oz/4 tbsp ground
  almonds
25g/1oz/2 tbsp caster
  sugar
1 egg yolk
15ml/1 tbsp cold water
1.5ml/¼ tsp almond
  essence
6/5g/1½lb cooking apples
25g/1oz/2 tbsp raisins

For the topping

115g/4oz/1 cup plain
  flour
1.5ml/¼ tsp ground
  mixed spice
50g/2oz/4 tbsp butter,
  cut in small cubes
50g/2oz/4 tbsp demerara
  sugar
50g/2oz/½ cup flaked
  almonds

1 To make the pastry, rub the butter into the flour until it
resembles breadcrumbs. Stir in the almonds and sugar. Whisk
the egg yolk, water and almond essence together and mix into
the dry ingredients to form a soft dough. Knead until smooth,
wrap, and leave to rest for 20 minutes.

2 For the topping, sift the flour and spice into a bowl and
rub in the butter. Stir in the sugar and almonds. Roll out the
pastry and use to line a 23cm/9in loose-based flan tin. Trim
the top and chill for 15 minutes.

3 Preheat a baking sheet in the oven at 190°C/375°F/Gas 5.
Peel, core and slice the apples thinly. Arrange in the flan in
overlapping, concentric circles, doming the centre. Sprinkle
with raisins.

4 Cover with the topping mixture, pressing it on lightly.
Bake on the hot baking sheet for 25–30 minutes, or until the
top is golden brown and the apples are tender (test them with
a fine skewer). Leave the flan to cool in the tin for 10 minutes
before serving.

Rhubarb and Cherry Pie

**The unusual partnership of rhubarb and cherries works
well in this pie.**

Serves 8

450g/1lb rhubarb, cut
  into 2.5cm/1in pieces
450g/1lb canned stoned
  tart red or black
  cherries, drained
275g/10oz/scant 1½ cups
  caster sugar
45ml/3 tbsp quick-
  cooking tapioca

For the pastry
275g/10oz/2½ cups plain
  flour
5ml/1 tsp salt
75g/3oz/6 tbsp cold
  butter, cut in pieces
50g/2oz/4 tbsp cold
  vegetable fat or lard,
  cut in pieces
50–120ml/2–4fl oz/
  ¼–½ cup iced water
milk, for glazing

1 For the pastry, sift the flour and salt into a bowl. Add the
butter and fat and rub in until the mixture resembles coarse
breadcrumbs. Stir in enough water to bind. Form into two
balls, wrap and chill for 20 minutes.

2 Preheat a baking sheet in the oven at 200°C/400°F/Gas 6.
Roll out one pastry ball and use to line a 23cm/9in pie dish,
leaving a 1cm/½in overhang.

3 Mix together the filling ingredients and spoon into the
pastry case.

4 Roll out the remaining pastry, cut out four leaf shapes, and
use to cover the pie leaving a 2cm/¾in overhang. Fold this
under the pastry base and flute. Roll small balls from the
scraps, mark veins in the leaves and use to decorate the pie.

5 Glaze the top and bake on the baking sheet until golden,
40–50 minutes.

Festive Apple Pie

Serves 8

900g/2lb cooking apples
15g/½oz/2 tbsp plain
  flour
115g/4oz/generous ½ cup
  caster sugar
25ml/1½ tbsp fresh
  lemon juice
2.5ml/½ tsp ground
  cinnamon
2.5ml/½ tsp mixed spice
1.5ml/¼ tsp ground
  ginger
1.5ml/¼ tsp grated
  nutmeg
1.5ml/¼ tsp salt

50g/2oz/4 tbsp butter,
  diced

For the pastry
275g/10oz/2½ cups plain
  flour
5ml/1 tsp salt
75g/3oz/6 tbsp cold
  butter, cut in pieces
50g/2oz/4 tbsp cold
  vegetable fat or lard,
  cut in pieces
50–120ml/2–
  4fl oz/¼–½ cup iced
  water

1 For the pastry, sift the flour and salt into a bowl. Add the
butter and fat, and rub in until the mixture resembles coarse
breadcrumbs. Stir in just enough water to bind. Form two
balls, wrap and chill for 20 minutes.

2 Roll out one ball and use to line a 23cm/9in pie dish.
Preheat a baking sheet in the oven at 220°C/425°F/Gas 7.

3 Peel, core and slice the apples. Toss with the flour, sugar,
lemon juice, spices and salt. Spoon into the pastry case and
dot with butter.

4 Roll out the remaining pastry. Place on top of the pie and
trim to leave a 2cm/¾in overhang. Fold this under the pastry
base and press to seal. Crimp the edge. Form the scraps into
leaf shapes and balls. Arrange on the pie and cut steam vents.

5 Bake on the baking sheet for 10 minutes. Reduce the heat
to 180°C/350°F/Gas 4 and bake for 40 minutes, until golden.

Black Bottom Pie

Serves 8

10ml/2 tsp gelatine
45ml/3 tbsp cold water
2 eggs, separated
150g/5oz/¾ cup caster
 sugar
15g/½oz/2 tbsp cornflour
2.5ml/½ tsp salt
475ml/16fl oz/2 cups
 milk
50g/2oz plain chocolate,
 finely chopped

30ml/2 tbsp rum
1.5ml/¼ tsp cream of
 tartar
chocolate curls, to
 decorate

For the crust
175g/6oz/2 cups
 gingernuts, crushed
65g/2½oz/5 tbsp butter,
 melted

1 Preheat the oven to 180°C/350°F/Gas 4. Mix the crushed
gingernuts and melted butter. Press evenly over the base and
side of a 23cm/9in pie plate. Bake for 6 minutes. Sprinkle the
gelatine over the water and leave to soften.

2 Beat the egg yolks in a large mixing bowl and set aside. In
a saucepan, combine half the sugar, the cornflour and salt.
Gradually stir in the milk. Boil for 1 minute, stirring
constantly. Whisk the hot milk mixture into the yolks, pour
back into the saucepan and return to the boil, whisking. Cook
for 1 minute, still whisking. Remove from the heat.

3 Pour 225g/8oz of the custard mixture into a bowl. Add the
chopped chocolate and stir until melted. Stir in half the rum
and pour into the pie crust. Whisk the softened gelatine into
the plain custard until dissolved, then stir in the remaining
rum. Set the pan in cold water to reach room temperature.

4 Beat the egg whites and cream of tartar until they peak
stiffly. Add the remaining sugar gradually, beating
thoroughly after each addition. Fold the custard into the egg
whites, then spoon over the chocolate mixture in the pie crust.
Chill until set, about 2 hours. Decorate with chocolate curls.

Pumpkin Pie

A North American classic, this pie is traditionally served at
Thanksgiving.

Serves 8

40g/1½oz/scant ½ cup
 pecan nuts, chopped
250g/9oz puréed
 pumpkin
475ml/16fl oz/2 cups
 single cream
130g/4½oz/¾ cup light
 brown sugar
1.5ml/¼ tsp salt
5ml/1 tsp ground
 cinnamon
2.5ml/½ tsp ground
 ginger

1.5ml/¼ tsp ground
 cloves
1.5ml/¼ tsp grated
 nutmeg
2 eggs

For the pastry
165g/5½oz/1⅓ cups plain
 flour
2.5ml/½ tsp salt
115g/4oz/½ cup lard or
 vegetable fat
30 – 45ml/2 – 3 tbsp iced
 water

1 Preheat the oven to 220°C/425°F/Gas 7. For the pastry, sift
the flour and salt into a mixing bowl. Rub in the fat until the
mixture resembles coarse breadcrumbs. Sprinkle in enough
water to form the mixture into a ball.

2 Roll out the pastry to a 5mm/¼in thickness. Use to line a
23cm/9in pie tin. Trim and flute the edge. Sprinkle the
chopped pecan nuts over the base of the case.

3 Beat together the pumpkin, cream, sugar, salt, spices and
eggs. Pour the pumpkin mixture into the pastry case. Bake for
10 minutes, then reduce the heat to 180°C/350°F/Gas 4 and
continue baking until the filling is set, about 45 minutes.
Leave the pie to cool in the tin, set on a wire rack.

Chocolate Nut Tart

This is a sophisticated tart – strictly for grown-ups!

Serves 6–8

225g/8oz sweet shortcrust pastry	45ml/3 tbsp sugar
200g/7oz/1¼ cups dry amaretti biscuits	200g/7oz plain cooking chocolate
90g/3½oz/⅔ cup blanched almonds	45ml/3 tbsp milk
50g/2oz/½ cup blanched hazelnuts	50g/2oz/4 tbsp butter
	45ml/3 tbsp amaretto liqueur or brandy
	30ml/2 tbsp single cream

1 Grease a shallow loose-based 25cm/10in tart tin. Roll out the pastry and use to line the tin. Trim the edge, prick the base with a fork and chill for 30 minutes.

2 Grind the amaretti biscuits in a blender or food processor. Tip into a mixing bowl. Set eight whole almonds aside and place the rest in the food processor or blender with the hazelnuts and sugar. Grind to a medium texture. Add the nuts to the amaretti, and mix well.

3 Preheat the oven to 190°C/375°F/Gas 5. In the top of a double boiler, melt the chocolate with the milk and butter. Stir until smooth.

4 Pour the chocolate mixture into the dry ingredients, and mix well. Add the liqueur or brandy and cream.

5 Spread the filling evenly in the pastry case. Bake for 35 minutes, or until the crust is golden brown and the filling has puffed up and is beginning to darken. Allow to cool to room temperature. Split the reserved almonds in half and use to decorate the tart.

Pecan Nut Tartlets

These delightful individual tartlets make an elegant dinner-party dessert.

Makes 6 10cm/4in tartlets

450g/1lb shortcrust pastry	275g/10oz/1¼ cups golden syrup
175g/6oz/1 cup pecan nut halves	2.5ml/½ tsp vanilla essence
3 eggs, beaten	115g/4oz/generous ½ cup caster sugar
25g/1oz/2 tbsp butter, melted	15ml/1 tbsp plain flour

1 Preheat the oven to 180°C/350°F/Gas 4. Roll out the pastry and use to line 6 10cm/4in tartlet tins. Divide the pecan nut halves between the pastry cases.

2 Combine the eggs with the butter, and add the golden syrup and vanilla essence. Sift over the caster sugar and flour, and blend. Fill the pastry cases with the mixture and leave until the nuts rise to the surface.

3 Bake for 35–40 minutes, until a skewer inserted in the centre comes out clean. Cool in the tins for 15 minutes, then turn out on to a wire rack.

Pear and Hazelnut Flan

A delicious flan for Sunday lunch. Grind the hazelnuts yourself if you prefer, or use ground almonds instead.

Serves 6 – 8

115g/4oz/1 cup plain
    flour
115g/4oz/¾ cup
    wholemeal flour
115g/4oz/½ cup
    sunflower margarine
45ml/3 tbsp cold water

For the filling
50g/2oz/½ cup self-
    raising flour
115g/4oz/1 cup ground
    hazelnuts

5ml/1 tsp vanilla essence
50g/2oz/4 tbsp caster
    sugar
50g/2oz/4 tbsp butter,
    softened
2 eggs, beaten
45ml/3 tbsp raspberry
    jam
400g/14oz can pears in
    natural juice
few chopped hazelnuts, to
    decorate

1 For the pastry, stir the flours together, then rub in the margarine until the mixture resembles fine breadcrumbs. Mix to a firm dough with the water.

2 Roll out the dough and use to line a 23–25cm/9–10in flan tin, pressing it up the sides after trimming, so the pastry sits a little above the tin. Prick the base, line with greaseproof paper and fill with baking beans. Chill for 30 minutes.

3 Preheat the oven to 200°C/400°F/Gas 6. Place the flan tin on a baking sheet and bake blind for 20 minutes. Remove the paper and beans after 15 minutes.

4 Beat all the filling ingredients together except for the jam and pears. If too thick, stir in some of the pear juice. Reduce the oven temperature to 180°C/350°F/Gas 4. Spread the jam on the pastry case and spoon over the filling.

5 Drain the pears and arrange them, cut-side down, in the filling. Scatter over the nuts. Bake for 30 minutes until risen, firm and golden brown.

Latticed Peaches

This elegant dessert may be prepared using canned peach halves when fresh peaches are out of season.

Serves 6
For the pastry
115g/4oz/1 cup plain
    flour
45ml/3 tbsp butter or
    sunflower margarine
45ml/3 tbsp natural
    yogurt
30ml/2 tbsp orange juice
milk, to glaze

For the filling
3 ripe peaches

45ml/3 tbsp ground
    almonds
30ml/2 tbsp natural
    yogurt
finely grated rind of
    1 small orange
1.5ml/¼ tsp almond
    essence

For the sauce
1 ripe peach
45ml/3 tbsp orange juice

1 Lightly grease a baking sheet. Sift the flour into a bowl and rub in the butter or margarine. Stir in the yogurt and orange juice to make a firm dough. Roll out half the pastry thinly and stamp out six rounds with a 7.5cm/3in biscuit cutter.

2 Skin the peaches, halve and remove the stones. Mix together the almonds, yogurt, orange rind and almond essence. Spoon into the hollows of each peach half and place, cut-side down, on the pastry rounds.

3 Roll out the remaining pastry thinly and cut into thin strips. Arrange the strips over the peaches to form a lattice, brushing with milk to secure firmly. Trim the ends. Chill for 30 minutes. Preheat the oven to 200°C/400°F/ Gas 6. Brush with milk and bake for 15–18 minutes, until golden brown.

4 For the sauce, skin the peach and halve it to remove the stone. Place the flesh in a food processor or blender, with the orange juice, and purée until smooth. Serve the peaches hot, with the peach sauce spooned around.

Surprise Fruit Tarts

These delicious and simple little tarts are the perfect summer treat.

Serves 6

4 large or 8 small sheets
  frozen filo pastry,
  thawed
65g/2½oz/5 tbsp butter
  or margarine, melted
250ml/8fl oz/1 cup
  whipping cream
45ml/3 tbsp strawberry
  jam
15ml/1 tbsp Cointreau or
  other orange-flavour
  liqueur
115g/4oz/1 cup seedless
  black grapes, halved

115g/4oz/1 cup seedless
  white grapes, halved
150g/5oz fresh pineapple,
  cubed, or drained
  canned pineapple
  chunks
115g/4oz/⅔ cup
  raspberries
30ml/2 tbsp icing sugar
6 sprigs fresh mint, to
  decorate

1 Preheat the oven to 180°C/350°F/Gas 4. Grease six cups of a bun tray. Stack the filo sheets and cut with a sharp knife or scissors into 24 squares 11cm/4½in.

2 Lay four squares of pastry in each of the six greased cups. Press the pastry firmly into the cups, rotating slightly to make star-shaped baskets. Brush the pastry baskets lightly with butter or margarine. Bake until the pastry is crisp and golden, 5–7 minutes. Cool on a wire rack.

3 In a bowl, lightly whip the cream until soft peaks form. Gently fold the strawberry jam and Cointreau into the cream.

4 Just before serving, spoon a little of the cream mixture into each pastry basket. Top with the fruit. Sprinkle with icing sugar and decorate each basket with a small sprig of mint.

Truffle Filo Tarts

The cups can be prepared a day ahead and stored in an air-tight container.

Makes 24 cups

3–6 sheets fresh or
  frozen (thawed) filo
  pastry, depending on
  size
45g/1½oz/3 tbsp unsalted
  butter, melted
sugar, for sprinkling
lemon rind, to decorate

Truffle mixture
250ml/8fl oz/1 cup
  double cream
225g/8oz bittersweet or
  semi-sweet chocolate,
  chopped
50g/2oz/4 tbsp unsalted
  butter, cut into pieces
30ml/2 tbsp brandy

1 Prepare the truffle mixture. In a saucepan over medium heat, bring the cream to the boil. Remove from the heat and add the chocolate, stirring until melted. Beat in the butter and add the brandy. Sieve into a bowl and chill for 1 hour.

2 Preheat the oven to 200°C/400°F/Gas 6. Grease a bun tray with 24 cups, each 4cm/1½in. Cut each filo sheet into 6cm/2½in squares. Cover with a damp dish towel. Keeping the filo sheets covered, place one square on a work surface. Brush lightly with melted butter, turn over and brush the other side. Sprinkle with a pinch of sugar. Butter another square and place it over the first at an angle. Sprinkle with sugar. Butter a third square and place over the first two, unevenly, so the corners form an uneven edge. Press the layered square into the tray. Continue to fill the tray.

3 Bake the filo cups for 4–6 minutes, until golden. Cool for 10 minutes on a wire rack in the tray. Remove from the tray and cool completely.

4 Stir the chocolate mixture, which should be just thick enough to pipe. Spoon the mixture into a piping bag fitted with a medium star nozzle and pipe a swirl into each cup. Decorate with lemon rind.

Apple Strudel

Ready-made filo pastry makes a good substitute for paper-thin strudel pastry in this classic Austrian dish.

Serves 10–12

75g/3oz/generous ½ cup
   raisins
30ml/2 tbsp brandy
5 eating apples
3 large cooking apples
90g/3½oz/generous ½
   cup dark brown sugar
5ml/1 tsp ground
   cinnamon
grated rind and juice of
   1 lemon

25g/1oz/½ cup dry
   breadcrumbs
50g/2oz/½ cup chopped
   pecan nuts or walnuts
12 sheets frozen filo
   pastry, thawed
175g/6oz/¾ cup butter,
   melted
icing sugar, for dusting

1 Soak the raisins in the brandy for 15 minutes.

2 Peel, core and thinly slice the apples. Combine with the rest of the filling ingredients, reserving half the breadcrumbs.

3 Preheat the oven to 190°C/375°F/Gas 5. Grease two baking sheets. Unfold the filo pastry and cover with a dish towel. One by one, butter and stack the sheets to make a six-sheet pile.

4 Sprinkle half the reserved breadcrumbs over the last sheet and spoon half the apple mixture at the bottom edge. Roll up from this edge, Swiss roll style. Place on a baking sheet, seam-side down and fold under the ends to seal. Repeat to make a second strudel. Brush both with butter.

5 Bake in the oven for 45 minutes, cool slightly, then dust with icing sugar.

Cherry Strudel

A refreshing variation on traditional apple strudel. Serve with whipped cream, if you like.

Serves 8

65g/2½oz/1¼ cups fresh
   breadcrumbs
175g/6oz/¾ cup butter,
   melted
200g/7oz/1 cup sugar
15ml/1 tbsp ground
   cinnamon

5ml/1 tsp grated lemon
   rind
450g/1lb/2 cups sour
   cherries, stoned
8 sheets filo pastry
icing sugar, for dusting

1 In a frying pan, fry the breadcrumbs in 65g/2½oz/5 tbsp of the butter until golden. Set aside.

2 In a large mixing bowl, toss together the sugar, cinnamon and lemon rind. Stir in the cherries.

3 Preheat the oven to 190°C/375°F/Gas 5. Grease a baking sheet. Unfold the filo sheets. Keep the unused sheets covered with damp kitchen paper. Lift off one sheet and place on a piece of greaseproof paper. Brush the pastry with butter. Sprinkle an eighth of the breadcrumbs over the surface.

4 Lay a second sheet of filo pastry on top, brush with butter and sprinkle with breadcrumbs. Continue until you have used up all the pastry.

5 Spoon the cherry mixture at the bottom edge of the strip. Starting at the cherry-filled end, roll up the dough Swiss roll style. Use the paper to flip the strudel on to the baking sheet, seam-side down. Carefully fold under the ends to seal. Brush the top with melted butter.

6 Bake the strudel for 45 minutes. Cool slightly, then dust with a fine layer of icing sugar.

Strawberry Tart

This tart is best assembled just before serving, but you can bake the pastry case and make the filling ahead.

Serves 6

350g/12oz rough-puff or puff pastry
225g/8oz/1 cup cream cheese
grated rind of ½ orange
30ml/2 tbsp orange liqueur or juice

45–60ml/3–4 tbsp icing sugar, plus extra for dusting (optional)
450g/1lb/4 cups ripe strawberries, hulled

1 Preheat the oven to 200°C/400°F/Gas 6. Roll out the pastry to about a 3mm/⅛in thickness and use to line a 28 x 10cm/11 x 4in rectangular flan tin. Trim the edges, then chill for 30 minutes.

2 Prick the base of the pastry all over. Line with foil, fill with baking beans and bake for 15 minutes. Remove the foil and beans and bake for 10 minutes, until the pastry is browned. Gently press down on the pastry base to deflate, then leave to cool on a wire rack.

3 Beat together the cheese, orange rind, liqueur or orange juice and icing sugar to taste. Spread the cheese filling in the pastry case. Halve the strawberries and arrange them on top of the filling. Dust with icing sugar, if you like.

Alsatian Plum Tart

Fruit and custard tarts, similar to a fruit quiche, are typical in Alsace. Sometimes they have a yeast dough base instead of pastry. You can use other seasonal fruits in this tart, or a mixture of fruit.

Serves 6–8

450g/1lb ripe plums, halved and stoned
30ml/2 tbsp kirsch or plum brandy
350g/12oz shortcrust or sweet shortcrust pastry
30ml/2 tbsp seedless raspberry jam

For the custard filling
2 eggs
25g/1oz/4 tbsp icing sugar
175ml/6 fl oz/¾ cup double cream
grated rind of ½ lemon
1.5ml/¼ tsp vanilla essence

1 Preheat the oven to 200°C/400°F/Gas 6. Mix the plums with the kirsch or brandy and set aside for about 30 minutes.

2 Roll out the pastry thinly and use to line a 23cm/9in pie tin. Prick the base of the pastry case all over and line with foil. Add a layer of baking beans and bake for 15 minutes until slightly dry and set. Remove the foil and the baking beans.

3 Brush the base of the pastry case with a thin layer of jam, then bake for a further 5 minutes. Remove the pastry case from the oven and transfer to a wire rack. Reduce the oven temperature to 180°C/350°F/Gas 4.

4 To make the custard filling, beat the eggs and sugar until well combined, then beat in the cream, lemon rind, vanilla and any juice from the plums.

5 Arrange the plums, cut-side down, in the pastry case and pour over the custard mixture. Bake for about 30–35 minutes until a knife inserted in the centre comes out clean. Serve the tart warm or at room temperature.

Almond Mincemeat Tartlets

Makes 36

275g/10oz/2½ cups plain
  flour
75g/3oz/¾ cup icing
  sugar
5ml/1 tsp ground
  cinnamon
175g/6oz/¾ cup butter
50g/2oz/½ cup ground
  almonds
1 egg yolk
45ml/3 tbsp milk
450g/1lb jar mincemeat
15ml/1 tbsp brandy or
  rum

For the lemon filling
115g/4oz/½ cup butter or
  margarine
115g/4oz/½ cup caster
  sugar
175g/6oz/1½ cups self-
  raising flour
2 large eggs
finely grated rind of
  1 large lemon

For the lemon icing
115g/4oz/1 cup icing
  sugar
15ml/1 tbsp lemon juice

1 Sift the flour, sugar and cinnamon into a bowl and rub in the butter until it resembles breadcrumbs. Add the ground almonds and bind with the egg yolk and milk to a soft, pliable dough. Knead until smooth, wrap and chill for 30 minutes.

2 Preheat the oven to 375°F/190°C/Gas 5. On a lightly floured surface, roll out the pastry and cut out 36 fluted rounds with a pastry cutter. Mix the mincemeat with the brandy or rum and put a small teaspoonful in the bottom of each pastry case. Chill.

3 For the lemon sponge filling, whisk the butter or margarine, sugar, flour, eggs and lemon rind together until smooth. Spoon on top of the mincemeat, dividing it evenly, and level the tops. Bake for 20–30 minutes, or until golden brown and springy to the touch. Remove and leave to cool on a wire rack.

4 For the lemon icing, sift the icing sugar and mix with the lemon juice to a smooth coating consistency. Spoon into a piping bag and drizzle a zig-zag pattern over each tart. If you're short of time, simply dust the tartlets with icing sugar.

Mince Pies with Orange Pastry

Homemade mince pies are so much nicer than shop-bought, especially with this flavoursome pastry.

Makes 18

225g/8oz/2 cups plain
  flour
30g/1½oz/scant ⅓ cup
  icing sugar
10ml/2 tsp ground
  cinnamon
150g/5oz/generous 1 cup
  butter

grated rind of 1 orange
about 60ml/4 tbsp iced
  water
225g/8oz/1½ cups
  mincemeat
1 egg, beaten, to glaze
icing sugar, for dusting

1 Sift together the flour, icing sugar and cinnamon. Rub in the butter until it resembles fine breadcrumbs. Stir in the grated orange rind.

2 Mix to a firm dough with the water. Knead lightly, then roll out to a 5mm/¼in thickness. Using a 7cm/2½in round biscuit cutter, stamp out 18 circles, then stamp out 18 smaller 5cm/2in circles.

3 Line two bun tins with the larger circles. Place a small spoonful of mincemeat into each pastry case and top with the smaller pastry circles, pressing the edges to seal.

4 Glaze the tops with egg and leave to rest in the fridge for 30 minutes. Preheat the oven to 200°C/400°F/Gas 6.

5 Bake for 15–20 minutes, or until golden brown. Remove to wire racks. Serve just warm, dusted with icing sugar.

Glacé Fruit Pie

Use half digestive and half gingernut biscuits for the crust, if you prefer.

Serves 10

15ml/1 tbsp rum
50g/2oz/4 tbsp mixed
  glacé fruit, chopped
475ml/16fl oz/2 cups
  milk
20ml/4 tsp gelatine
90g/3½oz/½ cup sugar
2.5ml/½ tsp salt
3 eggs, separated
250ml/8fl oz/1 cup
  whipping cream,
  whipped

chocolate curls, to
  decorate

For the crust

175g/6oz/2 cups
  digestive biscuits,
  crushed
75g/2½oz/5 tbsp butter,
  melted
15ml/1 tbsp sugar

1 Mix the digestive biscuits, butter and sugar. Press evenly over the base and sides of a 23cm/9in pie plate. Chill.

2 Stir together the rum and glacé fruit. Set aside. Pour 120ml/4fl oz/½ cup of the milk into a small bowl. Sprinkle over the gelatine and leave for 5 minutes to soften.

3 In the top of a double boiler, combine 50g/2oz/4 tbsp of the sugar, the remaining milk and salt. Stir in the gelatine mixture. Cook, stirring, until the gelatine dissolves. Whisk in the egg yolks and cook, stirring, until thick enough to coat the spoon. Pour the custard over the glacé fruit mixture, set in a bowl of iced water.

4 Beat the egg whites until they peak softly. Add the remaining sugar and beat just to blend. Fold a large dollop of the egg whites into the cooled gelatine mixture. Pour into the remaining egg whites and fold together. Fold in the cream.

5 Pour into the pie crust and chill until firm. Decorate with chocolate curls.

Chocolate Chiffon Pie

As the name suggests, this is a wonderfully smooth and light-textured pie.

Serves 8

200g/7oz plain chocolate,
  chopped
250ml/8fl oz/1 cup milk
15ml/1 tbsp gelatine
90g/3½oz/1 cup sugar
2 extra-large eggs,
  separated
5ml/1 tsp vanilla essence
1.5ml/¼ tsp salt
350ml/12fl oz/1½ cups
  whipping cream,
  whipped

whipped cream and
  chocolate curls, to
  decorate

For the crust

200g/7oz/2⅓ cups
  digestive biscuits,
  crushed
75g/3oz/6 tbsp butter,
  melted

1 Place a baking sheet in the oven and preheat to 180°C/350°F/Gas 4. Mix the biscuits and butter together and press over the base and sides of a 23cm/9in pie plate. Bake for 8 minutes.

2 Grate the chocolate in a blender or food processor. Place the milk in the top of a double boiler. Sprinkle over the gelatine and leave for 5 minutes to soften.

3 In the top of a double boiler, put 40g/1½oz/6 tbsp sugar, the chocolate and egg yolks. Stir until dissolved. Add the vanilla. Place the top in a bowl of ice and stir until the mixture reaches room temperature. Remove from the ice.

4 Beat the egg whites and salt until they peak softly. Add the remaining sugar and beat just to blend. Fold a dollop of egg whites into the chocolate mixture, then pour back into the whites and fold in.

5 Fold in the cream and pour into the pie crust. Freeze until just set, about 5 minutes, then chill for 3–4 hours. Decorate with whipped cream and chocolate curls.

Chocolate Pear Tart

Chocolate and pears have a natural affinity, well used in this luxurious pudding.

Serves 8

115g/4oz plain chocolate, grated	**For the pastry**
3 large firm, ripe pears	150g/5oz/1¼ cups plain flour
1 egg	1.5ml/¼ tsp salt
1 egg yolk	30ml/2 tbsp sugar
120ml/4fl oz/½ cup single cream	115g/4oz/½ cup cold unsalted butter, cut into pieces
2.5ml/½ tsp vanilla essence	1 egg yolk
45ml/3 tbsp caster sugar	15ml/1 tbsp lemon juice

1 For the pastry, sift the flour and salt into a bowl. Add the sugar and butter. Rub in until the mixture resembles coarse breadcrumbs. Stir in the egg yolk and lemon juice. Form a ball, wrap, and chill for 20 minutes.

2 Preheat the oven to 200℃/400℉/Gas 6. Roll out the pastry and use to line a 25cm/10in tart dish.

3 Sprinkle the pastry case with the grated chocolate.

4 Peel, halve and core the pears. Cut in thin slices crossways, then fan out slightly. Transfer the pears to the tart using a palette knife and arrange like wheel spokes.

5 Whisk together the egg and egg yolk, cream and vanilla. Ladle over the pears and sprinkle with sugar.

6 Bake on a baking sheet for 10 minutes. Reduce the heat to 180℃/350℉/Gas 4 and cook until the custard is set and the pears begin to caramelize, about 20 minutes more. Serve while still warm.

Pear and Apple Crumble Pie

You could use just one fruit in this pie if you prefer.

Serves 8

3 firm pears	5ml/1 tsp ground cinnamon
4 cooking apples	75g/3oz/6 tbsp cold butter, cut in pieces
175g/6oz/scant 1 cup caster sugar	
30ml/2 tbsp cornflour	
1.5ml/¼ tsp salt	**For the pastry**
grated rind of 1 lemon	150g/5oz/1¼ cups plain flour
30ml/2 tbsp fresh lemon juice	2.5ml/½ tsp salt
75g/3oz/generous ½ cup raisins	65g/2½oz/5 tbsp cold vegetable fat or lard, cut in pieces
75g/3oz/¾ cup plain flour	30ml/2 tbsp iced water

1 For the pastry, sift the flour and salt into a bowl. Add the fat and rub in until the mixture resembles breadcrumbs. Stir in enough water to bind. Form into a ball, roll out, and use to line a 23cm/9in pie dish, leaving a 1cm/½in overhang. Fold this under for double thickness. Flute the edge, then chill.

2 Preheat a baking sheet at 230℃/450℉/Gas 8. Peel, core and slice the fruit. Combine in a bowl with one-third of the sugar, the cornflour, salt, lemon rind and juice, and raisins.

3 For the crumble topping, combine the remaining sugar, flour, cinnamon and butter in a bowl. Rub in until the mixture resembles coarse breadcrumbs.

4 Spoon the filling into the pastry case. Sprinkle the crumbs over the top.

5 Bake on the baking sheet for 10 minutes, then reduce the heat to 180℃/350℉/Gas 4. Cover the pie loosely with foil and bake until browned, 35–40 minutes more.

Chocolate Lemon Tart

The unusual chocolate pastry complements the lemon filling superbly in this rich tart.

Serves 8–10

245g/8¾oz/1¼ cups
  caster sugar
6 eggs
grated rind of 2 lemons
160ml/5½fl oz/generous
  ⅔ cup fresh lemon
  juice
160ml/5½fl oz/generous
  ⅔ cup whipping cream
chocolate curls, to
  decorate

For the pastry
180g/6¼oz/generous
  1½ cups plain flour
30ml/2 tbsp cocoa
  powder
25g/1oz/4 tbsp icing
  sugar
2.5ml/½ tsp salt
115g/4oz/½ cup butter or
  margarine
15ml/1 tbsp water

1 Grease a 25cm/10in tart tin. For the pastry, sift the flour, cocoa powder, icing sugar and salt into a bowl. Set aside.

2 Melt the butter and water over a low heat. Pour over the flour mixture and stir until the dough is smooth.

3 Press the dough evenly over the base and sides of the tart tin. Chill while preparing the filling.

4 Preheat a baking sheet in the oven at 190°C/375°F/Gas 5. Whisk the sugar and eggs until the sugar is dissolved. Add the lemon rind and juice and mix well. Add the cream.

5 Pour the filling into the pastry case and bake on the hot baking sheet until the filling is set, 20–25 minutes. Cool on a wire rack, then decorate with chocolate curls.

Kiwi Ricotta Cheese Tart

A delicious filling in a rich pastry case creates an elegant dinner-party dessert.

Serves 8

75g/3oz/½ cup blanched
  almonds, ground
130g/3½ oz/½ cup sugar
900g/2lb/4 cups
  ricotta cheese
250ml/8fl oz/1 cup
  whipping cream
1 egg and 3 egg yolks
15ml/1 tbsp plain flour
pinch of salt
30ml/2 tbsp rum
grated rind of 1 lemon
30ml/2 tbsp lemon juice

30ml/2 tbsp honey
5 kiwi fruit

For the pastry
150g/5oz/1¼ cups
  plain flour
15ml/1 tbsp sugar
2.5ml/½ tsp each salt and
  baking powder
75g/3oz/6 tbsp butter
1 egg yolk
45–60ml/3–4 tbsp
  whipping cream

1 For the pastry, mix the flour, sugar, salt and baking powder. Add the butter and rub in. Mix in the egg yolk and cream to bind the pastry. Wrap and chill for 30 minutes.

2 Preheat the oven to 220°C/425°F/Gas 7. On a lightly floured surface, roll out the dough to a 3mm/⅛in thickness. Use to line a 23cm/9in springform tin. Prick the pastry all over with a fork. Line with crumpled greaseproof paper and fill with dried beans. Bake for 10 minutes. Remove the paper and beans and bake for another 6–8 minutes until golden. Reduce the oven temperature to 180°C/350°F/Gas 4.

3 Mix the almonds with 15ml/1 tbsp of the sugar. Beat the ricotta until creamy then add the cream, egg, yolks, remaining sugar, flour, salt, rum, lemon rind and 30ml/2 tbsp lemon juice. Beat, add the almonds and mix. Pour into pastry case and bake for 1 hour, until golden. Cool and chill. Mix the honey and remaining lemon juice. Halve the kiwis lengthways then slice. Arrange over tart and brush with the honey glaze.

Lime Tart

Use lemons instead of limes, with yellow food colouring, if
you prefer.

Serves 8
3 large egg yolks
400g/14oz can sweetened
  condensed milk
15ml/1 tbsp grated lime
  rind
120ml/4fl oz/½ cup fresh
  lime juice
green food colouring
  (optional)

120ml/4fl oz/½ cup
  whipping cream

For the base
115g/4oz/1⅓ cups
  crushed digestive
  biscuits
65g/2½oz/5 tbsp butter
  or margarine, melted

1 Preheat the oven to 180°C/350°F/Gas 4. For the base, place
the crushed biscuits in a bowl and add the butter or
margarine. Mix to combine.

2 Press the mixture evenly over the base and sides of a
23cm/9in pie dish. Bake for 8 minutes, then cool.

3 Beat the yolks until thick. Beat in the milk, lime rind and
juice and colouring, if using. Pour into the pastry case and
chill until set, about 4 hours. To serve, whip the cream. Pipe a
lattice pattern on top, or spoon dollops around the edge.

Fruit Tartlets

You could make one large fruit tart for an elegant dessert, if
you like.

Makes 8
175ml/6fl oz/¾ cup
  redcurrant jelly
15ml/1 tbsp fresh lemon
  juice
175ml/6fl oz/¾ cup
  whipping cream
675g/1½lb fresh fruit,
  such as strawberries,
  raspberries, kiwi fruit,
  peaches, grapes or
  currants, peeled and
  sliced as necessary

For the pastry
150g/5oz/generous ½ cup
  cold butter, cut in
  pieces
65g/2½oz/scant ½ cup
  dark brown sugar
45ml/3 tbsp cocoa
  powder
200g/7oz/1¾ cups plain
  flour
1 egg white

1 For the pastry, melt the butter, brown sugar and cocoa
over a low heat. Remove from the heat and sift over the flour.
Stir, then add enough egg white to bind. Form into a ball,
wrap, and chill for 30 minutes.

2 Grease eight 8cm/3in tartlet tins. Roll out the pastry
between two sheets of greaseproof paper. Stamp out eight
10cm/4in rounds with a fluted biscuit cutter.

3 Line the tartlet tins and prick the bases with a fork. Chill
for 15 minutes. Preheat the oven to 180°C/350°F/Gas 4.

4 Bake the pastry cases until firm, 20–25 minutes. Cool, then
turn out.

5 Melt the jelly with the lemon juice. Brush over the tartlet
bases. Whip the cream and spread thinly in the tartlet cases.
Arrange the fruit on top. Brush with the jelly glaze and serve.

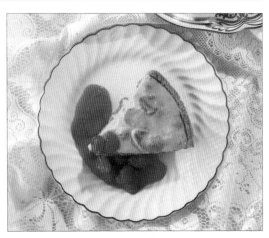

Chocolate Cheesecake Tart

You can use just digestive biscuits for the base of this tart, if you prefer.

Serves 8

350g/12oz/1½ cups
   cream cheese
60ml/4 tbsp whipping
   cream
225g/8oz/generous 1 cup
   caster sugar
50g/2oz/½ cup cocoa
   powder
2.5ml/½ tsp ground
   cinnamon
3 eggs

whipped cream and
   chocolate curls, to
   decorate

For the base
75g/3oz/1 cup crushed
   digestive biscuits
40g/1½oz/scant 1 cup
   crushed amaretti
   biscuits
75g/3oz/6 tbsp butter,
   melted

1 Preheat a baking sheet in the oven at 180°C/350°F/Gas 4. For the base, mix the crushed biscuits and butter in a bowl. Press the mixture over the base and sides of a 23cm/9in pie dish. Bake for 8 minutes. Leave to cool. Keep the oven on.

2 Beat the cream cheese and cream together until smooth. Beat in the sugar, cocoa and cinnamon until blended.

3 Add the eggs, one at a time, beating just enough to blend.

4 Pour into the biscuit base and bake on the baking sheet for 25–30 minutes. The filling will sink down as it cools. Decorate with whipped cream and chocolate curls.

Frozen Strawberry Tart

For a frozen raspberry tart, use raspberries in place of the strawberries.

Serves 8

225g/8oz/1 cup cream
   cheese
250ml/8fl oz/1 cup
   soured cream
500g/1¼lb/5 cups frozen
   strawberries, thawed
   and sliced

For the base
115g/4oz/1⅓ cups
   crushed digestive
   biscuits
15ml/1 tbsp caster sugar
65g/2½oz/5 tbsp butter,
   melted

1 For the base, mix together the biscuits, sugar and butter. Press the mixture over the base and sides of a 23cm/9in pie dish. Freeze until firm.

2 Blend together the cream cheese and soured cream. Reserve 90ml/6 tbsp of the strawberries. Add the rest to the cream cheese mixture.

3 Pour the filling into the biscuit base and freeze until firm, about 6–8 hours. To serve, spoon some of the reserved strawberries on top.

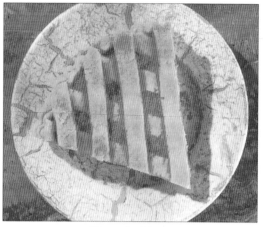

Treacle Tart

A very rich dessert, popular with all the family.

Serves 4–6

*175ml/6fl oz/¾ cup
  golden syrup
75g/3oz/1½ cups fresh
  white breadcrumbs
grated rind of 1 lemon
30ml/2 tbsp fresh lemon
  juice*

For the pastry
*175g/6oz/1½ cups plain
  flour
2.5ml/½ tsp salt
75g/3oz/6 tbsp cold
  butter, cut in pieces
40g/1½oz/3 tbsp cold
  margarine, cut in
  pieces
45–60ml/3–4 tbsp iced
  water*

1 For the pastry, sift together the flour and salt, add the fats and rub in until the mixture resembles coarse breadcrumbs. Stir in enough water to bind. Form into a ball, wrap and chill for 20 minutes.

2 Roll out the pastry and use to line a 20cm/8in pie dish. Chill for 20 minutes. Reserve the pastry trimmings.

3 Preheat a baking sheet in the oven at 200°C/400°F/Gas 6. In a saucepan, warm the syrup until thin and runny. Stir in the breadcrumbs and lemon rind. Leave for 10 minutes, then stir in the lemon juice. Spread in the pastry case.

4 Roll out the pastry trimmings and cut into 12 thin strips. Lay six strips on the filling, then lay the other six at an angle over them to form a lattice.

5 Bake on the baking sheet for 10 minutes. Lower the heat to 190°C/375°F/Gas 5. Bake until golden, about 15 minutes more. Serve warm or cold.

Almond Syrup Tart

Serves 6

*75g/3oz/1½ cups fresh
  white breadcrumbs
225g/8oz/1 cup golden
  syrup
finely grated rind of
  ½ lemon
10ml/2 tsp lemon juice
23cm/9in pastry case,
  made with basic, nut
  or rich shortcrust
  pastry*

*25g/1oz/4 tbsp flaked
  almonds
milk, to glaze (optional)
cream, custard, ice
  cream, to serve*

1 Preheat the oven to 200°C/400°F/Gas 6. Combine the breadcrumbs with the syrup and the lemon rind and juice.

2 Spoon into the pastry case and spread out evenly. Sprinkle the flaked almonds evenly over the top.

3 Brush the pastry with milk to glaze, if you like. Bake for 25–30 minutes, until the pastry and filling are golden brown.

4 Transfer to a wire rack to cool. Serve warm or cold, with cream, custard or ice cream.

Tarte Tatin

A special *tarte tatin* tin is ideal, but an ovenproof frying pan can be used quite successfully.

Serves 8–10

225g/½lb puff or
  shortcrust pastry
10–12 large Golden
  Delicious apples
115g/4oz/½ cup butter,
  cut into pieces

115g/4oz/½ cup
  caster sugar
2.5ml/½ tsp ground
  cinnamon
crème fraîche or whipped
  cream, to serve

1 On a lightly floured surface, roll out the pastry to a 28cm/11in round less than 5mm/¼in thick. Transfer to a lightly floured baking sheet and chill.

2 Peel, halve and core the apples, sprinkle with lemon juice.

3 In a 25cm/10in *tarte tatin* tin, cook the butter, sugar and cinnamon until the butter has melted and the sugar has dissolved. Cook for 6–8 minutes until the mixture is a medium caramel colour. Remove from the heat and arrange the apple halves, standing on their edges, in the tin.

4 Return the tin to the heat and simmer for 20–25 minutes until the apples are tender and coloured. Remove from the heat and cool slightly.

5 Preheat the oven to 230°C/450°F/Gas 8. Place the pastry over the apples and tuck the edges inside the tin around the apples. Pierce the pastry in two or three places, then bake for 25–30 minutes until the pastry is golden and the filling is bubbling. Cool in the tin for 10–15 minutes.

6 To serve, run a sharp knife around the edge of the tin to loosen the pastry. Cover with a serving plate and carefully invert the tin and plate together. It is best to do this over a sink in case any caramel drips. Lift off the tin and loosen any apples that stick with a palette knife. Serve the tart warm with crème fraîche or whipped cream.

Rich Chocolate Pie

A delicious pie generously decorated with chocolate curls.

Serves 8

75g/3oz plain chocolate
50g/2oz/4 tbsp butter or
  margarine
45ml/3 tbsp golden syrup
3 eggs, beaten
150g/5oz/⅔ cup caster
  sugar
5ml/1 tsp vanilla essence
115g/4oz milk chocolate
475ml/16fl oz/2 cups
  whipping cream

For the pastry
165g/5½oz/1⅓ cups plain
  flour
2.5ml/½ tsp salt
115g/4oz/½ cup lard or
  vegetable fat
30–45ml/2–3 tbsp iced
  water

1 Preheat the oven to 220°C/425°F/Gas 7. For the pastry, sift the flour and salt into a bowl. Rub in the fat until the mixture resembles coarse breadcrumbs. Add water until the pastry forms a ball.

2 Roll out the pastry and use to line a 20–23cm/8–9in pie tin. Flute the edge. Prick the base and sides of the pastry case with a fork. Bake until lightly browned, 10–15 minutes. Cool in the tin on a wire rack.

3 Reduce the oven temperature to 180°C/350°F/Gas 4. In the top of a double boiler, melt the plain chocolate, the butter or margarine and syrup. Remove from the heat and stir in the eggs, sugar and vanilla. Pour the chocolate mixture into the pastry case. Bake until the filling is set, 35–40 minutes. Cool in the tin on a wire rack.

4 For the decoration, use the heat of your hands to soften the milk chocolate slightly. Use a swivel-headed vegetable peeler to shave off short, wide curls. Chill until needed.

5 Before serving, lightly whip the cream until soft peaks form. Spread the cream over the surface of the chocolate filling. Decorate with the milk chocolate curls.

Red Berry Tart with Lemon Cream

This flan is best filled just before serving so the pastry remains mouth-wateringly crisp.

Serves 6–8

150g/5oz/1¼ cups plain
   flour
25g/1oz/4 tbsp cornflour
30g/1½oz/scant ⅓ cup
   icing sugar
90g/3½oz/7 tbsp butter
5ml/1 tsp vanilla essence
2 egg yolks, beaten

For the filling
200g/7oz/scant 1 cup
   cream cheese, softened
45ml/3 tbsp lemon curd
grated rind and juice of
   1 lemon
icing sugar, to taste
   (optional)
225g/8oz/2 cups mixed
   red berry fruits
45ml/3 tbsp redcurrant
   jelly

1 Sift the flour, cornflour and icing sugar together. Rub in the butter until the mixture resembles fine breadcrumbs.

2 Beat the vanilla into the egg yolks, then stir into the flour mixture to make a firm dough. Add cold water if necessary.

3 Roll out the pastry and use it to line a 23cm/9in round flan tin. Trim the edges. Prick the base and leave to rest in the fridge for 30 minutes.

4 Preheat the oven to 200°C/400°F/Gas 6. Line the flan with greaseproof paper and fill with baking beans. Place on a baking sheet and bake for 20 minutes, removing the paper and beans after 15 minutes. Leave to cool, then remove the pastry case from the flan tin.

5 Cream the cheese, lemon curd and lemon rind and juice, adding icing sugar if you wish. Spread the mixture into the base of the flan. Top with the fruits. Warm the redcurrant jelly and trickle over the fruits just before serving.

Peach Tart with Almond Cream

Serves 8–10

4 large ripe peaches,
   peeled
115g/4oz blanched
   almonds
15g/½oz/2 tbsp plain
   flour
100g/3¼oz/scant ¼ cup
   unsalted butter
115g/4oz/1 cup, plus
   2 tbsp caster sugar
1 egg, plus 1 egg yolk
1.5ml/¼ tsp vanilla
   essence, or
10ml/2 tsp rum

For the pastry
190g/6¼oz/generous
   1½ cups plain flour
2.5ml/½ tsp salt
100g/3¼oz/scant ¼ cup
   cold unsalted butter,
   diced
1 egg yolk
10–45ml/2–3 tbsp iced
   water

1 Sift the flour and salt into a bowl. Rub in the butter until the mixture resembles coarse breadcrumbs. Stir in the egg yolk and enough water to bind the pastry. Gather into a ball, wrap and chill for at least 20 minutes. Preheat a baking sheet in the centre of a 200°C/400°F/Gas 6 oven.

2 Roll out the pastry 3mm/⅛in thick. Transfer to a 25cm/10in pie dish. Trim the edge, prick the base and chill.

3 Grind the almonds with the flour. With an electric mixer, cream the butter and 115g/4oz/scant ¾ cup of the sugar until light and fluffy. Gradually beat in the egg and yolk. Stir in the almonds and vanilla or rum. Spread in the pastry case.

4 Halve the peaches and remove the stones. Cut crossways in thin slices and arrange on top of the almond cream like the spokes of a wheel. Keep the slices of each peach-half together. Fan out by pressing down gently at a slight angle.

5 Bake until the pastry browns, 10–15 minutes. Lower the heat to 180°C/350°F/Gas 4 and bake until the almond cream sets, about 15 minutes more. 10 minutes before the end of the cooking time, sprinkle with the remaining sugar.

Pear and Almond Cream Tart

This tart is equally successful made with nectarines, peaches, apricots or apples.

Serves 6

350g/12oz shortcrust or
   sweet shortcrust
   pastry
3 firm pears
lemon juice
15ml/1 tbsp peach
   brandy or cold water
60ml/4 tbsp peach jam,
   sieved

For the filling
90g/3½oz/generous
   ½ cup blanched whole
   almonds
50g/2oz/4 tbsp caster
   sugar
65g/2½oz/5 tbsp butter
1 egg, plus 1 egg white
few drops almond essence

1 Roll out the pastry and use to line a 23cm/9in flan tin. Chill. For the filling, put the almonds and sugar in a food processor or blender and pulse until finely ground but not pasty. Add the butter and process until creamy, then add the egg, egg white and almond essence and mix well.

2 Preheat a baking sheet in the oven at 190℃/375℉/Gas 5. Peel the pears, halve them, remove the cores and rub with lemon juice. Put the pear halves, cut-side down, on a board and slice thinly crossways, keeping the slices together.

3 Pour the filling into the pastry case. Slide a palette knife under one pear half and press the top to fan out the slices. Transfer to the tart, placing the fruit on the filling like spokes of a wheel.

4 Bake the tart on the baking sheet for 50–55 minutes, until the filling is set and well browned. Cool on a wire rack.

5 Heat the brandy or water with the jam. Brush over the top of the hot tart to glaze. Serve at room temperature.

Lemon Tart

This tart, a classic of France, has a refreshing tangy flavour.

Serves 8–10

350g/12oz shortcrust or
   sweet shortcrust
   pastry
grated rind of 2–
   3 lemons
150ml/¼ pint/⅔ cup
   freshly squeezed lemon
   juice

100g/3½oz/½ cup caster
   sugar
60ml/4 tbsp crème
   fraîche or double
   cream
4 eggs, plus 3 egg yolks
icing sugar, for dusting

1 Preheat the oven to 190℃/375℉/Gas 5. Roll out the pastry and use to line a 23cm/9in flan tin. Prick the base, line with foil and fill with baking beans. Bake for 15 minutes, or until the edges are dry. Remove the foil and beans, and bake for a further 5–7 minutes, until golden.

2 Beat together the lemon rind, juice and sugar, then gradually add the crème fraîche or double cream and beat until well blended. Beat in the eggs, one at a time, then beat in the egg yolks.

3 Pour the filling into the baked pastry case. Bake for about 15–20 minutes, until the filling is set. If the pastry begins to brown too much, cover the edges with foil. Leave to cool. Dust with icing sugar before serving.

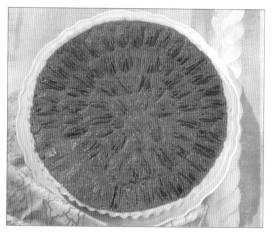

Maple Walnut Tart

Makes sure you use 100 per cent pure maple syrup in this decadent tart.

Serves 8

3 eggs
1.5ml/¼ tsp salt
50g/2oz/4 tbsp caster sugar
50g/2oz/4 tbsp butter, melted
250ml/8fl oz/1 cup pure maple syrup
115g/4oz/1 cup chopped walnuts
whipped cream, to decorate

For the pastry
65g/2½oz/9 tbsp plain flour
65g/2½oz/½ cup wholemeal flour
1.5ml/¼ tsp salt
50g/2oz/4 tbsp cold butter, cut in pieces
40g/1½oz/3 tbsp cold vegetable fat or lard, cut in pieces
1 egg yolk

1 For the pastry, mix the flours and salt in a bowl. Add the fats and rub in until the mixture resembles coarse breadcrumbs. Stir in the egg yolk and 30–45ml/2–3 tbsp iced water to bind. Form into a ball, wrap and chill for 20 minutes.

2 Preheat the oven to 220°C/425°F/Gas 7. Roll out the pastry and use to line a 23cm/9in pie dish. Use the trimmings to stamp out heart shapes. Arrange on the pastry case rim with a little water.

3 Prick the pastry base, line with greaseproof paper and fill with baking beans. Bake for 10 minutes. Remove the paper and beans and bake until golden, 3–6 minutes more.

4 Whisk together the eggs, salt and sugar. Stir in the butter and maple syrup. Set the pastry case on a baking sheet. Pour in the filling, then sprinkle with the nuts.

5 Bake until just set, about 35 minutes. Cool on a wire rack. Decorate with piped whipped cream.

Pecan Tart

Serve this tart warm, accompanied by ice cream or whipped cream, if you wish.

Serves 8

3 eggs
pinch of salt
200g/7oz/generous 1 cup dark brown sugar
120ml/4fl oz/½ cup golden syrup
30ml/2 tbsp fresh lemon juice
75g/3oz/6 tbsp butter, melted
150g/5oz/1¼ cups chopped pecan nuts
50g/2oz/½ cup pecan nut halves

For the pastry
175g/6oz/1½ cups plain flour
15ml/1 tbsp caster sugar
5ml/1 tsp baking powder
2.5ml/½ tsp salt
75g/3oz/6 tbsp cold unsalted butter, cut in pieces
1 egg yolk
45–60ml/3–4 tbsp whipping cream

1 For the pastry, sift together the flour, sugar, baking powder and salt. Add the butter and rub in until the mixture resembles coarse breadcrumbs.

2 Blend the egg yolk and whipping cream, then stir into the flour mixture.

3 Form the pastry into a ball, then roll out and use to line a 23cm/9in pie dish. Flute the edge and chill for 20 minutes.

4 Preheat a baking sheet in the oven at 200°C/400°F/Gas 6. Lightly whisk the eggs and salt. Mix in the sugar, syrup, lemon juice and butter. Stir in the chopped nuts.

5 Pour into the pastry case and arrange the pecan nut halves in concentric circles on top.

6 Bake on the baking sheet for 10 minutes. Reduce the heat to 160°C/325°F/Gas 3 and bake for 25 minutes more.

Velvety Mocha Tart

**A creamy smooth filling tops a dark light-textured base in
this wondrous dessert.**

Serves 8

*10ml/2 tsp instant
  espresso coffee
30ml/2 tbsp hot water
175g/6oz plain chocolate
25g/1oz bitter cooking
  chocolate
350ml/12fl oz/1½ cups
  whipping cream,
  slightly warmed
120ml/4fl oz/½ cup
  whipped cream, to
  decorate*

*chocolate coated coffee
  beans, to decorate*

For the base
*150g/5oz/2½ cups
  crushed chocolate
  wafers
30ml/2 tbsp caster sugar
65g/2½oz/5 tbsp butter,
  melted*

1 Combine the base ingredients. Press the mixture over the
base and sides of a 23cm/9in pie dish. Chill.

2 Dissolve the coffee in the water. Set aside.

3 Melt the chocolates in the top of a double boiler. Set the
base of the pan in cold water to cool.

4 Whip the cream until light and fluffy. Add the coffee and
whip until the cream just holds its shape.

5 When the chocolate is at room temperature, fold it gently
into the cream.

6 Pour into the biscuit base and chill until firm. Decorate
with piped whipped cream and chocolate coated coffee beans
just before serving.

Coconut Cream Tart

Serves 8

*140g/5oz desiccated
  coconut
140g/5oz/¾ cup caster
  sugar
25g/1oz/4 tbsp cornflour
1.5ml/¼ tsp salt
625ml/1 pint/2½ cups
  milk
65ml/2fl oz whipping
  cream
2 egg yolks
30g/1oz/2 tbsp unsalted
  butter*

*10ml/2 tsp vanilla
  essence*

For the pastry
*140g/5oz/1¼ cups plain
  flour
1.5ml/¼ tsp salt
45g/1½oz/3 tbsp cold
  butter, cut in pieces
30g/1oz/3 tbsp cold
  vegetable fat or lard
30–45ml/2–3 tbsp iced
  water*

1 Sift the flour and salt into a bowl, add the fats and rub in
until it resembles coarse breadcrumbs. With a fork, stir in just
enough water to bind the pastry. Gather into a ball, wrap and
chill for 20 minutes. Preheat the oven to 220°C/425°F/Gas 7.

2 Roll out the pastry 3mm/⅛in thick. Line a 23cm/9in pie
dish. Trim and flute the edges, prick the base, line with
crumpled greaseproof paper and fill with baking beans. Bake
for 10–12 minutes. Remove the paper and beans, reduce heat
to 180°C/350°F/Gas 4 and bake until brown, 10–15 minutes.

3 Spread 55g/2oz of the coconut on a baking sheet and toast
in the oven until golden, 6–8 minutes.

4 Put the sugar, cornflour and salt in a pan. In a bowl, whisk
the milk, cream and yolks. Add the egg mixture to the pan.

5 Cook over a low heat, stirring, until the mixture comes to
the boil. Boil for 1 minute, then remove from the heat. Add
the butter, vanilla and remaining coconut.

6 Pour into the pre-baked pastry case. When cool, sprinkle
toasted coconut in a ring in the centre.

Orange Tart

If you like oranges, this is the dessert for you!

Serves 8

200g/7oz/1 cup sugar
250ml/8fl oz/1 cup fresh
  orange juice, strained
2 large navel oranges
165g/5½oz/scant 1 cup
  whole blanched
  almonds
50g/2oz/4 tbsp butter
1 egg
15ml/1 tbsp plain flour
45ml/3 tbsp apricot jam

For the pastry

210g/7½oz/scant 2 cups
  plain flour
2.5ml/½ tsp salt
50g/2oz/4 tbsp cold
  butter, cut into pieces
40g/1½oz/3 tbsp cold
  margarine, cut into
  pieces
45–60ml/3–4 tbsp iced
  water

1 For the pastry, sift the flour and salt into a bowl. Add the butter and margarine and rub in until the mixture resembles coarse breadcrumbs. Stir in just enough water to bind the dough. Wrap and chill for 20 minutes. Roll out the pastry to a 5mm/¼in thickness. Use to line a 20cm/8in tart tin. Trim and chill until needed.

2 In a saucepan, combine 165g/5½oz/¾ cup of the sugar and the orange juice and boil until thick and syrupy. Cut the unpeeled oranges into 5mm/¼in slices. Add to the syrup. Simmer gently for 10 minutes. Put on a wire rack to dry. When cool, cut in half. Reserve the syrup. Place a baking sheet in the oven and heat to 200°C/400°F/Gas 6.

3 Grind the almonds finely in a blender or food processor. Cream the butter and remaining sugar until light and fluffy. Beat in the egg and 30ml/2 tbsp of the orange syrup. Stir in the almonds and flour.

4 Melt the jam over a low heat, then brush over the pastry case. Pour in the almond mixture. Bake on the baking sheet until set, about 20 minutes, then cool. Arrange overlapping orange slices on top. Boil the remaining syrup until thick and brush on top to glaze.

Raspberry Tart

A luscious tart with a custard topped with juicy berries.

Serves 8

4 egg yolks
65g/2½oz/generous
  4 tbsp caster sugar
45ml/3 tbsp plain flour
300ml/10fl oz/1¼ cups
  milk
1.5ml/¼ tsp salt
2.5ml/½ tsp vanilla
  essence
450g/1lb/2⅔ cups fresh
  raspberries
75ml/5 tbsp redcurrant
  jelly
15ml/1 tbsp orange juice

For the pastry

185g/6½oz/1⅓ cups plain
  flour
2.5ml/½ tsp baking
  powder
1.5ml/¼ tsp salt
15ml/1 tbsp sugar
grated rind of ½ orange
75g/3oz/6 tbsp cold
  butter, cut in pieces
1 egg yolk
45–60ml/3–4 tbsp
  whipping cream

1 For the pastry, sift the flour, baking powder and salt into a bowl. Stir in the sugar and orange rind. Add the butter and rub in until the mixture resembles breadcrumbs. Stir in the egg yolk and cream to bind. Form into a ball, wrap and chill.

2 For the filling, beat the egg yolks and sugar until thick and creamy. Gradually stir in the flour. Bring the milk and salt just to the boil, then remove from the heat. Whisk into the egg yolk mixture, return to the pan and continue whisking over a moderately high heat until just bubbling. Cook for 3 minutes to thicken. Transfer to a bowl. Stir in the vanilla, then cover with greaseproof paper.

3 Preheat the oven to 200°C/400°F/Gas 6. Roll out the pastry and use to line a 25cm/10in pie dish. Prick the base, line with greaseproof paper and fill with baking beans. Bake for 15 minutes. Remove the paper and beans, and bake until golden, 6–8 minutes more. Leave to cool. Spread an even layer of the custard filling in the pastry case and arrange the raspberries on top. Melt the jelly and orange juice in a pan and brush on top to glaze.

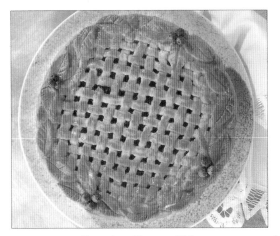

Lattice Berry Pie

Choose any berries you like for this handsome pie.

Serves 8

450g/1lb/about 4 cups
berries, such as
bilberries, blueberries
and blackcurrants
115g/4oz/generous ½ cup
caster sugar
45ml/3 tbsp cornflour
30ml/2 tbsp fresh lemon
juice
25g/1oz/2 tbsp butter,
diced

For the pastry
275g/10oz/2½ cups plain
flour
4ml/¾ tsp salt
115g/4oz/½ cup cold
butter, diced
40g/1½oz/3 tbsp cold
vegetable fat or lard,
diced
75–90ml/5–6 tbsp iced
water
1 egg, beaten with
15ml/1 tbsp water, for
glazing

1 For the pastry, sift the flour and salt into a bowl. Add the butter and fat and rub in until the mixture resembles coarse breadcrumbs. Stir in just enough water to bind. Form into two balls, wrap and chill for 20 minutes. Roll out one ball and use to line a 23cm/9in pie dish, leaving a 1cm/½in overhang. Brush the base with egg.

2 Mix all the filling ingredients together, except the butter (reserve a few berries for decoration). Spoon into the pastry case and dot with the butter. Brush egg around the pastry rim

3 Preheat a baking sheet at 220°C/425°F/Gas 7. Roll out the remaining pastry on a baking sheet lined with greaseproof paper. With a serrated pastry wheel, make 24 thin strips. Use the scraps to cut out leaf shapes, and mark veins. Weave the strips in a close lattice and transfer to the pie. Seal the edges and trim. Arrange the leaves around the rim. Brush with egg and bake for 10 minutes.

4 Reduce the heat to 180°C/350°F/Gas 4 and bake the pie for a further 40–45 minutes. Decorate with berries.

Plum Pie

Treat someone special with this lightly spiced plum pie.

Serves 8

900g/2lb red or purple
plums
grated rind of 1 lemon
15ml/1 tbsp fresh lemon
juice
115–175g/4–6oz/1–
1¼ cups caster sugar
45ml/3 tbsp quick-
cooking tapioca
1.5ml/¼ tsp salt
2.5ml/½ tsp ground
cinnamon
1.5ml/¼ tsp grated
nutmeg

For the pastry
275g/10oz/2½ cups plain
flour
5ml/1 tsp salt
75g/3oz/6 tbsp cold
butter, diced
50g/2oz/4 tbsp cold
vegetable fat or lard,
diced
50–120ml/2–4fl oz/
¼–½ cup iced water
milk, for glazing

1 For the pastry, sift the flour and salt into a bowl. Add the butter and fat and rub in until the mixture resembles coarse breadcrumbs. Stir in just enough water to bind the pastry. Form into two balls, wrap and chill for 20 minutes.

2 Preheat a baking sheet in the oven at 220°C/425°F/Gas 7. Roll out a pastry ball and use to line a 23cm/9in pie dish.

3 Halve and stone the plums, and chop roughly. Mix all the filling ingredients together, then transfer to the pastry case.

4 Roll out the remaining pastry, place on a baking sheet lined with greaseproof paper, and stamp out four hearts. Transfer the pastry lid to the pie using the paper.

5 Trim to leave a 2cm/¾in overhang. Fold this under the pastry base and pinch to seal. Arrange the hearts on top. Brush with milk and bake for 15 minutes. Reduce the heat to 180°C/350°F/Gas 4 and bake for a further 30–35 minutes.

Dorset Apple Cake

Serve this fruity apple cake warm, and spread with butter if liked.

Makes one 18cm/7in round cake

225g/8oz cooking apples, peeled, cored and chopped
juice of ½ lemon
225g/8oz/2 cups plain flour
7.5ml/1½ tsp baking powder
115g/4oz/½ cup butter, diced
165g/5½oz/scant 1 cup soft light brown sugar
1 egg, beaten
about 30–45ml/2–3 tbsp milk, to mix
2.5ml/½ tsp ground cinnamon

1 Preheat the oven to 180°C/350°F/Gas 4. Grease and line an 18cm/7in round cake tin.

2 Toss the apple with the lemon juice and set aside. Sift the flour and baking powder together, then rub in the butter, until the mixture resembles breadcrumbs.

3 Stir in 115g/4oz/¾ cup of the brown sugar, the apple and the egg, and mix well, adding sufficient milk to make a soft dropping consistency.

4 Transfer the dough to the prepared tin. In a bowl, mix together the remaining sugar and the cinnamon. Sprinkle over the cake mixture, then bake for 45–50 minutes, until golden. Leave to cool in the tin for 10 minutes, then transfer to a wire rack.

Parkin

The flavour of the cake will improve if it is stored in an air-tight container for several days or a week before serving.

Makes 16–20 squares

300ml/½ pint/1¼ cups milk
225g/8oz/5 tbsp golden syrup
225g/8oz/4 tbsp black treacle
115g/4oz/½ cup butter or margarine, diced
50g/2oz/scant ¼ cup dark brown sugar
450g/1lb/4 cups plain flour
2.5ml/½ tsp bicarbonate of soda
6.5ml/1¼ tsp ground ginger
350g/12oz/4 cups medium oatmeal
1 egg, beaten
icing sugar, for dusting

1 Preheat the oven to 180°C/350°F/Gas 4. Grease and line the base of a 20cm/8in square cake tin. Gently heat together the milk, syrup, treacle, butter or margarine and sugar, stirring until smooth. Do not allow the mixture to boil.

2 Stir together the flour, bicarbonate of soda, ginger and oatmeal. Make a well in the centre, pour in the egg, then slowly pour in the warmed mixture, stirring to make a smooth batter.

3 Pour the batter into the tin and bake for about 45 minutes, until firm to the touch. Cool slightly in the tin, then cool completely on a wire rack. Cut into squares and dust with icing sugar.

Banana Ginger Parkin

Parkin keeps well and really improves with keeping. Store it in a covered container for up to two months.

Makes 16–20 squares

200g/7oz/scant 2 cups plain flour
10ml/2 tsp bicarbonate of soda
10ml/2 tsp ground ginger
150g/5oz/1¼ cups medium oatmeal
50g/2oz/4 tbsp dark muscovado sugar

75g/3oz/6 tbsp sunflower margarine
150g/5oz/3 tbsp golden syrup
1 egg, beaten
3 ripe bananas, mashed
75g/3oz/¾ cup icing sugar
stem ginger, to decorate (optional)

1 Preheat the oven to 160°C/325°F/Gas 3. Grease and line an 18 x 28cm/7 x 11in cake tin.

2 Sift together the flour, bicarbonate of soda and ginger, then stir in the oatmeal. Melt the sugar, margarine and syrup in a saucepan, then stir into the flour mixture. Beat in the egg and mashed bananas.

3 Spoon into the tin and bake for about 1 hour, or until firm to the touch. Allow to cool in the tin, then turn out and cut into squares.

4 Sift the icing sugar into a bowl and stir in just enough water to make a smooth, runny icing. Drizzle the icing over each square and top with a piece of stem ginger, if you like.

Gooseberry Cake

This cake is delicious served warm with whipped cream.

Makes one 18cm/7in square cake

115g/4oz/½ cup butter
165g/5½oz/1⅓ cups self-raising flour
5ml/1 tsp baking powder
2 eggs, beaten
115g/4oz/generous ½ cup caster sugar
5–10ml/1–2 tsp rose water

pinch of freshly grated nutmeg
115g/4oz jar gooseberries in syrup, drained, juice reserved
caster sugar, to decorate
whipped cream, to serve

1 Preheat the oven to 180°C/350°F/Gas 4. Grease an 18cm/7in square cake tin, line the base and sides with greaseproof paper and grease the paper. Gently melt the butter, then transfer to a mixing bowl and allow to cool.

2 Sift together the flour and baking powder and add to the butter. Beat in the eggs, one at a time, the sugar, rose water and grated nutmeg, to make a smooth batter.

3 Mix in 15–30ml/1–2 tbsp of the reserved gooseberry juice, then pour half of the batter mixture into the prepared tin. Scatter over the gooseberries and pour over the remaining batter mixture.

4 Bake for about 45 minutes, or until a skewer inserted into the centre of the cake comes out clean.

5 Leave in the tin for 5 minutes, then turn out on a wire rack, peel off the lining paper and allow to cool for a further 5 minutes. Dredge with caster sugar and serve immediately with whipped cream, or leave the cake to cool completely before decorating.

Crunchy-topped Sponge Loaf

This light sponge makes a perfect tea-time treat.

Makes one 450g/1lb loaf

200g/7oz/scant 1 cup
  butter, softened
finely grated rind of 1
  lemon
150g/5oz/5 tbsp caster
  sugar
3 eggs
75g/3oz/¾ cup plain
  flour, sifted
150g/5oz/1¼ cups self-
  raising flour, sifted

For the topping
45ml/3 tbsp clear honey
115g/4oz/¾ cup mixed
  peel
50g/2oz/½ cup flaked
  almonds

1 Preheat the oven to 180°C/350°F/Gas 4. Grease and line a 450g/1lb loaf tin with greaseproof paper. Grease the paper.

2 Beat together the butter, lemon rind and sugar until light and fluffy. Blend in the eggs, one at a time.

3 Sift together the flours, then stir into the egg mixture. Fill the loaf tin.

4 Bake for 45 minutes, or until a skewer inserted into the centre comes out clean. Stand in the tin for 5 minutes. Turn the loaf out on to a wire rack, peel off the lining paper and leave to cool.

5 For the topping, melt the honey with the mixed peel and almonds. Remove from the heat, stir briefly, then spread over the cake top. Cool before serving.

Irish Whiskey Cake

Other whiskies could be used in this cake.

Makes one 23 x 13cm/9 x 5in cake

175g/6oz/1½ cups
  chopped walnuts
75g/3oz/generous ½ cup
  raisins, chopped
75g/3oz/scant ½ cup
  currants
115g/4oz/1 cup plain
  flour
5ml/1 tsp baking powder
1.5ml/¼ tsp salt
115g/4oz/½ cup butter

225g/8oz/scant 1½ cups
  caster sugar
3 eggs, separated, at
  room temperature
5ml/1 tsp grated nutmeg
2.5ml/½ tsp ground
  cinnamon
85ml/5 tbsp Irish
  whiskey
icing sugar, for dusting

1 Preheat the oven to 160°C/325°F/Gas 3. Base-line and grease a 23 x 13cm/9 x 5in loaf tin. Mix the nuts and dried fruit with 30ml/2 tbsp of the flour and set aside. Sift together the remaining flour, baking powder and salt.

2 Cream the butter and sugar until light and fluffy. Beat in the egg yolks.

3 Mix the nutmeg, cinnamon and whiskey. Fold into the butter mixture, alternating with the flour mixture.

4 Beat the egg whites until stiff. Fold into the whiskey mixture until just blended. Fold in the walnut mixture.

5 Fill the loaf tin and bake until a skewer inserted in the centre comes out clean, about 1 hour. Cool in the tin. To serve, dust with icing sugar over a template.

Autumn Dessert Cake

Greengages, plums or semi-dried prunes are delicious in this recipe.

Serves 6–8

115g/4oz/½ cup butter, softened	5ml/1 tsp baking powder
150g/5oz/5 tbsp caster sugar	2.5ml/½ tsp salt
3 eggs, beaten	675g/1½lb/3 cups stoned plums, greengages or semi-dried prunes
75g/3oz/¾ cup ground hazelnuts	60ml/4 tbsp lime marmalade
150g/5oz/1¼ cups shelled pecan nuts, chopped	15ml/1 tbsp lime juice
50g/2oz/½ cup plain flour	30ml/2 tbsp blanched almonds, chopped, to decorate

1 Preheat the oven to 180°C/350°F/Gas 4. Grease a 23cm/9in round, fluted tart tin.

2 Beat the butter and sugar until light and fluffy. Gradually beat in the eggs, alternating with the ground hazelnuts.

3 Stir in the pecan nuts, then sift and fold in the flour, baking powder and salt. Spoon into the tart tin.

4 Bake for 45 minutes, or until a skewer inserted into the centre comes out clean.

5 Arrange the fruit on the base. Return to the oven and bake for 10–15 minutes until the fruit has softened. Transfer to a wire rack to cool, then turn out.

6 Warm the marmalade and lime juice gently. Brush over the fruit, then sprinkle with the almonds. Allow to set, then chill before serving.

Apple Crumble Cake

In the autumn use windfall apples. Served warm with thick cream or custard, this cake doubles as a dessert.

Serves 8–10

For the topping

75g/3oz/⅔ cup self-raising flour	115g/4oz/1 cup self-raising flour, sifted
½ tsp ground cinnamon	2 cooking apples, peeled, cored and sliced
40g/1½oz/3 tbsp butter	50g/2oz/4 tbsp sultanas
25g/1oz/2 tbsp caster sugar	

To decorate

For the base

50g/2oz/4 tbsp butter, softened	1 red dessert apple, cored, thinly sliced and tossed in lemon juice
75g/3oz/6 tbsp caster sugar	25g/1oz/2 tbsp caster sugar, sifted
1 size 3 egg, beaten	pinch of ground cinnamon

1 Preheat the oven 180°C/350°F/Gas 4. Grease a deep 18cm/7in springform tin, line the base with greaseproof paper and grease the paper.

2 To make the topping, sift the flour and cinnamon into a mixing bowl. Rub the butter into the flour until it resembles breadcrumbs, then stir in the sugar. Set aside.

3 To make the base, put the butter, sugar, egg and flour into a bowl and beat for 1–2 minutes until smooth. Spoon into the prepared tin.

4 Mix together the apple slices and sultanas and spread them evenly over the top. Sprinkle with the topping.

5 Bake in the centre of the oven for about 1 hour. Cool in the tin for 10 minutes before turning out on to a wire rack and peeling off the lining paper. Serve warm or cool, decorated with slices of red dessert apple and caster sugar and cinnamon sprinkled over.

Light Fruit Cake

For the best flavour, wrap this cake in foil and store for a week before cutting.

Makes two 23 x 13cm/9 x 5in cakes

225g/8oz/1 cup prunes
225g/8oz/1⅓ cups dates
225g/8oz/1 cup currants
225g/8oz/generous 1½
   cups sultanas
250ml/8fl oz/1 cup dry
   white wine
250ml/8fl oz/1 cup rum
350g/12oz/3 cups plain
   flour
10ml/2 tsp baking
   powder
5ml/1 tsp ground
   cinnamon
2.5ml/½ tsp grated
   nutmeg
225g/8oz/1 cup butter, at
   room temperature
225g/8oz/scant 1¼ cups
   caster sugar
4 eggs, lightly beaten
5ml/1 tsp vanilla essence

1 Stone the prunes and dates and chop finely. Place in a bowl with the currants and sultanas. Stir in the wine and rum and leave, covered, for 2 days. Stir occasionally.

2 Preheat the oven to 150°C/300°F/Gas 2 with a tray of hot water in the bottom. Line two 23 x 13cm/9 x 5in loaf tins with greaseproof paper and grease the paper.

3 Sift together the flour, baking powder, ground cinnamon and grated nutmeg.

4 Cream the butter and sugar together until light and fluffy. Gradually add the eggs and vanilla. Fold in the flour mixture in three batches. Fold in the dried fruit mixture and its liquid.

5 Divide the mixture between the tins and bake until a skewer inserted in the centre comes out clean, about 1½ hours. Stand for 20 minutes, then unmould on to a wire rack.

Rich Fruit Cake

Makes one 23 x 8cm/9 x 3in cake

140g/5oz/½ cup currants
170g/6oz/generous 1 cup
   raisins
50g/2oz/½ cup sultanas
55g/2oz/4 tbsp glacé
   cherries, halved
3 tbsp sweet sherry
170g/6oz/¾ cup butter
200g/7oz/scant 1 cup
   dark brown sugar
2 size 1 eggs, at room
   temperature
200g/7oz/1¼ cups plain
   flour
10ml/2 tsp baking
   powder
10ml/2 tsp each ground
   ginger, allspice, and
   cinnamon
15ml/1 tbsp golden syrup
15ml/1 tbsp milk
55g/2oz/5 tbsp cut mixed
   peel
115g/4oz/1 cup chopped
   walnuts

For the decoration

120ml/4fl oz/½ cup
   orange marmalade
crystallized citrus fruit
   slices
glacé cherries

1 A day in advance, combine the dried fruit and cherries in a bowl. Stir in the sherry, cover and soak overnight.

2 Preheat the oven to 150°C/300°F/Gas 2. Line and grease a 23 x 8cm/9 x 3in springform tin with greaseproof paper. Place a tray of hot water on the bottom of the oven.

3 Cream the butter and sugar. Beat in the eggs, 1 at a time. Sift the flour, baking powder and spices together three times. Fold into the butter mixture in three batches. Fold in the syrup, milk, dried fruit and liquid, mixed peel and nuts.

4 Spoon into the tin, spreading out so there is a slight depression in the centre. Bake for about 2½–3 hours. Cover with foil when the top is golden to prevent over-browning. Cool in the tin on a rack.

5 Melt the marmalade over a low heat, then brush over the top of the cake. Decorate with the crystallized citrus fruit slices and glacé cherries.

Creole Christmas Cake

Makes one 23cm/9in cake

450g/1lb/3 cups raisins
225g/8oz/1 cup currants
115g/4oz/¾ cup sultanas
115g/4oz/½ cup no-soak
  prunes, chopped
115g/4oz/1 cup candied
  orange peel, chopped
115g/4oz/1 cup chopped
  walnuts
60ml/4 tbsp dark
  brown sugar
5ml/1 tsp vanilla essence
5ml/1 tsp ground
  cinnamon
1.5ml/¼ tsp each ground
  nutmeg and cloves

5ml/1 tsp salt
60ml/4 tbsp each rum,
  brandy and whisky
For the second stage
225g/8oz/2 cups plain
  flour
5ml/1 tsp baking powder
225g/8oz demerara sugar
225g/8oz/1 cup butter
4 eggs, beaten
For the topping
225g/8oz apricot
  jam, sieved
pecan halves and
  crystallized kumquat
  slices, to decorate

1 Put the first set of ingredients into a pan, mix and heat gently. Simmer over low heat for 15 minutes. Remove from the heat and cool. Transfer to a lidded jar and leave in the fridge for 7 days, stirring at least once a day.

2 Preheat the oven to 140°C/275°F/Gas 1. Line a 23cm/9in round cake tin with a double thickness of non-stick baking paper and grease it well. Beat the flour, baking powder, sugar and butter together until smooth, then gradually beat in the eggs until the mixture is well blended and smooth.

3 Fold in the fruit mixture and stir well to mix. Spoon the mixture into the prepared tin, level the surface and bake in the centre of the oven for 3 hours. Cover with foil and continue baking for 1 hour, until the cake feels springy. Cool on a wire rack then remove from the tin. Wrap in foil until needed. The cake will keep well for 1 year.

4 To decorate , heat the jam with 30ml/2 tbsp water, brush half over the cake. Arrange the nuts and fruit over the cake and brush with the remaining apricot glaze.

Light Jewelled Fruit Cake

If you want to cover this cake with marzipan and icing, omit the almond decoration.

Makes one 20cm/8in round or 18cm/7in square cake

115g/4oz/½ cup currants
115g/4oz/¾ cup sultanas
225g/8oz/1 cup mixed
  glacé cherries,
  quartered
50g/2oz/½ cup mixed
  peel, finely chopped
30ml/2 tbsp rum, brandy
  or sherry
225g/8oz/1 cup butter
225g/8oz/generous 1 cup
  caster sugar
finely grated rind of
  1 orange

grated rind of 1 lemon
4 eggs
50g/2oz/½ cup chopped
  almonds
50g/2oz/5 tbsp ground
  almonds
225g/8oz/2 cups plain
  flour

To decorate
50g/2oz/5 tbsp whole
  blanched almonds
  (optional)
15ml/1 tbsp apricot jam

1 A day in advance, soak the currants, sultanas, glacé cherries and mixed peel in the rum, brandy or sherry, cover and leave to soak overnight.

2 Grease and line a 20cm/8in round cake tin or an 18cm/7in square cake tin with a double thickness of greaseproof paper. Preheat the oven to 160°C/325°F/Gas 3. Beat the butter, sugar and orange and lemon rinds together until light and fluffy. Beat in the eggs, one at a time. Mix in the chopped almonds, ground almonds, soaked fruits (with the liquid) and the flour. Spoon into the cake tin and level the top. Bake for 30 minutes.

3 Arrange the almonds, if using, on top of the cake (do not press them into the cake or they will sink during cooking). Return the cake to the oven and cook for 1½–2 hours, or until the centre is firm to the touch. Let the cake cool in the tin for 30 minutes, then turn it out in its paper on to a wire rack. When cold, wrap foil over the paper and store in a cool place. To finish, warm, then sieve the jam and use to glaze the cake.

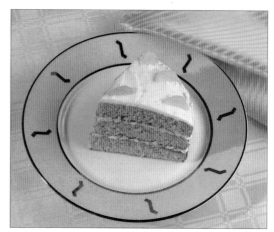

Angel Cake

This heavenly cake tastes simply divine!

Makes one 25cm/10in cake

130g/4½oz/generous
  1 cup sifted plain flour
30ml/2 tbsp cornflour
285g/10½oz/1½ cups
  caster sugar
10–11 egg whites
6.5ml/1¼ tsp cream of
  tartar

1.5ml/¼ tsp salt
5ml/1 tsp vanilla essence
1.5ml/¼ tsp almond
  essence
icing sugar, for dusting

1 Preheat the oven to 160°C/325°F/Gas 3. Sift the flours before measuring, then sift them four times together with 90g/3½oz/½ cup of the sugar.

2 Beat the egg whites until foamy. Sift over the cream of tartar and salt and continue to beat until the egg whites form soft peaks.

3 Add the remaining sugar in three batches, beating well after each addition. Stir in the vanilla and almond essences. Fold in the flour mixture in two batches.

4 Transfer to an ungreased 25cm/10in cake tin and bake until just browned on top, about 1 hour.

5 Turn the tin upside-down on to a wire rack and cool for 1 hour. Then invert on to a serving plate. Lay a star-shaped template on top of the cake, sift over some icing sugar and remove the template.

Spice Cake with Ginger Frosting

A rich three-layer cake with a creamy ginger frosting.

Makes one 20cm/8in round cake

300ml/10fl oz/1¼ cups
  milk
30ml/2 tbsp golden syrup
10ml/2 tsp vanilla
  essence
75g/3oz/¾ cup chopped
  walnuts
175g/6oz/¾ cup butter, at
  room temperature
285g/10½oz/1½ cups
  sugar
1 whole egg, plus 3 egg
  yolks
275g/10oz/2½ cups plain
  flour
15ml/1 tbsp baking
  powder
5ml/1 tsp grated nutmeg
5ml/1 tsp ground
  cinnamon

2.5ml/½ tsp ground
  cloves
1.5ml/¼ tsp ground
  ginger
1.5ml/¼ tsp mixed spice
stem ginger pieces, to
  decorate

For the frosting

175g/6oz/¾ cup cream
  cheese
25g/1oz/2 tbsp unsalted
  butter
200g/7oz/1⅓ cups icing
  sugar
30ml/2 tbsp finely
  chopped stem ginger
30ml/2 tbsp syrup from
  stem ginger

1 Preheat the oven to 180°C/350°F/Gas 4. Line and grease three 20cm/8in cake tins with greaseproof paper. In a bowl, combine the milk, golden syrup, vanilla and walnuts.

2 Cream the butter and sugar until light and fluffy. Beat in the egg and egg yolks. Add the milk mixture and stir well. Sift together the flour, baking powder and spices three times. Add to the butter mixture in four batches, folding in carefully.

3 Divide the cake mixture between the tins. Bake until the cakes spring back when touched lightly, about 25 minutes. Leave in the tins for 5 minutes, then cool on a wire rack. For the frosting, combine all the ingredients and beat until smooth. Spread the frosting between the layers and over the top. Decorate with pieces of stem ginger.

Lemon Coconut Layer Cake

Makes one 20cm/8in round cake

150g/5oz/1¼ cups plain
  flour, sifted with
  1.5ml/¼ tsp salt
8 eggs
370g/12¾oz/scant 2 cups
  caster sugar
15ml/1 tbsp grated
  orange rind
grated rind of 2 lemons
juice of 1 lemon
65g/2½oz/1¼ cups
  sweetened, shredded
  coconut
30ml/2 tbsp cornflour

250ml/8fl oz/1 cup water
75g/3oz/6 tbsp butter

For the frosting

115g/4oz/½ cup unsalted
  butter
115g/4oz/1 cup icing
  sugar
grated rind of 1 lemon
90–120ml/6–8 tbsp
  lemon juice
115g/4oz/2 cups
  sweetened shredded
  coconut

1 Preheat the oven to 180°C/350°F/Gas 4. Line and grease three 20cm/8in cake tins with greaseproof paper.

2 Place 6 of the eggs in a bowl set over hot water and beat until frothy. Beat in 165g/5½oz/¾ cup sugar until the mixture doubles in volume. Remove from the heat. Fold in the orange rind, half the lemon rind, 15ml/1 tbsp of the lemon juice and the coconut. Sift over the flour mixture and fold in well.

3 Divide the mixture between the cake tins. Bake until the cakes pull away from the sides of the tins, 25–30 minutes. Leave in the tins for 5 minutes, then cool on a wire rack.

4 Blend the cornflour with cold water to dissolve. Whisk in the remaining eggs until blended. In a pan, mix the remaining lemon rind and juice, water, remaining sugar and butter. Bring to the boil. Whisk in the cornflour, and return to the boil. Whisk until thick. Remove and cover with clear film.

5 Cream the butter and icing sugar. Stir in the lemon rind and enough lemon juice to obtain a spreadable consistency. Sandwich the cake layers with the lemon custard. Spread the frosting over the top and sides. Cover with the coconut.

Lemon Yogurt Ring

The glaze gives this dessert a refreshing finishing touch.

Serves 12

225g/8oz/1 cup butter, at
  room temperature
285g/10½oz/1½ cups
  caster sugar
4 eggs, separated
10ml/2 tsp grated lemon
  rind
90ml/6 tbsp lemon juice
250ml/8fl oz/1 cup
  natural yogurt
275g/10oz/2½ cups plain
  flour

10ml/2 tsp baking
  powder
5ml/1 tsp bicarbonate of
  soda
2.5ml/½ tsp salt

For the glaze

115g/4oz/1 cup icing
  sugar
30ml/2 tbsp lemon juice
45–60ml/3–4 tbsp
  natural yogurt

1 Preheat the oven to 180°C/350°F/Gas 4. Grease a 3-litre/5-pint/12½-cup *bundt* or fluted tube tin and dust with flour.

2 Cream the butter and caster sugar until light and fluffy. Add the egg yolks, one at a time, beating well after each addition. Add the lemon rind, juice and yogurt and stir .

3 Sift together the flour, baking powder and bicarbonate of soda. In another bowl, beat the egg whites and salt until they hold stiff peaks.

4 Fold the dry ingredients into the butter mixture, then fold in a dollop of egg whites. Fold in the remaining whites.

5 Pour into the tin and bake until a skewer inserted in the centre comes out clean, about 50 minutes. Leave in the tin for 15 minutes, then turn out and cool on a wire rack.

6 For the glaze, sift the icing sugar into a bowl. Stir in the lemon juice and just enough yogurt to make a smooth glaze.

7 Set the cooled cake on the wire rack over a sheet of greaseproof paper. Pour over the glaze and allow to set.

Carrot Cake with Geranium Cheese

Makes one 23 x 12cm/9 x 5in cake

115g/4oz/1 cup self-
raising flour
5ml/1 tsp bicarbonate of
soda
2.5ml/½ tsp ground
cinnamon
2.5ml/½ tsp ground
cloves
200g/7oz/generous 1 cup
soft brown sugar
225g/8oz/generous
1½ cups grated
carrot
150g/5oz/1 cup sultanas
150g/5oz/½ cup finely
chopped preserved
stem ginger

150g/5oz/generous 1 cup
pecan nuts
150ml/¼ pint/⅔ cup
sunflower oil
2 eggs, lightly beaten

For the topping
2–3 lemon-scented
geranium leaves
225g/8oz/2 cups icing
sugar
60g/2¼oz/generous
4 tbsp cream cheese
30g/1¼oz/generous
2 tbsp softened butter
5ml/1 tsp grated lemon
rind

1 For the topping, put the geranium leaves, torn into small
pieces, in a small bowl and mix with the icing sugar. Leave in
a warm place overnight for the sugar to take up the scent.

2 For the cake, sift the flour, bicarbonate of soda and spices
together. Add the sugar, carrots, sultanas, ginger and pecan
nuts. Stir well, then add the oil and beaten eggs. Mix with an
electric mixer for 5 minutes.

3 Preheat the oven to 180°C/350°F/Gas 4. Then grease a
23 x 12cm/9 x 5in loaf tin, line the base with greaseproof
paper, and grease the paper. Pour the mixture into the tin and
bake for about 1 hour. Remove the cake from the oven, leave
to stand for a few minutes, and then cool on a wire rack.

4 Meanwhile, make the cream cheese topping. Remove the
pieces of geranium leaf from the icing sugar and discard.
Place the cream cheese, butter and lemon rind in a bowl.
Using an electric mixer, gradually add the icing sugar, beating
well until smooth. Spread over the top of the cooled cake.

Carrot and Courgette Cake

If you can't resist the lure of a slice of iced cake, you'll love
this spiced sponge with its delicious creamy topping.

Makes one 18cm/7in square cake

1 carrot
1 courgette
3 eggs, separated
115g/4oz/¾ cup soft light
brown sugar
30ml/2 tbsp ground
almonds
finely grated rind of
1 orange
150g/5oz/1¼ cups
self-raising wholemeal
flour

5ml/1 tsp ground
cinnamon
5ml/1 tsp icing sugar, for
dusting
fondant carrots and
courgettes, to decorate

For the topping
175g/6oz/¾ cup low-fat
soft cheese
5ml/1 tsp clear honey

1 Preheat the oven to 180°C/350°F/Gas 4. Line an 18cm/7in
square tin with non-stick baking paper. Coarsely grate the
carrot and courgette.

2 Put the egg yolks, sugar, ground almonds and orange rind
into a bowl and whisk until very thick and light. Sift together
the flour and cinnamon and fold into the mixture together
with the grated vegetables. Add any bran left in the sieve.

3 Whisk the egg whites until stiff and carefully fold them in,
a half at a time. Spoon into the tin. Bake in the oven for 1 hour,
covering the top with foil after 40 minutes. Leave to cool in
the tin for 5 minutes, then turn out on to a wire rack and
remove the lining paper.

4 For the topping, beat together the cheese and honey and
spread over the cake. Dust with icing sugar and decorate with
fondant carrots and courgettes.

Banana Coconut Cake

Slightly over-ripe bananas are best for this perfect coffee-morning cake.

Makes one 18cm/7in square cake

115g/4oz/½ cup butter, softened
115g/4oz/generous ½ cup caster sugar
2 eggs
115g/4oz/1 cup self-raising flour
50g/2oz/½ cup plain flour
5ml/1 tsp bicarbonate of soda
120ml/4fl oz/½ cup milk

2 large bananas, peeled and mashed
75g/3oz/1½ cups desiccated coconut, toasted

For the topping
25g/1oz/2 tbsp butter
30ml/2 tbsp clear honey
115g/4oz/2 cups shredded coconut

1 Preheat the oven to 190°C/375°F/Gas 5. Grease a deep 18cm/7in square cake tin, line with greaseproof paper and grease the paper.

2 Beat the butter and sugar until smooth and creamy. Beat in the eggs, one at a time. Sift together the flours and bicarbonate of soda, sift half into the butter mixture and stir to mix.

3 Combine the milk and mashed banana and beat half into the egg mixture. Stir in the remaining flour and banana mixtures and toasted coconut. Transfer to the cake tin and smooth the surface.

4 Bake for 1 hour, or until a skewer inserted into the centre of the cake comes out clean. Leave in the tin for 5 minutes, then turn out on to a wire rack, peel off the paper and cool.

5 For the topping, gently melt the butter and honey. Stir in the shredded coconut and cook, stirring, for 5 minutes or until lightly browned. Remove from the heat and allow to cool slightly. Spoon the topping over the cake and allow to cool.

St Clement's Cake

A tangy orange-and-lemon cake makes a spectacular centrepiece when decorated with fruits and flowers.

Makes one 23cm/9in ring cake

175g/6oz/¾ cup butter
75g/3oz/⅓ cup soft light brown sugar
3 eggs, separated
grated rind and juice of 1 orange and 1 lemon
150g/5oz/1¼ cups self-raising flour
75g/3oz/6 tbsp caster sugar

15g/½ oz/2 tbsp ground almonds
350ml/12fl oz/1½ cups double cream
15ml/1 tbsp Grand Marnier
16 crystallized orange and lemon slices, silver dragées, sugared almonds and fresh flowers, to decorate

1 Preheat the oven to 180°C/350°F/Gas 4. Grease and flour a 900ml/1½ pint/3¾ cup ring mould.

2 Cream half the butter and all of the brown sugar until pale and light. Beat in the egg yolks, orange rind and juice and fold in 75g/3oz/⅔ cup flour.

3 Cream the remaining butter and caster sugar. Stir in the lemon rind and juice and fold in the remaining flour and ground almonds. Whisk the egg whites until stiff, and fold in.

4 Spoon the two mixtures alternately into the prepared tin. Using a skewer or small spoon, swirl through the mixture to create a marbled effect. Bake for 45–50 minutes until risen, and a skewer inserted in the cake comes out clean. Cool in the tin for 10 minutes then transfer to a wire rack to cool.

5 Whip the cream and Grand Marnier together until lightly thickened. Spread over the cake and swirl a pattern over the icing with a palette knife. Decorate the ring with the crystallized fruits, dragées and sugared almonds to resemble a jewelled crown. Arrange a few fresh flowers in the centre.

Apple Cake

Makes one ring cake

675g/1½lb apples, peeled,
   cored and quartered
500g/1lb 2oz/generous
   2½ cups caster sugar
15ml/1 tbsp water
350g/12oz/3 cups plain
   flour
9ml/1¾ tsp bicarbonate of
   soda
5ml/1 tsp ground
   cinnamon
5ml/1 tsp ground cloves
175g/6oz/generous 1 cup
   raisins

150g/5oz/1¼ cups
   chopped walnuts
225g/8oz/1 cup butter or
   margarine, at room
   temperature
5ml/1 tsp vanilla essence

For the icing

115g/4oz/1 cup icing
   sugar
1.5ml/¼ tsp vanilla
   essence
30–45ml/2–3 tbsp milk

1   Put the apples, 50g/2oz/4 tbsp of the sugar and the water in a saucepan and bring to the boil. Simmer for 25 minutes, stirring occasionally to break up any lumps. Leave to cool. Preheat the oven to 160°C/325°F/Gas 3. Thoroughly butter and flour a 1.75-litre/3-pint/7½-cup tube tin.

2   Sift the flour, bicarbonate of soda and spices into a bowl. Remove 30ml/2 tbsp of the mixture to another bowl and toss with the raisins and 115g/4oz/1 cup of the walnuts.

3   Cream the butter or margarine and remaining sugar together until light and fluffy. Fold in the apple mixture gently. Fold the flour mixture into the apple mixture. Stir in the vanilla and the raisin and walnut mixture. Pour into the tube tin. Bake until a skewer inserted in the centre comes out clean, about 1½ hours. Cool completely in the tin on a wire rack, then unmould on to the rack.

4   For the icing, put the sugar in a bowl and stir in the vanilla and 15ml/1 tbsp milk. Add more milk until the icing is smooth and has a thick pouring consistency. Transfer the cake to a serving plate and drizzle the icing on top. Sprinkle with the remaining nuts. Allow the icing to set.

Chocolate Amaretto Marquise

This light-as-air marquise is perfect for a special occasion, served with Amaretto cream.

Makes one heart-shaped cake

15ml/1 tbsp sunflower oil
75g/3oz/7–8 amaretti
   biscuits, crushed
25g/1oz/2 tbsp
   unblanched almonds,
   toasted and
   finely chopped
450g/1lb plain chocolate,
   broken into pieces
75ml/5 tbsp Amaretto
   liqueur

75ml/5 tbsp golden syrup
475ml/16fl oz/2 cups
   double cream
cocoa powder, to dust

For the Amaretto cream

350ml/12fl oz 1½ cups
   whipping or
   double cream
30–45 ml/2–3 tbsp
   Amaretto liqueur

1   Lightly oil a 23cm/9in heart-shaped or springform cake tin. Line the base with non-stick baking paper and oil the paper. In a small bowl, combine the crushed amaretti biscuits and the chopped almonds. Sprinkle evenly over the base of the tin.

2   Place the chocolate, Amaretto liqueur and golden syrup in a saucepan over very low heat. Stir frequently until the chocolate is melted and the mixture is smooth. Allow to cool for 6–8 minutes, until the mixture just feels warm.

3   Beat the cream until it just begins to hold its shape. Stir a large spoonful into the chocolate mixture, then quickly add the remaining cream and gently fold into the chocolate mixture. Pour into the prepared tin and tap the tin gently on the work surface to release any large air bubbles. Cover the tin with clear film and leave in the fridge overnight.

4   To unmould, run a thin-bladed sharp knife under hot water and dry carefully. Run the knife around the edge of the tin to loosen, place a serving plate over the tin, then invert to unmould. Carefully peel off the paper then dust with cocoa. Whip the cream and liqueur and serve separately.

Tangy Lemon Cake

The lemon syrup forms a crusty topping when completely cooled. Leave in the tin until ready to serve.

Makes one 900g/2lb loaf

175g/6oz/¾ cup butter
175g/6oz/scant 1 cup
   caster sugar
3 eggs, beaten
175g/6oz/1½ cups self-
   raising flour
grated rind of 1 orange
grated rind of 1 lemon

For the syrup
115g/4oz/generous ½ cup
   caster sugar
juice of 2 lemons

1 Preheat the oven to 180°C/350°F/Gas 4. Then grease a 900g/2lb loaf tin.

2 Beat the butter and sugar together until light and fluffy, then gradually beat in the eggs. Fold in the flour and the orange and lemon rinds.

3 Turn the cake mixture into the cake tin and bake for 1¼–1½ hours, until set in the centre, risen and golden. Remove the cake from the oven, but leave in the tin.

4 To make the syrup, gently heat the sugar in the lemon juice until melted, then boil for 15 seconds. Pour the syrup over the cake in the tin and leave to cool.

Pineapple and Apricot Cake

This is not a long-keeping cake, but it does freeze, well-wrapped in greaseproof paper and then foil.

Makes one 18cm/7in square or 20cm/8in round cake

175g/6oz/¾ cup unsalted
   butter
150g/5oz/generous ¾ cup
   caster sugar
3 eggs, beaten
few drops vanilla
   essence
225g/8oz/2 cups plain
   flour
1.5ml/¼ tsp salt
7.5ml/1½ tsp baking
   powder

225g/8oz/1¾ cups ready-
   to-eat dried apricots,
   chopped
115g/4oz/½ cup each
   chopped crystallized
   ginger and
   crystallized pineapple
grated rind and juice of
   ½ orange
grated rind and juice of
   ½ lemon
a little milk

1 Preheat the oven to 180°C/350°F/Gas 4. Double line an 18cm/7in square or 20cm/8in round cake tin. Cream the butter and sugar together until light and fluffy.

2 Gradually beat in the eggs with the vanilla essence, beating well after each addition. Sift together the flour, salt and baking powder, add a little with the last of the egg, then fold in the rest.

3 Gently fold in the apricots, ginger and pineapple and the fruit rinds, then add sufficient fruit juice and milk to give a fairly soft dropping consistency.

4 Spoon into the cake tin and smooth the top with a wet spoon. Bake for 20 minutes, then reduce the oven temperature to 160°C/325°F/Gas 3 and bake for a further 1½–2 hours, or until firm to the touch and a skewer comes out of the centre clean. Leave the cake to cool completely in the tin. Wrap in fresh paper before storing in an airtight tin.

Soured Cream Crumble Cake

The consistency of this cake, with its two layers of crumble, is sublime.

Makes one 23cm/9in square cake

115g/4oz/½ cup butter,
    at room temperature
130g/4½oz/scant ¾ cup
    caster sugar
3 eggs
210g/7½oz/scant 2 cups
    plain flour
5ml/1 tsp bicarbonate of
    soda
5ml/1 tsp baking powder
250ml/8fl oz/1 cup
    soured cream

For the topping
225g/8oz/1 cup dark
    brown sugar
10ml/2 tsp ground
    cinnamon
115g/4oz/1 cup finely
    chopped walnuts
50g/2oz/4 tbsp cold
    butter, cut into pieces

1 Preheat the oven to 180°C/350°F/Gas 4. Line the base of a 23cm/9in square cake tin with greaseproof paper and grease the paper and sides.

2 For the topping, place the brown sugar, cinnamon and walnuts in a bowl. Mix, then add the butter and rub in until the mixture resembles breadcrumbs.

3 To make the cake, cream the butter until soft. Add the sugar and beat until light and fluffy. Add the eggs, one at a time, beating well after each addition.

4 In another bowl, sift the flour, bicarbonate of soda and baking powder together three times. Fold the dry ingredients into the butter mixture in three batches, alternating with the soured cream. Fold until blended after each addition.

5 Pour half of the batter into the prepared tin and sprinkle over half of the topping. Pour the remaining batter on top and sprinkle over the remaining topping. Bake until browned, 60–70 minutes. Leave in the tin for 5 minutes, then turn out and cool on a wire rack.

Plum Crumble Cake

This cake can also be made with the same quantity of apricots or cherries.

Serves 8–10

150g/5oz/generous ½ cup
    butter or margarine,
    at room temperature
150g/5oz/¾ cup caster
    sugar
4 eggs, at room
    temperature
7.5ml/1½ tsp vanilla
    essence
150g/5oz/1¼ cups plain
    flour
5ml/1 tsp baking powder

675g/1½lb red plums,
    halved and stoned

For the topping
115g/4oz/1 cup plain
    flour
130g/4½oz/generous
    ¾ cup light brown
    sugar
7.5ml/1½ tsp ground
    cinnamon
75g/3oz/6 tbsp butter,
    cut in pieces

1 Preheat the oven to 180°C/350°F/Gas 4. Using greaseproof paper, line a 25 x 5cm/10 x 2in tin and grease the paper. For the topping, combine the flour, light brown sugar and cinnamon in a bowl. Add the butter and rub in until it resembles coarse breadcrumbs.

2 Cream the butter or margarine and sugar until light and fluffy. Beat in the eggs, one at a time. Stir in the vanilla. In three batches, sift, then fold in the flour and baking powder.

3 Pour the mixture into the tin. Arrange the plums on top and sprinkle with the topping.

4 Bake until a skewer inserted in the centre comes out clean, about 45 minutes. Cool in the tin.

5 To serve, run a knife around the inside edge and invert on to a plate. Invert again on to a serving plate so the topping is uppermost.

Pineapple Upside-down Cake

For an apricot cake, replace the pineapple slices with 225g/8oz/1¾ cups dried ready-to-eat apricots.

Makes one 25cm/10in round cake

115g/4oz/½ cup butter	grated rind of 1 lemon
200g/7oz/generous 1 cup dark brown sugar	pinch of salt
450g/1lb canned pineapple slices, drained	115g/4oz/generous ½ cup caster sugar
	75g/3oz/¾ cup plain flour
4 eggs, separated	5ml/1 tsp baking powder

1 Preheat the oven to 180°C/350°F/Gas 4. Melt the butter in a 25cm/10in ovenproof cast-iron frying pan. Then reserve 15ml/1 tbsp butter. Add the brown sugar to the pan and stir to blend. Place the pineapple on top in one layer. Set aside.

2 Whisk together the egg yolks, reserved butter and lemon rind until well blended. Set aside.

3 Beat the egg whites and salt until stiff. Gradually fold in the caster sugar, then the egg yolk mixture.

4 Sift the flour and baking powder together. Carefully fold into the egg mixture in three batches.

5 Pour the mixture over the pineapple. Bake until a skewer inserted in the centre comes out clean, about 30 minutes.

6 While still hot, invert on to a serving plate. Serve hot or cold.

Upside-down Pear and Ginger Cake

This light spicy sponge, topped with glossy baked fruit and ginger, makes an excellent pudding.

Serves 6–8

900g/2lb can pear halves, drained	2.5ml/½ tsp baking powder
120ml/8 tbsp finely chopped stem ginger	5ml/1 tsp ground ginger
120ml/8 tbsp ginger syrup from the jar	175g/6oz/1 cup soft light brown sugar
175g/6oz/1½ cups self-raising flour	175g/6oz/¾ cup butter, softened
	3 eggs, lightly beaten

1 Preheat the oven to 180°C/350°F/Gas 4. Base-line and grease a deep 20cm/8in round cake tin.

2 Fill the hollow in each pear with half the chopped stem ginger. Arrange, flat-sides down, in the base of the cake tin, then spoon over half the ginger syrup.

3 Sift together the flour, baking powder and ground ginger. Stir in the sugar and butter, add the eggs and beat until creamy, 1–2 minutes.

4 Spoon the mixture into the cake tin. Bake in the oven for 50 minutes, or until a skewer inserted in the centre of the cake comes out clean. Leave the cake in the tin for 5 minutes. Turn out on to a wire rack, peel off the lining paper and leave to cool completely.

5 Add the reserved ginger to the pear halves and drizzle over the remaining syrup.

Cranberry and Apple Ring

Tangy cranberries add an unusual flavour to this cake which is best eaten very fresh.

Makes one ring cake

225g/8oz/2 cups self-
    raising flour
5ml/1 tsp ground
    cinnamon
75g/3oz/⅓ cup light
    muscovado sugar
1 eating apple, cored and
    diced

75g/3oz/¾ cup fresh or
    frozen cranberries
60ml/4 tbsp sunflower oil
150ml/¼ pint/⅔ cup
    apple juice
cranberry jelly and apple
    slices, to decorate

1 Preheat the oven to 180°C/350°F/Gas 4. Lightly grease a 1-litre/1¾-pint/4-cup ring tin with oil.

2 Sift together the flour and ground cinnamon, then stir in the muscovado sugar.

3 Toss together the diced apple and cranberries. Stir into the dry ingredients, then add the oil and apple juice and beat together well.

4 Spoon the mixture into the prepared ring tin and bake for 35–40 minutes, or until the cake is firm to the touch. Turn out and leave to cool completely on a wire rack.

5 To serve, drizzle warmed cranberry jelly over the cake and decorate with apple slices.

Greek Honey and Lemon Cake

A wonderfully moist and tangy cake, you could ice it if you wished.

Makes one 19cm/7½in square cake

40g/1½oz/3 tbsp
    sunflower margarine
60ml/4 tbsp clear honey
finely grated rind and
    juice of 1 lemon
150ml/¼ pint/⅔ cup milk
150g/5oz/1¼ cups plain
    flour

7.5ml/1½ tsp baking
    powder
2.5ml/½ tsp grated
    nutmeg
50g/2oz/¼ cup semolina
2 egg whites
10ml/2 tsp sesame seeds

1 Preheat the oven to 200°C/400°F/Gas 6. Lightly oil and base-line a 19cm/7½in square deep cake tin.

2 Place the margarine and 45ml/3 tbsp of the honey in a saucepan and heat gently until melted. Reserve 15ml/1 tbsp lemon juice, then stir in the rest with the lemon rind and milk.

3 Sift together the flour, baking powder and nutmeg, then beat in with the semolina. Whisk the egg whites until they form soft peaks, then fold evenly into the mixture.

4 Spoon into the cake tin and sprinkle with sesame seeds. Bake for 25–30 minutes, until golden brown. Mix the reserved honey and lemon juice and drizzle over the cake while warm. Cool in the tin, then cut into fingers to serve.

Pear and Cardamom Spice Cake

Fresh pears and cardamoms – a classic combination – are used together in this moist fruit and nut cake.

Makes one 20cm/8in round cake

115g/4oz/½ cup butter
115g/4oz/generous ½ cup
  caster sugar
2 eggs, lightly beaten
225g/8oz/2 cups plain
  flour
15ml/1 tbsp baking
  powder
30ml/2 tbsp milk
crushed seeds from
  2 cardamom pods

50g/2oz/½ cup walnuts,
  chopped
15ml/1 tbsp poppy seeds
500g/1¼lb dessert pears,
  peeled, cored and
  thinly sliced
3 walnut halves, to
  decorate
clear honey, to glaze

1 Preheat the oven to 180°C/350°F/Gas 4. Grease and base-line a 20cm/8in round, loose-based cake tin.

2 Cream the butter and sugar until pale and light. Gradually beat in the eggs. Sift over the flour and baking powder and fold in with the milk.

3 Stir in the cardamom seeds, chopped nuts and poppy seeds. Reserve one-third of the pear slices, and chop the rest. Fold into the creamed mixture.

4 Transfer to the cake tin. Smooth the surface, making a small dip in the centre. Place the walnut halves in the centre of the cake and fan the reserved pear slices around the walnuts, covering the cake mixture. Bake for 1¼–1½ hours, or until a skewer inserted in the centre comes out clean.

5 Remove the cake from the oven and brush with the honey. Leave in the tin for 20 minutes, then transfer to a wire rack to cool before serving.

Spiced Honey Nut Cake

A combination of ground pistachio nuts and breadcrumbs replaces flour in this recipe, resulting in a light, moist sponge cake.

Makes one 20cm/8in square cake

115g/4oz/generous ½ cup
  caster sugar
4 eggs, separated
grated rind and juice of 1
  lemon
130g/4½oz/generous 1
  cup ground pistachios
50g/2oz/scant 1 cup
  dried breadcrumbs

For the glaze
1 lemon
90ml/6 tbsp clear honey
1 cinnamon stick
15ml/1 tbsp brandy

1 Preheat the oven to 180°C/350°F/Gas 4. Grease and base-line a 20cm/8in square cake tin.

2 Beat the sugar, egg yolks, lemon rind and juice together until pale and creamy. Fold in 115g/4oz/1 cup of the ground pistachios and the breadcrumbs.

3 Whisk the egg whites until stiff and fold into the creamed mixture. Transfer to the cake tin and bake for 15 minutes, until risen and springy to the touch. Cool in the tin for 10 minutes, then transfer to a wire rack.

4 For the syrup, peel the lemon and cut the rind into very thin strips. Squeeze the juice into a small pan and add the honey and cinnamon stick. Bring to the boil, add the shredded rind, and simmer fast for 1 minute. Cool slightly and stir in the brandy.

5 Place the cake on a serving plate, prick all over with a skewer, and pour over the cooled syrup, lemon shreds and cinnamon stick. Sprinkle over the reserved pistachios.

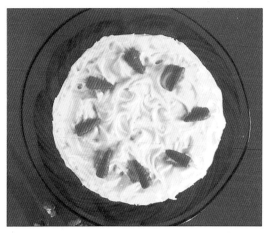

Clare's American Carrot Cake

Makes one 20cm/8in round cake

250ml/8fl oz/1 cup corn
oil
175g/6oz/1¼ cups
granulated sugar
3 eggs
175g/6oz/1½ cups plain
flour
7.5ml/1½ tsp baking
powder
7.5ml/1½ tsp bicarbonate
of soda
1.5ml/¼ tsp salt
7.5ml/1½ tsp ground
cinnamon
good pinch of grated
nutmeg
1.5ml/¼ tsp ground
ginger

115g/4oz/1 cup chopped
walnuts
225g/8oz/generous
1½ cups finely grated
carrots
5ml/1 tsp vanilla essence
30ml/2 tbsp soured
cream
8 tiny marzipan carrots,
to decorate

For the frosting

175g/6oz/1 cup full fat
soft cheese
25g/1oz/2 tbsp butter,
softened
225g/8oz/2 cups icing
sugar, sifted

1 Preheat the oven to 180°C/350°F/Gas 4. Grease and line two 20cm/8in loose-based round cake tins.

2 Put the corn oil and sugar into a bowl and beat well. Add the eggs, one at a time, and beat thoroughly. Sift the flour, baking powder, bicarbonate of soda, salt, cinnamon, nutmeg and ginger into the bowl and beat well. Fold in the chopped walnuts and grated carrots and stir in the vanilla essence and soured cream.

3 Divide the mixture between the cake tins and bake in the centre of the oven for about 65 minutes, or until a skewer inserted into the centre of the cakes comes out clean. Leave to cool in the tins on a wire rack. Meanwhile, beat all the frosting ingredients together until smooth.

4 Sandwich the cakes together with a little frosting. Spread the remaining frosting over the top and sides of the cake. Just before serving, decorate with the marzipan carrots.

Passion Cake

This cake is associated with Passion Sunday. The carrot and banana give it a rich, moist texture.

Makes one 20cm/8in round cake

200g/7oz/1¾ cups self-
raising flour
10ml/2 tsp baking
powder
5ml/1 tsp cinnamon
2.5ml/½ tsp freshly
grated nutmeg
150g/5oz/10 tbsp butter,
softened, or sunflower
margarine
150g/5oz/¾ cup soft
brown sugar
grated rind of 1 lemon
2 eggs, beaten
2 carrots, coarsely grated
1 ripe banana, mashed

115g/4oz/¾ cup raisins
50g/2oz/½ cup chopped
walnuts or pecan nuts
30ml/2 tbsp milk
6–8 walnuts, halved, to
decorate
coffee crystal sugar, to
decorate

For the frosting

200g/7oz/scant 1 cup
cream cheese, softened
30g/1½oz/scant ⅓ cup
icing sugar
juice of 1 lemon
grated rind of 1 orange

1 Line and grease a deep 20cm/8in round cake tin. Preheat the oven to 180°C/350°F/Gas 4. Sift the flour, baking powder and spices into a bowl. In another bowl, cream the butter and sugar with the lemon rind until it is light and fluffy, then beat in the eggs. Fold in the flour mixture, then the carrots, banana, raisins, chopped nuts and milk.

2 Spoon the mixture into the cake tin, level the top and bake for about 1 hour, until risen and the top is springy to touch. Turn the tin upside-down and allow the cake to cool in the tin for 30 minutes. Then turn out on to a wire rack. When cold, split the cake in half.

3 Cream the cheese with the icing sugar, lemon juice and orange rind, then sandwich the two halves of the cake together with half of the frosting. Spread the rest of the frosting on top and decorate with walnut halves and sugar.

Caribbean Fruit and Rum Cake

Definitely a festive treat, this spicy cake contains both rum and sherry.

Makes one 25cm/10in round cake

450g/1lb/2 cups currants
450g/1lb/2¾ cups raisins
225g/8oz/1 cup prunes, stoned
115g/4oz/¾ cup mixed peel
400g/14oz/2⅔ cups dark soft brown sugar
5ml/1 tsp mixed spice
90ml/6 tbsp rum, plus more if needed
300ml/½ pint/1¼ cups sherry, plus more if needed
450g/1lb/4 cups self-raising flour
450g/1lb/2 cups butter, softened
10 eggs, beaten
5ml/1 tsp vanilla essence

1 Finely chop the dried fruits and peel in a food processor. Combine them in a bowl with 115g/4oz/generous ½ cup of the sugar, the mixed spice, rum and sherry. Cover and leave for 2 weeks. Stir daily and add more alcohol if you wish.

2 Preheat the oven to 160°C/325°F/Gas 3. Grease and then line a 25cm/10in round cake tin with a double layer of greaseproof paper.

3 Sift the flour, and set aside. Cream together the butter and remaining sugar and beat in the eggs until the mixture is smooth and creamy.

4 Add the fruit mixture, then gradually stir in the flour and vanilla essence. Mix well, adding more sherry if the mixture is too stiff; it should just fall off the back of the spoon.

5 Spoon the mixture into the prepared tin, cover loosely with foil and bake for about 2½ hours, until the cake is firm and springy. Leave to cool in the tin overnight.

Thai Rice Cake

A celebration gâteau made from fragrant Thai rice covered with a tangy cream icing and topped with fresh fruits.

Makes one 25cm/10in round cake

225g/8oz/1¼ cups Thai fragrant rice
1 litre/1¾ pints/4½ cups milk
115g/4oz/½ cup caster sugar
6 cardamom pods, crushed open
2 bay leaves
300ml/½ pint/1¼ cups whipping cream
6 eggs, separated

For the topping
300ml/½ pint/1¼ cups double cream
200g/7oz/scant 1 cup quark
5ml/1 tsp vanilla essence
grated rind of 1 lemon
30g/1½oz/scant ¼ cup caster sugar
soft berry fruits and sliced star or kiwi fruit, to decorate

1 Grease and line a deep 25cm/10in round cake tin. Boil the rice in unsalted water for 3 minutes, then drain.

2 Return the rice to the pan with the milk, sugar, cardamom pods and bay leaves. Bring to the boil, then simmer for 20 minutes, stirring occasionally.

3 Allow to cool, then remove the bay leaves and any cardamom husks. Turn into a bowl. Beat in the cream and then the egg yolks. Preheat the oven to 180°C/350°F/Gas 4.

4 Whisk the egg whites until they form soft peaks and fold into the rice mixture. Spoon into the cake tin and bake for 45–50 minutes, until risen and golden brown. The centre should be slightly wobbly – it will firm up as it cools.

5 Chill overnight in the tin. Turn out on to a large serving plate. Whip the double cream until stiff, then mix in the quark, vanilla essence, lemon rind and sugar. Cover the top and sides of the cake with the cream, swirling it attractively. Decorate with soft berry fruits and sliced star or kiwi fruit.

Luxurious Chocolate Cake

This delicious chocolate cake contains no flour and has a light mousse-like texture.

Makes one 20cm/8in round cake

175g/6oz/¾ cup butter,
   softened
130g/3½oz/⅔ cup
   caster sugar
9 x 25g/1oz squares plain
   chocolate, melted

225g/8oz/2 cups ground
   almonds
4 eggs, separated
4 x 25g/1oz squares
   white chocolate,
   melted, to decorate

1 Preheat the oven to 180°C/350°F/Gas 4. Grease and base-line a 20cm/8in springform cake tin. Beat 115g/4oz butter and all the sugar until light and fluffy. Add two-thirds of the plain chocolate, the almonds and egg yolks and beat well.

2 Whisk the egg whites in another clean, dry bowl until stiff. Fold them into the chocolate mixture, then transfer to the tin and smooth the surface. Bake for 50–55 minutes or until a skewer inserted into the centre comes out clean. Cool in the tin for 5 minutes, then remove from the tin and transfer to a wire rack. Remove the lining paper and cool completely.

3 Place the remaining butter and remaining melted chocolate in a saucepan. Heat very gently, stirring constantly, until melted. Place a large sheet of greaseproof paper under the wire rack to catch any drips. Pour the chocolate topping over the cake, allowing the topping to coat the top and sides. Leave to set for at least 1 hour.

4 To decorate, fill a paper piping bag with the melted white chocolate and snip the end. Drizzle the white chocolate around the edges. Use any remaining chocolate to make leaves. Allow to set then place on top of the cake.

One-stage Chocolate Sponge

For family teas, quick and easy favourites like this chocolate cake are invaluable.

Makes one 18cm/7in round cake

175g/6oz/¾ cup soft
   margarine, at room
   temperature
115g/4oz/½ cup caster
   sugar
50g/2oz/4 tbsp golden
   syrup
175g/6oz/1½ cups self-
   raising flour, sifted
45ml/3 tbsp cocoa
   powder, sifted

2.5ml/½ tsp salt
3 eggs, beaten
a little milk, as required
150ml/¼ pint/⅔ cup
   whipping cream
15–30ml/1–2 tbsp fine
   shred marmalade
icing sugar, for dusting

1 Preheat the oven to 180°C/350°F/Gas 4. Lightly grease or line two 18cm/7in sandwich tins. Place the margarine, sugar, syrup, flour, cocoa, salt and eggs in a large bowl, and cream together until well blended. If the mixture seems a little thick, stir in 15–30ml/1–2 tbsp milk, until you have a soft dropping consistency.

2 Spoon the mixture into the prepared sandwich tins and bake for about 30 minutes, changing shelves if necessary after 15 minutes, until the tops are just firm and the cakes are springy to the touch.

3 Leave the cakes to cool for 5 minutes, then remove from the tins and leave to cool completely on a wire rack.

4 Whip the cream and fold in the marmalade, then use to sandwich the two cakes together. Sprinkle the top with sifted icing sugar.

One-stage Victoria Sandwich

This versatile sponge recipe can be used for all sorts of cakes.

Makes one 18cm/7in round cake

175g/6oz/1½ cups self-raising flour
pinch of salt
175g/6oz/¾ cup butter, softened
175g/6oz/scant 1 cup caster sugar
3 eggs

To finish
60 – 90ml/4 – 6 tbsp raspberry jam
caster sugar or icing sugar

1 Preheat the oven to 180°C/350°F/Gas 4. Grease two 18cm/7in sandwich tins, line the bases with greaseproof paper and grease the paper.

2 Whisk all the cake ingredients together until smooth and creamy. Divide the mixture between the cake tins and smooth the surfaces. Bake for 25 – 30 minutes, or until a skewer inserted into the centre of the cakes comes out clean. Turn out on to a wire rack, peel off the lining paper and leave to cool.

3 Place one of the cakes on a serving plate and spread with the raspberry jam. Place the other cake on top.

4 Cut out paper star shapes, place on the cake and dredge with sugar. Remove the paper to reveal the pattern.

Mocha Victoria Sponge

A light coffee- and cocoa-flavoured sponge with a ric buttercream topping.

Makes one 18cm/7in round cake

175g/6oz/¾ cup butter
175g/6oz/generous ¾ cup caster sugar
3 eggs
175g/6oz/1½ cups self-raising flour, sifted
15ml/1 tbsp strong black coffee
15ml/1 tbsp cocoa powder mixed with 15 – 30ml/1 – 2 tbsp boiling water

For the coffee buttercream
150g/5oz/generous ½ cup butter
15ml/1 tbsp coffee essence or 10ml/2 tsp instant coffee powder dissolved in 15 – 30ml/1 – 2 tbsp warm milk
275g/10oz/2½ cups icing sugar

1 Preheat the oven to 180°C/350°F/Gas 4. Grease and base-line two 18cm/7in round sandwich tins. For the sponge, cream the butter and sugar until light and fluffy. Add the eggs, one at a time, beating well after each addition. Fold in the flour.

2 Divide the mixture into two bowls. Fold the coffee into one and the cocoa mixture into the other.

3 Place alternate spoonfuls of each mixture side by side in the cake tins. Bake for 25 – 30 minutes. Turn out on to a wire rack to cool.

4 For the buttercream, beat the butter until soft. Gradually beat in the remaining ingredients until smooth.

5 Sandwich the cakes, base-sides together, with a third of the buttercream. Cover the top and side with the rest.

Lemon and Apricot Cake

This cake is soaked in a tangy lemon syrup after baking to keep it really moist.

Makes one 23 x 13cm/9 x 5in loaf

175g/6oz/¾ cup butter, softened
175g/6oz/1½ cups self-raising flour
2.5ml/½ tsp baking powder
175g/6oz/¾ cup caster sugar
3 eggs, lightly beaten
finely grated rind of 1 lemon
175g/6oz/1½ cups ready-to-eat dried apricots, finely chopped

75g/3oz/¾ cup ground almonds
40g/1½oz/6 tbsp pistachio nuts, chopped
50g/2oz/½ cup flaked almonds
15g/½oz/2 tbsp whole pistachio nuts

For the syrup
45ml/3 tbsp caster sugar
freshly squeezed juice of 1 lemon

1 Preheat the oven to 180°C/350°F/Gas 4. Grease and line a 23 x 13cm/9 x 5in loaf tin with greaseproof paper and grease the paper.

2 Place the butter in a mixing bowl. Sift over the flour and baking powder, then add the sugar, eggs and lemon rind. Beat for 1–2 minutes until smooth and glossy, then stir in the apricots, ground almonds and chopped pistachio nuts.

3 Spoon the mixture into the loaf tin and smooth the surface. Sprinkle with the flaked almonds and the whole pistachio nuts. Bake for 1¼ hours, or until a skewer inserted into the centre of the cake comes out clean. Check the cake after 45 minutes and cover with a piece of foil when the top is nicely browned. Leave the cake to cool in the tin.

4 For the lemon syrup, gently dissolve the sugar in the lemon juice. Spoon the syrup over the cake. When the cake is completely cooled, turn it carefully out of the tin and peel off the lining paper.

Cherry Batter Cake

This colourful tray bake looks pretty cut into neat squares or fingers.

Makes one 33 x 23cm/13 x 9in cake

225g/8oz/2 cups self-raising flour
5ml/1 tsp baking powder
75g/3oz/6 tbsp butter, softened
150g/5oz/scant 1 cup soft light brown sugar
1 egg, lightly beaten
150ml/¼ pint/⅔ cup milk
icing sugar, for dusting
whipped cream, to serve (optional)

For the topping
675g/1½lb jar black cherries or blackcurrants, drained
175g/6oz/1 cup soft light brown sugar
50g/2oz/½ cup self-raising flour
50g/2oz/¼ cup butter, melted

1 Preheat the oven to 190°C/375°F/Gas 5. Grease and line a 33 x 23cm/13 x 9in Swiss roll tin with greaseproof paper and grease the paper.

2 To make the base, sift the flour and baking powder into a mixing bowl. Add the butter, sugar, egg and milk. Beat until the mixture becomes smooth, then turn into the prepared tin and smooth the surface.

3 Scatter the drained fruit evenly over the batter mixture.

4 Mix together the remaining topping ingredients and spoon evenly over the fruit. Bake for 40 minutes, or until golden brown and the centre is firm to the touch.

5 Leave to cool, then dust with icing sugar. Serve with whipped cream, if wished.

Fruit Salad Cake

You can use any combination of dried fruits in this rich dark fruit cake.

Makes one 18cm/7in round cake

175g/6oz/1 cup roughly chopped mixed dried fruit, such as apples, apricots, prunes and peaches
250ml/8fl oz/1 cup hot tea
225g/8oz/2 cups wholemeal self-raising flour

5ml/1 tsp grated nutmeg
50g/2oz/⅓ cup dark muscovado sugar
45ml/3 tbsp sunflower oil
45ml/3 tbsp skimmed milk
demerara sugar, for sprinkling

1 Soak the dried fruits in the tea for several hours or overnight. Drain and reserve the liquid.

2 Preheat the oven to 180°C/350°F/Gas 4. Grease an 18cm/7in round cake tin and line the base with non-stick baking paper.

3 Sift the flour into a bowl with the nutmeg. Stir in the muscovado sugar, fruit and tea. Add the oil and milk, and mix well.

4 Spoon the mixture into the cake tin and sprinkle with demerara sugar. Bake for 50–55 minutes or until firm. Turn out on to a wire rack to cool.

Fairy Cakes with Blueberries

This luxurious treatment of fairy cakes means they will be as popular with adults as with children.

Makes 8–10

115g/4oz/½ cup soft margarine
115g/4oz/½ cup caster sugar
5ml/1 tsp grated lemon rind
pinch of salt
2 eggs, beaten

115g/4oz/1 cup self-raising flour, sifted
120ml/4fl oz/½ cup whipping cream
75–115g/3–4oz/¾– 1 cup blueberries
icing sugar, for dusting

1 Preheat the oven to 190°C/375°F/Gas 5. Cream the margarine, sugar, lemon rind and salt in a large bowl until pale and fluffy.

2 Gradually beat in the eggs, then fold in the flour until well mixed. Spoon the mixture into eight to ten paper cases on baking sheets and bake for 15–20 minutes, until just golden.

3 Leave the cakes to cool, then scoop out a circle of sponge from the top of each using the point of a small sharp knife, and set them aside.

4 Whip the cream and place a spoonful in each cake, plus a couple of blueberries. Replace the lids at an angle and sift over some icing sugar.

Jewel Cake

This pretty cake is excellent served as a tea-time treat.

Makes one 23 x 13cm/9 x 5in cake

115g/4oz/½ cup mixed
  glacé cherries, halved,
  washed and dried
50g/2oz/4 tbsp stem
  ginger in syrup,
  chopped, washed and
  dried
50g/2oz/5 tbsp chopped
  mixed peel
115g/4oz/1 cup self-
  raising flour
75g/3oz/¼ cup plain
  flour
25g/1oz/3 tbsp cornflour
175g/6oz/¾ cup butter

175g/6oz/scant 1 cup
  caster sugar
3 eggs
grated rind of 1 orange

To decorate

175g/6oz/1½ cups icing
  sugar, sifted
30–45ml/2–3 tbsp
  freshly squeezed
  orange juice
50g/2oz/¼ cup mixed
  glacé cherries, chopped
25g/1oz/2½ tbsp mixed
  peel, chopped

1 Preheat the oven to 180°C/350°F/Gas 4. Grease and line a 23 x 13cm/9 x 5in loaf tin and grease the paper.

2 Place the cherries, stem ginger and mixed peel in a polythene bag with 25g/1oz/4 tbsp of the self-raising flour and shake to coat evenly. Sift together the remaining flours and cornflour.

3 Beat together the butter and sugar until light and fluffy. Beat in the eggs, one at a time. Fold in the sifted flours with the orange rind, then stir in the dried fruit.

4 Transfer the mixture to the cake tin and bake for 1¼ hours, or until a skewer inserted into the centre comes out clean. Leave in the tin for 5 minutes, then cool on a wire rack.

5 For the decoration, mix the icing sugar with the orange juice until smooth. Drizzle the icing over the cake. Mix together the chopped glacé cherries and mixed peel, then use to decorate the cake. Allow the icing to set before serving.

Iced Paradise Cake

Makes one 23 x 13cm/9 x 5in cake

3 eggs
75g/3oz/scant ½ cup
  caster sugar
65g/12½oz/9 tbsp plain
  flour
15g/½oz/1 tbsp
  cornflour
90ml/6 tbsp dark rum
250g/9oz/1½ cups plain
  chocolate chips
30ml/2 tbsp golden syrup
30ml/2 tbsp water

400ml/14fl oz/1¾ cups
  double cream
115g/4oz/scant 1 cup
  desiccated coconut,
  toasted
25g/1oz/2 tbsp unsalted
  butter
30ml/2 tbsp single cream
50g/2oz/5 tbsp white
  chocolate chips, melted
coconut curls, to decorate
cocoa powder, for dusting

1 Preheat the oven to 200°C/400°F/Gas 6. Grease and flour two baking sheets. Line a 23 x 13cm/9 x 5in tin with clear film.

2 Whisk the eggs and sugar in a heatproof bowl until blended. Place over a pan of simmering water and whisk until pale and thick. Whisk off the heat until cool. Sift over the flour and cornflour and fold in. Pipe 30 8cm/3in sponge fingers on to the baking sheets. Bake for 8–10 minutes. Cool slightly on the sheets, then on a wire rack.

3 Line the base and sides of the loaf tin with sponge fingers. Brush with rum. Melt 75g/3oz/½ cup chocolate chips, syrup, water and 30ml/2 tbsp rum in a bowl over simmering water.

4 Whip the double cream until it holds its shape, stir in the chocolate mixture and toasted coconut. Pour into the tin and top with the remaining sponge fingers. Brush over the remaining rum. Cover with clear film and freeze until firm.

5 Melt the remaining chocolate, butter and cream as before, then cool slightly. Turn the cake out on to a wire rack. Pour over the icing to coat. Chill.

6 Drizzle the white chocolate in zigzags over the cake. Chill. Sprinkle with coconut curls and dust with cocoa powder.

Pound Cake with Red Fruit

This orange-scented cake is good for tea, or serve as a dessert with a fruit coulis.

Makes one 20 x 10cm/8 x 4in cake

450g/1lb/about 4 cups
  fresh raspberries,
  strawberries or stoned
  cherries, or a
  combination of any of
  these
175g/6oz/¾ cup caster
  sugar, plus
  15–30ml/1–2 tbsp,
  plus extra for
  sprinkling

15ml/1 tbsp lemon juice
175g/6oz/1½ cups plain
  flour
10ml/2 tsp baking
  powder
pinch of salt
175g/6oz/¾ cup unsalted
  butter, softened
3 eggs
grated rind of 1 orange
15ml/1 tbsp orange juice

1 Reserve a few whole fruits for decorating. In a blender or food processor, process the fruit until smooth. Add 15–30ml/1–2 tbsp sugar and the lemon juice, and process again. Strain the sauce and chill.

2 Grease the base and sides of a 20 x 10cm/8 x 4in loaf tin and line the base with non-stick baking paper. Grease the paper. Sprinkle with sugar and tip out any excess. Preheat the oven to 180°C/350°F/Gas 4.

3 Sift together the flour, baking powder and a pinch of salt. Beat the butter until creamy. Add the sugar and beat until light and fluffy. Add the eggs, one at a time, beating well after each addition. Beat in the orange rind and juice. Gently fold the flour mixture into the butter mixture in three batches, then spoon the mixture into the loaf tin and tap gently to release any air bubbles.

4 Bake for 35–40 minutes, until the top is golden and it is springy to the touch. Leave the cake in its tin on a wire rack for 10 minutes, then remove the cake from the tin and cool for 30 minutes. Remove the paper and serve slices of cake with a little of the fruit sauce, decorated with the reserved fruit.

Madeleine Cakes

These little tea cakes, baked in a special tin with shell-shaped cups, are best eaten on the day they are made.

Makes 12

165g/5½oz/generous
  1¼ cups plain flour
5ml/1 tsp baking powder
2 eggs
75g/3oz/½ cup icing
  sugar, plus extra for
  dusting

grated rind of 1 lemon or
  orange
15ml/1 tbsp lemon or
  orange juice
75g/3oz/6 tbsp unsalted
  butter, melted and
  slightly cooled

1 Preheat the oven to 190°C/375°F/Gas 5. Generously grease a 12-cup madeleine cake tin. Sift together the flour and the baking powder.

2 Beat the eggs and icing sugar until the mixture is thick and creamy and leaves ribbon trails. Gently fold in the lemon or orange rind and juice.

3 Beginning with the flour mixture, alternately fold in the flour and melted butter in four batches. Leave to stand for 10 minutes, then spoon into the tin. Tap gently to release any air bubbles. Bake for 12–15 minutes, rotating the tin halfway through cooking, until a skewer inserted in the centre comes out clean. Tip out on to a wire rack to cool completely and dust with icing sugar before serving.

Chocolate-orange Battenburg Cake

A tasty variation on the traditional pink-and-white Battenburg cake.

Makes one 18cm/7in long rectangular cake

115g/4oz/½ cup soft
  margarine
115g/4oz/½ cup caster
  sugar
2 eggs, beaten
few drops vanilla essence
15g/½oz/1 tbsp ground
  almonds
115g/4oz/1 cup self-
  raising flour, sifted

grated rind and juice of
  ½ orange
15g/½oz/2 tbsp cocoa
  powder, sifted
30–45ml/2–3 tbsp milk
1 jar chocolate and nut
  spread
225g/8oz white almond
  paste

1 Preheat the oven to 180°C/350°F/Gas 4. Grease and line an 18cm/7in square cake tin. Put a double piece of foil across the middle of the tin, to divide it into two equal oblongs.

2 Cream the margarine and sugar. Beat in the eggs, vanilla and almonds. Divide the mixture evenly into two halves. Fold half of the flour into one half, with the orange rind and enough juice to give a soft dropping consistency. Fold the rest of the flour and the cocoa into the other half, with enough milk to give a soft dropping consistency. Fill the tin with the two mixes and level the top.

3 Bake for 15 minutes, reduce the heat to 160°C/325°F/Gas 3 and cook for 20–30 minutes, until the top is just firm. Leave to cool in the tin for a few minutes. Turn out on to a board, cut each cake into two strips and trim evenly. Leave to cool.

4 Using the spread, sandwich the cakes together, Battenburg-style. Roll out the almond paste on a board lightly dusted with cornflour to a rectangle 18cm/7in wide and long enough to wrap around the cake. Wrap the paste around the cake, putting the join underneath. Press to seal.

Best-ever Chocolate Sandwich

A three-layered cake that would be ideal for a birthday party or a special high tea.

Makes one 20cm/8in round cake

115g/4oz/1cup plain
  flour
50g/2oz/½ cup cocoa
  powder
5ml/1 tsp baking powder
pinch of salt
6 eggs
225g/8oz/generous 1 cup
  caster sugar
10ml/2 tsp vanilla
  essence

115g/4oz/½ cup unsalted
  butter, melted
225g/8oz plain chocolate,
  chopped
75g/3oz/6 tbsp unsalted
  butter
3 eggs, separated
250ml/8fl oz/1 cup
  whipping cream
45ml/3 tbsp caster sugar

1 Preheat the oven to 180°C/350°F/Gas 4. Line three 20cm/8in round tins with greaseproof paper, grease the paper and dust with flour. Sift the flour, cocoa, baking powder and salt together three times.

2 Place the eggs and sugar in a heatproof bowl set over a pan of simmering water. Beat until doubled in volume, about 10 minutes. Add the vanilla. Fold in the flour mixture in three batches, then the butter.

3 Put the mixture in the tins. Bake until the cakes pull away from the tin sides, about 25 minutes. Transfer to a wire rack.

4 For the icing, melt the chocolate in the top of a double boiler. Off the heat, stir in the butter and egg yolks. Return to the heat and stir until thick.

5 Whip the cream until firm. In another bowl, beat the egg whites until stiff. Add the sugar and beat until glossy. Fold the cream, then the egg whites, into the chocolate mixture. Chill for about 20 minutes, then sandwich together and cover the cake with icing.

Chocolate Layer Cake

Makes one 23cm/9in cake

225g/8oz can cooked whole beetroot, drained and juice reserved
115g/4oz/½ cup unsalted butter, softened
550g/1lb 6oz/2½ cups light brown sugar
3 eggs
15ml/1 tbsp vanilla essence
75g/3oz unsweetened chocolate, melted
285g/10oz/2 cups plain flour
10ml/2 tsp baking powder
2.5ml/½ tsp salt
120ml/4fl oz/½ cup buttermilk
chocolate curls, to decorate (optional)

For the frosting
450ml/16fl oz/2 cups double cream
500g/1lb 2oz plain chocolate, chopped
15ml/1 tbsp vanilla essence

1 Preheat the oven to 180°C/350°F/Gas 4. Grease two 23cm/9in cake tins and dust with cocoa powder. Grate the beetroot and add it to its juice. Beat the butter, brown sugar, eggs and vanilla until pale and fluffy. Beat in the chocolate.

2 Sift together the flour, baking powder and salt. With the mixer on low speed and beginning and ending with flour mixture, alternately beat in flour and buttermilk. Add the beetroot and juice and beat for 1 minute. Fill the tins and bake for 30–35 minutes, until a skewer inserted in the centre comes out clean. Cool for 10 minutes, then unmould and cool.

3 To make the frosting, heat the cream until it just begins to boil, stirring occasionally to prevent scorching. Remove from the heat and stir in the chocolate, until melted and smooth. Stir in the vanilla. Strain into a bowl and chill, stirring every 10 minutes, for 1 hour.

4 Sandwich and cover the cake with frosting, and top with chocolate curls, if using. Allow to set for 20–30 minutes, then chill before serving.

Marbled Chocolate-peanut Cake

Serves 12–14

115g/4oz unsweetened chocolate, chopped
225g/8oz/1 cup unsalted butter, softened
225g/8oz/1 cup peanut butter
200g/6½oz/1 cup granulated sugar
220g/7oz/1 cup light brown sugar
5 eggs
285g/10oz/2 cups plain flour
10ml/2 tsp baking powder
2.5ml/½ tsp salt
125ml/4fl oz/½ cup milk
50g/2oz/5 tbsp chocolate chips

For the chocolate-peanut butter glaze
25g/1oz/2 tbsp butter, diced
25g/1oz/2 tbsp smooth peanut butter
45ml/3 tbsp golden syrup
5ml/1 tsp vanilla essence
175g/6oz plain chocolate, broken into pieces

1 Preheat the oven to 180°C/350°F/Gas 4. Grease and flour a 3-litre/5-pint/12-cup tube tin or ring mould. In the top of a double boiler, melt the chocolate.

2 Beat the butter, peanut butter and sugars until light and creamy. Add the eggs, one at a time, beating well after each addition. Sift together the flour, baking powder and salt. Add to the butter mixture alternately with the milk.

3 Pour half the batter into another bowl. Stir the melted chocolate into one half and stir the chocolate chips into the other half. Drop alternate large spoonfuls of the two batters into the tin or mould. Using a knife, pull through the batters to create a swirled marbled effect; do not let the knife touch the side or base of the tin. Bake for 50–60 minutes, until the top springs back when touched. Cool in the tin on a wire rack for 10 minutes. Then unmould on to the wire rack.

4 Combine the glaze ingredients and 15ml/1 tbsp water in a small saucepan. Melt over a low heat, stirring. Cool slightly, then drizzle over the cake, allowing it to run down the side.

Chocolate Fairy Cakes

Makes 24

115g/4oz good-quality
    plain chocolate, cut
    into small pieces
15ml/1 tbsp water
300g/10oz/2½ cups plain
    flour
5ml/1 tsp baking powder
2.5ml/½ tsp bicarbonate
    of soda
pinch of salt
300g/10oz/scant 1½ cups
    caster sugar

170g/6oz/¾ cup butter or
    margarine, at room
    temperature
150ml/¼ pint/⅔ cup milk
5ml/1 tsp vanilla essence
3 eggs
1 recipe quantity
    buttercream, flavoured
    to taste

1 Preheat the oven to 180°C/350°F/Gas 4. Grease and flour 24 deep bun tins, about 6.5cm/2¾in in diameter, or use paper cases in the tins.

2 Put the chocolate and water in a bowl set over a pan of almost simmering water. Heat until melted and smooth, stirring. Remove from the heat and leave to cool.

3 Sift the flour, baking powder, bicarbonate of soda, salt and sugar into a large bowl. Add the chocolate mixture, butter or margarine, milk and vanilla essence.

4 With an electric mixer on medium-low speed, beat until smoothly blended. Increase the speed to high and beat for 2 minutes. Add the eggs and beat for 2 more minutes.

5 Divide the mixture evenly among the prepared bun tins and bake for 20–25 minutes, or until a skewer inserted into the centre of a cake comes out clean. Cool in the tins for 10 minutes, then turn out to cool completely on a wire rack.

6 Ice the top of each cake with buttercream, swirling it into a peak in the centre.

Chocolate Mint-filled Cupcakes

For extra mint flavour, chop eight thin mint cream-filled after-dinner mints and fold into the cake batter.

Makes 12

225g/8oz/2 cups plain
    flour
5ml/1 tsp bicarbonate of
    soda
pinch of salt
50g/2oz/½ cup cocoa
    powder
150g/5oz/10 tbsp
    unsalted butter,
    softened
300g/10½oz/1½ cups
    caster sugar
3 eggs
5ml/1 tsp peppermint
    essence

250ml/8fl oz/1 cup milk

For the filling
300ml/10fl oz/1¼ cups
    double or whipping
    cream
5ml/1 tsp peppermint
    essence

For the glaze
170g/6oz plain chocolate
115g/4oz/½ cup unsalted
    butter
5ml/1 tsp peppermint
    essence

1 Preheat the oven to 180°C/350°F/Gas 4. Line a 12-cup bun tray with paper cases. Sift together the flour, bicarbonate of soda, salt and cocoa powder. In another bowl, beat the butter and sugar until light and creamy. Add the eggs, one at a time, beating well after each addition; beat in the peppermint. On low speed, beat in the flour mixture alternately with the milk, until just blended. Spoon into the paper cases.

2 Bake for 12–15 minutes, until a skewer inserted in the centre of a cake comes out clean. Transfer to a wire rack to cool. When cool, remove the paper cases.

3 For the filling, whip the cream and peppermint until stiff. Spoon into a piping bag fitted with a small plain nozzle. Pipe about 15ml/1 tbsp into each cake through the base.

4 For the glaze, melt the chocolate and butter, stirring until smooth. Remove from the heat and stir in the peppermint essence. Cool, then spread on top of each cake.

Rich Chocolate Nut Cake

Use walnuts or pecan nuts for the cake sides if you prefer.

Makes one 23cm/9in round cake

225g/8oz/1 cup butter
225g/8oz plain chocolate
115g/4oz/1 cup cocoa
    powder
350g/12oz/1¾ cups
    caster sugar
6 eggs
85ml/3fl oz/5 tbsp
    brandy

225g/8oz/2 cups finely
    chopped hazelnuts

For the glaze
50g/2oz/4 tbsp butter
150g/5oz bitter cooking
    chocolate
30ml/2 tbsp milk
5ml/1 tsp vanilla essence

1 Preheat the oven to 180°C/350°F/Gas 4. Line a 23 x 5cm/ 9 x 2in round tin with greaseproof paper and grease the paper. Melt the butter and chocolate in the top of a double boiler. Leave to cool.

2 Sift the cocoa into a bowl. Add the sugar and eggs and stir until just combined. Pour in the chocolate mixture and brandy. Fold in three-quarters of the nuts, then pour the mixture into the cake tin.

3 Set the tin in a roasting tin and pour 2.5cm/1in hot water into the outer tin. Bake until the cake is firm to the touch, about 45 minutes. Leave for 15 minutes, then unmould on to a wire rack. When cool, wrap in greaseproof paper and chill for at least 6 hours.

4 For the glaze, melt the butter and chocolate with the milk and vanilla in the top of a double boiler.

5 Place the cake on a wire rack over a plate. Drizzle the glaze over, letting it drip down the sides. Cover the cake sides with the remaining nuts. Transfer to a serving plate when set.

Multi-layer Chocolate Cake

For a change, sandwich the cake layers with softened vanilla ice cream. Freeze before serving.

Makes one 20cm/8in round cake

115g/4oz plain chocolate
175g/6oz/¾ cup butter
450g/1lb/2¼ cups caster
    sugar
3 eggs
5ml/1 tsp vanilla essence
175g/6oz/1½ cups plain
    flour
5ml/1 tsp baking powder

115g/4oz/1 cup chopped
    walnuts

For the filling and topping
350g/12fl oz/1½ cups
    whipping cream
225g/8oz plain chocolate
15ml/1 tbsp vegetable oil

1 Preheat the oven to 180°C/350°F/Gas 4. Line two 20cm/8in round cake tins with greaseproof paper and grease the paper.

2 Melt the chocolate and butter in the top of a double boiler. Transfer to a bowl and stir in the sugar. Add the eggs and vanilla and mix well. Sift over the flour and baking powder. Stir in the walnuts.

3 Pour the mixture into the cake tins. Bake until a skewer inserted in the centre comes out clean, about 30 minutes. Stand for 10 minutes, then unmould on to a wire rack to cool.

4 Whip the cream until firm. Slice the cakes in half horizontally. Sandwich them together and cover the cake with the cream. Chill.

5 To make the chocolate curls, melt the chocolate and oil in the top of a double boiler. Spread on to a non-porous surface. Just before it sets, hold the blade of a knife at an angle to the chocolate and scrape across the surface to make curls. Use to decorate the cake.

Chocolate Frosted Layer Cake

The contrast between the frosting and the sponge creates a dramatic effect when the cake is cut.

Makes one 20cm/8in round cake

225g/8oz/1 cup butter or margarine, at room temperature	10ml/2 tsp baking powder
285g/10½oz/1½ cups sugar	1.5ml/¼ tsp salt
4 eggs, separated	250ml/8fl oz/1 cup milk
10ml/2 tsp vanilla essence	**For the frosting**
385g/13½oz/3½ cups plain flour	150g/5oz plain chocolate
	120ml/4fl oz/½ cup soured cream
	1.5ml/¼ tsp salt

1 Preheat the oven to 180°C/350°F/Gas 4. Line two 20cm/8in round cake tins with greaseproof paper and grease the paper. Dust the tins with flour. Tap to remove any excess.

2 Cream the butter or margarine until soft. Gradually add the sugar and beat until light and fluffy. Beat the egg yolks, then add to the butter mixture with the vanilla.

3 Sift the flour with the baking powder three times. Set aside. Beat the egg whites with the salt until they peak stiffly.

4 Fold the dry ingredients into the butter mixture in three batches, alternating with the milk. Add a dollop of the egg white and fold in to lighten the mixture. Fold in the rest until just blended.

5 Spoon into the cake tins and bake until the cakes pull away from the sides, about 30 minutes. Leave in the tins for 5 minutes, then turn out on to a wire rack.

6 For the frosting, melt the chocolate in the top of a double boiler. When cool, stir in the soured cream and salt. Sandwich the layers with frosting, then spread on the top and side.

Devil's Food Cake with Orange

Makes one 23cm/9in round cake

50g/2oz/½ cup cocoa powder	120ml/4fl oz/½ cup soured cream
175ml/6fl oz/¾ cup boiling water	blanched orange rind shreds, to decorate
175g/6oz/¾ cup butter, at room temperature	
350g/12oz/2 cups dark brown sugar	**For the frosting**
3 eggs	285g/10½oz/1½ cups caster sugar
275g/10oz/2½ cups plain flour	2 egg whites
7.5ml/1½ tsp bicarbonate of soda	60ml/4 tbsp frozen orange juice concentrate
1.5ml/¼ tsp baking powder	15ml/1 tbsp lemon juice grated rind of 1 orange

1 Preheat the oven to 180°C/350°F/Gas 4. Line two 23cm/9in cake tins with greaseproof paper and grease the paper. In a bowl, mix the cocoa and water until smooth.

2 Cream the butter and sugar until light and fluffy. Add the eggs, one at a time, beating well after each addition. When the cocoa mixture is lukewarm, add to the butter mixture. Sift together the flour, soda and baking powder twice. Fold into the cocoa mixture in three batches, alternating with the soured cream. Pour into the tins and bake until the cakes pull away from the sides, 30–35 minutes. Stand for 15 minutes, then turn out on to a wire rack.

3 For the frosting, place all the ingredients in the top of a double boiler. With an electric mixer, beat until the mixture holds soft peaks. Continue beating off the heat until thick enough to spread.

4 Sandwich the cake layers with frosting, then spread over the top and side. Decorate with orange rind shreds.

French Chocolate Cake

This is typical of a French home-made cake – dense, dark and delicious. Serve with cream or a fruit coulis.

Makes one 24cm/9½in round cake

150g/5oz/5 tbsp caster sugar	5 eggs, separated
275g/10oz plain chocolate, chopped	40g/1½oz/¼ cup plain flour, sifted
175g/6oz/¾ cup unsalted butter, cut into pieces	pinch of salt
10ml/2 tsp vanilla essence	icing sugar, for dusting

1 Preheat the oven to 160°C/325°F/Gas 3. Butter a 24cm/9½in springform tin, sprinkle with sugar and tap out the excess.

2 Set aside 45ml/3 tbsp of the sugar. Place the chocolate, butter and remaining sugar in a heavy saucepan and cook over a low heat until melted. Remove from the heat, stir in the vanilla essence and leave to cool slightly.

3 Beat the egg yolks, one at a time, into the chocolate mixture, then stir in the flour.

4 Beat the egg whites with the salt until soft peaks form. Sprinkle over the reserved sugar and beat until stiff and glossy. Beat one-third of the whites into the chocolate mixture, then fold in the rest.

5 Pour the mixture into the tin and tap it gently to release any air bubbles.

6 Bake the cake for 35–45 minutes, until well risen and the top springs back when touched lightly. Transfer to a wire rack, remove the sides of the tin and leave to cool. Remove the tin base, dust the cake with icing sugar and transfer to a serving plate.

Almond Cake

Serve this wonderfully nutty cake with coffee, or, for a treat, with a glass of almond liqueur.

Makes one 23cm/9in round cake

225g/8oz/1⅓ cups blanched, toasted whole almonds	2.5ml/½ tsp almond essence
75g/3oz/5 tbsp icing sugar	25g/1oz/4 tbsp plain flour
3 eggs	3 egg whites
25g/1oz/2 tbsp butter, melted	15ml/1 tbsp caster sugar
	toasted whole almonds, to decorate

1 Preheat the oven to 160°C/325°F/Gas 3. Line a 23cm/9in round cake tin with greaseproof paper and grease the paper.

2 Coarsely chop the almonds and grind them with half the icing sugar in a blender or food processor. Transfer to a mixing bowl.

3 Beat in the whole eggs and remaining icing sugar until the mixture forms ribbon trails. Mix in the butter and almond essence. Sift over the flour and fold in.

4 Beat the egg whites until they peak softly. Add the caster sugar and beat until stiff and glossy. Fold into the almond mixture in four batches.

5 Spoon the mixture into the cake tin and bake until golden brown, 15–20 minutes. Decorate with toasted almonds.

Caramel Layer Cake

Makes one 20cm/8in round cake

275g/10oz/2½ cups plain flour
7.5ml/1½ tsp baking powder
175g/6oz/¾ cup butter, at room temperature
165g/5½oz/generous ⅔ cup caster sugar
4 eggs, beaten
5ml/1 tsp vanilla essence
120ml/4fl oz/½ cup milk whipped cream, to decorate

caramel threads, to decorate (optional)

For the frosting
285g/10½oz/1⅓ cups dark brown sugar
250ml/8fl oz/1 cup milk
25g/1oz/2 tbsp unsalted butter
45–75ml/3–5 tbsp whipping cream

1 Preheat the oven to 180°C/350°F/Gas 4. Line two 20cm/8in cake tins with greaseproof paper and grease the paper. Sift the flour and baking powder together three times.

2 Cream the butter and caster sugar until light and fluffy. Slowly mix in the beaten eggs. Add the vanilla. Fold in the flour mixture, alternating with the milk. Divide the batter between the cake tins and spread evenly. Bake until the cakes pull away from the sides of the tin, about 30 minutes. Stand in the tins for 5 minutes, then turn out and cool on a wire rack.

3 For the frosting, bring the brown sugar and milk to the boil, cover and cook for 2 minutes. Uncover and continue to boil, without stirring, until the mixture reaches 119°C/238°F (soft ball stage) on a sugar thermometer.

4 Remove the pan from the heat and add the butter, but do not stir it in. Leave to cool until lukewarm, then beat until the mixture is smooth. Stir in enough cream to obtain a spreadable consistency.

5 Sandwich the cake together with frosting and then cover the top and sides. Decorate with whipped cream, and caramel threads if liked.

Marbled Spice Cake

You could bake this cake in a 20cm/8in round tin if you do not have a kugelhopf.

Makes one ring cake

75g/3oz/6 tbsp butter, softened
115g/4oz/generous ½ cup caster sugar
2 eggs, lightly beaten
few drops vanilla essence
130g/4½oz/generous 1 cup plain flour
7.5ml/1½ tsp baking powder

45ml/3 tbsp milk
45ml/3 tbsp black treacle
5ml/1 tsp mixed spice
2.5ml/½ tsp ground ginger
175g/6oz/1½ cups icing sugar, sifted, to decorate

1 Preheat the oven to 180°C/350°F/Gas 4. Grease and flour a 900g/2lb kugelhopf or ring mould.

2 Cream together the butter and sugar until light and fluffy. Beat in the eggs and vanilla.

3 Sift together the flour and baking powder, then fold into the butter mixture, alternating with the milk.

4 Add the treacle and spices to one-third of the mixture. Drop alternating spoonfuls of the two mixtures into the tin. Run a knife through them to give a marbled effect.

5 Bake for 50 minutes, or until a skewer inserted into the centre comes out clean. Leave in the tin for 10 minutes, then turn out on to a wire rack to cool.

6 To decorate, make a smooth icing with the icing sugar and some warm water. Drizzle over the cake and leave to set.

Raspberry Meringue Gâteau

A rich hazelnut meringue filled with cream and raspberries makes a delicious combination of textures and tastes.

Serves 8

4 egg whites
225g/8oz/1 cup caster sugar
few drops vanilla essence
5ml/1 tsp malt vinegar
115g/4oz/1 cup toasted chopped hazelnuts, ground
300ml/½ pint/1¼ cups double cream
350g/12oz /2 cups raspberries

icing sugar, for dusting
raspberries and mint sprigs, to decorate

For the sauce
225g/8oz/1⅓ cups raspberries
45ml/3 tbsp icing sugar
15ml/1 tbsp orange liqueur

1 Preheat the oven to 180°C/350°F/Gas 4. Grease two 20cm/8in cake tins and line the bases with greaseproof paper.

2 Whisk the egg whites in a large bowl until they hold stiff peaks, then gradually whisk in the caster sugar a tablespoon at a time, whisking well after each addition.

3 Continue whisking the meringue mixture for a minute or two until very stiff, then fold in the vanilla essence, vinegar and the ground hazelnuts. Divide the meringue mixture between the prepared tins and spread level. Bake for 50–60 minutes, until crisp. Remove the meringues from the tins and leave to cool on a wire rack.

4 Meanwhile, make the sauce. Purée the raspberries with the icing sugar and orange liqueur in a blender or food processor, then press the purée through a nylon sieve to remove any pips. Chill the sauce until ready to serve.

5 Whip the cream then fold in the raspberries. Sandwich the meringue rounds with the raspberry cream. Dust with icing sugar, decorate with fruit and mint and serve with the sauce.

Strawberry Mint Sponge

This combination of fruit, mint and ice cream will prove popular with everyone.

Makes one 20cm/8in round cake

6–10 fresh mint leaves, plus extra to decorate
175g/6oz/¾ cup caster sugar
175g/6oz/¾ cup butter
175g/6oz/1½ cups self-raising flour
3 eggs

1.2 litres/2 pints/5 cups strawberry ice cream, softened
600ml/1 pint/2½ cups double cream
30ml/2 tbsp mint liqueur
350g/12oz/2 cups fresh strawberries

1 Tear the mint into pieces, mix with the sugar, and leave overnight. (Remove the leaves from the sugar before use.)

2 Preheat the oven to 190°C/375°F/Gas 5. Grease and line a 20cm/8in deep springform cake tin. Cream the butter and sugar, add the flour, and then the eggs. Pour the mixture into the tin.

3 Bake for 20–25 minutes, or until a skewer inserted in the centre comes out clean. Turn out on to a wire rack to cool. When cool, split into two layers.

4 Wash the cake tin and line with clear film. Put the cake base back in the tin. Spread with the ice cream, then cover with the top half of the cake. Freeze for 3–4 hours.

5 Whip the cream with the liqueur. Turn the cake out on to a serving plate and quickly spread a layer of whipped cream all over it, leaving a rough finish. Freeze until 10 minutes before serving. Decorate the cake with the strawberries and place fresh mint leaves around it.

Chestnut Cake

This rich, moist cake can be made up to 1 week in advance and kept, undecorated and wrapped, in an airtight tin.

Serves 8–10
150g/5oz/1¼ cups plain
　flour
pinch of salt
225g/8oz/1 cup
　butter, softened
150g/5oz/¾ cup caster
　sugar

425g/15oz can
　chestnut purée
9 eggs, separated
105ml/7 tbsp dark rum
300ml/½ pint/1¼ cups
　double cream
marron glacés and icing
　sugar, to decorate

1 Preheat the oven to 180°C/350°F/Gas 4. Grease and line a 20cm/8in springform cake tin.

2 Sift the flour and salt and set aside. Beat the butter and sugar together until light and fluffy. Fold in two-thirds of the chestnut purée, with the egg yolks. Fold in the flour and salt.

3 Whisk the egg whites in a clean, dry bowl until stiff. Beat a little of the egg whites into the chestnut mixture, until evenly blended, then fold in the remainder. Transfer the cake mixture to the tin and smooth the surface. Bake in the centre of the oven for about 1¼ hours, or until a skewer comes out clean. Leave in the tin and place on a wire rack.

4 Using a skewer, pierce holes over the cake. Sprinkle with 60ml/4 tbsp of rum, then cool. Remove the cake from the tin, peel off the lining paper and cut horizontally into two layers. Place bottom layer on a serving plate. Whisk the cream with the remaining rum, sugar and chestnut purée until smooth.

5 To assemble, spread two-thirds of the chestnut cream mixture over the bottom layer and place other layer on top. Spread some chestnut cream over the top and sides of the cake, pipe the remainder in large swirls round the edge of the cake. Decorate with chopped marron glacés and icing sugar.

Marbled Ring Cake

Glaze this cake with running icing if you prefer.

Makes one 25cm/10in ring cake
115g/4oz plain chocolate
350g/12oz/3 cups plain
　flour
5ml/1 tsp baking powder
450g/1lb/2 cups butter,
　at room temperature
725g/1lb 10oz/3¾ cups
　caster sugar

15ml/1 tbsp vanilla
　essence
10 eggs, at room
　temperature
icing sugar, for dusting

1 Preheat the oven to 180°C/350°F/Gas 4. Line a 25 x 10cm/10 x 4in ring mould with greaseproof paper and grease the paper. Dust with flour. Melt the chocolate in the top of a double boiler, stirring occasionally. Set aside.

2 Sift together the flour and baking powder. In another bowl, cream the butter, sugar and vanilla essence until light and fluffy. Add the eggs, two at a time, then gradually blend in the flour mixture.

3 Spoon half of the mixture into the ring mould. Stir the chocolate into the remaining mixture, then spoon into the tin. With a palette knife, swirl the mixtures for a marbled effect.

4 Bake until a skewer inserted in the centre comes out clean, about 1¾ hours. Cover with foil halfway through baking. Stand for 15 minutes, then unmould and transfer to a wire rack. To serve, dust with icing sugar.

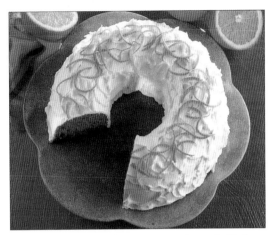

Chocolate and Nut Gâteau

Hazelnuts give an interesting crunchy texture to this delicious iced dessert.

Serves 6–8
75g/3oz/½ cup shelled
  hazelnuts
about 32 sponge fingers
150ml/¼ pint/¾ cup cold
  strong black coffee
30ml/2 tbsp brandy
450ml/¾ pint/1¾ cups
  double cream

75g/3oz/6 tbsp icing
  sugar, sifted
150g/5oz plain chocolate
icing sugar and cocoa
  powder, for dusting

1 Preheat the oven to 200°C/400°F/Gas 6. Spread out the hazelnuts on a baking sheet and toast them in the oven for 5 minutes until golden. Transfer the nuts to a clean dish towel and rub off the skins while still warm. Cool, then chop finely.

2 Line a 1.2 litre/2 pint/5 cup loaf tin with clear film and cut enough sponge fingers to fit the base and sides. Reserve the remaining fingers.

3 Mix the coffee and brandy in a shallow dish. Dip the sponge fingers briefly into the coffee mixture and return to the tin, sugary side down.

4 Whip the cream with the icing sugar until it forms soft peaks. Roughly chop 75g/3oz of the chocolate, and fold into the cream with the hazelnuts. Melt the remaining chocolate in a bowl set over a pan of barely simmering water. Cool, then fold into the cream mixture. Spoon into the tin.

5 Moisten the remaining biscuits in the coffee mixture and lay over the filling. Wrap and freeze until firm.

6 Remove from the freezer 30 minutes before serving. Turn out on to a serving plate and dust with icing sugar and cocoa.

Chocolate and Orange Angel Cake

This light-as-air sponge with its fluffy icing is the answer to a cake-lover's prayer.

Makes one 20cm/8in ring cake
25g/1oz/¼ cup plain
  flour
15g/½oz/2 tbsp cocoa
  powder
15g/½oz/2 tbsp cornflour
pinch of salt
5 egg whites
2.5ml/½ tsp cream of
  tartar

115g/4oz/scant ½ cup
  caster sugar
blanched and shredded
  rind of 1 orange, to
  decorate

For the icing
200g/7oz/1 cup caster
  sugar
1 egg white

1 Preheat the oven to 180°C/350°F/Gas 4. Sift the flour, cocoa powder, cornflour and salt together three times. Beat the egg whites in a large bowl until foamy. Add the cream of tartar, then whisk until soft peaks form.

2 Add the caster sugar to the egg whites a spoonful at a time, whisking after each addition. Sift a third of the flour and cocoa mixture over the meringue and gently fold in. Repeat twice more.

3 Spoon the mixture into a non-stick 20cm/8in ring mould and level the top. Bake for 35 minutes, or until springy when lightly pressed. Turn upside-down on to a wire rack and leave to cool in the tin. Carefully ease out of the tin.

4 For the icing, put the sugar in a pan with 75ml/5 tbsp cold water. Stir over a low heat until dissolved. Boil until the syrup reaches soft ball stage (119°C/238°F on a sugar thermometer). Remove from the heat. Whisk the egg white until stiff. Add the syrup in a thin stream, whisking all the time, until the mixture is very thick and fluffy.

5 Spread the icing over the top and sides of the cooled cake. Sprinkle the orange rind over the top of the cake and serve.

Chocolate Date Cake

A stunning cake that tastes wonderful. Rich and gooey –
it's a chocoholic's delight!

Serves 8

200g/7oz/scant 1 cup
fromage frais
200g/7oz/scant 1 cup
mascarpone
5ml/1 tsp vanilla essence,
plus few extra drops
icing sugar, to taste
4 egg whites
115g/4oz/½ cup caster
sugar

200g/7oz plain chocolate
175g/6oz/scant 1 cup
Medjool dates, stoned
and chopped
175g/6oz/1½ cups
walnuts or pecan
nuts, chopped

1 Preheat the oven to 180°C/350°F/Gas 4. Grease and base-
line a 20cm/8in springform cake tin.

2 To make the frosting, mix together the fromage frais and
mascarpone, add a few drops of vanilla essence and icing
sugar to taste, then set aside.

3 Whisk the egg whites until they form stiff peaks. Whisk in
30ml/2 tbsp of the caster sugar until the meringue is thick
and glossy, then fold in the remainder.

4 Chop 175g/6oz of the chocolate. Carefully fold into the
meringue with the dates, nuts and 5ml/1 tsp of the vanilla
essence. Pour into the prepared tin, spread level and bake for
about 45 minutes, until risen around the edges.

5 Allow to cool in the tin for about 10 minutes, then
unmould, peel off the lining paper and leave until completely
cold. Swirl the frosting over the top of the cake.

6 Melt the remaining chocolate in a bowl over hot water.
Spoon into a small paper piping bag and drizzle the chocolate
over the cake. Chill before serving.

Apple and Sultana Cake

This spicy, moist and fruity cake will be a popular teatime
treat for the whole family.

Serves 12

175g/6oz/¾ cup butter
175g/6oz/¾ cup soft light
brown sugar
3 eggs
225g/8oz/2 cups self-
raising wholemeal
flour
115g/4oz/1 cup self-
raising flour
5ml/1 tsp baking
powder, sifted

10ml/2 tsp ground
mixed spice
350g/12 oz cooking
apples, peeled, cored
and diced
175g/6oz/1 cup sultanas
75ml/5 tbsp skimmed
milk
30ml/2 tbsp demerara
sugar

1 Preheat the oven to 160°C/325°F/Gas 3. Lightly grease a
deep 20cm/8in round loose-based cake tin and line with non-
stick baking paper.

2 Place the butter, sugar, eggs, flours, baking powder and
spice in a large bowl and beat together until thoroughly
mixed. Fold in the apples, sultanas and enough milk to make
a soft dropping consistency.

3 Spoon the mixture into the prepared tin and level the
surface. Sprinkle the top with demerara sugar, then bake for
about 1½ hours, until risen, golden brown and firm to the
touch. Cool in the tin for a few minutes, then turn out onto a
wire rack to cook completely. Serve in slices.

Strawberry Shortcake Gâteau

A light biscuit-textured sponge forms the base of this summertime dessert.

Makes one 20cm/8in round cake

225g/8oz/2 cups fresh
   strawberries, hulled
30ml/2 tbsp ruby port
225g/8oz/2 cups self-
   raising flour
10ml/2 tsp baking
   powder
75g/3oz/6 tbsp unsalted
   butter, diced

40g/1½oz/3 tbsp caster
   sugar
1 egg, lightly beaten
15–30ml/1–2 tbsp milk
melted butter, for
   brushing
250ml/8fl oz/1 cup
   double cream
icing sugar, for dusting

1 Preheat the oven to 220°C/425°F/Gas 7. Grease and base-line two 20cm/8in round, loose-based cake tins. Reserve 5 strawberries, slice the rest and marinate in the port for about 1–2 hours. Strain, reserving the port.

2 Sift the flour and baking powder into a bowl. Rub in the butter until the mixture resembles fine breadcrumbs and stir in the sugar. Work in the egg and 15ml/1 tbsp of the milk to form a soft dough, adding more milk if needed.

3 Knead on a lightly floured surface and divide in two. Roll out each half, mark one half into eight wedges, and transfer to the cake tins. Brush with a little melted butter and bake for 15 minutes until risen and golden. Cool in the tins for 10 minutes, then transfer to a wire rack.

4 Cut the marked cake into wedges. Reserving a little cream for decoration, whip the rest until it holds its shape, and fold in the reserved port and strawberry slices. Spread over the cake. Place the wedges on top and dust with icing sugar.

5 Whip the remaining cream and use to pipe swirls on each wedge. Halve the reserved strawberries and use to decorate the cake.

Almond and Raspberry Swiss Roll

A light and airy sponge cake is rolled up with a fresh cream and raspberry filling for a decadent tea-time treat.

Makes one 23cm/9in long roll

3 eggs
75g/3oz/⅓ cup caster
   sugar
50g/2oz/½ cup plain
   flour
30ml/2 tbsp ground
   almonds

caster sugar, for dusting
250ml/8fl oz/1 cup
   double cream
225g/8oz/generous 1 cup
   fresh raspberries
16 flaked almonds,
   toasted, to decorate

1 Preheat the oven to 200°C/400°F/Gas 6. Grease a 33 x 23cm/13 x 9in Swiss roll tin and line with greaseproof and grease the paper.

2 Whisk the eggs and sugar in a heatproof bowl until blended. Place over a pan of simmering water and whisk until thick and pale. Whisk off the heat until cool. Sift over the flour and almonds and fold in gently.

3 Transfer to the prepared tin and bake for 10–12 minutes, until risen and springy to the touch. Invert the cake in its tin on to greaseproof paper dusted with caster sugar. Leave to cool, then remove the tin and lining paper.

4 Reserve a little cream, then whip the rest until it holds its shape. Fold in all but 8 raspberries and spread the mixture over the cooled cake, leaving a narrow border. Roll the cake up and sprinkle with caster sugar.

5 Whip the reserved cream until it just holds its shape, and spoon along the cake centre. Decorate with the reserved raspberries and toasted flaked almonds.

Orange and Walnut Swiss Roll

This unusual cake is tasty enough to serve alone, but you could also pour over some single cream.

Makes one 24cm/9½in long roll

4 eggs, separated
115g/4oz/generous ½ cup
    caster sugar
115g/4oz/1 cup very
    finely chopped
    walnuts
pinch of cream of tartar
pinch of salt
icing sugar, for dusting

For the filling
300ml/10fl oz/1¼ cups
    whipping cream
15ml/1 tbsp caster sugar
grated rind of 1 orange
15ml/1 tbsp orange-
    flavour liqueur

1 Preheat the oven to 180°C/350°F/Gas 4. Line a 30 x 24cm/12 x 9½in Swiss roll tin with greaseproof paper and grease the paper.

2 Beat the egg yolks and sugar until thick. Stir in the walnuts. Beat the egg whites with the cream of tartar and salt until stiffly peaking. Fold into the walnut mixture.

3 Pour the mixture into the prepared tin and level. Bake for 15 minutes. Invert the cake on to greaseproof paper dusted with icing sugar. Peel off the lining paper. Roll up the cake with the sugared paper. Leave to cool.

4 For the filling, whip the cream until softly peaking. Fold in the caster sugar, orange rind and liqueur.

5 Unroll the cake. Spread with the filling, then re-roll. Chill. To serve, dust with icing sugar.

Chocolate Swiss Roll

Makes one 33cm/13in long roll

225g/8oz plain chocolate
45ml/3 tbsp water
30ml/2 tbsp rum, brandy
    or strong coffee
7 eggs, separated
170g/6oz/scant 1 cup
    caster sugar

1.5ml/¼ tsp salt
350ml/12fl oz/1½ cups
    whipping cream
icing sugar, for dusting

1 Preheat the oven to 180°C/350°F/Gas 4. Line and grease a 38 x 33cm/15 x 13in Swiss roll tin with greaseproof paper.

2 Combine the chocolate, water and rum or other flavouring in the top of a double boiler, or in a heatproof bowl set over simmering water. Heat until melted. Set aside.

3 With an electric mixer, beat the egg yolks and sugar until thick. Stir in the melted chocolate.

4 In another bowl, beat the egg whites and salt until they hold stiff peaks. Fold a large dollop of egg whites into the yolk mixture to lighten it, then carefully fold in the rest of the egg whites.

5 Pour the mixture into the tin and smooth evenly with a palette knife. Bake for 15 minutes. Remove from the oven, cover with greaseproof paper and a damp cloth. Leave to stand for 1–2 hours. With an electric mixer, whip the cream until stiff. Set aside.

6 Run a knife along the inside edge of the tin to loosen the cake, then invert the cake on to a sheet of greaseproof paper that has been dusted with icing sugar.

7 Peel off the lining paper. Spread with an even layer of whipped cream, then roll up the cake with the help of the sugared paper. Chill for several hours. Before serving, dust with an even layer of icing sugar.

Apricot Brandy-snap Roulade

A magnificent combination of soft and crisp textures, this cake looks impressive and is easy to prepare.

Makes one 33cm/13in long roll

4 eggs, separated	**For the filling**
7.5ml/1½ tsp fresh	150g/5oz canned
orange juice	apricots, drained
115g/4oz/generous ½ cup	300ml/½ pint/1¼ cups
caster sugar	double cream
175g/6oz/1½ cups	25g/1oz/¼ cup icing
ground almonds	sugar
4 brandy snaps, crushed,	
to decorate	

1 Preheat the oven to 190°C/375°F/Gas 5. Base-line and grease a 33 x 23cm/13 x 9in Swiss roll tin. Beat together the egg yolks, orange juice and sugar until thick and pale, about 10 minutes. Fold in the ground almonds.

2 Whisk the egg whites until they hold stiff peaks. Fold into the almond mixture, then transfer to the Swiss roll tin and smooth the surface. Bake for 20 minutes, or until a skewer inserted into the centre comes out clean. Leave to cool in the tin, covered with a just-damp dish towel.

3 For the filling, process the apricots in a blender or food processor until smooth. Whip the cream and icing sugar until it holds soft peaks. Fold in the apricot purée.

4 Spread the crushed brandy snaps on a sheet of greaseproof paper. Spread one-third of the cream mixture over the cake, then invert on to the brandy snaps. Peel off the lining paper.

5 Use the remaining cream mixture to cover the whole cake, then roll up the roulade from a short end. Transfer to a serving dish.

Apricot and Orange Roulade

This sophisticated dessert is very good served with a spoonful of Greek yogurt or crème fraîche.

Makes one 33cm/13in long roll

For the roulade	**For the filling**
4 egg whites	115g/4oz/½ cup ready-
115g/4oz/½ cup golden	to-eat dried apricots
caster sugar	150ml/¼ pint/⅔ cup
50g/2oz/½ cup plain	orange juice
flour	
finely grated rind of 1	**To decorate**
small orange	10ml/2 tsp icing sugar
45ml/3 tbsp orange juice	shredded orange rind

1 Preheat the oven to 200°C/400°F/Gas 6. Base-line and grease a 33 x 23cm/13 x 9in Swiss roll tin.

2 To make the roulade, place the egg whites in a large bowl and whisk until they hold soft peaks. Gradually add the sugar, whisking hard between each addition. Fold in the flour, orange rind and juice. Spoon the mixture into the tin and spread it evenly.

3 Bake for 15–18 minutes, or until the sponge is firm and light golden in colour. Turn out on to a sheet of greaseproof paper and roll it up loosely from one short side. Leave to cool.

4 Roughly chop the apricots and place them in a pan with the orange juice. Cover and leave to simmer until most of the liquid has been absorbed. Purée the apricots in a food processor or blender.

5 Unroll the roulade and spread with the apricot mixture. Roll up, arrange strips of paper diagonally across the roll, sprinkle lightly with icing sugar, remove the paper and scatter with orange rind.

Classic Cheesecake

Dust the top of the cheesecake with icing sugar to decorate, if you wish.

Serves 8

50g/2oz/⅔ cup digestive biscuits, crushed
900g/2lb/4 cups cream cheese, at room temperature
245g/8¾oz/generous 1¼ cups sugar
grated rind of 1 lemon
45ml/3 tbsp lemon juice
5ml/1 tsp vanilla essence
4 eggs

1 Preheat the oven to 160°C/325°F/Gas 3. Grease a 20cm/8in springform tin. Place on a 30cm/12in circle of foil. Press it up the sides to seal tightly. Press the crushed biscuits into the base of the tin.

2 Beat the cream cheese until smooth. Add the sugar, lemon rind and juice, and vanilla, and beat until blended. Beat in the eggs, one at a time.

3 Pour into the prepared tin. Set the tin in a larger baking tray and place in the oven. Pour enough hot water in the outer tray to come 2.5cm/1in up the side of the tin.

4 Bake until the top is golden brown, about 1½ hours. Cool in the tin.

5 Run a knife around the edge to loosen, then remove the rim of the tin. Chill for at least 4 hours before serving.

Chocolate Cheesecake

Substitute digestive biscuits for the base to create a slightly different pudding.

Serves 10–12

275g/10oz plain chocolate
1.1kg/2½lb/5 cups cream cheese, at room temperature
200g/7oz/1 cup sugar
10ml/2 tsp vanilla essence
4 eggs
15ml/1 tbsp cocoa powder
175ml/6fl oz/¾ cup soured cream

For the base
200g/7oz/2⅓ cups chocolate biscuits, crushed
75g/3oz/6 tbsp butter, melted
2.5ml/½ tsp ground cinnamon

1 Preheat the oven to 180°C/350°F/Gas 4. Grease the base and sides of a 23 x 7.5cm/9 x 3in springform tin.

2 For the base, mix the biscuits with the butter and cinnamon. Press into the base of the tin.

3 Melt the chocolate in the top of a double boiler. Set aside.

4 Beat the cream cheese until smooth, then beat in the sugar and vanilla. Add the eggs, one at a time.

5 Stir the cocoa powder into the soured cream. Add to the cream cheese mixture. Stir in the melted chocolate.

6 Pour over the crust. Bake for 1 hour. Cool in the tin, then remove the rim. Chill before serving.

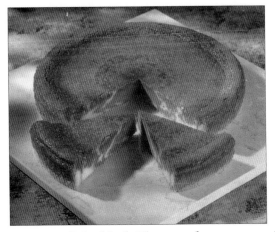

Marbled Cheesecake

Serves 10

900g/2lb/4 cups cream
  cheese, at room
  temperature
200g/7oz/1 cup
  caster sugar
4 eggs

5ml/1 tsp vanilla essence
50g/2oz/½ cup cocoa
  powder, dissolved in
  75ml/5 tbsp hot water
70g/2½oz/1 cup digestive
  biscuits, crushed

1 Preheat the oven to 180°C/350°F/Gas 4. Grease and base-line a 20 x 7.5cm/8 x 3in cake tin.

2 With an electric mixer, beat the cheese until smooth and creamy. Add the sugar and beat to incorporate. Beat in the eggs, one at a time. Do not overmix.

3 Divide the mixture between two bowls. Stir the vanilla into one, then add the chocolate mixture to the other. Pour a cupful of the vanilla mixture into the centre of the tin to make an even layer. Slowly pour over a cupful of chocolate mixture in the centre. Repeat, alternating cupfuls of the batter in a circular pattern until both are used up.

4 Set the tin in a larger baking tray and pour in hot water to come 3cm/1¼in up the sides of the cake tin. Bake until the top of the cake is golden, about 1½ hours. It will rise during baking but will sink later. Leave to cool in the tin on a rack.

5 To turn out, run a knife around the inside edge. Place a flat plate, bottom-side up, over the tin and invert on to the plate.

6 Sprinkle the crushed biscuits evenly over the base, gently place another plate over them, and invert again. Cover and chill for at least 3 hours, or overnight. To serve, cut slices with a sharp knife dipped in hot water.

Baked Cheesecake with Fresh Fruits

Vary the fruit decoration to suit the season for this rich, creamy dessert.

Serves 12

175g/6oz/2 cups
  digestive biscuits,
  crushed
50g/2oz/¼ cup unsalted
  butter, melted
450g/1lb/2 cups curd
  cheese
150ml/¼ pint/⅔ cup
  soured cream
115g/4oz/generous ½ cup
  caster sugar
3 eggs, separated
grated rind of 1 lemon

30ml/2 tbsp Marsala
2.5ml/½ tsp almond
  essence
50g/2oz/½ cup ground
  almonds
50g/2oz/scant ½ cup
  sultanas
450g/1lb prepared mixed
  fruits, such as figs,
  cherries, peaches and
  strawberries, to
  decorate

1 Preheat the oven to 180°C/350°F/Gas 4. Grease and line the sides of a 25cm/10in round springform tin. Combine the biscuits and butter and press into the base of the tin. Chill for 20 minutes.

2 For the cake mixture, beat together the cheese, cream, sugar, egg yolks, lemon rind, Marsala and almond essence until smooth and creamy.

3 Whisk the egg whites until stiff and fold into the cheese mixture with all the remaining ingredients, except the fruit, until evenly combined. Pour over the biscuit base and bake for 45 minutes, until risen and just set in the centre.

4 Leave in the tin until completely cold. Carefully remove the tin and peel away the lining paper.

5 Chill the cheesecake for at least 1 hour before decorating with the prepared fruits, just before serving.

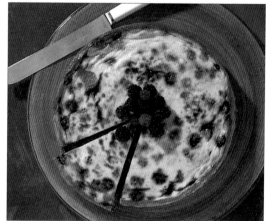

Tofu Berry "Cheesecake"

Strictly speaking, this summery "cheesecake" is not a cheese-cake at all, as it's based on tofu – but who would guess?

Serves 6
For the base
50g/2oz/4 tbsp margarine
30ml/2 tbsp apple juice
115g/4oz/1 cup bran
 flakes

For the filling
275g/10oz/1¼ cups tofu
 or low fat soft cheese
200g/7oz/scant 1 cup
 natural yogurt
15ml/1 tbsp/1 sachet
 powdered gelatine

60ml/4 tbsp apple juice

For the topping
175g/6oz/1½ cups mixed
 summer soft fruit,
 such as strawberries,
 raspberries,
 redcurrants,
 blackberries
30ml/2 tbsp redcurrant
 jelly
30ml/2 tbsp hot water

1 For the base, place the margarine and apple juice in a pan and heat gently until melted. Crush the cereal and stir it into the pan. Tip into a 23cm/9in round flan tin and press down firmly. Leave to set.

2 For the filling, place the tofu or cheese and yogurt in a food processor or blender and process until smooth. Dissolve the gelatine in the apple juice and stir into the tofu mixture.

3 Spread the tofu mixture over the chilled base, smoothing it evenly. Chill until set.

4 Remove the flan tin and place the "cheesecake" on a serving plate. Arrange the fruits over the top. Melt the redcurrant jelly with the hot water. Let it cool, and then spoon over the fruit to serve.

Baked Blackberry Cheesecake

This light cheesecake is best made with wild blackberries; if they're not available, use cultivated ones.

Serves 6
175g/6oz/¾ cup cottage
 cheese
150g/5oz/¾ cup natural
 yogurt
15ml/1 tbsp plain
 wholemeal flour
25g/1oz/2 tbsp golden
 caster sugar

1 egg
1 egg white
finely grated rind and
 juice of ½ lemon
200g/7oz/scant 2 cups
 fresh or frozen and
 thawed blackberries

1 Preheat the oven to 180°C/350°F/Gas 4. Lightly grease and base-line an 18cm/7in sandwich tin.

2 Place the cottage cheese in a food processor or blender and process until smooth. Place in a bowl, then add the yogurt, flour, sugar, egg and egg white, and mix. Add the lemon rind, juice and blackberries, reserving a few.

3 Tip the mixture into the tin and bake for 30–35 minutes, or until just set. Turn off the oven and leave the cake in it for a further 30 minutes.

4 Run a knife around the edge of the cheesecake and turn it out. Remove the lining paper and place the cheesecake on a warm serving plate.

5 Decorate the cheesecake with the reserved blackberries and serve warm.

Coffee, Peach and Almond Daquoise

Makes one 23cm/9in gâteau

5 eggs, separated
425g/15oz/scant 2 cups
  caster sugar
15ml/1 tbsp cornflour
175g/6oz/1½ cups
  ground almonds,
  toasted
135ml/4½fl oz/generous
  ½ cup milk
275g/10oz/1¼ cups
  unsalted butter, diced

45–60ml/3–4 tbsp
  coffee essence
2 x 400g/14oz cans peach
  halves in juice,
  drained
65g/2½oz/generous
  ½ cup flaked almonds,
  toasted
icing sugar, for dusting
few fresh mint leaves, to
  decorate

1 Preheat the oven to 150°C/300°F/Gas 2. Draw three 23cm/9in circles on to some greaseproof paper and place on baking sheets.

2 Whisk the egg whites until stiff. Gradually whisk in 275g/10oz/scant 1½ cups of the sugar until thick and glossy. Fold in the cornflour and almonds. Using a 1cm/½in plain nozzle, pipe circles of the mixture on to the paper. Bake for 2 hours. Turn on to wire racks to cool.

3 For the buttercream, beat together the egg yolks and remaining sugar until thick and pale. Heat the milk to boiling point and beat into the egg mixture. Return to the pan and heat until the mixture coats the back of a spoon. Strain into a large bowl and beat until lukewarm. Gradually beat in the butter until glossy. Beat in the coffee essence.

4 Trim the meringues and crush the trimmings. Reserve 3 peach halves, chop the rest and fold into half the buttercream with the crushed meringue. Use to sandwich the meringues together and place on a serving plate.

5 Ice the cake with the plain buttercream. Cover the top with flaked almonds and dust generously with icing sugar. Thinly slice the reserved peaches and use to decorate the cake edge with some mint leaves.

Mocha Brazil Layer Torte

Makes one 20cm/8in round cake

For the meringue

3 egg whites
115g/4oz/generous ½ cup
  caster sugar
15ml/1 tbsp coffee
  essence
75g/3oz/¾ cup Brazil
  nuts, toasted and
  finely ground
20cm/8in chocolate
  sponge cake

For the icing

175g/6oz/1 cup plain
  chocolate chips
30ml/2 tbsp coffee
  essence
30ml/2 tbsp water
600ml/1 pint/2½ cups
  double cream, whipped

To decorate

12 chocolate triangles
12 chocolate-coated coffee
  beans

1 Preheat the oven to 150°C/300°F/Gas 2. Draw two 20cm/8in circles on greaseproof paper and place on a baking sheet. Grease, base-line and flour a 20cm/8in round springform tin.

2 For the meringue, whisk the egg whites until stiff. Whisk in the sugar until glossy. Fold in the coffee essence and nuts. Using a 1cm/½in plain nozzle, pipe circles of the mixture on to the paper. Bake for 2 hours. Cool. Increase the oven temperature to 180°C/350°F/Gas 4.

3 For the icing, melt the chocolate chips, coffee essence and water in a bowl over a pan of simmering water. Remove from the heat and fold in the whipped cream.

4 Cut the cake into three equal layers. Trim meringue discs to the same size and assemble the cake with a layer of sponge, a little icing and a meringue disc, ending with sponge.

5 Reserve a little of the remaining icing, use the rest to cover the cake completely, forming a swirling pattern over the top. Using the reserved icing, and a piping bag with a star nozzle, pipe 24 small rosettes on top of the cake. Top alternately with the coffee beans and the chocolate triangles.

Fresh Fruit Genoese

This Italian classic can be made with any selection of seasonal fruits.

Serves 8–10

For the sponge
175g/6oz/1½ cups plain
  flour
pinch of salt
4 eggs
115g/4oz/½ cup
  caster sugar
90ml/6 tbsp orange-
  flavoured liqueur

For the filling and topping
600ml/1 pint/2½ cups
  double cream
60ml/4 tbsp vanilla sugar
450g/1lb mixed fresh
  fruits
150g/5oz/1¼ cups
  pistachio nuts,
  chopped
60ml/4 tbsp apricot jam,
  warmed and sieved

1 Preheat the oven to 180°C/350°F/Gas 4. Grease and line the base of a 20cm/ 8in springform cake tin.

2 Sift the flour and salt together three times, then set aside. Using an electric mixer, beat the eggs and sugar together for 10 minutes until thick and pale.

3 Fold the flour mixture gently into the egg and sugar mixture. Transfer the cake mixture to the prepared tin and bake for 30–35 minutes. Leave the cake in the tin for about 5 minutes, then transfer to a wire rack, remove paper and cool.

4 Cut the cake horizontally in to two layers, place the bottom layer on a plate. Sprinkle both layers with liqueur.

5 Add the vanilla sugar to the cream and whisk until the cream holds peaks. Spread two-thirds of the cream over the bottom layer and top with half of the fruit. Top with the second layer and spread the top and sides with the remaining cream. Press the nuts around the sides, arrange remaining fruit on top and brush with the apricot jam.

Fruit Gâteau with Heartsease

This gâteau would be lovely to serve as a dessert at a summer lunch party in the garden.

Makes one ring cake
90g/3½oz/½ cup soft
  margarine
100g/3½oz/scant ½ cup
  sugar
10ml/2 tsp clear honey
150g/5oz/1¼ cups self-
  raising flour
2.5ml/½ tsp baking
  powder
30ml/2 tbsp milk
2 eggs
15ml/1 tbsp rose water
15ml/1 tbsp Cointreau

To decorate
16 heartsease pansy
  flowers
1 egg white, lightly
  beaten
caster sugar
icing sugar
450g/1lb/4 cups
  strawberries
strawberry leaves

1 Preheat the oven to 190°C/375°F/Gas 5. Grease and lightly flour a ring mould. Put the soft margarine, sugar, honey, flour, baking powder, milk and eggs into a mixing bowl and beat well for 1 minute. Add the rose water and the Cointreau and mix well.

2 Pour the mixture into the mould and bake for 40 minutes. Allow to stand for a few minutes, and then turn out on to a serving plate.

3 Crystallize the heartsease pansies by painting them with the lightly beaten egg white and sprinkling with caster sugar. Leave to dry.

4 Sift icing sugar over the cake. Fill the centre of the ring with strawberries – if they will not all fit, place some around the edge. Decorate with the crystallized heartsease flowers and some strawberry leaves.

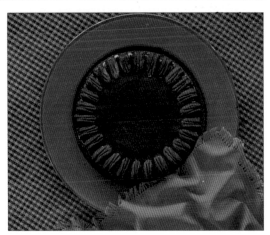

Nut and Apple Gâteau

Makes one 23cm/9in round cake

115g/4oz/1 cup pecan
  nuts or walnuts,
  toasted
50g/2oz/½ cup plain
  flour
10ml/2 tsp baking
  powder
1.5ml/¼ tsp salt

2 large cooking apples
3 eggs
225g/8oz/scant 1¼ cups
  caster sugar
5ml/1 tsp vanilla essence
175ml/6fl oz/¾ cup
  whipping cream

1 Preheat the oven to 160°C/325°F/Gas 3. Line two 23cm/9in cake tins with greaseproof paper and grease the paper.

2 Finely chop the nuts. Reserve 25ml/1½ tbsp of them and place the rest in a mixing bowl. Sift over the flour, baking powder and salt and stir.

3 Peel and core the apples. Cut into 3mm/⅛in dice, then stir into the flour mixture.

4 Beat the eggs until frothy. Gradually add the sugar and vanilla and beat until ribbon trails form, about 8 minutes. Fold in the flour mixture.

5 Pour into the cake tins and bake until a skewer inserted in the centre comes out clean, about 35 minutes. Leave to stand for 10 minutes, then turn out on to a wire rack to cool.

6 Whip the cream until firm. Use half for the filling. Pipe rosettes on the top and sprinkle over the reserved nuts.

Chocolate Pecan Nut Torte

This torte uses finely ground nuts instead of flour. Toast, then cool the nuts before grinding finely in a processor.

Makes one 20cm/8in round cake

200g/7oz plain chocolate,
  chopped
150g/5oz/10 tbsp
  unsalted butter, cut
  into pieces
4 eggs
100g/3½oz/½ cup caster
  sugar
10ml/2 tsp vanilla
  essence
115g/4oz/1 cup ground
  pecan nuts
10ml/2 tsp ground
  cinnamon

24 toasted pecan nut
  halves, to decorate
  (optional)

**For the chocolate
honey glaze**
115g/4oz plain chocolate,
  chopped
60g/2oz/¼ cup unsalted
  butter, cut into pieces
30ml/2 tbsp honey
pinch of ground
  cinnamon

1 Preheat the oven to 180°C/350°F/Gas 4. Grease a 20cm/8in springform tin, line with greaseproof paper, then grease the paper. Wrap the tin with foil.

2 Melt the chocolate and butter over a low heat, stirring until smooth. Set aside. Beat the eggs, sugar and vanilla until frothy. Stir in the melted chocolate and butter, ground nuts and cinnamon. Pour into the tin. Place in a large roasting tin and pour boiling water into the roasting tin, to come 2cm/¾in up the side of the springform tin. Bake for 25–30 minutes, until the edge of the cake is set, but the centre soft. Remove the foil and set on a wire rack.

3 For the glaze, melt the chocolate, butter, honey and cinnamon, stirring until smooth. Remove from the heat. If using, dip toasted pecan halves halfway into the glaze and place on greaseproof paper to set. Remove the cake from its tin and invert on to a wire rack. Remove the paper. Pour the glaze over the cake, tilting the rack to spread it. Use a palette knife to smooth the sides. Arrange the nuts on top.

Coconut Lime Gâteau

Makes one 23cm/9in round cake

225g/8oz/2 cups plain
  flour
12.5ml/2½ tsp baking
  powder
1.5ml/¼ tsp salt
225g/8oz/1 cup butter, at
  room temperature
225g/8oz/generous 1 cup
  caster sugar
grated rind of 2 limes
4 eggs
60ml/4 tbsp fresh lime
  juice

75g/3oz/1½ cups
  desiccated coconut

For the frosting
450g/1lb/generous 2 cups
  granulated sugar
60ml/4 tbsp water
pinch of cream of tartar
1 egg white, whisked
  stiffly

1   Preheat the oven to 180°C/350°F/Gas 4. Grease and base-line two 23cm/9in sandwich tins. Sift together the flour, baking powder and salt.

2   Beat the butter until soft. Add the sugar and lime rind and beat until pale and fluffy. Beat in the eggs, one at a time.

3   Gradually fold in the dry ingredients, alternating with the lime juice, then stir in two-thirds of the coconut.

4   Divide the mixture between the cake tins, even the tops and bake for 30–35 minutes. Cool in the tins on a wire rack for 10 minutes, then turn out and peel off the lining paper.

5   Bake the remaining coconut until golden brown, stirring occasionally. For the frosting, heat the sugar, water and cream of tartar until dissolved, stirring. Boil to reach 120°C/250°F on a sugar thermometer. Remove from the heat and, when the bubbles subside, whisk in the egg white until thick.

6   Sandwich and cover the cake with the frosting. Sprinkle over the toasted coconut. Leave to set.

Exotic Celebration Gâteau

Use any tropical fruits you can find to make a spectacular display of colours and tastes.

Makes one 20cm/8in ring gâteau

175g/6oz/¾ cup butter,
  softened
175g/6oz/scant 1 cup
  caster sugar
3 eggs, beaten
250g/9oz/2¼ cups self-
  raising flour
30–45ml/2–3 tbsp milk
90–120ml/6–8 tbsp
  light rum
425ml/14fl oz/scant
  2 cups double cream
25g/1oz/¼ cup icing
  sugar, sifted

To decorate
450g/1lb mixed fresh
  exotic and soft fruits,
  such as figs,
  redcurrants, star fruit
  and kiwi fruit
90ml/6 tbsp apricot jam,
  warmed and sieved
30ml/2 tbsp warm water
icing sugar

1   Preheat the oven to 190°C/375°F/Gas 5. Grease and flour a deep 20cm/8in ring mould.

2   Beat together the butter and sugar until light and fluffy. Gradually beat in the eggs, then fold in the flour and milk.

3   Spoon the mixture into the ring mould. Bake the cake for 45 minutes, or until a skewer inserted into the centre comes out clean. Turn out on to a wire rack and leave to cool.

4   Place the cake on a serving plate. Make holes randomly over the cake with a skewer. Drizzle over the rum and allow to soak in.

5   Beat together the cream and icing sugar until the mixture holds soft peaks. Spread all over the cake. Arrange the fruits in the hollow centre of the cake. Mix the apricot jam and water, then brush over the fruit. Sift over some icing sugar.

Chocolate and Fresh Cherry Gâteau

Makes one 20cm/8in round cake

115g/4oz/½ cup butter
150g/5oz/⅔ cup caster
   sugar
3 eggs, lightly beaten
175g/6oz/1 cup plain
   chocolate chips, melted
60ml/4 tbsp kirsch
150g/5oz/1¼ cups self-
   raising flour
5ml/1 tsp ground
   cinnamon
2.5ml/½ tsp ground
   cloves
350g/12oz fresh cherries,
   stoned and halved
45ml/3 tbsp morello
   cherry jam, warmed

5ml/1 tsp lemon juice

For the frosting

115g/4oz/⅔ cup plain
   chocolate chips
50g/2oz/¼ cup unsalted
   butter
60ml/4 tbsp double cream

To decorate

75g/3oz/½ cup white
   chocolate chips, melted
18 fresh cherries
few rose leaves, washed
   and dried

1 Preheat the oven to 160°C/325°F/Gas 3. Grease, base-line and flour a 20cm/8in round springform tin.

2 Cream the butter and 115g/4oz/½ cup of the sugar until pale. Beat in the eggs. Stir in the chocolate and half the kirsch. Fold in the flour and spices. Transfer to the tin and bake for 55–60 minutes, or until a skewer inserted in the centre comes out clean. Cool for 10 minutes then transfer to a wire rack.

3 For the filling, bring the cherries, remaining kirsch and sugar to the boil, cover, and simmer for 10 minutes. Uncover for a further 10 minutes until syrupy. Leave to cool.

4 Halve the cake horizontally. Cut a 1cm/½in deep circle from the base, leaving a 1cm/½in edge. Crumble into the filling and stir to form a paste. Fill and cover the cake base.

5 Sieve the jam and lemon juice. Brush all over the cake. For the frosting, melt all the ingredients. Cool, pour over the cake. Decorate with chocolate-dipped cherries and leaves.

Coffee Almond Flower Gâteau

This delicious cake can be made quite quickly. Ring the changes by using a coffee-flavoured sponge.

Makes one 20cm/8in round cake

475g/1lb 2oz/2¼ cups
   coffee-flavour butter
   icing
2 x 20cm/8in round
   sponge cakes with
   chopped nuts

75g/3oz plain chocolate
20 blanched almonds
4 chocolate-coated coffee
   beans

1 Reserve 60ml/4 tbsp of the butter icing for piping and use the rest to sandwich the sponges together and cover the top and side of the cake. Smooth the top with a palette knife and serrate the side with a scraper.

2 Melt the chocolate in a heatproof bowl over a pan of hot water. Remove from the heat, then dip in half of each almond at a slight angle. Leave to dry on greaseproof paper. Return the chocolate to the pan of hot water (off the heat) so it does not set. Remove and allow to cool slightly.

3 Arrange the almonds on top of the cake to represent flowers. Place a chocolate-coated coffee bean in the flower centres. Spoon the remaining melted chocolate into a greaseproof paper piping bag. Cut a small piece off the end in a straight line. Pipe the chocolate in wavy lines over the top of the cake and in small beads around the top edge.

4 Transfer the cake to a serving plate. Place the reserved buttercream in a fresh piping bag fitted with a No 2 writing nozzle. Pipe beads of icing all around the bottom of the cake, then top with small beads of chocolate.

Vegan Chocolate Gâteau

A rare treat for vegans, this gâteau tastes really delicious.

Makes one 20cm/8in gâteau

275g/10oz/2½ cups self-
  raising wholemeal
  flour
50g/2oz/½ cup cocoa
  powder
15ml/1 tbsp baking
  powder
250g/9oz/1¼ cups caster
  sugar
a few drops of vanilla
  essence
135ml/9 tbsp sunflower
  oil
350ml/12fl oz/1½ cups
  water

sifted cocoa powder, to
  decorate
25g/1oz/¼ cup chopped
  nuts, to decorate

For the chocolate fudge
50g/2oz/¼ cup soya
  margarine
45ml/3 tbsp water
250g/9oz/2¼ cups icing
  sugar
30ml/2 tbsp cocoa
  powder

1 Preheat the oven to 160°C/325°F/Gas 3. Grease and line a deep 20cm/8in round cake tin, and grease the paper.

2 Sift the flour, cocoa and baking powder into a large mixing bowl. Add the sugar and vanilla, then gradually beat in the oil and water to make a smooth batter. Pour the mixture into the cake tin and smooth the surface. Bake for 45 minutes, or until a skewer inserted into the centre of the cake comes out clean. Leave in the tin for 5 minutes, then turn out on to a wire rack and leave to cool. Cut the cake in half.

3 For the chocolate fudge, gently melt the margarine with the water. Remove from the heat, add the icing sugar and cocoa, and beat until smooth and shiny. Allow to cool until firm enough to spread and pipe.

4 Place a layer of cake on a serving plate and spread over two-thirds of the chocolate fudge. Top with the other layer of cake. Using a star nozzle, pipe chocolate fudge stars over the cake. Sprinkle with cocoa powder and chopped nuts.

Black Forest Gâteau

A perfect gâteau for a special tea party, or for serving as sumptuous dinner-party dessert.

Makes one 20cm/8in gâteau

5 eggs
175g/6oz/scant 1 cup
  caster sugar
50g/2oz/½ cup plain
  flour
50g/2oz/½ cup cocoa
  powder
75g/3oz/6 tbsp butter,
  melted

For the filling
75–90ml/5–6 tbsp
  kirsch

600ml/1 pint/2½ cups
  double cream
425g/15oz can black
  cherries, drained,
  stoned and chopped

To decorate
chocolate curls
15–20 fresh cherries,
  preferably with stems
icing sugar

1 Preheat the oven to 180°C/350°F/Gas 4. Base-line and grease two deep 20cm/8in round cake tins.

2 Beat together the eggs and sugar for 10 minutes, or until thick and pale. Sift over the flour and cocoa, and fold in gently. Trickle in the melted butter and fold in gently.

3 Transfer the mixture to the cake tins. Bake for 30 minutes, or until springy to the touch. Leave in the tins for 5 minutes, then turn out on to a wire rack, peel off the lining paper and leave to cool. Cut each cake in half horizontally and sprinkle with the kirsch.

4 Whip the cream until softly peaking. Combine two-thirds of the cream with the chopped cherries. Place a layer of cake on a serving plate and spread with one-third of the filling. Repeat twice, and top with a layer of cake. Use the reserved cream to cover the top and sides of the gâteau.

5 Decorate the gâteau with chocolate curls, fresh cherries and dredge with icing sugar.

Walnut Coffee Gâteau

Serves 8–10

140g/5oz/1¼ cups
  walnuts
150g/5½oz/generous
  ¾ cup caster sugar
5 eggs, separated
55g/2oz/scant 1 cup dry
  breadcrumbs
15ml/1 tbsp cocoa powder
15ml/1 tbsp instant coffee
30ml/2 tbsp rum or
  lemon juice

1.5ml/¼ tsp salt
90ml/6 tbsp redcurrant
  jelly, warmed
chopped walnuts, for
  decorating

For the frosting
225g/8oz plain chocolate
750ml/1¼ pint/3 cups
  whipping cream

1 For the frosting, combine the chocolate and cream in the top of a double boiler until the chocolate melts. Cool, then cover and chill overnight, or until the mixture is firm.

2 Preheat the oven to 180°C/350°F/Gas 4. Line and grease a 23 x 5cm/9 x 2in cake tin. Grind the nuts with 45ml/3 tbsp of the sugar in a food processor, blender or coffee grinder.

3 With an electric mixer, beat the egg yolks and remaining sugar until thick and lemon-coloured. Fold in the walnuts. Stir in the breadcrumbs, cocoa, coffee and rum or lemon juice.

4 In another bowl, beat the egg whites with the salt until they hold stiff peaks. Fold carefully into the walnut mixture. Pour the meringue batter into the tin and bake until the top of the cake springs back when touched, about 45 minutes. Allow the cake to stand for 5 minutes, then turn out and cool, before slicing the cake in half horizontally.

5 With an electric mixer, beat the chocolate frosting mixture on low speed until it becomes lighter, about 30 seconds. Brush some of the jelly over the cut cake layer. Spread with some of the chocolate frosting, then sandwich with the remaining cake layer. Brush the top of the cake with jelly, then cover the side and top with the remaining frosting. Make a starburst pattern with a knife and sprinkle chopped walnuts around the edge.

Sachertorte

A rich cake, ideal to serve as a treat for anyone who is a self-confessed chocoholic.

Makes one 23cm/9in round cake

115g/4oz plain chocolate
90g/3oz/⅓ cup unsalted
  butter, at room
  temperature
50g/2oz/¼ cup sugar
4 eggs, separated, plus 1
  egg white
1.5ml/¼ tsp salt
65g/2½oz/9 tbsp plain
  flour, sifted

For the topping
75ml/5 tbsp apricot jam
250ml/8fl oz/1 cup plus
  15ml/1 tbsp water
15g/½oz/1 tbsp unsalted
  butter
175g/6oz plain chocolate
75g/3oz/⅓ cup sugar
ready-made chocolate
  decorating icing

1 Preheat the oven to 160°C/325°F/Gas 3. Line and grease a 23cm/9in cake tin. Melt the chocolate in the top of a double boiler and set aside.

2 Cream the butter and sugar until light and fluffy. Stir in the chocolate, then beat in the egg yolks, one at a time.

3 Beat the egg whites with the salt until stiff. Fold a dollop of whites into the chocolate mixture to lighten it. Fold in the remaining whites in three batches, alternating with the sifted flour. Pour into the tin and bake until a skewer comes out clean, about 45 minutes. Turn out on to a wire rack.

4 Meanwhile, melt the jam with 15ml/1 tbsp of the water, then strain for a smooth consistency. For the frosting, melt the butter and chocolate in the top of a double boiler. In a heavy saucepan, dissolve the sugar in the remaining water, then boil until it reaches 107°C/225°F (thread stage) on a sugar thermometer. Plunge the base of the pan into cold water for 1 minute. Stir into the chocolate. Cool for a few minutes.

5 Brush the warm jam over the cake. Pour over the frosting and spread over the top and sides. Leave to set overnight. Decorate with chocolate icing.

Dundee Cake

This is the perfect recipe for a festive occasion when a lighter fruit cake is required.

Makes one 20cm/8in round cake

175g/6oz/¾ cup butter
175g/6oz/1 cup light
  soft brown sugar
3 eggs
225g/8oz/2 cups plain
  flour
10ml/2 tsp baking
  powder
5ml/1 tsp ground
  cinnamon
2.5ml/½ tsp ground
  cloves
1.5ml/¼ tsp grated
  nutmeg
225g/8oz/generous
  1½ cups sultanas

175g/6oz/generous 1 cup
  raisins
175g/6oz/¾ cup glacé
  cherries, halved
115g/4oz/¾ cup chopped
  mixed peel
50g/2oz/½ cup blanched
  almonds, chopped
grated rind of 1 lemon
30ml/2 tbsp brandy
115g/4oz/1 cup whole
  blanched almonds,
  to decorate

1 Preheat the oven to 160°C/325°F/Gas 3. Grease and line a 20cm/8in round deep cake tin. Cream the butter and sugar until pale and light. Add the eggs, 1 at a time, beating well after each addition.

2 Sift together the flour, baking powder and spices. Fold into the egg mixture alternately with the remaining ingredients, until evenly combined. Transfer to the cake tin. Smooth the surface, then make a small dip in the centre.

3 Decorate the top of the cake by pressing the blanched almonds in decreasing circles over the entire surface. Bake for 2–2¼ hours, until a skewer inserted in the centre of the cake comes out clean.

4 Leave to cool in the tin for 30 minutes then transfer the cake to a wire rack.

Vegan Dundee Cake

As it contains neither eggs nor dairy products, this cake is suitable for vegans.

Makes one 20cm/8in square cake

350g/12oz/scant 2½ cups
  wholemeal flour
5ml/1 tsp mixed spice
175g/6oz/¾ cup soya
  margarine
175g/6oz/1 cup dark
  muscovado sugar, plus
  30ml/2 tbsp
175g/6oz/generous 1 cup
  sultanas
175g/6oz/1 cup currants
175g/6oz/generous 1 cup
  raisins
75g/3oz/½ cup chopped
  mixed peel
150g/5oz/generous ½ cup
  glacé cherries, halved
finely grated rind of
  1 orange

30ml/2 tbsp ground
  almonds
25g/1oz/¼ cup blanched
  almonds, chopped
5ml/1 tsp bicarbonate
  of soda
120ml/4fl oz/½ cup soya
  milk
75ml/3fl oz/⅓ cup
  sunflower oil
30ml/2 tbsp malt vinegar

To decorate

mixed nuts, such as
  pistachios, pecan nuts
  and macadamia nuts
glacé cherries
angelica
60ml/4 tbsp clear honey,
  warmed

1 Preheat the oven to 150°C/300°F/Gas 2. Grease and double-line a deep 20cm/8in square loose-based cake tin.

2 Sift together the flour and mixed spice. Rub in the soya margarine. Stir in the sugar, dried fruits, mixed peel, cherries, orange rind, ground almonds and blanched almonds.

3 Dissolve the bicarbonate in a little of the milk. Warm the remaining milk with the oil and vinegar and add the bicarbonate mixture. Stir into the flour mixture.

4 Spoon into the tin and smooth. Bake for 2½ hours. Leave in the tin for 5 minutes, then cool on a rack. Decorate with the nuts, cherries and angelica and brush with the honey.

Panforte

This rich, spicy nougat-type cake is a Christmas speciality of Siena in Italy.

Makes one 20cm/8in round cake

275g/10oz/1⅔ cups mixed chopped exotic peel, to include lemon orange, citron, papaya and pineapple	5ml/1 tsp ground cinnamon
115g/4oz/1 cup unblanched almonds	1.5ml/¼ tsp each grated nutmeg, ground cloves and ground coriander
50g/2oz/½ cup walnut halves	175g/6oz/1 cup caster sugar
50g/2oz/½ cup plain flour	60ml/4 tbsp water
	icing sugar, for dusting

1 Preheat the oven to 180°C/350°F/Gas 4. Grease and base-line a 20cm/8in round loose-based cake tin with rice paper. Put the mixed peel and nuts in a bowl. Sift in the flour and spices and mix well.

2 Dissolve the caster sugar and water in a small saucepan, then boil until the mixture reaches 107°C/225°F on a sugar thermometer (thread stage). Pour on to the fruit mixture, stirring to coat well. Transfer to the cake tin, pressing into the sides with a metal spoon.

3 Bake for 25–30 minutes, until the mixture is bubbling. Cool in the tin for 5 minutes.

4 Use a lightly oiled palette knife to work around the edges of the cake to loosen it. Remove the cake from the tin, leaving the base in place. Leave to go cold, then remove the base and dust generously with icing sugar.

Kulich

This Russian yeast cake is traditionally made at Eastertime.

Makes two cakes

15ml/1 tbsp easy-blend dried yeast	½ vanilla pod, finely chopped
90ml/6 tbsp lukewarm milk	25g/1oz/2 tbsp each crystallized ginger, mixed peel, almonds and currants, chopped
75g/3oz/scant ½ cup caster sugar	
500g/1¼lb/5 cups plain flour	
pinch of saffron strands	**To decorate**
30ml/2 tbsp dark rum	75g/3oz/¾ cup icing sugar, sifted
2.5ml/½ tsp ground cardamom seeds	7.5–10ml/1½–2 tsp warm water
2.5ml/½ tsp ground cumin	drop of almond essence
50g/2oz/4 tbsp unsalted butter	2 candles
2 eggs plus 2 egg yolks	blanched almonds mixed peel

1 Blend together the yeast, milk, 25g/1oz/2 tbsp sugar and 50g/2oz/½ cup flour. Leave in a warm place for 15 minutes, until frothy. Soak the saffron in the rum for 15 minutes.

2 Sift together the remaining flour and spices and rub in the butter. Stir in the rest of the sugar. Add the yeast mixture, saffron liquid and remaining ingredients. Knead until smooth. Put in an oiled bowl, cover and leave until doubled in size.

3 Preheat the oven to 190°C/375°F/Gas 5. Grease, line and flour two 500g/1¼lb coffee tins or 15cm/6in clay flowerpots.

4 Punch down the dough and form into two rounds. Press into the tins or pots, cover and leave for 30 minutes. Bake for 35 minutes for the pots or 50 minutes for the tins. Cool.

5 Mix together the icing sugar, water and almond essence. Pour over the cakes. Decorate with the candles, nuts and peel.

Yule Log

This rich seasonal treat could provide an economical alternative to a traditional iced fruit cake.

Makes one 28cm/11in long roll

4 eggs, separated
150g/5oz/¾ cup caster
   sugar
5ml/1 tsp vanilla essence
pinch of cream of tartar
   (optional)
115g/4oz/1 cup plain
   flour, sifted

250ml/8fl oz/1 cup
   whipping cream
300g/11oz plain
   chocolate, chopped
30ml/2 tbsp rum or
   Cognac
icing sugar, for dusting

1 Preheat the oven to 190°C/375°F/Gas 5. Grease, line and flour a 40 x 28cm/16 x 11in Swiss roll tin.

2 Whisk the egg yolks with all but 25g/1oz/2 tbsp of the sugar until pale and thick. Add the vanilla essence.

3 Whisk the egg whites (with the cream of tartar if not using a copper bowl) until they form soft peaks. Add the reserved sugar and continue whisking until stiff and glossy.

4 Fold half the flour into the yolk mixture. Add a quarter of the egg whites and fold in to lighten the mixture. Fold in the remaining flour, then the remaining egg whites.

5 Spread the mixture in the tin. Bake for 15 minutes. Turn on to paper sprinkled with caster sugar. Roll up and leave to cool.

6 Bring the cream to the boil. Put the chocolate in a bowl and add the cream. Stir until the chocolate has melted, then beat until it is fluffy and has thickened to a spreading consistency. Mix a third of the chocolate cream with the rum or Cognac.

7 Unroll the cake and spread with the rum mixture. Re-roll and cut off about a quarter, at an angle. Arrange to form a branch. Spread the chocolate cream over the cake. Mark with a fork, add Christmas decorations and dust with icing sugar.

Chocolate Chestnut Roulade

A traditional version of Bûche de Nôel, the delicious French Christmas gâteau.

Makes one 33cm/13in long roll

225g/8oz plain chocolate
50g/2oz white chocolate
4 eggs, separated
115g/4oz/generous ½ cup
   caster sugar

For the chestnut filling
150ml/¼ pint/⅔ cup
   double cream

225g/8oz can chestnut
   purée
50–65g/2–2½oz/
   4–5 tbsp icing sugar,
   plus extra for dusting
15–30ml/1–2 tbsp
   brandy

1 Preheat the oven to 180°C/350°F/Gas 4. Line and grease a 23 x 33cm/9 x 13in Swiss roll tin.

2 For the chocolate curls, melt 50g/2oz of the plain and all of the white chocolate in separate bowls set over saucepans of hot water. When melted, spread on a non-porous surface and leave to set. Hold a long sharp knife at a 45-degree angle to the chocolate and push it along the chocolate, turning the knife in a circular motion. Put the curls on greaseproof paper.

3 Melt the remaining plain chocolate. Beat the egg yolks and caster sugar until thick and pale. Stir in the chocolate.

4 Whisk the whites until they form stiff peaks, then fold into the mixture. Turn into the tin and bake for 15–20 minutes. Cool, covered with a just-damp dish towel, on a wire rack.

5 Sprinkle a sheet of greaseproof paper with caster sugar. Turn the roulade out on to it. Peel off the lining paper and trim the edges of the roulade. Cover with the dish towel.

6 For the filling, whip the cream until softly peaking. Beat together the chestnut purée, icing sugar and brandy until smooth, then fold in the cream. Spread over the roulade and roll it up. Top with chocolate curls and dust with icing sugar.

Chocolate Christmas Cups

To crystallize cranberries for decoration, beat an egg white until frothy. Dip each berry in egg white then in sugar.

Makes about 35 cups

70–80 foil or paper sweet cases
275g/10oz plain chocolate, broken into pieces
175g/6oz cooked, cold Christmas pudding

75ml/3fl oz/⅓ cup brandy or whisky
chocolate leaves and a few crystallized cranberries, to decorate

1 Place the chocolate in a bowl over a saucepan of hot water. Heat gently until the chocolate is melted, stirring until the chocolate is smooth.

2 Using a pastry brush, brush or coat the base and sides of about 35 sweet cases. Allow to set, then repeat, reheating the melted chocolate if necessary, and apply a second coat. Leave to cool and set completely, 4–5 hours or overnight. Reserve the remaining chocolate.

3 Crumble the Christmas pudding in a small bowl, sprinkle with the brandy or whisky and allow to stand for 30–40 minutes, until the spirit is absorbed.

4 Spoon a little of the pudding mixture into each cup, smoothing the top. Reheat the remaining chocolate and spoon over the top of each cup to cover the surface of each cup to the edge. Leave to set.

5 When completely set, carefully peel off the cases and place in clean foil cases. Decorate with chocolate leaves and crystallized cranberries.

Eggless Christmas Cake

This simple cake contains a wealth of fruit and nuts to give it that traditional Christmas flavour.

Makes one 18cm/7in square cake

75g/3oz/½ cup sultanas
75g/3oz/½ cup raisins
75g/3oz/1½ cup currants
75g/3oz/scant ½ cup glacé cherries, halved
50g/2oz/¼ cup mixed peel
250ml/8fl oz/1 cup apple juice
25g/1oz/scant ¼ cup toasted hazelnuts
30ml/2 tbsp pumpkin seeds
2 pieces stem ginger in syrup, chopped

finely grated rind of 1 lemon
120ml/4fl oz/½ cup milk
50ml/2fl oz/¼ cup sunflower oil
225g/8oz/2 cups wholemeal self-raising flour
10ml/2 tsp mixed spice
45ml/3 tbsp brandy or dark rum
apricot jam, for brushing
glacé fruits, to decorate

1 Soak the sultanas, raisins, currants, cherries and mixed peel in the apple juice overnight.

2 Preheat the oven to 150°C/300°F/Gas 2. Grease and line an 18cm/7in square cake tin.

3 Add the hazelnuts, pumpkin seeds, ginger and lemon rind to the fruit. Stir in the milk and oil. Sift the flour and spice, then stir in with the brandy or rum.

4 Spoon into the cake tin and bake for about 1½ hours, or until the cake is golden brown and firm to the touch.

5 Turn out and cool on a wire rack. Brush with sieved apricot jam and decorate with glacé fruits.

Flourless Fruit Cake

This makes the perfect base for a birthday cake for anyone who needs to avoid eating flour.

Makes one 25cm/10in round cake

450g/1lb/1⅓ cups
  mincemeat
350g/12oz/2 cups dried
  mixed fruit
115g/4oz/½ cup ready-to-
  eat dried apricots,
  chopped
115g/4oz/⅔cup ready-to-
  eat dried figs, chopped
115g/4oz/½ cup glacé
  cherries, halved

115g/4oz/1 cup walnut
  pieces
225g/8oz/8–10 cups
  cornflakes, crushed
4 eggs, lightly beaten
410g/14½oz can
  evaporated milk
5ml/1 tsp mixed spice
5ml/1 tsp baking powder
mixed glacé fruits,
  chopped, to decorate

1 Preheat the oven to 150°C/300°F/Gas 2. Grease a 25cm/10in round cake tin, line the base and sides with a double thickness of greaseproof paper and grease the paper.

2 Put all the ingredients into a large mixing bowl. Beat together well.

3 Turn into the cake tin and smooth the surface.

4 Bake for about 1¾ hours or until a skewer inserted in the centre of the cake comes out clean. Allow the cake to cool in the tin for 10 minutes, then turn out on to a wire rack, peel off the lining paper and leave to cool completely. Decorate with the chopped glacé fruits.

Glazed Christmas Ring

Makes one 25cm/10in ring cake

225g/8oz/generous 1½
  cups sultanas
175g/6oz/generous 1 cup
  raisins
175g/6oz/generous 1 cup
  currants
175g/6oz/1 cup dried
  figs, chopped
90ml/6 tbsp whisky
45ml/3 tbsp orange juice
225g/8oz/1 cup butter
225g/8oz/1cup dark soft
  brown sugar
5 eggs
250g/9oz/2¼ cups plain
  flour
15ml/1 tbsp baking
  powder
15ml/1 tbsp mixed spice
115g/4oz/⅔ cup glacé
  cherries, chopped

115g/4oz/1 cup brazil
  nuts, chopped
50g/2oz/⅓ cup chopped
  mixed peel
50g/2oz/½ cup ground
  almonds
grated rind and juice
  1 orange
30ml/2 tbsp thick-cut
  orange marmalade

To decorate

150ml/¼ pint/⅔ cup
  thick-cut orange
  marmalade
15ml/1 tbsp orange juice
175g/6oz/1 cup glacé
  cherries
115g/4oz/⅔cup dried
  figs, halved
75g/3oz/½ cup whole
  brazil nuts

1 Put the dried fruits in a bowl, pour over 60ml/4 tbsp of the whisky and all the orange juice and marinate overnight.

2 Preheat the oven to 160°C/325°F/Gas 3. Grease and line a 25cm/10in ring mould. Cream the butter and sugar. Beat in the eggs. Sift together the remaining flour, baking powder and mixed spice. Fold into the egg mixture, alternating with the rest of the ingredients, except the whisky. Transfer to the tin and bake for 1 hour, then reduce the oven temperature to 150°C/300°F/Gas 2 and bake for a further 1¾–2 hours.

3 Prick the cake all over and pour over the reserved whisky. Cool in the tin for 30 minutes, then transfer to a wire rack. Boil the marmalade and orange juice for 3 minutes. Stir in the fruit and nuts. Cool, then spoon over the cake and leave to set.

Noel Christmas Cake

If you like a traditional royal-iced cake, this is a simple design using only one icing and easy-to-pipe decorations.

Makes one 20cm/8in round cake

20cm/8in round rich fruit cake	**Materials/equipment**
30ml/2 tbsp apricot jam, warmed and sieved	*23cm/9in round silver cake board*
750g/1¼lb/5¼ cups marzipan	*3 greaseproof paper piping bags*
900g/2lb/6 cups royal icing	*No 1 writing nozzle bags*
red and green food colouring	*2 x No 0 writing nozzles*
	44 large gold dragées
	2.5m/2½yd gold ribbon, 2cm/¾in wide
	2.5m/2½yd red ribbon, 5mm/¼in wide

1 Brush the fruit cake with apricot jam, cover with the marzipan and place on the cake board.

2 Flat-ice the top of the cake with two layers of royal icing and leave to dry. Ice the sides of the cake and peak the royal icing, leaving a space around the centre for the ribbon. Leave to dry. Reserve the remaining royal icing.

3 Pipe beads of icing around the top edge of the cake and place a gold dragée on alternate beads. Using a No 1 writing nozzle, write "NOEL" across the cake and pipe holly leaves, stems and berries around the top.

4 Secure the ribbons around the side of the cake. Tie a red bow and attach to the front of the cake. Use the remaining ribbon for the board. Leave to dry overnight.

5 Tint 30ml/2 tbsp of the royal icing bright green and 15ml/1 tbsp bright red. Using a No 0 writing nozzle, over-pipe "NOEL" in red, then the edging beads and berries. Overpipe the holly in green. Leave to dry.

Christmas Tree Cake

No piping is involved in this bright and colourful cake, making it an easy choice.

Makes one 20cm/8in round cake

45ml/3 tbsp apricot jam	*225g/8oz/1½ cups royal icing*
20cm/8in round rich fruit cake	*edible silver balls*
900g/2lb/6 cups marzipan	
green, red, yellow and purple food colouring	**Materials/equipment**
	25cm/10in round cake board

1 Warm, then sieve the apricot jam and brush the cake with it. Colour 675g/1½lb/4½ cups of the marzipan green. Use to cover the cake. Leave to dry overnight.

2 Secure the cake to the board with royal icing. Spread the icing halfway up the cake side. Press the flat side of a palette knife into the icing, then pull away sharply to form peaks.

3 Make three different-size Christmas tree templates. Tint half the remaining marzipan a deeper green than the top. Using the templates, cut out three tree shapes and arrange them on the cake.

4 Divide the remaining marzipan into three and colour red, yellow and purple. Use a little of each marzipan to make five 9cm/3in rolls. Loop them alternately around the top edge of the cake. Make small red balls and press on to the loop ends.

5 Use the remaining marzipan to make the tree decorations. Arrange on the trees, securing with water, if necessary. Finish the cake by adding silver balls to the Christmas trees.

Christmas Stocking Cake

A bright and happy cake that is sure to delight children at Christmas time.

Makes one 20cm/8in square cake

20cm/8in square rich	red and green food
fruit cake	colouring
45ml/3 tbsp apricot jam,	
warmed and sieved	**Materials/equipment**
900g/2lb/6 cups	25cm/10in square silver
marzipan	cake board
1.2kg/2½lb/7½ cups	1.25m/1½yd red ribbon,
sugarpaste icing	2cm/¾in wide
15ml/1 tbsp royal icing	1m/1yd green ribbon,
	2cm/¾in wide

1 Brush the cake with the apricot jam and place on the cake board. Cover with marzipan.

2 Set aside 225g/8oz/1½ cups of the sugarpaste icing. Cover the cake with the rest. Leave to dry. Secure the red ribbon around the board and the green ribbon around the cake with royal icing.

3 Divide the icing in half and roll out one half. Using a template, cut out two sugarpaste stockings, one 5mm/¼in larger all round. Put the smaller one on top of the larger one.

4 Divide the other half of the sugarpaste into two and tint one red and the other green. Roll out and cut each colour into seven 1 cm/½in strips. Alternate the strips on top of the stocking. Roll lightly to fuse and press the edges together. Leave to dry.

5 Shape the remaining white sugarpaste into four parcels. Trim with red and green sugarpaste ribbons. Use the remaining red and green sugarpaste to make thin strips to decorate the cake sides. Secure in place with royal icing. Stick small sugarpaste balls over the joins. Arrange the stocking and parcels on the cake top.

Marbled Cracker Cake

Here is a Christmas cake that is decorated in a most untraditional way!

Makes one 20cm/8in round cake

20cm/8in round rich	**Materials /equipment**
fruit cake	wooden cocktail sticks
45ml/3 tbsp apricot jam,	25cm/10in round cake
warmed and sieved	board
675g/1½lb/4½ cups	red, green and gold thin
marzipan	gift-wrapping ribbon
750g/1¾lb/5¼ cups	3 red and 3 green ribbon
sugarpaste icing	bows
red and green food	
colouring	
edible gold balls	

1 Brush the cake with the jam. Roll out the marzipan and use to cover the cake. Leave to dry overnight.

2 Form a roll with 500g/1¼lb/3¾ cups of the sugarpaste icing. With a cocktail stick, dab a few drops of red colouring on to the icing. Repeat with the green. Knead lightly. Roll out the icing until marbled. Brush the marzipan with water and cover with the icing. Position the cake on the cake board.

3 Colour half of the remaining sugarpaste icing red and the rest green. Use half of each colour to make five crackers, about 6cm/2½in long. Decorate each with a gold ball. Leave to dry on greaseproof paper.

4 Roll out the remaining red and green icings, and cut into 1cm/½in wide strips. Then cut into 12 red and 12 green diamonds. Attach them alternately around the top and base of the cake with water.

5 Cut the ribbons into 10cm/4in lengths. Arrange them with the crackers on the cake top. Attach the bows with softened sugarpaste icing, between the diamonds at the top cake edge.

Greek New Year Cake

A "good luck", foil-wrapped gold coin is traditionally baked into this cake.

Makes one 23cm/9in square cake

275g/10oz/2½ cups plain
  flour
10ml/2 tsp baking
  powder
50g/2oz/½ cup ground
  almonds
225g/8oz/1 cup butter,
  softened
175g/6oz/generous ¾ cup
  caster sugar, plus
  extra for sprinkling

4 eggs
150ml/¼ pint/⅔ cup
  fresh orange juice
50g/2oz/½ cup blanched
  almonds
15g/½oz/1 tbsp sesame
  seeds

1 Preheat the oven to 180°C/350°F/Gas 4. Grease a 23cm/9in square cake tin, line with greaseproof paper and grease the paper.

2 Sift together the flour and baking powder and stir in the ground almonds.

3 Cream the butter and sugar until light and fluffy. Beat in the eggs, 1 at a time. Fold in the flour mixture, alternating with the orange juice.

4 Spoon the mixture into the cake tin. Arrange the blanched almonds on top, then sprinkle over the sesame seeds. Bake for 50 minutes, or until a skewer inserted in the centre comes out clean. Leave in the tin for 5 minutes, then turn out on to a wire rack and peel off the lining paper. Sprinkle with caster sugar before serving.

Starry New Year Cake

Makes one 23cm/9in round cake

23cm/9in round Madeira
  cake
675g/1½lb/3 cups butter
  icing
750g/1¾lb/5¼ cups
  sugarpaste icing
grape violet and
  mulberry food
  colouring
gold, lilac shimmer and
  primrose sparkle
  powdered food
  colouring

Materials/equipment
fine paintbrush
star-shaped cutter
florist's wire, cut into
  short lengths
28cm/11in round
  cake board
purple ribbon with
  gold stars

1 Cut the cake into three layers. Sandwich together with three-quarters of the butter icing. Spread the rest thinly over the top and sides of the cake.

2 Tint 500g/1¼lb/3¼ cups of the sugarpaste icing purple with the grape violet and mulberry food colouring. Roll out and use to cover the cake. Leave to dry overnight.

3 Place the cake on a sheet of greaseproof paper. Water down some gold and lilac food colouring. Use a paintbrush to flick each colour in turn over the cake. Leave to dry.

4 For the stars, divide the remaining sugarpaste icing into three pieces. Tint one portion purple with the grape violet food colouring, one with the lilac shimmer and one with the primrose sparkle. Roll out each colour to 3mm/⅛in thick. Cut out ten stars in each colour and highlight the stars by flicking on the watered-down gold and lilac colours.

5 While the icing is soft, push the florist's wire through the middle of 15 of the stars. Leave to dry overnight. Put the cake on the board. Arrange the stars on top of the cake. Secure the unwired ones with water. Secure the ribbon around the base.

Simnel Cake

This is a traditional cake to celebrate Easter, but it is delicious at any time of the year.

Makes one 20cm/8in round cake

225g/8oz/1 cup butter, softened
225g/8oz/generous 1 cup caster sugar
4 eggs, beaten
500g/1¼lb/3⅓ cups mixed dried fruit
115g/4oz/½ cup glacé cherries
45ml/3 tbsp sherry (optional)

275g/10oz/2½ cups plain flour
15ml/1 tbsp mixed spice
5ml/1 tsp baking powder
675g/1½lb/4½ cups yellow marzipan
1 egg yolk, beaten
ribbons, sugared eggs and sugarpaste animals, to decorate

1 Preheat the oven to 160°C/325°F/Gas 3. Grease a deep 20cm/8in round cake tin, line with a double thickness of greaseproof paper and grease the paper.

2 Beat together the butter and sugar until light and fluffy. Gradually beat in the eggs. Stir in the dried fruit, glacé cherries and sherry, if using. Sift over the flour, mixed spice and baking powder, then fold in.

3 Roll out half the marzipan to a 20cm/8in round. Spoon half of the cake mixture into the cake tin and place the round of marzipan on top. Add the other half of the cake mixture and smooth the surface.

4 Bake for 2½ hours, or until golden and springy to the touch. Leave in the tin for 15 minutes, then turn out on to a wire rack, peel off the lining paper and leave to cool.

5 Roll out the reserved marzipan to fit the cake. Brush the cake top with egg yolk and place the marzipan on top. Flute the edges and make a pattern on top with a fork. Brush with more egg yolk. Put the cake on a baking sheet and grill for 5 minutes to brown the top lightly. Cool before decorating.

Easter Sponge Cake

This light lemon quick-mix sponge cake is decorated with lemon butter icing and cut-out marzipan flowers.

Makes one 20cm/8in round cake

3-egg quantity lemon-flavour quick-mix sponge cake
675g/1½lb/3 cups lemon-flavour butter icing
50g/2oz/½ cup flaked almonds, toasted

To decorate
50g/2oz/⅜ cup homemade or commercial white marzipan
green, orange and yellow food colouring

1 Preheat the oven to 160°C/325°F/Gas 3. Bake the cakes in two lined and greased 20cm/8in round sandwich tins for 35–40 minutes until they are golden brown and spring back when lightly pressed in the centre. Loosen the edges of the cakes with a palette knife, turn out, remove the lining paper and cool on a wire rack.

2 Sandwich the cakes together with one-quarter of the butter icing. Spread the side of the cake evenly with another one-quarter of butter icing.

3 Press the almonds on to the sides to cover evenly. Spread the top of the cake evenly with another one-quarter of icing. Finish with a palette knife dipped in hot water, spreading backwards and forwards to give an even lined effect.

4 Place the remaining icing into a nylon piping bag fitted with a medium-size gâteau nozzle and pipe a scroll edging.

5 Using the marzipan and food colouring, make six cut-out daffodils and ten green and eight orange cut-out marzipan flowers. Arrange them on the cake and leave the icing to set.

Easter Egg Nest Cake

Celebrate Easter with this colourfully adorned, fresh-tasting lemon sponge cake.

Makes one 20cm/8in ring cake

20cm/8in lemon sponge ring cake	pink, green and purple food colouring
350g/12oz/1½ cups lemon-flavour butter icing	small foil-wrapped chocolate eggs
225g/8oz/1½ cups marzipan	**Materials/equipment** 25cm/10in cake board

1 Cut the cake in half horizontally and sandwich together with one-third of the butter icing. Place on the cake board. Use the remaining icing to cover the cake. Smooth the top and swirl the side with a palette knife.

2 For the marzipan plaits, divide the marzipan into three and tint pink, green and purple. Cut each portion in half. Using one-half of each colour, roll thin sausages long enough to go around the base. Pinch the ends together, then twist the strands into a rope. Pinch the other ends to seal.

3 Place the coloured marzipan rope on the cake board around the cake.

4 For the nests, take the remaining portions of coloured marzipan and divide each into five. Roll each piece into a 16cm/6½in rope. Take a rope of each colour, pinch the ends together, twist to form a multi-coloured rope and pinch the other ends. Form into a circle. Repeat to make five nests.

5 Space the nests evenly on the cake. Place small chocolate eggs in the nests.

Mother's Day Bouquet

A piped bouquet of flowers can bring as much pleasure as a fresh one for a Mother's Day treat.

Makes one 18cm/7in round cake

675g/1½lb/3 cups butter icing	**Materials/equipment** serrated scraper
2 x 18cm/7in round sponge cakes	No 3 writing and petal nozzles
green, blue, yellow and pink food colouring	5 greaseproof paper piping bags

1 Reserve one-third of the butter icing for decorating. Sandwich together the two sponges with butter icing and place on a serving plate. Cover the top and side with the rest of the butter icing, smoothing the top with a palette knife and serrating the side using a scraper.

2 Divide the remaining butter icing into four bowls. Tint them green, blue, yellow and pink.

3 Decorate the top of the cake first. Use No 3 writing nozzles for the blue and green icing and petal nozzles for the yellow and pink. Pipe on the vase and flowers.

4 For the side decoration, spoon the remaining yellow icing into a fresh piping bag fitted with a No 3 writing nozzle. Pipe the stems, then the flowers and flower centres. Finish by piping green beads at the top and base edges of the cake.

Mother's Day Basket

Makes one 15cm/6in cake

175g/6oz/1½ cups self-
rising flour, sifted
175g/6oz/scant 1 cup
caster sugar
175g/6oz/¾ cup soft
margarine
3 eggs
900g/2lb/4 cups orange-
flavour butter icing

Materials/equipment

thin 15cm/6in round
silver cake board
greaseproof paper piping
bag
basketweave nozzle
foil
1m/1yd mauve ribbon,
1cm/½in wide
fresh flowers
0.5m/½yd spotted mauve
ribbon, 3mm/⅛in
wide

1 Preheat the oven to 160°C/325°F/Gas 3. Lightly grease
and base-line a 15cm/6in brioche mould. Place all the cake
ingredients in a bowl, mix together then beat for 1 – 2 minutes
until smooth. Transfer to the prepared mould and bake for
about 1¼ hours, or until risen and golden.

2 Place the cooled cake upside-down on the board. Cover
the sides with one-third of the butter icing. Using a
basketweave nozzle, pipe the sides with a basketweave
pattern.

3 Invert the cake on the board and spread the top with
butter icing. Pipe a shell edging with the basketweave nozzle.
Pipe the basketweave pattern over the cake top, starting at the
edge. Leave to set.

4 Fold a strip of foil several layers thick. Wrap the plain
ribbon around the strip and bend up the ends to secure the
ribbon. Form the foil into a handle and press into the icing.

5 Finish by tying a posy of fresh flowers with the spotted
ribbon and making a mixed ribbon bow for the handle.

Basket Cake

This is a perfect cake for a retirement gathering or other
special occasion.

Makes one basket-shaped cake

20cm/8in round
Madeira cake
450g/1lb/2 cups coloured
butter icing
chocolates or sweets and
ribbon for decoration

Materials/equipment

pastillage (gum paste)
2 greaseproof paper
piping bags, fitted
with a plain tube and
a basketweave tube
powder food colour

1 Cut a template from card to the same size as the top of the
cake, fold it in half and cut along the fold. Roll out pastillage
fairly thinlyand cut out two pieces for the lid, using the
templates as a guide. Leave to dry.

2 Coat the top of the cake with butter icing. Fill both piping
bags with butter icing and on the side of the cake and about
2.5cm/1in on to the top of the cake, pipe a plain vertical line,
then pipe short lengths of basketweave across the line. Pipe
another plain line along the ends of the basketweave strips.
Pipe the next row of basketweave strips in the spaces left
between the existing strips and over the new plain line.
Continue until the side of the cake and the area on the top is
completely covered.

3 Brush the underside of the pastillage lid with powder food
colour, then pipe a basketweave on top of the lid.

4 Divide the top of the cake in half and pipe a line of
basketweave along this central line. Use two or three pieces of
pastillage to support each lid half in an open position on the
cake. Fill the area under each lid half with chocolates or
sweets and decorate with ribbon.

Valentine's Heart Cake

This cake could also be used to celebrate a special birthday or anniversary.

Makes one 20cm/8in square cake

20cm/8in square light fruit cake	**Materials/equipment**
45ml/3 tbsp apricot jam, warmed and sieved	25cm/10in square cake board
900g/2lb/6 cups marzipan	5cm/2in heart-shaped cutter
1.5kg/3lb/9 cups royal icing	2.5cm/1in heart-shaped cutter
115g/4oz/¾ cup sugarpaste icing	4 greaseproof paper piping bags
red food colouring	No 1 and No 2 writing and No 42 star nozzles
	heart-patterned ribbon

1 Brush the cake with the apricot jam. Roll out the marzipan and use to cover the cake. Leave to dry overnight.

2 Secure the cake on the cake board with a little royal icing. Flat-ice the cake with three or four layers of smooth icing. Set aside some royal icing in an airtight container for piping.

3 Tint the sugarpaste icing red. Roll it out and cut 12 hearts with the larger cutter. Stamp out the middles with the smaller cutter. Cut four extra small hearts. Dry on greaseproof paper.

4 Using a No 1 writing nozzle, pipe wavy lines in royal icing around the four small hearts. Leave to dry. Using a fresh bag and a No 42 nozzle, pipe swirls around the top and base of the cake. Colour 15ml/1 tbsp of the remaining royal icing red and pipe red dots on top of each white swirl with the No 1 nozzle.

5 Secure the ribbon in place. Using a No 2 writing nozzle, pipe beads down each corner, avoiding the ribbon. Decorate the cake with the hearts, using royal icing to secure them.

Valentine's Box of Chocolates Cake

This cake would also make a wonderful surprise for Mother's Day.

Makes one 20cm/8in heart-shaped cake

20cm/8in heart-shaped chocolate sponge cake	**Materials/equipment**
275g/10oz/generous 2 cups marzipan	23cm/9in square piece of stiff card
120ml/8 tbsp apricot jam, warmed and sieved	pencil and scissors
900g/2lb/6 cups sugarpaste icing	23cm/9in square cake board
red food colouring	piece of string
225g/8oz/about 16–20 hand-made chocolates	small heart-shaped cutter
	length of ribbon and a pin
	small paper sweet cases

1 Place the cake on the card, draw around it and cut the heart shape out. It will be used to support the box lid. Cut through the cake horizontally just below the dome. Place the top section on the card and the base on the board.

2 Use the string to measure around the outside of the base. Roll the marzipan into a long sausage to the measured length. Place on the cake around the outside edge. Brush both sections of the cake with apricot jam. Tint the sugarpaste icing red and cut off one-third. Cut another 50g/2oz/8 tbsp portion from the larger piece. Set aside. Use the large piece to cover the base section of cake.

3 Stand the lid on a raised surface. Use the reserved one-third of sugarpaste icing to cover the lid. Roll out the remaining piece of icing and stamp out small hearts with the cutter. Stick them around the edge of the lid with water. Tie the ribbon in a bow and secure on top of the lid with the pin.

4 Place the chocolates in the paper cases and arrange in the cake base. Position the lid slightly off-centre, to reveal the chocolates. Remove the ribbon and pin before serving.

Double Heart Engagement Cake

For a celebratory engagement party, these sumptuous cakes make the perfect centrepiece.

Makes two 20cm/8in heart-shaped cakes

*350g/12oz plain
    chocolate
2 x 20cm/8in heart-
    shaped chocolate
    sponge cakes
675g/1½lb/3 cups coffee-
    flavour butter icing*

*icing sugar, for dusting
fresh raspberries, to
    decorate*

Materials/equipment
*2 x 23cm/9in heart-
    shaped cake boards*

1 Melt the chocolate in a heatproof bowl over a saucepan of hot water. Pour the chocolate on to a smooth, non-porous surface and spread it out with a palette knife. Leave to cool until just set, but not hard.

2 To make the chocolate curls, hold a large sharp knife at a 45-degree angle to the chocolate and push it along the chocolate in short sawing movements. Leave to set on greaseproof paper.

3 Cut each cake in half horizontally. Use one-third of the butter icing to sandwich the cakes together. Use the remaining icing to coat the tops and sides of the cakes.

4 Place the cakes on the cake boards. Generously cover the tops and sides of the cakes with the chocolate curls, pressing them gently into the butter icing.

5 Sift a little icing sugar over the top of each cake and decorate with raspberries. Chill until ready to serve.

Sweetheart Cake

Makes one 20cm/8in heart-shaped cake

*20cm/8in heart-shaped
    light fruit cake
30ml/2 tbsp apricot jam,
    warmed and sieved
900g/2lb/6 cups
    marzipan
900g/2lb/6 cups
    sugarpaste icing
red food colouring
225g/8oz/1½ cups royal
    icing*

*large and medium heart-
    shaped plunger
    cutters
1m/1yd red ribbon,
    2.5cm/1in wide
1m/1yd looped red
    ribbon, 1cm/½in wide
0.5m/½yd red ribbon,
    5mm/¼in wide
greaseproof paper piping
    bag
medium star nozzle
fresh red rosebud*

Materials/equipment
*25cm/10in silver heart-
    shaped cake board*

1 Brush the cake with apricot jam, place on the cake board and cover with marzipan. Cover the cake and board with sugarpaste icing. Leave to dry overnight.

2 Tint the sugarpaste icing red. Cut out 18 large and 21 medium-size hearts. Leave to dry on greaseproof paper.

3 Secure the wide ribbon around the cake board. Secure a band of the looped ribbon around the side of the cake with a bead of icing. Tie a bow with long tails and attach to the side of the cake with a bead of icing.

4 Using the star nozzle, pipe a row of royal icing stars around the base of the cake and attach a medium-size heart to every third star. Pipe stars around the cake top, and arrange large red hearts on each one.

5 Tie a bow on to the rosebud stem and place on the cake top just before serving.

Cloth-of-Roses Cake

This cake simply says "congratulations". It is a very pretty cake that is bound to impress your guests.

Makes one 20cm/8in round cake

20cm/8in round light
   fruit cake
45ml/3 tbsp apricot jam,
   warmed and sieved
675g/1½lb/4½ cups
   marzipan
900g/2lb/6 cups
   sugarpaste icing
yellow, orange and green
   food colouring

115g/4oz/¾ cup royal
   icing

Materials/equipment
25cm/10in cake board
5.5cm/2¼in plain cutter
petal cutter
thin yellow ribbon

1 Brush the cake with apricot jam. Cover with marzipan and leave to dry overnight.

2 Cut off 675g/1½lb/4½ cups of the sugarpaste icing and divide in half. Colour pale yellow and pale orange.

3 Make a greaseproof paper template for the orange icing by drawing a 25cm/10in circle round the cake board then, using the plain cutter, draw scallops around the circle.

4 Cover the cake side with yellow sugarpaste icing. Place the cake on the board. Using the template, cut out the orange sugarpaste icing. Place on the cake and bend the scallops slightly. Leave to dry overnight.

5 For the roses and leaves, cut off three-quarters of the remaining sugarpaste icing and divide into four. Tint pale yellow, deep yellow, orange, and marbled yellow and orange. Make 18 roses. Tint the remaining icing green. Cut out 24 leaves with a petal cutter. Dry on greaseproof paper.

6 Secure the leaves and roses with royal icing. Decorate the cake with the ribbon.

Rose Blossom Wedding Cake

Serves 80

23cm/9in square rich
   fruit cake
15cm/6in square rich
   fruit cake
75ml/5 tbsp apricot jam,
   warmed and sieved
1.5kg/3½lb/10½ cups
   marzipan
1.5kg/3½lb/10½ cups
   royal icing, to coat
675g/1½lb/4½ cups royal
   icing, to pipe
pink and green food
   colouring

Materials/equipment
28cm/11in square
   cake board
20cm/8in square
   cake board
No 1 writing and No 42
   nozzles
greaseproof paper piping
   bags
thin pink ribbon
8 pink bows
3–4 cake pillars
12 miniature roses
few fern sprigs

1 Brush the cakes with the jam and cover with marzipan. Leave to dry overnight, then secure to their boards with icing. Flat-ice the cakes with three or four layers, allowing each to dry overnight. Dry for several days.

2 For the sugar pieces, use the No 1 writing nozzle to pipe the double-triangle design in white icing on greaseproof paper. You will need 40 pieces, but make extra. Tint some icing pale pink and some very pale green. Using No 1 writing nozzles, pipe pink dots on the corners of the top triangles and green on the corners of the lower triangles. Leave to dry.

3 Use a pin to mark out the triangles on the tops and sides of each cake. Using a No 1 writing nozzle, pipe double white lines over the pin marks, then pipe cornelli inside all the triangles. With a No 42 nozzle, pipe white shells around the top and base edges of each cake, between the triangles.

4 Using No 1 writing nozzles, pipe pink and green dots on the cake corners. Secure the sugar pieces to the cakes and boards with icing. Attach the ribbons and bows. Assemble the cake with the pillars and decorate with roses and fern sprigs.

Basketweave Wedding Cake

This wonderful wedding cake can be made in any flavour.

Serves 150
25cm/10in, 20cm/8in
and 15cm/6in square
Madeira cakes
2.75kg/6lb/12 cups
butter icing

12 small greaseproof
piping bags
No 4 writing and
basketweave nozzles
1.5m/1½yd pale lilac
ribbon, 2.5cm/1in
wide
2.5m/2½yd deep lilac
ribbon, 5mm/¼in
wide
30 fresh lilac-coloured
freesias

Materials/equipment
30cm/12in square silver
cake board
20cm/8in and 15cm/6in
thin silver cake board
smooth scraper

1 Level the cake tops, then invert the cakes on to the boards
and cover with butter icing. Use a smooth scraper on the sides
and a palette knife to smooth the top. Leave to set for 1 hour.

2 Pipe a line of icing with the No 4 writing nozzle on to the
corner of the large cake, from the base to the top. Using the
basketweave nozzle, pipe a basketweave pattern (see above
photograph). Pipe all around the side of the cake and neaten
the top edge with a shell border, using the basketweave
nozzle. Repeat for the second cake.

3 To decorate the top of the small cake, start at the edge with
a straight plain line, then pipe across with the basketweave
nozzle, spacing the lines equally apart. When the top is
complete, work the design around the sides, making sure the
top and side designs align. Leave the cakes overnight to set.

4 Fit the wide and narrow lilac ribbons around the board.
Use the remaining narrow ribbon to tie eight small bows with
long tails. Trim off the flower stems.

5 Assemble the cakes. Decorate with the bows and flowers.

Chocolate-iced Anniversary Cake

This attractive cake is special enough to celebrate any
wedding anniversary.

Makes one 20cm/8in round cake
20cm/8in round Madeira
cake
475g/1lb 2oz/2¼ cups
chocolate-flavour
butter icing

selection of fresh fruits,
such as kiwi fruit,
nectarines, peaches,
apricots and Cape
gooseberries, peeled
and sliced as necessary

For the chocolate icing
175g/6oz plain chocolate
150ml/¼ pint/⅔ cup
single cream
2.5ml/½ tsp instant
coffee powder

Materials/equipment
No 22 star nozzle
greaseproof paper
piping bag
gold ribbon, about
5mm/¼in wide
florist's wire

To decorate
chocolate buttons,
quartered

1 Cut the cake horizontally into three and sandwich
together with three-quarters of the butter icing. Place on a
wire rack over a baking sheet.

2 To make the satin chocolate icing, put all of the ingredients
in a saucepan and melt over a very low heat until smooth.
Immediately pour over the cake to coat completely. Use a
palette knife, if necessary. Allow to set.

3 Transfer the cake to a serving plate. Using a No 22 star
nozzle, pipe butter icing scrolls around the top edge. Decorate
with chocolate button pieces and fruit.

4 Make seven ribbon decorations. For each one, make two
small loops from ribbon and secure the ends with a twist of
florist's wire . Cut the wire to the length you want and use to
position the decoration in the fruit. Remove before serving.

Silver Wedding Cake

Makes one 25cm/10in round cake

25cm/10in round rich or
  light fruit cake
60ml/4 tbsp apricot jam,
  warmed and sieved
1.2kg/2½lb/7½ cups
  marzipan
1.5kg/3lb/9 cups royal
  icing

For the petal paste

10ml/2 tsp gelatine
75ml/5 tbsp cold water
10ml/2 tsp liquid glucose
10ml/2 tsp white
  vegetable fat
450g/1lb/4 cups icing
  sugar, sifted
5ml/1 tsp gum
  tragacanth, sifted
1 egg white

Materials/equipment

30cm/12in round silver
  cake board
1.5m/1½yd white ribbon,
  2.5cm/1in wide
2m/2yd silver ribbon,
  2.5cm/1in wide
club cocktail cutter
tiny round cutter
greaseproof piping bag
No 1 writing nozzle
50 large silver dragées
1.5m/1½yd silver ribbon,
  5mm/¼in wide
7 silver leaves
"25" silver cake
  decoration

1 Brush the cake with apricot jam and cover with marzipan. Place on the board. Flat-ice the top and side of the cake with three or four layers of royal icing. Leave to dry overnight, then ice the board. Reserve the remaining royal icing. Secure the wider ribbons around the board and cake with icing.

2 For the petal paste, melt the first four ingredients in a pan set over a bowl of hot water. Mix the sugar, gum tragacanth, egg white and gelatine mixture to a paste and knead until smooth. Leave for 2 hours, then re-knead. Make 65 cut-outs using the two cutters. Leave to dry overnight.

3 Arrange 25 cut-outs around the top and secure with icing beads piped with a No 1 writing nozzle. Repeat at the base. Pipe icing beads between and press a dragée in each. Leave to dry. Thread the thin ribbon through. Arrange seven cut-outs and seven dragées in the centre. Position the leaves and "25".

Golden Wedding Heart Cake

Makes one 23cm/9in round cake

60ml/4 tbsp apricot jam
23cm/9in round rich
  fruit cake
900g/2lb/6 cups
  marzipan
900g/2lb/6 cups
  sugarpaste icing
cream food colouring
115g/4oz/¾ cup royal
  icing

Materials/equipment

28cm/11in round cake
  board

crimping tool
pins
small heart-shaped
  plunger tool
7.5cm/3in plain cutter
dual large and small
  blossom cutter
stamens
frill cutter
wooden cocktail stick
foil-wrapped chocolate
  hearts

1 Warm, then sieve the apricot jam and brush over the cake. Cover with marzipan and leave to dry overnight.

2 Tint 675g/1½lb/4½ cups of the sugarpaste icing very pale cream and cover the cake. Put on the board. Crimp the top edge. With pins, mark eight equidistant points around the top edge. Crimp slanting lines to the base. Emboss the base edge with the plunger. Use the plain cutter to emboss a circle on top.

3 Divide the remaining sugarpaste icing into two and tint cream and pale cream. Using half of each colour, make flowers with the blossom cutter. Make pinholes in the large flowers. Leave to dry then secure the stamens in the holes with royal icing.

4 Make eight frills with the rest of the sugarpaste icing using the frill cutter, and a cocktail stick to trim and fill the edges. Attach the frills with water next to the crimped lines on the cake side. Crimp the edges of the deeper coloured frills.

5 Secure the flowers on the top and side of the cake with royal icing. Place the chocolate hearts in the centre.

Marzipan Bell Cake

This cake can be easily adapted to make a christening cake if you leave out the holly decorations.

Makes one 18cm/7in round cake

18cm/7in round rich or light fruit cake	**Materials/equipment**
30ml/2 tbsp apricot jam, warmed and sieved	20cm/8in round silver cake board
900g/2lb/6 cups marzipan	crimping tool
green, yellow and red food colouring	bell and holly leaf cutter
	1m/1yd red ribbon, 2cm/¾in wide
	1m/1yd green ribbon, 5mm/¼in wide
	0.25m/¼yd red ribbon, 5mm/¼in wide

1 Brush the cake with apricot jam and place on the cake board. Tint two-thirds of the marzipan pale green. Use to cover the cake. Crimp the top edge of the cake to make a scalloped pattern.

2 Tint a small piece of remaining marzipan bright yellow, another bright red and the rest bright green. Make two yellow bells and clappers, 11 green holly leaves (veins marked with the back of a knife), two green bell ropes, 16 red holly berries and two bell-rope ends. Leave to dry.

3 Secure the wide red and fine green ribbons around the side of the cake with a pin. Tie a double bow from red and green fine ribbon and attach to the side with a pin.

4 Arrange the bells, clappers, bell ropes, holly leaves and berries on top of the cake and secure with apricot jam.

Christening Sampler

Serves 30

20cm/8in square rich fruit cake	**Materials/equipment**
45ml/3 tbsp apricot jam, warmed and sieved	25cm/10in square cake board
450g/1lb/3cups marzipan	fine paintbrush
675g/1½lb/4½ cups sugarpaste icing	small heart-shaped biscuit cutter
brown, yellow, orange, purple, cream, blue, green and pink food colouring	

1 Brush the cake with apricot jam. Roll out the marzipan, cover the cake and leave to dry overnight. Roll out 150g/5oz/1 cup of the sugarpaste icing to fit the cake top. Brush the top with water and cover with the icing.

2 Colour 300g/10oz/2 cups of the icing brown and roll out four pieces to the length and about 1cm/½in wider than the cake sides. Brush the sides with water and cover with icing, folding over the extra width at the top and cutting the corners at an angle to make the picture frame. Place on a cake board. With a fine paintbrush, paint over the sides with watered-down brown food colouring to represent wood grain.

3 Take the remaining icing and colour small amounts yellow, orange, brown, purple and cream and two shades of blue, green and pink. Leave a little white. Use these colours to shape the ducks, teddy bear, bulrushes, water, branch and leaves. Cut out a pink heart and make the baby's initial from white icing.

4 Mix the white and pink icings together for the apple blossom flowers. Make the shapes for the border. Attach the decorations to the cake with a little water.

5 Use the leftover colours to make "threads". Arrange in loops around the base of the cake on the board.

Teddy Bear Christening Cake

To personalize the cake, make a simple plaque for the top and pipe on the name of the new baby.

Makes one 20cm/8in square cake

20cm/8in square light fruit cake	**Materials/equipment**
45ml/3 tbsp apricot jam, warmed and sieved	*25cm/10in square cake board*
900g/2lb/6 cups marzipan	*crimping tool cornflour, for dipping*
800g/1¾lb/5¼ cups sugarpaste icing	*fine paintbrush wooden cocktail stick*
peach, yellow, blue and brown food colouring	*peach ribbon small blue ribbon bow*
115g/4oz/¾ cup royal icing	

1 Brush the cake with the apricot jam. Roll out the marzipan and use to cover the cake. Leave to dry overnight.

2 Colour 500g/1¼lb/3¾ cups of the sugarpaste icing peach, then roll it out. Brush the marzipan with water and cover the cake with the icing. Place the cake on the board. Using a crimping tool dipped in cornflour, crimp the top and base edges of the cake.

3 Divide the remaining sugarpaste into three. Leave one-third white and tint one-third yellow. Divide the last third in two, tint one half peach and the other blue.

4 Make flowers from the peach and blue sugarpaste. Leave to dry. Reserve the blue trimmings. Make a yellow teddy bear. Paint on its face with brown food colouring. Give it a blue button. Leave to dry. Make a blue blanket. Frill the white edge with a cocktail stick. Secure the frill to the blanket with water.

5 Decorate the cake with the ribbon, place the bear on top under its blanket, securing with royal icing. Secure the flowers and the bear's bow-tie in the same way.

Daisy Christening Cake

A ring of daisies sets off this pretty pink christening cake.

Makes one 20cm/8in round cake

20cm/8in round rich fruit cake	**Materials/equipment**
45ml/3 tbsp apricot jam, warmed and sieved	*25cm/10in round cake board*
675g/1½lb/4½ cups marzipan	*fine paintbrush 5cm/2in fluted cutter*
900g/2lb/6 cups royal icing	*wooden cocktail stick 2 greaseproof paper piping bags*
115g/4oz/¾ cup sugarpaste icing	*No 42 nozzle pink and white ribbon*
pink and yellow food colouring	

1 Brush the cake with the apricot jam. Roll out the marzipan and use to cover the cake. Leave to dry overnight.

2 Use a little royal icing to secure the cake to the board. Tint three-quarters of the royal icing pink. Flat-ice the cake with three or four layers, using white for the top and pink for the side. Allow each layer to dry overnight before applying the next. Set aside a little of both icings in airtight containers.

3 Make 28 daisies. For each daisy, shape a small piece of sugarpaste icing to look like a golf tee. Snip the edges and curl them slightly. Dry on greaseproof paper. Trim the stems and paint the edges pink and the centres yellow.

4 To make the plaque, roll out the remaining sugarpaste icing and cut out a circle with the fluted cutter. Roll a cocktail stick around the edge until it frills. Dry on greaseproof paper, then paint the name and the edges with pink food colouring.

5 Pipe twisted ropes around the top and base of the cake with the reserved white royal icing. Then pipe a row of stars around the top of the cake. Stick the plaque in the centre with royal icing. Stick on the daisies and decorate with the ribbons.

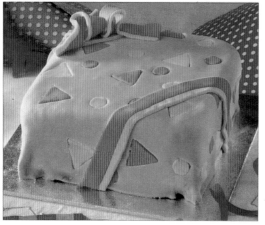

Birthday Parcel

Serves 10

15cm/6in square Madeira
  cake
275g/10oz/1⅓ cup
  orange-flavour butter
  icing
45ml/3 tbsp apricot jam,
  warmed and sieved
450g/1lb/3cups
  sugarpaste icing
blue, orange and green
  food colouring

icing sugar, for dusting

Materials/equipment
15–18cm/7–8in square
  cake board
small triangular and
  round cocktail cutters

1 Cut the cake in half horizontally and sandwich together with the butter icing. Brush the cake with apricot jam. Colour three-quarters of the sugarpaste icing blue. Divide the remaining sugarpaste icing in half and colour one half orange and the other half green. Wrap the orange and green sugarpaste separately in clear film and set aside. Roll out the blue icing on a work surface lightly dusted with icing sugar and use it to cover the cake. Position on the cake board.

2 While the sugarpaste covering is still soft, use the cocktail cutters to cut out triangles and circles from the blue icing, lifting out the shapes to expose the cake.

3 Roll out the orange and green icings and cut out circles and triangles to fill the exposed holes in the blue icing. Roll out the trimmings and cut three orange strips, 2cm/¾in wide and long enough to go over the corner of the cake and 3 very thin green strips the same length as the orange ones. Place the strips next to each other to make three striped ribbons, and secure the pieces together with a little water.

4 Place one striped ribbon over one corner of the cake, securing with a little water. Place a second strip over the opposite corner. Cut the remaining ribbon in half. Bend each half to make loops and attach both to one corner of the cake with water to form a loose bow.

Chocolate Fruit Birthday Cake

The marzipan fruits on this moist chocolate Madeira cak make an eye-catching decoration.

Makes one 18cm/7in square cake

18cm/7in square deep
  chocolate Madeira
  cake
45ml/3 tbsp apricot jam,
  warmed and sieved
450g/1lb/3 cups
  marzipan
450g/1lb/2cups chocolate
  fudge icing
red, yellow, orange, green
  and purple food
  colouring

whole cloves
angelica strips

Materials/equipment
20cm/8in square silver
  cake board
medium gâteau nozzle
nylon piping bag
0.75m/¾yd yellow
  ribbon, 1cm/½in wide

1 Level the cake top and invert. Brush with apricot jam.

2 Use two-thirds of the marzipan to cover the cake. Reserve the trimmings.

3 Place the cake on a wire rack over a tray and pour three-quarters of the chocolate fudge icing over, spreading with a palette knife. Leave for 10 minutes, then place on the board.

4 Using the reserved icing and a medium-size gâteau nozzle, pipe stars around the top edge and base of the cake. Leave to set.

5 Using the reserved marzipan, food colouring, cloves and angelica strips, model a selection of fruits.

6 Secure the ribbon around the sides of the cake. Decorate the top with the marzipan fruits.

Eighteenth Birthday Cake

A really striking cake for an eighteenth birthday. Change the shape if you don't have the tin.

Serves 80

33.5 x 20cm/13½ x 8in diamond-shaped deep rich or light fruit cake	**Materials/equipment** 38 x 23cm/15 x 9in diamond-shaped cake
45ml/3 tbsp apricot jam, warmed and sieved	board "18" template
1.1kg/2½lb/7½ cups marzipan	small greaseproof paper piping bag
1.6kg/3½lb/10½ cups sugarpaste	No 1 writing nozzle 2m/2yd white ribbon,
black food colouring	2.5cm/1in wide
30ml/2 tbsp royal icing	2m/2yd black ribbon, 3mm/⅛in wide

1 Make the cake using quantities for a 23cm/9in round cake. Brush with apricot jam. Cover in marzipan. Place on the cake board. Cover the cake using 1.2kg/2½lb/7½ cups sugarpaste icing. Knead the trimmings into the remaining sugarpaste and tint black.

2 Use two-thirds of the black sugarpaste to cover the board.

3 Use a quarter of the remaining sugarpaste to cut out a number "18" using a template. Use the rest to cut out a variety of bow ties, wine glasses and music notes. Leave to dry on greaseproof paper.

4 Tint the royal icing black. Using a No 1 writing nozzle, attach the cut-outs to the cake top and sides.

5 Tie four small bows with the black ribbon. Secure with icing to the top corners. Position and secure black ribbon around the cake base and white ribbon around the board.

Flickering Birthday Candle Cake

Flickering stripy candles are ready to blow out on this birthday cake for all ages.

Makes one 20cm/8in square cake

20cm/8in square Madeira cake	**Materials/equipment** 23cm/9in square cake
350g/12oz/1½ cups butter icing	board small round cutter
45ml/3 tbsp apricot jam, warmed and sieved	pink and purple food colouring pens
800g/1¾lb/5¼ cups sugarpaste icing	5mm/¼in wide jade-coloured ribbon
pink, yellow, purple and jade food colouring	
edible silver balls	

1 Cut the cake into three layers. Sandwich together with the butter icing and brush the cake with the apricot jam. Roll out 500g/1¼lb/3¾ cups of the sugarpaste icing and use to cover the cake. Position on the cake board.

2 Divide the remaining sugarpaste into four pieces and tint them pink, yellow, pale purple and jade.

3 Make the candles from jade and the flames from yellow icing. Press a silver ball into their bases. Position the candles and flames on the cake with a little water. Mould strips in yellow and purple icing to go round the candles. Secure with water. Cut small wavy pieces from the pink and purple icing for smoke, and arrange them, using water, above the candles.

4 Cut out yellow circles with the cutter for the side decorations. Mould small pink balls and press a silver ball into their centres. Attach using water.

5 Using food colouring pens, draw wavy lines and dots coming from the purple and pink wavy icings. Decorate the sides of the cake board with the ribbon, securing at the back with a little softened sugarpaste.

Flower Birthday Cake

A simple birthday cake decorated with piped yellow and white flowers and ribbons.

Makes one 18cm/7in round cake

18cm/7in round light
   fruit cake
30ml/2 tbsp apricot jam,
   warmed and sieved
675g/1½lb/4½ cups
   marzipan
1.2kg/2½lb/7½ cups royal
   icing
yellow and orange food
   colouring

petal nozzle, No 1 and
   2 writing nozzles, and
   medium star nozzle
greaseproof paper piping
   bags
1m/1yd white ribbon,
   2cm/¾in wide
2m/2yd coral ribbon,
   1cm/½in wide
25cm/10in coral ribbon,
   5mm/¼in wide

Materials/equipment

23cm/9in round silver
   cake board

1 Brush the cake with apricot jam and cover with marzipan. Place on the board.

2 Flat-ice the top and side of the cake with three layers of royal icing. Leave to dry, then ice the board. Reserve the remaining royal icing.

3 Tint one-third of the reserved royal icing yellow and 15ml/1 tbsp of it orange. Using the petal nozzle for the petals and No 1 writing nozzle for the centres, make four white narcissi with yellow centres and nine yellow narcissi with orange centres. Make nine plain white flowers with a snipped piping bag with yellow centres. When dry, secure to the top.

4 Use the star nozzle to pipe shell edgings to the cake top and base. Pipe "Happy Birthday" using the No 2 writing nozzle. Overlay in orange using the No 1 writing nozzle.

5 Secure the ribbons around the board and cake side. Finish with a coral bow.

Jazzy Chocolate Gâteau

This cake is made with Father's Day in mind, though you can make it for anyone who loves chocolate.

Serves 12–15

2 x quantity chocolate-
   flavour quick-mix
   sponge cake mix
75g/3oz/3 squares plain
   chocolate
75g/3oz/3 squares white
   chocolate
175g/6oz fudge frosting
115g/4oz/1 cup glacé
   icing

5ml/1 tsp weak coffee
8 tbsp chocolate hazelnut
   spread

Materials/equipment

2 x 20cm/8in round cake
   tins
greaseproof paper piping
   bag
No 1 writing nozzle

1 Preheat the oven to 160°C/325°F/Gas 3. Grease the cake tins, line the bases with greaseproof paper and grease the paper. Divide the cake mixture evenly between the tins and smooth the surfaces. Bake in the centre of the oven for about 20–30 minutes, or until firm to the touch. Turn out on to a wire rack, peel off the lining paper and leave to cool.

2 Melt the chocolates in two separate bowls, pour on to baking paper and spread evenly. As it begins to set, place another sheet of baking paper on top and turn the chocolate "sandwich" over. When set, peel off the paper and turn the chocolate sheets over. Cut out haphazard shapes of chocolate and set aside.

3 Sandwich the two cakes together using the fudge frosting. Place the cake on a stand or plate. Colour the glacé icing using the weak coffee and add enough water to form a spreading consistency. Spread the icing on top of the cake almost to the edges. Cover the side of the cake with chocolate hazelnut spread.

4 Press the chocolate pieces around the side of the cake and, using a piping bag fitted with a No 1 nozzle, decorate the top of the cake with "jazzy" lines over the glacé icing.

Petal Retirement Cake

Makes one 20cm/8in petal-shaped cake

20cm/8in petal-shaped deep light fruit cake	*foam sponge*
45ml/3 tbsp apricot jam, warmed and sieved	*large and small blossom plunger cutters*
900g/2lb/6 cups marzipan	*2m/2yd white ribbon, 2cm/¾in wide*
mulberry and pink food colouring	*2m/2yd fuchsia ribbon, 1cm/½in wide*
900g/2lb/6 cups sugarpaste icing	*2m/2yd fuchsia ribbon, 3mm/⅛in wide*
275g/10oz petal paste	*greaseproof paper piping bag*
15ml/1 tbsp royal icing	*No 1 writing nozzle*
	pink food colouring pen
Materials/equipment	*fresh flowers*
23cm/9in petal-shaped silver cake board	

1 Brush the cake with jam and put on the board. Cover with marzipan. Knead mulberry colouring into the sugarpaste icing. Use to cover the cake and board. Dry overnight.

2 Tint the petal paste with pink colouring. Roll and cut out a 5 x 2.5cm/2 x 1in rectangle. Fold in half and dry over a foam sponge to make the card. Make holes in the top edges of the fold for the ribbon. Cut out 30 large and four small plunger blossom flowers. Leave to dry.

3 Using the royal icing and a No 1 writing nozzle, secure the white and narrow fuchsia ribbons around the board and the medium ribbon around the cake base. Tie six small bows from the narrow ribbon for the base.

4 Attach the large flowers to the side of the cake with icing. Secure the small flowers to the board. Draw a design and write a message inside the card with the pen. Thread ribbon through the holes and tie a bow. Place on the cake top with the fresh flowers.

Pansy Retirement Cake

You can use other edible flowers such as nasturtiums, roses or tiny daffodils for this cake, if you prefer.

Makes one 20cm/8in round cake

20cm/8in round light fruit cake	**Materials/equipment**
45ml/3 tbsp apricot jam, warmed and sieved	*25cm/10in round cake board*
675g/1½lb/4½ cups marzipan	*2 greaseproof paper piping bags*
1.1kg/2½lb/7½ cups royal icing	*No 19 star and No 1 writing nozzles*
orange food colouring	*2cm/¾in wide purple ribbon*
about 7 sugar-frosted pansies (orange and purple)	*3mm/⅛in wide dark purple ribbon*

1 Brush the cake with the apricot jam. Roll out the marzipan and use to cover the cake. Leave to dry overnight.

2 Secure the cake to the cake board with a little royal icing. Tint a quarter of the royal icing pale orange. Flat-ice the cake with three layers of smooth icing. Use the orange icing for the top and the white for the side. Set aside a little of both icings in airtight containers for decoration.

3 Spoon the reserved white royal icing into a greaseproof paper piping bag fitted with a No 19 star nozzle. Pipe a row of scrolls around the cake top. Pipe a second row directly underneath the first row in the reverse direction. Pipe another row of scrolls around the base of the cake.

4 Spoon the reserved orange icing into a fresh piping bag fitted with a No 1 writing nozzle. Pipe around the outline of the top of each scroll. Pipe a row of single orange dots below the lower row of reverse scrolls at the top and a double row of dots above the base row of scrolls. Arrange the sugar-frosted pansies on top of the cake. Decorate the side with the ribbons.

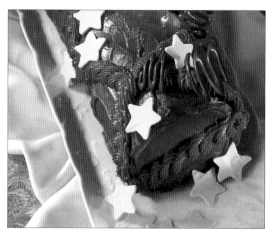

Hallowe'en Pumpkin Patch Cake

Celebrate Hallowe'en with this autumn-coloured cake, colourfully decorated with sugarpaste pumpkins.

Makes one 20cm/8in round cake

175g/6oz/generous 1 cup sugarpaste icing	**Materials/equipment**
brown and orange food colouring	*wooden cocktail stick*
2 x 20cm/8in round chocolate sponge cakes	*fine paintbrush*
	23cm/9in round cake board
675g/1/½lb/3 cups orange-flavour butter icing	*serrated scraper*
chocolate chips	*No 7 writing nozzle*
angelica	*greaseproof paper piping bag*

1 For the pumpkins, tint a very small piece of the sugarpaste icing brown, and the rest orange. Shape some balls of the orange icing the size of walnuts and some a bit smaller. Make ridges with a cocktail stick. Make stems from the brown icing and secure with water. Paint highlights on the pumpkins in orange. Leave to dry on greaseproof paper.

2 Cut both cakes in half horizontally. Use one-quarter of the butter icing to sandwich the cakes together. Place the cake on the board. Use two-thirds of the remaining icing to cover the cake. Texture the icing with a serrated scraper.

3 Using a No 7 writing nozzle, pipe a twisted rope pattern around the top and base edges of the cake with the remaining butter icing. Decorate with chocolate chips.

4 Cut the angelica into diamond shapes and arrange on the cake with the pumpkins.

Fudge-frosted Starry Roll

Whether it's for a birthday or another occasion, this sumptuous-looking cake is sure to please.

Makes one 33cm/13in long roll

23 x 33cm/9 x 13in Swiss roll sponge	*75g/3oz/6 tbsp butter or margarine*
175g/6oz/¾ cup chocolate butter icing	*65ml/4½ tbsp milk or single cream*
50g/2oz white chocolate	*7.5ml/1½ tsp vanilla essence*
50g/2oz plain chocolate	

For the fudge frosting	**Materials/equipment**
75g/3oz plain chocolate, broken into pieces	*small star cutter*
350g/12oz/3 cups icing sugar, sifted	*several greaseproof paper piping bags*
	No 19 star nozzle

1 Unroll the sponge and spread with the butter icing. Re-roll and set aside.

2 For the decorations, melt the white chocolate in a bowl set over a pan of hot water and spread on to a non-porous surface. Leave to firm, then cut out stars with the cutter. Leave to set on greaseproof paper. To make lace curls, melt the plain chocolate and then cool slightly. Cover a rolling pin with greaseproof paper. Pipe zigzags on the paper and leave on the rolling pin until cool.

3 For the frosting, stir all the ingredients over a low heat until melted. Remove from the heat and beat frequently until cool and thick. Cover the cake with two-thirds of the frosting, swirling with a palette knife.

4 With a No 19 star nozzle, use the remaining frosting to pipe diagonal lines on the cake.

5 Position the lace curls and stars. Transfer the cake to a serving plate and decorate with more stars.

Lucky Horseshoe Cake

This horseshoe-shaped cake, made to wish "good luck", is made from a round cake and the shape is then cut out.

Makes one 25cm/10in horseshoe cake

25cm/10in rich fruit cake	**Materials/equipment**
60ml/4 tbsp apricot jam, warmed and sieved	30cm/12in round cake board
800g/1¾lb/5¼ cups marzipan	crimping tool
1kg/2¼lb/6¾ cups sugarpaste icing	pale blue ribbon, 3mm/⅛in wide
peach and blue food colouring	scalpel
edible silver balls	large and small blossom cutters
115g/4oz/¾ cup royal icing	

1 Make a horseshoe template and use to shape the cake. Brush the cake with the apricot jam. Roll out 350g/12oz/ 2¼ cups of the marzipan to a 25cm/10in circle. Using the template, cut out the shape and place on the cake. Measure the inside and outside of the cake. Cover with the remaining marzipan. Place the cake on the board and leave overnight.

2 Tint 800g/1¾lb/5¼ cups of the sugarpaste icing peach. Cover the cake in the same way. Crimp the top edge.

3 Draw and measure the ribbon insertion on the template. Cut 13 pieces of ribbon fractionally longer than each slit. Make the slits through the template with a scalpel. Insert the ribbon with a painted tool. Leave to dry overnight.

4 Make a small horseshoe template. Tint half the remaining sugarpaste icing pale blue. Using the template, cut out nine blue shapes. Mark each horseshoe with a sharp knife. Cut out 12 large and 15 small blossoms. Press a silver ball into the centres of the larger blossoms. Leave to dry. Repeat with the white icing. Decorate the cake and board with the ribbon, horseshoes and blossoms, securing with royal icing.

Bluebird Bon-voyage Cake

This cake is sure to see someone off on an exciting journey in a very special way.

Makes one 20cm/8in round cake

450g/1lb/3 cups royal icing	edible silver balls
blue food colouring	**Materials/equipment**
800g/1¾lb/5¼ cups sugarpaste icing	No 1 writing nozzle
20cm/8in round Madeira cake	greaseproof paper piping bags
350g/12oz/1½ cups butter icing	25cm/10in round cake board
45ml/3 tbsp apricot jam, warmed and sieved	thin pale blue ribbon

1 Make two-thirds of the royal icing softer to use for the run-outs. Make the rest stiffer for the outlines and further piping. Tint the softer icing bright blue. Cover and leave overnight.

2 Make two different-size bird templates, and use to pipe the run-outs on greaseproof paper. Using a No 1 writing nozzle, pipe the outlines, and then fill in. You need four large and five small birds. Leave to dry for at least 2 days.

3 Tint two-thirds of the sugarpaste icing blue. Form all the icing into small rolls and place them alternately together on a work surface. Form into a round and lightly knead to marble.

4 Cut the cake horizontally into three and sandwich together with the butter icing. Place the cake on the board, flush with an edge, and brush with apricot jam. Roll out the marbled icing and use to cover the cake and board.

5 Using the No 1 writing nozzle and the stiffer royal icing, pipe a wavy line around the edge of the board. Position the balls evenly in the icing. Secure the birds to the cake with royal icing. Pipe beads of white icing for eyes and stick on a ball. Drape the ribbon between the beaks, securing with icing.

Ghost Cake

This children's cake is really simple to make yet very effective. It is ideal for a Hallowe'en party.

Serves 15–20

900g/2lb/6 cups
  sugarpaste icing
black food colouring
2 Madeira cakes, baked in
  an 18cm/7in square
  cake tin and a
  300ml/½ pint/1¼ cup
  pudding basin

350g/12oz/1½ cups
  butter icing

Materials/equipment
23cm/9in round cake
  board
fine paintbrush

1 Tint 115g/4oz/¾ cup of the sugarpaste icing dark grey and use to cover the cake board.

2 Cut two small corners off the large cake. Cut two larger wedges off the other two corners, then stand the cake on the board. Divide the larger trimmings in half and wedge around the base of the cake.

3 Secure the small cake to the top of the larger cake with butter icing. Completely cover both of the cakes with the remaining butter icing.

4 Roll out the remaining sugarpaste icing to an oval shape 50 x 30cm/20 x 12in. Lay it over the cake, letting the icing fall into folds around the sides. Gently smooth the icing over the top half of the cake and trim off any excess.

5 Using black food colouring and a fine paintbrush, paint two oval eyes on to the head.

Cat-in-a-Basket Cake

Makes one 15cm/6in round cake

800g/1¾lb/5¼ cups
  marzipan
red, green, yellow and
  brown food colouring
15cm/6in round deep
  sponge cake
30ml/2 tbsp apricot jam,
  warmed and sieved
50g/2oz/4 tbsp butter
  icing

50g/2oz/4 tbsp white
  sugarpaste icing

Materials/equipment
20cm/8in round cake
  board
fine paintbrush

1 Tint 350g/12oz/2 cups of the marzipan pink. Divide the rest in half and tint one half green and the other yellow. Brush the cake with the apricot jam and place it on the board.

2 Roll out the pink marzipan to a rectangle measuring 15 x 25cm/6 x 10in. Cut five 1cm/½in wide strips, about 24cm/9½in long, keeping them attached to the rectangle at one end. Roll out the green marzipan and cut it into 7.5cm/3in lengths of the same width. Fold back alternate pink strips and lay a green strip across widthways. Bring the pink strips over the green strip to form the weave. Keep repeating the process until the entire length is woven. Press lightly to join. Repeat with the rest of the rectangle and more strips of green marzipan.

3 Press the two pieces of basketweave on to the side of cake, joining them neatly. Model a yellow marzipan cat about 7.5cm/3in across. Leave to dry overnight.

4 Roll out the sugarpaste icing and place on the centre of the cake. Put the cat on top and arrange the icing in folds around it. Trim the edges neatly.

5 Make long ropes from any leftover pink and green marzipan. Twist together and press on to the top edge of the cake. Paint the cat's features in brown food colouring.

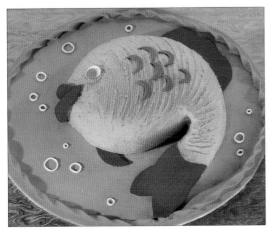

Fish-shaped Cake

A very easy, but colourful cake, perfect for a small child's birthday party.

Makes one fish-shaped cake

450g/1lb/3 cups
  sugarpaste icing
blue, orange, red, mauve
  and green food
  colouring
sponge cake, baked in a
  3.5 litre/6 pint/15 cup
  ovenproof mixing
  bowl
350g/12oz/1½ cups
  butter icing

1 blue Smartie

Materials/equipment
large oval cake board
2.5cm/1in plain biscuit
  cutter
greaseproof paper piping
  bag

1 Tint two-thirds of the sugarpaste icing blue, roll out very thinly and use to cover the dampened cake board.

2 Invert the cake and trim into the fish shape. Slope the sides. Place on the cake board.

3 Tint all but 15ml/1 tbsp of the butter icing orange. Use to cover the cake, smoothing with a palette knife. Score curved lines for scales, starting from the tail end.

4 Tint half the remaining sugarpaste icing red. Shape and position two lips. Cut out the tail and fins. Mark with lines using a knife and position on the fish. Make the eye from white sugarpaste and the blue Smartie.

5 Tint a little sugarpaste mauve, cut out crescent-shaped scales using a biscuit cutter and place on the fish. Tint the remaining sugarpaste green and cut into long thin strips. Twist each strip and arrange around the board.

6 To make the bubbles around the fish, place the reserved butter icing in a piping bag, snip off the end and pipe small circles on to the board.

Pink Monkey Cake

This cheeky little monkey could be made in any colour icing you wish.

Makes one 20cm/8in cake

20cm/8in round sponge
  cake
115g/4oz/½ cup butter
  icing
45ml/3 tbsp apricot jam,
  warmed and sieved
450g/1lb/3 cups
  marzipan
500g/1¼lb/scant 3¾ cups
  sugarpaste icing

red, blue and black food
  colouring

Materials/equipment
25cm/10in round cake
  board
2 candles and holders

1 Trace the outline and paws of the monkey from the photograph. Enlarge to fit the cake and cut a template.

2 Split and fill the cake with butter icing. Place on the cake board and use the template to cut out the basic shape of the monkey. Use the trimmings to shape the nose and tummy. Brush with apricot jam and cover with a layer of marzipan.

3 Tint 450g/1lb/3 cups of the sugarpaste icing pale pink and use to cover the cake. Leave to dry overnight.

4 Mark the position of the face and paws. Tint a little of the sugarpaste icing blue and use for the eyes. Tint a little icing black and cut out the pupils and tie.

5 Tint the remaining sugarpaste icing dark pink and cut out the nose, mouth, ears and paws. Stick all the features in place with water. Roll the trimmings into balls and place on the board to hold the candles.

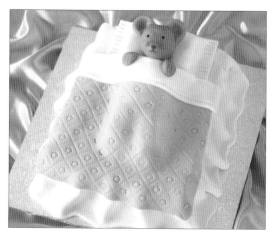

Porcupine Cake

Melt-in-the-mouth strips of chocolate flake give this porcupine its spiky coating.

Serves 15–20

2 chocolate sponge cakes, baked in a 1.2 litre/ 2 pint/5 cup and a 600ml/1 pint/2½ cup pudding basin
500g/1¼lb/2½ cups chocolate-flavour butter icing
cream, black, green, brown and red food colouring

5–6 chocolate flakes
50g/2oz/⅓ cup white marzipan

Materials/equipment
36cm/14in long rectangular cake board
wooden cocktail stick
fine paintbrush

1 Use the smaller cake for the head and shape a pointed nose at one end. Reserve the trimmed wedges.

2 Place the cakes side-by-side on the board, inverted, and use the trimmings to fill in the sides and top where they meet. Secure with butter icing.

3 Cover the cake with the remaining butter icing and mark the nose with a cocktail stick.

4 Make the spikes by breaking the chocolate flakes into thin strips and sticking them into the butter icing all over the body part of the porcupine.

5 Reserve a small portion of marzipan. Divide the remainder into three and tint cream, black and green. Tint a tiny portion of the reserved marzipan brown. Shape cream ears and feet, black-and-white eyes, and black claws and nose. Arrange all the features on the cake. Make green apples and highlight in red with a fine paintbrush. Make the stalks from the brown marzipan and push them in to the apples.

Mouse-in-Bed Cake

This cake is suitable for almost any age. Make the mouse well in advance to give it time to dry.

Makes one 20 x 15cm/8 x 6in cake

20cm/8in square sponge cake
115g/4oz/½ cup butter icing
45ml/3 tbsp apricot jam, warmed and sieved
450g/1lb/3 cups marzipan
675g/1½lb/4½ cups sugarpaste icing

blue and red food colouring

Materials/equipment
25cm/10in square cake board
flower cutter
blue and red food colouring pens

1 Cut 5cm/2in off one side of the cake. Split and fill the main cake with butter icing. Place on the cake board, brush with apricot jam and cover with a layer of marzipan. With the cake off-cut, shape a hollowed pillow, the torso and the legs of the mouse. Cover with marzipan and leave to dry overnight.

2 Cover the cake and pillow with white sugarpaste icing. Lightly frill the edge of the pillow with a fork. To make the valance, roll out 350g/12oz/2¼ cups of sugarpaste icing and cut into four 7.5cm/3in wide strips. Attach to the bed with water. Arrange the pillow and mouse body on the cake.

3 For the quilt, tint 75g/3oz/½ cup of sugarpaste icing blue and roll out to an 18cm/7in square. Mark with a diamond pattern and the flower cutter. Cover the mouse with the quilt.

4 Cut a 2.5 x 19cm/1 x 7½in white sugarpaste icing strip for the sheet, mark the edge and place over the quilt, tucking it under at the top edge.

5 Tint 25g/1oz/2 tbsp of marzipan pink and make the head and paws of the mouse. Put the head on the pillow, tucked under the sheet, and the paws over the edge of the sheet. Use food colouring pens to draw on the face of the mouse.

Teddy's Birthday

After the pieces have been assembled and stuck into the cake, an icing smoother is useful to flatten the design.

Makes one 20cm/8in round cake

20cm/8in round cake
115g/4oz/½ cup butter icing
45ml/3 tbsp apricot jam, warmed and sieved
350g/12oz/2 cups marzipan
450g/1lb/3 cups sugarpaste icing
brown, red, blue and black food colouring
115g/4oz/¾ cup royal icing
edible silver balls

Materials/equipment
25cm/10in round cake board
small greaseproof paper piping bags
No 7 shell and No 7 star nozzle
1.5m/1½yd red ribbon
2 candles and holders

1 Split and fill the cake with butter icing. Place on the cake board and brush with apricot jam. Cover with a layer of marzipan then a layer of sugarpaste icing. Using a template, mark the design on top of the cake.

2 Colour one-third of the remaining sugarpaste icing pale brown. Colour a piece pink, a piece red, some blue and a tiny piece black. Using the template, cut out the pieces and place in position on the cake. Stick down by lifting the edges carefully and brushing the undersides with a little water. Roll small ovals for the eyes and stick in place with the nose and eyebrows. Cut out a mouth and press flat.

3 Tie the ribbon around the cake. Colour the royal icing blue and pipe the border around the base of the cake with the shell nozzle and tiny stars around the small cake with the star nozzle, inserting silver balls. Put the candles on the cake.

Party Teddy Bear Cake

The teddy on this cake is built up with royal icing and coloured coconut.

Makes one 20cm/8in square cake

20cm/8in square sponge cake
115g/4oz/½ cup butter icing
45ml/3 tbsp apricot jam, warmed and sieved
450g/1lb/3 cups marzipan
350g/12oz/2 cups white sugarpaste icing
25g/1oz/⅓ cup desiccated coconut
blue and black food colouring

115g/4oz/¾ cup royal icing

Materials/equipment
25cm/10in square cake board
2 small greaseproof paper piping bags
small red bow
No 7 shell nozzle
1.5m/1½yd red ribbon
6 candles and holders

1 Cut the cake in half and sandwich together with butter icing. Place on the cake board and brush with apricot jam. Cover with a thin layer of marzipan and then white sugarpaste icing. Leave to dry overnight. Using a template, carefully mark the position of the teddy on to the cake.

2 Put the coconut into a bowl and mix in a drop of blue colouring to colour it pale blue. Spread a thin layer of royal icing within the outline of the teddy. Before the icing dries, sprinkle on some pale blue coconut and press it down lightly.

3 Roll out the sugarpaste trimmings and cut out a nose, ears and paws. Stick in place with a little royal icing. Tint some royal icing black and pipe on the eyes, nose and mouth. Use the bow as a tie and stick it in place. Pipe a white royal icing border around the base of the cake, tie the ribbon around the cake and position the candles on top.

Iced Fancies

These cakes are ideal for a children's tea-party. Ready-made cake decorating products may be used instead, if preferred.

Makes 16

115g/4oz/½ cup butter,
   at room temperature
225g/8oz/generous 1 cup
   caster sugar
2 eggs, at room
   temperature
175g/6oz/1½ cups plain
   flour
1.5ml/¼ tsp salt
7.5ml/1½ tsp baking
   powder
120ml/4fl oz/½ cup milk
5ml/1 tsp vanilla essence

For the icing
2 large egg whites
400g/14oz/3½ cups sifted
   icing sugar
1–2 drops glycerine
juice of 1 lemon
food colourings
coloured vermicelli, to
   decorate
crystallized lemon and
   orange slices, to
   decorate

1 Preheat the oven to 190°C/375°F/Gas 5. Line a 16-bun tray with paper cases.

2 Cream the butter and sugar until light and fluffy. Add the eggs, 1 at a time, beating well after each addition. Sift over and stir in the flour, salt and baking powder, alternating with the milk. Add the vanilla essence.

3 Half-fill the cups and bake for about 20 minutes, or until the tops spring back when touched. Stand in the tray to cool for 5 minutes, then unmould on to a wire rack.

4 For the icing, beat the egg whites until stiff. Gradually add the sugar, glycerine and lemon juice, and beat for 1 minute.

5 Tint the icing with different food colourings. Ice the cakes.

6 Decorate the cakes with coloured vermicelli and crystallized lemon and orange slices. Make freehand decorations using a paper piping bag.

Fairy Castle Cake

If the icing on this cake dries too quickly, dip a palette knife into hot water to help smooth the surface.

Makes one castle-shaped cake

20cm/8in round sponge
   cake
115g/4oz/½ cup butter
   icing
45ml/3 tbsp apricot jam,
   warmed and sieved
675g/1½lb/4½ cups
   marzipan
8 mini Swiss rolls
675g/1½lb/4½ cups royal
   icing
red, blue and green food
   colouring

jelly diamonds
4 ice cream cones
2 ice cream wafers
50g/2oz/1 cup desiccated
   coconut
8 marshmallows

Materials/equipment
30cm/12in square cake
   board
wooden cocktail stick

1 Split and fill the cake with butter icing, place in the centre of the board and brush with apricot jam. Cover with a layer of marzipan. Cover each of the Swiss rolls with marzipan. Stick four of them around the cake and cut the other four in half.

2 Tint two-thirds of the royal icing pale pink and cover the cake. Ice the extra pieces of Swiss roll and stick them around the top of the cake. Use a cocktail stick to score the walls with a brick pattern. Make windows on the corner towers from jelly diamonds. Cut the ice cream cones to make the tower spires and stick them in place. Leave to dry overnight.

3 Tint half the remaining royal icing pale blue and cover the cones. Use a fork to pattern the icing. Shape the wafers for the gates, stick to the cake and cover with blue icing. Use the back of a knife to mark planks.

4 Tint the coconut with a few drops of green colouring. Spread the board with the remaining royal icing and sprinkle over the coconut. Stick on the marshmallows with a little royal icing to make the small turrets.

Sailing Boat

For chocoholics, make this cake using chocolate sponge.

Makes one boat-shaped cake

20cm/8in square sponge cake	
225g/8oz/1 cup butter icing	**Materials/equipment**
	25cm/10in square cake board
15ml/1 tbsp cocoa powder	*rice paper*
4 large chocolate flakes	*blue and red powder tints*
115g/4oz/¾ cup royal icing	*paint brush*
	plastic drinking straw
blue food colouring	*wooden cocktail stick*
	2 small cake ornaments

1 Split and fill the cake with half of the butter icing. Cut 7cm/2¾in from one side of the cake. Shape the larger piece to resemble the hull of a boat. Place diagonally across the cake board. Mix the cocoa powder into the remaining butter icing and spread evenly over the top and sides of the boat.

2 Make the rudder and tiller from short lengths of flake and place them at the stern of the boat. Split the rest of the flakes lengthways and press on to the sides of the boat, horizontally, to resemble planks of wood. Sprinkle the crumbs over the top.

3 Cut two rice paper rectangles, one 14 x 16cm/5¾ x 6½in and the other 15 x 7.5cm/6 x 3in. Cut the bigger one in a gentle curve to make the large sail and the smaller one into a triangle. Brush a circle of blue powder tint on to the large sail. Wet the edges of the sails and stick on to the straw. Make a hole for the straw 7.5cm/3in from the bow of the boat and push into the cake.

4 Cut a rice paper flag and brush with red powder tint. Stick the flag on to a cocktail stick and insert into the top of the straw. Tint the royal icing blue and spread on the board in waves. Place the small ornaments on the boat.

Spiders' Cake

A spooky cake for any occasion, fancy dress or otherwise.

Makes one 900g/2lb cake

900g/2lb dome-shaped lemon sponge cake	*cocoa powder, for dusting*
225g/8oz/¾ cup lemon-flavour glacé icing	*chocolate vermicelli*
	2–3 liquorice wheels, sweet centres removed
black and yellow food colouring	*15g/½oz/2 tbsp sugarpaste icing*

For the spiders	**Materials/equipment**
115g/4oz plain chocolate, broken into pieces	*greaseproof paper*
	small greaseproof paper piping bag
150ml/¼ pint/⅔ cup double cream	*wooden skewer*
45ml/3 tbsp ground almonds	*20cm/8in cake board*

1 Place the cake on greaseproof paper. Tint 45ml/3 tbsp of the glacé icing black. Tint the rest yellow and pour it over the cake, letting it run down the side.

2 Fill a piping bag with the black icing and, starting at the centre top, drizzle it round the cake in an evenly-spaced spiral. Finish the web by drawing downwards through the icing with a skewer. When set, place on the cake board.

3 For the spiders, gently melt the chocolate with the cream, stirring frequently. Transfer to a bowl, allow to cool, then beat the mixture for 10 minutes, or until thick and pale. Stir in the ground almonds, then chill until firm enough to handle. Dust your hands with a little cocoa, then make walnut-size balls with the mixture. Roll the balls in chocolate vermicelli.

4 For the legs, cut the liquorice into 4cm/1½in lengths. Make holes in the sides of the spiders and insert the legs. For the spiders' eyes, tint a piece of sugarpaste icing black and form into tiny balls. Make larger balls with white icing. Stick on using water. Arrange the spiders on and around the cake.

Toy Telephone Cake

The child's name could be piped in a contrasting colour of icing, if you wish.

Makes one telephone-shaped cake

15cm/6in square sponge cake
50g/2oz/¼ cup butter icing
30ml/2 tbsp apricot jam, warmed and sieve
275g/10oz/2 cups marzipan
350g/12oz/2 cups sugarpaste icing yellow, blue, red and black food colouring liquorice strips
115g/4oz/¾ cup royal icing

Materials/equipment

20cm/8in square cake board
piping nozzle
small greaseproof paper piping bag
No 1 writing nozzle

1 Split and fill the cake with butter icing. Trim to the shape of a telephone. Round off the edges and cut a shallow groove where the receiver rests on the telephone. Place the cake on the board and brush with apricot jam.

2 Cover the cake with marzipan then sugarpaste icing. Tint half the remaining sugarpaste icing yellow, a small piece blue and the rest of the icing red. To make the dial, cut out an 8cm/3½in diameter circle in yellow and a 4cm/1½in diameter circle in blue. Stamp out 12 red discs for the numbers with the end of a piping nozzle and cut out a red receiver. Position on the cake with water.

3 Twist the liquorice around to form a curly cord and use royal icing to stick one end to the telephone and the other end to the receiver. Tint the royal icing black and pipe the numbers on the discs and the child's name on the telephone.

Bumble Bee Cake

The edible sugar flowers that are used to decorate this cake were bought ready-made.

Makes one bee-shaped cake

20cm/8in round sponge cake
115g/4oz/½ cup butter icing
45ml/3 tbsp apricot jam, warmed and sieved
350g/12oz/2¼ cups marzipan
500g/1¼ lb/3¾ cups sugarpaste icing yellow, black, blue and red food colouring
115g/4oz/¾ cup royal icing
50g/2oz/1 cup desiccated coconut

Materials/equipment

25cm/10in square cake board
6 sugarpaste daisies
1 paper doily
sticky tape
1 pipe cleaner

1 Split and fill the cake with butter icing. Cut in half to make semicircles, sandwich the halves together and stand upright on the cake board. Trim the ends to shape the head and tail. Brush with apricot jam and cover with a layer of marzipan. Tint 350g/12oz/2¼ cups of the sugarpaste icing yellow and use to cover the cake.

2 Tint 115g/4oz/¾ cup of the sugarpaste icing black. Roll out and cut three stripes, each 2.5 x 25cm/1 x 10in. Space evenly on the cake and stick on with water. Use the remaining icing to make the eyes and mouth, tinting the icing blue for the pupils and pink for the mouth. Stick on with water.

3 Tint the coconut with a drop of yellow colouring. Cover the cake board with royal icing then sprinkle with coconut. Place the daisies on the board.

4 To make the wings, cut the doily in half, wrap each half into a cone shape and stick together with sticky tape. Cut the pipe cleaner in half and stick the pieces into the cake, just behind the head. Place the wings over the pipe cleaners.

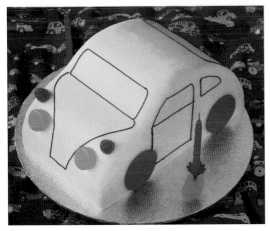

Toy Car Cake

You can add a personalized number plate with the child's name and age to the back of this car.

Makes one car-shaped cake

20cm/8in round sponge cake	*red and green sweets*
115g/4oz/½ cup butter icing	**Materials/equipment**
45ml/3 tbsp apricot jam, warmed and served	*25cm/10in round cake board*
450g/1lb/3 cups marzipan	*wooden cocktail stick cutters, 4cm/1½in and 2.5cm/1in*
500g/1¼lb/3¾ cups sugarpaste icing	*small greaseproof paper piping bag*
yellow, red and black food colouring	*No 1 writing nozzle*
30ml/2 tbsp royal icing	*2 candles and holders*

1 Split and fill the cake with the butter icing. Cut in half and sandwich the halves together. Stand upright and slice off pieces to create the windscreen and bonnet. Place on the cake board and brush with apricot jam.

2 Cut a strip of marzipan to cover the top of the cake to level the joins. Then cover the cake all over with marzipan. Tint 450g/1lb/3 cups of the sugarpaste icing yellow and use to cover the cake. Leave to dry overnight.

3 Mark the outlines of the doors and windows on to the car with a cocktail stick.

4 Tint the remaining sugarpaste icing red. Cut out four wheels with the larger cutter. Stick in place with water. Mark the hubs in the centre of each wheel with the smaller cutter.

5 Tint the royal icing black and pipe over the outline marks of the doors and windows. Stick on sweets for headlights with royal icing. Press the candles into sweets and stick to the board with royal icing.

Fire Engine Cake

This jolly fire engine is simplicity itself as the decoration are mainly bought sweets and novelties.

Makes one 20 x 10cm/8 x 4in cake

20cm/8in square sponge cake	*115g/4oz/4 tbsp royal icing*
115g/4oz/½ cup butter icing	*sweets*
45ml/3 tbsp apricot jam, warmed and sieved	*50g/2oz/1 cup desiccated coconut*
350g/12oz/2¼ cups marzipan	**Materials/equipment**
450g/1lb/3 cups sugarpaste icing	*25cm/10in round cake board*
red, black and green food colouring	*small greaseproof paper piping bag*
liquorice strips	*No 2 plain nozzle*
	2 silver bells
	3 candles and holders

1 Split and fill the cake with the butter icing. Cut in half and sandwich one half on top of the other. Place on the cake board and brush with apricot jam.

2 Trim a thin wedge off the front edge to make a sloping windscreen. Cover with marzipan. Tint 350g/12oz/2¼ cups of the sugarpaste icing red and use to cover the cake.

3 For the ladder, cut the liquorice into two strips and some short pieces for the rungs. Tint half the royal icing black and use some to stick the ladder to the top of the cake. Roll out the remaining sugarpaste icing, cut out windows and stick them on with a little water.

4 Pipe around the windows in black royal icing. Stick sweets in place for headlights, lamps and wheels and stick the silver bells on the roof. Tint the coconut green, spread a little royal icing over the cake board and sprinkle with the coconut. Stick sweets to the board with royal icing and press the candles into the sweets.

Sandcastle Cake

Crushed digestive biscuits make convincing-looking sand when used to cover this fun cake.

Makes one 15cm/6in round cake

2 x 15cm/6in round
  sponge cakes
115g/4oz/½ cup butter
  icing
45ml/3 tbsp apricot jam,
  warmed and sieved
115g/4oz/¾ cup digestive
  biscuits
115g/4oz/¾ cup royal
  icing

blue food colouring
shrimp-shaped sweets

Materials/equipment

25cm/10in square cake
  board
rice paper
plastic drinking straw
4 candles and holders

1 Split both of the cakes, then sandwich all the layers together with the butter icing. Place in the centre of the cake board. Cut 3cm/1¼in off the top just above the filling and set aside. Shape the rest of the cake with slightly sloping sides.

2 Cut four 3cm/1¼in cubes from the reserved piece of cake. Stick on the cubes for the turrets and brush with apricot jam.

3 Crush the digestive biscuits and press through a sieve to make the "sand". Press some crushed biscuits on to the cake, using a palette knife to get a smooth finish.

4 Colour some royal icing blue and spread on the board around the sandcastle to make a moat. Spread a little royal icing on the board around the outside edge of the moat and sprinkle on some crushed biscuit.

5 To make the flag, cut a small rectangle of rice paper and stick on to half a straw with water. Push the end of the straw into the cake. Stick candles into each turret and arrange the shrimp-shaped sweets on the board.

Clown Face Cake

Children love this happy clown whose frilly collar is surprisingly simple to make.

Makes one 20cm/8in cake

20cm/8in round
  sponge cake
115g/4oz/½ cup
  butter icing
45ml/3 tbsp apricot jam,
  warmed and sieved
450g/1lb/3 cups
  marzipan
450g/1lb/3 cups
  sugarpaste icing
115g/4oz/¾ cup
  royal icing
edible silver balls

red, green, blue and black
  food colouring

Materials/equipment

25cm/10in round
  cake board
small greaseproof paper
  piping bag
No 8 star nozzle
wooden cocktail stick
cotton wool
two candles and holders

1 Split and fill the cake with butter icing. Place on the cake board and brush with apricot jam. Cover with a thin layer of marzipan then with white sugarpaste icing. Mark the position of the features. Pipe stars around the base of the cake with some royal icing, placing silver balls as you work, and leave to dry overnight.

2 Make a template for the face and features. Tint half the remaining sugarpaste icing pink and cut out the face base. Tint and cut out all the features, rolling a sausage to make the mouth. Cut thin strands for the hair. Stick all the features and hair in place with a little water.

3 Tint the remaining sugarpaste icing green. Cut three strips 4cm/1½ in wide. Give each a scalloped edge and stretch by rolling a cocktail stick along it to make the frill. Stick on with water and arrange the frills, holding them in place with cotton wool until dry. Place the candles at the top of the head.

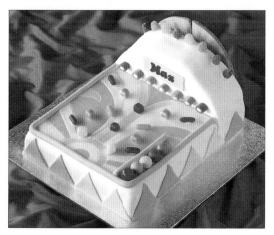

Pinball Machine

Serves 8–10

25cm/10in square sponge
  cake
225g/8oz/1½ cups butter
  icing
45ml/3 tbsp apricot jam,
  warmed and sieved
450g/1lb/3 cups
  marzipan
115g/4oz/¾cup royal
  icing
450g/1lb/3 cups
  sugarpaste icing

yellow, blue, green and
  red food colouring
sweets
2 ice cream fan wafers

Materials/equipment
20cm/8in round cake tin
30cm/12in square cake
  board
small greaseproof paper
  piping bag
No 1 writing nozzle

1   Split and fill the sponge cake with butter icing. Cut off a 5cm/2in strip from one side and reserve. Cut a thin wedge off the top of the cake, diagonally along its length, to end just above the halfway mark. This will give a sloping table.

2   Using the cake tin as a guide, cut the reserved strip of cake to make a rounded back for the pinball table. Brush the back and table with apricot jam, then cover separately with marzipan and place on the board. Stick them together with royal icing. Leave to dry overnight.

3   Cover with a layer of sugarpaste icing and leave to dry. Use a template to mark out the pinball design on the top of the cake. Colour the remaining sugarpaste icing yellow, blue, green and pink. Roll out the colours and cut to fit the design. Stick on the pieces with water and smooth the joins carefully.

4   Using royal icing, stick sweets on the cake as buffers, flippers, lights and knobs. Roll some blue sugarpaste icing into a long sausage and edge the pinball table and divider. Cut zig-zags for the sides and a screen for the back. Stick on with water. Stick the ice cream fans at the back of the screen. Load the pinball sweets. Add the child's name on the screen with run-out letters or piping.

Pirate's Hat

If you prefer, buy ready-made black sugarpaste icing rather than tinting it yourself.

Serves 8–10

25cm/10in round sponge
  cake
225g/8oz/1 cup butter
  icing
45ml/3 tbsp apricot jam,
  warmed and sieved
450g/1lb/3 cups
  marzipan
500g/1¼lb/3¾ cups
  sugarpaste icing

black and gold food
  colouring
chocolate money
jewel sweets

Materials/equipment
30cm/12in square cake
  board
fine paint brush

1   Split and fill the cake with butter icing. Cut in half and sandwich the halves together. Stand upright diagonally across the cake board and cut shallow dips from each end to create the brim of the hat. Brush with apricot jam.

2   Cut a strip of marzipan to lay over the top of the cake. Then cover the whole of the cake with a layer of marzipan. Tint 450g/1lb/3 cups of the sugarpaste icing black. Use to cover the cake.

3   Roll out the remaining sugarpaste icing and cut some 1cm/½in strips. Stick the strips in place with a little water around the brim of the pirate's hat and mark with the prongs of a fork to make a braid.

4   Make a skull and crossbones template and mark on to the hat. Cut the shapes out of the white sugarpaste icing and stick in place with water. Paint the braid strip gold and arrange the chocolate money and jewel sweets on the board.

Noah's Ark Cake

This charming cake is decorated with small animals, about 4cm/1½in high, available from cake decorating shops.

Makes one 20 x 13cm/8 x 5in cake

20cm/8in square sponge cake	115g/4oz/¾ cup royal icing
115g/4oz/½ cup butter icing	chocolate mint stick
45ml/3 tbsp apricot jam, warmed and sieved	**Materials/equipment**
450g/1lb/3 cups marzipan	25cm/10in square cake board
450g/1lb/3 cups sugarpaste icing	skewer
brown, yellow and blue food colouring	rice paper flag
	small animal cake ornaments

1 Split and fill the cake with butter icing. Cut off and set aside a 7.5cm/3in strip. Shape the remaining piece of cake to form the hull of the boat. Place diagonally on the cake board.

2 Use the set-aside piece of cake, to cut a rectangle 10 x 6cm/4 x 2½in for the cabin and a triangular piece for the roof. Sandwich together with butter icing or apricot jam.

3 Cover the three pieces with a layer of marzipan. Tint the sugarpaste icing brown and use most of it to cover the hull and cabin. Use the remaining brown icing to make a long sausage. Stick around the edge of the hull with water. Mark planks with the back of a knife. Leave to dry overnight.

4 Tint one-third of the royal icing yellow and spread it over the cabin roof with a palette knife. Roughen it with a skewer to create a thatch effect.

5 Tint the remaining royal icing blue and spread over the cake board, making rough waves. Stick a rice paper flag on to the chocolate mint stick and press on the back of the boat. Stick the small animals on to the boat with a dab of icing.

Balloons Cake

This is a simple yet effective cake design that can be adapted to suit any age.

Makes one 20cm/8in round cake

20cm/8in round cake	**Materials/equipment**
115g/4oz/½ cup butter icing	25cm/10in round cake board
45ml/3 tbsp apricot jam, warmed and sieved	2 small greaseproof paper piping bags
450g/1lb/3 cups marzipan	No 2 plain and No 7 star nozzles
450g/1lb/3 cups sugarpaste icing	1.5m/1½yd blue ribbon
red, blue, green and yellow food colouring	3 candles and holders
115g/4oz/¾ cup royal icing	

1 Split and fill the cake with butter icing. Place on the cake board and brush with apricot jam. Cover with a layer of marzipan then sugarpaste icing.

2 Divide the remaining sugarpaste icing into three pieces and tint pink, blue and green. Make a balloon template, roll out the coloured sugarpaste and cut out one balloon from each colour. Stick on to the cake with water and rub the edges gently to round them off.

3 Tint the royal icing yellow. With a plain nozzle, pipe on the balloon strings and a number on each balloon. Using the star nozzle, pipe a border around the base of the cake.

4 Tie the ribbon round the cake and place the candles on top.

Horse Stencil Cake

Use a fairly dry brush when painting the design on this cake and allow each colour to dry before adding the next.

Makes one 20cm/8in round cake

	Materials/equipment
20cm/8in round sponge cake	25cm/10in round cake board
115g/4oz/½ cup butter icing	spoon with decorative handle
45ml/3 tbsp apricot jam, warmed and sieved	fine paintbrush
450g/1lb/3 cups marzipan	horse and letter stencils
450g/1lb/3 cups sugarpaste icing	1.5m/1½yd blue ribbon
yellow, brown, black, red, orange and blue food colouring	7 candles and holders

1 Split and fill the cake with butter icing. Place on the cake board and brush with apricot jam. Cover with a layer of marzipan. Tint the sugarpaste icing yellow, roll out and use to cover the cake. Roll the trimmings into two thin ropes, long enough to go halfway round the cake. Brush water in a thin band around the base of the cake, lay on the ropes and press together. Pattern the border with the decorative spoon handle. Leave to dry overnight.

2 If you do not have a stencil, make one by tracing a simple design on to a thin piece of card and cutting out the shape with a craft knife. Place the horse stencil in the centre of the cake. With a fairly dry brush, gently paint over the parts you want to colour first. Allow these to dry completely before adding another colour, otherwise the colours will run into each other. Clean the stencil between colours.

3 When the horse picture is finished carefully paint on the lettering. Tie the ribbon around the side of the cake and place the candles on top.

Doll's House Cake

Serves 8–10

	Materials/equipment
25cm/10in square sponge cake	30cm/12in square cake board
225g/8oz/1 cup butter icing	pastry wheel
45ml/3 tbsp apricot jam, warmed and sieved	large and fine paintbrushes
450g/1lb/3 cups marzipan	wooden cocktail stick
450g/1lb/3 cups sugarpaste icing	small greaseproof paper piping bags
red, yellow, blue, black, green and gold food colouring	No 2 writing nozzle flower decorations
115g/4oz/¾ cup royal icing	

1 Split and fill the cake with butter icing. Cut triangles off two corners and use the pieces to make a chimney. Place on the cake board and brush with apricot jam. Cover with a layer of marzipan then sugarpaste icing.

2 Mark the roof with a pastry wheel and the chimney with the back of a knife. Paint the chimney red and the roof yellow.

3 Tint 25g/1oz/2 tbsp of sugarpaste icing red and cut out a 7.5 x 12cm/3 x 4½in door. Tint enough sugarpaste icing blue to make a fanlight. Stick to the cake with water. Mark windows, 6cm/2½in square, with a cocktail stick. Paint on curtains with blue food colouring. Tint half the royal icing black and pipe around the windows and the door.

4 Tint the remaining royal icing green. Pipe the flower stems and leaves under the windows and the climber up on to the roof. Stick the flowers in place with a little icing and pipe green flower centres. Pipe the house number or child's age, the knocker and handle on the door. Leave to dry for 1 hour, then paint with gold food colouring.

Treasure Chest Cake

Allow yourself a few days before the party to make this cake as the lock and handles need to dry for 48 hours.

Makes one 20 x 10cm/8 x 4in cake

20cm/8in square sponge cake	50g/2oz/1 cup desiccated coconut
115g/4oz/½ cup butter icing	115g/4oz/¾ cup royal icing
45ml/3 tbsp apricot jam, warmed and sieved	edible gold dusting powder
350g/12oz/2cups marzipan	edible silver balls
400g/14oz/2½ cups sugarpaste icing	chocolate money
brown and green food colouring	**Materials/equipment**
	30cm/12in round cake board
	fine paintbrush

1 Split and fill the cake with butter icing. Cut the cake in half and sandwich the halves on top of each other with butter icing. Place on the cake board.

2 Shape the top into a rounded lid and brush with apricot jam. Cover with a layer of marzipan. Tint 350g/12oz/2¼ cups of the sugarpaste icing brown and use to cover the cake.

3 Use the brown sugarpaste trimmings to make strips. Stick on to the chest with water. Mark the lid with a sharp knife.

4 Tint the coconut with a few drops of green colouring. Spread a little royal icing over the cake board and press the green coconut lightly into it to make the grass.

5 From the remaining sugarpaste icing, cut out the padlock and handles. Cut a keyhole shape from the padlock and shape the handles over a small box. Leave to dry. Stick the padlock and handles in place with royal icing and paint them gold. Stick silver balls on to look like nails. Arrange the chocolate money on the board.

Lion Cake

For an animal lover or a celebration cake for a Leo horoscope sign, this cake is ideal.

Makes one 28 x 23cm/11 x 9in oval cake

25 x 30cm/10 x 12in sponge cake	red and orange liquorice bootlaces
350g/12oz/1½ cups orange flavour butter icing	long and round marshmallows
orange and red food colouring	**Materials/equipment**
675g/1½lb/4½ cups yellow marzipan	30cm/12in square cake board
50g/2oz/generous 4 tbsp sugarpaste icing	cheese grater
	small heart-shaped cutter

1 With the flat side of the cake uppermost, cut it to make an oval shape with an uneven scallop design around the edge. Turn the cake over and trim the top level.

2 Place the cake on the cake board. Tint the butter icing orange and use it to cover the cake.

3 Roll 115g/4oz/¾ cup of marzipan to a 15cm/6in square. Place in the centre of the cake for the lion's face.

4 Grate the remaining marzipan and use to cover the sides and the top of the cake up to the face panel.

5 Tint the sugarpaste icing red. Use the heart-shaped cutter to stamp out the lion's nose and position on the cake with water. Roll the remaining red icing into two thin, short strands to make the lion's mouth, and stick on with water.

6 Cut the liquorice into graduated lengths, and place on the cake for the whiskers. Use two flattened round marshmallows for the eyes and two snipped long ones for the eyebrows.

Train Cake

This cake is made in a train-shaped tin, so all you need to do is decorate it.

Makes one train-shaped cake

train-shaped sponge cake,	**Materials/equipment**
about 35cm/14in long	*25 x 38cm/10 x 15in cake*
675g/1½lb/3 cups butter	*board*
icing	*2 fabric piping bags*
yellow food colouring	*small round and small*
red liquorice bootlaces	*star nozzles*
90–120ml/6–8 tbsp	*pink and white cotton*
coloured vermicelli	*wool balls*
4 liquorice wheels	

1 Slice off the top surface of the cake to make it flat. Place diagonally on the cake board.

2 Tint the butter icing yellow. Use half of it to cover the cake.

3 Using a round nozzle and a quarter of the remaining butter icing, pipe a straight double border around the top edge of the cake.

4 Place the red liquorice bootlaces on the piped border. Snip the bootlaces around the curves on the train.

5 Using a small star nozzle and the remaining butter icing, pipe small stars over the top of the cake. Add extra liquorice and piping, if you like. Use a palette knife to press on the coloured vermicelli all around the sides of the cake.

6 Pull a couple of balls of cotton wool apart for the steam and stick on the cake board with butter icing. Press the liquorice wheels in place for the wheels.

Number 7 Cake

Any combination of colours will work well for this cake with its marbled effect.

Makes one 30cm/12in long cake

23 x 30cm/9 x 12in	*blue and green food*
sponge cake	*colouring*
350g/12oz/1½ cups	*rice paper sweets*
orange-flavour butter	
icing	**Materials /equipment**
60ml/4 tbsp apricot jam,	*25 x 33cm/10 x 13in cake*
warmed and sieved	*board*
675g/1½lb/4½ cups	*small "7" cutter*
sugarpaste icing	

1 Place the cake flat-side up and cut out the number seven. Slice the cake horizontally, sandwich together with the butter icing and place on the board.

2 Brush the cake evenly with apricot jam. Divide the sugarpaste icing into three and tint one of the pieces blue and another green. Set aside 50g/2oz/scant ½cup from each of the coloured icings. Knead together the large pieces of blue and green icing with the third piece of white icing to marble. Use to cover the cake.

3 Immediately after covering, use the cutter to remove sugarpaste shapes in a random pattern from the covered cake.

4 Roll out the reserved blue and green sugarpaste icing and stamp out shapes with the same cutter. Use these to fill the stamped-out shapes from the cake. Decorate the board with some rice paper sweets.

Musical Cake

Creating a sheet of music on a cake requires very delicate piping work, so it is best to practise first.

Makes one 20 x 25cm/8 x 10in cake

25cm/10in square sponge cake
225g/8oz/1 cup butter icing
45ml/3 tbsp apricot jam, warmed and sieved
450g/1lb/3 cups marzipan
450g/1lb/3 cups sugarpaste icing
115g/4oz/¾ cup royal icing

black food colouring

Materials/equipment
25 x 30cm/10 x 12in cake board
wooden cocktail stick
2 small greaseproof paper piping bags
No 0 writing and No 7 shell nozzles
1.5m/1½yd red ribbon

1 Split and fill the cake with a little butter icing. Cut a 5cm/2in strip off one side of the cake. Place the cake on the cake board and brush with apricot jam. Cover with a layer of marzipan then sugarpaste icing. Leave to dry overnight.

2 Make a template and mark out the sheet of music and child's name with a cocktail stick.

3 Using white royal icing and a No 0 nozzle, begin by piping the lines and bars. Leave to dry.

4 Tint the remaining icing black and pipe the clefs, name and notes. With the shell nozzle, pipe a royal icing border around the base of the cake and tie a ribbon around the side.

Magic Rabbit Cake

Makes one 15cm/6in tall round cake

2 x 15cm/6in round cakes
225g/8oz/1 cup butter icing
115g/4oz/¾ cup royal icing
45ml/3 tbsp apricot jam, warmed and sieved
675g/1½lb/4½ cups marzipan
675g/1½lb/4½ cups sugarpaste icing

black and pink food colouring
edible silver balls

Materials/equipment
25cm/10in square cake board
2 small greaseproof paper piping bags
star nozzle
1.5m/1½yd pink ribbon

1 Split and fill the cakes with butter icing, then sandwich them one on top of the other. Stick on the centre of the cake board with a little royal icing. Brush with apricot jam. Use 450g/1lb/3 cups of the marzipan to cover the cake.

2 Tint the sugarpaste icing grey. Use about two-thirds of it to cover the cake. Roll out the rest to a 20cm/8in round. Cut a 15cm/6in circle from its centre. Lower the brim over the cake. Shape the brim sides over wooden spoon handles until dry.

3 Cut a cross in the 15cm/6in grey circle and place on the hat. Curl the triangles over a wooden spoon handle to shape. Smooth the join at the top and sides of the hat.

4 Tint the remaining marzipan pink and make the rabbit's head, about 5cm/2in wide with a pointed face. Mark the position of the eyes, nose and mouth. Leave to dry overnight.

5 Stick the rabbit in the centre of the hat with a little royal icing. Pipe a border of royal icing around the top and base of the hat and decorate with silver balls while still wet. Tint the remaining royal icing black and pipe the rabbit's eyes and mouth. Tie the ribbon round the hat.

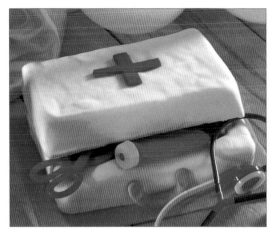

Nurse's Kit Cake

The box is easy to make and is simply filled with toy kit.

Makes one 20 x 17cm/8 x 6½in cake

35 x 20cm/14 x 8in chocolate sponge cake	**Materials/equipment** 25cm/10in square cake
120ml/4fl oz/½ cup apricot jam, warmed and sieved	board selection of toy medical equipment
675g/1½lb/4½ cups sugarpaste icing	
red food colouring	

1 Place the cake dome-side down and cut in half widthways.

2 To make the base of the nurse's box, turn one cake half dome-side up and hollow out the centre to a depth of 1cm/½in, leaving a 1cm/½in border on the three uncut edges. Brush the tops and sides of both halves with jam.

3 Tint 150g/5oz/generous ½ cup sugarpaste icing deep pink. Use a little to make a small handle for the box. Wrap in clear film and set aside. Cover the cake board with the rest of the pink icing. Tint 25g/1oz/2 tbsp of the sugarpaste icing red. Cover with clear film and set aside.

4 Tint the remaining icing light pink and divide into two portions, one slightly bigger than the other. Roll out the bigger portion and use to cover the base of the box, easing it into the hollow and along the edges. Trim, then position the base on the cake board.

5 Roll out the other portion and use to cover the lid of the box. Trim, then place on top of the base at a slight angle.

6 Stick the handle to the base of the box using water. Cut a small cross out of red icing and stick it on the lid. Place a few toy items under the lid, protruding slightly. Arrange some more items around the board and cake.

Ballerina Cake

Use flower cutters with ejectors to make the tiny flowers.

Makes one 20cm/8in round cake

20cm/8in round sponge cake	**Materials/equipment** 25cm/10in round cake
115g/4oz/½ cup butter icing	board small flower cutter
45ml/3 tbsp apricot jam, warmed and sieved	small circle cutter wooden cocktail stick
450g/1lb/3 cups marzipan	cotton wool fine paintbrush
450g/1lb/3 cups sugarpaste icing	3 small greaseproof paper piping bags
pink, yellow, blue and green food colouring	No 7 shell nozzle 1.5m/1½yd pink ribbon
115g/4oz/¾ cup royal icing	

1 Split and fill the cake with butter icing. Place on the board and brush with apricot jam. Cover with marzipan then sugarpaste icing. Leave to dry overnight. Divide the rest of the sugarpaste into three. Tint flesh tone, light pink and dark pink. Stamp out 15 pale pink flowers. Leave to dry.

2 Make a template of the ballerina. Mark her position on the cake. Cut out a flesh-tone body and dark pink bodice. Stick on with water, rounding off the edges.

3 Cut two dark pink underskirts, a pale pink top skirt and a dark pink bodice extension to make the tutu. Stamp out hollow, fluted circles, divide the circles into four and frill the fluted edges with a cocktail stick. Stick the tutu in place, supported with cotton wool. Cut out and stick on pale pink shoes. Leave to dry overnight.

4 Paint the ballerina's face and hair. Position 12 hoop and three headdress flowers. Tint some royal icing green and dark pink to complete the flowers and ballet shoes. Pipe a border around the base with the shell nozzle. Tie round the ribbon.

Monsters on the Moon

A great cake for little monsters! This cake is best eaten on the day of making.

Serves 12–15

1 quantity quick-mix
  sponge cake
500g/1¼lb/3¾ cups
  sugarpaste icing
225g/8oz/1½ cups
  marzipan
black food colouring
edible silver glitter
  powder (optional)
375g/12oz/¾ cups
  caster sugar

2 egg whites
60ml/4 tbsp water

Materials/equipment
ovenproof wok
various sizes of plain
  round and star cutters
30cm/12in round cake
  board
small monster toys

1 Preheat the oven to 180°C/350°F/Gas 4. Grease and line the wok. Spoon in the cake mixture and smooth the surface. Bake in the centre of the oven for 35–40 minutes. Leave for 5 minutes, then turn out on to a rack and peel off the paper.

2 With the cake dome-side up, use the round cutters to cut out craters. Press in the cutters to about 2.5cm/1in deep, then remove and cut the craters out of the cake with a knife.

3 Use 115g/4oz/¾ cup of the sugarpaste icing to cover the cake, pulling off small pieces and pressing them in uneven strips around the edges of the craters. Tint the remaining sugarpaste icing black. Roll out and cover the board. Stamp out stars and replace with marzipan stars of the same size. Dust with glitter powder, if using and place on the board.

4 Put the sugar, egg whites and water in a heatproof bowl over a pan of simmering water. Beat until thick and peaky. Spoon the icing over the cake, swirling it into the craters and peaking it unevenly. Sprinkle over the silver glitter powder, if using, then position the monsters on the cake.

Circus Cake

This colourful design is easy to achieve and is sure to delight young children.

Makes one 20cm/8in cake

20cm/8in round sponge
  cake
115g/4oz/½ cup butter
  icing
45ml/3 tbsp apricot jam,
  warmed and sieved
450g/1lb/3 cups
  marzipan
450g/1lb/3 cups
  sugarpaste icing
red and blue food
  colouring

115g/4oz/¾ cup royal
  icing
edible silver balls
3 digestive biscuits

Materials/equipment
25cm/10in round cake
  board
small greaseproof paper
  piping bag
No 5 star nozzle
5cm/2in plastic circus
  ornaments

1 Split and fill the cake with butter icing. Place on the cake board and brush with apricot jam. Cover with a layer of marzipan then sugarpaste icing.

2 Tint 115g/4oz/¾ cup sugarpaste icing pink, then roll into a rope and stick around the top edge of the cake with a little water.

3 Tint half the remaining sugarpaste icing red and half blue. Roll out each colour and cut into twelve 2.5cm/1in squares. Stick the squares alternately at an angle around the side of the cake with a little water. Pipe stars around the base of the cake with royal icing and stick in the edible silver balls.

4 Crush the digestive biscuits by pressing through a sieve to make the "sand" for the circus ring. Scatter over the top of the cake and place small circus ornaments on top.

Frog Prince Cake

Serves 8–10

20cm/8in round sponge
  cake
115g/4oz/½ cup butter
  icing
45ml/3 tbsp apricot jam,
  warmed and sieved
450g/1lb/3 cups
  marzipan
cornflour, for dusting
400g/1¼lb/3¾ cups
  sugarpaste icing

115g/4oz/¾ cup royal
  icing
green, red, black and gold
  food colouring

Materials/equipment
25cm/10in square cake
  board
glass
fine paintbrush

1 Split and fill the cake with butter icing. Cut in half and sandwich the halves together with apricot jam. Stand upright diagonally across the cake board. Brush the cake with apricot jam and cover with marzipan.

2 Tint 450g/1lb/3 cups of the sugarpaste icing green and cover the cake. Roll the remaining green sugarpaste icing into 1cm/½in diameter sausages. You will need two folded 20cm/8in lengths for the back legs and 14 10cm/4in lengths for the front legs and feet. Stick in place with a little royal icing. Roll balls for the eyes and stick in place.

3 Roll out the reserved sugarpaste icing and cut a 5 x 19cm/2 x 7½in strip. Cut out triangles along one edge to make the crown shape. Wrap around a glass dusted with cornflour and moisten the edges to join. Leave to dry.

4 Cut a 10cm/4in circle for the white shirt. Stick in place and trim the base edge. Cut white circles and stick to the eyes. Tint a little sugarpaste pink, roll into a sausage and stick on for the mouth. Tint the rest black and use for the pupils and the bow tie. Stick in place.

5 Paint the crown with gold food colouring, leave to dry, then stick into position with royal icing.

Ladybird Cake

Children will love this colourful and appealing ladybird, and it is very simple to make.

Serves 10–12

3-egg quantity quick-mix
  sponge cake
175g/6oz butter icing
60ml/4 tbsp lemon
  curd, warmed
icing sugar, for dusting

1kg/2¼ lb sugarpaste
  icing
food colourings
5 marshmallows
50g/2oz marzipan
2 pipe cleaners

1 Preheat the oven to 180°C/350°F/Gas 4. Grease and line the base of a 1.2 litre/2 pint/5 cup ovenproof bowl. Spoon in the cake mixture and smooth the surface. Bake for 55–60 minutes until a skewer comes out clean. Cool.

2 Cut the cake in half crossways and sandwich together with the butter icing. Cut vertically through the cake, about a third of the way in. Brush both pieces with the lemon curd.

3 Colour 450g/1lb of the sugarpaste icing red. Dust a work surface with icing sugar and roll out the icing to about 5mm/¼ in thick. Use to cover the larger piece of cake to make the body. Using a wooden skewer, make an indentation down the centre for the wings. Colour 350g/12oz of icing black, roll out three-quarters and use to cover the smaller piece of cake for the head. Place both cakes on a cakeboard, press together.

4 Roll out 50g/2oz icing and cut out two 5cm/2in circles for the eyes, stick to the head with water. Roll out the remaining black icing and cut out eight 4cm/1½ in circles. Use two of these for the eyes and stick the others on to the body.

5 Colour some icing green and squeeze through a garlic crusher to make grass. Flatten the marshmallows and stick a marzipan round in the centre of each. Colour pipe cleaners black and press a ball of black icing on to the end of each. Arrange grass on board, with the ladybird and decorations.

Spaceship Cake

Serves 10–12

25cm/10in square sponge
   cake
225g/8oz/1 cup butter
   icing
60ml/4 tbsp apricot jam,
   warmed and sieved
350g/12oz/2¼ cups
   marzipan
450g/1lb/3 cups
   sugarpaste icing

blue, red and black food
   colouring

Materials/equipment
30cm/12in square cake
   board
4 silver candles and
   holders
gold paper stars

1 Split and fill the sponge cake with butter icing. Cut a 10cm/4in wide piece diagonally across the middle of the cake, about 25cm/10in long. Shape the nose end and straighten the other end.

2 From the off-cuts make three 7.5cm/3in triangles for the wings and top of the ship. Cut two smaller triangles for the booster jets. Position the main body, wings and top of the cake diagonally across the board. Add extra pieces of cake in front of the top triangle. Brush the cake and booster jets with apricot jam, then cover with a layer of marzipan and sugarpaste icing.

3 Divide the remaining sugarpaste icing into three. Tint blue, pink and black. Roll out the blue icing and cut it into 1cm/½in strips. Stick around the base of the cake with water and outline the boosters. Cut a 2.5cm/1in strip and stick down the centre of the spaceship.

4 Roll out the pink and black sugarpaste icing separately and cut shapes, numbers and the child's name to finish the design. When complete, position the boosters.

5 Make small cubes with the off-cuts of sugarpaste icing and use to stick the candles to the cake board. Decorate the board with gold stars.

Racing Track Cake

This cake will delight eight-year-old racing car enthusiasts.

Serves 10–12

2 x 15cm/6in round
   sponge cakes
115g/4oz/½ cup butter
   icing
60ml/4 tbsp apricot jam,
   warmed and sieved
450g/1lb/3 cups
   marzipan
500g/1¼lb/3¼ cups
   sugarpaste icing
blue and red food
   colouring
115g/4oz/¾ cup royal
   icing

Materials/equipment
25 x 35cm/10 x 14in cake
   board
5cm/2in fluted cutter
2 small greaseproof paper
   piping bags
No 8 star and No 2 plain
   nozzles
8 candles and holders
2 small racing cars

1 Split and fill the cakes with a little butter icing. Cut off a 1cm/½in piece from the side of each cake and place the cakes on the cake board, cut edges together.

2 Brush the cake with apricot jam and cover with a layer of marzipan. Tint 450g/1lb/3 cups of the sugarpaste icing pale blue and use to cover the cake.

3 Mark a 5cm/2in circle in the centre of each cake. Roll out the remaining white sugarpaste icing and cut out two fluted 5cm/2in circles and stick them in the marked spaces.

4 Tint the royal icing red. Pipe a shell border around the base of the cake using the star nozzle. Pipe a track for the cars on the cake using the plain nozzle and stick the candles into the two white circles. Place the cars on the track.

Floating Balloons Cake

Makes one 20cm/8in round cake

20cm/8in round sponge or fruit cake, covered with 800g/1¾lb/ 5½ cups marzipan, if liked	**Materials/equipment**
	25cm/10in round cake board
	3 bamboo skewers, 25cm/10in, 24cm/ 9½in and 23cm/9in long
900g/2lb/6 cups sugarpaste icing	
red, green and yellow food colouring	small star cutter
3 eggs	greaseproof paper piping bags
2 egg whites	fine writing nozzle
450g/1lb/4 cups icing sugar	1m/1yd fine coloured ribbon
	8 candles

1 Place the cake on the board. Tint 50g/2oz/scant ½ cup of the sugarpaste icing red, 50g/2oz/scant ½ cup green and 115g/4oz/1 cup yellow. Cover the cake with the remaining icing. Use just under half the yellow icing to cover the board.

2 Using a skewer, pierce the eggs and carefully empty the contents. Wash and dry the shells. Cover them carefully with the tinted sugarpaste and insert a bamboo skewer in each. Use the trimmings to stamp out a star shape of each colour. Thread on to the skewers for the balloon knots.

3 Trace 16 balloon shapes on to baking paper. Beat the egg whites with the icing sugar until smooth and divide among four bowls. Leave one white and tint the others red, green and yellow. With the fine writing nozzle and white icing, trace round the balloon shapes. Thin the tinted icings with water. Fill the run-outs using snipped piping bags. Dry overnight.

4 Stick the run-outs around the side of the cake with icing. Pipe white balloon strings. Push the large balloons into the centre and decorate with the ribbon. Push the candles into the icing around the edge.

Number 6 Cake

Use the round cake tin as a guide to cut the square cake to fit neatly around the round cake.

Serves 10–12

15cm/6in round and 15cm/6in square sponge cakes	115g/4oz/¾ cup royal icing
115g/4oz/½ cup butter icing	
60ml/4 tbsp apricot jam, warmed and sieved	**Materials/equipment**
	25 x 35cm/10 x 14in cake board
450g/1lb/3 cups marzipan	2 small greaseproof paper piping bags
500g/1¼lb/3¾ cups sugarpaste icing	7.5cm/3in fluted cutter
yellow and green food colouring	No 1 plain and No 8 star nozzles
	plastic train set with 6 candles

1 Split and fill the cakes with butter icing. Cut the square cake in half and cut, using the round cake tin as a guide, a rounded end from one rectangle to fit around the round cake. Trim the cakes to the same depth and assemble the number on the cake board. Brush with apricot jam and cover with a thin layer of marzipan.

2 Tint 450g/1lb/3 cups of the sugarpaste icing yellow and the rest green. Cover the cake with the yellow icing. With the cutter, mark a circle in the centre of the round cake. Cut out a green sugarpaste icing circle. Stick in place with water and leave to dry overnight.

3 Mark a track the width of the train on the top of the cake. Tint the royal icing yellow and pipe the track with the plain nozzle. Use the star nozzle to pipe a border around the base and top of the cake. Pipe the name on the green circle and attach the train and candles with royal icing.

Spider's Web Cake

Make the marzipan spider several days before you need the
cake to give it time to dry.

Makes one 20cm/8in round cake

20cm/8in round deep
   sponge cake
225g/8oz/1 cup butter
   icing
45ml/3 tbsp apricot jam,
   warmed and sieved
30ml/2 tbsp cocoa
   powder
chocolate vermicelli
40g/1½oz/4 tbsp
   marzipan
yellow, red, black and
   brown food colouring

225g/8oz/1½ cups icing
   sugar
15–30ml/1–2 tbsp
   water

Materials/equipment
25cm/10in round cake
   board
2 small greaseproof paper
   piping bags
wooden cocktail stick
star nozzle
8 candles and holders

1 Split and fill the cake with half the butter icing. Brush the
sides with apricot jam, add the cocoa to the remaining butter
icing then smooth a little over the sides of the cake. Roll the
sides of the cake in chocolate vermicelli. Place on the board.

2 For the spider, tint the marzipan yellow. Roll half of it into
two balls for the head and body. Tint a small piece red and
make three balls and a mouth. Tint a tiny piece black for the
eyes. Roll the rest of the marzipan into eight legs and two
smaller feelers. Stick together.

3 Gently heat the icing sugar and water over a pan of hot
water. Use two-thirds of the glacé icing to cover the cake top.

4 Tint the remaining glacé icing brown and use it to pipe
concentric circles on to the cake. Divide the web into eighths
by drawing lines across with a cocktail stick. Leave to set.

5 Put the rest of the chocolate butter icing into a piping bag
fitted with a star nozzle and pipe a border around the web.
Put candles around the border and the spider in the centre.

Dart Board Cake

Makes one 25cm/10in round cake

25cm/10in round sponge
   cake
175g/6oz/¾ cup butter
   icing
5ml/3 tbsp apricot jam,
   warmed and sieved
450g/1lb/3 cups
   marzipan
450g/1lb/3 cups
   sugarpaste icing
115g/4oz/¾ cup royal
   icing

black, red, yellow and
   silver food colouring

Materials/equipment
30cm/12in round cake
   board
icing smoother
1cm/½in plain circle
   cutter
small greaseproof paper
   piping bag
No 1 writing nozzle
3 candles and holders

1 Split and fill the cake with butter icing and put on to the
board. Brush with jam and cover with marzipan. Colour some
of the sugarpaste icing black, a small piece red and the
remaining yellow. Cover the cake with black sugarpaste icing.
Cut a 20cm/8in circular template out of greaseproof paper.
Fold it in quarters, then divide each quarter into fifths.

2 Using the template, mark the centre and wedges on the
top of the cake with a sharp knife. Cut out ten wedges from
the yellow sugarpaste, using the template as a guide. Place on
alternate sections but do not stick in place yet. Repeat with
the black sugarpaste. Cut 3mm/⅛in off each wedge and swop
the colours. Mark a 13cm/5in circle in the centre of the board
and cut out 3mm/⅛in pieces to swop with adjoining colours.
Stick in place and use an icing smoother to flatten.

3 Use the cutter to remove the centre for the bull's eye.
Replace with a circle of red sugarpaste, cut with the same
cutter. Surround it with a strip of black sugarpaste. Roll the
remaining black sugarpaste into a long sausage to fit round
the base of the cake and stick in place with a little water. Mark
numbers on the board and pipe on with royal icing. Leave to
dry then paint with silver food colouring. Stick candles in at
an angle to resemble darts.

Camping Tent Cake

Makes one 20 x 10cm/8 x 4in cake

20cm/8in square sponge
  cake
115g/4oz/½ cup butter
  icing
45ml/3 tbsp apricot jam,
  warmed and sieved
450g/1lb/3 cups
  marzipan
500g/1¼lb/3¾ cups
  sugarpaste icing
  brown, orange, green,
  red and blue food
  colouring
115g/4oz/¾ cup royal
  icing

50g/2oz/1 cup desiccated
  coconut
chocolate mint sticks

Materials/equipment
25cm/10in square cake
  board
wooden cocktail sticks
fine paintbrush
4 small greaseproof paper
  piping bags
No 1 basketweave and
  plain nozzles

1 Split and fill the cake with butter icing. Cut the cake in half. Cut one half in two diagonally from the top right edge to the bottom left edge to form the roof of the tent. Stick the two wedges, back-to-back, on top of the rectangle with jam. Trim to 10cm/4in high and use the trimmings on the base. Place the cake diagonally on the board and brush with jam.

2 Cover with marzipan, reserving some for modelling. Tint 50g/2oz/scant ½ cup of the sugarpaste icing brown and cover one end of the tent. Tint the rest orange and cover the rest of the cake. Cut a semicircle for the tent opening and a central 7.5cm/3in slit. Lay over the brown end. Secure the flaps with royal icing. Put halved cocktail sticks in the corners and ridge.

3 Tint the coconut green. Spread the board with a thin layer of royal icing and sprinkle with the coconut.

4 Tint the reserved marzipan flesh-colour and use to make a model of a child. Paint on a blue T-shirt and leave to dry. Tint some royal icing brown and pipe on the hair with a basketweave nozzle. Tint the icing and pipe on the mouth and eyes. Make a bonfire with broken chocolate mint sticks.

Army Tank Cake

Create an authentic camouflaged tank by combining green and brown sugarpaste icing.

Makes one 25 x 15cm/10 x 6in cake

25cm/10in square sponge
  cake
225g/8oz/1 cup butter
  icing
45ml/3 tbsp apricot jam,
  warmed and sieved
450g/1lb/3 cups
  marzipan
450g/1lb/3 cups
  sugarpaste icing

brown, green and black
  food colouring
chocolate flake
liquorice strips
60ml/4 tbsp royal icing
round biscuits
sweets

Materials/equipment
25 x 35cm/10 x 14in
  cake board

1 Split and fill the sponge cake with butter icing. Cut off a 10cm/4in strip from one side of the cake. Use the off-cut to make a 15 x 7.5cm/6 x 3in rectangle, and stick on the top.

2 Shape the sloping top and cut a 2.5cm/1in piece from both ends between the tracks. Shape the rounded ends for the wheels and tracks. Place on the cake board and brush with apricot jam. Cover with a layer of marzipan.

3 Tint a quarter of the sugarpaste icing brown and the rest green. Roll out the green to a 25cm/10in square. Break small pieces of brown icing and place all over the green. Flatten and roll out together to give a camouflage effect. Turn the icing over and repeat.

4 Continue to roll out until the icing is 3mm/⅛in thick. Lay it over the cake and gently press to fit. Cut away the excess. Cut a piece into a 6cm/2½in disc and stick on the top with a little water. Cut a small hole in it for the gun and insert the chocolate flake. Stick liquorice on for the tracks, using a little black royal icing. Stick on biscuits for the wheels and sweets for the lights and portholes.

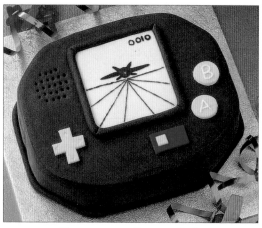

Computer Game Cake

Making a cake look like a computer is easier than you think. This cake is ideal for a computer game fanatic.

Makes one 14 x 13cm/5½ x 5in cake

15cm/6in square sponge
  cake
115g/4oz/½ cup butter
  icing
45ml/3 tbsp apricot jam,
  warmed and sieved
225g/8oz/1½ cups
  marzipan
275g/10oz/scant 2 cups
  sugarpaste icing

black, blue, red and
  yellow food colouring
royal icing, to decorate

Materials/equipment
20cm/8in square cake
  board
wooden cocktail stick
fine paintbrush
small greaseproof paper
  piping bag

1 Split and fill the cake with a little butter icing. Cut 2.5cm/1in off one side of the cake and 1cm/½in off the other side. Round the corners slightly. Place on the cake board and brush with apricot jam. Cover with a layer of marzipan.

2 Tint 225g/8oz/1½ cups of the sugarpaste black. Use to cover the cake. Reserve the trimmings. With a cocktail stick, mark the speaker holes and position of the screen and knobs.

3 Tint half the remaining sugarpaste pale blue, roll out and cut out a 6cm/2½in square for the screen. Stick in the centre of the game with a little water. Tint a small piece of sugarpaste red and the rest yellow. Use to cut out the switch and controls. Stick them in position with water. Roll the reserved black sugarpaste icing into a long, thin sausage and edge the screen and base of the cake.

4 With a fine paintbrush, draw the game on to the screen with a little blue colouring. Pipe letters on to the buttons with royal icing.

Chessboard Cake

To make this cake look most effective, ensure that the squares have very sharp edges.

Makes one 25cm/10in square cake

25cm/10in square sponge
  cake
225g/8oz/1 cup butter
  icing
60ml/4 tbsp apricot jam,
  warmed and sieved
800g/1¾lb/5¼ cups
  marzipan
500g/1¼lb/3¾ cups
  sugarpaste icing

black and red food
  colouring
edible silver balls
115g/4oz/¾ cup royal
  icing

Materials/equipment
30cm/12in square cake
  board
small greaseproof paper
  piping bag
No 8 star nozzle

1 Split and fill the cake with butter icing. Place on the board and brush with jam. Roll out 450g/1lb/3 cups of marzipan and use to cover the cake. Then cover with 450g/1lb/3 cups of the sugarpaste icing. Leave to dry overnight.

2 Divide the remaining marzipan into two, and tint black and red. To shape the chess pieces, roll 50g/2oz/4 tbsp of each colour into a sausage and cut into eight equal pieces. Shape into pawns.

3 Divide 75g/3oz/generous 4 tbsp of each colour into six equal pieces and use to shape into two castles, two knights and two bishops.

4 Divide 25g/1oz/2 tbsp of each colour marzipan in half and shape a queen and a king. Decorate with silver balls. Leave to dry overnight.

5 Cut 1cm/½in black strips of marzipan to edge the board and stick in place with water. Pipe a border round the base of the cake with royal icing. Place the chess pieces in position.

Kite Cake

The happy face on this cheerful kite is a great favourite with children of all ages.

Serves 10–12

25cm/10in square sponge cake
225g/8oz/1 cup butter icing
45ml/3 tbsp apricot jam, warmed and sieved
675g/1½lb/4½ cups sugarpaste icing
yellow, red, green, blue and black food colouring
450g/1lb/3 cups marzipan

115g/4oz/¾ cup royal icing

Materials/equipment

30cm/12in square cake board
wooden cocktail stick
small greaseproof paper piping bag
No 8 star nozzle
6 candles and holders

1 Trim the cake into a kite shape, then split and fill with butter icing. Place diagonally on the cake board and brush with apricot jam. Cover with a layer of marzipan

2 Tint 225g/8oz/1½ cups of the sugarpaste icing pale yellow and cover the cake. Make a template of the face, tie and buttons and mark on to the cake with a cocktail stick. Divide the rest of the sugarpaste icing into four and tint red, green, blue and black. Cut out the features and stick on with water.

3 Pipe a royal icing border around the base of the cake.

4 For the kite's tail, roll out each colour separately and cut two 4 x 1cm/1½ x ½in lengths in blue, red and green. Pinch each length to shape into a bow.

5 Roll the yellow into a long rope and lay it on the board in a wavy line from the narrow end of the kite. Stick the bows in place with water. Roll balls of yellow sugarpaste, stick on the board with a little royal icing and press in the candles.

Hotdog Cake

Makes one 23cm/9in long cake

23 x 33cm/9 x 13in Swiss roll sponge
175g/6oz/¾ cup coffee flavour butter icing
90ml/6 tbsp apricot jam, warmed and sieved
450g/1lb/3 cups sugarpaste icing
brown and red food colouring
15–30ml/1–2 tbsp toasted sesame seeds
115g/4oz/¾ cup glacé icing

Filling

175g/6oz sponge cake pieces
50g/2oz/¼ cup dark brown sugar
45ml/3tbsp orange juice
75ml/5tbsp honey

Materials/equipment

fine paintbrush
2 small greaseproof paper piping bags
napkin, plate, knife and fork

1 Unroll the Swiss roll, spread with butter icing, then roll up again. Slice the Swiss roll along the centre lengthways, almost to the base and ease the two halves apart.

2 Mix all the filling ingredients in a food processor or blender until smooth. Shape the mixture with your hands to a 23cm/9in sausage shape.

3 Tint all the sugarpaste icing brown. Set aside 50g/2oz/scant ½ cup and use the rest to cover the cake.

4 Paint the top of the "bun" with diluted brown food colouring to give a toasted effect. Position the "sausage".

5 Divide the glacé icing in half. Tint one half brown and the other red. Pipe red icing along the sausage, then overlay with brown icing. Sprinkle the sesame seeds over the "bun".

6 Cut the reserved brown sugarpaste icing into thin strips. Place on the cake with the joins under the "sausage". Place the cake on a napkin on a serving plate, with a knife and fork.

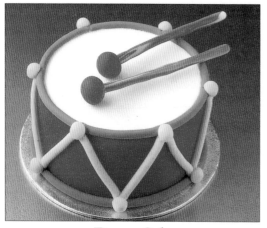

Drum Cake

This is a colourful cake for very young children. It even comes complete with drumsticks.

Makes one 15cm/6in round cake

15cm/6in round sponge cake	*red, blue and yellow food colouring*
50g/2oz/4 tbsp butter icing	*royal icing, for sticking*
45ml/3 tbsp apricot jam, warmed and served	**Materials/equipment**
350g/12oz/2cups marzipan	*20cm/8in round cake board*
450g/1lb/3 cups sugarpaste icing	

1 Split and fill the cake with a little butter icing. Place on the cake board and brush with apricot jam. Cover with a layer of marzipan and leave to dry overnight.

2 Tint half of the sugarpaste icing red and roll it out to 25 x 30cm/10 x 12in. Cut in half and stick to the side of the cake with water.

3 Roll out a circle of white sugarpaste icing to fit the top of the cake and divide the rest in half. Tint one half blue and the other yellow. Divide the blue into four pieces and roll into sausages long enough to go halfway round the cake. Stick around the base and top of the cake with a little water.

4 Mark the cake into six around the top and base. Roll the yellow sugarpaste icing into 12 strands long enough to cross diagonally from top to base to form the drum strings. Roll the rest of the yellow icing into 12 small balls and stick where the strings join the drum.

5 Knead together the red and white sugarpaste icing until streaky, then roll two balls and sticks 15cm/6in long. Leave to dry overnight. Stick together with royal icing to make the drumsticks and place on top of the cake.

Ice Cream Cones

Individual cakes make a change for a party. Put a candle in the special person's one.

Makes 9

115g/4oz/¾ cup marzipan	*coloured and chocolate vermicelli, wafers and chocolate sticks*
9 ice cream cones	
9 sponge fairy cakes	*sweets*
350g/12oz/1½ cups butter icing	
red, green and brown food colouring	**Materials/equipment**
	3 12-egg egg boxes
	foil

1 Make the stands for the cakes by turning the egg boxes upside down and pressing three balls of marzipan into evenly spaced holes in each box. Wrap the boxes in foil. Pierce the foil above the marzipan balls and insert the cones, pressing them in gently.

2 Gently push a fairy cake into each cone. If the bases of the cakes are too large, trim them down with a small, sharp knife. The cakes should be quite secure in the cones.

3 Divide the butter icing into three bowls and tint them pale red, green and brown.

4 Using a small palette knife, spread each cake with some of one of the icings, making sure that the finish on the icing is a little textured so it looks like ice cream.

5 To insert a wafer or chocolate stick into an ice cream, use a small, sharp knife to make a hole through the icing and into the cake, then insert the wafer or stick. Add the finishing touches to the cakes by sprinkling over some coloured and chocolate vermicelli. Arrange sweets around the cones.

Treasure Map

Makes one 20 x 25cm/8 x 10in cake

25cm/10in square sponge
   cake
225g/8oz/1½ cups butter
   icing
45ml/3 tbsp apricot jam,
   warmed and sieved
450g/1lb/3 cups
   marzipan
675g/1½lb/4½ cups
   sugarpaste icing
yellow, brown, paprika,
   green, black and red
   food colouring

115g/4oz/¾ cup
   royal icing

Materials/equipment
25 x 35cm/10 x 14in cake
   board
fine paintbrush
kitchen paper
4 small greaseproof paper
   piping bags
No 7 shell and No 1
   writing nozzles
6 candles and holders

1 Split and fill the cake with butter icing, cut it into a
20 x 25cm/8 x 10in rectangle and place on the cake board.
Brush with apricot jam. Cover with a layer of marzipan then
with 450g/1lb/3cups sugarpaste icing.

2 Colour the remaining sugarpaste icing yellow and cut out
with an uneven outline. Stick on to the cake with water and
leave to dry overnight. Mark the island, river, lake, mountains
and trees on the map.

3 With brown and paprika colours and a fine paintbrush,
paint the edges of the map to look old, smudging the colours
together with kitchen paper. Paint the island pale green and
the water around the island, the river and the lake pale blue.
Dry overnight before painting on the other details, otherwise
the colours will run.

4 Pipe a border of royal icing around the base of the cake
with a shell nozzle. Colour a little royal icing red and pipe the
path to the treasure, marked with an "X". Colour some icing
green and pipe on grass and trees. Finally colour some icing
black and pipe on a North sign with the writing nozzle.

Royal Crown Cake

This regal cake is sure to delight any prince or princess.

Serves 16–20

20cm/8in and 15cm/6in
   round sponge cake
175g/6oz/¾ cup butter
   icing
45ml/3 tbsp apricot jam,
   warmed and sieved
450g/1lb/3 cups
   marzipan
500g/1¼lb/3¾ cups
   sugarpaste icing
red food colouring

450g/1lb/3 cups royal
   icing
small black jelly sweets
4 ice cream fan wafers
edible silver balls
jewel sweets

Materials/equipment
30cm/12in square cake
   board
wooden cocktail sticks

1 Split and fill the cakes with butter icing. Sandwich one on
top of the other and place on the board. Shape the top cake
into a dome.

2 Brush the cake with apricot jam and cover with marzipan.
Set aside 115g/4oz/¾ cup of the sugarpaste icing and use the
rest to cover the cake.

3 Tint the reserved sugarpaste icing red, and use to cover the
dome of the cake. Trim away the excess.

4 Spoon rough mounds of royal icing around the base of the
cake and stick a black jelly sweet on each mound.

5 Cut the ice cream wafers in half. Spread both sides of the
wafers with royal icing and stick to the cake, smoothing the
icing level with the sides of the cake.

6 Use cocktail sticks to support the wafers until they are dry.
Put silver balls on top of each point and stick jewel sweets
around the side of the crown with a little royal icing.

Box of Chocolates Cake

This sophisticated cake is perfect for an adult's birthday and will delight chocolate lovers.

Makes one 15cm/6in square cake

15cm/6in square sponge cake	wrapped chocolates
50g/2oz/4 tbsp butter icing	**Materials/equipment**
30ml/2 tbsp apricot jam, warmed and sieved	20cm/8in square cake board
350g/12oz/2¼ cups marzipan	small paper sweet cases 1.30m/1½yd x
350g/12oz/2¼ cups sugarpaste icing	4cm/1½in-wide gold and red ribbon
red food colouring	

1 Split and fill the cake with butter icing. Cut a shallow square from the top of the cake, leaving a 1cm/¼in border around the edge. Place on the cake board and brush with apricot jam. Cover with a layer of marzipan.

2 Roll out the sugarpaste icing and cut an 18cm/7in square. Ease it into the hollow dip and trim. Tint the remaining sugarpaste icing red and use to cover the sides.

3 Put the chocolates into paper cases and arrange in the box. Tie the ribbon around the sides and tie a big bow.

Strawberry Cake

Makes one 900g/2lb cake

650g/1lb 7oz/scant 4½ cups marzipan	caster sugar, for dusting
green, red and yellow food colouring	**Materials/equipment**
30ml/2 tbsp apricot jam, warmed and sieved	30cm/12in round cake board
900g/2lb heart-shaped sponge cake	icing smoother teaspoon

1 Tint 175g/6oz/generous 1 cup of the marzipan green. Brush the cake board with apricot jam, roll out the green marzipan and use to cover the board. Trim the edges. Use an icing smoother to flatten and smooth the marzipan.

2 Brush the remaining apricot jam over the top and sides of the cake. Position the cake on the cake board. Tint 275g/10oz/scant 2 cups of the remaining marzipan red. Roll it out to 5mm/¼in thick and use to cover the cake, smoothing down the sides. Trim the edges. Use the handle of a teaspoon to indent the "strawberry" evenly and lightly all over.

3 For the stalk, tint 175g/6oz/generous 1 cup of the marzipan bright green. Cut it in half and roll out one portion into a 10 x 15cm/4 x 6in rectangle. Cut "V" shapes out of the rectangle, leaving a 2.5cm/1in border across the top, to form the calyx. Position on the cake, curling the "V" shapes to make them look realistic.

4 Roll the rest of the green marzipan into a sausage shape 13cm/5in long. Bend it slightly, then position it on the board to form the stalk.

5 For the strawberry pips, tint the remaining marzipan yellow. Pull off tiny pieces and roll them into tear-shaped pips. Place them in the indentations all over the strawberry. Dust the cake and board with sifted caster sugar.

Gift-wrapped Parcel

If you don't have a tiny flower cutter for the "wrapping paper" design, then press a small decorative button into the icing while still soft to create a pattern.

Makes one 15cm/6in square cake

15cm/6in square cake
50g/2oz/4 tbsp butter
 icing
45ml/3 tbsp apricot jam,
 warmed and served
450g/1lb/3 cups
 marzipan
350g/12oz/2¼ cups pale
 lemon yellow fondant
 icing

red and green food
 colouring
30ml/2 tbsp royal icing

Materials/equipment
20cm/8in square cake
 board
small flower cutter
 (optional)

1 Split and fill the cake with butter icing. Place on the cake board and brush with jam. Cover with half the marzipan, then yellow fondant and mark with a small flower cutter.

2 Divide the remaining marzipan in half, colour one half pink and the other pale green. Roll out the pink marzipan and cut into four 2.5 x 18cm/1 x 7in strips. Roll out the green marzipan and cut into four 1cm/½in strips the same length. Centre the green strips on top of the pink strips and stick on to the cake with a little water. Cut two 5cm/2in strips from each colour and cut a "V" from the ends to form the ends of the ribbon. Stick in place and leave to dry overnight.

3 Cut the rest of the green into four 2.5 x 7.5cm/1 x 3in lengths and the pink into four 1 x 7.5cm/½ x 3in lengths. Centre the pink on top of the green, fold in half, stick ends together and slip over the handle of a wooden spoon, dusted with cornflour. Leave to dry overnight.

4 Cut the ends in "V" shapes to fit neatly together on the cake. Cut two pieces for the join in the centre. Remove the bows from the spoon and stick in position with royal icing.

Sweetheart Cake

The heart-shaped run-outs can be made a week before the cake is made to ensure that they are completely dry.

Makes one 20cm/8in round cake

20cm/8in round sponge
 cake
115g/4oz/½ cup butter
 icing
45ml/3 tbsp apricot jam,
 warmed and served
450g/1lb/3 cups
 marzipan
675g/1½lb/4½ cups
 sugarpaste icing
red food colouring
115g/4oz/¾ cup royal
 icing

Materials/equipment
25cm/10in round cake
 board
spoon with decorative
 handle
small greaseproof paper
 piping bag
No 1 writing nozzle
8 candles and holders
1.5m/1½yd x 2.5cm/1in
 wide ribbon

1 Split and fill the cake with butter icing. Place on the cake board and brush with apricot jam. Cover with a layer of marzipan. Tint the sugarpaste icing pale pink and cover the cake and board. Mark the edge with the decorative handle of a spoon.

2 Tint the royal icing dark pink. Make a heart-shaped template and use to pipe the run-outs on greaseproof paper. Using a No 1 writing nozzle, pipe the outlines in a continuous line. Then fill in until the hearts are rounded. You will need eight for the cake top. Leave to dry for at least 2 days.

3 Arrange the hearts on top of the cake and place the candles in the centre. Tie the ribbon round the cake.

Rosette Cake

This cake is quick to decorate and looks truly professional.

Makes one 20cm/8in square cake

20cm/8in square sponge cake	**Materials/equipment**
450g/1lb/2 cups butter icing	25cm/10in square cake board
60ml/4 tbsp apricot jam, warmed and sieved	serrated scraper
mulberry red food colouring	piping bag
crystallized violets	No 8 star nozzle
	4 candles and holders

1 Split and fill the cake with a little butter icing. Place in the centre of the cake board and brush with apricot jam. Tint the remaining butter icing dark pink. Spread the top and sides with butter icing.

2 Using the serrated scraper, hold it against the cake and move it from side to side across the top to make waves. Hold the scraper against the side of the cake, resting the flat edge on the board and draw it along to give straight ridges along each side.

3 Put the rest of the butter icing into a piping bag fitted with a No 8 star nozzle. Mark a 15cm/6in circle on the top of the cake and pipe stars around it and around the base of the cake. Place the candles and violets in the corners.

Number 10 Cake

This is a very simple cake to decorate. If you can't master the shell edge, pipe stars instead.

Makes one 20cm/8in tall round cake

20cm/8in and 15cm/6in round sponge cakes	**Materials/equipment**
450g/1lb/2 cups butter icing	25cm/10in round cake board
75ml/5 tbsp apricot jam, warmed and sieved	wooden cocktail stick
coloured vermicelli	plastic "10" cake decoration
cream food colouring	small greaseproof paper piping bag
	No 7 shell and No 7 star nozzles
	10 candles and holders

1 Split and fill both cakes with a little butter icing. Brush the sides with apricot jam. When cold, spread a layer of butter icing on the sides then roll in coloured vermicelli to cover.

2 Tint the rest of the icing cream, spread over the top of each cake. Place the small cake on top of the large cake. Using a cocktail stick, make a pattern in the icing on top of the cake.

3 Using the remaining icing, pipe around the base of the cakes and around the edge. Stick the "10" decoration in the centre of the top tier and two candles on either side. Arrange the other candles evenly around the base cake.

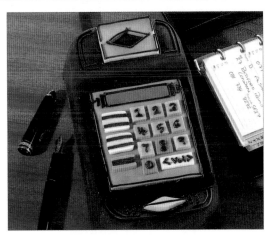

Shirt and Tie Cake

Makes one 19 x 26.5cm/7½ x 10½in cake

coffee sponge cake, baked
in a 19 x 26.5cm/
7½ x 5in loaf tin
350g/12oz/1½ cups
coffee-flavour butter
icing
90ml/6 tbsp apricot jam,
warmed and sieved
good 1kg/2lb 6oz/7 cups
sugarpaste icing
blue food colouring
125g/4oz/1 cup icing
sugar, sifted

45–60ml/3–4 tbsp water

Materials/equipment
30 x 39cm/15½ x 12in
cake board
steel ruler
small greaseproof paper
piping bag
small round nozzle
card collar template
"Happy Birthday"
decoration
tissue paper (optional)

1 Cut the cake in half horizontally and sandwich together
with the butter icing. Brush the cake with apricot jam. Colour
675g/1½lb/4½ cups sugarpaste icing light blue and roll out to
about 5mm/¼in thick. Use to cover the whole cake. Trim
away any excess icing. Place the cake on the cake board.

2 Using a steel ruler, make grooves down the length and
sides of the cake, about 2.5cm/1in apart. Mix the icing sugar
and water to make a glacé icing to pipe into the grooves.

3 To make the collar, roll out 225g/8oz/1½ cups sugarpaste
icing to a 40.5 x 10cm/16½ x 4in rectangle. Lay the piece of
card for the collar on top. Brush water around the edges, then
carefully lift one edge over the card to encase it completely.
Trim the two short ends to match the angles of the card. Lift
the collar and gently bend it round and position on the cake.

4 Colour 175g/6oz/1 cup sugarpaste icing dark blue. Cut
off one-third and shape into a tie knot. Position the knot. Roll
out the rest to about 5mm/¼in thick. Cut out a tie piece to fit
under the knot and long enough to hang over the edge of the
cake. Position the tie piece, tucking it under the knot and
securing in place with a little water. Finish the cake with the
"Happy Birthday" decoration and tissue paper, if using.

Mobile Phone Cake

Makes one 23 x 13cm/9 x 5in cake

sponge cake, baked in a 23
x 13cm/9 x 5in loaf tin
30ml/2 tbsp apricot jam,
warmed and sieved
375g/13oz/2¼ cups
sugarpaste icing
black food colouring
10 small square sweets
2 striped liquorice sweets
30–45ml/2–3 tbsp icing
sugar
2.5–5ml/½–1 tsp water

Materials/equipment
25 x 18cm/10 x 7in cake
board
diamond-shaped biscuit
cutter
small piece of foil
small greaseproof paper
piping bag
small round nozzle

1 Turn the cake upside-down. Make a 2.5cm/1in diagonal
cut 2.5cm/1in from one end. Cut down vertically to remove
the wedge. Remove the middle of the cake to the wedge
depth up to 4cm/1½in from the other end.

2 Place the cake on the board and brush with apricot jam.
Tint 275g/10oz/1¼ cups of the sugarpaste icing black. Use to
cover the cake, smoothing it over the carved shape. Reserve
the trimmings.

3 Tint 75g/3oz/ ½ cup of the sugarpaste icing grey. Cut a
piece to fit the hollowed centre, leaving a 1cm/½in border,
and another piece 2.5cm/1in square. Stamp out the centre of
the square with the cutter. Secure all the pieces on the cake
with water.

4 Position the sweets and the foil for the display pad. For the
glacé icing, mix the icing sugar with the water and tint black.
With the small round nozzle, pipe border lines around the
edges of the phone, including the grey pieces of sugarpaste.
Pipe the numbers on the keys.

5 Roll a sausage shape from the reserved black sugarpaste
for the aerial. Indent one side of the top with a knife and
secure the aerial with water.

Heart Cake

Makes one 20cm/8in heart-shaped cake

3 egg whites
350g/12oz/1¼ cups
caster sugar
30ml/2 tbsp cold water
30ml/2 tbsp fresh lemon
juice
1.5ml/¼ tsp cream of
tartar
red food colouring
20cm/8in heart-shaped
sponge cake

85–115g/3–4oz/¾–1 cup
icing sugar

Materials/equipment
30cm/12in square cake
board
small greaseproof piping
bag
small nozzle

1 Make the icing by combining 2 of the egg whites, the caster sugar, water, lemon juice and cream of tartar in the top of a double boiler or in a bowl set over simmering water. With an electric mixer, beat until thick and holding soft peaks, about 7 minutes. Remove from the heat and continue beating until the mixture is thick enough to spread. Colour the icing pale pink.

2 Put the cake on the cake board and spread the icing evenly on the cake. Smooth the top and sides. Leave to set for 3–4 hours, or overnight.

3 Place 1 tbsp of the remaining egg white in a bowl and whisk until frothy. Gradually beat in enough icing sugar to make a stiff mixture suitable for piping.

4 Spoon the white icing into a piping bag and pipe the decorations on the top and sides of the cake as shown in the photograph above.

Bowl-of-Strawberries Cake

The strawberry theme of the painting is carried on into the moulded decorations on this summery birthday cake.

Makes one 20cm/8in petal-shaped cake

350g/12oz/1½ cups
butter icing
red, yellow, green and
claret food colouring
20cm/8in petal-shaped
Madeira cake
45ml/3 tbsp apricot jam,
warmed and sieved
675g/1½lb/4½ cups
sugarpaste icing
yellow powder tint

Materials/equipment
25cm/10in petal-shaped
cake board
paint palette or small
saucers
fine paintbrushes
thin red and green
ribbons

1 Tint the butter icing pink. Cut the cake horizontally into three. Sandwich together with the butter icing. Brush the cake with apricot jam. Use 500g/1¼lb/3¾ cups of the sugarpaste icing to cover the cake. Place on the cake board and leave to dry overnight.

2 For the strawberries, tint three-quarters of the remaining sugarpaste icing red, and equal portions of the rest yellow and green. Make the strawberries, securing with water if necessary. Leave to dry on greaseproof paper.

3 Put the red, green, yellow and claret food colouring in a palette and water them down slightly. Paint the bowl and strawberries, using yellow powder tint to highlight the bowl.

4 Decorate the cake with the ribbons. Secure two strawberries to the top of the cake, and arrange the others around the base.

Barley Twist Cake

Makes one 20cm/8in round cake

20cm/8in round sponge cake	blue food colouring
115g/4oz/½ cup butter icing	pink dusting powder
45ml/3 tbsp apricot jam, warmed and sieved	**Materials/equipment**
450/1lb/3 cups marzipan	25cm/10in round cake board
450g/1lb/3 cups pale yellow sugarpaste icing	wooden cocktail stick
115g/4oz/¾ cup white sugarpaste icing	fine paintbrush
115g/4oz/¾ cup royal icing	No 1 plain nozzle
	small greaseproof paper piping bags
	6 small blue bows

1 Split and fill the cake with butter icing. Place on the board and brush with jam. Cover with marzipan, then yellow sugarpaste icing, extending it over the board. Mark six equidistant points around the cake with a cocktail stick.

2 Colour 40g/½oz/1 tbsp of white sugarpaste icing pale blue and roll out thinly. Moisten a paintbrush with water and brush lightly over it. Roll out the same quantity of white icing, lay on top and press together. Roll out to a 20cm/8in square.

3 Cut 5mm/¼in strips, carefully twist each one, moisten the six marked points around the cake with water and drape each barley twist into place, pressing lightly to stick to the cake.

4 Cut out a jersey shape from white icing and stick on with water. Roll some icing into a ball and colour a small amount dark blue. Roll into two tapering 7.5cm/3in needles with a small ball at the end. Dry overnight. Stick the needles and ball in position. Using royal icing and a No 1 nozzle, pipe the stitches and wool in position. Pipe a white border around the base of the cake. Stick small bows around the edge of the cake with a little royal icing and carefully brush the knitting with red powder tint.

Tablecloth Cake

Makes one 20cm/8in round cake

20cm/8in round sponge cake	**Materials/equipment**
115g/4oz/½ cup butter icing	25cm/10in round cake board
45ml/3 tbsp apricot jam, warmed and sieved	spoon with decorative handle
450g/1lb/3 cups marzipan	8 wooden cocktail sticks
675g/1½lb/4½ cups sugarpaste icing	sharp needle
115g/4oz/¾ cup royal icing	skewer
red food colouring	8 red ribbon bows
	small greaseproof paper piping bags
	No 2 and No 0 plain nozzles

1 Split and fill the cake with butter icing. Place on the board and brush with apricot jam. Cover with a layer of marzipan. Tint 450g/1lb/3 cups of the sugarpaste icing red and cover the cake and board. Roll the rest of the red fondant into a thin rope long enough to go round the cake. Stick around the base of the cake with water. Mark with the decorative handle of a spoon. Leave to dry overnight.

2 Roll out the remaining icing to a 25cm/10in circle and trim. Lay this icing over the cake and drape the "cloth" over the wooden cocktail sticks set at equidistant points.

3 Mark a 10cm/4in circle in the centre of the cake. Make a template of the flower design and transfer to the cake with a needle. Use a skewer to make the flowers; the red colour should show through.

4 Remove the cocktail sticks and stick on the bows with royal icing. With a No 2 plain nozzle and white royal icing pipe around the circle in the centre. With a No 0 plain nozzle, pipe small dots around the edge of the cloth. Colour some royal icing red and pipe a name in the centre.

Pizza Cake

Quick and easy, this really is a definite winner for pizza fanatics everywhere.

Makes one 23cm/9in round cake

23cm/9in shallow sponge cake
350g/12oz/1½ cups butter icing
red and green food colouring
175g/6oz/generous 1 cup yellow marzipan

25g/1oz/4 tbsp sugarpaste icing
15ml/1 tbsp desiccated coconut

Materials/equipment
25cm/10in pizza plate
cheese grater
leaf cutter

1 Place the cake on the pizza plate. Tint the butter icing red and spread evenly over the cake, leaving a 1cm/½in border.

2 Knead the marzipan for a few minutes, to soften slightly, then grate it like cheese, and sprinkle all over the top of the red butter icing.

3 Tint the sugarpaste icing green. Use the leaf cutter to cut out two leaf shapes. Mark the veins with the back of a knife and place on the pizza cake.

4 For the chopped herbs, tint the desiccated coconut dark green. Then scatter over the pizza cake.

Flowerpot Cake

Makes one round cake

Madeira cake, baked in a 1.2-litre/2-pint/5-cup pudding basin
175g/6oz/½ cup jam
175g/6oz/¾ cup butter icing
30ml/2 tbsp apricot jam, warmed and sieved
575g/1¼lb/4¼ cups sugarpaste icing
125g/4oz/¾ cup royal icing

dark orange-red, red, silver, green, purple and yellow food colouring
2 chocolate flakes, coarsely crushed

Materials/equipment
fine paintbrush
wooden spoon

1 Slice the cake into three layers and stick together again with jam and butter icing. Cut out a shallow circle from the cake top, leaving a 1cm/½in rim. Brush the outside of the cake and rim with apricot jam. Tint 400g/14oz/2¼ cups of the sugarpaste orange-red and cover the cake, moulding it over the rim. Reserve the trimmings. Leave to dry.

2 Use the trimmings to make decorations and handles for the flowerpot. Leave to dry on greaseproof paper. Sprinkle the chocolate flakes into the pot for soil.

3 Tint a small piece of sugarpaste very pale orange-red. Use to make a seed bag. When dry, paint on a pattern in food colouring. Tint two small pieces of icing red and silver. Make a trowel and dry over a wooden spoon handle.

4 Tint the remaining icing green, purple and a small piece yellow. Use to make the flowers and leaves, attaching together with royal icing. Score leaf veins with the back of a knife. Leave to dry on greaseproof paper.

5 Attach all the decorations to the flowerpot and arrange the plant, seed bag and trowel with soil, seeds and grass made from leftover tinted sugarpaste.

Glittering Star Cake

With a quick flick of a paintbrush you can give a sparkling effect to this glittering cake.

Makes one 20cm/8in round cake

20cm/8in round rich fruit cake	silver, gold, lilac shimmer, red sparkle, glitter green and primrose sparkle food colouring and powder tints
40ml/2½ tbsp apricot jam, warmed and sieved	
675g/1½lb/4½ cups marzipan	
450g/1lb/4 cups sugarpaste icing	**Materials/equipment**
115g/4oz/¾ cup royal icing	paintbrush
	25cm/10in round cake board

1 Brush the cake with the apricot jam. Use two-thirds of the marzipan to cover the cake. Leave to dry overnight.

2 Cover the cake with the sugarpaste icing. Leave to dry.

3 Place the cake on a large sheet of greaseproof paper. Dilute a little powdered silver food colouring and, using a loaded paintbrush, flick it all over the cake to give a spattered effect. Allow to dry.

4 Make templates of two different-size moon shapes and three irregular star shapes. Divide the remaining marzipan into six pieces and tint silver, gold, lilac, pink, green and yellow. Cut into stars and moons using the templates as a guide, cutting some of the stars in half.

5 Place the cut-outs on greaseproof paper, brush each with its own colour powder tint. Allow to dry.

6 Secure the cake on the board with royal icing. Arrange the stars and moons at different angles all over the cake, attaching with royal icing, and position the halved stars upright as though coming out of the cake. Allow to set.

Racing Ring Cake

Serves 12

ring mould sponge cake	113g/4½oz packet liquorice Catherine wheels
350g/12oz/1½ cups butter icing	
500g/1lb 2oz/4⅛ cups sugarpaste icing	
125g/4oz/¾ cup royal icing, for fixing	**Materials/equipment**
black, blue, yellow, green, orange, red, purple food colouring	25cm/10in round cake board
selection of liquorice sweets, dolly mixtures and teddy bears	wooden kebab skewer fine paintbrush

1 Cut the cake in half horizontally and fill with some butter icing. Cover the outside with the remaining butter icing.

2 Use 350g/12oz/2¼ cups of sugarpaste icing to coat the top and inside of the cake. Use the trimmings to roll an oblong for the flag. Cut the skewer to 12.5cm/5in and fold one end of the flag around it, securing with water. Paint on the pattern with black food colouring. Colour a ball of icing black, and stick on top of the skewer. Make a few folds and leave to dry.

3 Colour the remaining sugarpaste icing blue, yellow, green, orange, red and a very small amount purple. Shape each car in two pieces, attaching in the centre with royal icing where the seat joins the body of the car. Add decorations and headlights and attach dolly mixture wheels with royal icing. Place a teddy bear in each car and leave to set.

4 Unwind the Catherine wheels and remove the centre sweets. Fix them to the top of the cake with royal icing. Secure one strip round the bottom. Cut some of the liquorice into small strips and attach round the middle of the outside of the cake with royal icing. Arrange small liquorice sweets around the bottom of the cake. Position the cars on top of the cake on the tracks and attach the flag to the outside with royal icing.

Artist's Cake

Making cakes is an art in itself, and this cake proves it!

Makes one 20cm/8in square cake

20cm/8in square rich
  fruit cake
45ml/3 tbsp apricot jam,
  warmed and sieved
450g/1lb/3 cups
  marzipan
800g/1¾lb/5¼ cups
  sugarpaste icing
115g/4oz/¾ cup royal
  icing

chestnut, yellow, blue,
  black, silver, paprika,
  green and mulberry
  food colouring

Materials/equipment
25cm/10in square cake
  board
fine paintbrush

1 Brush the cake with the apricot jam. Cover in marzipan and leave to dry overnight.

2 Make a template of a painter's palette that will fit the cake top. Tint 175g/6oz/generous 1 cup of the sugarpaste very pale chestnut. Cut out the palette shape, place on greaseproof paper and leave to dry overnight.

3 Tint 450g/1lb/3 cups of the sugarpaste icing dark chestnut. Use to cover the cake. Secure the cake on the board with royal icing. Leave to dry.

4 Divide half the remaining sugarpaste icing into seven equal parts and tint yellow, blue, black, silver, paprika, green and mulberry. Make all the decorative pieces for the box and palette, using the remaining white sugarpaste for the paint tubes. Leave to dry on greaseproof paper.

5 Paint black markings on the paint tubes and chestnut wood markings on the box.

6 Position all the sugarpaste pieces on the cake and board using royal icing. Leave to dry.

Liquorice Sweet Cake

Makes one 20cm/8in square cake

20cm/8in and 15cm/6in
  square Madeira cakes
675g/1½lb/3 cups butter
  icing
45ml/3 tbsp apricot jam,
  warmed and sieved
350g/12oz/2¼ cups
  marzipan
800g/1¾lb/5¼ cups
  sugarpaste icing

egg-yellow, black, blue
  and mulberry food
  colouring

Materials/equipment
25cm/10in square cake
  board
4.5cm/1¾in round cutter

1 Cut both cakes horizontally into three. Fill with butter icing, reserving a little to coat the smaller cake. Wrap and set aside the smaller cake. Brush the larger cake with apricot jam. Cover with marzipan and secure on the cake board with butter icing. Leave to dry overnight.

2 Tint 350g/12oz/2¼ cups of the sugarpaste icing yellow. Take 115g/4oz/¾ cup of the sugarpaste icing and tint half black and leave the other half white. Cover the top and one-third of the sides of the cake with yellow sugarpaste icing.

3 Use the white icing to cover the lower third of the sides of the cake. Use the black icing to fill the central third.

4 Cut the smaller cake into three equal strips. Divide two of the strips into three squares each. Cut out two circles from the third strip, using a cutter as a guide.

5 Tint 115g/4oz/¾ cup of the remaining sugarpaste black. Divide the rest into four equal portions, leave one white and tint the others blue, pink and yellow.

6 Coat the outsides of the cake cut-outs with the reserved butter icing. Use the tinted and white sugarpaste to cover the pieces to resemble sweets. Make small rolls from the trimmings. Arrange on and around the cake.

Sun Cake

Makes one 20cm/8in star-shaped cake

2 x 20 x 5cm/8 x 2in	**Materials/equipment**
sponge cakes	40cm/16in square cake
25g/1oz/2 tbsp unsalted	board
butter	fabric piping bag
450g/1lb/4 cups sifted	small star nozzle
icing sugar	
120ml/4fl oz/½ cup	
apricot jam	
30ml/2 tbsp water	
2 large egg whites	
1–2 drops glycerine	
juice of 1 lemon	
yellow and orange food	
colouring	

1 Cut one of the cakes into eight wedges. Trim the outsides to fit round the other cake. Make butter icing with the butter and 25g/1oz/2 tbsp of the icing sugar. Place the whole cake on a 40cm/16in board and attach the sunbeams with the butter icing.

2 Melt the jam with the water and brush over the cake.

3 For the icing, beat the egg whites until stiff. Gradually add the icing sugar, glycerine and lemon juice, and beat for 1 minute. Tint yellow and spread over the cake. Tint the remaining icing bright yellow and orange. Pipe the details on to the cake.

Strawberry Basket Cake

Makes one small rectangular cake

sponge cake baked in a	**Materials/equipment**
450g/1lb/3 cup loaf tin	small star nozzle
45ml/3 tbsp apricot jam,	small greaseproof paper
warmed and sieved	piping bag
675g/1½lb/4½ cups	10 plastic strawberry
marzipan	stalks
350g/12oz/1½cups	30 x 7.5cm/12 x 3in strip
chocolate-flavour	foil
butter icing	30cm/12in thin red
red food colouring	ribbon
50g/2oz/4 tbsp caster	
sugar	

1 Level the top of the cake and make it perfectly flat. Score a 5mm/¼in border around the edge and scoop out the inside to make a shallow hollow.

2 Brush the sides and border edges of the cake with apricot jam. Roll out 275g/10oz/scant 2 cups of the marzipan, cut into rectangles and use to cover the sides of the cake, overlapping the borders. Press the edges together to seal.

3 Using the star nozzle, pipe vertical lines 2.5cm/1in apart all around the sides of the cake. Pipe short horizontal lines of butter icing alternately crossing over and then stopping at the vertical lines to give a basketweave effect. Pipe a decorative line of icing around the top edge of the basket to finish.

4 Tint the remaining marzipan red and mould it into ten strawberry shapes. Roll in the caster sugar and press a plastic stalk into each top. Arrange in the "basket"

5 For the basket handle, fold the foil into a thin strip and wind the ribbon around it to cover. Bend up the ends and then bend into a curve. Push the ends into the sides of the cake. Decorate with bows made from the ribbon.

Banana Gingerbread Slices

Bananas make this spicy bake delightfully moist. The flavour develops on keeping, so store the gingerbread for a few days before cutting, if possible.

Makes 20 slices

275g/10oz/2½ cups plain flour	60ml/4 tbsp corn oil
20ml/4 tsp ground ginger	30ml/2 tbsp molasses or black treacle
10ml/2 tsp mixed spice	30ml/2 tbsp malt extract
5ml/1 tsp bicarbonate of soda	2 eggs, beaten
115g/4oz/½ cup soft light brown sugar	60ml/4 tbsp orange juice
	3 ripe bananas
	115g/4oz/scant 1 cup raisins or sultanas

1 Preheat the oven to 180°C/350°F/Gas 4. Line and grease a 28 x 18cm/11 x 7in baking tin.

2 Sift the flour, spices and bicarbonate of soda into a mixing bowl. Spoon some of the mixture back into the sieve, add the brown sugar and sift the mixture back into the bowl.

3 Make a well in the centre of the dry ingredients and add the oil, molasses or treacle, malt extract, eggs, and orange juice. Mix thoroughly.

4 Mash the bananas in a bowl. Add to the gingerbread mixture with the raisins or sultanas. Mix well.

5 Scrape the mixture into the prepared tin. Bake for 35–40 minutes or until the centre springs back when the surface of the cake is lightly pressed.

6 Leave the gingerbread in the tin to cool for 5 minutes, then turn onto a wire rack, remove the lining paper and leave to cool completely. Cut into 20 slices to serve.

Banana and Apricot Chelsea Buns

Old favourites get a new twist with a delectable filling.

Serves 9

225g/8oz/2 cups strong plain flour	**For the filling**
10ml/2 tsp mixed spice	1 large ripe banana
2.5ml/½ tsp salt	175g/6oz/1 cup ready-to-eat dried apricots
25g/1oz/2 tbsp soft margarine	30ml/2tbsp soft light brown sugar
7.5ml/1½ tsp easy-blend dried yeast	
50g/2oz/¼ cup caster sugar	**For the glaze**
90ml/6 tbsp hand-hot milk	30ml/2tbsp caster sugar
1 egg, beaten	30ml/2tbsp water

1 Grease an 18cm/7in square cake tin. Prepare the filling. Mash the banana in a bowl. Using kitchen scissors, snip in the apricots, then stir in the brown sugar. Mix well.

2 Sift the flour, spice and salt into a mixing bowl. Rub in the margarine, then stir in the yeast and sugar. Make a well in the centre and pour in the milk and the egg. Mix to a soft dough, adding a little extra milk if necessary.

3 Turn the dough onto a floured surface and knead for 5 minutes until smooth and elastic. Roll out to a 30 x 23cm/12 x 9in rectangle. Spread the filling over the dough and roll up lengthways like a Swiss roll, with the join underneath. Cut into 9 pieces and place cut side downwards in the prepared tin. Cover and leave in a warm place until doubled in size.

4 Preheat the oven to 200°C/400°F/Gas 6. Bake the buns for 20–25 minutes until golden brown. Meanwhile make the glaze: mix the caster sugar and water in a small saucepan. Heat, stirring, until dissolved, then boil for 2 minutes. Brush the glaze over the buns while still hot, then remove from the tin and cool on a wire rack.

Lemon Sponge Fingers

These sponge fingers are perfect for serving with fruit salads or light, creamy desserts.

Makes about 20

2 eggs	50g/2oz/½ cup plain
75g/3oz/6 tbsp caster	flour, sifted
sugar	caster sugar, for
grated rind of 1 lemon	sprinkling

1 Preheat the oven to 190°C/375°F/Gas 5. Line two baking sheets with non-stick baking paper. Whisk the eggs, sugar and lemon rind together with a hand-held electric whisk until thick and mousse-like: when the whisk is lifted, a trail should remain on the surface of the mixture for at least 30 seconds.

2 Carefully fold in the flour with a large metal spoon using a figure-of-eight action.

3 Place the mixture in a piping bag fitted with a 1cm/½in plain nozzle. Pipe into finger lengths on the prepared baking sheets, leaving room for spreading.

4 Sprinkle the fingers with caster sugar. Bake for 6–8 minutes until golden brown, then remove to a wire rack to cool completely.

Variation
To make Hazelnut Fingers, omit the lemon rind and fold in 25g/1oz/¼ cup toasted ground hazelnuts and 5ml/1 tsp mixed spice with the flour.

Apricot and Almond Fingers

These delicious almond fingers will stay moist for several days, thanks to the addition of apricots.

Makes 18

225g/8oz/2 cups self-	30ml/2 tbsp malt extract
raising flour	2 eggs, beaten
115g/4oz/½ cup soft light	60ml/4 tbsp skimmed
brown sugar	milk
50g/2oz/⅓ cup semolina	60ml/4 tbsp sunflower oil
175g/6oz/1 cup ready-to-	few drops of almond
eat dried apricots,	essence
chopped	30ml/2 tbsp flaked
30ml/2 tbsp clear honey	almonds

1 Preheat the oven to 160°C/325°F/Gas 3. Grease and line a 28 x 18cm/11 x 7in baking tin. Sift the flour into a bowl and stir in the sugar, semolina and apricots. Make a well in the centre and add the honey, malt extract, eggs, milk, oil and almond essence. Mix well until combined.

2 Turn the mixture into the prepared tin, spread to the edges and sprinkle with the flaked almonds.

3 Bake for 30–35 minutes or until the centre springs back when lightly pressed. Invert the cake on a wire rack to cool. Remove the lining paper if necessary and cut into 18 slices with a sharp knife.

Cook's Tip
If you cannot find ready-to-eat dried apricots, soak chopped dried apricots in boiling water for 1 hour, then drain them and add to the mixture. This works well with other dried fruit too. Try ready-to-eat dried pears or peaches for a change.

Raspberry Muffins

Unlike English muffins, which are made from a yeast mixture and cooked on a griddle, these American muffins are baked, giving them a light and spongy texture.

Makes 10–12

275g/10oz/2¹/₂ cups plain
   flour
15ml/1 tbsp baking
   powder
115g/4oz/¹/₂ cup caster
   sugar

1 egg
250ml/8fl oz/1 cup
   buttermilk
60ml/4 tbsp sunflower oil
150g/5oz/1 cup
   raspberries

1 Preheat the oven to 200°C/400°F/Gas 6. Arrange 12 paper cases in a deep muffin tin. Sift the flour and baking powder into a mixing bowl, stir in the sugar, then make a well in the centre.

2 Mix the egg, buttermilk and oil together in a jug, pour into the bowl and mix quickly until just combined.

3 Add the raspberries and lightly fold in with a metal spoon. Spoon into the paper cases to within a third of the top.

4 Bake the muffins for 20–25 minutes until golden brown and firm in the middle. Remove to a wire rack and serve while still warm.

Cook's Tip
This is a fairly moist mixture which should only be lightly mixed. Over-mixing toughens the muffins and breaks up the fruit. Use blackberries, blueberries or blackcurrants instead of raspberries if you prefer.

Date and Apple Muffins

These tasty muffins are delicious with morning coffee or breakfast. You will only need one or two per person as they are very filling.

Makes 12

150g/5oz/1¹/₄ cups self-
   raising wholemeal
   flour
150g/5oz/1¹/₄ cups self-
   raising white flour
5ml/1 tsp ground
   cinnamon
5ml/1 tsp baking powder
25g/1oz/2 tbsp soft
   margarine
75g/3oz/6 tbsp soft light

brown sugar
250ml/8fl oz/1 cup apple
   juice
30ml/2 tbsp pear and
   apple spread
1 egg, lightly beaten
1 eating apple
75g/3oz/¹/₂ cup chopped
   dates
15ml/1 tbsp chopped
   pecan nuts

1 Preheat the oven to 200°C/400°F/Gas 6. Arrange 12 paper cases in a deep muffin tin. Put the wholemeal flour in a mixing bowl. Sift in the white flour with the cinnamon and baking powder. Rub in the margarine until the mixture resembles breadcrumbs, then stir in the brown sugar.

2 In a bowl, stir a little of the apple juice with the pear and apple spread until smooth. Add the remaining juice, mix well, then add to the rubbed-in mixture with the egg. Peel and core the apple, chop the flesh finely and add it to the bowl with the dates. Mix quickly until just combined.

3 Divide the mixture among the muffin cases. Sprinkle with the chopped pecans.

4 Bake the muffins for 20–25 minutes until golden brown and firm in the middle. Turn onto a wire rack and serve while still warm.

Filo and Apricot Purses

Filo pastry is very easy to use and is low in fat. Always keep a packet in the freezer ready for rustling up a speedy teatime treat.

Makes 12

115g/4oz/1 cup ready-to-
  eat dried apricots
45ml/3 tbsp apricot
  compôte
3 amaretti biscuits,
  crushed

3 sheets of filo pastry
20ml/4 tsp soft
  margarine, melted
icing sugar, for dusting

1 Preheat the oven to 180°C/350°F/Gas 4. Grease two baking sheets. Chop the apricots, put them in a bowl and stir in the apricot compôte. Mix in the amaretti biscuits.

2 Cut the filo pastry into 24 13cm/5in squares, pile the squares on top of each other and cover with a clean dish towel to prevent the pastry from drying out.

3 Lay one pastry square on a flat surface, brush lightly with melted margarine and lay another square diagonally on top. Brush the top square with melted margarine. Spoon a small mound of apricot mixture in the centre of the pastry, bring up the edges and pinch together in a money-bag shape. The margarine will help to make the pastry stick.

4 Repeat with the remaining filo squares and filling to make 12 purses in all. Arrange on the prepared baking sheets and bake for 5–8 minutes until golden brown. Dust with icing sugar and serve warm.

Cook's Tip
The easiest way to crush the amaretti biscuits is to put them in a plastic bag and roll with a rolling pin.

Filo Scrunchies

Quick and easy to make, these are ideal to serve at teatime. Eat them warm or they will lose their crispness.

Makes 6

5 apricots or plums
4 sheets of filo pastry
20ml/4 tsp soft
  margarine, melted

50g/2oz/¼ cup demerara
  sugar
30ml/2 tbsp flaked
  almonds
icing sugar, for dusting

1 Preheat the oven to 190°C/375°F/Gas 5. Cut the apricots or plums in half, remove the stones and slice the fruit thinly.

2 Cut the filo pastry into 12 18cm/7in squares. Pile the squares on top of each other and cover with a clean dish towel to prevent the pastry from drying out. Remove one square and brush it with melted margarine. Lay a second filo square on top, then, using your fingers, mould the pastry into neat folds.

3 Lay the scrunched filo square on a baking sheet. Make five more scrunchies in the same way, working quickly so that the pastry does not dry out. Arrange a few slices of fruit in the folds of each scrunchie, then sprinkle generously with demerara sugar and almonds.

4 Bake the scrunchies for 8–10 minutes until golden brown, then loosen from the baking sheet with a palette knife. Place on a platter, dust with icing sugar and serve immediately.

Cook's Tip
Filo pastry dries out very quickly. Keep it covered as much as possible with clear film or a dry cloth to limit exposure to the air, or it will become too brittle to use.

Coffee Sponge Drops

These light biscuits are delicious on their own, but taste even better with a filling made by mixing low-fat soft cheese with chopped stem ginger.

Makes about 24

50g/2oz/¹/₂ cup plain
  flour
15ml/1 tbsp instant
  coffee powder
2 eggs
75g/3oz/6 tbsp caster
  sugar

For the filling (optional)
115g/4oz/¹/₂ cup low fat
  soft cheese
40g/1¹/₂oz/¹/₄ cup
  chopped stem ginger

1 Preheat the oven to 190°C/375°F/Gas 5. Line two baking sheets with non-stick paper. Sift the flour and coffee powder together.

2 Combine the eggs and caster sugar in a heatproof bowl. Place over a saucepan of simmering water. Beat with a hand-held electric whisk until thick and mousse-like: when the whisk is lifted a trail should remain on the surface of the mixture for at least 30 seconds.

3 Carefully fold in the sifted flour mixture with a large metal spoon, being careful not to knock out any air.

4 Spoon the mixture into a piping bag fitted with a 1cm/¹/₂in plain nozzle and pipe 4cm/1¹/₂in rounds on the prepared baking sheets. Bake for 12 minutes. Cool on a wire rack. Sandwich together in pairs with a ginger-cheese filling (above) or a coffee icing, if you like.

Variation
To make Chocolate Sponge Drops, replace the coffee with 30ml/2 tbsp reduced-fat cocoa powder.

Oaty Crisps

These biscuits are very crisp and crunchy – ideal to serve with morning coffee.

Makes 18

175g/6oz/1¹/₂ cups rolled
  oats
75g/3oz/6 tbsp soft light
  brown sugar

1 egg
60ml/4 tbsp sunflower oil
30ml/2 tbsp malt extract

1 Preheat the oven to 190°C/375°F/Gas 5. Grease two baking sheets. Mix the oats and brown sugar in a bowl, breaking up any lumps in the sugar.

2 Add the egg, oil and malt extract, mix well, then leave to soak for 15 minutes.

3 Using a teaspoon, place small heaps of the mixture on the prepared baking sheets, leaving room for spreading. Press into 7.5cm/3in rounds with a dampened fork.

4 Bake the biscuits for 10–15 minutes until golden brown. Leave to cool for 1 minute, then remove with a palette knife and cool on a wire rack.

Variation
Add 50g/2oz/¹/₂ cup chopped almonds or hazelnuts to the mixture. You can also add some jumbo oats to give a coarser texture.

Snowballs

These light and airy morsels make a good accompaniment
to yogurt ice cream.

Makes about 20

2 egg whites
115g/4oz/¹/₂ cup caster
*   sugar*
15ml/1 tbsp cornflour,
*   sifted*

5ml/1 tsp white wine
*   vinegar*
1.5ml/¹/₄ tsp vanilla
*   essence*

1 Preheat the oven to 150°C/300°F/Gas 2 and line two
baking sheets with non-stick baking paper. Whisk the egg
whites in a grease-free bowl, using a hand-held electric whisk,
until very stiff.

2 Add the caster sugar, a little at a time, whisking until the
meringue is very stiff. Whisk in the cornflour, vinegar and
vanilla essence.

3 Using a teaspoon, mound the mixture into snowballs on
the prepared baking sheets. Bake for 30 minutes.

4 Cool on the baking sheets, then remove the snowballs
from the paper with a palette knife.

Variation
*Make Pineapple Snowballs by lightly folding about
50g/2oz/¹/₃ cup finely chopped semi-dried pineapple
into the meringue.*

Caramel Meringues

Muscovado sugar gives these meringues a marvellous
caramel flavour. Take care not to overcook them, so that
they stay chewy in the middle.

Makes about 20

115g/4oz/¹/₂ cup
*   muscovado sugar*
2 egg whites

5ml/1 tsp finely chopped
*   walnuts*

1 Preheat the oven to 160°C/325°F/Gas 3. Line two baking
sheets with non-stick paper. Press the sugar through a metal
sieve into a bowl. Whisk the egg whites in a grease-free bowl
until very stiff and dry, then add the sieved brown sugar,
about 15ml/1 tbsp at a time, whisking it in the meringue until
it is thick and glossy.

2 Spoon small mounds of the mixture onto the prepared
baking sheets. Sprinkle with the walnuts.

3 Bake for 30 minutes, then leave to cool for 5 minutes on
the baking sheets. Transfer the meringues to a wire rack to
cool completely.

Cook's Tip
*For an easy sophisticated filling, mix 115g/4oz/¹/₂ cup
low-fat soft cheese with 15ml/1 tbsp icing sugar. Chop
2 slices of fresh pineapple and add to the mixture.
Sandwich the meringues together in pairs.*

Chocolate Banana Cake

A delicious sticky chocolate cake, moist enough to eat without the icing if you want to cut down on the calories.

Serves 8

225g/8oz/2 cups self-raising flour
45ml/3 tbsp fat-reduced cocoa powder
115g/4oz/½ cup soft light brown sugar
30ml/2 tbsp malt extract
30ml/2 tbsp golden syrup
2 eggs, beaten
60ml/4 tbsp skimmed milk

60ml/4 tbsp sunflower oil
2 large ripe bananas

For the icing
175g/6oz/1½ cups icing sugar, sifted
30ml/2 tbsp fat-reduced cocoa powder, sifted
15–30ml/1–2 tbsp warm water

1 Preheat the oven to 160°C/325°F/Gas 3. Line and grease a deep 20cm/8in round cake tin. Sift the flour into a mixing bowl with the cocoa powder. Stir in the sugar.

2 Make a well in the centre and add the malt extract, golden syrup, eggs, milk and oil. Mix well. Mash the bananas thoroughly and stir them into the mixture until thoroughly combined.

3 Spoon the mixture into the prepared tin and bake for 1–1¼ hours or until the centre of the cake springs back when lightly pressed. Remove the cake from the tin and turn on to a wire rack to cool.

4 Make the icing: put the icing sugar and cocoa in a mixing bowl and gradually add enough water to make a mixture thick enough to coat the back of a wooden spoon. Pour over the top of the cake and ease to the edges, allowing the icing to dribble down the sides.

Spiced Apple Cake

Grated apple and dates give this cake a natural sweetness. It may not be necessary to add all the sugar.

Serves 8

225g/8oz/2 cups self-raising wholemeal flour
5ml/1 tsp baking powder
10ml/2 tsp ground cinnamon
175g/6oz/1 cup chopped dates
75g/3oz/scant ½ cup soft light brown sugar

15ml/1 tbsp pear and apple spread
120ml/4fl oz/½ cup apple juice
2 eggs, beaten
90ml/6 tbsp sunflower oil
2 eating apples, cored and grated
15ml/1 tbsp chopped walnuts

1 Preheat the oven to 180°C/350°F/Gas 4. Line and grease a 20cm/8in deep round cake tin. Sift the flour, baking powder and cinnamon into a mixing bowl, then mix in the dates and make a well in the centre.

2 Mix the sugar with the pear and apple spread in a small bowl. Gradually stir in the apple juice. Add to the dry ingredients with the eggs, oil and apples. Mix thoroughly.

3 Spoon into the prepared cake tin, sprinkle with the walnuts and bake for 60–65 minutes or until a skewer inserted into the centre of the cake comes out clean. Invert on a wire rack, remove the lining paper and leave to cool.

Cook's Tip
It is not necessary to peel the apples – the skin adds extra fibre and softens on cooking.

Irish Whiskey Cake

This moist rich fruit cake is drizzled with whiskey as soon as it comes out of the oven.

Serves 10

115g/4oz/scant 1 cup
  sultanas
115g/4oz/scant 1 cup
  raisins
115g/4oz/½ cup currants
115g/4oz/½ cup glacé
  cherries
175g/6oz/1 cup soft light
  brown sugar

300ml/½ pint/1¼ cups
  cold tea
1 egg, beaten
300g/11oz/2½ cups self-
  raising flour, sifted
45ml/3 tbsp Irish
  whiskey

1 Mix the dried fruit, cherries, sugar and tea in a large bowl. Leave to soak overnight until the tea has been absorbed.

2 Preheat the oven to 180°C/350°F/Gas 4. Line and grease a 1kg/2¼lb loaf tin. Add the egg and flour to the fruit mixture and beat thoroughly until well mixed.

3 Pour into the prepared tin and bake for 1½ hours or until a skewer inserted into the centre comes out clean.

4 Prick the top of the cake with a skewer and drizzle over the whiskey while still hot. Allow to stand for 5 minutes, then remove from the tin and cool on a wire rack.

Cook's Tip
If time is short use hot tea and soak the fruit for two hours instead of overnight.

Fruit and Nut Cake

A rich fruit cake that matures with keeping.

Serves 12–14

175g/6oz/1½ cups self-
  raising wholemeal
  flour
175g/6oz/1½ cups self-
  raising white flour
10ml/2 tsp mixed spice
15ml/1 tbsp apple and
  apricot spread
45ml/3 tbsp clear honey
15ml/1 tbsp molasses

90ml/6 tbsp sunflower oil
175ml/6fl oz/¾ cup
  orange juice
2 eggs, beaten
675g/1½lb/4 cups luxury
  mixed fruit
115g/4oz/½ cup glacé
  cherries, halved
45ml/3 tbsp split
  almonds

1 Preheat the oven to 160°C/325°F/Gas 3. Line and grease a deep 20cm/8in cake tin. Tie a band of newspaper around the outside of the tin and stand it on a pad of newspaper on a baking sheet.

2 Combine the flours in a mixing bowl. Stir in the mixed spice and make a well in the centre.

3 Put the apple and apricot spread in a small bowl. Gradually stir in the honey and molasses. Add to the bowl with the oil, orange juice, eggs and mixed fruit. Stir with a wooden spoon to mix thoroughly.

4 Scrape the mixture into the prepared tin and smooth the surface. Arrange the cherries and almonds in a decorative pattern over the top. Bake for 2 hours or until a skewer inserted into the centre of the cake comes out clean. Turn on to a wire rack to cool, then remove the lining paper.

Cook's Tip
For a less elaborate cake, omit the cherries, chop the almonds roughly and sprinkle them over the top.

Frosted Angel Cake

Served with fromage frais and fresh raspberries, this makes a light dessert.

Serves 10

40g/1¹/₂oz/scant ½ cup cornflour	225g/8oz/1 cup caster sugar, plus extra for sprinkling
40g/1¹/₂oz/scant ½ cup plain flour	5ml/1 tsp vanilla essence
8 egg whites	icing sugar, for dusting

1 Preheat the oven to 180°C/350°F/Gas 4. Sift both flours into a bowl.

2 Whisk the egg whites in a large grease-free bowl until very stiff, then gradually add the sugar and vanilla essence, whisking until the mixture is thick and glossy.

3 Fold in the flour mixture with a large metal spoon. Spoon into an ungreased 25cm/10in angel cake tin, smooth the surface and bake for 40–45 minutes.

4 Sprinkle a piece of greaseproof paper with caster sugar and set an egg cup in the centre. Invert the cake tin over the paper, balancing it carefully on the egg cup. When cold, the cake will drop out of the tin. Transfer it to a plate, dust generously with icing sugar and serve.

Variation
Make a lemon icing by mixing 175g/6oz/1¹/₂ cups icing sugar with 15–30ml/1–2 tbsp lemon juice. Drizzle the icing over the cake and decorate with lemon slices and mint sprigs or physalis.

Peach Swiss Roll

This is the perfect cake for a summer afternoon tea in the garden.

Serves 6–8

3 eggs	15ml/1 tbsp boiling water
115g/4oz/¹/₂ cup caster sugar	90ml/6 tbsp peach jam
75g/3oz/¾ cup plain flour, sifted	icing sugar, for dusting (optional)

1 Preheat the oven to 200°C/400°F/Gas 6. Line and grease a 30 x 20cm/12 x 8in Swiss roll tin. Combine the eggs and sugar in a bowl. Beat with a hand-held electric whisk until thick and mousse-like: when the whisk is lifted a trail should remain on the surface of the mixture for at least 30 seconds.

2 Carefully fold in the flour with a large metal spoon, then add the boiling water in the same way.

3 Spoon into the prepared tin, spread evenly to the edges and bake for 10–12 minutes until the cake springs back when lightly pressed.

4 Spread a sheet of greaseproof paper on a flat surface, sprinkle it with caster sugar, then invert the cake on top. Peel off the lining paper.

5 Make a neat cut two-thirds of the way through the cake, about 1 cm/½ in from the short edge nearest you – this will make it easier to roll. Trim the remaining edges.

6 Spread the cake with the peach jam and roll up quickly from the partially-cut end. Hold in position for a minute, making sure the join is underneath. Cool on a wire rack. Dust with icing sugar before serving, if you like.

Pear and Sultana Tea Bread

This is an ideal tea bread to make when pears are plentiful
There's no better use for autumn windfalls.

Serves 6–8

25g/1oz/3 cups rolled oats	115g/4oz/1 cup self-raising flour
50g/2oz/¼ cup soft light brown sugar	115g/4oz/scant 1 cup sultanas
30ml/2 tbsp pear or apple juice	2.5ml/½ tsp baking powder
30ml/2 tbsp sunflower oil	10ml/2 tsp mixed spice
1 large or 2 small pears	1 egg

1 Preheat the oven to 180°C/350°F/Gas 4. Line a 450g/1lb
loaf tin with non-stick paper. Put the oats in a bowl with the
sugar, pour over the pear or apple juice and oil, mix well and
leave to stand for 15 minutes.

2 Quarter, core and grate the pear(s). Add to the bowl with
the flour, sultanas, baking powder, spice and egg. Using a
wooden spoon, mix thoroughly.

3 Spoon the tea bread mixture into the prepared loaf tin.
Bake for 55–60 minutes or until a skewer inserted into the
centre comes out clean.

4 Invert the tea bread on a wire rack and remove the lining
paper. Leave to cool.

Cook's Tip
*Health-food shops sell concentrated pear juice, ready
for diluting as required.*

Banana and Ginger Tea Bread

The bland creaminess of banana is given a delightful lift
with chunks of stem ginger in this tasty tea bread. If you
like a strong ginger flavour add 5ml/1 tsp ground ginger
with the flour.

Serves 6–8

175g/6oz/1½ cups self-raising flour	50g/2oz/⅓ cup drained stem ginger, chopped
5ml/1 tsp baking powder	60ml/4 tbsp skimmed milk
40g/1½oz/3 tbsp soft margarine	2 ripe bananas, mashed
50g/2oz/¼ cup soft light brown sugar	

1 Preheat the oven to 180°C/350°F/Gas 4. Line and grease a
450g/1lb loaf tin. Sift the flour and baking powder into a
mixing bowl.

2 Rub in the margarine until the mixture resembles
breadcrumbs, then stir in the sugar.

3 Add the ginger, milk and mashed bananas and mix to a
soft dough.

4 Spoon into the prepared tin and bake for 40–45 minutes.
Run a palette knife around the edges to loosen them, turn the
tea bread onto a wire rack and leave to cool.

Variation
*To make Banana and Walnut Tea Bread, add 5ml/1 tsp
mixed spice and omit the chopped stem ginger. Stir in
50g/2oz/½ cup chopped walnuts and add
50g/2oz/scant ½ cup sultanas.*

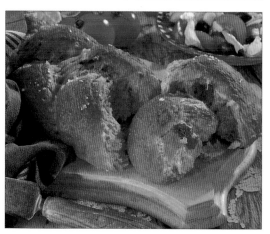

Olive and Oregano Bread

This is an excellent accompaniment to all salads and is very good with grilled goat's cheese.

Serves 8–10

15ml/1 tbsp olive oil
1 onion, chopped
450g/1lb/4 cups strong
  white flour
10ml/2 tsp easy-blend
  dried yeast
5ml/1 tsp salt
1.5ml/¼ tsp black pepper
50g/2oz/⅓ cup pitted
  black olives, roughly
  chopped

15ml/1 tbsp black olive
  paste
15ml/1 tbsp chopped
  fresh oregano
15ml/1 tbsp chopped
  fresh parsley
300ml/½ pint/1¼ cups
  hand-hot water

1 Lightly oil a baking sheet. Heat the olive oil in a frying pan and fry the onion until golden brown.

2 Sift the flour into a mixing bowl. Add the yeast, salt and pepper. Make a well in the centre. Add the fried onion (with the oil), the olives, olive paste, herbs and water. Gradually incorporate the flour and mix to a soft dough, adding a little extra water if necessary.

3 Turn the dough onto a floured surface and knead for 5 minutes until smooth and elastic. Shape into a 20cm/8in round and place on the prepared baking sheet. Using a sharp knife, make criss-cross cuts over the top, cover and leave in a warm place until doubled in size. Preheat the oven to 220°C/425°F/Gas 7.

4 Bake the olive and oregano loaf for 10 minutes, then lower the oven temperature to 200°C/400°F/Gas 6. Bake for 20 minutes more, or until the loaf sounds hollow when tapped underneath. Cool on a wire rack.

Sun-dried Tomato Plait

This makes a marvellous centrepiece for a summer buffet.

Serves 8–10

225g/8oz/2 cups
  wholemeal flour
225g/8oz/2 cups strong
  white flour
5ml/1 tsp salt
1.5ml/¼ tsp black pepper
10ml/2 tsp easy-blend
  dried yeast
pinch of sugar
300ml/½ pint/1¼ cups
  hand-hot water

115g/4oz/¾ cup drained
  sun-dried tomatoes in
  oil, chopped, plus
15ml/1 tbsp oil from
  the jar
25g/1oz/¼ cup freshly
  grated Parmesan
  cheese
30ml/2 tbsp red pesto
2.5ml/½ tsp coarse
  sea salt

1 Lightly oil a baking sheet. Put the wholemeal flour in a mixing bowl. Sift in the white flour, salt and pepper. Add the yeast and sugar. Make a well in the centre and add the water, the sun-dried tomatoes, oil, Parmesan and pesto. Gradually incorporate the flour and mix to a soft dough, adding a little extra water if necessary.

2 Turn the dough onto a floured surface and knead for 5 minutes until smooth and elastic. Shape into 3 33cm/13in long sausages.

3 Dampen the ends of the three sausages. Press them together at one end, plait them loosely, then press them together at the other end. Place on the baking sheet, cover and leave in a warm place until doubled in size. Preheat the oven to 220°C/425°F/Gas 7.

4 Sprinkle the plait with coarse sea salt. Bake for 10 minutes, then lower the oven temperature to 200°C/400°F/Gas 6 and bake for a further 15–20 minutes, or until the loaf sounds hollow when tapped underneath. Cool on a wire rack.

Cheese and Onion Herb Stick

An extremely tasty bread which is very good with soup or salads. Use a strong cheese to give plenty of flavour.

Makes 2 sticks, each serving 4 – 6

15ml/1 tbsp sunflower oil
1 red onion, chopped
450g/1lb/4 cups strong
  white flour
5ml/1 tsp salt
5ml/1 tsp mustard
  powder
10ml/2 tsp easy-blend
  dried yeast
45ml/3 tbsp chopped
  fresh herbs, such as
  thyme, parsley,
  marjoram or sage
75g/3oz/¾ cup grated
  reduced-fat Cheddar
  cheese
300ml/½ pint/1¼ cups
  hand-hot water

1 Lightly oil two baking sheets. Heat the oil in a frying pan and fry the onion until well browned.

2 Sift the flour, salt and mustard powder into a mixing bowl. Stir in the yeast and herbs. Set aside 30ml/2 tbsp of the cheese. Add the rest to the flour mixture and make a well in the centre. Add the water with the fried onions and oil; gradually incorporate the flour and mix to a soft dough, adding a little extra water if necessary.

3 Turn the dough onto a floured surface and knead for 5 minutes until smooth and elastic. Divide the mixture in half and roll each piece into a stick 30cm/12in in length.

4 Place each bread stick on a baking sheet, make diagonal cuts along the top and sprinkle with the reserved cheese. Cover and leave until doubled in size. Preheat the oven to 220°C/425°F/Gas 7.

5 Bake the loaves for 25 minutes or until the bread sounds hollow when tapped underneath.

Focaccia

This Italian flatbread is best served warm. It makes a delicious snack with olives and feta cheese.

Serves 8

450g/1lb/4 cups strong
  white flour
5ml/1 tsp salt
1.5ml/¼ tsp freshly
  ground black pepper
10ml/2 tsp easy-blend
  dried yeast
300ml/½ pint/1¼ cups
  hand-hot water
pinch of sugar
15ml/1 tbsp pesto
115g/4oz/⅔ cup pitted
  black olives, chopped
25g/1oz/3 tbsp drained
  sun-dried tomatoes in
  oil, chopped, plus
  15ml/1 tbsp oil from
  the jar
5ml/1 tsp coarse sea salt
5ml/1 tsp chopped fresh
  rosemary

1 Lightly oil a 30 x 20cm/12 x 8in Swiss roll tin. Sift the flour, salt and pepper into a bowl. Add the yeast and sugar and make a well in the centre.

2 Add the water with the pesto, olives and sun-dried tomatoes (reserve the oil). Mix to a soft dough, adding a little extra water if necessary.

3 Turn the dough onto a floured surface and knead for 5 minutes until smooth and elastic. Roll into a rectangle measuring 33 x 23cm/13 x 9in. Lop over the rolling pin and place in the prepared tin. Leave to rise until doubled in size. Preheat the oven to 220°C/425°F/Gas 7.

4 Using your fingertips, make indentations all over the dough. Brush with the oil from the sun-dried tomatoes, then sprinkle with the salt and rosemary. Bake for 20 – 25 minutes until golden. Remove to a wire rack and serve warm.

Spinach and Bacon Bread

This bread is so good that it is a good idea to make double the quantity and freeze one of the loaves.

Makes 2 loaves, each serving 8

15ml/1 tbsp olive oil
1 onion, chopped
115g/4oz rindless smoked bacon rashers, chopped
675g/1¹/₂lb/6 cups plain flour
7.5ml/1¹/₂ tsp salt
2.5ml/¹/₂ tsp grated nutmeg

1 sachet easy-blend dried yeast
475ml/16fl oz/2 cups hand-hot water
225g/8oz chopped spinach, thawed if frozen
25g/1oz/¹/₄ cup grated reduced-fat Cheddar cheese

1 Lightly oil two 23cm/9in cake tins. Heat the oil in a frying pan and fry the onion and bacon for 10 minutes until golden brown.

2 Sift the flour, salt and nutmeg into a mixing bowl, add the yeast and make a well in the centre. Add the water. Tip in the fried bacon and onion, with the oil, then add the well-drained spinach. Gradually incorporate the flour and mix to a soft dough.

3 Turn the dough onto a floured surface and knead for 5 minutes until smooth and elastic. Divide the mixture in half. Shape each half into a ball, flatten slightly and place in a tin, pressing the dough so that it extends to the edges.

4 Mark each loaf into six wedges and sprinkle with the cheese. Cover loosely with a plastic bag and leave in a warm place until each loaf has doubled in size. Preheat the oven to 200°C/400°F/Gas 6.

5 Bake the loaves for 25–30 minutes or until they sound hollow when tapped underneath. Cool on a wire rack.

Parma Ham and Parmesan Bread

This nourishing bread can be made very quickly, and is a meal in itself when served with a tomato and feta salad.

Serves 8

225g/8oz/2 cups self-raising wholemeal flour
225g/8oz/2 cups self-raising plain flour
5ml/1 tsp salt
5ml/1 tsp freshly ground black pepper
75g/3oz Parma ham, chopped

30ml/2 tbsp chopped fresh parsley
25g/1oz/2 tbsp freshly grated Parmesan cheese
45ml/3 tbsp Meaux mustard
350ml/12fl oz/1¹/₂ cups buttermilk
skimmed milk, to glaze

1 Preheat the oven to 200°C/400°F/Gas 6. Flour a baking sheet. Put the wholemeal flour in a bowl and sift in the plain flour, salt and pepper. Stir in the ham and parsley. Set aside about half of the grated Parmesan and add the rest to the flour mixture. Make a well in the centre.

2 Mix the mustard and buttermilk in a jug, pour into the bowl and quickly mix to a soft dough.

3 Turn onto a well-floured surface and knead very briefly. Shape into an oval loaf and place on the baking sheet.

4 Brush the loaf with milk, sprinkle with the reserved Parmesan and bake for 25–30 minutes until golden brown. Cool on a wire rack.

Cook's Tip
When chopping the ham, sprinkle it with flour so that it does not stick together. Do not knead the mixture as for a yeast dough, or it will become tough. It should be mixed quickly and kneaded very briefly before shaping.

Austrian Three-Grain Bread

A mixture of grains gives this close-textured bread a delightful nutty flavour.

Makes 1 large loaf

225g/8oz/2 cups strong white flour
7.5ml/1½ tsp salt
225g/8oz/2 cups malted brown flour
225g/8oz/2 cups rye flour
75g/3oz/½ cup medium oatmeal
1 sachet easy-blend dried yeast
45ml/3 tbsp sunflower seeds
30ml/2 tbsp linseeds
475ml/16fl oz/2 cups hand-hot water
30ml/2 tbsp malt extract

1 Sift the plain flour and salt into a mixing bowl and add the remaining flours, oatmeal, yeast and sunflower seeds. Set aside 5ml/1 tsp of the linseeds and add the rest to the flour mixture. Make a well in the centre.

2 Add the water to the bowl with the malt extract. Gradually incorporate the flour and mix to a soft dough, adding extra water if necessary.

3 Flour a baking sheet. Turn the dough onto a floured surface and knead for 5 minutes until smooth and elastic. Divide it in half. Roll each half into a sausage, about 30cm/12in in length. Twist the two pieces together, dampen each end and press together firmly.

4 Lift the loaf onto the prepared baking sheet. Brush with water, sprinkle with the remaining linseeds and cover loosely with a large plastic bag (balloon it to trap the air inside). Leave in a warm place until doubled in size. Preheat the oven to 220°C/425°F/Gas 7.

5 Bake the bread for 10 minutes, then lower the oven temperature to 200°C/400°F/Gas 6 and cook for 20 minutes more, or until the loaf sounds hollow when tapped underneath. Allow to cool on a wire rack.

Rye Bread

Rye bread is popular in Northern Europe and makes an excellent base for open sandwiches.

Makes 2 loaves, each serving 10

350g/12oz/3 cups wholemeal flour
225g/8oz/2 cups rye flour
115g/4oz/1 cup strong white flour
7.5ml/1½ tsp salt
1 sachet easy-blend dried yeast
30ml/2 tbsp caraway seeds
475ml/16fl oz/2 cups hand-hot water
30ml/2 tbsp molasses
30ml/2 tbsp sunflower oil

1 Grease a baking sheet. Put the flours in a bowl with the salt and yeast. Set aside 5ml/1 tsp of the caraway seeds and add the rest to the bowl. Mix well, then make a well in the centre.

2 Add the water to the bowl with the molasses and oil. Gradually incorporate the flour and mix to a soft dough, adding a little extra water if necessary.

3 Turn the dough on to a floured surface and knead for 5 minutes until smooth and elastic. Divide the dough in half and shape into two 23cm/9in long oval loaves.

4 Flatten the loaves slightly and place them on the baking sheet. Brush them with water and sprinkle with the remaining caraway seeds. Cover and leave in a warm place until doubled in size. Preheat the oven to 220°C/425°F/Gas 7.

5 Bake the loaves for 30 minutes until they sound hollow when tapped underneath. Allow to cool on a wire rack.

Soda Bread

Finding the bread bin empty need never be a problem when your repertoire includes a recipe for soda bread. It takes only a few minutes to make and needs no rising or proving. If possible, eat soda bread warm from the oven as it does not keep well.

Serves 8
450g/1lb/4 cups plain flour
5ml/1 tsp salt
5ml/1 tsp bicarbonate of soda
5ml/1 tsp cream of tartar
350ml/12fl oz/1½ cups buttermilk

1 Preheat the oven to 220°C/425°F/Gas 7. Flour a baking sheet. Sift the dry ingredients into a mixing bowl and make a well in the centre.

2 Add the buttermilk and mix quickly to a soft dough. Turn onto a floured surface and knead lightly. Shape into a round about 18cm/7in in diameter; place on the baking sheet.

3 Cut a deep cross on top of the loaf and sprinkle with a little flour. Bake for 25–30 minutes, then transfer to a wire rack to cool.

Cook's Tip
Soda bread needs a light hand. The ingredients should be bound together quickly in the bowl and kneaded very briefly. The aim is just to get rid of the largest cracks, as the dough becomes tough if handled for too long.

Malt Loaf

This is a rich and sticky loaf. If it lasts long enough to go stale, try toasting it for a delicious teatime treat.

Serves 8
350g/12oz/3 cups plain flour
1.5ml/¼ tsp salt
5ml/1 tsp easy-blend dried yeast
pinch of caster sugar
30ml/2 tbsp soft light brown sugar
175g/6oz/generous 1 cup sultanas
150ml/¼ pint/⅔ cup hand-hot skimmed milk
15ml/1 tbsp sunflower oil
45ml/3 tbsp malt extract

To glaze
30ml/2 tbsp caster sugar
30ml/2 tbsp water

1 Sift the flour and salt into a mixing bowl, stir in the yeast, pinch of sugar, brown sugar and sultanas, and make a well in the centre. Add the hot milk with the oil and malt extract. Gradually incorporate the flour and mix to a soft dough, adding a little extra milk if necessary.

2 Turn onto a floured surface and knead for about 5 minutes until smooth and elastic. Lightly oil a 450g/1lb loaf tin.

3 Shape the dough and place it in the prepared tin. Cover with a damp dish cloth and leave in a warm place until doubled in size. Preheat the oven to 190°C/375°F/Gas 5.

4 Bake the loaf for 30–35 minutes or until it sounds hollow when tapped underneath.

5 Meanwhile, make the glaze by dissolving the sugar in the water in a small pan. Bring to the boil, stirring, then lower the heat and simmer for 1 minute. Brush the loaf while hot, then transfer it to a wire rack to cool.

Banana and Cardamom Bread

The combination of banana and cardamom is delicious in this soft-textured moist loaf.

Serves 6

10 cardamom pods
400g/14oz/3¹/₂ cups
   strong white flour
5ml/1 tsp salt
5ml/1 tsp easy-blend
   dried yeast

150ml/¹/₄ pint/²/₃ cup
   hand-hot water
30ml/2 tbsp malt extract
2 ripe bananas, mashed
5ml/1 tsp sesame seeds

1 Grease a 450g/1lb loaf tin. Split the cardamom pods. Remove the seeds and chop the pods finely.

2 Sift the flour and salt into a mixing bowl, add the yeast and make a well in the centre. Add the water with the malt extract, chopped cardamom pods and bananas. Gradually incorporate the flour and mix to a soft dough, adding a little extra water if necessary.

3 Turn the dough onto a floured surface and knead for 5 minutes until smooth and elastic. Shape into a plait and place in the prepared tin. Cover loosely with a plastic bag (ballooning it to trap the air) and leave in a warm place until well risen. Preheat the oven to 220°C/425°F/Gas 7.

4 Brush the plait lightly with water and sprinkle with the sesame seeds. Bake for 10 minutes, then lower the oven temperature to 200°C/400°F/Gas 6. Cook for 15 minutes more, or until the loaf sounds hollow when tapped underneath. Remove to a wire rack to cool.

Swedish Sultana Bread

A lightly sweetened bread that goes very well with the cheeseboard and is also excellent toasted as a tea bread.

Serves 10

225g/8oz/2 cups
   wholemeal flour
225g/8oz/2 cups strong
   white flour
5ml/1 tsp easy-blend
   dried yeast
5ml/1 tsp salt
115g/4oz/scant 1 cup
   sultanas

50g/2oz/¹/₂ cup walnuts,
   chopped
15ml/1 tbsp clear honey
150ml/¹/₄ pint/²/₃ cup
   hand-hot water
175ml/6fl oz/³/₄ cup
   hand-hot skimmed
   milk, plus extra for
   glazing

1 Grease a baking sheet. Put the flours in a bowl with the yeast, salt and sultanas. Set aside 15ml/1 tbsp of the walnuts and add the rest to the bowl. Mix lightly and make a well in the centre.

2 Dissolve the honey in the water and add it to the bowl with the milk. Gradually incorporate the flour, mixing to a soft dough and adding a little extra water if necessary.

3 Turn the dough onto a floured surface and knead for 5 minutes until smooth and elastic. Shape into a 28cm/11in long sausage shape. Place on the prepared baking sheet.

4 Make diagonal cuts down the length of the loaf, brush with milk, sprinkle with the remaining walnuts and leave in a warm place until doubled in size. Preheat the oven to 220°C/425°F/Gas 7.

5 Bake the loaf for 10 minutes, then lower the oven temperature to 200°C/400°F/Gas 6 and bake for 20 minutes more or until the loaf sounds hollow when tapped underneath. Remove to a wire rack to cool.

Poppy Seed Rolls

Pile these soft rolls in a basket and serve them for breakfast
or with dinner.

Makes 12

oil for greasing	hand-hot skimmed
450g/1lb/4 cups strong	milk
white flour	1 egg, beaten
5ml/1 tsp salt	
5ml/1 tsp easy-blend	**For the topping**
dried yeast	1 egg, beaten
300ml/¹/₂ pint/1¹/₄ cups	poppy seeds

1 Lightly grease two baking sheets with the oil. Sift the flour
and salt into a mixing bowl. Add the yeast. Make a well in the
centre and pour in the milk and the egg. Gradually
incorporate the flour and mix to a soft dough.

2 Turn the dough on to a floured surface and knead for
5 minutes until smooth and elastic. Cut into 12 pieces and
shape into rolls.

3 Place the rolls on the prepared baking sheets, cover loosely
with a large plastic bag (ballooning it to trap the air inside)
and leave in a warm place until the rolls have doubled in size.
Preheat the oven to 220°C/425°F/Gas 7.

4 Glaze the rolls with beaten egg, sprinkle with poppy seeds
and bake for 12–15 minutes until golden brown.

Variations
*Vary the toppings. Linseed, sesame and caraway seeds
all look good; try adding caraway seeds to the dough,
too, for extra flavour.*

Granary Baps

These make excellent picnic fare and are also good buns for
hamburgers.

Makes 8

oil for greasing	15ml/1 tbsp malt extract
450g/1lb/4 cups malted	300ml/¹/₂ pint/1¹/₄ cups
brown flour	hand-hot water
5ml/1 tsp salt	15ml/1 tbsp rolled oats
10ml/2 tsp easy-blend	
dried yeast	

1 Lightly oil a large baking sheet. Put the malted flour, salt
and yeast in a mixing bowl and make a well in the centre.
Dissolve the malt extract in the water and add it to the well.
Gradually incorporate the flour and mix to a soft dough.

2 Turn the dough on to a floured surface and knead for 5
minutes until smooth and elastic. Divide it into eight pieces.
Shape into balls and flatten with the palm of your hand to
make 10cm/4in rounds.

3 Place the rounds on the prepared baking sheet, cover
loosely with a large plastic bag (ballooning it to trap the air
inside), and leave in a warm place until the baps have
doubled in size. Preheat the oven to 220°C/425°F/Gas 7.

4 Brush the baps with water, sprinkle with the oats and bake
for 20–25 minutes or until they sound hollow when tapped
underneath. Cool on a wire rack.

Variation
*To make a large loaf, shape the dough into a round,
flatten it slightly and bake for 30–40 minutes. Test by
tapping the base of the loaf – if it sounds hollow, it is
cooked.*

Wholemeal Herb Triangles

These make a good lunchtime snack when stuffed with ham and salad and also taste good when served with soup.

Makes 8

225g/8oz/2 cups
   wholemeal flour
115g/4oz/1 cup strong
   plain flour
5ml/1 tsp salt
2.5ml/¹/₂ tsp bicarbonate
   of soda
5ml/1 tsp cream of tartar
2.5ml/¹/₂ tsp chilli
   powder

50g/2oz/¹/₄ cup soft
   margarine
250ml/8fl oz/1 cup
   skimmed milk
60ml/4 tbsp chopped
   mixed fresh herbs
15ml/1 tbsp sesame seeds

1 Preheat the oven to 220°C/425°F/Gas 7. Flour a baking sheet. Put the wholemeal flour in a mixing bowl. Sift in the remaining dry ingredients, including the chilli powder, then rub in the margarine.

2 Add the milk and herbs and mix quickly to a soft dough. Turn onto a lightly floured surface. Knead very briefly or the dough will become tough.

3 Roll out to a 23cm/9in circle and place on the prepared baking sheet. Brush lightly with water and sprinkle with the sesame seeds.

4 Cut the dough round into 8 wedges, separate slightly and bake for 15–20 minutes. Transfer the triangles to a wire rack to cool. Serve warm or cold.

Variation
Sun-dried Tomato Triangles: replace the mixed herbs with 30ml/2 tbsp chopped, drained sun-dried tomatoes in oil, and add 15ml/1 tbsp mild paprika, 15ml/1 tbsp chopped fresh parsley and 15ml/1 tbsp chopped fresh marjoram.

Caraway Bread Sticks

Ideal to nibble with drinks, these can be made in a wide variety of flavours, including cumin seed, poppy seed and celery seed, as well as the coriander and sesame variation given below.

Makes about 20

225g/8oz/2 cups plain
   flour
2.5ml/¹/₂ tsp salt
2.5ml/¹/₂ tsp easy-blend
   dried yeast

10ml/2 tsp caraway seeds
150ml/¹/₄ pint/²/₃ cup
   hand-hot water
pinch of sugar

1 Grease two baking sheets. Sift the flour, salt, yeast and sugar into a mixing bowl, stir in the caraway seeds and make a well in the centre. Add the water and gradually mix the flour to make a soft dough, adding a little extra water if necessary.

2 Turn onto a lightly floured surface and knead for 5 minutes until smooth and elastic. Divide the mixture into 20 pieces and roll each one into a 30cm/12in stick.

3 Arrange the bread sticks on the baking sheets, leaving room to allow for rising. Leave for 30 minutes until well risen. Meanwhile, preheat the oven to 220°C/425°F/Gas 7.

4 Bake the bread sticks for 10–12 minutes until golden brown. Cool on the baking sheets.

Variation
Coriander and Sesame Sticks: replace the caraway seeds with 15ml/1 tbsp crushed coriander seeds. Dampen the bread sticks lightly and sprinkle them with sesame seeds before baking.

Curry Crackers

These spicy, crisp little biscuits are ideal for serving with drinks or cheese.

Makes 12

50g/2oz/¹/₂ cup plain
   flour
5ml/1 tsp curry powder
1.5ml/¹/₄ tsp chilli
   powder

1.5ml/¹/₄ tsp salt
15ml/1 tbsp chopped
   fresh coriander
30ml/2 tbsp water

1 Preheat the oven to 180°C/350°F/Gas 4. Sift the flour, curry powder, chilli powder and salt into a mixing bowl and make a well in the centre. Add the chopped coriander and water. Gradually incorporate the flour and mix to a fine dough.

2 Turn onto a lightly floured surface, knead until smooth, then leave to rest for 5 minutes.

3 Cut the dough into 12 pieces and knead into small balls. Roll each ball out very thinly to a 10cm/4in round.

4 Arrange the rounds on two ungreased baking sheets. Bake for 15 minutes, turning over once during cooking.

Variations
These can be flavoured in many different ways. Omit the curry and chilli powders and add 15ml/1 tbsp caraway, fennel or mustard seeds. Any of the stronger spices such as nutmeg, cloves or ginger will give a good flavour but you will only need to add 5ml/1 tsp.

Oatcakes

These are traditionally served with cheese, but are also delicious topped with thick honey for breakfast.

Makes 8

175g/6oz/1 cup medium
   oatmeal, plus extra for
   sprinkling
pinch of bicarbonate of
   soda

2.5ml/¹/₂ tsp salt
15g/¹/₂oz/1 tbsp butter
75ml/5 tbsp water

1 Preheat the oven to 150°C/300°F/Gas 2. Grease a baking sheet. Put the oatmeal, bicarbonate of soda and salt in a mixing bowl.

2 Melt the butter with the water in a small saucepan. Bring to the boil, then add to the oatmeal and mix to a moist dough.

3 Turn on to a surface sprinkled with oatmeal and knead to a smooth ball. Turn a large baking sheet upside down, sprinkle it lightly with oatmeal and place the ball of dough on top. Dust with oatmeal; roll out thinly to a 25cm/10in round.

4 Cut the round into eight sections, ease apart slightly and bake for 50–60 minutes until crisp. Leave to cool on the baking sheet, then remove the oatcakes with a palette knife.

Cook's Tip
To get a neat circle, place a 25cm/10in cake board or plate on top of the oatcake. Cut away any excess dough with a palette knife, then remove the board or plate.

Chive and Potato Scones

These little cakes should be fairly thin, soft and crisp. They are delicious served for breakfast.

Makes 20

450g/1lb potatoes
115g/4oz/1 cup plain flour, sifted
30ml/2 tbsp olive oil
30ml/2 tbsp snipped chives

salt and freshly ground black pepper
low-fat spread, for topping

1 Cook the potatoes in a saucepan of boiling salted water for 20 minutes, then drain thoroughly. Return the potatoes to the clean pan and mash them. Preheat a griddle or heavy-based frying pan over low heat.

2 Tip the hot mashed potatoes into a bowl. Add the flour, olive oil and chives, with a little salt and pepper. Mix to a soft dough.

3 Roll out the dough on a well-floured surface to a thickness of 5 mm/¼ in and stamp out rounds with a 5cm/2in scone cutter, re-rolling and cutting the trimmings.

4 Cook the scones, in batches, on the hot griddle or frying pan for about 10 minutes until they are golden brown. Keep the heat low and turn the scones once. Spread with a little low-fat spread and serve immediately.

Cook's Tip
Use floury potatoes such as King Edwards. The potatoes must be freshly cooked and mashed and should not be allowed to cool before mixing. Cook the scones over low heat so that the outside does not burn before the inside is cooked.

Ham and Tomato Scones

These make an ideal accompaniment for soup. If you have any left over the next day, halve them, sprinkle with cheese, and toast under the grill.

Makes 12

225g/8oz/2 cups self-raising flour
5ml/1 tsp mustard powder
5ml/1 tsp paprika, plus extra for topping
2.5ml/½ tsp salt
25g/1oz/2 tbsp soft margarine
50g/2oz Black Forest ham, chopped

15ml/1 tbsp snipped fresh basil
50g/2oz/⅓ cup drained sun-dried tomatoes in oil, chopped
90–120ml/3–4fl oz/ ⅓–½ cup skimmed milk, plus extra for brushing

1 Preheat the oven to 200°C/400°F/Gas 6. Flour a large baking sheet. Sift the flour, mustard, paprika and salt into a bowl. Rub in the margarine until the mixture resembles breadcrumbs.

2 Stir in the ham, basil and sun-dried tomatoes; mix lightly. Pour in enough milk to mix to a soft dough. ·

3 Turn the dough onto a lightly floured surface, knead lightly and roll out to a 20 x 15cm (8 x 6in) rectangle. Cut into 5cm/2in squares and arrange on the baking sheet.

4 Brush sparingly with milk, sprinkle with paprika and bake for 12–15 minutes. Transfer to a wire rack to cool.

Cook's Tip
Scone dough should be soft and moist and mixed for just long enough to bind the ingredients together. Too much kneading makes the scones tough.

Drop Scones

Children love making – and eating – these little scones.

Makes 18

225g/8oz/2 cups self-
    raising flour
2.5ml/¹/₂ tsp salt
15ml/1 tbsp caster sugar

1 egg, beaten
300ml/¹/₂ pint/1¹/₄ cups
    skimmed milk
oil for brushing

1 Preheat a griddle, heavy-based frying pan or an electric frying pan. Sift the flour and salt into a mixing bowl. Stir in the sugar and make a well in the centre.

2 Add the egg and half the milk and gradually incorporate the surrounding flour to make a smooth batter. Beat in the remaining milk.

3 Lightly grease the griddle or pan. Drop tablespoons of the batter onto the surface, leaving them until they bubble and the bubbles begin to burst.

4 Turn the drop scones with a palette knife and cook until the underside is golden brown. Keep the cooked drop scones warm and moist by wrapping them in a clean napkin while cooking successive batches. Serve with jam.

Variation
*For a savoury version of these tasty scones, add
2 chopped spring onions and 15ml/1 tbsp freshly
grated Parmesan cheese to the batter. Serve with
cottage cheese.*

Pineapple and Spice Drop Scones

Making the batter with pineapple or orange juice instead of milk cuts down on fat and adds to the taste. Semi-dried pineapple has an intense flavour that makes it ideal to use in baking.

Makes 24

115g/4oz/1 cup self-
    raising wholemeal
    flour
115g/4oz/1 cup self-
    raising white flour
5ml/1 tsp ground
    cinnamon
15ml/1 tbsp caster sugar

1 egg, beaten
300ml/¹/₂ pint/1¹/₄ cups
    pineapple juice
75g/3oz/¹/₂ cup semi-
    dried pineapple,
    chopped
oil for greasing

1 Preheat a griddle, heavy-based frying pan or an electric frying pan. Put the wholemeal flour in a mixing bowl. Sift in the white flour, ground cinnamon and sugar and make a well in the centre.

2 Add the egg with half the pineapple juice and gradually incorporate the surrounding flour to make a smooth batter. Beat in the remaining juice with the chopped pineapple.

3 Lightly grease the griddle or pan. Drop tablespoons of the batter onto the surface, leaving them until they bubble and the bubbles begin to burst.

4 Turn the drop scones with a palette knife and cook until the underside is golden brown. Keep the cooked scones warm and moist by wrapping them in a clean napkin while cooking successive batches.

Cook's Tip
*Drop scones do not keep well and are best eaten freshly
cooked. These taste good with cottage cheese.*

Peach and Amaretto Cake

Try this delicious cake for dessert, with reduced-fat fromage frais, or serve it solo for afternoon tea.

Serves 8
3 eggs, separated
175g/6oz/¾ cup caster sugar
grated rind and juice of 1 lemon
50g/2oz/⅓ cup semolina
40g/1½oz/scant ½ cup ground almonds
25g/1oz/¼ cup plain flour

For the syrup
75g/3oz/6 tbsp caster sugar
90ml/6 tbsp water
30ml/2 tbsp Amaretto liqueur
2 peaches or nectarines, halved and stoned
60ml/4 tbsp apricot jam, sieved, to glaze

1 Preheat the oven to 180°C/350°F/Gas 4. Grease a 20cm/8in round loose-bottomed cake tin. Whisk the egg yolks, caster sugar, lemon rind and juice in a bowl until thick, pale and creamy, then fold in the semolina, almonds and flour until smooth.

2 Whisk the egg whites in a grease-free bowl until fairly stiff. Using a metal spoon, stir a generous spoonful of the whites into the semolina mixture to lighten it, then fold in the remaining egg whites. Spoon into the prepared cake tin.

3 Bake for 30–35 minutes, then remove the cake from the oven and carefully loosen the edges. Prick the top with a skewer and leave to cool slightly in the tin.

4 Meanwhile, make the syrup. Heat the sugar and water in a small pan, stirring until dissolved, then boil without stirring for 2 minutes. Add the Amaretto liqueur and drizzle slowly over the cake.

5 Remove the cake from the tin and transfer it to a serving plate. Slice the peaches or nectarines, arrange them in concentric circles over the top and brush with the glaze.

Chestnut and Orange Roulade

A very moist roulade – ideal to serve as a dessert.

Serves 8
3 eggs, separated
115g/4oz/½ cup caster sugar
½ x 439g/15½oz can unsweetened chestnut purée
grated rind and juice of 1 orange
icing sugar, for dusting

For the filling
225g/8oz/1 cup low-fat soft cheese
15ml/1 tbsp clear honey
1 orange

1 Preheat the oven to 180°C/350°F/Gas 4. Line and grease a 30 x 20cm/12 x 8in Swiss roll tin. Whisk the egg yolks and sugar in a mixing bowl until thick and creamy. Put the chestnut purée in a separate bowl. Whisk the orange rind and juice into the purée, then whisk into the egg mixture.

2 Whisk the egg whites until fairly stiff. Stir a generous spoonful of the whites into the chestnut mixture to lighten it, then fold in the remaining egg whites. Spoon the mixture into the prepared tin and bake for 30 minutes until firm. Cool for 5 minutes, then cover with a clean damp dish cloth and leave until cold.

3 Meanwhile, make the filling. Put the soft cheese in a bowl with the honey. Finely grate the orange rind and add to the bowl. Peel away all the pith from the orange, cut the fruit into segments, chop roughly and set aside. Add any juice to the bowl, then beat until smooth. Mix in the orange segments.

4 Sprinkle a sheet of greaseproof paper with icing sugar. Turn the roulade out onto the paper; peel off the lining paper. Spread the filling over the roulade and roll up like a Swiss roll. Transfer to a plate and dust with icing sugar.

Cinnamon and Apple Gâteau

Make this lovely gâteau for an autumn teatime treat.

Serves 8

3 eggs
115g/4oz/¹/₂ cup caster
  sugar
75g/3oz/¾ cup plain flour
5ml/1 tsp ground
  cinnamon

For the filling and topping
4 large eating apples

15ml/1 tbsp water
60ml/4 tbsp clear honey
75g/3oz/¹/₂ cup sultanas
2.5ml/¹/₂ tsp ground
  cinnamon
350g/12oz/1¹/₂ cups low-
  fat soft cheese
60ml/4 tbsp reduced-fat
  fromage frais
10ml/2 tsp lemon juice

1 Preheat the oven to 190°C/375°F/Gas 5. Line and grease a 23cm/9in sandwich cake tin. Whisk the eggs and sugar until thick, then sift the flour and cinnamon over the surface and carefully fold in with a large metal spoon.

2 Pour into the prepared tin and bake for 25–30 minutes or until the cake springs back when lightly pressed. Cool on a wire rack.

3 To make the filling, peel, core and slice three of the apples and cook them in a covered pan with the water and half the honey until softened. Add the sultanas and cinnamon, stir well, replace the lid and leave to cool.

4 Put the soft cheese in a bowl with the fromage frais, the remaining honey and half the lemon juice; beat until smooth. Split the sponge cake in half, place the bottom half on a plate and drizzle over any liquid from the apples. Spread with two-thirds of the cheese mixture, then top with the apple filling. Fit the top of the cake in place.

5 Swirl the remaining filling over the top of the sponge. Quarter, core and slice the remaining apple, dip the slices in the remaining lemon juice and use to decorate the edges.

Lemon Chiffon Cake

Lemon mousse makes a tangy and delicious sponge filling.

Serves 8

1 lemon sponge cake mix
lemon glacé icing
shreds of blanched
  lemon rind

For the filling
2 eggs, separated
75g/3oz/6 tbsp
  caster sugar

grated rind and juice of
  1 small lemon
20ml/4 tsp water
10ml/2 tsp gelatine
120ml/4fl oz/¹/₂ cup
  reduced-fat fromage
  frais

1 Preheat the oven to 180°C/350°F/Gas 4. Line and grease a 20cm/8in loose-bottomed cake tin, add the sponge mixture and bake for 20–25 minutes until firm and golden. Cool on a wire rack, then split in half. Return the lower half of the cake to the clean cake tin and set aside.

2 Make the filling. Whisk the egg yolks, sugar, lemon rind and juice in a bowl until thick, pale and creamy. In a grease-free bowl, whisk the egg whites to soft peaks.

3 Sprinkle the gelatine over the water in a bowl. When spongy, dissolve over simmering water. Cool slightly, then whisk into the yolk mixture. Fold in the fromage frais. When the mixture begins to set, fold in a generous spoonful of the egg whites to lighten it, then fold in the remaining whites.

4 Spoon the lemon mousse over the sponge in the cake tin. Set the second layer of sponge on top and chill until set.

5 Carefully transfer the cake to a serving plate. Pour the glacé icing over the cake and spread it evenly to the edges. Decorate with the lemon shreds.

Strawberry Gâteau

It is difficult to believe that a cake that tastes so delicious can be low fat.

Serves 6

2 eggs
75g/3oz/6 tbsp caster sugar
grated rind of ½ orange
50g/2oz/½ cup plain flour

grated rind of ½ orange
30ml/2 tbsp caster sugar
60ml/4 tbsp reduced-fat fromage frais
225g/8oz strawberries, halved and chopped
25g/1oz/¼ cup chopped almonds, toasted

For the filling
275g/10oz/1¼ cups low-fat soft cheese

1 Preheat the oven to 190°C/375°F/Gas 5. Line a 30 x 20cm/12 x 8in Swiss roll tin with non-stick baking paper.

2 In a bowl, whisk the eggs, sugar and orange rind until thick and mousse-like, then fold in the flour lightly. Turn the mixture into the prepared tin. Bake for 15–20 minutes or until firm and golden. Cool on a wire rack, removing the lining paper.

3 Meanwhile, make the filling. In a bowl, mix the soft cheese with the orange rind, sugar and fromage frais until smooth. Divide between two bowls. Add half the strawberries to one bowl. Cut the sponge widthways into three equal pieces and sandwich together with the strawberry filling. Place on a serving plate.

4 Spread the plain filling over the top and sides of the cake. Press the toasted almonds over the sides and decorate the top with the remaining strawberry halves.

Tia Maria Gâteau

A feather-light coffee sponge with a creamy liqueur-flavoured filling spiked with stem ginger.

Serves 8

75g/3oz/¾ cup plain flour
30ml/2 tbsp instant coffee powder
3 eggs
115g/4oz/½ cup caster sugar

15ml/1 tbsp Tia Maria
50g/2oz/⅓ cup stem ginger, chopped

For the icing
225g/8oz/2 cups icing sugar, sifted
10ml/2 tsp coffee essence
5ml/1 tsp fat-reduced cocoa
coffee beans (optional)

For the filling
175g/6oz/¾ cup low-fat soft cheese
15ml/1 tbsp clear honey

1 Preheat the oven to 190°C/375°F/Gas 5. Line and grease a 20cm/8in round cake tin. Sift the flour and coffee powder together.

2 Whisk the eggs and sugar in a bowl until thick and mousse-like, then fold in the flour mixture lightly. Turn the mixture into the prepared tin. Bake for 30–35 minutes or until firm and golden. Cool on a wire rack.

3 Make the filling. Mix the soft cheese with the honey in a bowl. Beat until smooth, then stir in the Tia Maria and ginger. Split the cake in half horizontally and sandwich together with the Tia Maria filling.

4 Make the icing. In a bowl, mix the icing sugar and coffee essence with enough water to make an icing which will coat the back of a wooden spoon. Pour three-quarters of the icing over the cake. Stir the cocoa into the remaining icing, spoon it into a piping bag fitted with a writing nozzle and drizzle the mocha icing over the coffee icing. Decorate with coffee beans, if desired.

Quick-mix Sponge Cake

Choose either chocolate or lemon flavouring for this light and versatile sponge cake, or leave it plain.

Makes 1 x 20cm/8in round cake

115g/4oz/1 cup self-
* raising flour*
5ml/1 tsp baking powder
115g/4oz/½ cup soft
* margarine*
115g/4oz/½ cup
* caster sugar*
2 eggs

For the flavourings
Chocolate: 15ml/1 tbsp
* cocoa powder blended*
* with 15ml/1 tbsp*
* boiling water*
Lemon: 10ml/2 tsp
* grated lemon rind*

1 Preheat the oven to 160°C/325°F/Gas 3. Grease a 20cm/8in round cake tin, line the base with greaseproof paper and grease the paper.

2 Sift the flour and baking powder into a bowl. Add the margarine, sugar and eggs with the chosen flavourings, if using.

3 Beat with a wooden spoon for 2–3 minutes. The mixture should be pale in colour and slightly glossy.

4 Spoon the mixture into the cake tin and smooth the surface. Bake in the centre of the oven for 30–40 minutes, or until a skewer inserted into the centre of the cake comes out clean. Turn out onto a wire rack, remove the lining paper and leave to cool completely.

Genoese Sponge Cake

This sponge cake has a firm texture due to the addition of butter and is suitable for cutting into layers for gâteaux.

Makes 1 x 20cm/8in round cake

4 eggs
125g/4oz/½ cup caster
* sugar*
75g/3oz/6tbsp unsalted
* butter, melted and*
* cooled slightly*
75g/3oz/¾ cup plain
* flour*

For the flavourings
Citrus: 10ml/2 tsp grated
* orange, lemon or*
* lime rind*
Chocolate: 50g/2oz plain
* chocolate, melted*
Coffee: 10ml/2 tsp coffee
* granules, dissolved*
* in 5ml/1 tsp*
* boiling water*

1 Preheat the oven to 180°C/350°F/Gas 4. Base line and grease a 20cm/8in round cake tin.

2 Whisk the eggs and caster sugar together in a heatproof bowl until thoroughly blended. Place the bowl over a saucepan of simmering water and continue to whisk the mixture until thick and pale.

3 Remove the bowl from the saucepan and continue to whisk until the mixture is cool and leaves a thick trail on the surface when beaters are lifted.

4 Pour the butter carefully into the mixture, leaving any sediment behind.

5 Sift the flour over the surface. Using a plastic spatula, carefully fold the flour, butter and any flavourings into the mixture until smooth and evenly blended. Scrape the mixture into the prepared tin, tilt to level and bake for 30–40 minutes, until firm to the touch and golden. Cool on a wire rack.

Madeira Cake

Enjoy this cake in the traditional way with a large glass of
Madeira or a schooner of sherry.

Serves 6–8

225g/8oz/2 cups plain
  flour
5ml/1 tsp baking powder
225g/8oz/1 cup butter or
  margarine, at room
  temperature

225g/8oz/1 cup caster
  sugar
grated rind of 1 lemon
5ml/1 tsp vanilla essence
4 eggs

1 Preheat the oven to 160°C/325°F/Gas 3. Base line and
grease a 20cm/8in cake tin.

2 Sift the flour and baking powder into a bowl. Set the
mixture aside.

3 Cream the butter or margarine, adding the caster sugar
about 30ml/2 tbsp at a time, until light and fluffy. Stir in the
lemon rind and vanilla. Add the eggs one at a time, beating
for 1 minute after each addition. Add the flour mixture and
stir until just combined.

4 Pour the cake mixture into the prepared tin and tap lightly
to level. Bake for about 1¼ hours, or until a metal skewer
inserted in the centre comes out clean.

5 Cool in the tin on a wire rack for 10 minutes, then turn the
cake out onto a wire rack and leave to cool completely.

Swiss Roll

Vary the flavour of the Swiss roll by adding a little grated
orange, lime or lemon rind to the mixture.

Serves 6–8

4 eggs, separated
115g/4oz/½ cup caster
  sugar
115g/4oz/1 cup plain
  flour
5ml/1 tsp baking powder

**For a chocolate
flavouring**
Replace 25ml/1½ tbsp of
  the flour with
25ml/1½ tbsp cocoa
  powder

1 Preheat the oven to 180°C/350°F/Gas 4. Base line and
grease a 33 x 23cm/13 x 9in Swiss roll tin. Whisk the egg
whites until stiff. Beat in 30ml/2 tbsp of the caster sugar.

2 Beat the egg yolks with the remaining caster sugar and
15ml/1 tbsp water for about 2 minutes until the mixture is
pale and leaves a thick ribbon trail.

3 Sift together the flour and baking powder. Carefully fold
the beaten egg yolks into the egg whites, then fold in the flour
mixture.

4 Pour the mixture into the prepared tin and gently smooth
the surface. Bake in the centre of the oven for 12–15 minutes,
or until the cake starts to come away from the edges of the tin.

5 Turn out onto a piece of greaseproof paper lightly
sprinkled with caster sugar. Peel off the lining paper and cut
off any crisp edges. Spread with jam, if wished, and roll up,
using the greaseproof paper as a guide. Leave to cool
completely on a wire rack.

Rich Fruit Cake

Make this cake a few weeks before icing, wrap well and store in an airtight container to mature.

Makes 1 x 20cm/8in round or 18cm/7in square cake

375g/12oz/1¾ cups currants
250g/9oz/scant 2 cups sultanas
150g/5oz/1 cup raisins
90g/3½ oz/scant ½ cup glacé cherries, halved
90g/3½ oz/scant 1 cup almonds, chopped
65g/2½ oz/scant ½ cup mixed peel
grated rind of 1 lemon
40ml/2½ tbsp brandy
250g/9oz/2¼ cups plain flour, sifted
6.5ml/1¼ tsp mixed spice
2.5ml/½ tsp grated nutmeg
65g/2½ oz/generous ½ cup ground almonds
200g/7oz/scant 1 cup soft margarine or butter
225g/8oz/1¼ cups soft brown sugar
15ml/1 tbsp black treacle
5 eggs, beaten

1 Preheat the oven to 140°C/275°F/Gas 1. Grease a deep 20cm/8in round or 18cm/7in square cake tin, line the base and sides with a double thickness of greaseproof paper and grease the paper.

2 Combine the ingredients in a large mixing bowl. Beat with a wooden spoon for 5 minutes until well mixed.

3 Spoon the mixture into the prepared cake tin. Make a slight depression in the centre.

4 Bake in the centre of the oven for 3–3½ hours. Test the cake after 3 hours. If it is ready it will feel firm and a skewer inserted in the centre will come out clean. Cover the top loosely with foil if it starts to brown too quickly.

5 Leave the cake to cool completely in the tin. Then turn out. The lining paper can be left on to help keep the cake moist.

Light Fruit Cake

For those who prefer a slightly less dense fruit cake, here is one that is still ideal for marzipanning and icing.

Makes 1 x 20cm/8in round or 18cm/7in square cake

225g/8oz/1 cup soft margarine or butter
225g/8oz/1 cup caster sugar
grated rind of 1 orange
5 eggs, beaten
300g/11oz/2¾ cups plain flour
2.5ml/½ tsp baking powder
10ml/2 tsp mixed spice
175g/6oz/¾ cup currants
175g/6oz/generous 1 cup raisins
175g/6oz/generous 1 cup sultanas
50g/2oz/⅓ cup dried, ready-to-eat apricots
115g/4oz/⅔ cup mixed peel

1 Preheat the oven to 150°C/300°F/Gas 2. Grease a deep 20cm/8in round or 18cm/7in square cake tin, line the base and sides with a double thickness of greaseproof paper and grease the paper.

2 Combine all the ingredients in a large mixing bowl, snipping in the apricots in strips, using kitchen scissors. Beat thoroughly with a wooden spoon for 3–4 minutes, until thoroughly mixed.

3 Spoon the mixture into the cake tin. Make a slight depression in the centre. Bake in the centre of the oven for 2½–3¼ hours. Test the cake after 2½ hours. If it is ready it will feel firm and a skewer inserted in the centre will come out clean. Test at intervals if necessary. Cover the top loosely with foil if it starts to brown too quickly.

4 Leave the cake to cool completely in the tin. Then turn out. The lining paper can be left on to help keep the cake moist.

Marzipan

Marzipan can be used on its own, under an icing or for modelling.

Makes 450g/1lb/3 cups
225g/8oz/2 cups ground
   almonds
115g/4oz/½ cup caster
   sugar
115g/4oz/1 cup icing
   sugar, sifted

5ml/1 tsp lemon juice
a few drops of almond
   essence
1 (size 4) egg, or
   1 (size 2) egg white

1 Stir the ground almonds and sugars together in a bowl until evenly mixed. Make a well in the centre and add the lemon juice, almond essence and enough egg or egg white to mix to a soft but firm dough, using a wooden spoon.

2 Form the marzipan into a ball. Lightly dust a surface with icing sugar and knead the marzipan until smooth. Wrap in clear film or store in a polythene bag until needed. Tint with food colouring if required.

Sugarpaste Icing

Sugarpaste icing is wonderfully pliable and can be coloured, moulded and shaped in imaginative ways.

Makes 350g/12oz/2¼ cups
1 egg white
15ml/1 tbsp liquid
   glucose, warmed
350g/12oz/3 cups icing

sugar, sifted

1 Put the egg white and glucose in a mixing bowl. Stir them together to break up the egg white.

2 Add the icing sugar and mix together with a palette knife, using a chopping action, until well blended and the icing begins to bind together. Knead the mixture with your fingers until it forms a ball.

3 Knead the sugarpaste on a work surface lightly dusted with icing sugar for several minutes until smooth, soft and pliable. If the icing is too soft, knead in some more sifted sugar until it reaches the right consistency.

Marzipan Roses

To decorate a cake, shape the roses in a variety of colours and sizes then arrange on top.

Form a small ball of coloured marzipan into a cone shape. This forms the central core which supports the petals. To make the petals, take a piece of marzipan about the size of a large pea, and make a petal shape which is thicker at the base. Wrap the petal around the cone, pressing the petal to the cone to secure. Bend back the ends of the petal to curl. Repeat with more petals, each overlapping. Make some petals bigger until the required size is achieved.

Royal Icing

Royal icing gives a professional finish. This recipe makes
enough icing to cover the top and sides of an 18cm/7in cake.

Makes 675g/1½ lb/4½ cups
3 egg whites
about 675g/1½ lb/6 cups
   icing sugar, sifted
7.5ml/1½ tsp glycerine
a few drops of lemon
   juice
food colouring (optional)

1 Put the egg whites in a bowl and stir lightly with a fork to
break them up.

2 Add the icing sugar gradually, beating well with a wooden
spoon after each addition. Add enough icing sugar to make a
smooth, shiny icing that has the consistency of very stiff
meringue.

3 Beat in the glycerine, lemon juice and food colouring, if
using. Leave for 1 hour before using, covered with damp clear
film, then stir to burst any air bubbles.

Storing
*The icing will keep for up to three days, stored in a
plastic container with a tight-fitting lid in a fridge.*

Icing consistencies
*This recipe is for an icing consistency suitable for flat
icing a marzipanned rich fruit cake. When the spoon is
lifted, the icing should form a sharp point, with a slight
curve at the end, known as "soft peak". For piping, the
icing needs to be slightly stiffer. It should form a fine
sharp peak when the spoon is lifted.*

Butter Icing

The creamy rich flavour and silky smoothness of butter
icing is popular with both children and adults.

Makes 350g/12oz/1½ cups
75g/3oz/6 tbsp soft
   margarine or butter,
   softened
225g/8oz/2 cups icing
   sugar, sifted
5ml/1 tsp vanilla essence
10–15ml/2–3 tsp milk

For the flavourings
Chocolate: Blend 15ml/
   1 tbsp cocoa powder
   with 15ml/1 tbsp hot
   water. Cool before
   beating into the icing.

Coffee: Blend 10ml/2 tsp
   coffee powder with
   15ml/1 tbsp boiling
   water. Omit the milk.
   Cool before beating the
   mixture into the icing.

Lemon, orange or lime:
   Substitute the vanilla
   essence and milk with
   lemon, orange or lime
   juice and 10ml/2 tsp
   of finely grated citrus
   rind. Omit the rind if
   using the icing for
   piping. Lightly tint
   the icing with food
   colouring, if wished.

1 Put the margarine or butter, icing sugar, vanilla essence
and 5ml/1 tsp of the milk in a bowl.

2 Beat with a wooden spoon or an electric mixer, adding
sufficient extra milk to give a light, smooth and fluffy
consistency. For flavoured butter icing, follow the instructions
above for the flavour of your choice.

Storing
*The icing will keep for up to three days in an airtight
container stored in a fridge.*

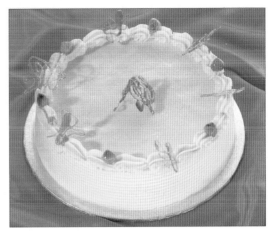

Fudge Frosting

A darkly delicious frosting, this can transform a simple sponge cake into one worthy of a very special occasion. Spread fudge frosting smoothly over the cake or swirl it. Or be even more elaborate with a little piping – it really is very versatile. This recipe makes enough to fill and coat the top and sides of a 20cm/8in or 23cm/9in round sponge cake.

Makes 350g/12oz/1½ cups

50g/2oz squares plain chocolate
225g/8oz icing sugar, sifted
50g/2oz/4 tbsp butter

45ml/3 tbsp milk or single cream
5ml/1 tsp vanilla essence

1 Break or chop the chocolate into small pieces. Put the chocolate, icing sugar, butter, milk or cream and vanilla essence in a heavy-based saucepan.

2 Stir over a very low heat until both the chocolate and the butter have melted. Remove the mixture from the heat and stir until evenly blended.

3 Beat the icing frequently as it cools until it thickens sufficiently to use for spreading or piping. Use the icing immediately and work quickly once it has reached the right consistency.

Storing
This icing should be used straightaway.

Crème au Beurre

The rich, smooth, light texture of this icing makes it ideal for spreading, filling or piping onto cakes and gâteaux for all occasions.

Makes 350g/12oz/1½ cups

60ml/4 tbsp water
75g/3oz/6 tbsp caster sugar
2 egg yolks
150g/5oz/generous ½ cup unsalted butter, softened

For the flavourings
Citrus: replace water

with orange, lemon or lime juice and 10ml/ 2 tsp grated rind
Chocolate: add 50g/2oz plain chocolate, melted
Coffee: add 10ml/2 tsp instant coffee granules, dissolved in 5ml/1 tsp boiling water, cooled

1 Bring the water to the boil, remove from the heat and stir in the sugar. Heat gently, stirring, until the sugar has dissolved. Then boil rapidly until the mixture becomes syrupy, or reaches the "thread" stage. To test, place a little syrup on the back of a dry teaspoon. Press a second teaspoon on to the syrup and gently pull apart. The syrup should form a fine thread. If not, return to the heat, boil rapidly and re-test a minute later.

2 Whisk the egg yolks together in a bowl. Continue to whisk while slowly adding the sugar syrup. Whisk until thick, pale and cool.

3 Beat the butter until light and fluffy. Add the egg mixture gradually, beating well after each addition, until thick and fluffy. For Chocolate or Coffee Crème au Beurre, fold in the flavouring at the end. If you prefer a citrus flavour, follow the instructions above.

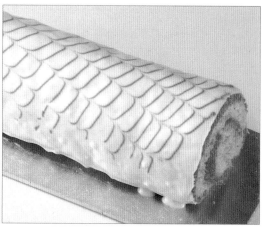

American Frosting

A light marshmallow icing which crisps on the outside when left to dry, this versatile frosting may be swirled or peaked into a soft coating.

Makes 350g/12oz/1½ cups
1 egg white
30ml/2 tbsp water
15ml/1 tbsp golden syrup
5ml/1 tsp cream of tartar
175g/6oz/1½ cups icing sugar, sifted

1 Place the egg white with the water, golden syrup and cream of tartar in a heatproof bowl. Whisk together well until thoroughly blended.

2 Stir the icing sugar into the mixture and place the bowl over a saucepan of simmering water. Whisk until the mixture becomes thick and white.

3 Remove the bowl from the saucepan and continue to whisk the frosting until cool and thick, and the mixture stands up in soft peaks. Use immediately to fill or cover cakes.

Glacé Icing

An instant icing for quickly finishing the tops of large or small cakes.

Makes 350g/12oz/1½ cup
225g/8oz/2 cups icing sugar
30–45ml/2–3 tbsp hot water
food colouring (optional)

For the flavourings
Citrus: replace the water with orange, lemon or lime juice
Chocolate: sift 10ml/2 tsp cocoa powder with the icing sugar
Coffee: replace the water with strong, liquid coffee

1 Sift the icing sugar into a bowl. Using a wooden spoon, gradually stir in enough water to obtain the consistency of thick cream.

2 Beat until white and smooth, and the icing thickly coats the back of the spoon. Tint with a few drops of food colouring, if desired, or flavour the icing as suggested above. Use immediately to cover the top of the cake.

Simple Piped Flowers

Bouquets of iced blossoms, such as roses, pansies and bright summer flowers make colourful cake decorations.

For a rose, make a fairly firm icing. Colour the icing. Fit a petal nozzle into a paper piping bag, half-fill with icing and fold over top to seal. Hold the piping bag so the wider end is pointing at what will be the base of the rose and hold a cocktail stick in the other hand. Pipe a small cone shape around the tip of the stick, pipe a petal half way around the cone, lifting it so it is at an angle and curling outwards, turning the stick at the same time. Repeat with more petals so they overlap. Remove from stick and leave until dry.

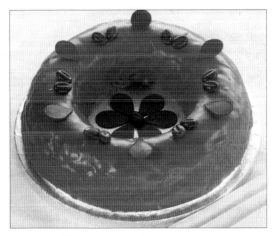

Butterscotch Frosting

Makes 675g/1½ lb/3 cups

75g/3oz/6 tbsp unsalted
  butter
45ml/3 tbsp milk
25g/1oz/2 tbsp soft light
  brown sugar
15ml/1 tbsp black treacle
350g/12oz/3 cups icing
  sugar, sifted

For the flavourings
Citrus: replace the treacle
  with golden syrup and
  add 10ml/2 tsp finely
  grated orange, lemon
  or lime rind
Chocolate: sift 15ml/
  1 tbsp cocoa powder
  with the icing sugar
Coffee: replace the treacle
  with 15ml/1 tbsp
  coffee granules

1 Place the butter, milk, sugar and treacle in a bowl over a
pan of simmering water. Stir until the butter and sugar melt.

2 Remove the bowl and stir in the icing sugar. Beat until
smooth and glossy. For flavouring, follow instructions above.

3 Pour over the cake, or cool for a thicker consistency.

Chocolate Fudge Icing

A rich glossy icing which sets like chocolate fudge, this is
versatile enough to smoothly coat, swirl or pipe, depending
on the temperature of the icing when it is used.

Makes 450g/1lb/2 cups

115g/4oz plain chocolate,
  in squares
50g/2oz/¼ cup unsalted
  butter

1 egg, beaten
175g/6oz/1½ cups icing
  sugar, sifted

1 Place the chocolate and butter in a heatproof bowl over a
saucepan of hot water.

2 Stir occasionally with a wooden spoon until both the
chocolate and butter are melted. Add the egg and beat well.

3 Remove the bowl from the saucepan and stir in the icing
sugar, then beat until smooth and glossy.

4 Pour immediately over the cake for a smooth finish, or
leave to cool for a thicker spreading or piping consistency.

Making Caramel

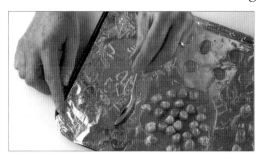

Caramel has endless uses – for dipping fruits and nuts,
crushing for cake coating, or drizzling into shapes.

Place 150ml/¼ pint/⅔ cup water in a saucepan. Bring to the
boil, remove from the heat and stir in 175g/6oz/¾ cup
caster sugar. Heat gently until the sugar has dissolved.
Bring the syrup to the boil, boil rapidly until the bubbles
begin to subside and the syrup begins to turn a pale golden
brown. For praline, add 75g/3oz/¾ cup toasted almonds to
the caramel, shake to mix, then pour onto a sheet of oiled
foil on a baking sheet. Cool, then crush with a rolling pin,
or process in a food processor until finely ground.

Apricot Glaze

It is a good idea to make a large quantity of apricot glaze, especially when making celebration cakes.

Makes 450g/1lb/1½ cups
*450g/1lb/1½ cups apricot
  jam
45ml/3 tbsp/ water*

1 Place the jam and water in a saucepan. Heat gently, stirring occasionally until melted. Boil rapidly for 1 minute, then rub through a sieve, pressing the fruit against the sides of the sieve with the back of a wooden spoon. Discard the skins left in the sieve. Use the warmed glaze to brush cakes before applying marzipan, or use for glazing fruits on gâteaux and cakes.

Glossy Chocolate Icing

A rich smooth glossy icing, this can be made with plain or milk chocolate.

Makes 350g/12oz/1¼ cups
*175g/6oz plain chocolate
150ml/¼ pint/⅔ cup
  single cream*

1 Break up the chocolate into small pieces and place it in a saucepan with the cream.

2 Heat gently, stirring occasionally, until the chocolate has melted and the mixture is smooth.

3 Allow the icing to cool until it is thick enough to coat the back of a wooden spoon. Use it at this stage for a smooth glossy icing, or allow it to thicken to obtain an icing which can be swirled or patterned with a cake decorating scraper.

Sugar-frosting Flowers

Choose edible flowers such as pansies, primroses, violets, roses, freesias, tiny daffodils or nasturtiums.

Lightly beat an egg white in a small bowl and sprinkle some caster sugar on a plate. Wash the flowers then dry on kitchen paper. If possible leave some stem attached. Evenly brush both sides of the petals with the egg white. Hold the flower by its stem over a plate lined with kitchen paper, sprinkle it evenly with the sugar, then shake off any excess. Place on a flat board or wire rack covered with kitchen paper and leave to dry in a warm place. Use to decorate a cake.

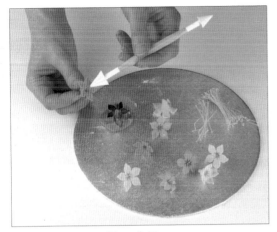

Petal Paste

Makes 500g/1¼lb

10ml/2 tsp gelatine	sugar, sifted
25ml/1½ tsp cold water	5ml/1 tsp gum
10ml/2 tsp liquid glucose	tragacanth
10ml/2 tsp white	1 egg white
vegetable fat	
450g/1lb/4 cups icing	

1 Place the gelatine, water, liquid glucose and white fat in a heatproof bowl over a saucepan of hot water until melted, stirring occasionally. Remove the bowl from the heat.

2 Sift the icing sugar and gum tragacanth into a bowl. Make a well in the centre and add the egg white and the gelatine mixture. Mix together to form a soft malleable white paste.

3 Knead on a surface dusted with icing sugar until smooth, white and free from cracks. Place in a plastic bag or wrap in clear film, sealing well to exclude all the air. Leave for about two hours before use, then knead again and use small pieces at a time, leaving the remaining petal paste well sealed.

Meringue Frosting

Makes 450g/1lb/1½ cups

2 egg whites	grated orange, lemon
115g/4oz/1 cup icing	or lime rind.
sugar, sifted	Chocolate: 50g/2oz plain
150g/5oz/⅔ cup unsalted	chocolate, melted
butter, softened	Coffee: 10ml/2 tsp coffee
	granules, blended with
For the flavourings	5ml/1 tsp boiling
Citrus: 10ml/2 tsp finely	water, cooled

1 Whisk the egg whites in a clean, heatproof bowl, add the icing sugar and gently whisk to mix well. Place the bowl over a saucepan of simmering water and whisk until thick and white. Remove the bowl from the saucepan and continue to whisk until cool and the meringue stands up in soft peaks.

2 Beat the butter in a separate bowl until light and fluffy. Add the meringue gradually, beating well after each addition, until thick and fluffy. Fold in the chosen flavouring, using a palette knife, until evenly blended. Use immediately for coating, filling and piping onto cakes.

Marbling

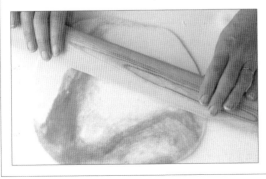

Sugarpaste, or fondant, lends itself to tinting in all shades and marbling is a good way to colour the paste.

Using a cocktail stick, add a few drops of the chosen edible food colour to some sugarpaste icing. Do not knead the food colouring fully into the icing.
When the sugarpaste is rolled out, the colour is dispersed in such a way that it gives a marbled appearance. Marbled sugarpaste icing can be used to cover novelty cakes. Several colours can be used in the same icing to give an interesting multi-coloured effect.